STYLES AND TYPES
OF
NORTH AMERICAN
ARCHITECTURE

Also by the author:

Images of American Living
The Comfortable House
Reading the Visible Past

STYLES AND TYPES OF NORTH AMERICAN ARCHITECTURE

Social Function and Cultural Expression

ALAN GOWANS

IconEditions

An Imprint of HarperCollins*Publishers*

STYLES AND TYPES OF NORTH AMERICAN ARCHITECTURE: SOCIAL FUNCTION AND CULTURAL EXPRESSION. Copyright © 1992 by Alan Gowans. All rights reserved. Printed in the United States of America. No part of this book may be used or reproduced in any manner whatsoever without written permission except in the case of brief quotations embodied in critical articles and reviews. For information address HarperCollins Publishers, 10 East 53rd Street, New York, NY 10022.

FIRST EDITION

Designed by Abigail Sturges

Library of Congress Cataloging-in-Publication Data

Gowans, Alan.
    Styles and types of North American architecture : social function
  and cultural expression / Alan Gowans. — 1st ed.
        p.   cm.
    Includes bibliographical references and index.
    ISBN 0-06-433276-4
    1. Architecture—North America.   2. Architecture and society—
  North America.   3. Interior architecture—North America.
  4. Decoration and ornament—North America.   5. North America—
  Civilization.   I. Title.
  NA703.G69   1991
  720′.103′097—dc20   89-46531

  92 93 94 95 96 CC/CW 10 9 8 7 6 5 4 3 2 1

CONTENTS

7 American Imperial Modern, c. 1950–c. 1980   271

8 An Imperial Underground: Popular/Commercial Styles in Architecture and Furniture, 1940s–1980s   319

PREFACE

Images of American Living was written in the late 1950s and early 1960s. The Modern movement was at its height and influenced every aspect of architectural thought. Cultural expression was the most history it would tolerate. When Corbusier wrote that "style is a unity of principle animating all the work of an epoch, the result of a state of mind which has its own special character" or Mies that "architecture is the translation of its epoch into space," they meant not only that their Modernism expressed the spirit of its times, but also that no time needing a different cultural expression would ever again arise. Theirs was the climactic era of history: with their creations, architectural history was to cease. Studying history in any way other than as a prelude to Modernism was a waste of time—which meant in practice that studying architectural history was a waste of time altogether, and it was in fact banned from many American architectural schools.

Now Modernism is in decline, and perspectives on the past have changed accordingly. Data of all sorts on North American architecture and furniture have mounted dramatically; new professional bodies dedicated to their study have been founded, and flourish. It's a different world; accordingly, this is a different book.

The text runs on three levels: text proper, notes, picture captions. Each involves a variant approach to the study of North American architecture.

The text proper has nine chapters, each devoted to a major stylistic category, taken up in chronological order. Each chapter begins with some representative examples put in a historical and geographical setting; from these examples I propose definitions of each style and identify its characteristics. There follows an account of each style's social function: what it did in and for the society of its time; how it was applied to various historic architectural types; and what substyles it engineered. Finally, I look at its continuing cultural expression—its legacy to our own times, for each major style has left some.

Supplementing this are notes that provide not only specific documentation and bibliographic references, but also a more informal commentary on various matters taken up in the text. Picture captions have two roles. They document illustrations of key monuments and the homelier, lesser-known examples from the author's collection (assembled over a thirty-year period, identified as IMG:NAL = National Images of North American Living). They also provide supplementary data by referring to relevant works that could not be illustrated for lack of space.

All sorts of people have contributed to this work over the many years it has been under way. To acknowledge all of them is not possible; but to some I owe special debts of gratitude: to Lamia Docemato, Head of Reader Services at the National Gallery, for all her bibliographical help; to Ed Gibson of Simon Fraser, with whose encouragement and collaboration an early version of *Styles and Types* was conceived; to Will Morgan for an invitation to the Morgan Professorship at the University of Louisville, where I first offered this material as a course; to the Canada Council for travel funds and the University of Victoria for generous leave provisions, which made possible eighteen months of field research, spent traveling all over the United States and Canada; to Henry A. Millon and the Center for Advanced Study at the National Gallery, where the categorization system was put in order; to Dennis Alan Mann for an invitation to spend a semester at the University of Cincinnati Architecture School, where it was further refined; to Lilien Robinson for an invitation to The George Washington University, where the course took approximately the form of this book. For help in obtaining illustrations and information, I am indebted to Ken Ames, Cary Carson, Ulysses Dietz, Jean France, Terry Guernsey, Richard Lindemann, William B. Rhoades, David Schuyler, Ann Serio, and Dianne Pilgrim, among others. For helpful conversations and general stimulation, special thanks to, among others, John Crosby Freeman, Leonard Eaton, Ingemarie Hays, Don Hibbard, Roger Kennedy, Peirce Lewis, Richard Longstreth, Tom McCormick, Karal Ann Marling, J. M. Neil, David Schuyler, Martin Segger, Dell Upton, Charles Wicke, and Wilbur Zelinsky. My thanks also to Kathy Buckalew, for printing photographs from IMG:NAL slides so competently—no easy task. Above all, thanks to Cass Canfield, Jr.; his faith in this project made it a reality, and his advice at all stages has been invaluable.

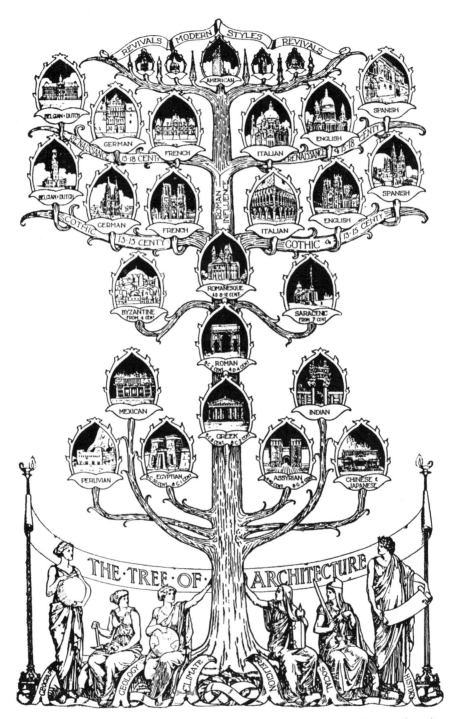

Title page to Sir Banister Fletcher's History of Architecture on the Comparative Method, *first published in London in 1896. It was unrivaled as a textbook for architectural history until superseded in the 1940s by Siegfried Giedion's* Space, Time and Architecture, *now come back into wide use because of its comprehensive presentation of stylistic details. In this frontispiece, made by the author himself, we see line-of-progress architectural history exemplified: a straight line runs from the trunk to the treetop, which is crowned by the Flatiron Building in New York of the early 1900s—the apex toward which all history grows. All other cultures are branches, side roads leading nowhere. Postmodernist thought questions whether history can or should be conceived as leading so directly to any one culmination.*

INTRODUCTION

Style and Type—
On Reading History in Architecture

It's a commonplace to say that architecture is a historical record of civilization, that it is "politics in three dimensions," and the like. But how was that record written? How is it to be read? An older answer was: by cultural expression, understanding how building forms reflect the spirit of successive historical eras. Every era has its own distinctive style, and architecture is one manifestation of it, along with furniture, music, dress, speech. From one era to another threads a line of progress, leading ever onward through history to culminate in Us.

The framework for historical study of architecture provided by concepts of line-of-progress and cultural expression is still useful, indeed essential. But the correspondences that they require are not as simple as sometimes implied. For historic architecture is much more than a reflection of tastes past, of transitory whims which time has conveniently congealed for examination. It always involved much more than merely utilitarian construction to meet some direct or physical need, or expression of materials and constructional techniques, no matter how eloquent or eye-catching such technological expressions might be. Architecture was always *about* something. Specifically, it was about values held by the people who had it built—their attitudes to life, their assumptions (sometimes conscious, sometimes not) about what is real and what is important.[1] These not only determine what people like in art at any given time, but, more importantly, on them necessarily rest all the fundamental institutions of any society at any given time. Architecture historically was always a prime means of reinforcing those values—of promoting, transmitting, even formulating them. It did so by means of forms understood within given societies as visual metaphors of value and thence of the validity of institutions they underlie. Such visual metaphors

were created through combinations of styles and types.

All buildings belong to some type, and the historic types of architecture can be best categorized in terms of the institutions they were made to serve. For example, Monument/Tomb is an ancient architectural type, made from earliest times to serve institutions by which the past of a society is commemorated; all societies have had such institutions because without any relation of past to future there can be no society at all. Another ancient architectural type is Sanctuary/Shrine, which also serves an institution universal in all societies. This study posits eight other historic architectural types, which since time immemorial have stood for and served institutions universally: Wall/Fort (defense), Shelter (conservation), Homestead (family), Palace (government), Public Works, Mansion (class status), Shop (commerce), Amenities (communal life). Within each basic type, there are broad subtypes and specific subtypes (listed in the appendix). Under Monument/Tomb comes, for example, the broad subtype Pillar/Stele, within which are war memorials, monuments to culture heroes, signs, graffiti, and flagpoles; subtype Tomb, with tombstones, mausolea, funerary sculpture; subtype Plot/Park, with cemetery parks, civic parks, monumental and/or ornamental fountains, gardens, lawn ornaments, and popular and private sculpture in public places, including Chamber of Commerce monuments, crèches, mailboxes. The Amenities type includes (among others) subtype Public Service, including hospitals and public libraries, and subtype Public Social/Recreational, such as clubs or lodges, theaters, and museums. At the very least, the list in the appendix gives some idea of the vast complexity of the architectural landscape of North America.

Each historical architectural type has had, and

Social function, not physical function, is what determines the form and significance of a visual metaphor, hence what architecture is. The Tomb of the Living King at Samarkand (USSR) is architecture not because its forms are grand or magnificent or because they serve a physical function effectively—in fact this complex has no physical function; nobody lives or works in it. It is architecture because it serves to memorialize the institution of kingship central to the Islamic society that built this group in the fourteenth century: since time immemorial such domical shapes, sequences of forms, and distinctive color schemes have had associations in the Levant and Central Asia with beliefs about the sacred, the royal, and the eternal. Inscriptions reinforce the meaning, as is common in most architecture at most times. Conversely, the shelter in the foreground of this 1974 photograph is a utilitarian building (and would be so anywhere) not because its forms are mean or its materials poor, not because of the lowly physical function it serves, but because it serves only that immediate function by forms unassociated with any public meaning or institutions. (IMG:NAL)

continues to require, a characteristic set of basic elements. If the type is to create an effective visual metaphor of the institution it stands for, its basic elements must evoke appropriate psychic recall (associations conscious or unconscious), attitudes, reactions, emotions.[2] Notions of what is appropriate have varied from era to era, and in every era— except for Modern, just past—have been debated and discussed. While there has never been general agreement, there has always been a kind of consensus.[3] It is expressed, in necessarily simplistic and tentative terms, in the accompanying table. Collectively these characteristics embody the social function of architecture types; how well any one of them, any single building, carries out its required social function is determined by its style.

Besides belonging to types and subtypes, all buildings except utilitarian structures can also be categorized in terms of style. Whereas "type" is a matter of physical use and social function, "style" is constituted by visual effects, of three sorts: ornament, proportion, and shapes. Certain combinations of these bring certain ideas and associations to mind, sometimes in conscious literary ways, sometimes subliminally; that is how styles historically have "worked." On that premise, eight basic styles found in North American buildings above the utilitarian level are posited here, each with numerous substyles (again listed in the appendix). Colonial styles, whose associations historically were a prime means for transmitting ideas, attitudes, and values from the Old to the New World, were succeeded by Classical Revival styles, which by contrast promoted principles of the American Revolution and the new government emerging from it, through allusion to what was taken to be its primary inspiration, the republics of classical antiquity. Picturesque styles of various sorts promoted, among

Basic Architectural Types: Functions, Qualities, Process, Elements

Basic Type	Physical Function	Social Function	Evocative Qualities	Psychic Process	Basic Elements
A. Monument and Tomb	None	Commemoration; before any semiotic patterns, memory must lift minds above stream of immediate events	Reverence (inspiration; exhortation)	Up/down; high/low	Upright/plot/mound/arch
B. Shrine and Sanctuary	Setting for ceremonies/rituals binding community	Perpetuate over generations values/belief systems	Awe; decorum	Mass/void; solid/ephemeral; heavy/light	Upright/plot/mound/arch, all elaborated plus roof
C. Wall and Fort	Guard against attacks	Provide security for work/leisure	Safety	Within/without	Wall and door; porch/arcade; curtain
D. Shelter	Protects man, food, beasts, tools	Perpetuates traditional spaces	"Rightness" (through traditional proportions)	Same as C	Same as C
E. Homestead	Facilities for family-raising	Visual metaphor of institution of the family	Roots; sense of belonging	Naturalness (as compared to artificiality of palace); way things are	Same as C and D, plus hearth/chimney
F. Palace	Living and working space for rulers	Visual metaphor of legitimate and necessary authority	Dignity	Artificiality/order; high/low	Tower; stair; controlled sequential spaces
G. Public Works	Physical foundations of civilized life	Promote social trust; advertise merits of regime	Stability; permanence; reliability	Solid/flimsy; permanent/transient	Not applicable
H. Mansion	Same as E, plus servants	Proclaims superior social status	Luxury	Have/have not	Selections from E and F, plus ornament
J. Shop	Facility for distributing goods or services	Promotes material well-being	Openness; availability	Open/closed; void/solid; simple/complex	Compartmentalized spaces, defined
K. Amenities	Facilities for community welfare and recreation	Promote human well-being	Graciousness; (generous, as compared to niggardly) comfortable	Rich/barren; spacious/cramped	Any of the above

Table suggesting ways historic architectural types have been conceived in terms of social function: evocative qualities that have made them "work" in and for society at given times; psychic processes involved in creating such qualities; and some basic interrelationships of architectural forms and spaces.

other things, romantic images of luxury attainable through free-enterprise capitalism. Modern styles insinuated the primacy of scientific attitudes. And so on.

Each basic style category, again, has numerous substyles. Under the basic Picturesque, for instance, is a range of substyles from Italianate through Second Empire to Queen Anne, Shingle, and Richardsonian Romanesque, all distinguished by emphasis on certain eye-catching qualities; under the basic Classical Revival are such substyles as Roman Revival, Greek Revival, Egyptian Revival, and a wide range of vernaculars.

A basic premise of this study is that it is the relation of style to type, substyle to subtype, that determines the effectiveness of any architecture; that is, creates visual metaphors and makes them effective or not. Inherent in this premise are implications for both understanding North American architecture in the past and practicing it in the Postmodern present, when opportunities for exploring and employing this kind of basic style/type vocabulary have opened up as rarely before.

Notes

1. Three or four decades ago the matter couldn't have been stated so baldly; then dominant were such definitions as Le Corbusier's "L'architecture, c'est un jeu savant, correct, et magnifique des volumes assemblés sous la lumière" (*Vers une Architecture,* Paris, 1923, p. 6) and Nikolaus Pevsner's *Outline of European Architecture,* distinguishing Lincoln Cathedral as architecture from a bicycle shed, which was "mere building," because the cathedral was "designed with a view to aesthetic appeal." On such facile subjective reasonings a later era now looks back in wonder, retorting that even if a bicycle shed had magnificent forms—a princely shed with grand Doric colonnades or rich fan-vaulting—it would still not be architecture; that the Parthenon would be architecture even if its grand play of volumes in light turned out—as is indeed the case—to be entirely incidental to its builders' purposes. For a building becomes architecture only when its forms refer in some way to an area of meaning. As J. Mordaunt Crook recently wrote with great felicity (in *The Dilemma of Style,* University of Chicago Press, 1987, p. 116), "Architecture is not simply a mechanical contrivance but an essay in the art of communication, a complex web of memories and messages."

2. Only a jejeune sort of popular science mentality could have imagined that style as it had developed and existed in world architecture for thousands of years could be permanently discarded. Throughout the high noon of Modernism, evidence was being assembled from all sorts of fields—biology and psychology most notably, but also physics—that the mind is less a tabula rasa than a reservoir: our psychic nature harbors a vast mass of images that has accumulated over millions of years of living development and become fixed in the organism. Such insights were applied in Priscilla Roberts's pioneering historical study *The Revolutions of 1848* (Princeton University Press, 1952): deep unconscious assumptions held by the revolutionaries themselves inhibited them at critical moments from implementing the drastic changes their rational minds proposed. If any, all, or part of such speculations are true, then style in architecture is an integral part of the human heritage and cannot be discarded at will.

3. It was a frequent subject for speculation by Renaissance architects and theoreticians, among them Alberti and Francesco di Giorgio; it was of prime concern to eighteenth-century academics (François Blondel) and Revolutionaries (Ledoux, Boullée) alike. Still in the early twentieth century leading American architects were aware of it: Louis Sullivan's concept that "Form follows function" referred to a metaphysical kind of function and not, as Modernist mechanistic enthusiasms would have it, to physical function. "Thus the St. Nicholas Hotel 'idea' hung on the banquet hall, the Ryerson Tomb . . . the eternal cycle of life, and the Transportation Building . . . 'holiday' excitement" (Robert Twombley, *Louis Sullivan,* New York: Viking, 1987, p. 278). Frank Lloyd Wright's many comparable concepts have been set out in Norris Kelly Smith, *Frank Lloyd Wright: A Study in Architectural Content* (New York, 1968; reprint, Watkins Glen, N.Y.: American Life Foundation, 1974).

Modernism killed interest in the subject among high-style architects for two generations. But concern for effects on the public has continually preoccupied Popular/Commercial designers. A seminal study for architectural thinking has been the civil engineer David P. Billington's "Structures and Machines—the Two Sides of Technology," in *Soundings* (Fall 1974), which defined the difference between structures and machines in terms of their psychological effects. Structures such as roads, bridges, waterworks, and powerplants were by their nature static, immovable, long-lived, and permanent, changing features and techniques only slowly. In contrast, machines such as cars, trains, pumps, motors, television sets, and computers were by their nature dynamic, short-lived, and disposable, continually becoming obsolescent. Structures are generally on a big scale, unique, and custom-made for given sites, requiring a long time to build; machines are generally small-scaled, mass-produced, built quickly for private consumption. "Our society has stressed change," Billington concluded. "We have become as restless as machines. . . . We have neglected such ideals as repose, permanence, uniqueness of scale, and patience. . . . In short, the value and qualities of structures need to be reaffirmed." Such thoughts as these could be effective guidelines for designing buildings of the Public Works type.

STYLES AND TYPES
OF
NORTH AMERICAN
ARCHITECTURE

1.1. Reconstruction of Martin's Hundred settlement on the James River near Williamsburg, Virginia, as it looked in March 1622 before the Indian attack that destroyed it. Painting by Richard Schlecht (© National Geographic Society) based on research in Ivor Noël Hume's book Martin's Hundred *(New York: Knopf, 1982). White settlement in North America usually began with such a brief recapitulation of European prehistory; here early seventeenth-century Englishmen relived the beginnings of their civilization, in the era before Charlemagne.*

1
UTILITARIAN BUILDING:
INFRASTRUCTURE OF CIVILIZATION

Utilitarian Building
in Its Time and Place

American history is a part of world history. American architecture is a chapter in world architecture. Utilitarian buildings were the first on the American landscape, as they were everywhere in the world.

Utilitarian building is the basis of all historical architecture, the bottom layer on all landscapes. It is the first kind of building people do anywhere, and has no defined range in time and space. It does not belong in any line of progress from one historical point to another. It lies outside history, timeless. Utilitarian is by far the oldest category of building, going back to crude windbreaks and cave-mouth barriers prehistoric aeons ago; it is also contemporary, as every late-twentieth-century landscape has its share of roads and trails, sheds and shelters, bridges and tunnels and fences built in direct physical response to some need. And no doubt utilitarian will be the last kind of human building as the world ends.

Thus the history of North American architecture does not begin when the Spaniards arrived. Others had come long before them. Thousands of years before Columbus, settlement began via a land bridge from extreme northeast Asia; that there were other significant arrivals—from Polynesia, China, Japan, or the Mediterranean, in various times and places—is at the very least an open question. Why not begin a book on American architecture, then, with the buildings of these peoples, the "first Americans"? That it has not been done is certainly not for lack of interest in the topic or awareness of its importance, still less because Indians happened to come out losers from recent centuries of wars to command the continent. Rather,

the kinds of architecture built by Europeans and Indians were products of totally different mindsets; there is no continuity between them. What Octavio Paz called in his review of Schele and Miller's *Blood of Kings* (*New York Review of Books*, 26 February 1987) "the psychological paralysis, the torpor that immobilized Mesoamerican societies when they confronted the Spaniards" remained a constant factor; "they lacked the intellectual and historical categories in which to place these beings who had come from no one knew where." And the whites had no place for Indians in their cosmology, either. Beings without concepts of individuality or personal property, who tortured themselves and others mercilessly and who seemed unable to conceive abstract propositions, fitted into neither liberal Enlightenment views about the goodness of mankind, nor rationalist confidence in the powers of the human mind to comprehend all the world and match the angels at last, nor traditional Christianity premised on self-awareness of sin. So they could not live together. Histories of their architecture are separate enterprises, or different chapters in a study of world history in architecture.

Everywhere in world history the infrastructure of utilitarian building involved a record of some kind of conquest. So it was in North America. Perhaps there was once a time when occupation of a land did not involve displacing peoples already there. But that time lies far back in prehistory, and in any event involved a conquest of sorts. Throughout all of recorded history, settling a land has meant occupying it and defending it against anyone already on the ground. And the first manifestation of conquest, whether over nature or animals or earlier occupiers, is necessarily some kind of utilitarian structures defended by walls, fences, ditches, or forts. So it had been in the Americas before any whites arrived; and when they came, they continued a long tradition of their own, for conquest of the Americas was a terminal phase of a much wider expansion of Indo-European peoples that had begun thousands of years before in Eurasia.[1] The landscape shaped by the first white settlement of America was the last of a long series of comparable records, which everywhere began with fort-like settlements constructed of whatever materials were available—poles and palisades in forests, sod on prairies, stone in deserts, adobe where suns were hot enough to bake.

Most such architectural landscapes have long since vanished. A few can be reconstructed, thanks to archaeology—like the fort and straggling shelters of Wolstenholme Towne on Martin's Hundred near Williamsburg, reconstructed as it was just before the Indian massacre that destroyed it in 1622 *[1.1]*. Excavation here showed that, however makeshift the materials, the design of the fortifications incorporated sophisticated European experiences of fort planning to provide covering fields of fire. This was also true of its legendary predecessor Fort Raleigh, the "Lost Colony" of 1585, excavated by J. C. Harrington on Roanoke Sound in North Carolina in the 1940s. Such primitive, utilitarian stages of settlement were usually brief; by 1676, just fifty years after fragile Wolstenholme Towne was sacked, the colony of Virginia was supplying (according to Wilcomb Washburn's *The Governor and the Rebel,* 1957, p. 9) over 100,000 pounds sterling annual revenue to the British treasury!

Sometimes white conquest of North America is evoked by obscure surviving "pioneer monuments," often nearly submerged in suburban sprawl. One such monument is the small fenced and treed plot outside Susanville in one of California's far northeast valleys, where settler Peter Lassen was "killed by Indians 1857" and his grave marked by a wooden upright with cross-piece, set into a mound *[1.2]*. Everything here is utilitarian, to be sure: plain wire fence, simple turnstile of iron and wood, plank bridge over roadside ditch. Yet in this simple arrangement, elemental instances of three primary and timeless types of historic architecture are coalesced: Monument, Sanctuary, Fort. Upright and mound are the primordial forms of Monument; sacred space (including, as so often in America, a grove)[2] the primordial essence of Sanctuary; fence and ditch the primordial elements of Fort. All are capable to some degree of evoking, as all such types should, emotions of reverence, awe,

and security (or resentment and hostility, depending on circumstances) in anyone of elementary sensitivity.

Any utilitarian form can thus be invested with associations or otherwise acquire a social, as distinct from physical, function. Even so supremely prosaic a utilitarian form as the rail, snake, or worm fence, made with a single simple tool and assembled in the most direct manner to provide protection for and from animals, could on occasion come to have a social function quite distinct from its original physical one: as symbol of sturdy yeoman virtue helping to elect, among others, Abraham ("Old Abe the Rail-Splitter") Lincoln; as symbol of heroism from its associations with the Civil War (many are the haunting photos of the dead piled up against such fences at Antietam, Gettysburg, New Market *[1.3]*). When it comes to definition, then, utilitarian is far from simple.

Definition and Identifying Characteristics

There is no such thing as a utilitarian architecture; there is only utilitarian building. Utilitarian building may be defined as structures made to serve physical functions only, for some immediate material purpose, without style (that is, without combinations of ornament, shape, or proportioned forms deliberately chosen for effect or dictated by folk custom).

Utilitarian building does not automatically produce architecture, sooner or later; nor is its appearance on a landscape necessarily an indication of civilization inevitably to come, for it has none of those associations, symbolisms, signings, or interactions with higher thought which are at once the cause and result of civilization. Utilitarian building is, rather, the infrastructure of civilization. On the economic life made possible by roads and bridges, trails and barriers, shelters and forts civilization can be built; such utilitarian structures are its prerequisites but not its manifestation. For it is only when humans begin to see their shelters and services in symbolic terms, as analogically related to the ideas and practices and rituals of the institutions on which their lives center, that architecture proper can appear.

Defined as the most direct and easiest way of accommodating some physical function, utilitarian building cannot be identified by any particular material or shape or proportion. Any and all sorts of construction can be involved in it, from the simplest assemblages of boards and nails to the most complex technological marvels. What characterizes buildings as utilitarian is intent. And intent is not of course verifiable by sight. You can't tell by looking; you have to *know* what a utilitarian building was done for, and the knowledge is acquired from experience at various stages of life, especially childhood. Indeed, to study the beginnings of a civilization in its utilitarian building is to study our own beginnings—ontogeny repeats phylogeny.

Similar principles apply in furniture. Utilitarian furniture is not to be identified by any particular materials or techniques, but by intent and use.

"Utilitarian furniture" usually brings to mind something primitive, like the "unhewed trees" the founders of Jamestown sat upon, according to John Smith's *Advertisements for the Unexperienced Planters of New England, or anywhere* (London, 1631), or the table legs made "from the perfectly straight limbs of any tree" or chairs from "sticks of ash . . . the pieces should be an inch and a half or two inches thick, and should have the bark peeled off" prescribed in C. P. Dwyer's *Immigrant Builder, or Practical Hints to Handy-Men* for men who wanted to "plan and construct dwellings in the bush, on the prairie, or anywhere . . . in Wood, Earth, and Gravel" (Philadelphia, 1872). "Survivals of utilitarian furniture" thus often mean the early-twentieth-century "log

1.2. Peter Lassen's grave and "sanctuary grove" outside Susanville, California. Original monument c. 1858; stone shaft of c. 1880 with inscription preserved under wooden shelter; the whole restored with surrounding fence, c. 1960. (IMG:NAL)

1.3. Monument to the 54th Regiment of Pennsylvania volunteers, on the 1862 Civil War battlefield at New Market, Virginia. Originally erected c. 1880, restored with snake/rail/worm fence, c. 1965. (IMG:NAL)

style" vogue in vacation and summer cottages, or furnishings of historic restorations like James Marshall's Cabin at Coloma ("where California began" with his gold strike in 1849), or stools made of wooden slabs standing on three or four rough-hewn sticks around the servants' table of a New England kitchen (as in the John Ward house in Salem), or perhaps some WPA photograph from the 1930s of tenement kitchens with trestle tables and exposed sink pipes.

These "survivals" overlook some of utilitarian furniture's most common manifestations, in portable, collapsible furniture for temporary use, like the folding chairs carried to picnics or to parade routes [1.4]. Such furniture and all its counterparts in card tables and canvas stools and bookcases that can be dismantled—utilitarian because made to meet an immediate purpose by the most direct means—became common from the mid-nineteenth century on, along with many other kinds of convertible furniture in varieties of Picturesque styles (cf. Chapter 5). Some versions of it, given appropriately "scientific" pedigrees, jargon names, and manifestos, later rose in the world to become masterpieces of Modern design. But the original utilitarian forms have continued on the market, changed only in material from wood and canvas to aluminum and plastic.

Social Function

By definition, utilitarian buildings have only a physical function and cannot therefore have a social

1.4. This "Folding Camp Chair" of wood and canvas, one of many such items illustrated in the 1905 American and Canadian Sportsmen's Encyclopaedia, *is sturdily and definably utilitarian: its construction is dictated by physical function alone, and its use is occasional and seasonal (for beach, backyard, porch).*

function proper; that is, they cannot deliberately and regularly involve any sort of visual metaphor of ideas which perpetuate civilization, cannot transmit its attitudes and values, and cannot make the world more intelligible or beautiful to beholders. Of course in practice social functions do in fact devolve upon them by circumstance.

Substyles

Structures without ornament, mimetic shapes, or traditional proportions cannot have style, since those are the basic elements required for style formation. What you do find in utilitarian structures, as a sort of counterpart, are certain visual effects or patterns produced by materials used in a utilitarian way.

Such "stylistic effects" include textural or pattern effects of sod and earth, thatch and branch, log, timber, board/siding/picket, shingle, adobe/mud brick, brick, tile, mortarless stone, rubble, fieldstone, cobblestone, cut-stone masonry, sheet metal, iron, concrete block, cast/ferroconcrete, glass, stucco, artificial facings like permastone, exposed post-and-lintel in wood or concrete or iron, and molded materials like concrete shells or pisé. In utilitarian building these effects are not consciously stylistic nor used in any symbolic way, but they constitute base elements which can be and often have been used in styles proper.

Modern architecture, especially in its earlier and more enthusiastic days, was frequently described as simply the direct use of materials and the honest expression of structure. What is the difference between that high style and simple utilitarian building? Most notably, of course, the materials and structure of Modern architecture were selected with a keen eye to their effects on beholders. But more philosophically, structure and materials were important to Modernists for their own sakes, as stylistic elements, whereas in utilitarian building they are only means to an end. Thus in his *Space, Time and Architecture* of 1941, for decades the Bible of Modernism, Siegfried Giedion cited balloon timber-framing and prefabricated metal skeleton construction as examples of lost opportunities for nineteenth-century America to take the lead in developing a "functional" architecture whose style would derive directly from its technology. But this is to misunderstand what those inventions were about. They were ingenious devices for meeting immediate needs for quickly produced houses and

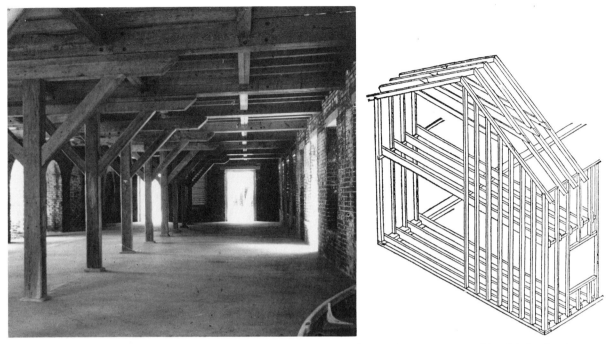

1.5. The art of architecture begins with a construction technology, and goes on from there. In utilitarian building, by contrast, the technology of structure and materials is all there is. Thus the shape of the timbers used to build this sail-drying shed at Nelson's Dockyard in Antigua c. 1790, during Britain's long Caribbean wars with America and France, was determined wholly by the building's function. Their shapes would never acquire symbolic significance from such utilitarian uses. But ages before, shapes much like them had been employed to construct homes for Aryan gods and chiefs, become symbols reproduced mimetically in stone, and ultimately refined into the orders of Greek, Indian, and Persian architecture. (IMG:NAL)

1.6. An immense improvement on traditional timber-framing was the technique developed in Chicago in the 1830s called "balloon-framing," from its lightness compared to traditional mortice- and tenon-pinned construction. As the easiest and cheapest way to build, it soon became the normal basis for wooden buildings throughout America. But it always remained a utilitarian means to an end, merely providing a frame that could be overlaid with details or proportioned to any stylistic formula. (George E. Woodward, The Country Gentleman, *15 April 1860, from Paul Sprague, "Origin of Balloon Framing," in* Journal of the Society of Architectural Historians *40/2 [1981]:312)*

shops.[3] In nineteenth-century America (and the West generally), mechanization had not yet taken command, machines did not yet dictate to their human inventors. Balloon- and metal-framed buildings took whatever shape their constructors chose to give them, not what scantlings and girders decreed [1.5, 1.6, 1.7].

Also the Modernist self-conscious usage of materials so as to bring out their character (the metalness of steel, the chunkiness of concrete) was in fact the direct opposite of utilitarian usage. Where physical function requires it, utilitarian buildings disguise the nature of their materials, and their structure too: fieldstone walls are plastered for protection from frost, wooden trussed bridges are roofed against rot, steel bridges painted against corrosion, concrete walls paneled on the inside to make rooms warmer, and so on.

Application of Utilitarian Building to Architectural Types

On only three basic architectural types can utilitarian building be to any real degree satisfactory: Public Works, Shelter/Shed/Factory, and Fort.

Utilitarian public works on occasion can command a kind of majesty, when the directness of utilitarian building produces effects of substantiality appropriate to structures that form the physical foundations of society. One familiar example would be those tall and dramatic watertowers of metal or concrete that often so dominate the approaches or skyline of small towns as to constitute monuments to their community enterprise [1.8]. Another would be atomic energy plants, whose huge cooling towers—utilitarian forms dictated directly by materials and physical function—dominate landscapes for

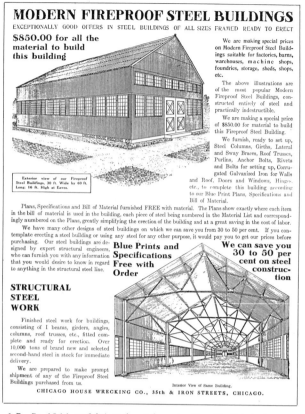

MODERN FIREPROOF STEEL BUILDINGS
EXCEPTIONALLY GOOD OFFERS IN STEEL BUILDINGS OF ALL SIZES FRAMED READY TO ERECT

$850.00 for all the material to build this building

We are making special prices on Modern Fireproof Steel Buildings suitable for factories, barns, warehouses, machine shops, foundries, storage, sheds, shops, etc.

The above illustrations are of the most popular Modern Fireproof Steel Buildings, constructed entirely of steel and practically indestructible.

We are making a special price of $850.00 for material to build this Fireproof Steel Building.

We furnish, ready to set up, Steel Columns, Girths, Lateral and Sway Braces, Roof Trusses, Purlins, Anchor Bolts, Rivets and Bolts for setting up, Corrugated Galvanized Iron for Walls and Roof, Doors and Windows, Hinges, etc., to complete this building according to our Blue Print Plans, Specifications and Bill of Material.

Exterior view of our Fireproof Steel Buildings, 30 ft. Wide by 60 ft. Long; 16 ft. High at Eaves.

Plans, Specifications and Bill of Material furnished FREE with material. The Plans show exactly where each item in the bill of material is used in the building, each piece of steel being numbered in the Material List and correspondingly numbered on the Plans, greatly simplifying the erection of the building and at a great saving in the cost of labor.

We have many other designs of steel buildings on which we can save you from 30 to 50 per cent. If you contemplate erecting a steel building or using any steel for any other purpose, it would pay you to get our prices before purchasing. Our steel buildings are designed by expert structural engineers, who can furnish you with any information that you would desire to know in regard to anything in the structural steel line.

Blue Prints and Specifications Free with Order

We can save you 30 to 50 per cent on steel construction

STRUCTURAL STEEL WORK

Finished steel work for buildings, consisting of I beams, girders, angles, columns, roof trusses, etc., fitted complete and ready for erection. Over 10,000 tons of brand new and selected second-hand steel in stock for immediate delivery.

We are prepared to make prompt shipment of any of the Fireproof Steel Buildings purchased from us.

Interior View of Same Building.

CHICAGO HOUSE WRECKING CO., 35th & IRON STREETS, CHICAGO.

1.7. By 1911 prefabricated metal construction like this had become common. Advertised by the Chicago House Wrecking Company as "designed by expert structural engineers" and applicable to "factories, barns, warehouses, machine shops, foundries, storage sheds, shops, &c.," it remained a utilitarian technology and never became a "style."

miles around and evoke so wide a range of emotions, from awe to horror. Roads on occasion have a kind of majesty too, especially those which have some sort of national associations, like survivors of the old National Roads and the later twentieth-century interstates. But majesty is most often found in utilitarian bridges.

Bridges show utilitarian building at its most visually effective. Many small bridges, early and late, have been so visually attractive as to make their utilitarianism debatable *[1.9, 1.10]*. Shouldn't those wonderful early Federal arched stone bridges like "Burnside's" over Antietam Creek or the Perikomen River bridge at Collegeville, Pennsylvania, be looked on as a variety of Colonial vernacular? Shouldn't those nineteenth-century covered bridges of the old Eastern states or early-twentieth-century arched concrete spans be considered works

of Romantic art, especially since most no longer serve their original practical purpose? As for really big-scale bridges, here is utilitarian building at its visual best: the Eads over the Mississippi at St. Louis *[1.11]*, the Brooklyn Bridge over the East River (cf. 4.48), and the Golden Gate Bridge over San Francisco Bay *[1.12]*. Soaring, swinging thrusts of pylons and cables and arches so articulate the structure of such bridges as to make them "beautiful" in the classic Greek sense of intelligible to the beholding mind and eye—"great sights" in the primordial sense.

Utilitarian building is appropriate enough to Shed/Shelter as to give many of its subtypes some kind of symbolic significance and hence social function. So simple and naturally utilitarian a structure as the mass-produced privy, for example—nobody lives in one, nobody works in one, it has no association with any institution fundamental to society—in practice has become so identifiable by a "traditional" shape resulting from physical function as to become a symbol in a wide range of Popular/Commercial arts from postcards to mass-produced portables (chapter 8). Early factories and mills derived forms from barns that belonged to recognizable vernacular traditions *[1.13]*; mid- and later nineteenth-century factories became emblems of industrial enterprise and took variants of historic styles accordingly; and twentieth-century factories often took self-consciously Modern styles as emblems of scientific endeavor (chapters 2, 6, 7). The specialized physical functions of their relatives the grain elevators produced distinctive shapes that early acquired more than utilitarian value: high, wooden, upended rectangles standing tall over Great Plains almost immediately became a Western prairie image in song and story and paint; massive complexes of concrete cylinders and cubes at major shipping centers *[1.14]* inspired Modernists to adulation[4] and emulation. None of this, however, prevented their disappearance when agribusiness demanded clusters of metal drums, in shape recalling the very earliest round, wooden-staved elevators of the 1870s, connected by feeder pipes and strutted towers.

As for Fort type, no matter how simple its elements, nonmaterial values of various kinds accrue naturally to them. Only in the most immediate and temporary situations—wooden or wire fences seasonally protecting garden plots or grazing lands, for instance—do they remain strictly utilitarian. Often, though not necessarily, such values derive

1.8. The town water tank, standing in the main (and only) public square of Pocahontas, Illinois, was built to meet a severely and strictly practical need. Yet, simply by its central location and by being the village's largest man-made object, it also serves something of the traditional social function of the Monument type. Announcing the hamlet's presence from afar, it becomes a monument to community resources and community aspirations, much like ceremonial fountains in other times and cultures. (IMG:NAL 1986)

1.9. Detail of a four-arched cut-stone bridge over the Perikomen River at Collegeville, Pennsylvania. Such bridges were common in the early decades of the nineteenth century. This detail shows the easternmost of the three buttresses, which were designed with

projections to deflect flood debris and ice floes as well as to provide springing for the arch, whose keystone is here visible. Benjamin Latrobe sketched this one, as a thing of beauty seen on his American travels, soon after it was opened on 4 November 1799. (IMG:NAL)

1.10. Guy Rothwell and Fred Orht, engineer/designers, built this reinforced concrete bridge in 1921 over Anahulu Stream at a point where it flows into the Pacific Ocean at Haleiwa, Hawaii. It was one of a number of similar bridges on the new Kamehameha Highway circling Oahu; most have now been replaced. Though proportions were dictated strictly by physical function, it would be hard to improve upon them by conscious design. (IMG:NAL)

1.11 (left). This stereopticon view of the Eads Bridge, one of many Keystone Views cards from the 1880s, shows the only great bridge to be named after a designer: Captain James B. Eads, who used steelmaking capacities developed in the Civil War to put spans over the Mississippi between St. Louis and East St. Louis high enough for shipping to pass beneath. An accompanying text invites children to marvel at both its technology (described in detail) and its "magnificence."

1.12 (below, left). The Golden Gate Bridge, like the Brooklyn Bridge an American icon almost from the day it was finished (in 1937), was designed by Irving Morrow (consulting architect) and Joseph Straus (chief engineer), to carry US 101 from the city of San Francisco to the peninsula opposite, and then north along the Pacific Coast. (IMG:NAL)

1.13 (below, right). Utilitarian factory buildings in various stages of ruin—abandoned once their immediate use ended—like this "Old Hundred" Mill and Mine in the Silverton region of San Juan County, Colorado, can be seen throughout the Rocky Mountains. (Colorado State Advertising & Publicity)

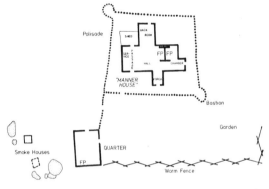

1.14. *An example of the visual qualities that gave grain elevators their title "cathedrals of the plains" is this cluster of concrete silos at Paoli in eastern Colorado, built c. 1929. At left is a small wooden elevator, characteristic of the period c. 1900–20. Both forms are now obsolete. (IMG:NAL)*

1.15. *Plan of "The Clifts," ancestor of "Stratford," seat of the Lees of Virginia, as reconstructed by Fraser D. Neiman, in "Domestic Architecture at the Clifts Plantation,"* Common Places, *figure 3. Note corner "bastions" connected by a palisade "erected in 1675 in response to the depredations of the Susquehannock Indians . . . dismantled soon afterward," and the "worm fence" protecting the garden.*

from those geometric shapes inherent in most Fort design, which are perceptible in the corner towers at Martin's Hundred *[1.1]* or a half-century later at "The Clifts" *[1.15]*. They are well developed a half-century after that in Governor Spottswood's Arsenal at Williamsburg, on which Governor Keith of Pennsylvania complimented him, as successive *Williamsburg Guides* record, for being "so well acquainted with Figures, and so good a Mathematician that his Skill in Architecture is yet to be seen in Virginia by the building of an elegant safe Magazine" *[1.16]*. In our own times the half-cylindrical metal-sheet Quonset hut, a utilitarian solution to an immediate problem if ever there was one (the World War II need for cheap, mass-producible, quickly erected shelters for stores and personnel), somehow became a shape symbolic of American resourcefulness and adaptability; people were proud to live in them or use them for small businesses.[5]

Use of utilitarian building for other types—such as Sanctuary, Shop, Amenities, Homestead, Mansion, or Palace (Government)—involves various degrees of contradiction in terms.

Obviously utilitarian forms are not very satisfactory for Sanctuary, whose function is in essence nonpractical (trance, ritual, worship, meditation—none of these exercises are dictated by material practicality). A utilitarian Sanctuary would be makeshift at best, like the pile of stones which, according to Genesis, served the patriarch Jacob to commemorate a spiritual experience. A more recent example is the grove, plank benches, and canvas tents which, according to Ellen Weiss,[6] seemed after the high spiritual excitement of a successful religious revival to be infused with a spiritual aura ("Surely the Lord is in this place") and was preserved accordingly. "At meeting's end, money was raised to purchase the lumber used for the benches and [preaching] stand and the decision taken to keep this now sa-

1.16. The Arsenal (Magazine) at Williamsburg, 1715. A high wall around it, built during the French and Indian wars (1754–63), pulled down in the nineteenth century, but rebuilt by Colonial Williamsburg, helped create the within/without effect essential for the psychological functioning of Fort types in and for society. Inherent in the Fort type is a symbolic statement of the presence of authority; this became explicit during the Revolutionary disturbances at Williamsburg. (IMG:NAL)

1.17. The Wesleyan Grove campsite on Martha's Vineyard in 1858. (H. Vincent, History of the Wesleyan Grove Camp Meeting, *1858, reproduced in Ellen Weiss,* City in the Woods.)

cred spot as a permanent one for camp meetings" *[1.17].* Examples of utilitarian buildings on sites so hallowed can still be found *[1.18].*

Obviously utilitarian forms of Shop have their uses on temporary occasions: as roadside fruit stands, tables at church socials, small ticket booths for a high school's football games—anywhere that assertion of an agent's reputation and reliability is not essential (that is, by an appearance of richness or at least solvent stability), or complicated transactions of goods and services are not required. Attempts to run a permanent business enterprise

from utilitarian premises would be clearly self-defeating.

Less obvious is the possiblity of an Amenities type in utilitarian quarters. It seems paradoxical, since an amenity is by definition something above and beyond strict community necessity. You can live and die without going to a hospital or having a concert hall or library or clubhouse in your community. But the paradox of a "utilitarian Amenity" can be instructive; to come across some shedlike structure of plywood or tar paper or corrugated tin lettered "Community Hall" in the Indian or Hispanic

1.18. Faith Tabernacle Camp, on Maryland Route 7 between the communities of Elkton and North East, which was made primarily *to serve for shelter during camp meetings held at irregular intervals. (IMG:NAL)*

section of some desolate town is to appreciate how impoverished is a community without community pride, how necessary are buildings styled to assert and maintain it.

A "utilitarian Homestead" also seems a contradiction in terms, as the idea of home obviously involves implications of permanence, roots, and psychic if not physical comfort. Yet such associations can and do attach to temporary utilitarian buildings. Not, perhaps, to those pits in the Delaware riverbank or the Pilgrims' "wigwams," beloved only in fatuous pioneer legend. But certainly to log cabins, adobes, prairie "soddies," and the like—history and survivors alike attest to that *[1.19, 1.20]*.

Only the idea of Mansion or Palace in utilitarian forms involves a complete contradiction in terms. You could imagine a school being housed temporarily in some kind of shed (like surplus army huts used on campuses just after World War II) or a shed serving government facilities on some primitive frontier (Judge Roy Bean's "Jersey Lily" Pecos County courthouse in Langtry, Texas, which included a bar and billiard room, is a historic example). But such structures can convey nothing of superior social status, hence they cannot have the social function of Mansion nor serve to inculcate authority. Nor can they have the social function of Palace. All higher social functions, in fact, demand architecture.

At what precise point in historic time utilitarian structures began to be elaborated into visual metaphors of ideas is of course unknowable. But by the

time North America was settled, any building above stark subsistence level betrayed some traces of those innate preferences for particular proportions and combinations of masses and voids which from the beginning of history collectively constituted instinctive metaphors of "rightness" for their makers and thus helped create distinctive self-awareness for each people, race, and nation emerging into civilization. Thus in Virginia, Massachusetts, Quebec, Mexico, Peru—everywhere—this process was repeated in the sixteenth, seventeenth, and eighteenth centuries, but only for instants of time. In every tiny patch of settlement hacked out by Europeans, the first utilitarian structures were almost instantly replaced by others, hardly more technologically advanced, which had proportions and combinations distinct not only from comparable buildings by the native Indians, but also from each other. At this point the first Colonial styles proper could appear.

Utilitarian Building as Continuing Cultural Expression

By definition utilitarian building, not being specially related to any one era, cannot involve the kind of cultural expression made by architecture belonging to some particular style, either vernacular or high. What utilitarian building expresses, if intelligently read, is its technology.

Though the earliest structures to appear in white

settlements in North America may have looked much like and been much more utilitarian than those of the Indians (which, however primitive they looked to Europeans, were products of long tradition), they manifested a different technology—iron axes and saws and nails instead of Neolithic arrowheads and choppers. Another kind of technological expression in utilitarian building is represented by structures used in sugar-processing and by wind-

mills, water races, and the like, which recall how in the seventeenth and eighteenth centuries water and wind were still the principal power sources for Western civilization, as they had been for every other since civilization first appeared. And the technology of our own culture is expressed, for better or worse, in hydroelectric dams, atomic energy plants, transmission towers parading across hill and dale, and, most dramatically, in the apparatus of

1.19. Log cabin on the grounds of "Farmington" outside Louisville, Kentucky, originally built c. 1790 and so antedating erection of the well-known house (1807) built for Lucy Speed and her husband John on plans supplied, according to tradition, by Thomas Jefferson (both houses refurbished in the 1970s). Log cabins were a "first dwelling" on most sites and, like this one, were then preserved by conversion to other uses. Log cabins, however temporary their builders' dwelling intentions, were often informed by traditional folk-building principles of proportion and quasi-symmetry related to traditional vernaculars of the British Isles.

1.20. Comparable proportions and symmetry inform the William B. Ide homestead built c. 1849 of adobe brick outside Red Bluff, California, however different its materials from the "Farmington" cabin. (IMG:NAL)

agribusiness. About the latter, Peirce Lewis has written[7] what is perhaps the best description of the continuing cultural expression of utilitarian building:

> I remember, several springs ago, driving across the Llano Estacado of North Texas. . . . It was still early, and the irrigation was going full tilt. Gigantic silver monsters, half a section long, were crawling across the dark red earth, casting great arcs of water that shattered the white Texas sunlight into a cascade of diamonds. Everything was geometry and primal color—circles and planes and cylinders and parabolas and swirling prisms of transparent light. It was superb—dazzling. Then there are the new grain elevators, huge steel spiders with silver tentacles reaching down to grain bins or railroad cars or Mack trucks that look dwarfed underneath the giant that feeds them. Like the old-fashioned elevators of the plains, you can see these new ones a long way away . . . exuberant pieces of silver jewelry—the kind wrought by Scandinavians, not Navajos. Close up, they are as handsome as elegant pieces of abstract sculpture.

> The new landscapes are everywhere you go. Machines crawl across the Dakota prairies, leaving marvellous forms behind them. Fields are strewn with mows of hay like great rough loaves of brown bread, or bales of straw that look like huge improbable disks of Shredded Wheat. . . . The farm machinery is wonderful, too. Partly it's just color: the splendid primary reds and yellows and greens of those New Holland combines and Ferguson tractors. But it's form as well. Those great cotton-pickers with their air-conditioned cabs and built-in stereo sets are more than mere machines; they are architecture, where form follows function more truly than in most buildings, and with no trace of archness or apology.

> I know, I know. Those irrigation pumps are greedy parasites, sucking dry the aquifers of Texas and Nebraska, and those silver grain elevators are probably owned by some faceless cartel, making profits to buy guns for terrorists in unknown places halfway around the world. And the machinery spells the ruin of a culture. The small farmer has sold out or gone broke. . . . But . . . Must one admire an artist to admire his art?

Notes

1. In a world context, American history began in the second millennium B.C., with bands of Indo-European speakers infiltrating, overrunning, ultimately imposing their language family and its outlook on most of Europe, large parts of the Near East, India, and Ceylon. They became Persians and Hindus, Gauls and Greeks, Romans and Italians, Spaniards, French, Germans, British, and, finally, Americans. Such was the stuff indeed of much nineteenth-century American "universal history." Though such views have lost their appeal nowadays, the facts remain: exhibited in the museum at Little Bighorn, Montana, is a list of countries of origin of U. S. Seventh Cavalry personnel who perished during "Custer's Last Stand" (actually, of course, "the North American Indians' Last Stand"); it includes almost every nation of Europe.

2. J. B. Jackson, in "The Sacred Groves of America" (in his extraordinary collection of essays *The Necessity for Ruins and Other Topics* (Amherst: University of Massachusetts Press, 1980), recalls how many place names still survive in the United States with a component "Grove," indicating the presence, formerly and sometimes still, of a camp-meeting site. They were equivalents of the kinds of spaces revered as shrines in every culture, from Monte Alban and La Venta to Olympia and Ise.

3. In the fall of 1832 several factors converged, writes Paul E. Sprague: "The sudden and rapid growth of Chicago which generated a demand . . . , a shortage of timber and skilled carpenters, and an abundance of machine-cut nails and of small trees near Chicago suitable of being worked into scantling." The first balloon-framed building, according to Sprague, was a warehouse erected by George Snow "near the mouth of the Chicago River entirely out of scantling and nails" ("The Origin of Balloon Framing," *Journal of the Society of Architectural Historians* 40/2 [1981]:319). See also H. Ward Jandl, ed., *The Technology of Historic American Buildings: Studies of the Materials, Craft Processes, and the Mechanization of Building Construction* (Washington, D.C., 1983).

4. "The overall impact of . . . grain elevators, . . . silos, . . . coal sheds . . . can almost stand comparison with the buildings of Old Egypt."

So wrote the then obscure Walter Gropius, in "Die Entwicklung moderner Industriebaukunst," in the *Jahrbuch des deutschen Werkbunds* for 1913, using as one illustration a "Kornsilo und Elevator, Montreal." He was not concerned by the total difference in social function between the kinds of architecture he was comparing; he was interested only in the coincidence of great size and geometric shape.

5. The Quonset hut, according to an article by Tim Clark in *Yankee* (November 1985), was invented in Rhode Island by a team led by architect Otto Brandenberger and originally produced at Quonset Point from 1941 on. Its improvement over the Nissen hut of World War I, invented by British Col. Peter Nissen, consisted in all-curved walls rather than curved roof and straight walls; this meant that sandbags could be built almost over the whole structure without crushing it. Strictly utilitarian, then; but Quonset Hut village at Davisville, Rhode Island, a surviving part of now-defunct Camp Endicott, built in 1942, is on the National Register of Historic Places, and all sorts of people take special pride in Quonset hut dwellings or stores acquired as surplus property after World War II and duly personalized.

6. Ellen Weiss, *City in the Woods: Life and Design of an American Camp Meeting on Martha's Vineyard* (New York: Oxford University Press, 1987), p. 25.

7. Peirce Lewis, "Facing Up to Ambiguity: The Traditional Family Farm Is Disappearing," *Landscape* 26/1 (1982):80–81.

2.1. In 1866, at the very height of the Picturesque vogue in high-style American architecture, Currier and Ives ("Printmakers to the American People") scored a tremendous success with a series of four prints of "The American Homestead." They offered a different form for each of the seasons, but each was supposed to represent "colonial style." The episode attests unmistakably to the continuing popularity of "Colonial," even if specific substyles were not well differentiated: Spring here shows a vague coalescence of Southern Cabin with shingled Cape Cod.

2
COLONIES AND COLONIAL STYLES

Colonial Styles
in Their Times and Places

What is conventionally called the colonial era refers to a period between systematic colonization of the Americas by European powers begun in the sixteenth century and achievement of independence by the United States in 1776. This colonization took varied forms, but its fundamental principle was everywhere similar: transference of distinctive social and political institutions from the Old World to the New; specifically, transferring cultures produced by and for societies structured upon a principle of hereditary class distinctions.[1] Spanish, French, Dutch, Swedish, and English were the first such "Colonial" arts to appear. But they were by no means the last. All sorts of other peoples immigrated to the United States after independence—from southern and eastern Europe, from the Near and Far East, from India and Malaysia—and insofar as their arts were used to transfer and perpetuate homeland cultures, Colonial is a proper designation for them as well.[2]

Colonial styles constitute a second layer, after utilitarian building, on the American landscape. Sometimes they represent actual survivals (refurbished and/or restored in varying degrees), sometimes they are complete recreations, sometimes they survive only in the ephemeral form of old prints and photographs. But in whatever forms, Colonial styles—especially Colonial English—have been the most consistently popular of historic American styles. Only at the height of the mid-nineteenth-century vogue for picturesqueness did they drop completely out of elite taste-making favor. (Louisa Tuthill's 1848 *History of Architecture from the Earliest Times,* reprinted by Garland, 1988, commented about colonial "wooden enormities" being "happily all of such perishable materials that

they will not much longer remain to annoy travellers in 'search of the picturesque' throughout the beautiful villages of New England.") But the prints of Currier and Ives bear witness to their continuous appeal on the popular level *[2.1],* and by the 1890s Colonial was back in high fashion, never thereafter to lose appeal. In Popular/Commercial form, Colonial styles easily outlasted Modernism's attempts to put the American population at large into steel and glass and concrete houses in the alleged spirit of its times, and their forms have been a major Postmodernist source of "historicist quotations" (see chapter 9).

Colonial styles survive on the late-twentieth-century landscape most commonly in the form of homesteads *[2.2, 2.3, 2.4]* in folk-vernacular rather than high styles from the homeland. These forms had developed out of utilitarian building by the shaping of proportions and spaces into patterns made familiar, hence desirable, hence self-evidently "right" by generations of family (folk) living.[3] To atavistic shapes, proportions, and techniques inherited by Colonial homesteads from Europe, little was added either from Native American examples (except in New Spain, a special case) or from African proportional systems, except in certain kinds of eighteenth-century vernacular housing.[4] For in general what settlers of every sort, of every colonizing power, above all wanted to do, once they got past that first brief utilitarian stage of survival-shelter building, was to transplant their familiar Old World—all its traditions and especially familiar architectural settings and furnishings—to the New as fast and faithfully as possible. They wanted to recreate the environment they had known, the environment that told them who they were, what their place in the world was.

From this impulse derives the colonial habit of

2.2. *Until quite recently, the isolation of Maryland's Eastern Shore helped conserve much Colonial feeling in its landscape; a good deal remains still, as seen in this view down Cockey Lane in Stevensville. In the foreground is the Cray house, a characteristic one-and-a-half-story Delmarva type of homestead built c. 1809–15. (IMG:NAL)*

2.3. *Homesteads in diverse colonial folk traditions are enduring elements on the American landscape. This one, set amid sugarcane fields outside Saint Martinville, represents Louisiana's original French tradition, reinforced by deportees from Acadia in Nova Scotia, plus influences coming down the Mississippi from New France's heartland on the Saint Lawrence. (IMG:NAL)*

2.4. *A colonial homestead in the making, photographed just off Interstate 10 outside Lordsburg, New Mexico, in November 1980. The builders are recently come across the Mexican border; their home and farmstead look almost utilitarian but in fact echo a kind of homestead built in this area while it was still part of New Spain. (IMG:NAL)*

naming New World towns after familiar Old World localities—New Amsterdam, New London, New Paltz. It is responsible for the consistent sets of proportions that give unity to colonial styles of any given region, informing homesteads and courthouses and churches alike. Through inherited, familiar kinds of space, stubbornly maintained through all switches of materials—from Old World sod and stone to New World boards and bricks and logs—patterns of regional settlement can be traced from the Appalachians to the Far West. Such familiar shapes, proportions, and spaces function in effect as visual metaphors of self-evident "rightness"—that sense of Us being right and Them being wrong which lies at the heart of all civilizations from the beginning. To that sense, embodied in such forms, the appeal of colonial survivals on the landscape owes much.

Prominent among survivors of the colonial era on the landscape are many variants of the palace type, opposite yet complementary architectural type to the homestead: palaces proper, for rulers; legislative palaces, for governmental deliberations; surrogate palaces, most commonly in the form of great churches functioning as visual metaphors if not actual seats of governmental authority. Of palaces proper, Pennsylvania's old Statehouse, which became Independence Hall *[2.5]*, and the two at Williamsburg (the Governor's Palace and the Capitol) are most famous *[2.73]*. Of surrogate palaces—which in a colonial context principally means churches functioning as images of all the authority, hierarchy, and continuity early colonists lacked and wanted—the Spanish mission churches are most famous *[2.6]*, but there are examples from every colonial culture, early and late *[2.7, 2.8]*. All forms and subtypes of the palace type have in colonial cultures a common function: to provide focal points for the societies that built them as a visual metaphor of principles of authority inherited from their homelands. They also deliberately contrast with homestead types, through the elaboration of ornament and plans, which visually state differences between rulers and ruled, between governing classes and those they govern. This contrast is typical of all Colonial styles, manifesting a paramount principle of the colonial era, the structuring of societies on hereditary class lines.

Also to be found on the American landscape are remains of middle-class Colonial styles—houses displaying the kind of regularity and applied ornament that distinguished churches and governors'

palaces, but on a scale closer to homesteads. In old colonial English territories especially, such buildings regularly became mansions that proclaimed superior class status. They soon rivaled palaces proper and thereby manifested intimations of revolution; for this reason, mansion was considered to be the core type in older American architectural history writing *[2.9, 2.10]*. If mansions do not seem quite as important today, it is perhaps because all remains and visual records of the colonial past—as of all the American past—have come to be seen as historically significant. There is no artifact beneath study in the colonial or any other period. All, read in terms of their diverse principles, characteristics,

2.5. "Independence Hall, the most historic place in the nation," the Philadelphia Convention and Visitors Bureau captions this picture and so, of course, it is; this is the country's most famous colonial building. In its present form Independence Hall belongs essentially to the 1740s; but it has a complicated later history, and its restoration in 1826 could be considered the beginning of the nineteenth-century Colonial Revival. Its ceremonial mall setting is, however, a manifestation of mid-twentieth-century attitudes.

2.6. In most colonial cultures, churches served as principal authority images, functioning as palace surrogates. This role was very obvious in New Spain, where mission churches, whose size makes a dramatic contrast with the homesteads, remain the culture's most conspicuous remains. The most famous example is San Xavier del Bac at Tucson, which still dramatically dominates the Arizona landscape. Originally begun 1783, completed c. 1791, it had some practical alterations in the early 1900s (schoolrooms, rear additions), then in 1949 a series of restorations that produced "a look of completion that it never had before" (Bernard Fontana, Biography of a Desert Church [Tucson: San Xavier Church; reprint from The Smoke Signal, Spring 1961], p. 16). (Metropolitan Tucson Convention & Visitors Bureau)

2.7. Quite comparable in social function to the more famous Spanish missions of the Southwest and California is the Mission of the Sacred Heart for the Coeur d'Alene Indians at Cataldo, Idaho. Begun in 1848 and finished in 1853, it was built by the band following directions of Father Anthony Ravalli (who was, among other things, a competent sculptor) and was part of an ambitious scheme for a model community based on ideas common to all social thinking in class-structured states. In general form the Cataldo mission recalls a church form established by the Jesuit Order in the sixteenth century and intended to make the strongest possible contrast with its rude environment. Completed just seven years before the first permanent non-Indian settlement in Idaho and abandoned in the 1880s when the band moved away, it was preserved and restored as a colonial monument by the Idaho Bicentennial Commission in 1973–75. (IMG:NAL)

2.8. Makiki Japanese Christian Church in Honolulu was built in 1904 (additions 1915 and 1932) on the model of a Japanese castle (Otakasaka in Kochi). It refers to Christianity being brought to Japan in the sixteenth century and therefore being not altogether foreign. It is also a "mighty fortress" symbol of authority and thus a focal point for this community. (IMG:NAL)

2.9. *The most famous of all colonial mansions—given that Monticello and Mount Vernon were remodeled in post-colonial times—was the grand Palatial Georgian house that John Hancock built in 1740 on Beacon Hill in Boston to celebrate his rise from humble beginnings to status of merchant prince and, ultimately, Founding Father of the new Republic. The house was torn down in 1863, but not before careful measured drawings had been made of it. From Robert Sears,* Pictorial Description of the United States *(New York, 1848).*

2.10. *Like most Colonial English mansions, the Hancock house differed only in degree from an official seat of authority. Compare it, for example, with the old Rhode Island Statehouse in Newport, completed in 1739. (Photograph by John T. Hopf, courtesy of Newport County Chamber of Commerce)*

and social functions, can contribute to American history in architecture.

Social Function

To understand the social function of Colonial architecture requires an understanding of the principles that justified structuring society along hereditary class lines—not always easy for us third- and fourth-generation heirs of democratic revolutionaries, who proclaimed these principles falsehoods, to be ever vigilantly rooted out of the popular mind. Yet history is history. Throughout the Renaissance and Baroque eras in Europe, from around 1350 into the eighteenth century, intellectual and moral

consenses held that human beings were by nature selfish, envious, jealous, deceitful, willful, cruel, capricious; that unchecked expression of such natures would therefore result in private mischief of all sorts as well as public strife, chaos, and misery; that for the happiness of all in this world, and salvation in the next, it was essential to curb the private expression of such instincts through religious institutions and control their public expression through social institutions that would regulate behavior. Appropriate behavior is not the same for everyone, whence it follows that different classes in society need to be distinguished carefully. Therefore, the best society is one structured along class lines. Reason is here supported, so the argument continues, by Revelation: justification for the "grand principle of subordination" can be found in revealed Scripture, properly interpreted.

The good society, therefore, was a pyramid. At its apex should stand a Godly Prince—a ruler, that is, in whose person was manifested upon earth that divine Mind by which the Universe was made, whose state church validated his claims. Associated with the godly prince were nobles who shared the ruler's attributes and so were uniquely qualified to lead armies, governments, and ecclesiastical establishments. At the pyramid's base was the mass of peasants and laborers. Their toil produced those goods which are the material base of all society, but they had no hand in its use or distribution because no wisdom had been vouchsafed to them, only low cunning, like the animals in their folklore. Between these two came a middle class; theirs was the duty of refining and distributing goods and services. The core of this class was merchants (who commonly operated out of cities or burgs, whence "burghers," "bourgeoisie"). But it also comprised artisans to shape the products of peasants' and laborers' toil into shoes and hats and furniture and armor and whatever else society required, as well as people to interpret the state's purposes, like clerks and lower clergy, teachers and scholars. Qualities from classes both above and below it were to be found in the middle.

For the peace and welfare of society it seemed essential that each class perform its proper functions, "do my duty in that station of life to which it hath pleased God to call me," as the old Anglican Prayer Book phrased it. Each must be constantly aware of its "place," of the differences, that is, between one class and another. These differences, and thereby the whole class-structured state, were maintained by a system of defined rights, privileges, and duties that distinguished each class. Such distinctions were established by law, by custom, and by "outward ordinances." Each class was supposed to have a distinctive dress: "What!" says the patrician Flavius to some artisans in the first speech of *Julius Caesar*, "know you not, / Being mechanical, you ought not walk / Upon a labouring day without the sign / Of your profession?" Each class was supposed to have a distinctive accent in speech and manner of address. "Speak," Flavius says to one of them, "What trade art thou?"—in pre-democratic English usage, patricians speak to artisans in the second person singular, as they would to children or pets or other inferiors. Each class had distinctive manners and rules for social interchange. Some

countries maintained class distinctions more rigorously than others—eighteenth-century Germany far more than England, for example[5]—and in all of them, architecture was a prime means of doing so.

Architecture most effectively proclaimed class distinctions by a contrast between the unselfconscious "naturalness" of the homestead type and the "artificiality" of the palace. "Natural" involved direct expression of materials and texture (where such does not conflict with physical function), and "artificial" involved refinement of materials by polishing and shaping in some obvious way, use of decorative detail, and deliberate symmetry. It is a contrast fundamental and common to all Colonial architecture. Where the Colonial homestead was small, the palace was ostentatiously grand (big in relative scale, or absolutely, though keeping proportions derived from a matrix common to the homestead, so as not to be alien). Where the homestead was natural, with exposed structure and materials—timber, plank, stone, brick, wattle, shingle, adobe, tabby—worked only to a minimum and painted only for protection, palace types displayed lots of applied ornament and used materials in deliberately artificial ways. To contrast with the additive haphazardness of the peasant homestead, product of years and generations of family living, the palace was designed on some demonstrable sort of rational principles, with geometric regularity and symmetry. Where the homestead was timeless and rooted in regional soil, the palace made reference—by association of shapes, both ornamental and architectural—to eras governed by Godly Princes and their delegates by supernatural authority and reason. Usually the reference was to Roman rulers, but it could be to Jewish kings like David or Solomon (as was common in the Middle Ages and also in Spain's sixteenth-century Escorial) or to a ruler's own illustrious predecessors, real or by appropriation (as Louis XIV put statues of Charlemagne and Saint Louis IX of France on Les Invalides in the 1670s). If possible, the palace type should be approached by some sequential devices—capacious stairways with railings, courtyards, platforms—to emphasize the gravity of nearing so important a personage, in contrast to the homestead of a peasant, set flush on the ground, with only a doorsill to cross at best.

Between palace and homestead types came middle-class dwellings. Like the class itself (which maintained relationships with both the class above and the one below), middle-class architecture combined qualities of both palace and homestead. It displayed something of the regularity and applied ornament of the palace, but on a smaller scale, closer to that of the homestead. During the sixteenth and seventeenth centuries, when Europe was colonizing America, the middle classes were only just emerging from the inconspicuous position they had occupied throughout most of history. In some countries their emergence to power and influence was going on faster than others, a situation plainly reflected in Colonial architecture. In New France or New Spain middle-class architecture was nowhere near as important as in the English colonies. There, toward the end of the colonial period, middle-class houses began to rival palaces, most markedly on the Virginia plantations, but in the town houses of New England and New York as well (a gradation exactly paralleled in eighteenth-century furniture, as will be seen). Many became mansions, manifesting the aspiration to higher class status that fueled the Revolution.

This social function of Colonial architecture was never so neatly and deliberately carried out as a bald description of it might suggest; social function is always subject to accidental and unpredictable factors. Nor was it always conscious. Certainly the vernacular forms of houses and barns in diverse regions and nations came about not by design but over centuries of trial and error—social logic. The design of palaces, churches, and comparable architectural types was of course more deliberate. There was general agreement among consensus-setters, and had been for centuries, that balance and symmetry and ornament were essential for such buildings; what had earlier been the rule for churches spread to palaces as they increased in relative social significance. Exactly what proportions were adopted, exactly from what ornament ought to be derived, varied with times and tastes; thus were created the Colonial substyles.

Substyles

Within the category "Colonial" belong all those styles developed in the colonizing nations of Europe and brought by immigrants to North America as metaphors of their cultures. A glance at colonial remains on the landscape demonstrates how numerous and varied these styles were. It is easy to tell a Colonial Spanish church like San Xavier del Bac from a Japanese one like Makiki in Honolulu, to tell a Colonial Spanish homestead from a Colonial English one, and both from Colonial French, and so on. Centuries ago each nationality had, in fact, developed distinctive forms and proportions for palaces, homesteads, and other building types, ranging all the way from medieval vernaculars in sheds and barns, to Renaissance/Baroque high styles for churches and palaces.

What was considered right proportions, what details were characteristic, varied from one colonial culture to another. But no single form can be pointed to as surely identifying one particular Colonial style. "Flemish gambrel" roofs or "Colonial French" flared eaves can be found in Connecticut on occasion, for example; comparable Baroque elements appear on occasion in Colonial English and Colonial Spanish, and so on. The point is that colonial buildings cannot be understood in isolation from each other. Because they belonged in and were built for a class-structured society, the characteristics of buildings for any one class need always to be compared and contrasted to both buildings for the same class and buildings for others.

It would almost be true to say that every racial and ethnic group in the world contributed to the peopling of North America, sooner or later, and thus in theory the number of Colonial substyles should be limitless. But in practice, English colonies so dominated all others that the story of Colonial substyles other than English is a record of assimilation and exotic remains.

Furthermore, whereas in theory all Colonial styles should display a full complement of substyles—vernacular, high, urban, and other intermediates—and examples of their application to all basic architectural types, in practice again that was true only of Colonial English. Others are represented by just a few substyles and subtypes. The explanation is differing backgrounds and colonizing motivations. Colonial Spanish architecture predominantly served a missionary effort. Colonial French architecture served the interests of an aggressively authoritarian state. Colonial North European architecture served the predominantly mercantile interests of New Netherlands and New Sweden. Colonial German architecture in the beginning was largely made by and for refugees, or small individualistic religious groups. Most post-Revolution immigrants found the country's cultural patterns already so set as to admit no more than odd bits to the mosaic, like peasant homestead styles or distinctive settings for national or minority religions lasting a generation or two.

Colonial Spanish

Imperial Spain! Union of Castile and Aragon under Ferdinand and Isabella in the late fifteenth century, Europe's premier power throughout the sixteenth, Europe's first mature class-structured dynastic nation-state, first to exploit the New World—all this was given visual metaphor in the Escorial Palace near Spain's new capital of Madrid and in the rebuilding of Rome's Capitoline hill and mighty basilica to Saint Peter, financed by the conquests in New Spain.

Impetus for those conquests, and model for their colonization, was the final reconquest of the Iberian peninsula from Moslems who had overrun nearly all of it in the eighth century. Granada, last of the Moorish kingdoms, surrendered to Ferdinand and Isabella in 1492. There the bodies of those Catholic kings lie buried in the Royal Chapel, and there it was that Isabella commissioned Christopher Co-

lumbus to find new worlds to conquer, new infidels to convert. He found them in the New World. New Spain was conquered on the pattern of the reconquest of Old Spain—"natives" (Moors in the Old World, Indians in the New) were to be converted so as to become the "peasant" base of a class structure capped by lords and soldier-adventurers from the old country. Grasp this controlling model, and the distinctive characteristics of Colonial Spanish architecture in the New World become self-evident. Here the palace/homestead contrast central to all colonial cultures appears at its starkest: palaces and their church-surrogates splendid in high styles from the homeland; homesteads insignificant in folk vernaculars; middle-class mansions scarce and nondescript until near the end.

Those characteristics are to be seen at their most dramatic in the oldest-settled parts of New Spain, especially Mexico between 1500 and 1650. By the time Spain's empire was expanding into what be-

2.11. Taos pueblo, outside Santa Fe, was begun long before Columbus. It is the most famous example of the "pueblo style" and exhibits the distinctive adobe brick smoothed over by mud and plaster, walls with rounded ends, and the roof rafters projecting at uneven lengths. Native homestead style of the region, it had a long and continuing afterlife in Academic and Popular/Commercial form. (New Mexico State Tourist Bureau)

came the American states of Florida, Texas, Arizona, New Mexico, and California during the 1700s until around 1820, their supporting convictions had weakened. But a controlling class-structured state model prevailed throughout.

"Homestead" in New Spain most commonly meant a native peoples' dwelling. It was the counterpart to European peasant homesteads in the class-structured state system, the product of Spanish efforts to reproduce their Old World in their New, an admirable visual metaphor of the process whereby conversion plus apprenticeship was to turn native peoples into approximations of Spanish peasants. At first, and in some places still, they were actual Precolumbian forms, with materials varying according to region of the Americas, from the grass-and-branch huts in the Maya country of Yucatan (whose distinctive shape you see everywhere mimetically reproduced as a central element in Precolumbian Maya high architecture), to substantial structures of adobe (sun-dried brick) in the American Southwest *[2.11]*. By the nineteenth century such dwellings usually had acquired a few European elements and a slightly more European look *[2.12]*, but theirs was never a folk vernacular with much distinctive character or attractiveness, always remaining a rather nondescript cross between the poorer elements of both Indian and European. Homesteads so built had a short survival span, but multiplied at such a rate as to become ever more prominent on the landscape of the American Southwest [cf. 2.4].

At the other end of the colonial social axis came palace. Of palaces proper the Southwest and California had nothing comparable to even modest examples like the Montejos Mansion in Merida of 1594, with its plan and Plateresque ornament so elegantly recalling splendors of the Escorial, or Cortes's retirement palace in Cuernava, let alone Mexico City; nothing comparable either to those grand ceremonial settings prescribed for palaces and their church surrogates from Cortes's time on[6]—nothing like Mexico City's Zocalo or even the great fountain at Chiapa de Corzo in Chiapas *[2.13]*. There is a grand space in front of San Xavier in Tucson *[2.6]*, but it functions as a parking lot; only vestigial too at San Xavier is the balcony for Holders of Authority,[7] which distinguishes the Colonial Spanish palace proper as found in Mexico. What convention calls Governor's Palace in outposts like San Antonio, Santa Fe, or Monterey were not even in a high style but, at best, some vernacu-

2.12. *Adobe homestead in the vicinity of Los Angeles, built c. 1840, demolished c. 1900. (University of California at Los Angeles Library, Special Collections)*

lar version of an urban Colonial Spanish style that hardly conveyed any effective image of governmental authority, let alone majesty *[2.14]*. In reality they were no more than impoverished mansions, and mansions only in comparison to Indian homesteads.

Lack of anything between palace and homestead types until very late in the history of New Spain is, indeed, one of its most striking aspects. Of these late mansions the Vallejo Adobe ranch near Petaluma, California, begun in 1834 and restored in 1951, gives some idea *[2.15]*. In plan it was based on palace types—four sides surrounding an open atrium—but was built of the same materials (wood and adobe) as a lower-class homestead. Its general appearance was a mixture of Spanish and incoming American characteristics, appropriate for the Spanish-American families for whom such late middle-class mansions were erected.[8] The Colonial Spanish mansion described in Helen Hunt Jackson's 1884 novel *Ramona* that so attractively portrayed California—"pastel-tinted hacienda with tile roofs, carved woodwork, cantilevered balconies, and glazed galleries opening onto brick-paved verandahs and walled gardens"—was a myth not clothed in architectural reality until the early-twentieth-century Academic Spanish Colonial Revival. Only the myth of the Colonial Spanish mission churches was to some extent real.

To Americans, the California missions have always been the best-known examples of the Colonial Spanish architecture. Their prestige goes back to awed reactions of early Anglo explorers like Jedediah Smith or Harrison Rogers, who spent months struggling through wildernesses of rocks, stinging

2.13. *Chiapa de Corzo fountain in state of Chiapas, Mexico. It is a transplantation of the tradition of grand civic monuments proclaiming governmental authority from Old to New Spain, involving a secularization of domical symbolism, from baptistry (eternal life, new beginnings, etc.). It is a transplantation, too, of a particular,* mudejar, *building technique from Seville to southern Mexico. Begun 1557, completed 1562, restored 1944. (IMG:NAL)*

2.14. *Present appearance of the Palace of the Governors at Santa Fe, New Mexico. Only a few walls of the 1609 building survived to 1890, when the first major restoration was undertaken; the* portales *in Pueblo style seen here were added as part of a more or less hypothetical restoration in 1914; still more recent is a patio behind, created by recent constructions assuming a Spanish palace/mansion prototype. (State of New Mexico Economic Development and Tourism Department, Santa Fe)*

2.15. *The country mansion of General Mariano Guadalupe Vallejo, Mexican War hero and American supporter in California, was originally built 1834–36 on an open square plan as the largest adobe house in northern California; the east wing of the square was destroyed by fire c. 1900. This view of the Vallejo Adobe or Casa Grande on its hilltop still captures something of its original grand presence. (IMG:NAL, 1968)*

LEFT·TOWER·NEVER·
COMPLETED·BVT·
CERTAINLY·PROPOSED·
BY·PADRE·PEYRI·

·DOTTED·LI
·SKY-LINE·A

CHVRCH·FACHADA·OF
BRICK·STVCCOED

BALVSTRADE·OF·BRICK

BRICK·STVCCOED

2.16. Proposed restoration of Mission San Luis Rey de Francia in Oceanside, San Diego County, California, as originally intended c. 1800. The building was repaired in 1892 and 1930. (HABS)

sand, cataracts, precipices, and swamps, to emerge finally and find themselves in a mission like San Gabriel, which in 1826 had two thousand acres under cultivation with wheat, peas, beans, corn, and hundreds of trees (apple, pear, peach, olive, orange) and shipped out annually to Europe some fifty thousand dollars worth of skins, tallow, and soap. By 1905 French traveler Jules Huret found the missions objects of a cult; Californians, he observed, professed an absurd veneration for "these walls without history and without architecture, near-secular," to which they paid "the same respect which we experience before our cathedrals of the Middle Ages or the ruins of the Parthenon."[9] Today such awe does seem a bit ridiculous, when the California missions are compared to their Mexican counterparts and especially in view of the extraordinary vicissitudes most of them have undergone. For example, San Miguel Arcangel, before its reconsecration in 1878, had been a church only from 1816 to 1818 (though the mission was founded in 1797) and then successively a saloon, dance hall, sewing machine agency, and store; its present appearance dates only from a restoration in 1928. San Antonio de Padua in Jolon (built 1810–12) had become an abandoned ruin, "stabilized" in 1903, and its present appearance dates from a restoration in 1948–49. Yet the "mission legend" rested on a sure instinct: churches were by far the most important architectural type everywhere in New Spain throughout its history.

It was in churches and monasteries that the high styles of Spain were best and most insistently represented. There were three successive styles, recognizable by different combinations of elements common to all Spanish building—openings marked by metal grillwork, framed in elaborate masses of plant- and shell-work ornament, tiled roofs, pilasters, pediments, and gables shaped more or less directly on classical Antiquity via Italian Renaissance models. Earliest was the sixteenth-century Plateresque, composed of elements drawn to a considerable extent from silverwork, magnificently represented in Mexico (for example, the great church/monasteries at Acolman and Huejotzingo) but only vestigially further north. This was followed by considerably more elaborate Churrigueresque, which took its name from the seventeenth-century Spanish master Daniel Churriguera. Examples abound in Mexico—the cathedrals of Oaxaca and Mexico City (Sagrario), Chapel of the Third Order at Cuernavaca—but there are examples further north as well, more modest but not insignificant: San Jose in San Antonio, San Xavier del Bac in Tucson. The third was the Spanish style of eighteenth-century classicism, with details like pilasters, entablatures, and round-headed windows drawn from sixteenth-century Italian Renaissance pattern books, most favored for the California missions [2.16].

High styles were of crucial ideological importance to the Spanish colonial enterprise because they established and proclaimed authority. They

2.17. *Interior of San Xavier del Bac, looking toward altar, photographed at Christmas 1980. The San Xavier mission was founded by Jesuits in 1700; Franciscans replaced them after 1767; and the present church was built under them, traditionally to designs by two "architects," the Gaona brothers. The artisans were mainly Subaipari, and later Papago, Indians. Construction is mainly of kiln-dried clay brick covered with white limestone plaster; interior decorative forms are largely of the same material. The Franciscans left the mission in 1822 and returned in 1911; the intervening deterioration was repaired subsequently. (IMG:NAL)*

2.18. *Chest made for a Spanish mission in northern New Mexico, about the middle of the eighteenth century, probably by Indian artisans; five feet long, two high, two wide. Such a form was already obsolete in English Colonial furniture on the Atlantic seaboard. (Museum of International Folk Art, Santa Fe)*

are found in architectural types making direct statements of power, like the Castillo de San Marcos in Saint Augustine, Florida, begun in 1672 with lavish royal support as a riposte to the founding of Charleston in 1670 and as a proclamation of Spanish authority in territories farther south. And of course they appear on palaces proper. Where they are most insistently applied and most tenaciously maintained, however, is on the sanctuary type in New Spain—churches, monasteries, shrines. No matter how coalesced their forms, how constricted their available resources, how remote their locations, sanctuaries retained a high style, or some approximation to one. For they had the compelling function of fostering and affirming conversions, of transmitting religious culture from the Old world to the New, on which the life of New Spain ultimately depended. They had therefore to be so designed as to promote the Faith—to attract, to invite, to invoke feelings of awe and decorum. Successive Spanish high styles had been invented to do just that, impelled by the need to meet Protestant Reformation challenges to Catholic authority. Hence these styles were maintained in early Mexico and on the wilderness frontiers of New Spain, right to the end.

To experience how Colonial Spanish high styles work in and for society, look at San Xavier del Bac in Tucson *[2.6, 2.17]*. At first the formula seems simple. An exterior with concentrations of lavish ornament set against plain expanses prepares entrants for the lavish interior, where masses of fantastically indented columns and flying cherubim, volutes, sprays, baldachins, cornucopia, flowers and fruit, saints and crucifixes suddenly loom up in the glittering flicker of candlelight at the end of cavernous naves made of thick adobe walls and solid square pillars. All this is intended to persuade the worshiper of the aweful majesty of the new God whom the Spaniards had introduced to replace older Indian deities and is tailored for peoples accustomed to understanding power in terms of size and the luxuriant architectural forms of Aztec or Maya complexes.

But the persuasion involved was subtler than such an obvious device supposes. For much of this rich architectural display, especially its ornamental element, was the work of Indians. In some cases, like San Miguel in Santa Fe and San Esteban del Rey in Acoma, Indians did all of it. A strong admixture of native building traditions and artistic attitudes is precisely what distinguished Spanish from other early American Colonial styles. Of special interest are the two sorts of mind-set involved. Native peoples trained in crafts by Spanish artisans or priests subtly altered the principles and forms of Spanish arts and architecture. For instance, in a little piece like the chest illustrated here *[2.18]*, two quite different mentalities, two quite different perceptions, were involved. The basic motifs plainly are Spanish; their treatment plainly is not. The heraldic composition of Renaissance-derived floral forms and the rampant Castilian lion are descended from the medieval and *mudejar* heritage of Spain established in the New World centuries before. But they are not conceived, executed, or "seen" like their originals. Forms that brought ideas of lions or leaves to European minds remained for Indians variants of those patterns of line and color that their peoples had perceived and reproduced over countless past generations; they proceeded to interpret and modify the forms accordingly. The result was a visual manifestation of those fundamental differences in perception of reality, in ways of structuring experience, which characterized meetings between Europeans and Indians from the very first, and persisted. It provides the basic stylistic pattern for architecture as well.

It is tempting to overemphasize the importance of the native element in Colonial Spanish arts because of its ethnic or aesthetic interest. But to do so is to misunderstand their social function. Their purpose was not to encourage artistic self-

expression among native peoples; it was to mold their lives. Therefore, while the attitudes, aptitudes, and perceptions of Indian craftsmen are everywhere evident in these assemblages of naive, stubby, stiff forms with little real understanding of human anatomy or awareness of sophisticated Renaissance laws of proportion, they nonetheless have an overall interrelationship that produces final effects quite different from the additive repetition of mimetic elements and motifs in Maya temples or Pueblo pottery design. Throughout the Colonial Spanish mission church, no matter how simple or how lavish, a controlling balance and order is perceptible: in bell towers that toll off ordered rounds of days; in courtyards and atria with surrounding walls that control, measure, and define space; in ornament massed around doors and windows so as to create a psychological contrast between openness and closedness, a dramatization of barriers penetrated in calculated sequence— each point of passage from court to porch to interior being demarcated by ornament, like systematic theological argument.

Thus the complex as a whole constitutes a succession of constriction-and-release experiences. They contrast a world securely ordered by Reason—in the persons of the Godly Prince and "those in authority under him," who include the mission fathers—with chaos outside, where reigns the natural lawless life of peasants or Indians—red in tooth and claw; nasty, brutish, and short. And in so doing they

2.19. *Our Lady of Guadeloupe Church in Fabens, Texas. Its cornerstone records dedication in 1941 under the titular Nuestra Señora de Guadeloupe, obviously for a congregation coming predominantly from Mexico. In 1980 it still had two Sunday services in Spanish. Thus, although technically the stylistic forms are Academic or Popular/Commercial Colonial Spanish Revival, in social function it is as colonial in the original sense as any earlier style. (IMG:NAL)*

prepare mind and eye to accept the convictions on which rested all the fundamental institutions of New Spain.

Every historical civilization, every culture, has always rested on a set of mental attitudes; it was the endurance of these attitudes, rather than survival of altered and restored physical structures, that was embodied alike in the magnificent cathedrals and monasteries of Mexico, and the humblest California missions. It endures still. No matter how commonly the history of New Spain is treated as something done and finished, long ago overrun by the progress of American civilization, in fact the architectural landscape of the American Southwest proves otherwise. Still today new churches with social functions comparable to the old missions are being built there *[2.19]*; they have a similar relationship to the neighboring homesteads *[2.4]* and recreate the traditional palace/homestead pattern of New Spain in only slightly modified form. It is an ongoing

demonstration of how tenacious are the patterns of mind in society, and how architecture works to promote and preserve them.

Colonial French

Colonial French, like Colonial Spanish, had its high styles and vernaculars, interacting to transmit an Old World class-structured state to the New. But there were distinctive differences that called for distinctively different forms.

The state served by French high styles of the seventeenth and early eighteenth centuries was the largest, most compact, most powerful, and most aggressive in Europe. France's culminating visual metaphor was the great palace built by and for its dynastic prince, Louis XIV. Versailles was much more systematic and geometrically rational than the Escorial, therefore much more self-consciously compelling in its sequence of tension-and-release

2.20. *Dominating Quebec City in this 1980 view across the Saint Lawrence is the Château Frontenac CPR Hotel, begun in the 1890s to designs of Bruce Price, whose reputation was made on resort hotels in the Adirondacks and Maine. Set on the old site of* Governor Frontenac's palace, it asserted the dominance of an Anglo-Scottish establishment in the city and nation. In earlier decades Quebec's skyline had been dominated by the gleaming silver roofs and the spire of the East Wing of French Université Laval,

experiences. Its enactment of power began on one side, with roads converging from all parts of the kingdom onto a palace courtyard enveloped by successive wings that reached out to meet them, continued on the other with mile after mile of landscaped grounds—successive terraces, clipped parks, fountains, treed *allées.* The little capitals of Louis XIV's overseas empire—Quebec, Montreal, New Orleans, Basse-Terre in Guadeloupe—all had their miniature Versailles. Still preserved in Quebec are remnants of the Governor's Garden laid out in 1635; the Grande Allée, originally laid out to run from the Governor's Palace to the Jesuit base at Sillery some miles away, is still one of Quebec's main avenues. Of New Orleans's counterparts only a vestige survives, in the form of a Place d'Armes now called Jackson Square.

None of New France's palaces proper remain. On the site of Quebec's Governor's Palace stands now the Château Frontenac Hotel, a different sort of palace, built to manifest a different sort of rule *[2.20]*. New Orleans's Governor's Palace was never built. Basse-Terre's is long gone, and the Château Vaudreuil in Montreal was demolished around 1830.

Church architecture originally functioned in New France as in New Spain—as a surrogate palace, asserting royal authority by proxy. For long the biggest church in Quebec was the Jesuits' *[2.21]*. There also was a basilica—"large and magnificent," Bishop Laval called it on his arrival in the 1650s; a smaller church for the Récollet Order, which recruited in Canada; a royal hospital with chapel; a handsome Ursuline convent. For New Orleans a similar complement of palace surrogates had been planned, though none were ever more than partially realized.

Between New France and New Spain there was a critical difference, however: the native Indian element in New France's population was negligible.

designed in unmistakably Québécois forms by Charles Baillairgé in the 1870s (right). That in its turn had been intended to upstage a Customs House built on the shoreline in First British Empire classical style of the 1830s (its effect reinforced by the 1910s Post Office [center] in an Academic version of the same). Such swings of visual ascendancy between French and English buildings make an architectural statement about the rivalry of races that gives Canadian architecture its unique interest. (IMG:NAL)

2.21. "*A View of the Jesuits College and Church. [built 1666, repaired 1765, demolished 1807]. Drawn on the SPOT by Richd. Short. Engraved by C. Grignion*" *was made by an officer in the forces occupying Quebec after its capture in 1759. The original intent of the print was to gratify a middle-class British public with evidence of the conquering power of British arms; this stronghold of papal and French aggression has been riddled with holes from British cannon. Moderns would more likely see in such a scene significant evidence of cultural patterns in New France. This was by far its largest institutional complex, complementing the cathedral, which stood just behind Short as he drew the scene, and the Governor's Palace just off to the right.*

The social authority that palaces and basilicas were built to assert on the Saint Lawrence and the Mississippi was over populations of European origin, not Indians. It followed that when the French Crown lost its overseas possessions in the Seven Years War (1756–63), palaces and basilicas correspondingly lost their social function as palace surrogates, and thereupon became mostly redundant. Parish churches took over their function as metaphors of social order, often indicating the transfer by their forms *[2.22]*.

As examples of how buildings work in and for the societies that built them, Quebec parish churches from the 1760s Conquest to the 1960s Quiet Revolution have few equals in North American architecture.[10] They are of special interest too as demonstrations of how social function determines what qualities are appropriate for given architectural types to express. Because they were not built to serve congregations of recent converts needing to be kept in line and reminded of their new status, the interiors of Quebec parish churches were not overwhelmingly awesome, like those in New Spain. Awe they inculcated, to be sure; but it was balanced by decorum, appropriately creating and expressing the dignity and stability of long-established ways of life *[2.23]*.

Having a peasant class come from Europe meant that New France would have French vernacular styles of homestead. They appeared first in the Saint Lawrence valley, then New Orleans, later down the Mississippi into the Missouri country and elsewhere.[11] Although New France had a middle class larger than New Spain's and represented by some surviving urban row houses in Quebec and Montreal, New France's principal impact and legacy on the North American landscape has been the rural homestead.

2.22. *Quebec's venerable Jesuit Church is recalled thirty miles up-river in the central facade of Deschambault (anciently Deschambault-la-Blanche) parish church, designed in 1834 by diocesan architect Thomas Baillairgé (who was responsible for more than thirty churches in the Quebec diocese). It was completed in 1836 and had flanking facade towers to recall the design of a new cathedral Baillairgé had proposed for the diocese of Montreal, and was topped by* clochers *that followed the model of the Anglican Cathedral of Quebec (which in turn followed Saint Martin-in-the-Fields, London)—a combination of three sources intended to image the harmonious fusion of the two founding races in Lower Canada. This was hardly agreeable to the spirit of Quebec's Quiet Revolution in the 1960s; and during it, the* clochers *seen in this photo of c. 1955 were replaced by the more "authentic Québécois" forms seen now. (IMG:NAL)*

2.23. *Not far from Deschambault is Cap Santé, another ancient parish, home of the great historian, archivist, and author Gérard Morisset, whose* Le Cap-Santé, Ses Eglises et Son Trésor *is a Quebec classic (1944, reprinted 1980). Its huge church, one of the largest in the country when built and still impressive, was conceived by curé Joseph Fillion, begun under his direction in 1754, and pushed to completion in 1763 despite campaigns of the Seven Years War raging around. Like many Quebec churches, it is a great monument to one dedicated individual, and a monument, too, to the spirit of* la survivance. *Compared to Colonial Spanish interiors like San Xavier del Bac's, it's all French clarity and structured order—not designed to overawe converts, but to keep fundamental verities central in the lives of a rural peasantry become sturdy farmers. (IMG:NAL)*

2.24 (top). *Just outside Cap Santé village the Marcotte homestead has stood for eight generations or more; it may have been begun as early as 1745–50 by a grandson of Jacques Marcot, who began farming this land in 1703. In 1797 Jean-François dit Petit Jean Marcot, put a date-plaque over the door, and in the 1980s two generations of Marcottes were still living in it. Characteristic of the Québecois homestead is the squarish plan, steep roof, irregular fenestration, and plastered fieldstone walls, which are whitewashed every dozen years. The house had a back or "weekday" door opening onto the farmland and the "Sunday" or main door seen here that opened onto the Chemin du Roi and the Saint Lawrence. At some time in the nineteenth century an open porch was added for rocking, relaxing, and visiting; in 1914 a roof was put over it, but the whole was removed c. 1955. Otherwise the homestead remains pristine, even to original interior arrangements: on the ground floor is one large central living parlor with a couple of rooms partitioned off on either side; the attic story is completely open and used for storage, not living (no insulation), hence no dormers. (IMG:NAL)*

2.25. *The resemblance between the Louis Bolduc house, built c. 1770 in Sainte Genevieve, Missouri, and the plans and proportions of homesteads in the Saint Lawrence Valley, where this region's first settlers came from, is unmistakable, although it is visually disguised by the gallery around all four sides and the stone kitchen built into it. It is, however, built of frame instead of stone and preserves in parts a* construction de pieux *long obsolete in Canada. Restored 1956–57, including garden, orchard, and eight-foot fence of cedar logs, by the National Society of Colonial Dames of America under the direction of Ernest Allen Connally. (IMG:NAL)*

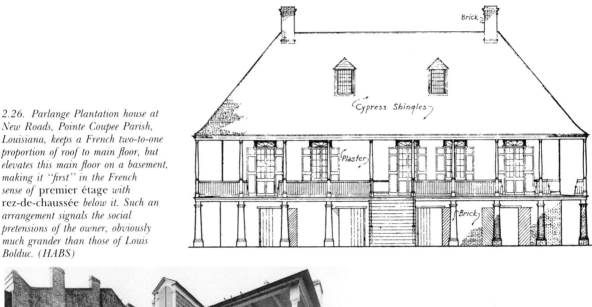

2.26. Parlange Plantation house at New Roads, Pointe Coupee Parish, Louisiana, keeps a French two-to-one proportion of roof to main floor, but elevates this main floor on a basement, making it "first" in the French sense of premier étage *with* rez-de-chaussée *below it. Such an arrangement signals the social pretensions of the owner, obviously much grander than those of Louis Bolduc. (HABS)*

2.27. Legend attributed "Madam John's Legacy" on Dumaine Street in New Orleans to a Captain Jean Pascal, around 1728, and so made it a focal point of "French heritage." It is indeed very similar to eighteenth-century homesteads in Quebec and Montreal. But in fact it seems to have been built after 1788 by an American, Robert Jones, for a Spanish officer, but why in this style is unrecorded (restored 1973). Most architecture in the "French Quarter" of New Orleans, built under American rule, has only a superficial Frenchness; its principal feature is wrought-iron balconies prefabricated in New York. (Louisiana State Museum)

Representative of the basic homestead form brought from France is the Marcotte house at Cap Santé *[2.24]*. There were later variations, of course. Chimneys came increasingly to be put on the gable ends of rural farmhouses, rather than located in the middle, less for practical reasons, apparently (there is a famous example on the Ile d'Orléans of fake chimneys added in the eighteenth century to a seventeenth-century farmhouse) than for prestige, to appropriate the massive firebreak walls of middle-class urban house forms. Porches too became popular sometime in the eighteenth century, added to the front and covered by projections from the main roof *[2.25]*. Raised basements developed; their effect was to constitute a "main" or "première" story—actually a second story in the English sense *[2.26, 2.27]*.

This vernacular Colonial French homestead, tenaciously perpetuated, offers a classic example of what geographers call "cultural spoor," evidence from material culture of patterns in peopling the continent. In Louisiana, French as an official language was legislated out of existence after the Civil War, but a good many Colonial French homesteads are still to be seen in rural areas *[2.3]* and a Popular/Commercial Colonial French style is vigorously promoted for all sorts of Louisiana buildings. Canada is of course the premier example. Not only has the traditional form survived in the core parishes of the Saint Lawrence valley, but a belt of peasant-vernacular homesteads traces a prodigious expansion of French-speakers out of that "cradle" from the 1850s through the 1950s. It runs west into the Ottawa valley and Northern Ontario, Manitoba, Saskatchewan, Alberta; north to Chicoutimi, the Saguenay, and Lac Saint-Jean; east through the Gaspé and into northern New Brunswick—and is everywhere accompanied by a trail of boarded-up Anglican and Presbyterian churches, crumbling Colonial English houses, huge spanking Catholic churches. Vestiges of New France are to be recognized in New England too, though not by the forms of homesteads, but by their color. Wherever in that region you see houses painted lilac, lime green, puce, red, or yellow, in contrast to trim white Yankee farmhouses, you will likely find in front of them mailboxes lettered "Paradee" (Paradis), "Shapley" (Chabot), Morris (Morriset), Longway (Langevin). Together they provide evidence of owners whose ancestors never experienced the Revolution with its classical white temple-house ideal, and therefore retained the continental eighteenth-century habit

of painting houses in bright colors; and who then brought that older tradition with them when they took up farmlands abandoned by New Englanders who moved to the west or to life in the suburbs. In so many ways, a colonial past lives on into a twentieth-century American present!

Colonial North European

New Netherlands (which early subsumed its short-lived rival New Sweden and in turn was soon subsumed into the English colonial system) was not designed for the aggrandizement of a monarch, like New France. It was conceived as a series of bases to facilitate the elaborate operations of commercial trading companies. Their enterprises spanned the globe: New Amsterdam (New York) on the Hudson and Fort Kasimir (New Castle) on the Delaware were links in a mercantile net extending around the Caribbean, with counterparts in the East Indies and Sri Lanka.

For such permanent population as these ports required, a minimum of institutional framework was provided. Governmental buildings were so un-

2.28. When Robert Sears picked the Albany Female Academy's monumental Greek Revival temple for inclusion in his Pictorial Description of the United States *(New York, 1848), it was*   *just a dozen years old. The little stepped-gable Dutch mercantile house beside it was a couple of centuries older, and already a rare survivor of its type in old New Netherlands territory.*

important that the Dutch seventeenth-century high style, with arrays of Renaissance pilasters, volutes, and statuary, was never transplanted at all; New Amsterdam's major official building was a Town Hall in the much plainer mercantile mansion style, featuring elaborately stepped brickwork gables. Some tiny tower-like churches called "candle snuffers"—examples survived into the nineteenth century at Bushwick on Long Island and Bergen in New Jersey—may have been intended as vestigial versions of an official Dutch church form developed in the seventeenth century and represented by the four great squarish domed churches that geographically marked the cardinal points of the home capital of Amsterdam. In the eighteenth century some rectangular churches were built for Dutch Reformed or Swedish Lutheran congregations descended from seventeenth-century populations; they were distinguished from English Protestant churches by blockier proportions and exotic (in this context) features like jerkin-headed roofs. Surviving examples have been heavily restored to conform with expected rather than proven appearances—old Swedes in Wilmington is one example, the "Old Dutch Church" at Tarrytown, New York (restored in 1897 on its "two-hundredth anniversary") is another. But nowhere in New Netherlands were there churches as significant as those the Dutch built in other colonies—Colombo, for example—where conversion or religious assertion was a factor in colonization. In New Netherlands that seems never to have been the case; the Dutch objective there was primarily to make money. It follows that the chief representative of Dutch high styles in North America was the mercantile mansion.

Mansions combining store and residence were common in seaports all around the North Sea and the Baltic. Elaborate front gables with stepped brickwork proclaiming their pretensions in Holland, north Germany, and Sweden were at one time common in Dutch-settled areas of America. Old prints are now all that is left of any of them, unfortunately; and even in them they were often depicted in connection with something else *[2.28]*.

The far fewer examples of Colonial Dutch urban style in the countryside have fared a little better. Famed is the earliest part of Medway, near Charleston, whose stepped gable is attributed to one "Jan van Arssens, seigneur de Weirnhoudt," in the 1680s *[2.29]*. But it has been very largely incorporated into later additions to Medway and serves principally as a reminder of how close Charleston's

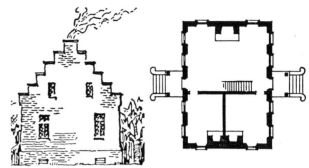

2.29. Conjectural restoration of the original form of Medway Plantation near Charleston, South Carolina, in 1686; elevation by H. C. Forman, in The Architecture of the Old South; *plan by Samuel G. Stoney,* Plantations of the Carolina Low Country.

connections once were to the Dutch mercantile empire in the West Indies. Another is Fort Crailo on the eastern shore of the Hudson in Rensselaer, New York *[2.30]*. Its elaborate stepped brickwork side gables proclaimed the headquarters of a vast plantation, which was to be peopled with more or less forced labor, owned and operated by Kiliaen van Rensselaer. According to Roger Kennedy, Fort Crailo was "at the outset a traders' refuge from the Indians, and later an overseers' refuge from unruly tenants . . . a fortress against enemies without and within."[12] It was, in short, a bastion of capitalist enterprise, which ultimately extended twenty-four miles along the Hudson. Among such huge and sparsely populated "patroon" estates (in 1700 the Livingston grant of sixteen by twenty-four miles had only four or five cottages on it, the Cortland holdings only four or five vassal families, and Frederick Phillips's estate about twenty families), free farmers squeezed in where they could. Yet their exploited situation did not prevent them from acting on the immemorial human impulse to establish status in their homesteads by borrowing elements from the class above them—in this case, from mansion/palace types like Fort Crailo. Such an explanation accounts for the form of the Leendert Bronck house near West Coxsackie in Greene County *[2.31]*. Built in 1738 next to a low stone house of the 1670s, it sported an elaborate brick gable complete with "mouse-tooth" brickwork, thus recalling the style of Fort Crailo and, distantly, the fine urban houses of New Amsterdam's rich merchants—and by association identifying the rural builder with their glories and aspirations. But Leendert

2.30. Fort Crailo, Rennselaer, New York, began as a trading post and family seat by Kiliaen van Rensselaer in 1642, to which era the end gables with inset stepwork presumably belong. It was extensively remodeled in the eighteenth century as a mansion proper, with a rear wing added in 1762, and extensively restored by the state of New York after 1924, to which era presumably its more romantic features belong—like the narrow diamond-mullioned medieval windows and the Dutch half-shutters. (New York State Department of Economic Development)

2.31. Bronck houses at West Coxsackie, New York. The earlier one of stone is by Pieter Bronck, c. 1663; the later one of brick is by Leendert Bronck, c. 1738. Maintained by the Greene County Historical Society.

Bronck's house was, by 1738, decidedly old-fashioned in style; Greene County was even more out of the mainstream then than now. By this time the traditional Colonial North European homestead could be much better upgraded in class by emulating the incoming Georgian Palatial style of the now dominant English.

Like New France, New Netherlands had its peasant class and vernacular homestead types. Originally that meant a "primitive"—in the sense of primevally naturalistic—structure consisting of a long, low, rectangular room, usually unpartitioned, such as may be seen at Skansa in Stockholm or in the Scottish countryside, usually with later amenities like whitewash; or in remoter regions of Ireland without any amenities at all, just huts of turf and piled-up flat stones. Such structures were assuredly transplanted to New World areas settled by North Europeans, along with a distinctive barn-building tradition. But only barns have survived *[2.32, 2.33]*. Upward mobility was just too strong: you might keep your barn unaltered, but not your house.

What happened to houses—and incidentally, what *real* upward mobility meant—is suggested by the "Van Cortlandt Manor" *[2.34]*.

Stepanus Van Cortlandt acquired an estate from Indians in 1697, and his original house functioned as a fort protecting the estate from them. By the mid-eighteenth century it had become a manor, and the Van Cortlandts began redesigning their house appropriately. A larger structure was built on top of the original homestead, which thus came to serve as basement for an upper, principal floor (a *première étage*, as developed for seventeenth-century palaces like Versailles). This main floor had regularized apertures, whose symmetry would set it apart from the haphazard openings of tenants' huts, establishing the traditional palace/homestead contrast. A flight of steps was built up to the new main door (a twentieth-century restoration is presumably fairly close to the original), ultimately recalling (though at a great remove in elaboration!) Michelangelo's redesign of the steps of the Capitol in Rome to impress visitors with the solemnity of the approach to the presence of Greatness. For the Van Cortlandts, all of this no doubt was done more by social instinct than conscious invention—but that is how architecture has traditionally performed its social functions.

That such a remodelling had the desired social effect was proved by imitation, in the form of the "Dutch Colonial" or "Flemish Colonial" house, which developed during the eighteenth century in those parts of New Netherlands where the patroon system did not hold and independent, upwardly mobile farmers could appear.

When the "Dutch Colonial cottage" was rediscovered by Colonial Revivalists at the turn of the twentieth century, much labor was expended upon trying to find a prototype for it in the Netherlands. None ever was found,[13] because this house was a New World development, a response to New World conditions and specifically to conditions in the old territories of New Netherlands. What this house really represents is one of a number of local folk variants of the Georgian style. That explains both its lack of a European prototype and its many otherwise baffling inconsistencies. To an original core—the North European peasant homestead reproduced by the desperately poor first settlers imported by merchant-developers—all sorts of things began happening once these settlers' descendants became independent enough to improve their properties. A second room, perhaps a third, would be added. Walls were rebuilt in more

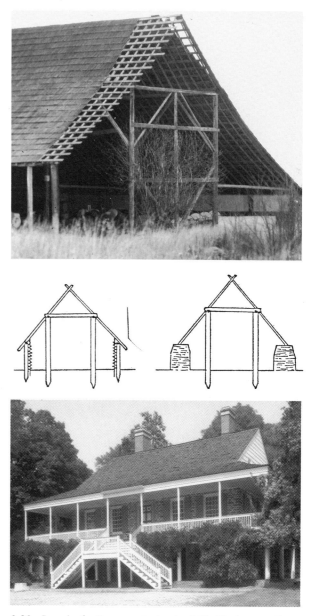

2.32. *Barn in the Dungeness peninsula of Washington near the Scandinavian settlement of Carlsborg, founded c. 1880. Traditional construction is exposed by demolition underway in 1971. (IMG:NAL)*

2.33. *Cross-section of halls from the eighth to the eleventh centuries in Leens, Groningen province, Holland: left, with wattled walls; right, resting on sod walls. (A. Zeppelius)*

2.34. *"Van Cortlandt Manor," Croton, New York, in its present appearance as a historic site, maintained in crisp condition with extensive surrounding gardens by Sleepy Hollow Restorations. It has a flanking building which was restored in the 1930s with flaring eave believed to be typical of Dutch/Flemish Colonial building in the Hudson Valley. (IMG:NAL)*

2.35. *Morton homestead, Essington, Pennsylvania, in the old territory of New Sweden. Its assemblage from several parts is obvious; they date from 1654, 1698, and 1806. (IMG:NAL)*

2.36. *Zabriskie–von Steuben house in North Hackensack, New Jersey. It was begun in 1737 as a single-room house of brownstone with straight gabled roof by miller John Zabriskie; extended to the south by another room added by his sons John and Peter; in the 1770s a third room was added to the north and the whole unified by a classic example of "Flemish gambrel" roof. As the Zabriskies were Loyalists, their house was confiscated during the Revolution and presented to Baron von Steuben as a token of Patriot esteem; he never lived here, and in 1797 the Zabriskie bought it back. (IMG:NAL)*

regular stonework or were clapboarded. Sometimes all the rooms would be covered with a single roof; sometimes each had a roof of its own [2.35, 2.36]. The various parts might even be at different levels. Sometimes there were dormers with straight roofs, sometimes not. Perhaps the two most distinctive features of this Colonial Dutch house were a gambreled roof (though far from every house was gambreled) and a veranda along the front (though not every house had one).

As late as the 1950s Colonial Revivalists would distinguish with some confidence between Flemish, Swedish, and English Colonial styles of gambrel roof. That confidence can no longer be shared. Gambrels of all sorts can be found throughout the English colonies; it was in fact a common English Georgian vernacular feature. Verandas too are hardly an invention of the old territory of New Netherlands. They appear almost everywhere in mid-eighteenth-century America; while functionalist theory likes to explain them as some kind of response to climate and convenience, it is far more likely (in terms of the way traditional architecture works) that these virtues were discovered afterward and that the primary motivation for the veranda was status, a symbol borrowed from similar features developed on seventeenth-century palaces.

Many problems of interpretation vanish once the social function of houses like this is taken into account. At all times and places, but especially in states structured on class lines, homesteads can be remodeled in the direction of mansions; that is, conceived not only to serve the institution of the family, but also to proclaim status in society. For that purpose elements from palace types are borrowed for them. That is in fact how urban or middle-class styles came into existence—midway between peasant vernacular and princely high style. The "Dutch/Flemish Colonial" is such a creation; it is not some exotic import but a home-grown product of status-seeking.

The same principle can be recognized in the interiors of such houses, where it governs the style of furniture. It may be seen very well in the bedroom from the Hardenbergh house in Kerhonkson, New York, now in the Winterthur Museum [2.37]. Some elements here remain from the peasant homestead: the basically medieval exposed beams and rafters in the ceiling constitute a framework comparable to the North European homestead core apparent on the exterior. There are crude elements in the furniture also. But as a whole this interior is anything but crude; it has

paneling so articulated in relation to the fireplace as to suggest some direct copying of high-style Georgian design. The clothes chest is an old-fashioned seventeenth-century piece, but still hardly one that might be found in a peasant homestead. There is nothing even faintly utilitarian about it, and its stenciling and drapery design, though folkish, reflect high-style Georgian design, as do the fashionable Delft artifacts.

By the mid-nineteenth century this kind of house had lost its function of proclaiming upward mobility; it just looked old-fashioned. So architectural developers of the period began advertising how they might bring such houses up to date. *Woodward's Country Homes* of 1866 explains in before-and-after pictures how a French Second Empire country villa might be created in "a 'presto change' that will almost defy the keen eyes of the old settlers to recognize any trace of the ancient landmark that for fifty years has overlooked the beautiful valley of

2.37. Bedroom of the Hardenbergh house from Kerhonkson, New York, as restored c. 1980 to the period c. 1763, in the Winterthur Museum. The old-fashioned character of the great exposed ceiling beams, the clothes chest with seventeenth-century trompe l'oeil *ornament and big ball feet, and the styling of the Queen Anne chairs all complement the exterior character of "Dutch Colonial" homesteads of the time. (Courtesy The Henry Francis du Pont Winterthur Museum)*

the Tenakill." Paradoxically, such a transformation restored the earlier social function of such houses even while obliterating their outward forms, for it made them once again symbols of upward mobility ("our place in the country, in the latest style"). And when, later in the century, Second Empire was no longer the latest style, when that style's proclamation of new wealth was coming to seem *gauche* and the well-to-do were demanding the sophisticated simplicity and restraint of Academic versions of historic styles, the older forms reappeared too. Academic "Dutch/Flemish Colonial" came to be one of the most popular styles for suburban houses after 1900, evidence that you had made it in the city and so could afford a move to the more healthful and beautiful suburbs.

Colonial German

Though sharing many features with Colonial North European, Colonial German needs to be considered in a distinct category, because of the scale and diversity of German immigration.

Occupying the strategic center of Europe, and constituting by far Europe's largest homogeneous population block, the Germanies for a thousand years were potentially the most powerful of all European states. But this was disguised until the later nineteenth century by extraordinary political fragmentation. The magnitude of German presence in the New World was comparably disguised by its arrival in two waves. The first, in the eighteenth century, centered in Pennsylvania; it had a high percentage of peasant refugees and religious

sectaries with very persistent medieval traditions. A second, in the nineteenth, settled predominantly in the expanding Midwest—Cincinnati, Saint Louis, Milwaukee, Chicago—and contained a high percentage of skilled artisans of every sort, from brewers to cabinet-makers and tailors, as well as political idealists.

Toward the end of the nineteenth century, three quite diverse legacies from the first German wave attracted those Americans beginning to be interested in their colonial past. First, its lingering medieval craft tradition appealed to enthusiasts of Romantic Nationalism, those Progressives promoting the Arts-and-Crafts revival. "Colonial German" proportions were discovered, and forms like flat dormers, hall-kitchens focused on wide hearths with great summer beams, and plain plastered walls so thick that small windows are set in deep splayed reveals, reappeared. There was also renewed interest in brightly painted ornament on furniture and pottery, which often included folk saws and sayings in quaint *fraktur* lettering. From this interest come period rooms from the 1750s like those at the Winterthur Museum or the Philadelphia Museum's Mueller kitchen from Milbach in Lebanon County, or the "Schifferstadt" house at Frederick, Maryland—not to mention Popular/Commercial vulgarizations aplenty (cf. 8.15). The second legacy is Pennsylvania German barns, those strikingly distinctive rural landmarks which are for cultural geographers indubitably the best demonstration of migration patterns within North America *[2.38]*. The third is the communal buildings for dissenting sect communities *[2.39, 2.40]*, which were beloved and restored especially during those fits of utopian enthusiasms the twentieth century has been prone to: the Society of the Solitary at Ephrata, Pennsylvania; Moravian communities at Bethlehem in Pennsylvania and Old Salem in North Carolina; Indiana's Rappite community at New Harmony.[14]

Most representative of the second wave were churches, breweries, and concert halls created by and for German communities in Midwestern cities. Mutter Gottes Kirche, for example, just across the Ohio from Cincinnati in Covington, Kentucky, has a plan, towers, decorative details, and windows brought directly from Germany, especially Bavaria *[2.41]*. To learn that this was painter Frank Duveneck's home parish is to be reminded why so many nineteenth-century American artists trained in Germany: German was their first language. Cincinnati's Music Hall of 1876–78, designed by local architect

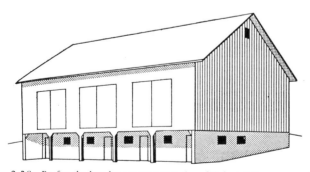

2.38. *By far the best-known representative of Colonial German are the great bank barns characteristically set into hillsides, with three great loading doors on the opposite side supported by the posts of a forebay on the bottom level. Their presence attests to German spread outward from Pennsylvania into the Midwest, southwest Virginia, and Ontario; this diagram is from Peter Ennals, "Nineteenth-century Ontario Barns,"* Canadian Geographer *16 (1972):257–70.*

Samuel Hannaford, was predominantly a product of the German community's musical traditions; it was inspired by Clara Baur, born in Cincinnati, a graduate of the music academy in Stuttgart, and founder of the Cincinnati Conservatory of Music along with philanthropist Reuben Springer *[2.42]*. German impact on American life is also architecturally evidenced by the style of many prominent breweries: German Renaissance at the Genessee in Rochester, New York; German Romanesque cupolas and turrets at the Heurich in Washington, D.C. (fondly recalled in old lithographs, where it sits proudly by the Potomac, on a site now occupied by the Kennedy Center, with the Capitol's far smaller dome in the distance); German Rococo at the Pearl in San Antonio, Texas *[2.43]*. All serve as reminders of how German beer superseded English ales and French wines as America's commonest drink by

2.39 (top). *"The Cloisters" housed a celibate community founded by Johann Conrad Beissel at Ephrata, Pennsylvania, in 1735: Saal for men at left (1741), Sharon (Sisters' House) in 1743. In general outline and many details these structures followed a prototype of large, multifamily dwellings of South Germany. It has been a museum since 1934, when the community was formally dissolved. (IMG:NAL)*

2.40. *This view of the Moravian chapel (1751) at Bethlehem, Pennsylvania, with the Bell house behind it (1740s) typifies the atmosphere of Moravian buildings of the 1740s through the 1760s; they now make a startling contrast with the huge Bethlehem Steel plant across the river. Prototype for most was the large, multifamily German homestead, which in this context took over social functions of palace, school, and sanctuary types. (IMG:NAL)*

2.41. *The present Mutter Gottes Kirche (Church of the Annunciation of the Ever Virgin Mary Mother of God) was built in 1870–71 in Covington, Kentucky, on the site of an earlier church built shortly after the parish was founded in 1841 by about thirty German Catholic families. Its size alone attests to the scale of intervening German immigration into the Cincinnati area. The interior was renovated as a Golden Jubilee project in 1891, and a Mass of Thanksgiving was offered for the artisans and artists, who included Johann Schmitt, Wenceslaus Thien, Ferdinand Muer, Paul Deschwanden, and also "Krienhagen, Schroder, and Donnenfelser." The church was famous for both its architecture and its choir. (IMG:NAL)*

2.42. *The completion date of 1877 is inscribed in decorative cypher over the main door of the Cincinnati Conservatory of Music, and its use is indicated by capitals featuring musical instruments. The style is technically Gothic Revival, and there is as usual in nineteenth-century records no documentation on why architect Samuel Hannaford chose or was instructed to use it. But it may be surmised that Gothic was taken to refer to "German culture"; Gothic had acquired such connotations in Germany, as nineteenth-century completion of Cologne Cathedral on its medieval plans attests. (IMG:NAL)*

the later nineteenth century (about the time that the percentage of the population descended from German stock surpassed the proportion descended from English).

What the two waves of German settlement have in common is their comparative invisibility, their comparative neglect in American studies. It came about in various ways.

Evidence for early German immigration was often lost by conflation with other groups. Thus Germans in Pennsylvania were generally known as "Dutch" by conflation with "deutsch." Or the German houses in New Paltz on the Hudson—a name derived directly from *Pflaz,* "the Palatinate," with even the German pronunciation of "ts" for "z" being retained—came to be called "French" because they were "built by refugees from Calais," which is like saying New England Puritans were Dutch because they embarked for the New World from Amsterdam.[15]

Such misidentifications hardly bothered early German settlers, who did not care what the outside world called them if only they could be left alone.

Their spirit was especially manifest in those great stone farmhouses that still stand out on the southeastern Pennsylvania countryside. To the casual eye they conform to English Georgian style, if a bit old-fashioned, but in fact they are just as distinctive Colonial German images of upward mobility as the far more famous "Dutch/Flemish Colonial" of northern New Jersey and Long Island. For example, the Peter Wentz house near Norristown *[2.44]* sports a good many Georgian-looking elements borrowed from the reigning mansion style of its time: symmetry, regular fenestration, simulations of ashlar stonework by plaster covering fieldstone, and even a naive rendering of the early Georgian high-style balcony (as on the Williamsburg Governor's Palace, fifty years before). But on the inside Georgian features are nowhere to be seen. Both plan and decoration are Germanic (as an early 1980s restoration shows very well). The whole is indeed a classic illustration of the principles laid out in Henry Glassie's essay on hidden Germanic features throughout Delaware Valley housing.[16] By such means settlers from this first German wave

2.43. The main building of the famous Pearl Brewery in San Antonio, Texas, built c. 1900 in German Rococo style by an architect named Beckmann, otherwise apparently lost to history. (Pearl Brewing Company; Zintgraff Photographers)

2.44. *The Peter Wentz house near Norristown, Pennsylvania (actually between Center Square and Worcester), was begun around 1758 and restored in the 1980s to its condition in 1777, "when George Washington slept here." The technique of sponge painting used for its interior walls is described in the* Bulletin of the Association for Preservation Technology *7/2 (1975): 124–30; the exterior has some even more remarkable anachronisms. (IMG:NAL)*

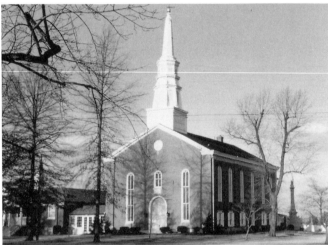

2.45. *The little church at Trappe, built in 1743 under Heinrich Melchior Mühlenberg, who came from a theological chair in Hanover to organize Lutheran congregations here and at New Hanover, New Providence, and elsewhere, looks quite Germanic: jerkin-headed roof, rough stone walls, clumsily patterned hand-forged ironware, hand-hewn timbers with folk decoration of cut-out hearts and crude "capitals." The church that replaced it for worship c. 1850 could stand anywhere, though its attenuated Romanesque forms often had Germanic connotations in the early nineteenth century. Twentieth-century Sunday school buildings at left in Academic Colonial Revival complete an image of assimilation. (IMG:NAL, 1966)*

preserved their roots, but also hid the extent of their contribution to American life.

The pressures operating on all settlers to assimilate into mainstream American culture are evident in German architecture even of this first wave. One can see it by comparing the original church at Trappe, Pennsylvania, with its nineteenth-century successor, for instance [2.45], or by comparing nineteenth- with eighteenth-century architecture at Bethlehem. Where it is most evident, perhaps, is in cemeteries of German-settled areas (Aaronsburg, Pennsylvania, is a good example); there you can trace the Anglicization of names, for instance. Counterpart to such Anglicization was the acceptance of German traditions as simple American ones: who today remembers that beer was not Colonial English in origin, or that music was not a major part of early-nineteenth-century American life? And it has taken later twentieth-century schol-

arship to recall how much German accent craftsmen like John Henry Belter gave nineteenth-century American furniture.

Assimilation was pushed to the point of oblivion by the violent anti-German campaign accompanying American entry into World War I. Attempts to counter it can still be seen on the landscape. A "National German-American alliance" erected a monument at Valley Forge in 1915, the war's second year, to keep in the public eye Baron von Steuben's contributions to the American Revolution and to reinforce the effect of a monument to von Steuben "erected by the Congress of the United States" in 1910 in Lafayette Park, opposite the White House. In 1917 Harvard University's Busch-Reisinger Museum was donated by "Americans of German ancestry" to remind their compatriots of German contributions to American culture. Unfortunately, that was the year America declared war

2.46. *Greek Orthodox Church of the Assumption in Wauwatosa was completed in 1961 on plans made by Frank Lloyd Wright in 1956. The three-dimensional logo in front introduces formal themes of the church behind, intended (especially low, blue saucer dome) to recall Justinian's great Church of Holy Wisdom in Constantinople (completed 537; now Aya Sofia Museum, Istanbul) and so transplant and maintain a formal link with Byzantine church tradition over fourteen centuries. Yet Wright's characteristic proportions, spatial sense, and distinctive abstraction of detail remain in evidence too. (IMG:NAL)*

2.47. *Around 1900 the last great settlement of unoccupied North American land occurred when Ukrainians took up farms on the western end of the Great Plains, a great many on the Canadian side of the border, whose geography strongly resembles the Ukraine. Their onion-domed churches and sod-roofed homesteads are still prominent on that landscape. This one, built c. 1905 of logs covered by wattle-and-daub plaster, with roof (later shingled), central hearth, low walls, and small windows, could be seen abandoned in a field near Mundare in central Alberta in 1980. Nearby stood its replacement—a trim split-level ranch, entirely indistinguishable from any other suburban house of the 1960s. (IMG:NAL)*

against Germany, when throughout the country German-sounding names for streets and towns were being changed and German ancestry disowned. Yet the evidence from material culture could not be altered. "Books," as Glassie concluded, "may not tell us, but buildings do."

Later Colonial Styles: East European, South European, Far and Near Eastern, Other

Later Colonial styles have much the same social function as those introduced by colonizing powers before the Revolution, but they were brought over when patterns of American civilization were more firmly fixed. Because the architecture that these later arrivals built for themselves (as distinct from the earlier structures they simply moved into) came after the colonial period proper, it has customarily been considered a variant of whatever Picturesque or Academic or Popular/Commercial styles were then dominant. Some does indeed properly belong there, but much does not. Nineteenth- or twentieth-century buildings obviously intended to recall Baroque churches in Poland, castles in Japan, or mosques in the Levant, in order to keep homeland traditions alive for some immigrant group, are just as Colonial in social function as mission churches in seventeenth-century Mexico or *bauernhauser* in eighteenth-century Pennsylvania. Nor does it matter, in this respect, whether the designer was a local artisan or a world-famous architect: the eighteenth-century Russian church Louis Sullivan designed in 1903 for a Russian Orthodox congregation in Chicago was colonial in social function; so was Frank Lloyd Wright's 1964 Byzantine-style church for a Greek Orthodox congregation near Milwaukee *[2.46]*.

Like earlier Colonial styles, these are represented principally by homestead and sanctuary building

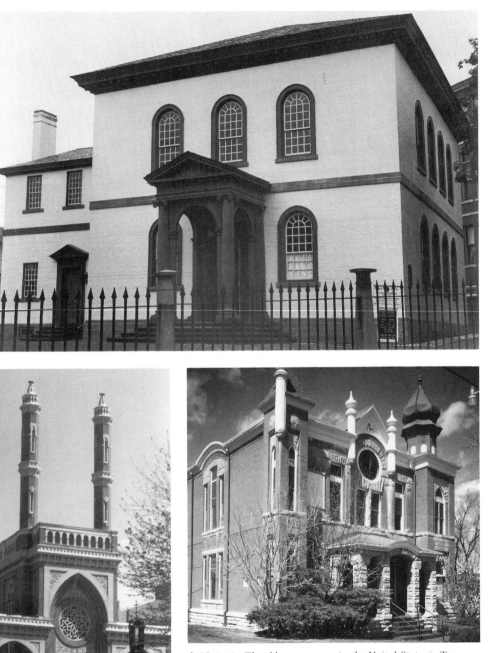

2.48 *(top). The oldest synagogue in the United States is Touro (Temple Jeshuath Israel) in Newport, Rhode Island, built in 1763 to designs by Peter Harrison. (Photograph by John T. Hopf, courtesy of Newport County Chamber of Commerce)*

2.49. *Plum Street Temple of B'nai Yeshurun Reformed Congregation was built in Cincinnati, 1865, under the leadership of Rabbi Mayer Wise. (IMG:NAL)*

2.50 *(left). Temple Aaron was built for a Jewish community in the Colorado mining town of Trinidad, to the designs of two local builders, the Rhapp brothers, in 1888–89. (IMG:NAL)*

types; one serves a community's enduring sense of self-awareness, the other authority of community mores and values. Homesteads in distinctive vernaculars were rarer than in the early colonization period because fewer of the new groups settled on the land; more came straight to cities and found housing already there. A notable exception was East European vernacular (Ukrainian, Czecho-Slovak, Russian) homesteads on the Great Plains *[2.47]*. But all were represented by high styles from the homeland applied to primary community foci like churches, synagogues, mosques, and graveyard monuments, often too community halls.

The first major examples of later Colonial high styles occur on synagogues. What Carol Krinsky has so admirably noted as the special problem of stylistic identity faced by nineteenth-century builders of synagogues in Europe[17] appeared in America too, and with another twist, when the first great wave of Jewish immigration from 1836 on (establishing about twenty-five congregations in New York alone within twenty years, representing every sort of Jewish ritual from all parts of Europe) began to build. It can be appreciated very well by comparing a famous pre-Revolutionary synagogue, Touro in Newport, with the Rabbi Wise (Plum Street) Temple in Cincinnati of 1865–66 or Temple Aaron in Trinidad, Colorado, of 1887–89 *[2.48, 2.49, 2.50]*.

Stylistic details of the Touro Synagogue were indistinguishable from those of the many public buildings of diverse sorts by the prolific Peter Harrison, the most famous architect in New England. Where it differed was in the absence of all elements signifying "public"—no towers, no spires, no portico, no formal approachway. The design proclaimed a building for a private community, Rhode Island citizens of Jewish religion. Many later nineteenth-century synagogues were similar: Kahal Kadosh Beth Elohim on Hasell Street in Charleston of 1840–41, for instance, is hardly distinguishable from any church in the reigning Greek Revival style (and not so incidentally, perhaps, was "the cradle of Reform Judaism in America").

But not all mid-nineteenth-century Jews were happy about such a proclamation of imminent assimilation. Many wanted to assert some kind of distinctive tradition by some kind of distinctive style. It was the same problem as in Europe, but in America assimilation was much more common. Israel Joseph Benjamin, who came from Moldavia to the United States in 1858 to study the state of Judaism in America, noted how "the political position of the

Jews kept pace with their rapid commercial development. . . . Israelites were represented, not only in all the states in municipal and state offices, but they were also members of Congress, in the Senate as well as the House of Representatives." (Just before Benjamin's arrival, Rabbi Raphall of the Polish B'nai Yeshurun in New York—the same denomination that built Plum Street Temple in Cincinnati—had given an eloquent prayer at the opening of Congress.) George Combe, the Philadelphia diarist (and gentile) commented how "Jews fall in love with, and marry, pretty Christian women, and within three generations the Jew is sunk and the family merges into the general population." American Jews, Combe declared, were so influenced by the American "spirit of free discussion" that they "altogether wear the chains of Judaism so loosely, that probably their brethren in Europe would disown them."[18] In such a situation, synagogues in styles distinctive enough to become metaphors of apartness had a signficant social role in maintaining community coherence.

Technically the Plum Street and Aaron synagogues might be classifiable as substyles of Gothic Revival and Picturesque, respectively. But they did not conform to any norm of those styles. They did not look like any of the churches or civic buildings in their towns; they looked like themselves. That is because they obviously had what is here defined as a Colonial social function, that is, to keep alive awareness and self-consciousness of a special society.

After the Civil War, immigration to feed industrialization began expanding older and newer American cities alike, at a furious rate and from new sources.[19] In Pittsburgh and Saint Louis, Chicago and Gary, Syracuse and Baltimore and Buffalo, sanctuaries began appearing in later Colonial East European styles. Built for Czechs (the "Bohemians" of Willa Cather's novels), Poles, and Russians, their distinctive domes and towers recalled Prague and Cracow, Lodz and Kiev. Many still survive *[2.51]*; characteristic of the present state of many others is Saint Stanislaus Kostka, erected in the late 1870s on the southeast corner of Noble and Evergreen Streets in the heart of the old Polish district of Chicago. It once served a community reputed to number 400,000, but by the 1960s it looked forlorn and dilapidated, with one belfry fallen and its neighborhood desolate. But like so many seemingly sorry spectacles on the American landscape, this is a monument not to failure but to success—to pa-

2.51. The small Minnesota town of Browerville has preserved its Polish congregation's church of Saint Joseph very well. A Polish eagle prominently adorns the facade, the onion dome still glitters, and a miniature pilgrimage site created in 1932 by Joseph Kisielewski still stands in front. But it is now part of a larger consolidated parish. (IMG:NAL)

2.52. Chinese laborers on the Southern Pacific and Western Pacific railroads erected this Joss House (Bok Kai Temple) at Marysville, California, about 1875; it still stands crammed against the Yuba River levee, over which the tracks run, although in recent years a more formal entrance has been added on the town side, along with a general refurbishing. The features that served most effectively its colonial social function of transplanting culture—scarlet columns, wooden bracketing, inscriptions, pictures, and joss sticks—were all on the interior, or discreetly obscured by the levee bank. (IMG:NAL)

2.53. Lum Sai Ho Tong was begun in Honolulu in 1899 and rebuilt in 1953. In both cases it created a visual metaphor of Chinese institutions transplanted to the New World, by a general form going back at least to Han times (pottery towers in graves A.D. c. 200 look much like this; they too presumably served as images of great families) and specific details identifiably "Chinese" in a Western setting: red, green, and yellow colors and curved eaves with distinctive bracketing systems. (IMG:NAL)

rishioners who became prosperous and moved to affluent suburbs.

Colonial South European churches, Italian and Greek, followed in a few decades. The Italian ones were commonly in Renaissance and Baroque high styles already familiar in America, while the Greeks perpetuated their more novel Byzantine traditions [2.46]. Italian or Greek vernacular styles generally appeared on restaurants, and are there more properly characterized as Popular/Commercial. Like the food generally served, the architectural style usually was more a response to the American public's stereotyped expectations than genuine transplantations of homeland traditions, more advertisements than visual metaphors of institutional values.

The same distinction holds for Late Colonial Far Eastern styles. It was not the vernacular or Popular/Commercial versions of them that promoted endurance and maintenance of transplanted Far Eastern communities, but the higher styles on buildings that stood for central institutions of their societies: Confucian temples, like the fine one at Marysville, California, from the 1860s [2.52], built by and for railroad laborers (and of even greater importance since the Red Guards' "Cultural Revolution" purge of the 1960s destroyed almost all bona fide ancient architecture in China itself); Tong buildings like Lum Sai Ho Tong in Honolulu [2.53]; Japanese Shinto shrines in Hawaii as well as Christian churches built in Colonial Far Eastern styles by congregations of Chinese or Japanese descent; or the tiled roofs and posts and distinctive turned-up eaves in pagoda-like successions that have preserved homeland culture in the "Chinatowns" of Western cities.

Newer Late Colonial styles keep appearing steadily. The first mosque in the United States was built in the 1950s on Massachusetts Avenue in the nation's capital· as a general Islamic Center; now enough Moslems are in the capital to dispute over which branch of Islam should claim it [2.54]. Other mosques appear constantly, as do Sikh temples. To study Colonial architecture in all its ramifications is indeed to find the panorama of a "Nation of Nations" [2.55]. It is also to study a kind of Colonial architecture which, far from ending in the eighteenth century, still has a vital role to fulfill in and for society.

Colonial English

The most diverse and numerous settlements in the New Word were English: the commonwealth/Puri-

2.54. *The Islamic Center of Washington was founded in 1949 on the initiative of ambassadors of Egypt, Turkey, Iran, and later Pakistan, who wanted to establish an Islamic presence in the nation's capital. The building, on Massachusetts Avenue's "embassy row," was completed in 1955. Its principal architect was an Italian, Mario Rossi, who later became a convert to Islam. The basic model was mosques in Cairo and Alexandria, but motifs from Syria, Lebanon, and Turkey (notably tilework donated in 1969) are evident as well. (IMG:NAL)*

2.55. *The McKees Rocks district outside Pittsburgh has a unique assemblage of ethnic sanctuaries; this is the Sri Venkateswara Hindu Temple begun in 1976 on models of temple designs in central southern India. Over the succeeding decade artisans came from India each summer to give details exactitude. The sculptures of idols and decorative black granite came from India as well. As of 1987, most services were still performed in Sanskrit. (Courtesy Pittsburgh Historic Landmarks Foundation)*

tan colony of New England; the mid-Atlantic haven of Quakers, Scots-Irish, and Germans centered on Philadelphia; the royalist/Anglican colonies of Virginia and South Carolina. Their motives were even more mixed: commercial/mercantilist like New Netherlands and New Sweden; nationally-assisted plantation enterprise, like New France and New Spain; religious utopianism, like many German groups; refuge from the two revolutions and a civil war that wracked England. Their populations were in consequence far greater and more upwardly mobile. And their types and styles of architecture were correspondingly more complicated.

Palace and homestead types interacted in English Colonial architecture as elsewhere. Distinctive to the English colonies is the greater variety of styles employed on them, the relatively small proportion of peasant huts, and the greater number of buildings compared with any other colonies. Neither public buildings nor churches were grand, relative to the size of the English communities, as they were in New France or New Spain. Mansions, on the other hand, were both grander and far more numerous than in any other colony, which testifies, of course, to the predominance of private adventurers

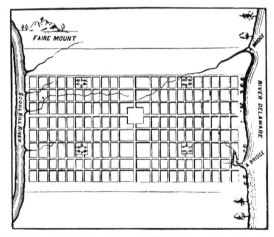

2.56. The 1682 Holme Plan of Philadelphia made minimal provision for public spaces: four little parks, barely larger than ordinary blocks, and a central one only slightly larger at the intersection of Market and Broad streets (site first of the waterworks, then of the [present] City Hall). The streets were narrow and natural topography ignored in order to provide easily saleable lots and so facilitate business. But Nature was not forgotten: east-west streets were named after native trees, Locust, Mulberry, Pine, Spruce, Walnut. North-south streets carried numbers, so that lots could be easily located. This system and its nomenclature were widely copied throughout the area.

and merchants and, by extension, to the extraordinary opportunities for upward mobility in English as compared to other colonial societies. Preachers and governors might talk all they wanted about class structure being ordered by God—"Good Order is the Strength and Beauty of the World. The Prosperity both of the Church and State depends very much upon it. And can there be order, where Men transgress the Limits of their Station, and intermeddle in the Business of Others?"[20]—but ordinary folk knew better. They knew that if you made money, you could "transgress the Limits of your Station" with ease and stay at the top, "Where *wealth* is hereditary, *power* is hereditary, for *wealth* is *power.* . . . The *rich* are *nobility,* and the *poor, plebians,*" as a Maryland farmer put it in that same decade.[21] The great Colonial English mansions are visual metaphors of this situation.

So too are Colonial English city plans. While most of them included some kind of public square with statues or other gestures acknowledging government authority (Williamsburg and Annapolis being especially noteworthy), their principal object, compared to other colonies, seemed to be division of land into parcels for easy sale. Philadelphia as laid out by Thomas Hulme in 1682 was perhaps most representative; it had four small public parks spaced around a central square like the five of dominoes, but these were mere punctuation points on a regular grid spreading evenly from the Delaware River side to the Schuylkill *[2.56].* "Within the first year," noted chronicler Israel Acrelius in his *History of New Sweden,* "the city contained eighty houses, and after twenty years was amazed at its own strength and greatness." Perhaps it was amazed as well by the discovery, as valid now as then, how great were the fortunes to be made buying and selling real estate.

Forts in the English colonies were represented not by great imperial outlays like the Castillo di San Marcos, but by dockyards maintained as private commercial ventures (with fierce rivalry) for building, outfitting, and repairing men-o-war and merchant ships. On such bases rested the seapower of the First British Empire.

Unique to the English colonies, for all practical purposes, was the way private enterprise and public welfare were perceived as closely interrelated. "Town hall" and other governmental buildings were often synonymous with "market," and both with philanthropy, so that Bonner's 1743 map of Boston can carry an inscription like: "Faneuil Hall

2.57. Newport's Redwood Library was funded in 1758 by Abraham Redwood, a Quaker merchant from Antigua, and built to the designs of Peter Harrison, who here followed a scheme devised by Palladio in the sixteenth century, and traceable to Alberti in the fifteenth, for widening a temple form by side aisles so that it could serve as a church or other public building. It was the continent's first building devoted exclusively to library purposes. (Photo by John T. Hopf, courtesy Newport County Chamber of Commerce)

2.58. Carpenters' Hall in Philadelphia was begun in the fall of 1770 on designs by Benjamin Loxley and Robert Smith, to serve the Carpenters' Company as a meeting hall and rentable space. Organizations taking advantage of it included the Library Company of Philadelphia, which occupied the second floor 1772–90, the Continental Congress (1774), and at various times the U.S. Custom House, Bank of the United States, Second Bank of the United States, Bank of Pennsylvania, and Franklin Institute. In 1798 a memorable event occurred: the first bank robbery in the United States (an inside job; $160,000 was stolen). The Carpenters' Company is now a club of executives in the building industry; it still owns the hall, although maintenance is by the National Park Service as part of Independence National Historical Park. (IMG:NAL)

Market House, handsom large brick building. Worthy of the generous founder Peter Faneuil who in 1742 gave it to the town for the use of a market." Only in the English colonies would you find something like the Redwood Library in Newport, Rhode Island, which was the gift of a private citizen, the merchant Abraham Redwood, to his community and is still standing *[2.57]*. Only in them would you find the combination of public and private interests represented by Carpenters' Hall in Philadelphia, which also still stands *[2.58]*. Built just at the end of the colonial era by the Carpenters' Company of the City and County of Philadelphia (which was not

a union but a guild, an association of master builders founded in 1724 on the model of the Worshipful Company of Carpenters in London), by private means for private purposes (to fix minimum prices for jobs and other business), it nevertheless contrived to be one of the most impressive structures in the city and housed the most famous public assembly of its time, the First Continental Congress of 1774 (for a fee—the Company turned a profit by renting out rooms to other tenants).

Styles and substyles were also far more complicated in Colonial English than elsewhere. Time and upward mobility coalesced many of them. The

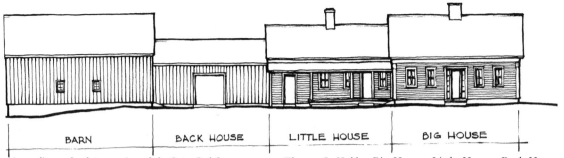

2.59. *An earlier and a later version of the Cape Cod form, contiguous with two farm buildings, constitute a complex characteristic of the period c. 1820–50 in New England. From* Thomas C. Hubka, Big House, Little House, Back House, Barn *(Hanover, N.H.: University Press of New England, 1987).*

"base vernacular" appeared with the first settlements and was soon reduced to the level of sheds (ice houses, toolsheds, slave quarters, and the like) or at best to very temporary housing; homesteads proper steadily took on greater regularity, balance, and system, moving in the direction of what would become Georgian.[22]

An early example of this process—recognized and named as early as 1801 by President Timothy Dwight of Yale—was the Cape Cod Cottage. It was a basically square unit that could be multiplied to a one-and-a-half- or two-room (double house) unit, and then, by contiguous additions, indefinitely [2.59]. It had a low cubical effect, a roof that was usually straight-gabled and not too steep, and walls commonly clapboarded in southern New England and shingled in the north. Spreading out from its hearth, the Cape Cod melded easily with other homestead vernaculars approximating Georgian, most notably the British Cabin.

A second famous example is the New England saltbox, whose name derived from the shape that resulted when a lean-to was added to a main building. Simple one-story versions of this saltbox form

2.60. *At one time the classic saltbox form, as in the Stanley-Whitman house in Farmington, Connecticut (begun by Samuel Whitman c. 1660; lean-to added c. 1760, modern museum wing added during a 1935 restoration), was taken as the normal seventeenth-century New England house form. Indeed, New England did have more of these substantial houses than other English colonies, because the great 1620–40 immigration gave the region's population stability and prosperity; but inventories reveal that small, low homestead types were far more common.*

2.61. *Room from the Hart house in Ipswich, Massachusetts restored as a typical seventeenth-century New England interior. Drops on the sideboard complementing the exterior and other luxurious decorative features made this something more than an* ordinary interior for its time; indeed, something closer to a mansion for its time and place (in England such medievalizing would already have been old-fashioned). (Courtesy of The Henry Francis du Pont Winterthur Museum)

existed and once were common, like the Clemence house in Johnston, Rhode Island. But within a generation the classic saltbox had appeared, as a two-and-a-half-story structure, distinguished by its second story overhanging the first, as in the Stanley-Whitman house in Farmington, Connecticut *[2.60].* The overhang in this context seems to have been more ideological than structural. It originated in towns, where it had the practical function of protecting pedestrians on sidewalks below (like the pent eaves of the Philadelphia house form *[2.64]).* But it soon became another urban feature adopted in the countryside to proclaim upward mobility, as in the Bronck house in West Coxsackie, the Wentz homestead in Norristown, the Gagnon homestead on the Ile d'Orléans, which added fake side chimneys to attain the "urban look" of a Quebec City row house with firebreak end walls, or like the Philadelphia pent eave itself reproduced throughout the Delaware Valley *[2.65].* The salt-

box's characteristic overhang with elaborately carved drops underneath functioned primarily not to image the homestead's social function of family-raising, but to proclaim class status. It thus came to constitute, for its time and place, more a mansion type than a homestead at all—an impression confirmed by interior furnishings of comparable ostentation *[2.61]* and by the fact that in its time and place the classic saltbox was a dwelling for the town's leading citizens.

Long considered Southern counterparts to the New England Cape Cod and saltbox were the hall-and-parlor and Southern Cabin stylistic forms. The classic Southern homestead was supposed to be a two-room house, composed of a "hall" (in the old sense of "Great Hall") and adjacent "parlor," with a sleeping loft above, a relatively steep roof, and, as its most distinctive feature, an outside chimney on one or both sides, frequently with stepped brick edges *[2.62].* Out of this form the

2.62. *The Adam Thoroughgood house near Norfolk was restored in the late 1920s as a paradigm of homesteads in the Old South and dated to c. 1640; more recent research has questioned the date and seen such a solid brick house as far more the exception than the rule in seventeenth-century Virginia. (IMG:NAL)*

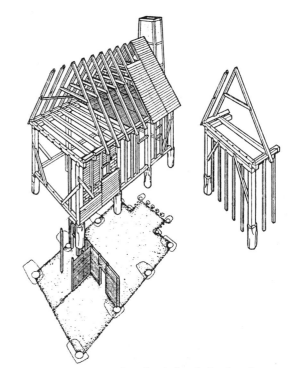

2.63. *Isometric reconstruction of typical early Southern house form, with posts set directly into the ground. From Cary Carson, Norman Barks, William Kelso, Garry Stone, and Dell Upton, "Impermanent Architecture in the Southern American Colonies," Winterthur Portfolio 16/2–3 (1981).*

Southern Cabin was supposed to have developed, through the addition of a porch running across the front in the mid-eighteenth century and the universal adoption of indigenous materials (logs, planks, etc.) by the early nineteenth century, when Jefferson described them as "wretched" but "fortunately, short-lived" in a famous passage from *Notes on Virginia*. Henry Glassie, in *Patterns in the Material Folk Culture of the Eastern United States*, proposed to distinguish a number of Southern Cabin variants, such as a "double pen." A later generic form of this homestead became the South's peculiar image, celebrated in song and story, and is still found at all levels in the later twentieth century: as a Popular/Commercial suburban style; as a creation of folk ingenuity, reproduced through improvised porches attached to mobile homes; and in the background of L'il Abner panels.

More recent research has suggested that two other early homestead forms may be even more characteristically Southern. One is that distinctive long, low box, often a single room extended by additions to the front (a porch) and back (a shed),

which goes under the generic name "shotgun house" and for which John Michael Vlach, among others, has claimed particular associations with and influences from the black slave population.[23] The other is that impermanent house frame erected by early Southern planters [2.63] which Cary Carson, among others, identified from archaeological evidence in southern Maryland as "the ordinary beginner's house."[24] A well-known example would be "The Clifts," a later seventeenth-century forerunner of Stratford [cf. 1.15]. By this time distinctive regional house forms were appearing in both Virginia and Maryland. Together, these two forms might conceivably be seen as the early South's peculiar version of the homestead/palace metaphor common to all class-structured states, with the slaves constituting a peasant class, the planters an aristocracy.

Yet another characteristically Southern form of homestead was a vernacular often found in the Delmarva region. It was at least one-and-a-half stories in height, was relatively narrow in width, and had the hall-and-parlor floor plan, an outside chimney, and a gambrel roof. (It used to be called an "English" gambrel, but the gambrel technique is now usually considered to have been determined more by carpentry techniques common in all seaboard colonies than by any one national tradition [2.2].

Distinctively urban stylistic forms for homesteads appeared early in the English colonies; archaeology reveals a row of them already in Jamestown, Virginia, derived from Elizabethan London. Longest-lasting and most distinctive of these forms—because it so neatly combined approximations to high-style symmetry with vernacular proportions and materials—was the urban spec (speculatively built) house introduced by the founders and early builders of Philadelphia [2.64].[25] The spec house seems to have been created by the builder Nicholas Barbon to meet the housing crisis after London's Great Fire of 1666. Its basic characteristic was use of a replicable unit of several sizes to allow for speedy construction. Identifying features were symmetrically arranged windows and dormers, a pent eave (literally "hanging," as it could be attached to the wall by a hook, for quick replacement when worn out) over the sidewalk in front, and blank side walls. So useful was this style that it continued to be built into the nineteenth century, not only in Philadelphia, but also in surrounding cities such as Chester, Wilmington, Norristown, and Bristol. It early acquired some symbolic significance as an image of equality within the City of Brotherly Love, so a generic version of it appears in the background of Benjamin West's 1773 painting *Penn's Treaty with the Indians*, now in the Pennsylvania Academy of Fine Arts.[26] Ultimately it became, alas, a sign of tenements.

So decisive an indication of urbanity was the Philadelphia spec house that farmhouses all around the city, on both sides of the Delaware River, reproduced it—in stone northwest of the city, in brick throughout the clay belt to the southeast. Sometimes it was replicated almost without change, producing the curious sight of farmhouses in open countryside with blank walls for nonexistent contiguous row houses and pent eaves for nonexistent city sidewalks. Usually there were variants induced by local circumstances and builders. Cove-corniced eaves might be run all around, for instance [2.65]. Across the river in South Jersey the Philadelphia spec house combined with traditions from New Sweden of gambrel-roofed, contiguous-room dwellings and ornamental brickwork to produce a distinctive Salem County variant [2.66]. Most such

2.64. A famous Philadelphia spec house: the Betsy Ross house on Arch Street, built "before 1756," shows characteristic pent eave and street facade. (IMG:NAL)

2.65. "Primitive Hall," a horizontally elongated form of the Philadelphia house built deep in the countryside off Street Road near Coatsville, Pennsylvania. Restored, with pent eaves and cove cornice, c. 1960. (IMG:NAL)

variants died out before 1800.[27] Much more tenacious was the I-form, an amalgam of Southern homestead forms and Philadelphia's easily reproducible urban house form that spread out of its mid-Atlantic hearth all over the nation, and lasted long enough to appear in catalogs of early-twentieth-century mass-produced suburban houses *[2.67]*.

The I-form was given its classic definition by the cultural geographer Fred Kniffen of Louisiana State, who described it as

compounded from the old English unit consisting of one room and end chimney . . . recorded full-blown for the Delaware-Chesapeake section by at least the late 17th century.[28]

He adds:

Certain qualities all "I" houses unfailingly had in common: gables to the side, at least two rooms in length,

one room deep, and two full stories in height . . . these few essentials constitute the basic type, beyond which there are several varieties. . . . Once formed, the "I" type joined the movement southward along the Appalachian axis, swung westward as far as Texas and northward across the Ohio, there joining a trickle that had come westward through Pennsylvania.

More frequently than not, the I-form had a one-story porch running the full, or nearly full, length of the long side.

Finally, once enlarged beyond the standard four rooms (two up, two down), the Philadelphia spec form inevitably became a critical element in the formation of Basic Georgian; that is, approximations on homesteads of those basic qualities of symmetry and regularity of plan, even on occasion some of the more elaborate and symbolic decorative elements, which had become signal elements in the high style known as Georgian. Basic Georgian indeed had become by the mid-eighteenth century

2.66. William and Sarah Hancock house at Hancock's Bridge across the Delaware in Salem County is another Philadelphia house form translated to the country. Its blank wall, designed for contiguous row houses, was employed here and elsewhere in Salem County for a grand statement in glazed red and blue bricks on the founding of a landed family, via commemorative initials, date, and elaborate patterning. (HABS, c. 1936)

2.67. The I-form in its heartland, on a surviving rural patch between two highways, near Principio, Maryland. (IMG:NAL)

the most common style for urban homesteads, occurring in modular units of one-third (two windows above, lined up over window plus door below), two-thirds (three windows above, lined up over two windows plus door below), or full (five windows above, lined up over a central door with two windows on either side) *[2.68]*. As a middle-class mean between elaborately ornamented, large-scaled high-style Georgian palace types or mansions and unornamented, small-scaled folk/vernacular homesteads, Basic Georgian was a cultural expression of a class-structured society; but its widespread adoption testified to the molding force of upward mobility.

General adoption of Georgian forms was preceded by several intermediate stylistic forms, which were less effective for proclaiming class status. One was the two- and three-story saltbox form with overhangs. Varieties of fortified building forms represented another; the bawn is an early example,[29] with the best being Stratford Hall *[2.69]*, which has been so eloquently analyzed by Roger Kennedy.[30] A third was the cross-axial plan. Its projecting two-story porches recalled the gatehouse/antechambers of medieval palaces and their counterparts in Renaissance/Baroque styles perpetuated in country manors and comparable small-palace forms in England. They were thus appropriate signals of special pretension. This social function was enhanced by the porches often bearing ornament in the form of spindles and drops (comparable to the saltbox's overhangs and drops), elaborate gables, coats of arms, and other appurtenances of the successful landed family *[2.70]*. As such the cross-axial plan had peculiar appropriateness in the colonies. In the seventeenth-century South, there were numerous examples of cross-axial mansions (and other types as well, such as the Third State House at Jamestown and the 1676 Maryland State House at Saint Mary's City). Bacon's Castle is the only survivor, though others are known *[2.71]*. But examples could be found in all the colonies[31] and a few famous ones remain. Medway, outside Charleston, begun in 1686, was made into a cross-axial plan (disguised by still later additions) when Thomas Smith anticipated becoming Landgrave (Proprietary Governor) of South Carolina.

The West Indies have preserved far more, thanks to early-nineteenth-century economic stagnation and low population growth. Nicolas Abbey (c. 1660) and Drax Hall (c. 1675) on Barbados are recognizable cross-plans, despite later accretions, while on Bermuda a dozen remain, including the Old Statehouse and the Town Hall in Saint Georges.

But the social function of cross-axial plans with their porches was much more effectively carried out by elements of the High Georgian style: doorways, porticos, freestanding double porches, formal interior entrance halls—all with correspondingly appropriate ornament.[32] By 1700 they were accordingly being superseded almost everywhere by High Georgian styles, which carried associations with upper-class palace architecture irresistibly attractive to classes below.

The appearance of Georgian coincided with, announced, and assisted the culmination of a three-phase pattern of settlement. All colonies experienced something similar. Their first decades were a time of weeding out the unfit. Windbags, sluggards, snobs, and the muddleheaded, regardless of hereditary rank, failed; they died, went back to England, or became poor white trash. A kind of native

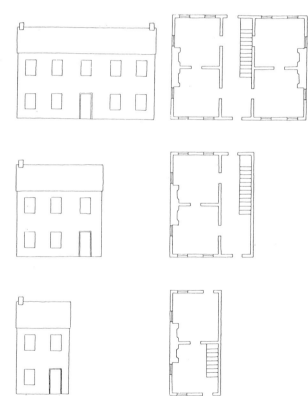

2.68. *Diagrams and plans of full, two-thirds, and one-third Georgian house forms, from Henry C. Glassie, "Eighteenth Century Cultural Process in Delaware Valley Folk Building,"* Winterthur Portfolio *7 (1972).*

2.69. *Stratford Hall in Westmoreland County in Virginia's
Northern Neck, near the small town of Montross, looking up from
the Potomac River. Since rivers were highways, bringing visitors
as well as transporting tobacco and other plantation products, this
would have been the original formal view; it was landscaped
accordingly, on principles of Capability Brown, who worked on
many contemporary estates in England. Stratford was built in the
1720s to be the seat of a great landed family, of which a
deliberate visual metaphor was the Great Hall connecting the two
wings; there portraits of the founders (Thomas Lee and his wife)
face each other across the formal space. Stratford went out of the
Lee family after its heir, Robert Edward, married the daughter of
George Washington Parke Custis and moved to the Custis
Mansion in Arlington. Since 1929 it has been administered as a
public trust by the Robert E. Lee Foundation. (IMG:NAL)*

2.70. *"View of Greenspring House near Jamestown," drawn by
Benjamin H. Latrobe in July 1796. During his Virginia travels
in 1796–98, Latrobe drew several such cross-axial mansions that
caught his eye as romantic antiquities, not long for this world.
Greenspring, built c. 1649 by Governor Sir William Berkeley, was
in fact demolished just after this drawing was made. Latrobe's
diary noted that the building was well preserved despite a
Revolutionary War action fought on the grounds, except for "an
arcade which has falled down. The porch has some clumsy
ornamental brickwork about it of the stile of James the Ist"* (From
Edward C. Carter II, Latrobe's View of America,
1795–1820 *[New Haven, Conn.: Yale University Press, 1985],
p. 100.) (Courtesy of Maryland Historical Society, Baltimore)*

aristocracy developed in succeeding decades, composed of people who had achieved eminence in the colony less because of any social distinctions brought from England than because they had proved tough, bold, hardworking, shrewd, lucky. Those who made the wilderness produce most rose above their fellows proportionately and found emblems for their success appropriate to their station in such architectural metaphors as saltbox and cross-plan forms. But by another generation colonies were producing enough for real wealth, and with it genuine class distinctions began to appear. Enter, at this point, High Georgian.

The style—called variously "Georgian" (from its rough coincidence with the reigns of the first three King Georges of England), "Palladian" (from the great influence on it of the sixteenth-century writings of Andrea Palladio), or, in its own time, "Renaissance," "Italian," or "Roman" (alluding to its source, the so-called rebirth of antiquity promoted by Italian Renaissance humanists two or three centuries before)—began to take definitive form toward the end of the seventeenth century and became steadily more uniform as the eighteenth century progressed. At its most elaborate, on many public buildings and mansions around 1750–1775, the style can properly be called palatial Georgian/Palladian. In its latest phases—and the style did not die out until the early decades of the nineteenth century (see chapter 3)—it was almost a vernacular.

To a late-twentieth-century temper Georgian/Palladian is not very congenial; although Postmodernists have taken many quotes from it, its heavy reliance on books and light emphasis on personality runs counter to architectural trends over the last hundred years. But as historical documentation, Georgian/Palladian has peculiar significance. First, as an unparalleled example of the mysterious workings of cultural lag. Dissemination of successive Georgian/Palladian styles through diverse colonial classes and regions occurred over very predictable spans of time,[33] which cannot be explained by simple mechanical calculations of time elapsed in exchanges of correspondence across the ocean, nor by any demonstrable influence from guidebooks;[34] cultural lag obviously has to do with deep layers of mind.[35] Even more, Georgian/Palladian is unrivaled as a record of the kind of mind-set that led a rising middle class of great merchants to challenge and ultimately unseat an aristocracy.

The constant elements in Georgian/Palladian throughout its history were both a reflection and an

2.71. Bacon's Castle, so called from its role in Nathaniel Bacon's rebellion against the Governor of Virginia in 1676, was built as Claremont Manor by Arthur Allen around 1655. Allen came to Virginia around 1632 and patented huge tracts of land in Surry County; this house proclaimed his manorial status via a cross-plan on the model of an English manor, like Greenspring. When the form lost that social function, the projecting entrance porch was bricked up and served as a quasi-bay window. But the elaborate Jacobean gable, another status symbol, remained. (IMG:NAL)

agent of that impulse toward social order noticeable throughout eighteenth-century literature, music, manners, and emerging scientific thought. Elements systematically conveying ideas and associations of authority were polished and coordinated decade after decade, so that challenges to royal authority that were not explicitly written out until the revolutionary pamphleteering of the 1760s and the declarations of the 1770s had been inherent in American architecture long before, in both plans and ornament.

Symmetry and regularity of plan, fenestration, and facade elevations, signaling "imposed order,"

2.72. *Foster-Hutchinson house, Boston, begun c. 1688 by Colonel John Foster from Buckinghamshire. It was occupied by Thomas Hutchinson as Lieutenant Governor and Governor of Massachusetts on grounds that it was more magnificent than his official residence. It was severely damaged in the Stamp Act riot of 1765, and demolished in 1833. (*Stark's Antique Views of Ye Towne of Boston, *1907)*

2.73. *Reconstruction of the Governor's Palace at Williamsburg. In its time the building imaged both the affluence and political stability achieved in a hundred years' settlement—and a power structure that rested ultimately on massive introduction of black slavery in response to a failing supply of indentured white labor, by the 1660s. Nothing remained of it after fire in 1781 destroyed the main building and the Civil War destroyed the flankers. Reconstruction was based primarily on an engraving from between* 1732 and 1747, *presumed to represent the palace as built by contractor Henry Cary in 1706 for Governor Francis Nicholson. The reconstruction that architects Perry, Shaw & Hepburn began in December 1931 and completed by April 1934 also took into account a plan drawn by Thomas Jefferson and excavations of the foundation. The flankers are based on eighteenth-century Virginia homestead styles. (*IMG:NAL)*

began to appear even in homesteads by the turn of the eighteenth century. But you could see them most obviously and deliberately in palace types and mansions, such as the Foster-Hutchinson house on North Square in Boston, begun around 1688 *[2.72]*. Besides size, it was distinguished from its neighbors by a number of features anticipating High Georgian: pronounced symmetry created by a central entrance axis and flanking sets of windows, themselves internally balanced by mullions; and such ornamental features derived from the Italian Renaissance as matching pilasters molded into the brickwork, roof balustrade, and cupola. A vertical axis is visually created by setting this cupola above the main entrance, which is further accented by a balcony directly above. Collectively all these elements make up an image of authority far more effective than cross-axial plans or saltbox shapes or pent eaves, and, of course, decisively contrasting with the haphazard naturalness of older homestead forms. Its symmetry and balance proclaim the Divine Reason supposed to be incarnate in persons "set in authority over us" in a class-structured social system. Its horizontal lines, decisively rejecting the lingering medieval verticality of earlier seventeenth-century architecture, make visual metaphor of stable hierarchical order. The balcony is an ancient authority sign, transferred to royal and noble palaces from "balconies of appearance" originating with the medieval papacy. The cupola is a Renaissance version of the dome, most venerable of all shapes imaging sacred and royal authority, developed over millennia out of sky and tomb forms. All these features, combining to proclaim Thomas Foster's rise from humble origins to high rank in the colony (judgeship, membership in the Governor's Council), made the house eminently suitable as a residence for Governor Hutchinson later on. How effective an authority symbol it was may be estimated by its being so repeated a target of mobs demonstrating against royal authority in this most fractious of colonies.

A more effective, more mature metaphor of authority was the Governor's Palace at Williamsburg *[2.73]*. It had most of the same elements, but arranged (following prototypes in England and ultimately Michelangelo's Capitol in Rome) so that subjects were *forced* to experience the ruler's power by a controlled sequence of spatial experiences. They could not just walk straight into the presence of royalty or its surrogate; they had to walk around, through constrictions, out into wider spaces again,

in a pattern prearranged by the authority they were experiencing. The effect of such a sophisticated design in a remote province like Virginia must have been enormous. But the novelty did not last long. Soon enough, the rising planter class was emulating and surpassing these governors' palaces with mansions in Palatial Georgian styles that soon became and long remained icons of political and social power: King Carter's Corotoman, Mann Page's Rosewell, the Byrds' Westover, the Burwells' Carter's Grove, the Harrisons' Berkeley, and many more *[2.74, 2.75]*. And by the middle and late eighteenth century, Georgian/Palladian mansions, albeit usually more modest, were being built for sea captains, merchants of every description, even tanners in remote places like Appoquinimink Creek in the tiny Province of Delaware. They varied in detail, but were all governed by the same canon *[2.76]*. This cultural expression is indeed for late-twentieth-century architectural historians the principal interest of this body of building, which once constituted the main theme of American architecture. It is a history of the Revolution in three dimensions.

A similar purpose, with similar historical interest, can be recognized in Palatial Georgian's characteristic ornamental elements. Porticos big and small, robust and delicate, and pediments, cornices, pilasters, "Palladian" or "Venetian" windows, ornamental iron railings, fanlights over doorways all come ultimately from ancient Rome via the Italian Renaissance through the medium of builders' guides, and all ultimately allude to sources of authority and social status *[2.77–2.80]*. Since something very like that social function for them revived in the early twentieth century, few indeed are the historical examples of Colonial that have not undergone some Colonial Revival "improvements."

From early in the eighteenth century, Palatial Georgian/Palladian became the normal and invariable style for official buildings of all sorts—not only mansions but homesteads, not only official palace types like state- and court-houses, but others perceived as having public character, such as universities, schools *[2.81]*, customs houses, libraries *[2.57]*, and insofar as they had a public social function, churches.

All high-style Colonial English architecture drew on homeland models. Little if any of it was as faithful to them as furniture, however, and it is in furniture that the style's eighteenth-century evolution can best be seen *[2.82]*. At a time when the best architecture in America was still being designed by

2.74. *According to the brochure from which this illustration is taken, "Carter's Grove was one of the plantations that anchored the world of the Virginia planter aristocracy. This group of some 100 families dominated the colony's productive economy, its political offices, and its social life, and from this culture came a generation of enlightened and accomplished leaders." Many of* these family names are still prominent in Virginia, West Virginia, and national politics. Carter's Grove near Williamsburg was built in 1750–51 by Carter Burwell, employing Richard Baylis as woodworker and David Minetree as contractor. Like many other such houses, it was "improved" in a 1920s restoration that raised its roof and added a third floor.

Berkeley Datestone

2.75. *"Berkeley," says the brochure from which these drawings are excerpted, "has no peer among the James River plantations as a center of historical interest and as a beautifully restored example of the mansions that graced Virginia's 'Golden Age.' . . . The land . . . was part of a grant . . . by King James I to the Berkeley Company. . . . On December 4, 1619, the settlers stepped ashore . . . and celebrated the first Thanksgiving Day more than a year before the Pilgrims arrived in New England. . . . It was as the home of the Harrison family that Berkeley achieved its greatness. The early Georgian mansion . . . was built in 1726 by [the father of] Benjamin Harrison, signer of the Declaration of Independence, thrice Governor of Virginia. . . . Colonel Harrison's younger son William Henry . . . was elected President of the United States. . . . The Harrison family was yet to produce another President in Benjamin, grandson of William Henry." Datestone commemorating the family-founding builders (Benjamin and Ann Harrison) is a sophisticated Georgian counterpart to the big initials and dates on homesteads in Salem County, New Jersey [2.66].*

2.76. *This fine brick mansion built c. 1773 for successful tanner William Corbit in Appoquinimink Creek, now Odessa, Delaware, featured woodwork by Robert May of Philadelphia and the local usage of black shutters above and white below. Like almost all the famous Georgian mansions familiar in American architectural history, this one has had some twentieth-century restoration; unlike all too many, its restoration was minimal and judicious. (IMG:NAL)*

itinerant carpenters and bookish gentlemen ama-
teurs, American painting was entirely imitative, and
sculpture was a matter of figureheads and tombstones, furniture produced by professional craftsmen in competent command of their medium was
following at an entirely consistent remove the sequence of English styles: William and Mary (in England c. 1685–1700; in America c. 1700–25), Queen
Anne (in England, including Early Georgian, c.
1700–40; in America c. 1725–50), Chippendale (in
England c. 1740–65; in America c. 1750–85), and
Adamesque/Federal (in America c. 1785–c. 1820),
corresponding to English "neoclassical" styles like
Adam, Sheraton, and Heppelwhite.

In Palladian Georgian's regular and orderly development the eighteenth-century mind is admirably manifested, especially its fascination with the
idea of law. Newton's Law of Gravity, Samuel Johnson's *Dictionary* establishing laws of the English language, Montesquieu's *Spirit of the Laws* were all
products of an underlying conviction that everything in life, from theology to mechanics, could be
ultimately knowable in, and reducible to, terms
of what that age called philosophic reason, and
ours science. The relationship of everything to
everything else could be reexamined in the light of
overriding abstract principles owing nothing to theological or feudal preconceptions, unprejudiced by
spiritual concerns—what we might call psychological factors. As long as that conviction remained
strong, Palladian Georgian would remain a dominant style; no other style could so satisfy the ideal
of a built environment totally balanced, wholly ordered, all in sharp three-dimensional light and
shadow, every part uniformly manifesting the powers of Man's reasoning mind.

Palladian High Georgian was also an appropriate
style for churches, insofar as the sanctuary type
functioned in the English colonies as elsewhere for
transmission and preservation of cultural identity.
Five principal stylistic forms can be identified in
sanctuary types of the English colonies. They correspond to those diverse effects requisite for different
social strata in the several colonies: (1) traditional
tower and nave, inherited from medieval ages; (2)
rectangular meetinghouse, towerless and otherwise
unornamented; (3) New England Puritan meetinghouse; (4) Wren/Gibbs High Georgian; (5) Southern Plantation Anglican.

Naves with tower attached had been the norm
for parish churches in England, and elsewhere on
the continent, for hundreds of years before English

2.77. *The most common element in palatial Georgian/Palladian
style is what in the eighteenth century was called a Venetian
window and is now more commonly called Palladian, from its
inventor or first popularizer, the sixteenth-century architect Andrea
Palladio.*

2.78. *Interior doorways like this mid-eighteenth-century example
at Morven in Princeton, New Jersey, with pilasters, keystone arch,
and fanlight, are characteristically lighter and smaller than exterior
doorways. Photograph by Elizabeth G. C. Menzies shows
restoration of c. 1930.*

2.79. Fireplace walls were interior focal points in the eighteenth as in earlier centuries. This elaborate example occurs in Boxwood Hall, Elizabeth, New Jersey, c. 1750. It is characteristic of Colonial interiors to have been tidied up and otherwise improved during the Colonial Revival earlier this century. (Photograph by M.W. Barish)

2.80. Since the 1960s, more systematic research has drastically altered the appearance given to many famous Georgian mansions by Colonial Revival restorations earlier in the century. Thus the newly (1986) restored entrance hall of Gunston Hall, the mansion George Mason built near Lorton, Virginia, in 1755 and lavishly ornamented with woodwork fashioned by English expert William Buckland, offers many surprises to those familiar with the earlier restoration of the 1910s. "Originally the center hall, in front of its pilaster-supported double arch, had been decorated with twelve additional pilasters, a pair flanking each door and window. . . . These twelve fluted pilasters had supported a complete Doric entablature, including a missing frieze under the remaining cornice. . . . Paint analysis indicates white oil base paint . . . on the woodwork . . . wallpaper between the pilasters in the hall" (Mary Lee Allen, "A New Look at Gunston Hall," Fairfax Chronicles 11/4 [1987]).

settlers came to America. They reproduced it as a matter of course, and this form remained a stereotypical norm in North America throughout the nineteenth and most of the twentieth century. Saint Luke's, Smithfield, in Surrey County, Virginia, from the 1680s, is probably the best-known early American example *[2.83].* [36] Towers were often added later, as at Williamsburg's Burton Parish. Its basic rectangle was built in 1711–15, and its pews were laid out in a ranking that manifested and furthered the class-structured social system governing Virginia (and all other English colonies): proper places all prescribed for parishioners, councillors, members of the House of Burgesses, and students from the College of William and Mary (in the balcony). But the tower was not added until 1769–71. Not until 1820 did Immanuel Church in New Castle, Delaware, get a tower added to its original small rectangle, begun in the 1680s *[2.84, 2.85].* Saint James Goose Creek, near Beaufort, South Carolina, of c. 1711, though elegant enough (as shown by an interior restored in the 1960s with royal arms, Commandment tablets, and the pelican emblem of

2.81. *Engraved between 1732 and 1747 on the upper part of the Bodleian plate were buildings of the College of William and Mary at Williamsburg (chartered 1693), said in Hugh Jones's* Present State of Virginia *(1732) to have been "first modelled by Sir Christopher Wren, adapted to the Nature of the County." Adapted indeed; but how much is attributable to Wren is hardly the point. The "Wren Building" was an image of the new social order created by the Glorious Revolution, and the mindset of its creators. On such an intellectual model (and to some extent architectural, too) Harvard College began shaping itself in the 1720s; later Brown at Providence and the College of New Jersey at Princeton acquired comparable buildings (designed by Robert Smith of Philadelphia). Thus young colonial aristocrats could pass from a mansion to a college to the halls of a capitol, perchance even to a Governor's Palace, in the same Georgian/Palladian architectural environment.*

2.82. *Drawings from Moreton Marsh,* The Easy Expert, *of case pieces from four quarters of the eighteenth century, illustrating consistency of evolution within the framework of the Georgian/Palladian style. Thomas Chippendale wrote in* A Gentleman and Cabinet Maker's Director *(first edition, 1754), "Without an acquaintance with this science [architectural geometry] and some knowledge of the rules of perspective, the cabinetmaker cannot make the designs of his work intelligible, nor shew, in a little compass, the whole conduct and effect of the piece."*

| 1700–1720 | 1730–1755 | 1760–1775 | 1780–1800 |

the Society for the Propagation of the Gospel in Foreign Parts prominently displayed), never got its tower at all. Saint Anne's in Middletown, Delaware, is another example.

Many sanctuary types were built by congregations who did not want the "public" sign made by a tower, with or without steeple [2.84]. Stricter sects of Baptists as a matter of course. Likewise Quakers, and Jews—only increasing size and scale manifested the expanding prosperity and social influence of their communities (e.g., Greater Meetinghouse opposite the Town Hall in Philadelphia; Touro synagogue, in Newport, Rhode Island [2.48]. Presbyterians usually—witness towerless Old Drawyer's Church near Odessa, Delaware [2.86], or Old Tennent in Monmouth County, New

Jersey of 1751, with only the tiniest of cupolas stuck onto the roof above one end and main entrance in a side wall.

By the Revolution, the same upward social mobility manifested in the steady shift of homestead types toward Georgian affected sanctuary types also. Many previously plain meetinghouses sprouted sizeable cupolas, towers, and steeples. The trend was most notable in New England. There, Puritans, who had originally shunned "steeple-houses" in what they believed to have been the spirit of early Christians, had invented for their meetinghouses a two-story cubical structure on a squarish plan, capped by a pyramidal roof [2.87] whose principal inspiration seems to have come from traditional small English town/

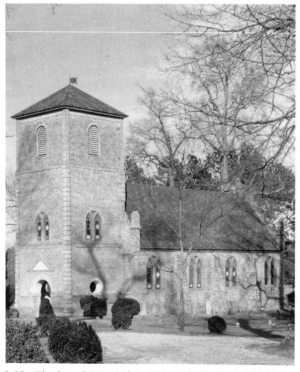

2.83. *The date of Saint Luke's (Episcopal) church, Smithfield, Virginia, has been much disputed; consensus now seems to date the whole, not just the upper part of the tower, from the 1680s. Such a church could well have been built in England at the same period; flat east ends (this one with stepped brick gable) distinguished English churches from medieval cathedrals through the eighteenth century. Pointed arches of the medieval Gothic style survived in rural England also through the seventeenth century. The interior was restored in the 1950s on the assumption church dated from 1632, hence as an example of usage at the time of Laudian High Church reform, with rood screen and the rest—quite different from 1680s usage. (IMG:NAL)*

2.84. *The original small rectangle that was the eighteenth-century Immanuel Church on the Green in New Castle, Delaware, has since been overpowered by additions—first a heavy tower and steeple added in Gothic style (at his own expense) by William Strickland in 1820, then a south cross-aisle by Stephen Button of Philadelphia just after the Civil War. It is a typical history for a Colonial Anglican church. (IMG:NAL)*

2.85. *The interior of Immanuel Church was refurbished in the 1930s, about the same time as the Delaware State Capitol at Dover, which shows the same delicate kind of Colonial Revival taste, was built. This view shows the old section of the church, looking toward altar, as it looked in the 1950s; the same elements as in Saint Luke's are recognizable, but in different scale and proportion to each other. Destroyed by fire 1 February 1980; restored 1981–82. (IMG:NAL)*

2.86. *Old Drawyer's Church in Odessa, Delaware, built for a Scotch-Irish Presbyterian congregation. Woodwork by Robert May, who was working for William Corbit at the same time and place (1773) (see 2.76). (HABS)*

2.87. *Something of the simplicity of design intended to create a visual image of society purged from corruption is evident in this engraving of the 1702 First Meeting House in West Springfield, Massachusetts, before its demolition in c. 1870. (From C. A. Place, "From Meeting House to Church in New England,"* Old-Time New England, *1922)*

2.88. *In the foreground of this picture is the squarish bulk of Old Ship Meetinghouse at Hingham, Massachusetts, begun in 1681, enlarged in 1731 and again in 1755, relegated to civic functions shortly thereafter, when the new church in the background was built. The meetinghouse was restored as a historical monument in 1930. (IMG:NAL)*

market halls—an expression of the consistent Puritan refusal to recognize a separation of "secular" from "religious" activities. But in the theocracy that such a conviction necessarily produced when the Puritans became an establishment in New England, whatever served as their meetinghouse necessarily functioned also as a public building, and so public "signs" soon began appearing on it: tower-like structures and/or cupolas. By the early eighteenth century the old form was rapidly being superseded by more conventional rectangular, towered, and steepled designs. At Hingham you can see old and new styles of meetinghouse together, as the successor to Old Ship was erected directly across the street [2.88].

But the older style had a long afterlife. Because the original meetinghouses had normally been used not only for worship, but also for assemblies of every kind, including school, its old form retained associations with government and education long after it was no longer used for worship. So in regions settled by emigrants from Massachusetts, it was common to find the old Puritan meetinghouse shape being perpetuated, as if by instinct, for use in

capitols [2.89], courthouses (Burlington County Courthouse, Mount Holly, New Jersey, 1796; the first courthouse in Independence, Missouri, c. 1836); town halls (Port Hope, Ontario, of c. 1845); universities; high schools; even fire stations.

Of course the most conspicuous sanctuary types in the English colonies were those erected for the Church of England, "by law established." They took what can best be called the Wren/Gibbs style of Palladian High Georgian. Examples once stood in prominent central places of every colonial capital—architectural declarations of the authority, the uniformity, and the acknowledged source of the body of laws that bound them all together—just as, in the colonial cities of the Roman Empire, there had stood a recognizable facsimile of the Temple of Capitoline Jupiter.

The First British Empire's definitive image was a distinctive form of church first devised by Sir Christopher Wren to replace medieval churches lost in London's Great Fire of 1666, but brought to polished systematic form by James Gibbs for Saint Martin-in-the-Fields, as completed in 1718 [2.90, 2.91]. Saint Martin's was not just another London

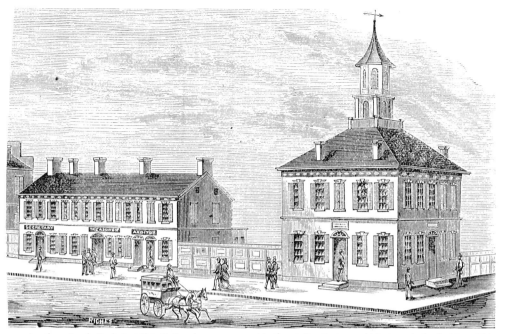

2.89. An engraving from Jacob Studer's 1873 Columbus, Ohio *showing the Third Ohio Capitol, built in 1814 and burned in 1852, on the main street with the old State Offices (1815, demolished 1857) beside it. Through such a distinctively New England building form, patterns of settlement in the Old* Northwest Territories could be traced; the first two Ohio capitols, at Chillicothe and Zanesville, were of this type, and so was the second (1813–50) Indiana capitol at Corydon, a stone building that still stands.*

parish church. It was the official church of the Admiralty—seat of the sea power on which Britain's First Empire rested—and the parish church of the sovereign. It was a symbol, then, and designed as such by Gibbs (in consensus with the parish Building Committee, of course, this being the 1710s)—to project an image of that Protestant establishment come to power in the Glorious Revolution of 1689 and consolidated by the Hanoverian succession in 1714. Every element made a meaningful contribution.[37]

Saint Martin's tower was not an addition to a rectangular body, of the traditional sort; it was set within the body of the church, so that its base formed a kind of proto-vestibule. Such an arrangement allowed for a full front portico, whose model was plain: the Roman Pantheon, in unmistakable allusion to the great empire to which some Britons were beginning to compare themselves. Rising above that portico was a tower composed of tiers of geometric shapes, whose height recalled something of traditional English Gothic towers and spires (deliberately, for Gibbs knew "steeples are Gothick"), but whose specific forms were taken from Renais-

sance Italy. It culminated in a steeple; but its most prominent feature was a clock—since medieval times the mark of an establishment ordering the community's hours. On the exterior, resolute Protestantism was proclaimed by a roof-level balustrade and row of urns anchoring the building firmly to the ground and visually refuting the soaring claims of Italian Baroque churches. A double row of windows in the side walls not only reinforced this horizontal accent, but, more significantly, also announced galleries within—to mark this as a preaching, rather than sacramentally ordered, church. Saint Martin's form proclaimed, then, the State Church of sober William of Orange rather than fervent and feckless James II; the Church of stoutly Protestant Anne; and now, Church of the stolid Hanoverians and those who put them on a constitutional throne. It was not a reworked medieval church, nor a revised Roman one, but something definitely new and appropriate to its function in and for the new establishment.

On the interior arcades with giant columns, to which the balconies are attached, and arcades springing from a detached piece of entablature above the capitals would remind empire-building Englishmen not so much (if at all) of Brunelleschi, the creative artist, as of the Medicis, for whom Brunelleschi worked and for whose churches of San Lorenzo and Santo Spirito he perfected this motif. For England's eighteenth-century establishment, composed not only of hereditary aristocrats but also of self-made merchant lords, the Medicis were admired prototypes and models (as they have been for comparable classes ever since): rich, competent in business and finance, yet much more than mere money grubbers; they were civic leaders and great patrons of art and architecture, capable not only of amassing wealth but of creating a great state. Ostentatiously set in a flat east end—since the early Middle Ages English churches of importance traditionally had flat east ends—was the most prominent of all emblematic elements in this substyle: the Palladian, or what they would have called it in the eighteenth century, Venetian window, a conscious mark, as Howard Stutchbury has pointed out, of "admiration of the Whig society for the Venetian constitution and its reflection in the way of life of an aristocracy similarly dependent upon sea-borne trade as much as upon inherited landed wealth."[38]

By such a combination of key signal elements, Saint Martin's in all respects became an especially compelling visual metaphor of the goals and justifications of the First British Empire, promoted by an oligarchy based upon sea power and at every

2.90. *Elevation and plan of the Church of Saint Martin-in-the-Fields, London, as it appeared in James Gibbs's* Book of Architecture, *1728.*

2.91. *Interior of Saint Martin-in-the-Fields as restored in 1958 to state depicted in watercolor by Thomas Malton of c. 1770. (IMG:NAL, 1965)*

point interrelated with the interests and ambitions of a rising mercantile class. Or more precisely, perhaps, a visual metaphor of the basic values and justifications of that empire—a metaphor of British law and institutions, and the supernatural verities held to underlie them. To replicate such a metaphor in the capital city of every colony was as natural to the eighteenth-century British Empire as was replication of imperial images in the Roman Empire of antiquity. Not, of course, an exact literal copy in the "DOS-diskcopy" sense; rather, a replication in the sense of one of a series of visible and tangible signs, none exactly similar to the next but all referring to a common truth outside themselves, a truth that is abstract and unchanging, as the law is compared to individual suits in lawcourts, as the Church is compared to individual congregations.

Thus, Christ Church in Philadelphia (begun c. 1728, completed 1744; some alterations 1836; refurbishings in 1950s and 1970s) is not an exact copy of Saint Martin's or any other church in England *[2.92]*. Nor was it the invention of physician John Kearsley, who was a warden in charge of the building program. Christ Church merely assembled enough key elements of Saint Martin's to call the London church to mind. It has an ordered sequence of tower stages quite like an alternate design in Gibbs's *Book of Architecture,* a balustrade, urns, a Venetian window formed in brick in the east end, interior giant columns with attached galleries, an arcade with detatched entablature, but no portico.

The same was true of Saint Paul's in New York (begun 1760s, spire and portico added 1790s) *[2.93]*, Saint Michael's in Charleston (begun 1752, considerably rebuilt after 1886, refurbished 1938) *[2.94]*, King's College Chapel in Boston (1749–54), and Saint Paul's in Halifax (begun 1750, remodeled 1866). None exactly resembles the other; all indubitably recall their common prototype; all, therefore, have the common social function of proclaiming law and religion common to all the British colonies.

That function remained valid in British North America after the Revolution. The single most striking witness to Saint Martin's continuing effectiveness as a metaphor of the Old Empire is Quebec's Holy Trinity Cathedral of 1803 *[2.95, 2.96]*. Its "architect," as in the old colonies, was a leading supporter of the British connection[39]; its interior is crammed with memorabilia—tablets commemorating imperial service, tattered battle flags, and behind the pulpit a white marble monument to Jacob

2.92. *Interior of Christ Church, Philadelphia, restored to its original whiteness 1953–70. Executed from Gibbs's prescription, beginning c. 1727, under the direction of Dr. John Kearsley, physician and leading contributor; the spire was added in the 1750s by Robert Smith, following Gibbs, perhaps via a Scottish intermediary. It was altered to Classical Revival taste in 1836, under Thomas U. Walter. (IMG:NAL)*

Mountain, first Anglican bishop of Quebec, who angrily denounced the covert consecration of French Catholic Bishop Briand in France: "How can there be two bishops in the same city?" And Saint Martin's social function was continued too in a whole series of little Anglican churches in Nova Scotia *[2.97]* erected under the aegis of Bishop Charles Inglis, a Loyalist/Tory who was formerly of Trinity Parish New York. Its outline, and something of its associations were still discernible in the first cathedrals of Toronto and Montreal.

After the Revolution the Georgian/Palladian forms of Saint Martin's could no longer function in the United States as metaphors of the British Empire, of course. But they could function as metaphors of "leading denomination," and in that capacity survived, and indeed thrived.

Already in 1775 First Baptist meetinghouse in Providence assembled elements from the Saint Martin's prototype to proclaim "leading denomina-

2.93 (top, left). Saint Paul's was begun in 1760 as a chapel of ease for Trinity Parish, in what was then the northern outskirts of the capital of New York. It was "completed" in 1790 under James Crommelin Lawrence, who added a spire and portico from Gibbs's book; the latter was put at the back of the church because busy Broadway had now made this the principal entrance (to this day one enters at the altar end). It thus obscured the Palladian east-end window. (IMG:NAL)

2.94 (left). Saint Michael's was begun in 1753 in Charleston, capital of South Carolina, "on the Plan of one of Mr. Gibson's designs." It was rebuilt in 1886; the chancel was redecorated 1906; and in 1938 paint was stripped off interior woodwork "to reveal natural dark cedar." Executed by local builder Samuel Cardy. (IMG:NAL)

2.95 (top, right). Holy Trinity Cathedral, a simplified version of Saint Martin's, erected 1803 under the supervision of career officer Major William Robe. It was flanked in the early twentieth century by two other architectural statements of English presence and power in the capital of French Canada: Château Frontenac [2.20] and Price Tower, built in 1929 and for thirty years Quebec's only skyscraper. (IMG:NAL)

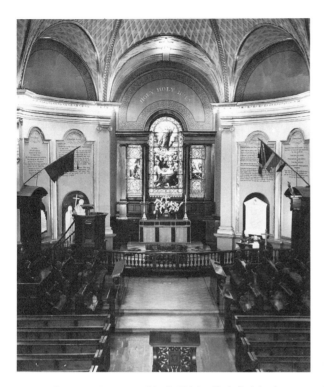

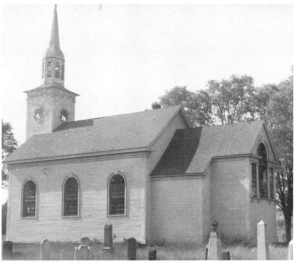

2.96. *The east end interior of Holy Trinity Cathedral is also a somewhat simplified version of Saint Martin's. By the 1860s the model's original symbolic compulsion was fading, and awe was emphasized over decorum by replacing the original white and gold color scheme with darkened wood and stained glass effects derived from the Gothic Revival. This happened as well to the interiors of Christ Church in Philadelphia and Saint Michael's in Charleston; there, however, the original effects have been restored. (IMG:NAL)*

2.97 *(top, right). The tiny church of Saint Mary's in Auburn was one of three similar Nova Scotia churches (along with Saint Stephen's, Chester [dem. 1840], and Saint John's, Cornwallis, near Williams) built in the 1790s with exaggerated east-end Palladian windows dramatizing the loyalties of designer and consecrator Bishop Charles Inglis, late of Trinity Parish, New York. (IMG:NAL)*

2.98 *(right). Joseph Brown, designer of mansions for Providence's leading family (his own), chose for its leading denomination (his own) a mix of elements from Gibbs's* Book of Architecture *that he had not used in his domestic building. This view shows Palladian window on the east end of the First Baptist Meetinghouse, and on the west a spire taken from one of the alternative designs for Saint Martin's. On the interior, Saint Martin's arcades were adapted to a squarish meetinghouse plan. (IMG:NAL)*

tion" or "principal church" *[2.98]*. This was a lead followed prolifically in later decades (Congregational churches at Middlebury and Bennington, Vermont, in 1805 and 1807, for example). Even closer allusions to Saint Martin's appeared in the 1810s and 1820s in Connecticut, proclaiming Congregationalist hopes of becoming an established church there; examples include Center and North churches in New Haven *[2.99]* and the "famous four": Milford, Southington, Cheshire, and Litchfield. But the really climactic monument, in terms of social function, was Kawaiahao Church in Honolulu *[2.100]*.

The Saint Martin's prototype also became a common stylistic form for courthouses; John Brown was tried and hanged in one—the Jefferson County Courthouse at Charles Town in West Virginia (1836, remodeled 1872).

This paradoxical imagery of an idealized Puritan New England derived from the official First Empire Anglican style finally passed into the Colonial Revival. That process began as early as Arlington Street Church on the south side of Boston Common, built by the old elite in 1859, when the first effects of the mighty Irish inrush were beginning to be felt. It was still going on in the 1920s, when the Wren/Gibbs form symbolized "patriotic old American" in Memorial Church on the Harvard campus; "patriotic new American" at the seminary chapel Cardinal Mundelein built at Saint Mary of the Lake forty miles from Chicago to assert the loyalties of his largely German-descended diocese [40]; and "leading denomination in the South" at the chapel Arthur Loomis designed for the Southern Baptist Seminary in Louisville. By stages the form passed into Popular/Commercial usages: in the South remain-

2.99. Churches on the New Haven Green: Trinity Episcopal, begun 1814 in Gothic by Ithiel Town (foreground); and two Congregational churches making claims to preeminence via Saint Martin's architectural forms: Center (First Congregational) of 1812 by Town via Asher Benjamin's adaptations of Gibbs; and North, designed 1812, completed 1815, by Ebenezer Johnson of New Haven. (IMG:NAL)

2.100. Kawaiahao Church in the historic center of Honolulu was designed by missionary Hiram Bingham and built 1839–42 by Hawaiians converted to New England Congregationalism. Insofar as practical under the circumstances (lime kilns, coral rock quarries, and appropriately cut timbers all had to be improvised), its forms recalled those Wren/Gibbs-derived churches which Congregationalists in New England had adapted to proclaim "leading denomination" at the time the missions were sent out. (IMG:NAL)

2.101. *Christ Church, Lancaster County, monument to Robert "King" Carter of Virginia. Front view as it was before restorations of 1970s. (IMG:NAL)*

2.102. *East end of Christ Church, showing sarcophagi of Robert "King" Carter and his two wives. One theory suggests that these were originally located inside, as in comparable family memorial churches in Britain. (HABS, c. 1950. The fence and frame structure are gone, but sarcophagi remain in the same place.)*

ing a meaningful form into the 1980s, in the North mainly reduced to a stereotyped Christmas card and crèche image.

An interesting contrast to the official Wren/ Gibbs Anglican church style was a form developed especially in plantations on the Northern Neck of Virginia between the Rappahannock and the Potomac (incidentally the region from which so many Founding Fathers came). It was a cube with four more or less equal arms, so that the plan approximates a Greek cross. It had no towers nor evidence of planning for any, galleries only at the ends of the arms, or none, elaborate brick moldings around doors and windows, and a pyramidal roof. The archetype is Christ Church in Lancaster County, known as King Carter's Church, whose date for completion generally is given as 1732, but which may have been begun as early as 1728 or 1722, or as late as 1735–36 *[2.101, 2.102]*. Its elegant proportions alone would mark it as having special significance; in "King Carter's Church"[41] I argued that its distinctive plan derived from a special type of family memorial church which had been developed (via an ancient tradition of central-type quasi-domical mausolea going back almost to the beginnings of architectural history) in the decades after the Glorious Whig Revolution of 1689 to celebrate the swift rise of many hitherto obscure families to great social prominence and political power. The Fox family memorial at Farley in Wiltshire is one exam-

ple; the Queensberry family memorial at Durisdeer in Dumfriesshire is another. King Carter's rise in the New World had been comparably meteoric; the form would have seemed entirely appropriate for his purposes. Quite a number of churches in Virginia from the same period as King Carter's were built on cruciform plans. Whether they also were family mausolea is doubtful, especially since very comparable churches can be found from the same period elsewhere—Saint Thomas-in-the-East near Morant Bay in Jamaica has a startling resemblance to King Carter's, for instance. In any event King Carter's Church remains one of the great monuments to eighteenth-century American architecture at its aesthetic best, and the body of plantation churches in this style is a telling witness to that founding of great landed families on which the Old Empire, and therefore the Republic that superseded it, was based.

Colonial Architecture as Continuing Cultural Expression

From the colonial era American civilization inherited two traits that are still among its most distinctive characteristics.

One is the American assumption that everyone has a right to a home and some land. Lots of Americans in the colonial era did not in fact have a home

2.103. *George Washington's Mount Vernon, land side, as created by additions and enlargements to the original 1740s house in c. 1759. (IMG:NAL)*

2.104. *Palladian window wall in the large dining room of Mount Vernon, planned in 1773, completed 1787. As restored in the 1970s, the glass is clear and looks out onto the landscaped grounds, while the mirrors reflect windows at the other end. Note the cover cornice and delicate Adamesque/Rococo plasterwork. (Courtesy of the Mount Vernon Ladies' Association)*

2.105. River side of Mount Vernon, showing the famous portico added in the 1780s. (IMG:NAL)

of their own, nor land; the same is true today. But the assumption remains; it is more than an assumption, it is an *expectation,* a *right.*

The most dramatic manifestation of this attitude was the mass-prefabrication of suburban houses on their own lots in 1890–1930 and later. Nothing like it was seen in the world before—thousands upon thousands of people of all classes insisting upon homes of their own, and getting them. Nor did it end with the 1930s. Mobile homes continued to manifest the same impulse, and so did the enormous popularity of television shows like *Dallas* or *Dynasty,* whose central image was indeed the creation of a landed family in a home of its own, amassing its own acres and possessions. This is all the more striking once you realize that fiction in this case followed fact, that the Ewings of Southfork *were* the Kennedys of Hyannisport, even to their casts' physical features.

A second characteristic of American civilization descended from the colonial era is restlessness. The famous observation that De Tocqueville made in his American travels during the 1830s is still valid as ever; the American is one who

> builds a house in which to spend his old age, and . . . sells it before the roof is on; he plants a garden and lets it just as the trees are coming into bearing; he brings a field into tillage and leaves other men to gather the crops . . . he settles in a place, which he soon afterwards leaves to carry his changeable longings elsewhere.

Not of course that Americans were shiftless; rather, they were constantly seeking self-improvement by changes of some kind—moving, upgrading, whatever. And if we had to choose a single building that would best express *both* fundamental American assumptions—that home ownership is one fundamental right, and another is to keep continuously upgrading it—there could hardly be a better choice than Mount Vernon on the Potomac, a few miles east of Washington, D.C. *[2.103–2.105].*

Like all Colonial mansions, Mount Vernon presents a visual metaphor of enduring, purposeful family-founding—as often a mercantile as a landed family, though in this case both, for the Washingtons understood "estate" in both senses. Like most Colonial mansions that image was not cast in elegantly correct Palladian Georgian forms.[42] What makes Mount Vernon a consummate expression of colonial culture continuing into the present is, rather, just the opposite: its curiously unfinished quality, even in its present hallowed setting. And that is not because it was arrested somehow in the process of completing some ideal and permanent composition; rather, Mount Vernon had no point of completion; it was forever being added onto.

The unprepossessing farmhouse begun around 1740 by Lawrence Washington (who also bestowed its name, after a now-forgotten British naval hero) and acquired in 1754 by his half-brother George got its first major enlargement and facelift just before Washington's marriage in 1759 to widow Martha Dandridge Custis. At that time it gained an extra half-story, exterior surfacing of channeled boards sanded to imitate stone, an entrance hall, dining room, and west parlor. An effort to tie the whole together by attached design elements—most notably a full pediment inserted in the wall, without pilasters or correspondence to the windows—was hardly successful. Nor was unity of design furthered by more enlargements projected for 1773—library with master bedroom above and a great banquet hall with Palladian window (finished inside only after the war)—which were to mark Washington's growing civic responsibilities as Virginia burgess, Truro parish vestryman and Pohick church warden, justice of the peace, and prospective delegate to the first Virginia Provincial Convention and the First Continental Congress. The whole was pulled together only from the river front, and only after the war, by the addition of the two-story porch fronting the Potomac and the octagonal cupola. These features changed the building from a colonial English mansion to a Roman Revival monumental icon appropriate to its owner's status as first President of the new Republic. He was in fact rarely home; Edward Savage's popular portrayal of the Washington Family of 1790 showed the general "at home" dressed in full military uniform and spurs, ready to leave on a moment's notice at the nation's call.[43]

Of course no changes or additions ever made Mount Vernon into a big, imposing mansion by contemporary European standards. Compared to the seats of English nobility like Kedleston or Stowe, it and all its neighbors—Gunston Hall, Berkeley, Westover—were pathetically tiny places. The contrast dramatizes how audacious was the challenge their owners made to the mighty British Empire by their declaration of Independence: "they *don't* necessarily do things better in Europe." In twentieth-century America, especially after the 1940s, when European Modernism came in, that attitude seemed reversed forever, and all comprehension of Mount Vernon's iconic symbolism lost. Yet it has been preserved on the popular level. And if nowadays Mount Vernon the icon chiefly occurs in the form of roadside restaurants, shopping centers, and middle-class housing developments, that is more than simply ironic; it is an ironic recognition that the ideals of Mount Vernon are still those of a mute majority of Americans.

Notes

1. "American culture in this early period becomes most fully comprehensible when seen as the exotic far western periphery, a marchland, of the metropolitan European culture system." "Proposition 4" of Bernard Bailyn's *The Peopling of British North America* (New York: Knopf, 1986), p. 112.

2. On the diversity of colonial arts, see also Dell Upton, ed., *America's Architectural Roots: Ethnic Groups That Built America* (Washington, D.C.: The Preservation Press, 1986). In a review (*Journal of the Society of Architectural Historians 47/3 [1988]: 316–17*) Bryan F. Le Beau comments: "Upton is correct in noting that serious scholarship is lacking on the ethnic architecture of [Italians, Greeks, Poles, and Jews] . . . like the Irish or Chinese, who are included, they may have left their mark on American interiors rather than exteriors."

3. On a principle aptly expressed by Amos Rapoport in *House Form and Culture: Foundations of Cultural Geography* (Englewood Cliffs, NJ: Prentice-Hall, 1969, p. 47): "Given a certain climate, the availability of certain materials, and the constraints and capabilities of given level of technology, what finally determines the form of a dwelling and molds the spaces and their relationships is the vision that people have of the ideal life."

4. The best case has been made by John Vlach, "The Shotgun House and African Architectural Legacy," in *Common Places,* ed. Dell Upton and J. Vlach (Athens: University of Georgia Press, 1985); see also his "Afro-American Domestic Artifacts in 18th-Century Virginia," *Material Culture* 19 (1987):3–23.

5. It is hard for moderns to imagine just how rigidly nobility and bourgeoisie [middle class] were separated by unbreachable compartments, not only in autocratic countries like France, Prussia, and Austria, but in England and even (!) the American colonies—as has been emphasized in America, in Jackson Turner Main's classic *The Social Structure of Revolutionary America* (Princeton, N.J.: Princeton University Press, 1965) and, more recently, John Corrigan, *The Hidden Balance* (Cambridge: Cambridge University Press, 1987). Corrigan cites examples like "James Bollocke, a Taylor" in Virginia being fined for arranging to race his horse against one owned by "Mr. Matthew Slader," "it being contrary to Law for a Labourer to make a race, being a sport only for Gentlemen."

6. "After felling the trees you must begin to clear the site and then, following the plan I have made, you must mark out the public places . . . : the plaza, church, town hall and jail, market and slaughterhouse, hospital. . . ."

Cortes in 1525, quoted in John McAndrew, *The Open-Air Churches of Sixteenth-Century Mexico* (Cambridge, Mass.: Harvard University Press, 1965), chapter III, "New Towns."

7. Originating as far back as the "balcony of appearances" invented for the Papal Jubilee of 1300; for examples see Adolf Reinle, *Zeichensprache der Architektur: Symbol, Darstellung und Brauch* in *der Baukunst des Mittelalters und der Neuzeit* (Zurich and Munich: Artemis, 1976). Every Colo-

nial style in North America had examples of this element in palaces or mansions, or both; the Governor's Palace at Williamsburg is best known.

8. On the sociological background of such Anglo-Spanish mansions in northern California generally, and Monterey in particular, see Harold Kirker, "The Role of Hispanic Kinships in Popularizing the Monterey Style 1836–1846," *JSAH* 43/3 (1984): 250–55, and David Gebhard, "California's Monterey Tradition," *JSAH* 46/2 (1987): 161–62, with an extensive bibliographical footnote.

9. On the California missions as they appeared to early-nineteenth-century explorers from the United States—whose impressions undoubtedly helped create the later legend—see Page Smith, *The Nation Comes of Age* (New York: McGraw-Hill, 1981), 442–52. Jules Huret's observations appeared in *En Amérique, de San Francisco au Canada* (Paris, 1907), p. 22.

10. It was Gérard Morisset who first recognized the uniqueness of Quebec parish churches and photographed and documented them in his *Inventaire des Oeuvres d'Art de la Province de Québec*. All serious studies of them rest on his work. He recognized the "Conefroy plan" as derived from Laval's parish churches, how it worked to perpetuate traditions in the early nineteenth century, and how Thomas Baillairgé developed it. Like most of his generation he had little taste for the Gothic Revival and later styles in Quebec; he had no interest, for example, in how a parish church like the one curé Hercule Dorion saw through to completion at Yamachiche in 1855 brought into the parishes architectural forms carrying ideological messages from Montreal's visual metaphors of French Catholicism: the great triple-arched facade from Notre-Dame, *La Paroisse*, and the dome from the scaled-down model of Saint Peter's that Bishop Bourget wanted for his cathedral, to signify devotion to the Holy See. And so forth . . . These and many other examples of parish churches are to be found in my *Building Canada* (Toronto: Oxford University Press, 1966), which, though obsolete in approach and obsolescent in much factual data, remains a useful pictorial survey.

11. There are of course many other pockets of French-speaking settlement within the United States. Some have attracted attention unwarranted by their significance, thanks to recent ethnic enthusiasms: "French Prairie" in Oregon is a good example. Interest in others goes farther back. New Orleans's exotic associations are legendary. The Missouri settlements around Sainte Geneviève and Saint Charles and Kaskaskia on the Illinois side attracted attention early enough for the old Saint Clare courthouse from Cahokia, Illinois, to be dismantled and exhibited at the St. Louis Fair in 1904, then reassembled on its old site. A good account of them is given in "The Missouri" volume of the Federal Writers Project on American Rivers (1941, pp.260ff).

12. Roger Kennedy, *Architecture, Men, Women, and Money* (New York: Random House, 1985), p.65.

13. That the form had no counterpart in the Netherlands was pointed out by Aymar Embury II in the *International Studio* article that launched the Dutch Colonial Re-

vival in 1908, by Fiske Kimball in the famous study *Domestic Architecture of the American Colonies* in 1922, and by everyone since. In eighteenth-century usage among builders in English colonies, "Dutch roof" was often merely a synonym for "gambrel," though presumably it acquired such a designation from some association.

14. For early writings on German ethnic arts, see Henry Kinzer Landis, *Early Kitchens of the Pennsylvania Germans* (Norristown, Pa: German Folklore Society, 1939), recapitulated in T. T. Waterman's 1941 *Dwellings of Colonial America* and Hugh Morrison's 1952 *Early American Architecture*. On Pennsylvania German barns, see Charles H. Dornbusch and John K. Heyl, *Pennsylvania German Barns* (Norristown, Pa: German Folklore Society, 1958), who describe over half a dozen subtypes; or, for a random example of later writings, Peter O. Wacker, "Traditional House and Barn Types in New Jersey: Keys to Past Culturogeographic Regions and Settlement History," *Geoscience and Man* 5 (1970): 163–76, which characteristically traces patterns of German versus Dutch settlement by distribution of "bank" versus "Dutch" barns. On utopian communities, see Dolores M. Hayden, *Seven American Utopias* (Cambridge, Mass.: The MIT Press, 1976).

15. On the jumble of nationalities represented in emigrants from "the Palatinates," see Bailyn, *Peopling of British North America*, p. 34 and notes 31–36. An early New York settlement wedged between patroonships, New Paltz illustrates the spotty transmission of architectural types in non-English Colonial styles. Its principal remains are a number of substantial old farmhouses with distinctive proportions, narrow rather than broad fronts, sharply sloping roofs, and massive walls. They look superficially French, but their feel is quite different. They are in fact typical peasant homesteads from the Rhine and Neckar regions of Germany. But their complementary types—palaces, churches, town houses—are not to be found in New Paltz (or anywhere else in America, for that matter). For those, you have to go to Old Pfalz, the Palatinate centered on Heidelburg.

16. "The plan is like that of peasant dwellings in Switzerland and the Rhine Valley. Its depth and proportions, products of the late medieval Continent, are not completely incompatible with the Georgian intent. . . . The flattish roof and external quasi-symmetry fool scholars into assigning its origin to England and neoclassicism. But its shell masks an aged Continental interior. . . . If the viewer rumbling by on the road does not look too critically, he thinks he is seeing the latest word, a Georgian house with a formal hall; that is the impression the builder wished to convey while his wife went about her work inside in the old way, speaking German to her offspring" (Henry Glassie, "Eighteenth Century Cultural Process in the Delaware Valley," *Winterthur Portfolio* [1972]; reprinted in Upton and Vlach, eds., *Common Places*, pp.394–425).

17. See Carol Krinsky, *Synagogues of Europe: Architecture, History, Meaning* (New York: The Architectural History Foundation, and Cambridge, Mass.: The MIT Press, 1985).

18. Quotations from discussion of Jewish life and in-

fluence in pre–Civil War America in Page Smith, *The Nation Comes of Age,* pp.533, 534.

19. On later nineteenth-century immigration to the United States, I am following William N. Parker, "Native Origins of Modern Industry," in D. C. Klingaman and R. K. Vedder, eds., *Essays on The Economy of the Old Northwest,* pp.243ff.

20. Charles Chauncey, *Seasonable Thoughts on the State of Religion in New England* (Boston, 1743).

21. Main, *The Social Structure of Revolutionary America,* pp.229–30. Nowadays, when questioning authority has become a favorite and favored academic pursuit, it is easy to overlook the revolutionary nature of Main's thesis, proposed at the height of Colonial Revival enthusiasms, that other factors besides patriotic altruism motivated Colonial Americans.

22. The intrinsic design process of vernacular building has generated an extensive literature over the last few decades. It has been usefully summarized in a review of Donald A. Hutslar's *Architecture of Migration* by Bernard L. Herman, in *JSAH* 46/4 (1987):437–38. I have found particularly useful Part One of Michael Owen Jones, *Exploring Folk Art* (Ann Arbor: U.M.I. Research Press, 1987), and Frazer D. Neiman, "Domestic Architecture at Clifts Plantation: The Social Context of Early Virginia Building," in Upton and Vlach, eds., *Common Places,* pp.292–312.

23. The considerable literature on slave housing has been conveniently summarized by Dell Upton, "New Views of the Virginia Landscape," *Virginia Magazine of History & Biography* 96/4 (1988):438–39. The issue is complicated by the disappearance of all evidence for "dormitories" and huts mentioned by historians, so that what this component of colonial class-structured architecture was actually like must be conjectured from hypothetical influences on later lower-class and workers' housing.

24. On "post" and "earth-fast" construction for even plantation houses of some pretensions, the classic article is Cary Carson, Norman F. Barks, William M. Kelso, Garry Wheeler Stone, and Dell Upton, "Impermanent Architecture in the Southern American Colonies," *Winterthur Portfolio* 16/2–3 (1981):135–96.

25. Study of Philadelphia row houses began early, with John F. Watson, *Annals of Philadelphia,* in 1830. One of them, the Letitia Street House—alleged to have belonged to Penn's daughter—was the subject of a pioneer scholarly study of American houses, by Fiske Kimball in *Philadelphia Museum Bulletin* 27 (May 1932). The later history of row houses is conveniently summarized by William B. Murtagh, "The Philadelphia Row House," *Journal of the Society of Architectural Historians* 16/4 (1957):8ff. Before 1700 a three-family dwelling was recorded in Philadelphia, and by 1722, four tenement houses on Front Street. See further G. B. Tatum, *Penn's Great Town.*

26. The painting was not intended to be a literal record of events nor of the first Philadelphia houses. Rather, it is an icon glorifying William Penn. This explains why its composition is modeled on Raphael's Vatican Stanze frescoes, especially the *School of Athens,* whose theme is the reconciliation of opposites, and why the figure of William Penn is modeled on a figure of Christ in one of Raphael's tapestry designs, *Feed My Lambs.* Association of early houses with ideas of equality follows naturally.

27. See further "The Mansions of Alloway's Creek," in Upton and Vlach, eds., *Common Places.* The stylistic form that developed in and around Salem County functioned primarily for homesteads, signifying the founding of a family with land, a permanent family on its homestead acres. But taken to the frontier it can signify "First Family of a Region," as it does, for example, in the William Whitley House in Stanford, Kentucky. The Whitley house dates from 1791–92; on the seaboard, even in Salem County, New Jersey, such a style would indicate someone incorrigibly *retardataire,* but in a frontier region like this, it could and did signify "first family."

28. Fred B. Kniffen, "Folk Housing: Key to Diffusion," *Annals of the Association of American Geographers* 55 (1965):549–77. A catalyst is probably to be found in the social function of houses like "Belair" of c. 1672; in its original rural setting (in Passyunk, now a rundown southwest section of the present city), this big vertical version of the Philadelphia spec house, in brick, must have had an air of grandeur, giving it great appeal as an image of successful settlement on the land. This quality was early cited in Eberlein and Hubbard's presentation of "Belair" in *American Georgian Architecture* (Philadelphia, 1952).

29. The bawn is a house with strong walls and other defensible features originally developed as a rallying-point for sixteenth- and early seventeenth-century settlements in Ulster and thought to be represented in the American colonies by the Whitfield house at Guilford, Connecticut. It was a short-lived form; for what proved useful in the confined territory of Ulster against native Irish proved unnecessarily elaborate in the expanding territories of New England and the far less systematic hostility of native Indians.

30. "[The Lees'] house seems at first glance as backward-looking as the literary tastes of the scholar of the family, Richard Lee (1647–1714) . . . 'a belated Elizabethan' . . . retaining as it does the shape of a border fortress" (Roger Kennedy, *Architecture, Men, Women and Money,* pp.87–89). Stratford is, he maintains, a form deriving from West Indian raised plantation houses. The H-form, providing entrances that could in theory be defended from their wings against attack, perhaps betray a mentality inherited from Stratford's predecessor, "The Clifts," which had a wooden wall and bastions all around. Another proto-Georgian fortress form is "Mulberry" in South Carolina of 1714, whose little corner towers presumably recall what once were necessary bastions.

31. A number of examples from old prints of New England and Philadelphia are reproduced in Edmund V. Gillon's useful *Early Illustrations and Views of Early American Architecture* (New York: Dover, 1971); others are recorded in H. C. Forman, *Architecture of the Old South* (Cambridge, Mass.: Harvard University Press, 1934).

32. Substitution of Georgian features for older metaphors of authority like overhangs and cross-axial plans explains a feature that puzzled many early commentators

on Colonial English; see, for example Joseph Jackson's comment in his 1924 *American Colonial Architecture* (Philadelphia: David McKay, 1924), repeated in Amelia F. Miller, *Connecticut River Doorways* (Boston: Boston University, for the Dublin Seminar for New England Folklife, 1983, p.88): "Proportion seems to have been forgotten, for many of the doorways and doors are excellent in themselves but they are appended to houses that are unfitted for them by design and general character."

33. In "The Classical Mind as Regional and Class Expression," *Images of American Living* (Philadelphia: J. B. Lippincott, 1964), pp.173–223, I developed an elaborate system for scoring this dissemination in a quasi-scientific manner.

34. Bernard Bailyn's *The Peopling of British North America* describes how early cultural lag began: John Winthrop I had been on the cutting edge of new ideas in England; John Winthrop II kept anxiously writing to England to find out how things were going, aware that he was falling behind and worried about it; but the third generation hardly cared what was new in that now remote land and sank happily into a state of contented provincialism, their tastes and ideas ever slower to change. So it went on every successive North American frontier, from Vermont to Kentucky to the far western islands off British Columbia. Since Fiske Kimball's *Domestic Architecture of the American Colonies and of the Early Republic* (1922) emphasizing how major an element in style transmission were design books (twenty-three published between 1725 and 1735 alone), their tardy appearance in the colonies has been very often cited to account for lag in architectural styles. Yet the facts warrant no such assumption.

35. One proof is that cultural lag still exists and is still predictable in our own time of instant communication. Anyone who has lived and traveled widely in North America will have come across regions as much as twenty-odd years out of date. What makes a region out of date are outdated mental presuppositions accepted as self-evidently true. Conceptual screens are thereby set up, through which all perception of day-to-day experience is filtered. New attitudes, ideas, or tastes cannot penetrate as long as the screen is there. And it may well last lifetimes, thus affecting tastes and transmissions of styles in architecture and furniture over generations.

36. Richest, at least in associations with the First British Empire, is Saint Peter's Cathedral in Saint George's, Bermuda, begun in 1621 but extant mostly from the eighteenth century. It is laden with tablets and monuments recording the vicissitudes of empire-building history. On its plate, see *Bermuda Historical Quarterly* 11/1 (1954): 10–41; on its tablets, *Bermuda Historical Quarterly* 21/1 (1964).

37. On the social function of Saint Martin's, see my "Paradigmatic Social Function in Anglican Church Architecture of the Fifteen Colonies," *Studies in the History of Art* (Washington, D.C.: National Gallery of Art, and Baltimore: Johns Hopkins University) 20 (1989):75–95; on the building, see Terry Friedman, *James Gibbs* (New Haven, Conn.: Yale University Press, 1984).

38. Howard E. Stutchbury, *The Architecture of Colen Campbell* (Manchester: Manchester University Press, 1967), chapter 1, "Wren's Successors and the New 'National Taste.'"

39. The architect was Col. Sir William Robe (1765–1820), who directed construction by mason Edward Cannon for the English community in Quebec. His life of imperial service is described in a long plaque in Bermuda. Its text, given in "Wall Tablets in St. Peter's Church, St. Georges, Bermuda," *Bermuda Historical Quarterly* 21/1 (1964), primarily commemorates Lt. Col. Thomas Congreve Robe, third son of Sir William, who died of yellow fever in Bermuda, 21 September 1853. Sir William married Sarah Watt of Quebec and had five sons, all of whom died on active service in various Empire wars, and four daughters, all of whom were named after various battles and none of whom married.

40. This use of Academic Colonial English is described and illustrated, with many other examples, by William B. Rhoads, "The Colonial Revival and the Americanization of Immigrants," in *The Colonial Revival in America,* ed. Alan Axelrod (New York: Norton, for the Winterthur Museum, 1985). Henry Ford's Greenfield Village at Dearborn outside Detroit had a similar social function, according to Rhoads; it was epitomized by its reproduction of Independence Hall as the museum building's centerpiece.

41. Victoria (British Columbia): University of Victoria Maltwood Museum, 1969. My essay "Paradigmatic Social Function" expands on some of the themes here.

42. "Anglo-Palladianism's importance has probably been overemphasized by architectural historians, who have an unwavering allegiance to the articulate few over the silent majority. In fact, Anglo-Palladianism was an aesthetic faith wholeheartedly accepted only by a few even in England, although many architects used Palladian forms from time to time. Yet historians of 18th-century southern architecture have tended to see Anglo-Palladianism everywhere, even though Palladio's own work was rarely mentioned in America before Thomas Jefferson's time" (Dell Upton, "New Views of the Virginia Landscape," *The Virginia Magazine of History & Biography,* 96/4 [1988]:426–27).

43. This was observed by Barry Schwartz in *George Washington: The Making of an American Symbol* (New York: The Free Press, 1987).

3.1. In the mid-1830s, when John Caspar Wild recorded this view of Third and Vine streets, Cincinnati was the rising Midwest's principal city, full of fine mansions. In the background appears one with a double porch that makes a poor (though common) substitute for a portico; in the foreground is a truly commanding image of success in the new republic. Indeed it imposes a sequence of spatial experiences hardly different from palace types in the old class-structured society: an abutment with delicately recessed arcade sets it off from the sidewalk, forcing visitors to enter up a high flight of stairs and so experience in due solemnity the great spread of grandly scaled Doric columns and formal entrance door. The wings are not temples but are designed in the Colonial homestead style, which in some ways makes the main mansion all the grander by contrast. All of this is long gone. (Courtesy of the Cincinnati Historical Society)

3

AN ARCADIAN LAND AND ITS CLASSICAL REVIVAL STYLES, c. 1800–1840

Classical Revival Styles in Their Time and Place

The American Revolution had two distinct aspects. One was a simple revolt against rule by an outside power, a fight of the sort waged by the Dutch against Spain a century before or the Swiss against Austria a century before that. The other was a struggle waged on high ideological principles, part of that broad European movement still called by its own name, "The Enlightenment." Its deepest impulse was to make human life, and particularly human government, confirm more to principles of what in that era was called Reason, and in ours mechanistic abstract causal thought.

In the popular mind—and in the mind of many intellectuals of the time too—those principles were best exemplifed in the ancient republics of Greece and Rome. Certainly the new American constitution took over names like "Senate" and based ideas like popular assemblies on Roman and Greek precedent; some enthusiasts spoke of their new Republic as a reincarnation of the republics of classical antiquity. It followed that the ideal landscape for the new Republic would evoke Arcadia, the classical paradise: rolling pastoral hillsides dotted with neat temples and tidy groves, town streets lined with porticoes and arcades in classical orders and dotted with statues honoring civic heroes. And the new Republic did indeed bring such landscapes into existence, especially in the 1820s and 1830s, the heyday of the Classical Revival styles [3.1]. Charles Dickens described them with a keen eye after his 1842 visit:

> Every little colony of houses has its church and schoolhouse peeping from among the roofs and shady trees; every house is the whitest of the white; every Venetian blind the greenest of the green; every fine day's sky the bluest of the blue. . . . All the buildings looked as if they had been built and painted that morning, and could be taken down on Monday with very little trouble. In the keen evening air, every sharp outline looked a hundred times sharper than ever. (*American Notes,* Chapter 5)

He caught the same enchanting kind of naiveté that marks "American primitive" paintings from the 1820s and 1830s [3.2]. There was an innocent optimism about the years between the end of the 1812–15 war with Britain and the dark premonitions of war between the states in the 1850s. The land was rich and empty; there was room for everybody. Never before in history had personal freedom been so great, so widespread; never before had slavery come to seem so odious. Nearly everybody could dream of a satisfying life, with some certainty of enjoying one, given hard work, good health, and a bit of luck. You could even have some certainty of getting rich, or at least "comfortably fixed." The first generation of painters trained and working in the United States, best represented by William Sidney Mount and George Caleb Bingham in the 1840s, captured this as an Arcadian age when all things were being made over and the curse of work was being lifted from human backs and brows.[1] But the greatest visual metaphors of American Arcadia were in the architecture of the new Republic, which could appropriately be called National Democratic Classical Revival. And it was a creation not paralleled elsewhere.

The newness of the American landscape as noted by Dickens in 1842 was not a poetic fiction. One of the great periodic rebuildings of the country[2] had just occurred. Even older structures were being transformed by the addition of porticoes in classical

3.2. Painting of the Sargent family in their home somewhere around Boston, c. 1800. Samuel Green Sargent was a successful merchant with an office at Spear's Wharf on Boston Harbor; he was a descendant of William Sargent, who came to America from Northampton, England, in 1638 and settled in Malden, Massachusetts. The unknown artist shows him with a harmonious family and material evidence of success, most notably shield-back side chairs from the third "improved" edition of George Hepplewhite's Cabinet Maker and Upholsterer's Guide *published in London in 1794 (and thus the latest Classical fashion), the Martha Washington or lolling chair on which his wife sits, and two birdcages matching the chairs in style. (National Gallery of Art, Washington, D.C., gift of Edgar William and Bernice Chrysler Garbisch)*

forms and proportions, or just by being painted classical white.

Not much Arcadian scenery remains now. It takes some imagination to visualize the world Dickens and these itinerant primitive painters saw in the wilderness of skyscrapers and billboards, diners and developments and decaying Victorian mansions that buries most of classical America today. Here and there patches survive in something like an original setting. In the hills of western New England or northern Georgia, in the valleys of the Mohawk or the Wabash or the Ohio, through the old Mississippi plantation country, along remaining patches of the old National Roads through the Great Plains and on to the Far West, you can still sometimes come upon the occasional neat pedimented farmhouse or pillared mansion, glinting white and gold in a sunset's rays, against a background of emerald fields and purple valleys and the ruddy gray haze of wooded slopes—a landscape idyllic in the manner of Poussin or Claude. Then for an instant you catch a glimpse of America when the Republic was new, of that lost nation of "templ'd hills" and Revolutionary ideals modeled on classical antiquity.

Urban counterparts to these rural scenes have suffered even worse from time. Occasional blocks remain in something like their original condition in New York, Philadelphia, Savannah, or villages like Middletown in western Maryland; here and there you find a dramatic Classical Revival monument like the Louisville Waterworks *[3.63]* or the Masonic Temple in Mendocino *[3.3]*. But the only really effective record is in prints. Only there are

we fully aware how dramatic a visual impact the new style made in its own time, how vividly it dramatized the impact upon American life of the revolutionary break from Britain *[3.1]*. Before 1820 American cities had looked in the main like provincial versions of British ones. The National Democratic Classical Revival changed that image forever—a visual counterpart to the change in language that introduced hundreds of "Americanisms" at this same time. Great temples out of scale to their surroundings occasionally appeared in early-nineteenth-century British cities, but as schools or museums or concert halls. In American cities they appeared regularly, and they were the mansions of private citizens—merchants, plantation owners, even tinkers and tailors come up in the world. They represented a fundamentally new kind of society. Foreigners might sneer at the naïveté of such pretensions; but in the first flush of well-established National Democracy, Americans were not as sensitive and subservient to foreign tastes as some of their descendants became. American Classical Revival landscapes were creations of the nation that led the March of Mankind, in their opinion; and what foreigners smiled at condescendingly today, they would be imitating tomorrow.

One of the best survivals of the American Classical Revival spirit in landscape is in Washington, creation of the Revolution. Those splendid wide streets and circles that Charles L'Enfant laid out with General Washington's encouragement and supervision are still there, even improved in effect by the early-twentieth-century McMillan Commis-

3.3. View of Ukiah and Lansing streets in Mendocino, California, showing the Masonic Hall of 1866–72, whose vestigial classical form gave some dignity to an early rowdy California community. Its tower, vaguely modeled on the Choragic Monument of Lysikrates, was designed by Master Mason Erick Albertson, who also carved the curious cupola figures showing Father Time and a (presumably allegorical) Maiden. The Corinthian and Doric columns have brass decorations made by George Hagemeyer, also a charter brother. By the 1860s Masonic halls in the East were no longer often designed in Classical Revival styles, but in the West cultural lag has preserved the older form. (IMG:NAL)

sion's work, still witnessing to aspirations for a new Rome on the Potomac *[3.4].* At the apex the United States Capitol still stands as it did in 1832 when veteran traveler Frances Trollope was "struck with admiration and surprise" by it, "so finely too, high, and alone" on its hill *[3.5].* Successive enlargements to plan and dome have only made the Capitol a more powerful symbol *[3.6].* So potent has it been that forty-seven of the fifty state capitols unmistakably emulate it, not to mention innumerable county courthouses and city halls *[3.7–3.9].* All manifest a deep popular understanding (not always shared by architects, it seems) of how architectural symbolism works: legislative buildings of similar forms manifest continuity and community of laws, or, more simply, One Nation, Undivided.[3]

At the other end of the Mall from the Capitol is Lincoln's majestic Memorial—classical too, albeit in the later, Academic form. Between them rises Washington's obelisk. This is grand cityscape. Poignant, however, is the word for the temple with curiously thick Greek columns that rises on a bluff directly across the Potomac, variously called the Lee Mansion, the Custis Mansion, or Arlington House *[3.10].* For here, in 1861, General Robert E. Lee had to act out a truly Greek tragedy. Here he had to decide, like an Aeschylean hero, between two courses of action—both honorable, both compelling, yet in such contradiction that either would bring inevitable ruin and retribution. Should he accept command of the Union armies, put a quick end to the war, and save a hundred thousand lives? He does not believe in secession, nor in slavery. Or should he take command of the armies of the newly

seceded Confederacy? To refuse is to betray his native state and make war on his own people. This is the stuff of epic tragedy, in an epic setting still— for Lee's estate, seized as war reparations, remains the center of Arlington National Cemetery.

I know of at least one little island of Classical Revival imagery that remains intact. It is in St. Louis. Here, an image of the ideals and tastes of the Arcadian republic has been perfectly preserved. Rows of little temple-houses stand each on its own

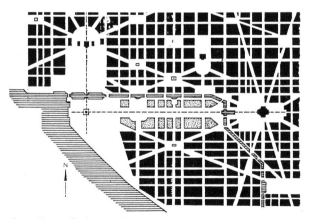

3.4. Pierre Charles L'Enfant's plan for the development of the city of Washington in 1792 emphasized the separation of executive (in its round park, top left) and legislative (in its rectangle-and-square space, far right) branches, both set on an axis with the monument to Washington. Space for a National Cathedral was significantly smaller and not on any axis or in the key triangle (upper section, right of center). The Potomac River flowed almost up to the monument site. In 1909 its course was changed and the Mall's width doubled over infilled land, so that the Lincoln Memorial balanced it.

3.5. *West front of the United States Capitol. The Capitol's long and complicated history focuses on its dome. First an ostensibly geometric shape (a low saucer, under Benjamin Latrobe), then a kind of pot (under Charles Bulfinch), it became the soaring structure that now dominates the building, and the city of Washington, in the middle of the Civil War. It was completed in 1863 under engineer Montgomery C. Meigs, who, it has been claimed, discovered blueprints for the dome of Saint Isaac's cathedral in Leningrad and applied them. Less plausible is the suggestion that Meigs's model was Saint Paul's in London. What matters is the dome's proportions relative to the wings of the building as expanded in the 1850s to Thomas U. Walter's designs and the visual metaphor of legislative representation thereby created: the states, by their two senators each, and the population at large, by representatives from electoral districts fixed by census, are joined by a dome that is on an axis to the White House. Significantly, perhaps, the Supreme Court, behind, does not sit on a relevant axis. (IMG:NAL)*

3.6. *Samuel F. B. Morse's painting* The Old House of Representatives *shows that chamber as it was in the 1830s, being prepared for an evening session; it admirably exemplifies how this architecture furthered the religious veneration accorded processes of democratic government. Morse's minister father sits in the gallery at far right with a representative of an Indian tribe whose rights had been protected by Congress; a dim religious light fills the whole. It could well illustrate John Quincy Adams's diary entry for 20 February 1831, in which a routine roll-call became "to a reflective mind a very striking exemplification of the magnificent grandeur of this nation and of the sublime principles upon which our Government is founded. The forms and proceedings of the House . . . the colossal emblem of the union over the Speaker's chair, the historic Muse at the clock, the echoing pillars of the hall . . . would form the subject for a descriptive poem." (Corcoran Gallery of Art, Washington, D.C.)*

3.7. *The Vermont State Capitol, Montpelier, exhibits the naive classicism of the early Republic, with a fine gold dome. Originally built 1833–56 to Ammi B. Young's designs; rebuilt 1857–59. (IMG:NAL)*

3.8 (below, right). *The Colorado State Capitol, Denver, has the thin, vertically proportioned Picturesque Classicism characteristic of the 1870s and 1880s. Begun in 1886 to designs of the self-taught architect Elijah E. Myers and completed in 1908. Myers also provided capitols for Michigan and Texas. (State of Colorado Advertising and Publicity Department)*

3.9 (below, left). *The Missouri State Capitol, Jefferson City, exemplifies the majestic, learned, early-twentieth-century Academic Roman Revival style. It was designed by Evarts Tracy and Egerton Swartout, long associated with the style's premier practitioners, McKim, Mead and White. (Missouri Resources Division)*

3.10. The Custis-Lee Mansion, originally known as Arlington House, was very deliberately sited on a bluff on the Virginia side of the Potomac, to overlook the new federal city. Its forms are as ideological as its siting. It was built on George Hadfield's designs for eccentric George Washington Park Custis, the general's grandson by adoption and the self-appointed guardian of the Washington tradition of liberty over equality. In the architecture of early Greek city-states Custis saw liberty's prime affirmation; hence he subordinated the house proper to its huge portico with great squat columns in what he took to be archaic Greek style (the model being Paestum in southern Italy). The whole was conceived as a rebuke to the Roman style promoted by the "egalitarian" third president, Thomas Jefferson. (IMG:NAL)

3.11. Street of mausolea in Bellefontaine Cemetery. Bellefontaine was laid out in romantic Gothic Revival style by Almerin Hotchkiss, surveyor and constructor of Greenwood Cemetery in Brooklyn, c. 1850; but it soon became most remarkable for its streets of Classical Revival temple-house mausolea. Like the obelisk/column, the mausoleum ultimately was not a tomb form at all; it was a house form. At first round temples were favored for mausolea, but soon a "standard" small temple-house became the norm, comparable to the "standard" small Classical Revival house of the 1820s and 1830s. It is characteristic of funeral arts at all times and places to be very much behind the times, as these are. (IMG:NAL)

spacious plot, each proclaiming individual success and virtue in some good Classical Revival style—Roman, Greek, Egyptian. Here a democratic equality such as imagined in those ancient republics survives reincarnate; a few are more equal than others, perhaps, but none too far out of line. In this place, liberty and equality are finally reconciled, and forever, because here all has been safe from the corroding effects of time and history. Here is the National Democratic Classical Revival metaphor of society at its best: each virtuous citizen in his virtuous temple-house. Only all of them are dead. The place is Bellefontaine Cemetery *[3.11]*.[4]

Definition and Identifying Characteristics

Classical Revival styles were created by employing combinations of details and shapes borrowed directly from classical antiquity (generally, Rome and Greece) for the conscious purpose of alluding to literary or historical ideas: democracy, liberty, republican government, civic virtue.

As even this cursory glance at Classical Revival architecture will show, there was really no such thing as "correct" copying of models from antiquity. America differed far too radically from the ancient world in social usage and climate. But educated architects—and architects in something like a modern sense now begin to appear, alongside and as contrasted to educated gentlemen—could and did strive for some studied consensus as to what constituted acceptable combinations of Greek or Roman (and occasionally Egyptian) forms, in given situations and for given architectural types.

Most of these forms were drawn from books. The earliest books were by travelers who had rendered their drawings on the spot: *The Antiquities of Athens* by Stuart and Revett, Robert Adam's *Ruins of the Palace of Diocletian at Spalatro,* and the like. There were also publications on Roman architecture that had been available at least since Palladio's time, two centuries before *[3.12]*. All were very large, very expensive, very exclusive. But by the early nineteenth century a multitude of builders' guides became available which drew upon these originals and were much smaller (some pocket-size), easily obtainable, and relatively cheap. Earliest was the *American Builder's Companion* published in 1806 in Boston by "Asher Benjamin, Architect and Carpenter." It claimed to be *A New System of Architecture Particularly*

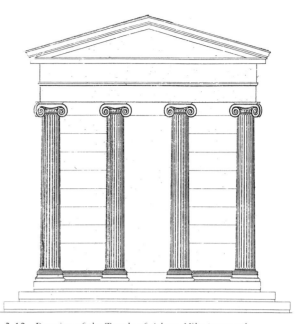

3.12. Drawing of the Temple of Athena Nike (proposed reconstruction) on the Acropolis in Athens, from James Stuart and Nicholas Revett, The Antiquities of Athens, Measured and Delineated. A new edition. And: Antiquities of Athens and Other Places in Greece, Sicily, &c., Supplementary of the Antiquities of Athens, *four volumes in two (London: Priestley and Weale, 1825–1830). It was this edition rather than the original (published 1792–1795, with supplementary edition appearing in 1816) that was the American Greek Revival's principal sourcebook.*

Adapted to the Present Style of Building in the United States of America and included a text explaining how to get correct proportions and interrelationships plus plans and elevations for meetinghouses, banks, town houses, and mansions, as well as details of fireplaces, cornices, and the like. So successful and so widely used were it and later guides by Benjamin (and others, particularly Minard Fever) that historians are still questioning the extent to which buildings should be attributed to him or to more prominent architects like Bulfinch or Ithiel Town. Such controversies result in large part from a pattern of development from elite to mass usage, or better, perhaps, toward an ever broader, ever more general kind of symbolic usage—in short, construction of visual metaphors to communicate ideas on a lowest common denominator.

As will become evident when we consider substyles, Classical Revival forms were in the beginning used primarily to create images of simplicity, purity, and Reason in general—geometric shapes,

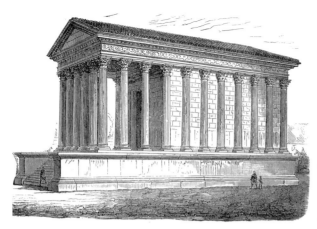

3.13. *To honor the divinity of the Roman Empire, as embodied in Augustus and his family, temples were built after the ancient Etruscan model, on a high platform approached by a flight of steps up the front. The most famous extant example is the Maison Carrée (Square House) at Nîmes (Roman Nemausus) in Provence, begun about* A.D. *2 and originally dedicated to Augustus' deceased nephews Gaius and Lucius.*

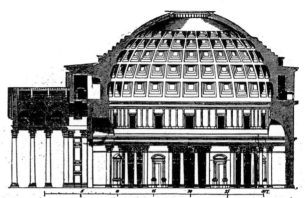

3.14. *Reconstructed section of the Pantheon in Rome, begun by Hadrian in the second century* A.D., *still extant in the eighteenth century, although converted into a church. It offered a dome and portico combination on which innumerable eighteenth- and nineteenth-century buildings were modeled.*

or abstractions and stylizations of forms from preceding styles. Later, specific imitations of forms supposed to be found in classical antiquity came to predominate, with connotations of Roman gravity, Greek culture, Egyptian wisdom, and the like. Necessarily, these later forms had to be drawn from a few ancient models (well known to anyone with any cultural pretensions), adapted to North American architectural types, and usually simplified so as to be easily replicable by workmen with little formal training and minimal skills (especially as the Classical Revival spread into remoter areas of the country). Any random perusal will spot them all easily: the Roman temple forms of the Maison Carrée (rectangular body plus portico, the whole set on a flight of steps [3.13] or the Pantheon (portico plus dome [3.14]; Jefferson's version of it at Monticello is the most familiar [3.45]); Greek temples with columns around all four sides, like the Parthenon in Athens, with eight columns across the front, or the Theseon with six, the whole set on a three-step platform. Few American Classical Revival buildings pretended to replicate such models exactly; most drew details and general effects from them and from others like the famous Athenian Erechtheon (for Ionic details), the Choragic Monument of Lysikrates ([3.65, 3.66], for "classical" towers or cupolas), or the Athena Nike Temple ([3.12] for little wings so commonly added to temple-house mansions). Another com-

mon model, the Column of Trajan, had long been known from Masonic usage. One fertile source for Egyptian Revival details was the Temple of Horus at Edfu [3.15].

Classical Revival furniture comparably copied a few types and forms known from vases and from the first excavations at Pompeii. Architectural interiors in this style normally conform to exteriors (that is, a Greek Revival exterior would normally have Greek Revival furniture [3.54]).

In general the trend of Classical Revival substyles is toward greater ornamentation, decade by decade, until all blur insensibly into Picturesque Italianate and Second (French) Empire. After the plainness of its first, Revolutionary Democratic, substyle, fluting returns to columns generally, entablatures and cornices regain ornamental richness, windows get more elaborate framing and pediments, and porches become more lavish. Proportions and "feel" become in general more robust (this is particularly apparent in furniture, as Empire is succeeded by "butcher" Phyfe). Increasing "vulgarity" is another way of putting it, and perhaps the better one, for it befits the Classical Revival's developing social function to address the broad masses rather than the architecturally erudite and politically sophisticated. It also corresponds to an expression of ever-increasing wealth; this function is so much better performed by Picturesque styles that their dominance after c. 1845 is inevitable. Until then, there is little mixing of substyles in any deliberate way (they were regularly mixed up on the popular level, of course). A given architect may design in many different styles (Roman, Greek, and Egyptian Revival, Gothic Revival) depending on the required associations for a given building; but mixing styles in the same building is a sign of the Picturesque.

Social Function

The broad social function of Classical Revival styles was to proclaim, more or less deliberately and consciously, the values and convictions underlying the democratic revolutions of 1776 in America and 1789 in France. These ideals were not always understood in the same way at all times by all proponents. Nor were they always consistent, within themselves or with each other. Consequently we should hardly expect a consistent social function throughout Classical Revival arts.

Classical Revival arts might at one time and place be persuasive, at others proclaim established conviction. The Battle Monument in Baltimore, for example *[3.16]* is persuasive: commissioned in 1815 to commemorate an event in the War of 1812 while that war was still going on and the issue undecided,

it was intended to proclaim to waverers that "Our flag is still there." By contrast, the Washington Monument in Baltimore, as conceived in 1809 and erected in the 1820s *[3.17]* was a monument to established conviction: it announced the success of the new country and its democratic ideals. They are executed in appropriately different Classical Revival substyles.

Furthermore, a building might function for one person as a visual metaphor of the ideals of the Enlightenment—Reason, social equality, secularism; for another, as a commemoration of ancient Roman civic virtue and heroism reincarnate; for a third, as just a war monument, Us beating Them. The choice of substyle usually was determined by primary social function and indicates what that function was conceived to be—granted, of course, that no art can do more than suggest how it is to be interpreted.

American Classical Revival styles had the function of promoting the values and self-definition of a new nation-state "conceived in liberty and dedicated to the proposition that all men are created equal." They created visual metaphors of the Declaration of Independence, if you like. Some of the ambivalence of these styles, their curious combination of pomposity and naiveté, may be traceable to

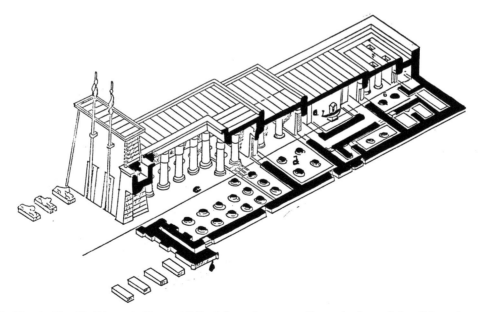

3.15. Late Egyptian temples, like this one to Horus at Edfu, fall well within Graeco-Roman times (begun 237 B.C. under the Greek king Ptolemy III, completed 212 B.C., final decoration completed 147, vestibule 122, final touches 57) but in form mimetically perpetuate primeval forms of mud and reed palaces in predynastic times, many thousands of years before. It has entrance towers (pylons), reed-palm (cavetto) cornices and capitals, bundled-reed columns, as well as divisions into three areas corresponding to ancient social arrangements: inner sanctum (chief's harem), hall for priests (chief's servants), courtyard for reception of visitors.

3.16. Lost in the shadow of Baltimore's commercial downtown, not far from its new Harborfront complex, is a premier sculptural example of the Revolutionary Democratic substyle: the Battle Monument, commissioned in 1814 to commemorate the repulse of the British attack on Baltimore (which also produced the national anthem). Begun 1815, entirely complete by 1825, it commemorated not generals or leaders but free citizens banded together in defense of their rights and laws (symbolized by fasces). (IMG:NAL)

3.17. To the relatively new city of Baltimore went the honor of erecting the nation's first great public monument to George Washington, built 1819–29 to the designs of Charlestonian architect Robert Mills. Twenty years later Mills designed another for Washington City, which featured an obelisk rising from within a great Greek Doric circular colonnade. The Monument, as it is known to this day in the District of Columbia, was begun in 1848 (coincidentally, the year of democratic revolutions all over Europe), but the obelisk was not completed until 1884 and the colonnade never completed at all. (IMG:NAL)

this social function. For it must be obvious that the Declaration is not to be understood literally.

People are neither born nor created equal. To say they are is a statement of faith, not fact. As to rights, none are in fact inalienable: liberty must stop somewhere well short of anarchy; one individual's pursuit of happiness must necessarily be limited by another's; life is something no government ever claimed the right to take away without due process. So what is the practical meaning of the Declaration that Classical Revival styles are to proclaim? Generations of readers have instinctively translated its eighteenth-century Deistic terms into the older medieval scholastic language from which it came. For "all men" read "all souls" and then continue: all souls have been created immortal by God, Who has also given them free access to grace at all times; any human government that interferes

with these God-given rights is invalid and must be resisted.

Deceit was not involved here. Jefferson and his committee did not use this older theological language directly, because it had become odious to their generation from its abuse during two centuries of ruinous religious wars and because it was irrelevant to them. In retrospect, we see them groping toward a new formulation of ancient truths, in terms of what their generation called Reason. But they were not yet fully conscious of it. Nor could they propose to base a new nation on speculations untried up to then, in fact never known in the world before. From this derives their (to us) curiously naive reliance on the precedent of classical antiquity and the application of classical details to every possible architectural type, no matter how fundamentally non-classical. A striking visual metaphor of this situation is the original Supreme Court chamber in the United States Capitol, where Latrobe's avant-garde simplified abstract classical details deck out a basically medieval Gothic rib-vaulted structure.

Only against this background can we understand how someone as learned and smart as Jefferson could be predisposed to see such close analogies between the new Republic in America and the ancient Republic of Rome. Jefferson's generation must certainly have been aware how long the learned had been scoffing at notions of Romans being paragons of virtue: "Nobody but a schoolboy in his declamation," Samuel Johnson thundered, "should whine over the Commonwealth of Rome, which grew great only by the misery of the rest of mankind. The Romans [were] . . . a people who, while they were poor robbed mankind, and as soon as they became rich, robbed one another."[5] For that matter, they could have remembered from Shakespeare's *Julius Caesar* how thin was the line between Roman virtue and Roman villiny. Or reflected on the desirability of reincarnating a civilization in which a *normal* mode of judicial punishment was crucifixion. All this was for them overridden by a hidden agenda—hidden, indeed, from themselves.

The makers of the American Revolution held as self-evident truth an intuitive conviction that mankind[6] could control its own destiny and mold worlds to its will. To bolster this conviction, it was useful to maintain that mankind had been on the verge of doing this before. Two thousand years ago, human society had been brought as close to perfection as ever imagined; the belief is spelled out in the first page of Gibbon's *Decline and Fall of the Roman Empire.* Then the great chance aborted. Gibbon explained how, summing up his generation's understanding of the calamity: "barbarism" and "religion" had undone that world, somehow. But our age is wiser. We have Reason. It won't happen again. Under our new government, based on Reason, the heroes and statesmen, the grandeur of Rome and the wisdom of Greece will return forever. The process has already begun. In the heroes and statesmen of the Revolution, the selfless patriotism of Horatii and Cincinnati live again. In the new Senate on the Potomac, the old Senate on the Tiber is reborn. In new cities dotted all over the new Republic's newest lands, names drawn from lands of classical antiquity witness to the rebirth.[7] Just so, ancient Rome's monuments will reappear in

the form of courthouses and capitols and official mansions of the new United States. Succeeding to Rome's destiny, America inherits Rome's arts, and it will be the function of those arts to assist that destiny.

Only thus can be comprehended the notion that Greek and Roman history constituted a vast reservoir of examples applicable to the new Republic—how to legislate, how to orate, how to make war (after each battle in the Peloponnesian War, Thucydides describes how the contending Greek states erected monuments to their dead heroes; with that history in mind, Baltimore's Battle Monument was commissioned immediately after the British bombardment in 1814). Only thus can be comprehended the corresponding insistence on stuffing privies and schoolhouses, mansions and hotels, churches and banks into temple-house shells, at sad expense to practical convenience. Or the extraordinary willingness of that generation to perceive in their Classical Revival architecture conscious, literary, and romantic associations with such abstractions (and absurdities) as "Greek liberty," "Roman virtue," "Egyptian wisdom."

Only if you were committed in some deep recesses of the mind to values that are unhistorical and self-contradictory, could you read such unhistorical and contradictory meanings into a style as the Republic's first generations read into their Classical Revival arts. Only if you understand how Classical Revival styles so worked in and for society can our generation hope to understand them.

Applications of the Classical Revival to Architectural Types

Of all architectural types, the monument was preeminently suited to Classical Revival treatment. Conversely, Classical Revival enthusiasts tended to think of all architecture—outside and in—in terms of occasions to celebrate, and monuments to commemorate, the new kind of human beings that democratic institutions must infallibly produce: the Virtuous Citizen, selflessly devoted to the Public Good.

"Every man in a republic," noted Benjamin Rush in 1787, "is public property. . . . His time, and talents—his youth—his manhood—his old age—nay more life, all belong to his country." This cult of the hero was no American monopoly; it was part of an international movement that climaxed in the revolutions of 1848.[8] But it was most fully realized

3.18. Throughout the history of the Republic, heroes have been commemorated standing on columns. Here is a monument in that form (though in the rough-hewn quasi-Romanesque style in favor at the time it was completed, 3 May 1890) at Coloma, California, to James W. Marshall, "whose discovery of gold January 24 1848 in the tailrace of Sutter's Mill at Coloma started the great rush of the Argonauts." The hero's finger points to the spot where he found gold. (IMG:NAL)

in America, where the Classical Revival as an ideological instrument reached its fullest expression as well.

This occurred first in monuments. In memorial and triumphal columns, arches, obelisks, and the like, historical associations were reinforced by such visual effects as uprightness and unyielding stability, which admirably expressed the nature of the virtuous doings of democratic citizens alike in peace and war, beginning of course with George Washington *[3.17, 3.18]*. Then it was realized in city plans and parks. The country's new capital was one great collective monument to Virtuous Citizens, beginning with the hero after whom it was named, and everywhere embellished, in the words of its designer Charles L'Enfant, with

> statues, columns, obelisks, or any other ornaments . . . to perpetuate not only the memory of such individuals whose counsels or military achievements

were conspicuous in giving liberty and independence to this country, but also those whose usefulness hath rendered them worthy of general imitation, to invite the youth of succeeding generations to tread in the paths of those sages or heroes whom their country has thought proper to celebrate.[9]

To announce the home, or rather mansion, of the Virtuous Citizen, classical porticoes were ideal. Columned fronts had been developing throughout the eighteenth century as a signal of social pretension (out of the seventeenth-century cross-plan porch and other sources); to identify them with Greek or Roman temple fronts was natural and inevitable. They remained mansion signals throughout the South until the Civil War *[3.19–3.21]*. In the North there were also grand classical mansions with giant porticoes *[3.22]*, but they were far outnumbered by variants manifesting upward mobility. Sometimes these were small temple-houses with smaller flanking temple-wings *[3.23]*, but most often were rudimentary intimations of classical forms only: modest porches with pillars or merely temple-house proportions with some hint of a pediment via a return of the eaves *[3.24]*. In those simpler forms Classical Revival homesteads complemented classical names like Rome, Syracuse, Utica, Ovid, Carthage, Romulus, Troy, Sparta, Ithaca, to mark population movements out of New York into Ohio, Michigan, Illinois.

For government buildings—capitols, courthouses, city halls—the appropriateness of Classical Revival styles was obvious. Where could Virtuous Citizens of the new Republic better assemble to govern themselves than within temple-houses associated with the noble assemblies of classical antiquity? Or, if the required space were too complex for accommodation within a single shape, suitable combinations of classical elements could be easily composed, each and all capable of being conceived and read as metaphors of legitimate democratic authority. So rows of columns "march" in solemn dignity along a street front (as in the Fifteenth Street front of the Treasury that Robert Mills designed for President Jackson *[3.25]*), each an individual with a "life" of its own, "standing" in firm dignity on its "feet," "pushing up" against the weight it carries (as the Greeks had perceived long ago, and refined their columns' mimetic shapes into appropriately scaled and proportioned orders accordingly). Yet each column "contributes" to the whole via a common platform (of Law) below and common entablature (institutions) at the top. Great

3.19 (right). Dunleith, one of the mansions featured in the brochure of the "Natchez Pilgrimage" tour, "Where The Old South Still Lives." Its date is here given as "after 1855." (IMG:NAL)

3.20 (below). One of the most elegant and sophisticated of all Southern plantation houses is remote Waverley, near West Point in deep rural Mississippi. It is an H-plan with a center octagon ringed by flying staircases. Completed c. 1852 by owner George Hampton Young, it made a dramatic image of "great landed family," complete with its own family shrine in the form of a niche for officiating clergy at christenings and weddings and for biers at funerals. Waverley remained in the family as the center of a working plantation until 1913, then stood empty until 1962, when the house, but not the plantation, was restored. (IMG:NAL)

3.21 (bottom). Neither sophistication nor elegance marked the Gamble Mansion at Ellenton near Bradenton; but it nonetheless serves as a useful reminder of Florida's early days, before the state was transformed by the great tourist and retirement boom of the 1920s and the refugee influx of the 1960s. Robert Gamble built it as a frontier mansion in 1845, during the great expansion of Southern territories, and its identifying colonnade and pediment were the simplest sort of Classical Revival signs. Judah P. Benjamin, a principal aide and advisor to Jefferson Davis, fled here when the Confederacy collapsed in 1865, and from here he escaped to England by sea, outrunning a Union gunboat. In 1925 the house was acquired by the United Daughters of the Confederacy and made into the only state Confederate shrine in Florida (the Judah P. Benjamin Memorial), perhaps in riposte to the Northern influx beginning in that decade. (Florida State News Bureau)

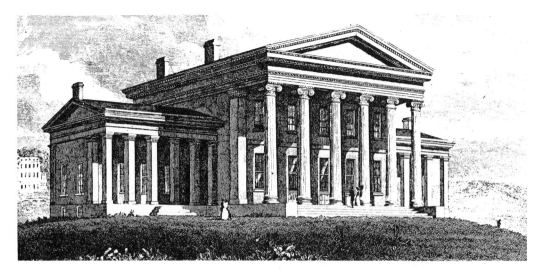

3.22 (top). The Bowers house, Northampton, Massachusetts, is a classic Northern temple-house in high-style Greek Ionic, with matching temple-house wings. Built to designs of Ithiel Town, c. 1830; long demolished. (From E. V. Gillon, Jr., Early Illustrations . . . of American Architecture *[New York: Dover, 1971]).*

3.23 (above). This temple-house with wings outside Canandaigua, New York, built c. 1840, is what this era would have called a "farmers' and mechanics' home." It is finished in the cobblestone technique characteristic of the region south of Lake Ontario and is the very image of Lincoln's faith in freedom of opportunity: "We do wish the humblest man an equal chance to get rich with everybody else. When one starts poor, as most do in the race of life, free society is such that he knows he can better his condition." (IMG:NAL)

3.24 (right). This classical vernacular farmhouse near Tecumseh, Michigan, is characteristic of buildings in the new states carved out of the old Northwest Territories from the 1840s through the 1860s. (IMG:NAL)

3.25. United States Treasury from the south; begun 1836 by Robert Mills; addition by Thomas U. Walter, 1869. The anthropomorphism of the Classical Revival colonnade is here plain: columns march along all sides of the building, some freestanding, some attached, others in pilaster form; but despite their individual differences, they are attached to each other and interdependent. The effect is reinforced by a barricade closing off Fifteenth Street for some event; the barriers also have a marching effect, but it is temporary and utilitarian, as contrasted with the eternal dignity of Mills's formal colonnades. (IMG:NAL)

domes arching over or dominating a complex can image due subordination of parts to the whole for the common good (so Lincoln conceived it, when he pressed the new United States Capitol dome to completion during the Civil War [3.5], a perceptual instinct shared throughout the Union then and later [3.7–3.9]. Classical arches and arcades, formal doorways, staircases, balustrades—all make ideal elements for composing a series of spatial experiences that can impress visitors with due respect for the precincts they enter, as Jefferson demonstrated at his University of Virginia campus [3.47].

Equally appropriate are the associations of Classical Revival forms applied to public works. American bridges, roads, and waterworks could justly have borne the proud inscription *Senatus Populusque Romanus*, for they too were monuments to a Virtuous Citizenry, Senate and People, cooperating for the Public Good [3.41]. The same was true of fort types, as demonstrated by the 1819–22 Pentagon at Baton Rouge, for example [3.26]. The temple-house form was readily adaptable to the more straightforward kinds of commercial buildings— small stores, small offices, especially banks—most common in the early Republic and could admirably accommodate the three basic spaces this type demands—for customers, for storage, for interaction of the two [3.61]. It also admirably expressed the increased prestige accruing to this type now that

the top layer of the class-structured state was gone, leaving only two of its three classes, with the former middle one ascendant.

For other architectural types, Classical Revival styles were not as obviously effective. The ancient religious associations of temple-house forms made them inherently unsuitable for housing a Christian church or Jewish synagogue, however often it might be done. But Classical Revival forms were appropriate for "reformed" religious bodies—those (and their numbers were increasing throughout the nineteenth century) in the process of transforming themselves into agencies dedicated to the elimination of "irrational" elements in the new Republic, such as slavery or, for that matter, vestiges of supernaturally religious belief [3.70, 3.71].

Public amenities were another ambiguous area for Classical Revival styles. On the one hand, they might proclaim freedom in the sense of freedom from crippling handicaps such as deafness or blindness [3.66]. On the other, there was some unsettling implication of failure in the erection, by a nation dedicated to limitless pursuit of happiness, of large and prominent Classical Revival (the National Democratic style) structures for lunatic asylums or hospitals: "It is," in the words of a British visitor of the 1830s, "an *unpopular duty* to expose the imperfections of any American institution, hence the actual conditions of some of these establishments (for the

3.26. *View inside the court of the Pentagon at Baton Rouge, Louisiana; it is enclosed by four blocks arranged in pentagonal form, with the fifth side left open. Each block has a range of* two-story columns. The effect is a kind of "military village" corresponding to Jefferson's "academic village" at his University of Virginia (IMG:NAL).

poor, the criminal, and the insane) is really unknown to the great body of upper classes of the city [New York], who would otherwise be disposed towards their improvement."[10]

In a society dedicated to steady improvement toward perfection, cemeteries in Classical Revival forms would be practically a contradiction in terms. Monuments to undying fame you might have, mausolea commemorating the Virtuous Citizen's community service from one generation to another; but the cemetery type itself is too unsettling a reminder that death is the ultimate end of all individual endeavors, no matter how improved. So, as Wilbur Zelinsky has ably pointed out, town plans in the early Republic rarely if ever included civic cemeteries.[11] The formal planned cemetery was a product of Gothic Revival romantic impulses; thus, even as archetypically Classical Revival mausolea as those in St. Louis's Bellefontaine Cemetery *[3.11]* or the Egyptian tomb for General Jacob Gould in Rochester's Mount Hope stand on curving avenues laid out on Picturesque lines.

As for shelter types, barns and other outbuildings might appropriately be built in proportions alluding to a Classical Revival mansion, consciously or by the operations of a folk aesthetic *[3.27]*; so too might factory subtypes, which long maintained classical allusions *[3.28]*. But if and when they take on some formal Classical Revival style, the result is pompous if not absurd; Bremo is the most famous

example *[3.29]*. Yet the attempt indicates how wonderfully adaptable Classical Revival styles became to the needs of National Democratic expression.

Substyles

Classical Revival substyles were the result of, as well as instruments to achieve, the adaptation of almost entirely inappropriate models to the needs of North American living.

What comes first to mind about the architecture of Greece or Rome or Egypt is temples; "Classical Revival" meant construction of temples. But neither Greeks nor Romans ever lived in temples, nor ever did business in them. They used temples as storehouses, despite what Andrea Palladio, the sixteenth-century architect revered by Classical Revivalists as their principal authority on the subject—his 1558 guidebook to Rome was still being used in the 1820s!—had said. Palladio had argued that "houses of the gods" were simply elaborated versions of the houses all mankind had lived in "when we were in a state of innocence," that is, before what Christians called The Fall or what eighteenth-century Enlightenment philosophers called corruption of man's natural goodness by civilization. It followed that if new democratic institutions were about to restore human purity and abolish Original Sin, a temple would be the proper form for citizens of a revived classical republic to live and work in.[12] The

3.27. Resemblances may be fortuitous between a classical basilica with its nave and lower side aisles and this barn built in Oregon near Warrenton, c. 1890; possibly both represent shapes originating in an ancient folk aesthetic. But a similar aesthetic produced Classical Revival vernaculars like the Basilica form of homestead [3.76]. (IMG:NAL)

3.28. A plaque tell us that Slater's Mill on the Blackstone River in Pawtucket, Rhode Island, was "birthplace of the Cotton Manufacturing Industry in America. Founded by Samuel Slater, Moses Brown, and William Macy." As built in 1793 the structure was utilitarian, perhaps tinged by folk proportions traditional in English shelter/shed types; it was brought up to date by a cupola over the main entrance gable, which, though also serving the practical purpose of announcing working hours, was given a quasi-classical shape. The original was replaced by the present one in 1823–35. In the background of this view, an Academic Colonial Revival cupola and a factory from the 1880s attest to the continuing prosperity brought by the industrialization of Rhode Island. (IMG:NAL)

3.29. Bremo, for those lucky enough to see it (the estate, in Fluvanna County, Virginia, is still in private hands), gives the best possible idea of what Upper South plantations in the early Federal period were like. Its farm buildings were completed before the main house [3.36, 3.37]; this main barn was perhaps begun as early as spring 1816 and completed with cupola and columns in August 1817. Frederick Nichols in Howard Adams, The Eye of Jefferson (Washington, D.C.: National Gallery of Art, 1976), p. 283, cites a letter from Jefferson to owner/builder John Hartwell Cocke, advising that "Tuscan order would do for the barns." On either side of the portico, the arcaded wall treatment differs. (IMG:NAL)

3.30. Fort Hill, John C. Calhoun's house at Clemson, South Carolina. In 1825 the rising South Carolina lawmaker acquired a plantation and house built by a Presbyterian minister around 1803; he enlarged it and named it Fort Hill. It was restored by the South Carolina Division of the United Daughters of the Confederacy and Clemson University, on whose campus it now stands. (Clemson Chamber of Commerce)

logic was attractive, but the facts were wrong. And the practical difficulties were formidable. Consequently the only exact copy of a temple ever built in America is the Parthenon at Nashville, Tennessee, as completed in the 1920s *[cf. 6.60.]* Instead, Classical Revivalists adapted the forms of classical antiquity to create very distinctive combinations that became substyles.

Buildings of colonial or even utilitarian character were "classicized" by the addition of porches or pediments or cupolas with some classical detail. Palladian buildings, with only slight modifications, could be made to look like and function in and for society as Classical Revival styles. Combinations of simplified classical elements—sometimes to the point of geometric abstractions—were commonly used by avant-gardists in the early revivals to make "Revolutionary" metaphors. Or buildings that literally were in the last, Adamesque-Federal phase of eighteenth-century Classicism were adapted for such purposes. Then there were Roman, Greek, and Egyptian Revival temple buildings proper—never "pure," but fairly consistent. Simplifications of such shapes by local builders, especially for homesteads, produced a number of stylistic forms that were loosely drawn from classical precedents but were in fact American inventions—"classical squares," "classical cottages," "shot-guns," and "basilicas." And from beginning to end there was a body of vernacular building incorporating some

vestigial details and/or shapes ultimately deriving from the Classical Revivals.

"Classicizing Touches": Proportions and Additions

All sorts of buildings could be given a "classical touch" by altering proportions or adding a few bits vaguely resembling Greek or Roman forms. For example, the primary stylistic form of Indiana's second capitol at Corydon, and Ohio's third at Columbus, is obviously the old Puritan meetinghouse *[2.89]*. But it needed some kind of classical character to be fully appropriate for a capitol in the new Republic; this was supplied by adding a cupola and doorway frames with classical pilasters and pediment. Slater's Mill in Pawtucket, where Moses Brown founded Rhode Island's textile industry in 1793, was basically utilitarian, an expanded barn; to help make it acceptable to his peers, and to overcome a prejudice widespread in the early Republic against manufacturing (as encouraging mobs, urban decay, and immorality),[13] Brown went to the expense of adding a cupola and framing the facade openings in vaguely classical detail *[3.28]*.

Appended Porch/Portico Substyles

Appending a porch or portico to buildings had been a way to give buildings an appearance of in-

3.31. Like Jefferson, Andrew Jackson remodeled his home while President. The Hermitage outside Nashville, Tennessee, was built in 1819. President Jackson commissioned Robert Mills to make a visual metaphor of his new position, and so Mills did, in 1836, by adding a portico of two-story Greek Corinthian columns to the long side, which gave a Classical Revival veneer to a traditional form. At The Hermitage this traditionalism is heightened by an obvious contrast between the naturalness of peasant outbuildings and the measured grandeurs of the mansion/palace. It is not so much the Roman Republic that comes to rebirth in a design like this as the class-structured state cast in new forms. (Tennessee Tourist Development)

3.32. In the mid-Atlantic states, porches functioning visually as Classical porticoes were ubiquitously appended to Georgian houses (sometimes masking Germanic interiors). Often, as here on Main Street in Middletown, Maryland, they formed a kind of classical colonnade. (IMG:NAL)

creased stability and size, hence greater dignity, long before the Classical Revival made such appendages interpretable as "classical touches" and thereby ideologically fashionable. All sorts of Colonial homestead and Georgian stylistic forms had them. Washington's Mount Vernon is a famous example *[2.105]*; most common were vernaculars of the sort that appear in Wild's views of Cincinnati *[3.1]*. It was easy to make an ordinary dwelling into a Classical Revival mansion of sorts, functioning as an instant authority symbol, by appending to it a

porch or portico decked out in some more or less classical detail. This kind of substyle was especially popular in the South, perhaps because creation of instant authority symbols was more requisite there; famous examples include the Tuscan porch attached to Fort Hill by John C. Calhoun, archapologist of slavery and secession *[3.30]*, and the grander Corinthian portico attached to the Hermitage outside Nashville by Andrew Jackson, whose famous denunciation of Calhoun's and South Carolina's policies noted that he was a "fellow South

Carolinian" *[3.31]*. But there are many in the North, too, including especially interesting variants on the vernacular level in the mid-Atlantic area *[3.32]*.

High Georgian/Palladian with Classical Revival Social Function

By definition, the Classical Revival meant taking models directly from antiquity rather than second-hand, via the Italian Renaissance and Andrea Palladio's *Four Books of Architecture* of the 1550s, as eighteenth-century designers had done. But this was too fine a point to be consistently maintained. Even such a Classical Revival style leader as Thomas Jefferson, renowned for adapting his Virginia State Capitol directly from the Roman temple in Nîmes, in many other ways was better described as an "innovative [Revolutionary] Palladian."[14] To many architecturally literate people just after the Revolution, there seemed no particular reason why Palladian or later Georgian in general should be given up. After all, those great Whig lords who had made the revolution of 1689 in the name of liberty had proclaimed it in great Palladian-style palaces. For revolutionary Americans of conservative mind

3.33. *The popular understanding of architecture as symbol is indicated by the appearance on American currency of Monticello, Lincoln Memorial, Treasury, Capitol, Independence Hall, and, on the twenty-dollar bill, the White House as icons of government and history. The view shows the south front, with the portico added in 1824 to the first public building in the new United States capital, begun in 1792. Irish Palladian James Hoban designed the original and supervised its rebuilding after the British attack in 1814; in the south and north porticoes (1829) Benjamin Latrobe and Jefferson were also involved. Among the more notable subsequent developments were the reconstruction in 1902 of the main floor, its redecoration, and the addition of low east and west wings (partly visible in the engraving) by McKim, Mead and White.*

3.34. *George Washington himself planned four government offices to flank the presidential mansion and so symbolize the executive branch. Amateur watercolorist and early tourist Anne-Marguérite-Henriette Rouillé de Marigny, Baroness Hyde de Neuville, made this view of them in 1820. Looking south from Pennsylvania Avenue she saw the north front of the White House with State (left) and War (right) department buildings in the foreground; behind them are Treasury (left) and Navy (right). First occupied were Treasury (1800, then including State) and War, designed by George Hadfield and rebuilt under James Hoban's direction in 1816. Treasury (1836, enlarged 1869) now has replaced the two left buildings and the Old Executive Office (built as State, War, and Navy) the two right ones. (New York Public Library)*

that style was still legitimately associated with British liberties claimed in the Puritan Revolution of 1641, affirmed in the Glorious Revolution of 1689, confirmed in the revolution of 1776. So in 1782 Benjamin West, then president of the Royal Academy in London but professedly loyal to his American origins in Pennsylvania, could paint *Cromwell Dissolving the Long Parliament,* with Cromwell's pose and action clearly resembling those in portraits of Washington. Architects used Palladian and late Georgian style with comparable ideological intent *[3.36–3.38]*.

The most famous example of this substyle was the White House and the four buildings for the Departments of Treasury, War, State, and Navy that flanked it *[3.33, 3.34]*. But both in the North and South, Palladian seemed an appropriate style for mansions proclaiming Classical Revival ideals of the Virtuous Citizen in the new Republic *[3.36–3.38]*. Two architects are particularly associated with it: Philip Hooker of Albany and Charles Bulfinch of Boston. Both used the style for fine mansions, churches, and other public buildings (like the Massachusetts General Hospital) to celebrate their new state capitals' rise in wealth and civic dignity; Bulfinch used it for the capitol buildings of Connecticut and Massachusetts *[3.35]*. The style's counterparts in furniture were most commonly found in the same region *[3.2]*. But Georgian/Palladian with a Classical Revival social function was found all over the country, used to some extent by every architect of importance. Jefferson's personal, as distinct from public, taste, as evidenced in his furnishings for Monticello, was for Louis Seize, the French version of Palladian. A list of other notable figures whose work could pass for being in the new Classical Revival taste, but whose actual forms were predominantly or entirely Palladian in architecture and Adamesque-Federal in furniture, would include Gabriel Manigault of Charleston, Samuel McIntire of Salem, the younger John McComb of New York, the senior Robert Cary Long in Baltimore, and Asher Benjamin of Boston.

Revolutionary Democratic: The Avant-Garde Substyle

Revolutionary Democratic, the most self-consciously ideological of all Classical Revival substyles, was the first to appear. Its origins were in mid-eighteenth-century Enlightenment Europe, and most of its practitioners in America were in fact Europeans attracted by the general promise of the future in a new democratic land. Many were drawn

3.35. *Until the 1870s Connecticut had two state capitals, one at Hartford and another at New Haven, both with several successive statehouses. What stands as the old statehouse at Hartford was built 1793–97, with a cupola added or rebuilt 1827–29; it is usually attributed to Charles Bulfinch. After the new permanent capitol was built at Hartford, this old statehouse became an administrative building and was then restored as a museum in 1911–21, under Academic Colonial Revival impulse. The peculiar significance of this building is that it was evidently designed after Federal Hall in New York, as remodeled by L'Enfant for use as capitol of the United States, thus inaugurating the trend to have state capitol designs follow the national capitol. Also significant is the anonymity of this building: it attests to the lingering colonial concept of the gentleman-designer, in contrast to the Boston Statehouse begun just a few years later, in 1795, where Bulfinch was paid as the architect and marched as such in the inaugural procession.*

3.36. *Elevation for the main house at Bremo, Fluvanna County, Virginia; drawing attributed to Cornelia Jefferson Randolph, Jefferson's daughter. (Courtesy of Alderman Library, University of Virginia)*

3.37 *(below). River side of Bremo, showing connected pavilions. (IMG:NAL)*

3.38 *(bottom). Gore Place, built 1805–6 to designs of Jacques LeGrand in Waltham, Massachusetts. Rear view showing the curved ballroom wall. Ovals in conjunction with flat, recessed blind arches characterize the last phase of Georgian/Palladian style and often coalesce, as here, with Revolutionary Democratic forms. (IMG:NAL)*

here by the encouragement of Thomas Jefferson this substyle's most vigorous native promoter.

Revolutionary Democratic has three distinctive traits. First, it is characterized by simplification and abstraction of forms derived from antiquity. Thus portico columns tend to be stubby and unfluted, acroteria reduced to earlike shapes, and domes flat and saucerlike. From this derives a second obvious characteristic: simple geometric shapes. Finally, there is an emphasis on whiteness or at least monochromatic effects; not only columns but also walls and pediments appear in some uniform off-white, buff, or gray. Within these general parameters forms could range from the robustly sculptural to delicate, even fragile. Of the first, the best example was Calverton outside Baltimore, whose facade was derived from designs by the French avant-gardist Claude-Nicolas Ledoux and featured a freestanding sculptural group on a lintel with fully three-dimensional niche space behind *[3.39]*. Examples of the second were more numerous, with William Jay's mansions of the late 1810s and early 1820s in Savannah *[3.40]* being outstanding.

Probably the two best extant examples of this Revolutionary Democratic substyle are the Custis-Lee Mansion *[3.10]* in Arlington and the Unitarian Church in Baltimore *[3.41]*. Both demonstrate its characteristic simple geometric shapes, unfluted columns, monochromy, and wall composition of inset blind arcades of exceedingly simple abstract form. Both were also designed, as so often with this style, by avant-garde European architects, in one case the Englishman George Hadfield, in the other the still enigmatic Frenchman Maximilien Godefroy. Thanks to a recent restoration, the Unitarian Church once again sports emblematic pedimental sculpture like that on Calverton.

The Revolutionary Democratic substyle appeared, of course, in Philadelphia, then the country's biggest city, seat of the revolution-making Continental Congress. The cosmopolitan Englishman Benjamin Henry Latrobe, who liked to think of himself as not only the country's first but also only trained professional architect, had several commissions there. He was responsible for the first Bank of Pennsylvania building; his presentation drawing shows it as a little white geometric jewel, exquisitely simplified to make the strongest possible contrast with the out-of-date Philadelphia spec-house forms on the street around. It is an image of high-minded commerce liberating individual initiative *[3.42]*. The basic scheme—central squarish domed space

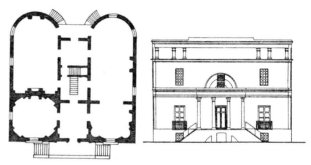

3.39. Calverton mansion outside Baltimore, long ago demolished and known only from an old photograph, was the country's most dramatic example of Revolutionary Democratic avant-garde styling. Built c. 1818 by Robert Cary Long, Sr., and J.-J. Ramée, on the model of Claude-Nicolas Ledoux's 1780s Hôtel Guimard in Paris.

3.40. Plan and elevation of the Alexander Telfair house (now Art Gallery of Savannah), 1819–20, one of a number of houses—the Bulloch and Scarborough are most outstanding—in which William Jay experimented with various avant-garde combinations of geometrical forms for the rising aristocracy of Georgia's growing new mercantile city.

with porticoes on either end—became standard for small banks over the next fifty years, even if, to Latrobe's chagrin, his Revolutionary Democratic style proved to be too erudite, too elitist, for adaptation by the Bank of the United States (cf. 3.60). Latrobe was architect too of the Philadelphia Waterworks, a subtle demonstration of a Virtuous Citizenry cooperating for the common good. Along the Schuylkill River he ranged delicately white little temples with unfluted columns housing intake machinery, but designed the main pumping station in big, blocky geometric shapes *[3.43]* that made stud-

3.41. Baltimore's First Unitarian Church was built in 1818 of brick covered by stucco, to designs of Maximilien Godefroy. It has a gilded terra cotta "Angel of Truth" by Antonio Capellano (sculptor on the Battle Monument) above its entrance pediment, a white portico remarkably similar to the background of Jacques-Louis David's Oath of the Horatii, and an interior recalling some of Etienne-Louis Boullée's French Revolutionary visionary proposals for halls and churches from the 1770s and 1780s—in short, it was one of the most avant-garde buildings in the country. The original exterior was largely restored in 1954, but to get some feel for the original interior (only a pulpit by Godefroy survived an 1893 remodeling), one needs to visit Eutaw Place Temple (Oheb Shalom Congregation), designed by local traditionalist architect Joseph E. Sperry in 1892–93. (IMG:NAL)

3.42. Banks were the most visible symbol of the new government's promised liberties in practice: freedom to better oneself by untrammeled enterprise. Benjamin Latrobe, commissioned to design a main Philadelphia office for the new Bank of Pennsylvania, rose to the occasion with the very latest and subtlest avant-garde geometrical forms. His presentation drawing, showing a sober Quaker and foppish couple standing together in the portico waiting for the doors to open, practically illustrates Voltaire's famous quip about exchanges being more religious places than many a church, where Jew and gentile, Anglican and agnostic, meet to do business in the service of Mankind. (Maryland Historical Society)

3.43. The central square where Philadelphia's City Hall has stood since the 1870s was first occupied by a pumping station of the Philadelphia Waterworks, designed by Benjamin Latrobe. This print of c. 1825 shows it surrounded by Lombardy poplars; they were much favored for Classical Revival landscaping because of a resemblance in shape to "classical" trees like Mediterranean cypress. In later decades this species suffered from a plague of caterpillars and had to be cut down, with a resultant change in landscape comparable only to the loss of American elms in the 1960s and 70s. (From George Bishop Tatum, Penn's Great Town [Philadelphia: University of Pennsylvania Press, 1961])

ied allusion to such Parisian avant-garde designs as Ledoux's Barrière [Customs House] de la Villette.

The most famous and influential of all were the architectural works of Thomas Jefferson, author of the Declaration of Independence, Governor of Virginia, third President. The most ideologically conscious of all the Revolutionary leaders, he was also the greatest promoter of the Revolutionary Democratic substyle, although, as Latrobe among others somewhat bitterly observed, he was not always a consistent user of it himself. (But, then, consistency is not a quality politicians can afford, nor architects either, as Latrobe ought to have known.)

It was Jefferson's idea to model Virginia's new post-Revolutionary capitol in Richmond on an actual Roman temple, the Maison Carrée, as a kind of monument sculpture to dramatize the new state of Virginia *[3.44]*.[15] Some departures from the model were obviously necessary for practical reasons. To transform a box designed to store offerings to some god and so lighted only from one front door into an American legislative building, Jefferson designed a tripartite interior with nicely curving walls in keeping with avant-garde taste for geometric subtleties; he also added windows, heating, and a gallery (which collapsed in 1870). Other departures were stylistic, introduced to make the temple a suitably Revolutionary Democratic icon. Geometric simplicity was to be emphasized by painting the brick-and-wood building entirely white, and columns were unfluted and heavier than the original. Instead of the Maison Carrée's Roman Corinthian capitals, the Richmond capitol used a kind of Ionic one, drawn, apparently, from Freemasonic teachings about distinctive virtues exuded by the several orders: Doric proclaims strength; Corinthian, beauty; Ionic, wisdom, with the latter eminently more suitable for legislators, obviously.[16] It is a highly symbolic building, and never more so than as seen in Matthew Brady's 1865 photograph of it standing in lonely majesty amidst the ruins of a conquered city.

Having set a model for state capitols (which was not followed in others, the domed United States Capitol being preferred), Jefferson undertook to provide a model for mansions by making over Monticello, his home since the 1770s, in the new Revolutionary Democratic mode *[3.45]*.[17] This enterprise had heavy ideological motivation. For Monticello as a dwelling, even as an ordinary mansion, was perfectly adequate. Its Palladian style was not out of date (as later Virginia mansions like Bremo show),[18] and its practicality was outstand-

3.44. *When the capital of Virginia was moved from Williamsburg to Richmond in 1780 (during the Revolutionary War), a new, independent, non-colonial image was obviously required. Then-governor Thomas Jefferson proposed three new government buildings, one each for legislative, judicial, and executive branches, in classical temple form. After his departure as Minister to France in 1784, the legislature decided to put all three offices in one big temple, and wrote Jefferson for a design. He obliged and presented, with the collaboration of archaeological authority Charles-Louis Clérisseau, plans and a model based upon the Roman temple at Nîmes (Maison Carrée). Construction began August 1785, and was completed—with brick substituted for the specified marble columns and other adaptations to practical usage—in 1788. The whole sits on a hill grandly overlooking the James River. Furnishings, including desks and draperies, were also designed by Jefferson. Interior remodeled after 1870; wings added 1904–6; restoration of Hall of Delegates 1929. (IMG:NAL)*

ing: Jefferson had designed and installed recessed beds and coordinated sliding doors, an automatic dumbwaiter, an indoor weather vane, and a "chaise desk"; he had also integrated his service buildings under a terrace and set the main floor on low brick arches for cooling.

From a practical point of view, the alterations carried out between 1796 and 1808 seemed deleterious. They provided no new living spaces; and to add a functionally useless dome and portico, Jefferson had to destroy his own large and airy second-floor library room, substituting for it cramped and awkward spaces next to his bedroom. He had, in effect, to split his house into two separate parts connected only by an open balcony, and plunge his drawing room into gloom. What the remodeling—especially the addition of the octagon dome, an entirely new element—accomplished was to make his mansion into an icon. The Palladian plantation house was transformed into a much more elaborate metaphor of the Democratic Leader than Washing-

3.45. *Monticello, garden front. The home that Thomas Jefferson made into a companion icon to Mount Vernon by rebuilding, in 1796–1809, the original Palladian mansion (c. 1769–c. 1780). (IMG:NAL)*

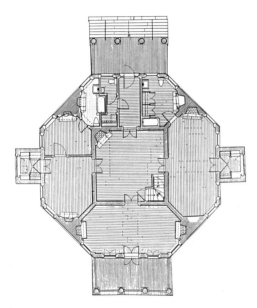

3.46. *First-floor plan and north elevation of Poplar Forest, Jefferson's most systematic exercise in geometric design, begun 1806. (HABS)*

ton had created with his Mount Vernon portico; Monticello became a very subtle version of the Pantheon in Rome.

Monticello's success as a public icon is attested to by its presence on United States coins and bills, which is appropriate, for like all persuasive architectural images throughout history, its ultimate function was to justify power to the possessor. Just as castles and palaces of class-structured states had been designed and ornamented so as to show forth the rightness of power acquired by heredity, so systematic geometric order in a presidential mansion could be read as Reason justifying power acquired

by democratic politics. To that principle Jefferson's other mansion, Poplar Forest, attested even more strikingly *[3.46]*.

Finally, Jefferson designed the model university, again for his own state, in his own town *[3.47]*. The design is complex and its formal origins have been much discussed. But the motivation was obviously ideological, not aesthetic. The University of Virginia was a cosmological statement, an image of what Daniel Boorstin called "the lost world of Thomas Jefferson."[19] How lost that world was by the 1890s is sadly revealed by alterations and "improvements" in the name of restoration at that

3.47. The University of Virginia at Charlottesville, originating as Albemarle Academy, became by legislative action the new nation's first state university in 1816. Between 1819 and 1826 Jefferson oversaw the building of an "academical village" campus for it, designed to look totally unlike any colonial college, most especially Jefferson's own alma mater, William and Mary. A library, not a chapel or a classroom/residence, is its focal point. Rows of temples   *inculcated, according to Masonic belief, various virtues through their various orders; in them masters, slaves, and students lived together under a rule of law, a microcosm of the society of the state of Virginia and by extension of the new nation. In the foreground of this aerial view is Cabell Hall, designed in the 1890s by McKim, Mead and White at the same time they restored the library. (Courtesy of University of Virginia)*

time; the subtleties of the campus's original concept survive only in records.

The focus of the campus was an image of the Enlightenment faith in Reason: a great geometric shape, composed of a dome set on a high drum, called the Rotunda, which served as the university library. The Rotunda resembled, and could well have been inspired by, projects for monuments to Isaac Newton, discoverer of the universe's immutable laws *[3.48]*. To its drum a portico entrance was attached; in this a vague resemblance to the Pantheon in Rome was perceptible.[20] Restorers McKim, Mead and White took care of that "vague-

3.48. As designed, Jefferson's Rotunda had a much more prominent dome, a cosmic ball actually. The relationship to cosmic allusions in other avant-garde architecture of the time is explained by Adolf Max Vogt in this excerpt from a plate in Russiche und französische Revolutionsarchitektur *(Cologne: Dumont, 1974); Vogt's book shows a comparison with Boullée's 1784 Monument to Newton (center) and Goethe's 1777 monument to Agathe Tyche at Weimar (right).*

ness" in a notable display of the insistence on "correctness" and failure to recognize specific iconographic symbolism so characteristic of Academic styles generally (see chapter 6); they made the style Academic Roman Revival, in other words, instead of Revolutionary Democratic.

Extending from the sides of the Rotunda platform, parallel rows of pavilions edged the campus. In these little temple-houses in diverse Classical Revival substyles might be seen images of collective life ordered by reason; this campus was a little world unto itself, an "academical village," in Jefferson's words, and nothing like the "fetid dens" housing older universities.[21] More immediately, their diverse columns and arches and pediments put the whole range of classical orders before students' eyes and kept the whole panorama of Roman republican virtues before their minds. In these temples too was an architectural exemplification of the "fasces" principle of Federal union: each building preserving individual differences and excellences,

but deriving full meaning only in contributing to the common whole. As all these diverse facades took common orientation from the Rotunda, emblem of Reason, so a common body of law and culture based upon Reason—Truths held to be self-evident, as Jefferson's Declaration had put it— might unify all the diverse peoples settled in the new United States.

This whole ordered, reasonable cosmos was shut off from the chaotic realities of time and history in the outside world by a wall, which emphasized this separation by a highly artificial form, elegantly serpentine. In this sense there was something monastic about the concept of this campus, as one can still feel at Monticello, high on its steep little mountain. Perhaps the beginnings of all new movements in human thought have needed nurturing in some such protective situation. Certainly a new movement in thought was what the Revolutionary Democratic style was all about.

Architecture Parlante

At the opposite pole from Revolutionary Democratic subtleties was *architecture parlante* (speaking architecture), an extreme form of democratic expression whereby the literal meaning of buildings, and their use, was conveyed to everyone, high and low, by representational shapes. It was peculiarly associated with the ideologically-minded French architects LeDoux and Boullée, who devised cenotaphs in the shape of giant coffins, woodcutters' homes as stacks of cordwood, and the like. One might have supposed this style to have been popular in the early Republic, but evidence is decidedly lacking. Perhaps that is because a building might be perceived both as a representational shape and as abstract geometry—Jefferson's Rotunda, for instance, or Latrobe's Pump House in Philadelphia. Or perhaps, by analogy with later times, it is simply because nobody thought examples worth recording; our roadsides abounded for sixty years with Popular/Commercial *architecture parlante* before it was noticed (see chapter 8).

Round/Octagon Substyle

Round, hexagonal, pentagonal, or octagon shapes were among the most common employed by avant-garde Classical Revival designers; they were also among the easiest to copy in simplified, vulgarized forms. So of all Classical Revival styles, round/octagon was the most long-lived.

Round/octagon shapes appeared very early as a

3.49. Science building and observatory at Amherst College, erected in 1848. Since the 1920s, when science took command and got great separate buildings for all its main branches here and at every other institution of higher learning, this structure has been home for the Department of Music. (Courtesy of Amherst College)

3.50. The Octagon, a mansion built in Washington in 1798–1800 to William Thornton's designs, more recently home of the American Institute of Architects. Since the 1970s it has been overpowered by the massive cliff and cave shapes devised by The Architects Collaborative of Cambridge. (IMG:NAL)

3.51. The cosmic implications of domes, balls, and hexagonal or octagonal shapes had a long subliminal life; this tollhouse built in the 1830s at the start of the National Road in Lavale, Maryland, has many precedents in eighteenth-century tollhouses. Restored c. 1980. (IMG:NAL)

shorthand summary of all the enthusiasm for a universe run by Reason—in Jeffersonian plans for a chapel at Williamsburg in the 1770s, as well as thirty years later for his Poplar Forest *[3.46].* From this came the frequent adoption of round/octagon shapes for buildings associated with science, which continued as late as Amherst College's 1848 observatory *[3.49].* Pleasing associations with science were long retained on the popular level, as attested by Orson Squire Fowler's promotion of octagons in his 1854 *A Home for All,* on pseudo-scientific grounds of greater healthfulness, convenience, and functional efficiency. But they were even more pleasantly combined with broader Classical Revival concepts of absolute, perfect forms, as Fowler reports: "Some forms are constitutionally more beautiful than others . . . A square house is more beautiful than a triangular one, and an octagon or

duodecagon than either . . . the octagon form is more beautiful as well as capacious, and more consonant with the predominant or governing form of Nature—the spherical." So doubly blessed, round/octagon forms could be appropriately given to just about every architectural type: to Latrobe's Congressional Cemetery monuments honoring congressmen who died in office, or George Hadfield's round Van Ness mausoleum in Georgetown; to mansions like the famous Octagon designed by William Thornton in 1798–1800 *[3.50];* to churches (one of 1813 in Richmond, Vermont, has sixteen sides, apparently associated with celestial harmony); to barns; to tollhouses on National Roads *[3.51]* and thence to railroad stations *[3.52]*[22]; to schools *[3.53].* As for houses, round and octagon forms continued to appear on all levels from the simplest round shapes to cobblestoned octagons to

3.52. The Baltimore & Ohio's old Mount Clare station of c. 1840, preserved in its Railroad Museum in Baltimore, derived in form from antecedent tollhouses. (IMG:NAL)

3.53. A state historical marker tells us that the octagonal Sodom School near Montandon in central Pennsylvania was built in 1863 and served as a school until 1915. To many moderns, an incongruous coexistence of Classical Revival with biblical tradition; but this is not the only case. The frequency of Sodom and Gomorrah as North American place-names (chosen at random from the Good Book) attests to an ability to take the sacredness of the Bible so literally as to drain it of meaning and so, paradoxically, make it nonadversarial to Greek or Roman Revival ideas or architecture. (IMG:NAL)

such elaborate examples as Longwood, whose fantastically intricate Moorish-style jacket disguised a correspondingly intricate plan *[4.41, 4.42]*.

Roman Revival Proper

A deliberate revival of Roman architecture on a mass popular level hardly began until the 1820s. During that decade it gradually replaced both simplified versions of Palladian or Adamesque-Federal and subtly geometric avant-garde abstractions as the Classical Revival norm. But it never displaced usage of appended porch/portico as a Classical Revival substitute; and it was itself superseded in the 1830s as the most popular classical style by Greek Revival proper *[3.12–3.15, 3.57–3.59]*. A building or piece of furniture may generally be recognized as Roman Revival proper by details of the Roman orders and, on occasion, in furniture especially, by "Roman" features like lions' feet, eagles' wings, and effects of marble with gilt accessories *[3.54]*.

There was always, of course, something heavy-handed about Roman Revival symbolism, beginning with the Great Seal of the United States and its all-seeing eye, pyramid, and *novus ordo seclorum*. When Empire-style furniture first began displacing Adamesque-Federal delicacies around 1810, critics called its overbearing, sculptural forms accented with brass and marble "bombastic, pedantic, trashy . . . a chaos of symbols and effigies."[23] But this very obviousness gave Empire furniture and Roman Revival architecture their popular appeal.

Some of the best-known monuments of the period fall into this substyle. Baltimore's Washington Monument, in the form of a huge column carrying an effigy, was not quite as simple in the original design by Mills as it now appears; but it was uncomplicated enough *[3.17]*.[24] Countless naive imitations attest to its popularity: the Ethan Allen monument in Burlington, Vermont, for instance; or the wonderful but now forgotten column topped by a naively modeled figure bending in beatific blessing over the treetops of what is now solid bush, erected in 1852–55 on a hillside near Pottsville, Pennsylvania, "by the citizens of Schuylkill County and Bequeathed to their Children. A Record of Gratitude for his Illustrious Service." "Whose?," I asked a contemporary citizen. "Mr. Potts," he supposed. So much for Fame Undying; this column commemorates Senator Henry Clay of Kentucky, the Great Compromiser of 1850. Later columns honored heroes of the Civil War, the Spanish-American War, and World War I, as well as firemen, businessmen, and civic leaders [3.18].

Unambiguous Roman Revival temples could compose monumental homes fit for such heroes to live in or could house their offices or other business ventures [3.55, 3.56]. What constituted "Roman" was never precisely defined, of course. Architects in general, and a good many local builders, could tell the broad difference between Roman and Greek orders; but as to finer points of distinction between, say, the Tuscan order in Roman Revival proper and as used in Georgian/Palladian or between Roman and Greek stylobates or entablature treatment, well, they were wobbly. Somehow this kind of exactitude was never deemed necessary by local carpenters, nor, one may add, by compilers of the guidebooks they fol-

3.54. *Parlor from the Rufus King house at Albany, New York, built c. 1830, demolished c. 1925, reconstructed as "the Empire Parlor" in the Winterthur Museum. There was always a naive quality about the Roman Revival, even in such high-style efforts as this. Here a kind of showroom was created to display the owner's wealth and devotion to the ideals of antiquity as fashionably understood, by assemblages of details derived with* *literal pedantry from archaeological evidence: white marble table tops and colonettes, with gilt metal adornments; lyres and caryatids and scrolls; eagles on the looking glass, gilt George Washington on the mantelpiece clock, more or less Grecian urns on side tables, and a more or less Roman harp in the "music corner." The interior is a perfect complement to the Classical Revival temple-house. (Courtesy of The Henry Francis du Pont Winterthur Museum)*

3.55. One of the first railroads in the United States was the West Feliciana, chartered in 1831 to carry cotton from plantations in and around Woodville in Wilkinson County to the Mississippi at Saint Francisville, Louisiana. Its office and banking house was built in 1834; it also served such passengers as might want to travel this predominantly freight road. In this photo the plaster has fallen off most of the columns, exposing their brick core. (IMG:NAL)

3.56. Quincy Market was begun in 1825 on plans of Alexander Parris to expand the market area around Faneuil Hall in Boston. It fronted on the harbor and was originally flanked by huge barn-like warehouses that made its classical character even more emphatic: classical porticoes on either end and a dome in the middle (like banks of the same period) admirably expressed the concept of exchange central to the concept of shop types of architecture at all times and places. This photograph, taken in 1973, shows the market as restored a few years earlier. It has since been incorporated into an elaborate urban marketplace "park." (IMG:NAL)

lowed. In most architectural types, Roman Revival was not so much superseded by Greek as rolled into it. Only in capitols, where connotations of Revival styles were most self-conscious, was the break at all clean.

Greek Revival Proper

"The Greek mania here is at its height," the New York correspondent of *The Architectural Magazine* wrote to London in December 1834, "as you infer from the fact that everything is a Greek temple from privies in the back court, through the various grades of prison, theatre, church, custom-house, and state house."

The precise differences between Greek and Roman were understood to be that Greek Doric columns had no bases and were usually fluted whereas Roman Doric columns usually had bases but no fluting; that Greek Doric had no encircling ring below the capital like Roman or Tuscan Doric; that Greek Ionic had volutes on only two sides whereas in Roman Ionic they appeared on all four; that Greek was, in general, more ornamented with brackets and acanthus scrolls and the like *[3.57, 3.58]*. Still more clouded was the distinction between Greek and Roman Corinthian (if any); not until around 1925 in fact was it firmly established that the Greeks did not generally use Corinthian until the Hellenistic age *[3.59]*.

Niceties of definition were not a problem for Greek Revival enthusiasts and need not bother us either, once we realize that the associated ideas were what mattered. Especially after Roman had been adopted by Napoleon's Imperial France, Greek preeminently stood for liberty.[25]

For banks, Greek Revival proclaimed liberty in

the especially direct and practical form of a new degree of personal autonomy. Thanks to the new Republic's banking laws, it was now possible as never before for an individual to save money and thereby experience freedom in the only sense that directly mattered: freedom to tell the boss to go to hell and to move, to use a nest egg to start a new life or a new profession. American banks in the form of Greek temples, in contrast to the older kind of palace forms still used for exchanges and banks in England (and in Canada until after 1867), made

that claim dramatically, beginning with the Second Bank of the United States in Philadelphia.[26] Bank President Nicholas Biddle specified only "purest Grecian" for it, as well as for his own mansion in nearby Andalusia, by which he meant no Palladian or avant-garde variants. And he commissioned what he wanted from native Americans, not Europeans: his bank was designed by William Strickland of Navesink, New Jersey, his mansion by Thomas U. Walter of Philadelphia. Biddle's Greek Revival bank *[3.60]* proved enormously popular and easily dis-

3.57 (left). The two orders recognized by American builders as specifically Greek were the Doric and Ionic. Both ultimately originated as mimetic imitations of wooden shapes that had acquired symbolic significance by ancestral associations with gods and burial. Greek Ionic could be distinguished from Roman by the erudite, but sturdy proportions, and sparse ornament made Greek Doric very distinctive. At the beginning of the nineteenth century it was still remembered that classical orders generally had been so refined, beginning in the fifth century B.C., as to admirably express relationships between weight and load and so help humanize buildings for beholders, and that this was indeed their real importance. By the end of the century this function had been forgotten, details like geison (i), metope (g), triglyph (h), architrave (f), abacus block (a), echinus block (b) were memorized by rote, so that there was little complaint when Modernists discarded the whole apparatus.

3.58 (center). Greek Ionic capital from the Tennessee State Capitol at Nashville [cf. 3.65].

3.59 (right). Capital from the Child house, built in the 1840s by Hugh Hastings, using designs from Minard Lafever's 1832 Beauties of Modern Architecture, *was supposed to be Greek Corinthian; but since nobody was quite sure then exactly what that meant, the effect is rather a composite of Ionic and Roman Corinthian. Jonathan Child was an early mayor of Rochester and related by marriage to the city's founder, Nathaniel Rochester. Other parts of Child's imposing mansion were in Ionic order from Lafever's book, as were many other mansions in Rochester and elsewhere in upstate New York. (IMG:NAL)*

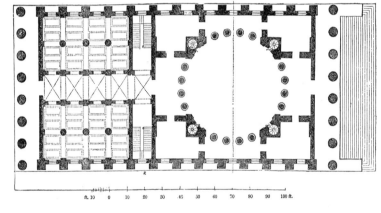

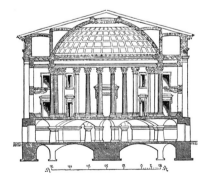

3.60 (above). Second Bank of the United States, commissioned from William Strickland by Nicholas Biddle, built 1818–24. Philadelphia City Hall architect John McArthur made some alterations in mid-nineteenth century; it was restored to the 1818 concept in the late 1970s. (IMG:NAL)

3.61 (left). Bank, market, custom house—a simple Classical Revival formula could effectively be applied to all such shop types: portico at either end, central dome, space between allocated to office spaces. Here it is applied by Town and Davis to the old New York Custom House, later New York's Subtreasury (1862–1925), still later an architectural monument to the first National Capitol Federal Hall (Federal Hall National Memorial). Section showing the interior dome (generally speaking, buildings with domes exposed were supposed to be Roman; without, Greek). (From Louis Torres, "Samuel Thompson and the Old Custom House," Journal of the Society of Architectural Historians *20/4 (1961):187.*

placed Latrobe's precedent in the Bank of Pennsylvania *[3.42].* It was copied all over the country *[3.61],* and, in Academic Classical forms, continued well into the twentieth century to provide a kind of democratic equivalent to the Gibbsian church of the old regime. On every public square it offered a paradigmatic emblem of the new constitution's blessings and assurances.[27]

Greek Revival also meant liberty when President Andrew Jackson had Robert Mills design the new United States Treasury building in that style *[3.25];* in this case, though, it meant freedom for government from interference by business interests, a freedom won in his long "Bank Wars" with Biddle, so dramatically described in Arthur Schlesinger's *Age of Jackson.*

Another kind of liberty proclaimed by Greek Revival forms was the opportunity to learn. Europeans sneered (and still do) at the multitude of small colleges that had sprung up by mid-century all over the United States. In 1848 there were twenty-five

"colleges" and "universities" in the state of Tennessee alone, and the total for the country ran into many hundreds, ranging all the way from what would become Ivy League universities like Brown and Princeton to every sort of small denominational college and outright degree-mills. What seemed their common aspiration to erect Greek Revival temple-style buildings had its ludicrous aspect, as old prints of them show. But these humble places gave many a bright boy from the backwoods—and girls too—a start toward higher education elsewhere that was quite unknown in countries like England or Germany or even Canada, where opportunities were limited to a few elitist institutions *[3.62].*

Greek Revival could proclaim free access to water, as it did in the elaborate Louisville Waterworks of 1855 *[3.63].* There is something faintly ludicrous, again, about a standpipe transformed, as here, into a gigantic Corinthian column ringed with an array of life-size water gods and nymphs, sug-

3.62. *Wealthy citizens donated temples to the gods in antiquity; so did citizens in early-nineteenth-century America. Just as Herodes Atticus funded completion of the Temple of Zeus Olympios beneath the Athenian Acropolis, so Stephen Girard funded a gigantic (for the time) temple to Reason in Philadelphia. By statute, no clergyman was permitted to set foot on the Girard College grounds.*

The building's size made an enormous impression on contemporaries; here Louisa C. Tuthill uses it as frontispiece for her History of Architecture from the Earliest Times *(Philadelphia, 1848; reprint by New York: Garland, 1988, with introduction by Lamia Doumato).*

gesting that the lower Ohio River is another Tiber, until you consider what it was like to bring all your water needs up to your dwelling in pails and what a consequent blessing it was to have water you could get from a tap, even in a remote place in the Midwest.

The greatest freedom offered by the new Republic was the freedom to develop to one's full human potential. Greek Revival style manifested it in many different ways. For instance, consider the very simple vernacular Greek Revival styling of Richardson's Inn at Bushnell Basin on the Erie Canal, which was an 1818 farmhouse enlarged around 1830 to accommodate canal traffic and then restored in 1979 *[3.64]*. This is the simplest sort of Greek Revival, recognizable principally by its proportions, eave-returns, and yellow-and-white color scheme. Yet such styling effectively proclaimed how the Erie Canal enlarged the whole country's potential, by opening up the Midwest not only to merchandise but even more to immigration (Frank Lloyd Wright's family got to Wisconsin by this route, for example). It also at one stroke made New York City the nation's financial capital and first metropolis.

3.63. *The Louisville Waterworks of 1855 was a much more ostentatious and naive celebration of the triumph of cooperative citizenry than the ones designed by Latrobe for Philadelphia. The temple that houses its machinery is sturdy, with lush-looking Corinthian columns; besides, it sports a standpipe in the form of a giant column rising from a circular colonnade, on which are water gods and nymphs appropriate to the perception of the lower Ohio River as a second Tiber. (IMG:NAL)*

3.64. *Accommodations for officials and senior workmen while construction on the Erie Canal was under way should in theory have been temporary but in fact came to constitute America's first "roadside" inns, ancestors of Ramada, Best Western, and Holiday chains. Richardson's Inn on Bushnell Basin in Pittsford near Rochester was a c. 1830 enlargement of an 1818 farmhouse. Used as a hotel from 1830 until 1917, it was restored in 1979, complete with the bright yellows, blues, and whites typical of Classical Revival taste. (IMG:NAL)*

A far more elaborate Greek Revival building with a similiar message is the Old Patent Office in Washington (now housing national art collections), commissioned from Robert Mills immediately after passage of the Patent Act in 1836, and for long second only in size among government buildings to the Capitol itself. It occupies a whole block, indeed precisely the space where L'Enfant had suggested a National Cathedral might stand. And that is entirely appropriate, for the Patent Office was a kind of cathedral to liberty, to the freedom of discovery—or, more precisely, to the possibility of exploiting an invention; without that, incentive to invent is much limited, and human potential by so much diminished. With this freedom, a new world of innovation became possible, and was realized.

The climax of the Greek Revival style, and intimations of its decline, appears in two elaborate buildings from the mid-1840s. The Tennessee State Capitol at Nashville by William Strickland, built 1845–55, is a design of almost incredible complexity, with porticoes on different sides varying somewhat, all sorts of imposing stairways, and the whole capped by an overscaled version of the Choragic Monument of Lysikrates *[3.65]*; but somehow

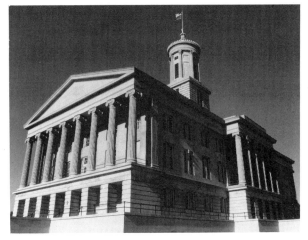

3.65. William Strickland capped his Tennessee State Capitol, 1845–55, with a much-enlarged rendering of the Choragic Monument of Lysikrates. It was a wise design decision, since a dome capable of dominating such a complex on such a site would have been grotesque. A decade before, Strickland used a smaller version of the same monument to cap his Merchants' Exchange in Philadelphia. Like all effective icons, a galaxy of monuments attesting to the kind of humans produced by the new constitution soon clustered around Strickland's creation: they honored local heroes, like Carmack and Sam Davis, and national ones, like Jackson and Polk. (IMG:NAL)

3.66. The Indiana Institution for the Blind, built in 1847, was a grand statement of concern for the handicapped and otherwise disadvantaged. It recalled civic buildings like Strickland's Tennessee State Capitol in its ingenious melding of miscellaneous elements into a grand whole. Unfortunately, such complex buildings rarely survived into the twentieth century; this one, long demolished, was recorded in Gleason's Pictorial Drawing Room Companion *in the early 1850s and reprinted in E. V. Gillon's* Illustrations of Early American Architecture *(New York: Dover, 1971).*

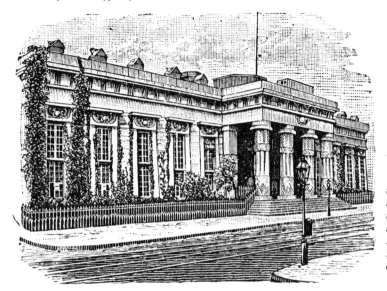

3.67. *"The Tombs" was an apt nickname for New York City Prison, designed by John Haviland in 1838. It looked like a prison; the requisite inside/outside effects of the fort type are fully met. In this respect, as well as the ostentatious heaviness of its Egyptian features, it made a considerable contrast to earlier Classical Revival prisons, such as the Burlington County prison of 1803 in Mount Holly, New Jersey, by Robert Mills, whose walls are almost delicate by comparison. Mills's prison survives, but "The Tombs" was demolished in 1938.*

3.68. *The First (now Downtown) Presbyterian Church in Nashville was designed in Egyptian Revival style by Strickland and built 1849–51. Even more remarkable than the original design is the faithful adherence to it in later years; the existing facade was not in fact completed until 1871, the interior painting dates from 1881–82, the stained glass windows from 1887, the choir screen and pulpit from 1894, and the new organ case from 1913. The only other comparable example of the spirit of a Romantic Revival style persisting over so many later decades is the Old Louisiana capitol at Baton Rouge (chapter 4). (IMG:NAL)*

the parts don't work together, like the Union of those same years. The same can be said of the Indiana Institution for the Blind in Indianapolis of 1847 *[3.66].* Yet even in its decline the style could carry significant ideological freight. For what could be more appropriate than a style with the Greek Revival's associations with liberty for an institution dedicated to providing freedom, and a new degree of independence, to people who in earlier societies had been abandoned as hopeless permanent burdens on themselves and their families?[28]

Egyptian Revival

What early-nineteenth-century Americans knew about Egypt, they knew from several sources, each of which gave Egyptian architecture different associations.[29] All this knowledge was fragmentary. The Egyptian Revival style consisted of fragments too: pylons (canted towers), columns composed of mimetic reproductions of bundled papyrus, and "cavetto" or overarching cornices *[3.15].*

Egypt was known first from the Hebrew, or Old Testament part of Protestant bibles. There it figured primarily as a land of bondage, from which came the common use of Egyptian Revival for prisons: around 1836 John Haviland designed "The Tombs" for New York, and Thomas U. Walter an Egyptian wing for debtors at Moyamensing in Phil-

adelphia *[3.67].* That Egyptian could also be used as a style for synagogues (Mikveh Israel of 1824 and Beth Israel of around 1849 in Philadelphia) might seem inconsistent; but consistency rarely distinguishes Romantic associationism. The reference here is to a Near Eastern heritage and to immemorial wisdom. The latter appealed to Protestants too, of course; witness the First Presbyterian Church of Nashville, which Strickland designed around 1859 while working on the Tennessee Capitol and which is probably the finest Egyptian Revival design extant *[3.68].*

From Herodotus on, Greek writers recalled the fabled scientific wisdom of Egypt, manifest in embalming. From this heritage derived Latrobe's proposal of Egyptian style for the Library of Congress (1808) and the Egyptian buildings for medical colleges at Richmond, Virginia, and Cleveland, Ohio, in the 1840s and 1850s. Egypt was also the exotic land where Caesar and Antony met Cleopatra, so Egyptian was appropriate for theaters, though more in the later than the earlier nineteenth century. But Egypt's agelessness had most impressed classical writers, and through them the moderns; "forty centuries look down upon you," Napoleon was supposed to have exhorted his troops. This enduring presence informed Egyptian public works (like the old Croton Reservoir, New York) and,

3.69. Entrance gate to Grove Street Cemetery, designed by Henry Austin and built 1845–49. It stands opposite the Yale campus. The inscription reads "The Dead Shall Be Raised," but the street sign insists "One Way." (IMG:NAL)

3.70. Mixed effects are the result of the complicated history of the Roman Catholic Cathedral of Baltimore. Originally designed in 1809 in Latrobe's avant-garde Classical style, it was finally dedicated in 1821, then enlarged and altered in 1863, under the direction of his son. It also shows the result of trying to meet difficult symbolic requirements: supposed to look up-to-date, it also serves as a reminder that not all patriotic Americans were Protestants by combining allusions to the Pantheon as a Classical Revival monument with allusions to the Pantheon as a church (which it was through the seventeenth century). (IMG:NAL)

above all, Egyptian tombstones and cemetery gates (Grove Street Cemetery in New Haven, c. 1830 *[3.69]*; Greenmount in Baltimore, c. 1845; the Jacob Gould tomb in Mount Hope Cemetery, Rochester).

But more than anything else the Egyptian Revival recalls that naive early-nineteenth-century America ready to venerate anything biblical, in the spirit of the little old lady who burst into tears every time she heard the word "Mesopotamia" or the pioneers who so devoutly named townships and villages Sodom and Gomorrah *[3.53]*.

Classical Mixes and Variants

Given the incompatibility of Greek and Roman models with nineteenth-century North American architectural types, mixing was inevitable, no matter how consciously high-style architects professed to avoid it.

To transform Hadrian's Pantheon into an acceptable Roman Catholic Cathedral for Baltimore, Latrobe had to combine fashionable avant-garde shallow niche-arches in the side walls with an ordinary Roman Revival portico and add two towers recalling those fronting the Pantheon when it was itself a church *[3.70]*. For the Round Top (Presbyterian) Church in Providence, J. C. Bucklin combined a Georgian brick box with a four-column Greek Doric

portico and a strange melon-shaped dome, capping everything with a version of the Choragic Monument of Lysikrates *[3.71]*.

In the early nineteenth century a new luxurious type of multistory hotel began to appear—the kind of "rentable mansions" for which the country would soon be famous. To fit them into Classical Revival stylistic molds demanded the most innovative sort of variation. Isaiah Rogers's Tremont House of 1818–30 in Boston essentially stuck a Doric portico onto a standard eighteenth-century institutional form that could just as easily have been a college or a jail. Asher Benjamin's Exchange Coffee House of 1806–9 went much further, anticipating later nineteenth-century solutions to skyscraper design by separating capping dome from entrance porticoes by a series of intermediate stories *[3.72]*.

But of course the principal cause of mixing and variations of Classical Revival styles was simply provinciality. Distinctions were confused enough in the first place without expecting near-architects and non-architects to comprehend them. So all sorts of strange combinations appear, even in older regions like the mid-Atlantic states, where the appended porch/portico had always been the commonest way of getting Classical Revival effects. As for the Far West, vernacular mixes were a norm.

One might speak of the style at this point as

dying. Or it may be seen as expanding into another level of society and taking on a new vernacular life, thus passing into the living substratum of culture.

Classical Vernacular Stylistic Shapes: Classical Square, Classical Cottage, Shotgun, Basilica

In the 1830s and 1840s as now, whatever effect architecture may have had on the population at large was made by overall forms and identifying shapes far more than by any stylistic details, let alone historical or literary associations with such details. For that population the most articulate and the only meaningful praise of any building has always been "it looks right, somehow." Throughout history an unselfconscious sense of what is right has been the basis of vernacular architecture. For this reason the homestead in every historical culture has been a metaphor of "rightness" and "roots," and ultimately a visual metaphor of national/racial/tribal/regional tradition. In nineteenth-century America this process can be traced in actual operation.

As formal Classical Revival architecture began to appear in the country, there arose alongside it buildings by local artisans that employed the broad shapes and general visual effects of the high style. Through them the Classical Revival style came to speak for the mass of inarticulate Americans. This vernacular developed a number of distinctive stylis-

3.71. Mixed effects also characterize Round Top (Presbyterian) Church in Providence, Rhode Island. J. C. Bucklin's name is attached to this 1837 combination of Palatial Georgian brick box with an entrance portico of four Greek Doric columns, capped by a melon-shaped gold dome bearing a motif drawn from the Choragic Monument of Lysikrates. But it looks like the work of a committee. (IMG:NAL)

3.72. The Exchange Coffee House in Boston, built 1806–9 and burned only ten years later, represented an interesting early effort at designing a tall-building hotel. Architect-carpenter Asher Benjamin, who had just published his American Builder's Companion, *tried to preserve allusions to the standard portico-and-dome motif, plus various elements from his own designs. It is an important attempt to master a design problem ultimately solved by the tripartite scheme invented for grand Academic Roman Revival hotels a century later. (Engraving by Thomas Wrightman in* Omnium Gatherum, *I [1809], from Jack Quinan, "Asher Benjamin,"* Journal of the Society of Architectural Historians *38/3 [1982])*

3.73. Classical Cottage (small Classical Square) form built as manse for Saint Andrew's Presbyterian Church at Niagara-on-the-Lake, Ontario. This first capital of Upper Canada was architecturally an American Classical Revival town like those in *upper New York state just across the river; the church was and is a fine example of Greek Revival, derived from Asher Benjamin. (IMG:NAL)*

tic forms. All were derived from the Classical Revival's distant foreign sources but were native to the country—like Americans themselves, indeed. The most prominent of such forms were the Classical Square, the Classical Cottage, the Shotgun, and the Basilica. They originated at no fixed point, nor can they be said to have disappeared, though over later decades they metamorphosed according to whatever Picturesque or Academic or Popular/Commercial taste happened to be ascendant.

Single or double cubes with pyramidal caps, the whole set on an elevated platform, constituted a Classical Square. Its composition of basic geometric shapes was highly agreeable to early Classical Revival taste. Jefferson is credited with a number of versions of the single cube, or Classical Cottage—for example, the 1793 Madison house in Orange County, Virginia (now The Residence at Woodberry Forest School), and Farmington (the Speed house), outside Louisville, of 1807. Evolution of the Classical Cottage into vernacular forms is traceable in copious examples *[3.73].* The same is true of a two-story (double-cube) version; its best early high-style representative was Latrobe's 1818–1820 Brentwood, outside Washington. This bigger version took somewhat longer to evolve into a vernacular *[3.74],* but by the early decades of the twentieth century a resultant Big Foursquare stylistic form rivaled in popularity the Small Foursquare descended from the Classical Cottage among providers of mass-prefabricated suburban houses.[30] (See further, chapter 6.)

The Shotgun was originally a fairly complicated kind of vernacular, combining one- and two-story elements *[3.75].* But it has come, from endless repetition in later suburban and company-town forms, to mean no more than a long, rectangular, one-story house, indistinguishable from cheap mass-produced descendants of the vernacular temple-house.

From the formal high-style temple-house with wings was derived the Basilica vernacular, so called (by architectural historians, not local populations) because of the resemblance of this much-simplified shape to early Christian churches with nave and side aisles *[3.76].*

Vestigial Classical Revival

At what point buildings with few or no specific Greek or Roman details, whose derivation is evidenced only by general orientation, are no longer classifiable as vernacular and are called merely vestigial is an academic question. As far as forms are concerned, these buildings are of little importance. Yet they are immensely significant cultural expressions. To recognize how a Vestigial Classical Revival was maintained well into the twentieth century for schools (the legendary "little red schoolhouse" *[3.77, 3.78]*), barracks, and all sorts of humbler federal works, is to learn something more than aesthetic about enduring American attitudes. For ultimate evidence of how upward mobility became a universal norm of life in the new country, consider how via a Vestigial Classical Revival even the hum-

3.74 (left). Buena Vista in Albemarle County just north of Charlottesville, Virginia, built during the Civil War (1862), hence entirely of materials fabricated on the plantation and necessarily simplified in design too. It is a double cube with appended portico recalling, but not able to emulate, high-style mansions like Latrobe's Brentwood, thereby anticipating mass-prefabricated big foursquares. (IMG:NAL)

3.75 (below). Shotgun (locally also called Gunshot) houses in the Butchertown district of Louisville, Kentucky, c. 1855. The detailing is already Italianate. (IMG:NAL)

3.76 (bottom). Basilica form Classical Revival house on Plymouth Road outside Ann Arbor, Michigan, c. 1835–40, photographed in 1963; demolished c. 1965. This is still a very common form throughout rural Michigan. (IMG:NAL)

3.77 (top). As in homesteads, in schools a classical revival vernacular and/or vestigial forms survived almost into our own times because the classic "little red schoolhouse" was the outward metaphor of a deep underlying ideology. It survived, in fact, over about the same period as the basic principle embodied in Jefferson's University of Virginia: that schools existed to train good citizens for the nation. That is, it survived until after World War I, though it began to disappear fast in the 1920s. The form betrayed its quasi-religious character: like the factory, the small schoolhouse form kept haunting overtones of the meetinghouse. A few have survived as icons, like this schoolhouse in Stone Lagoon, in northern California above Eureka, built in 1897 and preserved in the pioneer setting of that period. (IMG:NAL)

3.78. More often, the old schoolhouse form is to be found, if at all, in ruinous condition, like this one photographed in 1975 by the side of U.S. 30 in the vicinity of Hiawatha, Kansas. It had already been abandoned for some time, and unless soon thereafter rescued by someone renovating it for a home or studio, has long since fallen to pieces—whether along with the values it represented is, of course, arguable. (IMG:NAL)

blest homestead came to be conceived as a way-station toward a mansion. Of the colonial class-structured state's contentment "in that station of life to which it hath pleased Providence to call me" nothing is left, obviously. Vestigial Classical Revival truly manifests a new era.

The Classical Revival as Continuing Cultural Expression

Any culture is layered, and its arts record the layering process. Early child art records common beginnings. Then come arts manifesting those broad general assumptions of right and wrong and those deep meanings of words on which the great societies of human history have been built. They are followed by conscious high arts, those deliberate styles which set off one era of civilization from another. Each layer leaves something deep in the culture, as it leaves remains on the architectural landscape, unless and until, of course, all culture and works of a given civilization are obliterated.

We have considered what enduring cultural characteristics bequeathed from the colonial era might be manifested on the landscape; comparably enduring characteristics can be gleaned from the Arcadian land where Classical Revival styles were dominant. They took form preeminently in the monument, with its generating concept of the hero. A multitude of surviving Classical Revival monuments attest still to their era's admiration for the Individual who Accomplishes. And that has remained a strikingly American cultural trait.

There is other evidence of the same legacy: to say that "where two or three Americans are gathered together there will always be an award" is a jest, but it also attests to a very real encouragement of achievement. The "classical attitude" has been continually manifest in a willingness not merely to tolerate competition but to foster opportunities to compete on a broad scale. Furthermore, this classical respect for accomplishment, building upon an admiration for philanthrophy instilled in colonial times, has provided an array of public foundations without parallel in any other nation.[31]

Other enduring aspects of Classical America are not so unarguably beneficial. That admiration for amateurism which is expressed in proliferation of Classical Revival vernaculars, for example. It is very much in the spirit of Classical democracy to be well-rounded; specialization, according to Socrates, "leaves a man no leisure to attend to his friends' interests, or the public interest"—it is undemocratic to be too learned at anything. Such an attitude meant that American universities long put their emphasis on broad humanistic interests, achieving very remarkable results, especially during the Progressive era at state universities in the Midwest. It could also mean a triumph of egalitarian mediocrity, with consequent shortage of highly skilled people and need to import them from countries whose educational systems better encouraged and rewarded specialization.

Another legacy of dubious value was an assumption of a national moral superiority that Americans could and indeed ought to export. "What is common to every caste and class"—this is Page Smith summarizing twelve hundred pages of history from 1820 through the 1850s—"is the conviction that, frequently as they may deviate from it, there is a moral order in the universe." He continues:

> That order is clearly ascertainable, verifiable, unimpeachable. It manifests itself in every area of human experience. All questions—social, political, literary, or artistic—may be referred to it in the confident expectation of an unequivocal answer. . . . It is the only principle of coherence in a chaotic society. Republican governments and democratic principles are perhaps its most striking manifestations.[32]

And, of course, those find expression in the common use of Classical Revival by all classes and all regions, as *the* National Democratic style. In due course, under pressures of impending civil war, the particular symbolism of the Classical Revival lost its power; the high style dissolved into the ideological incoherence of Italianate and later Picturesque styles. But the fundamental idea the Classical Revivals first expressed, that the American Republic is a nation of Virtuous Citizens, never died. It merely changed its mode of expression. Abolitionists saw themselves as incarnating moral order even as they worked to wreck the Union; there is an obvious and direct connection between them and the moral fervor of Progressivism, so well expressed in the compulsively moral design theories of a Sullivan or a Wright. Nor was that the end. That same moral fervor blazed up again, in its old Puritan seat, when the Bauhaus came to Boston with its doctrines of salvation by scientific purity. Thereafter Modern zeal to remake the world compounded the old itch of Virtuous Classical Citizens to export their righteousness to selected global spots of iniquity.

Notes

1. This theme in painting is the counterpart to a major theme in American literature: an examination of the assumption that somehow, thanks to establishment of democratic institutions in a new land, paradise has returned. See, for example, David W. Noble, *The Eternal Adam and the New World Garden* (New York: George Braziller, 1968) or R. W. B. Lewis, *The American Adam* (Chicago: University of Chicago Press, 1959).

2. "National Rebuilding" is a term that comes originally from W. G. Hoskins, "The Rebuilding of Rural England 1570–1640," *Past and Present* 4/11 (1953):44–59. It was used to describe the replacement of the South's original impermanent architecture in the early eighteenth century by Cary Carson et al., "Impermanent Architecture in the Southern American colonies," *Winterthur Portfolio* 16 (1981):135–96. New England's comparable rebuilding was completed before the end of the seventeenth century. Both were "subsumed by the first truly nationwide rebuilding, in the early nineteenth century. Only at that point, say the period 1820–1850, would the trend lines for New England and the Old South finally converge." This is further evidence of the Classical Revival functioning as an instrument of national unity.

3. Emulations, not imitations: designs, that is, enough like the national capitol to bring it at once to mind. Nowadays, the ancient principle of similarily shaped buildings manifesting similar institutions and the ideas behind them operates openly only at the Popular/Commercial level—similar shapes identifying members of fast-food or cosmetic chains, models of famous buildings sold as tourist souvenirs. On other levels it operates also, but subliminally. In their *Temples of Democracy* (New York: Harcourt Brace, 1976) H. R. Hitchcock and William Seale noted (pp.265–66) a 1927 *Architectural Forum* article that declared "The American people are very largely committed to the firm belief that a state capitol must be designed . . . in Classic fashion, replete with colonnades . . . surmounted by a dome." "In the long history of American state capitols," they wrote, "not a single capitol commissioner has recorded any awareness of the architectural symbolism of American democracy. It was . . . laymen capitol builders—lawyers, businessmen, farmers, politicians—who valiantly defended the symbols."

4. Charles C. Savage, *Architecture of the Private Streets of St. Louis* (Columbia: University of Missouri Press, 1987), has pointed out that Bellefontaine Cemetery was surely one of the inspirations for St. Louis's famous "private streets." As founded in 1849 (by James Yeatman after the cholera epidemic in which his wife died) the cemetery park was supposed to be rustic in style; but, "in keeping with everything else in St. Louis, which resisted any kind of zoning throughout the 19th century," it was soon built in Classical Revival mausolea for the most part, despite its curving roads. See also John Albury Bryan, *A Walk Through Bellefontaine Cemetery* (St. Louis, 1957).

5. James Boswell, *The Life of Samuel Johnson* (London, 1791), quoting Johnson in 1756, at age forty-seven.

6. A mind-set coming out of the eighteenth-century

Enlightenment, of course, was premised on mechanistic abstract causality, but never quite so baldly stated as that—only in retrospect so plainly motivated. At the time, the new world was to be an inevitable result of applying Reason to human affairs (cf. Carl Becker, *The Heavenly City of the Eighteenth-Century Philosophers* [New Haven, Conn.: Yale University Press, 1957; original 1932]), of studying Nature and so freeing human minds of "superstition" (see Paul Hazard, *La Crise de la conscience européene* [Paris: Boivin, 1935]; and *La Pensée européene au XVIIIème siècle, de Montesquieu à Lessing* [Paris, 1946]; translated as *The European Mind in the Eighteenth Century* [New Haven, Conn.: Yale University Press, 1954]).

Involved here too was enthusiasm for the Greeks as precursors of science, beginning at least with Copernicus and still evidenced in John William Draper's mid-nineteenth-century popularizations of the religion of science, *Intellectual Development of Europe* and *History of the Conflict Between Religion and Science*.

7. In place-naming after the Revolution we sense a definite "American Adam in Eden" variant. "We live at the origin of things," Peter S. Onuf quotes from a letter of one "P. W." in *The Independent Chronicle* for 25 August 1785 (*Statehood and Union: A History of the Northwest Ordinance* [Bloomington: Indiana University Press, 1987]). Boundaries for sixteen new states (not to exceed 150 square miles each) were specified in that 1784 legislation; in a letter of that year (to Francis Hopkinson on 3 May; Julian P. Boyd, *The Papers of Thomas Jefferson* [Princeton, N.J.: Princeton University Press, 1950–1982], vol. 7, p. 205) Jefferson proposed such names for them as Polypotamia, Illinoia, Michania, Metropotamia, Pelisipia, and Washington. The settlers themselves simply consulted their memories and atlases of ancient history, sprinkling their new landscapes with Romes, Carthages, Ithacas, Senecas, Troys. Wilbur Zelinsky has written with his usual wit and incisiveness on this matter in "Classical Town Names in the United States: The Historical Geography of an American Idea," *Geographical Review* 57 (1967): 463–95; and "Nationalism in the American Place-Name Cover," *Names* 30 (1983): 1–28.

8. Rush, quoted by Barry Schwartz, *George Washington* (New York: The Free Press, 1987), p. 119. Priscilla Robertson's classic *Revolutions of 1848: A Social History* (Princeton, N.J.: Princeton University Press, 1952) documents this hero cult, draws attention to its psychological roots and therefore limitations, and observes its potential for transformation into a totalitarian state cult.

9. L'Enfant, in a letter of 1791, quoted by J. J. Jusserand, in *With Americans of Other Days* (Philadelphia, 1916), p. 151.

10. Quoted in Page Smith, *The Nation Comes of Age* (New York: McGraw-Hill, 1981), p. 89.

11. Wilbur Zelinsky has made some relevant and significant discoveries in his "Unearthly Delights: Cemetery Names as a Key to the Map of the Changing American Afterworld," in M. Bowden and D. Lowenthal, eds., *Geographies of the Mind: Papers in Geosophy in Honor of John K. Wright* (New York: Oxford University Press, 1975), pp. 171–95.

12. Chapter 14 of Roger Kennedy's *Architecture, Men, Women, and Money* (New York: Random House, 1985) gives a useful summary of the origins of Classical Revival forms; relevant in this context also are the works of Joseph Rykwert, *On Adam's Hut in Paradise: The Idea of the Primitive Hut* (New York: Museum of Modern Art, 1972), and *The First Moderns: The Architects of the Eighteenth Century* (Cambridge, Mass.: The MIT Press, 1980). At least one primeval temple still stands, on the grounds of Forsmark in Sweden's Uppsala province; it was designed by a professor with the wonderfully appropriate name of Olof Tempelman.

13. William H. Pierson, Jr., has written perceptively about this problem, in the context of Slater Mill, in *American Buildings and Their Architects: Technology and the Picturesque* (New York: Oxford University Press, 1978).

14. As he was designated by Buford Pickens in "Mr. Jefferson as Revolutionary Architect," *Journal of the Society of Architectural Historians* 34/4 (1975): 175–98.

15. Jefferson had been the last governor of Virginia to live in the old Governors' Palace at Williamsburg, and about 1779 made some plans for modernizing it, although it no doubt was to him almost as much a "rude misshapen Pile . . . a brick kiln" as the "Wren Building" at the College of William and Mary. What he thought of the Williamsburg capitol can be imagined. Shortly thereafter the palace was totally destroyed—a fate that also befell many later and lesser objects of avant-garde distaste. The new capitol's iconic character was well recognized at the time: Isaac Weld in his *Travels Through the States of North America* (London, 1799) observed how "from the opposite side of the [James] river this building appears extremely well, as its defects cannot be observed at that distance" (p. 108); and the perceptive Latrobe captured its spirit in drawings like numbers 28 and 37 in *Latrobe's View of America* (Edward C. Carter II, ed. [New Haven, Conn.: Yale University Press, 1985]).

16. The importance of Freemasonry in the Revolution and early Republic is often underestimated. Jefferson was a member of "the Craft," as was Washington, as was everybody of social importance in those times. As late as the 1910s and 1920s Freemasons were still erecting huge and expensive buildings, in Academic Classical Revival styles; but by then Freemasonry had become much more of a benevolent and fraternal organization, much less a kind of religion, than it was at first. In Jefferson's time its teachings were taken very seriously. There is a fine collection of nineteenth-century Masonic materials in the Wilbur Library of the University of Vermont in Burlington.

17. Monticello is, of course, one of the most discussed buildings in American architecture and there is by no means uniformity of opinion about its history and motivations. I follow here mainly Buford Pickens, "Mr. Jefferson," and Gene Waddell, "The First Monticello," *Journal of the Society of Architectural Historians* 46/1 (1987).

18. Bremo was once regularly attributed to Jefferson; but see data from Peter Hodson, *The Design and Building of Bremo 1815–1820* (Birmingham, Ala.: Privately printed; M.A. thesis, 1967, University of Virginia), who is followed by Howard Adams, *The Eye of Jefferson* (Washington, D.C.:

National Gallery of Art, 1976), p. 283.

19. Daniel Boorstin, *The Lost World of Thomas Jefferson* (Boston: Beacon Press, 1948).

20. See Adolf Max Vogt, *Russische und französische Revolutionsarchitektur* (Cologne: Dumont, 1974), pp. 137–39; his argument is that all such designs as the Rotunda represented "a compromise," imposed by practicality, "between the 'Egyptian' and the 'Greek' possibilities of architecture in stone. . . . A strongly geometric 'Egyptian' core is overlaid [for practical reasons] with a 'Greek' hull" (pp. 125–29). Pure geometry appears only in designs like Goethe's Weimar monuments and "decorative" elements like those "cosmic balls" on the platform at Thomas de Thomon's Leningrad Bourse—and, on the finials on the privies at Monticello! A kind of icon of this age's veneration of Reason in architectural design is Louis-Etienne Boullée's proposed Monument to Reason. The design is published by Klaus Lankheit, *Der Tempel der Vernunft: Unveröffentlichte Zeichnungen von Boullée* (Basel, 1973).

21. This famous phrase occurs in a letter of 6 May 1810 from Jefferson to trustees of a lottery of East Tennessee College, and is quoted by Mary Woods, "Thomas Jefferson and the University of Virginia," *Journal of the Society of Architectural Historians* 44/3 (1985), footnote 17.

22. That the first railroad stations derived an octagonal form directly from preceding octagonal tollhouses was first pointed out, I believe, in Carroll L. V. Meeks, *The Railroad Station* (New Haven, Conn.: Yale University Press, 1955).

23. Quotation from *Edinburgh Review* (1807), referring to the introduction in England of the Empire style through Thomas Hope's *Household Furniture and Interior Decorations* (London: Longman, Hurst, Rees and Orme, 1807).

24. Formal models for the Washington Monument might have included the Nelson Column in London and in Montreal and, ultimately, Trajan's Column in Rome; but the ideological inspiration probably came through Whig associations of the form with liberty—as in a 140-foot column erected by George Bowes in 1750–57 on his Gibside estate, which carried a 12-foot gilded statue of British Liberty (see Nicholas Pevsner, *Buildings of England: County Durham* [London: Penguin, 1953], p. 153)—via a general revival of columnar monuments in early-eighteenth-century England in apparent connection with Freemasonry.

25. In an 1811 "Anniversary Oration" before the Society of Artists in Philadelphia, Latrobe explained how a new Greece was developing "in the woods of America": "Greece was free; in Greece every citizen felt himself an important . . . part of his republic."

26. Prior to the Revolution stock exchanges were the principal representatives of this commercial building type. Early stock exchanges (like that of London, 1562) looked like monasteries with cloisters. Toward the end of the eighteenth century in England they took on Palatial Georgian forms and styles derived from aristocratic mansions (like the Bristol Exchange, 1760s) and in due course these were transplanted (Exchange and Custom House at Charleston, 1767–71). In Canada this English precedent was maintained (like so much else) well into the nineteenth century; examples are still to be seen in Toronto, Kingston, and Montreal. The First Bank of the United States of 1797 still had a Georgian stock-exchange form, but already the veneer of a classical portico, which its designer, Samuel Blodgett of New Hampshire, grandly described in the *Gazette of the United States* for 23 December 1797 as "a truly Grecian edifice . . . its proportions nearly corresponding to the front of the celebrated Roman temple at Nismes [sic]."

27. Right down to the Second World War, small temple-house banks remained, along with Classical courthouses, the principal visual metaphor for smaller American communities of the institutions established in 1789. You could see them in surviving banks from the Classical Revival Proper, then dramatically in Academic Roman and Greek versions that reappeared in the 1880s, even before Picturesque taste had run its course. They flourished with confident exuberance down to 1929—in small versions on remote Main Streets, perched atop metropolitan skyscrapers, proclaiming American expansionism in Hawaii, even in prefabricated forms springing up (to American designs) along the railroads of the Canadian West. So tenacious was the temple-house bank that, in subliminal Classical forms, it survived even the tyrannical Modernism of the 1950s. But in the 1960s larger banks abruptly abandoned it, in favor of walls sheathed in mirrors as if to disguise their existence, or massive featureless chunks of masonry as if under siege. Local independent banks, evidently more courageous, have perpetuated temple-houses in Popular/Commercial forms down to the present (chapters 6, 7, 8).

28. The connection between this new kind of freedom and the more conventional political sort is emphasized by the fact that Samuel Ward Howe, first director of the Boston Institute for the Blind and pioneer in the field, had actually fought in the Greek War of Independence.

29. "Although there are Egyptian Revival monuments from Ireland to Tasmania, it is only in the United States that a significant number were constructed," we are told by the chief authority on the subject, Richard G. Carrott, in *The Egyptian Revival: Its Sources, Monuments, and Meaning 1808–1858* (Berkeley: University of California Press, 1978).

30. Numerous illustrations of Big and Small Foursquares can be found in my book *The Comfortable House* (Cambridge, Mass.: The MIT Press, 1986), pp. 84–93.

31. "In a development of American capitalism not foreseen by Karl Marx . . . no other nation in the world has such an array of aggregations of private wealth devoted to public purposes; no other nation has given them, once created, such freedom of action; and in no other have foundations played such a significant role in the nation's life" (Waldemar A. Nielsen, *The Golden Donors* [New York: Dutton, 1985], p. 11).

32. Page Smith, *The Nation Comes of Age* (New York: McGraw-Hill, 1981), p. 1041.

4.6. A lithographed "Birds Eye View of Greenwood Cemetery near New York [Brooklyn]" from the 1860s already shows a preponderance of Classical Revival columns and obelisks among the monuments in this otherwise prototypical romantic Gothic Revival park, with winding avenues, paths, ponds, and greensward dappled with shade from leafy copses. (Library of Congress)

4
REACTION, NOSTALGIA, PROTEST: GOTHIC REVIVAL STYLES, c. 1820–c. 1860

The Gothic Revival in Its Time and Place

What historians call the Gothic Revival proper was significant in American architecture for only a short period and was represented by a relatively small number of buildings erected to serve the social needs and tastes of a limited segment of society. An early Gothic Revival boomlet reflecting the style's turn-of-the-century popularity in England had practically petered out by the 1820s.[1] After the Civil War, Gothic proper appeared on only a few buildings, created for special occasions or special aesthetic interests. So Gothic represented a significant national expression only between 1835 and 1860. It never came close to rivaling the Classical Revivals in general popularity and use. But Gothic was much more than just an episode in the history of taste; it manifested vital undercurrents of thought and social attitudes that found little other expression and that have continued vital up to the present, first in Picturesque, then in Academic, now in Popular/Commercial forms.

Like the Classical Revivals which overlapped it in time, the Gothic Revival was a romantic movement, making conscious literary allusions to a period in the past. But its ambience was different. Gothic Revival styles were a gut reaction against that rule of Reason that lay at the heart of the Classical Revivals. Classical appealed for justification to an era when Reason had allegedly prevailed, Gothic to an era when it allegedly had not. The motivations for the Gothic Revival were emotional and individualistic rather than political and social. Gothic Revival styles spoke to and for an aspect of the human condition that the Classical Revivals had neglected.

The Gothic Revival made its most dramatic contrast to Classical Revival taste in high-style interiors, where everything seemed different—shapes angular and crinkly, colors muted, rich, and dark. Those interiors survive only in studied restorations (Lyndhurst on the Hudson, for example) or in actual museum installations [4.1]. But many of the architectural landscapes the Gothic Revival created still survive [4.39, 4.40].

In theory the Gothic Revival created unobtrusive landscapes. Modest dells with little spired churches and chocolate-painted farmhouses nestled into them projected an air of romantic pastness that contrasted with the immediate civic connotations and monumental assertions of Classical Revival buildings [4.2]. But in practice that seldom happened [4.3, 4.4]. Surviving Gothic Revival landscapes are dominated by monuments on hilltops or otherwise commanding great vistas, quite like Classical ones, and are often as not painted stark white too. The basically classical cast of popular taste overpowered Gothic Revival principles on all but the most official high-style buildings. It even affected *them* eventually—witness the Mall in Washington, transformed by A. J. Downing during the 1850s from L'Enfant's cold geometry to a maze of winding paths and clumps of trees and shrubbery, only to be transformed back fifty years later, more or less by popular demand.

Parks, civic and burial, zoological and arboreal, were the second great legacy of the Gothic Revival to the American landscape. It encouraged a "park impulse" that met a real social need for some antidote to the Classical Revival's over-insistence on geometry, reason, order, balance, symmetry, precision. It asserted another side of human nature, by emphasis on curving avenues, greenery in natural states, unexpected vistas, and the like; it also met a

4.1. Small upstairs bedroom from Walnut Wood, a mansion designed by Alexander Jackson Davis about 1846 in Bridgeport, Connecticut, for Henry K. Harral, prosperous saddler, professedly forward-looking Anglophile, successful politician (thrice elected mayor). From 1866 until its demolition in 1957, Walnut Wood was owned by sewing-machine manufacturer and Connecticut legislator Nathaniel Wheeler (whose portrait appears over the mantel) and his son Archer. The Smithsonian Institution acquired this room and furniture from the city of Bridgeport, along with decorative objects by Ellen Wheeler, and exhibited them as here in its Growth of the United States *exhibition in the 1970s. (Photograph courtesy of National Museum of American History)*

4.2. Great master and mentor of the American Gothic Revival was Andrew Jackson Downing. Here are Figures 19 and 20 from his enormously influential Treatise on the Theory and Practise of Landscape Gardening with a View to the Improvement of Country Residences, *published in 1841: "View of a Country Residence, as frequently seen," and "View of the same Residence, improved."*

4.3. This fine farmhouse near Centerville on Maryland's Eastern Shore has evidently been "improved" according to Downing's ideas; but whether its setting ever underwent similar improvement is not evident. Today, certainly, it dominates the flat land all around. (IMG:NAL)

practical need for some immediate means of escape from congested urban conditions induced by industrialization from the early 1800s on. Central Park in New York, whose evolution has been so ably documented by Charles Beveridge and David Schuyler,[2] was the era's grand example *[4.5]*. Extant as well are the cemeteries that so admirably complemented civic parks—functioning, indeed, as such themselves *[4.6, on p. 130; 4.7]*. But from their beginnings, what was erected in these cemeteries tended overwhelmingly to be celebrations, in classical forms, of classical virtues and successes *[3.11]*. As for civic parks, their original functions have been largely vitiated by worldly successes, though in this case not so much by intrusive monuments as by increasing availability of cars and thus an alternative mass escape from congestion.

The third great legacy from the Gothic Revival to the American landscape is the suburb. Of suburbs from its own time, little physically remains. In West Orange, New Jersey, you can still see a gatehouse with stubby tower and medieval-looking turret that once stood guard over Llewellyn Park, first grand country escape for commuters to New York, and that still guards an elite and exclusive housing area *[4.8, 4.9]*. But the rural solitudes that once isolated it are all gone, long ago engulfed by North Jersey's endless suburban sprawl. Deep within every pre–Civil War American city, not far from its core, you can usually find some remains of what used to be an elegant outer ring where the rich built early Picturesque mansions on spacious lawns. But the mansions have long since decayed or been remodeled

4.4. Just as the main street of Mendocino is dominated by its Masonic Hall [3.3], so approach to this quintessentially California north coast town from the south was dominated by its Presbyterian church, built 1867–68 by San Francisco architects S. C. Bugbee & Son to overlook the old coast road (Pacific Street), which used to come up from the river flats. The road is now abandoned, but the church still stands on its bluff; it is the oldest active church in California and a notable example of the Presbyterian Gothic style in wood. The interior was restored in the mid-1960s. The manse beside it is a foursquare (frequently used for clergy residences of all sorts), dating from 1909. (IMG:NAL)

4.5. Plan for Central Park in New York (59th Street is at the left, 110th Street at the right) as proposed by Frederick Law Olmstead and his assistant Calvert Vaux in 1858. Olmstead was appointed director of the proposed new park in 1857 and kept a connection with it until near its completion in 1877. He called it "a democratic development of the highest significance, on which much of the progress of art and aesthetic culture in this country is *dependent." It would reassure Europeans and Southerners skeptical of American egalitarian democracy "that a republic could keep civil order, guarantee justice, and provide the means for elevating all classes of the population." (From Beveridge and Schuyler,* Creating Central Park)

4.7. *In Cambridge's Mount Auburn Cemetery, begun in 1831, graves were combined with experimental gardens. It was planned and built by the Boston Horticultural Society under active inspiration of prominent Boston physician Dr. Jacob Bigelow, who initiated the Rural Cemetery Movement (and thus in good American entrepreneurial fashion took care of both ends of his business). Mount Auburn remains the most livable part of Cambridge. This view shows one of its ponds, rolling hillsides, and shrubbery, dominated as usual by a Classical Revival monument, in this case the Academic Roman Revival tomb of Mary Baker Eddy, founder of the Christian Science Church. (IMG:NAL)*

(usually both), and the grounds long since been sub- and sub-sub-divided. Far more enduring is the suburban mental attitude the Gothic Revival engendered, attested by countless weekend gardeners and golfers and barbecuers and joggers who take for granted a right of access to country pleasures no matter how huge the metropolis where their living may be earned.

Most immediate of all Gothic Revival legacies is the parkway in all its variants, from scenic highway to Interstate. The term "parkway" first appeared in an 1866–67 report by Frederick Law Olmsted and Calvert Vaux on approaches to Central Park.[3] It designated a contrast to the "avenues" or "boulevards" of European city planners: the parkway was not so much a street as a sort of indefinite

4.8. *The primary inspiration for early garden suburbs came from Andrew Jackson Downing. The first of them was Llewellyn Park in West Orange, New Jersey, financed by chemical manufacturer Llewellyn P. Haskell. As in all such early communities, its entrances were all guarded by gatehouses, so as to preserve Downing's aristocratic concept of "a retreat for a man to exercise his own rights and privileges," which included the kind of eccentricities popularly associated with the Gothic Revival (atheists holding marriage ceremonies under a great tree, public scandals of various sorts). Thus Llewellyn Park, like Central Park, would help obviate what Olmsted called "the constant practise of heart-hardening and taste-smothering habits . . . to be found in our great Eastern cities." The suburb, however, was for a cultured minority, who had unearned income enough to buy and live in houses so remote. (IMG:NAL)*

4.9. All buildings in "The Community of Improved Residences" which was Llewellyn Park were designed by Alexander Jackson Davis and built between 1852 and 1869 in various substyles of the Gothic Revival. It was of course the perfect stylistic expression for a "cultured minority." The New York Illustrated News

showed its readers these "castellated" glories of Castlewood House in 1860. Only one of Davis's villas has survived, however—a cottage built for landscape painter Edward W. Nicholls and later boyhood home of Charles Follen McKim, the famous Academic Classical Revival architect.

extension of city parks. Just so were the first automobile parkways conceived, and perhaps not by accident they were most prominent in the New York metropolitan area: Merritt Parkway, Saw Mill Parkway, Garden State Parkway, and the rest. In lightly populated areas such roads had some chance of survival—Oregon's Columbia River Scenic Highway is still scenic, for instance *[4.10].*

But in general, parkways lost their rural character by a kind of inner necessity: the more successfully they brought cities out into the countryside, the more surely were they destroyed. Scenic bypasses begot congested commercial strips; replicated further out, they soon became clogged gauntlets once again. But the instinct has never been killed. If there are still many stretches of Interstates that

4.10. The original character of parkways is best preserved, perhaps, in Oregon's Columbia River Scenic Highway, constructed 1913–15 to designs of Samuel C. Lancaster (1864–1941). In this view over the Columbia River, an interstate "parkway" (I-80) appears far below. (IMG:NAL)

run unimpeded over natural prairie and mountain, thank those impulses to accept and enjoy Nature instead of always trying to control it that first surfaced with the Gothic Revival.

Definition and Identifying Characteristics

In a narrow sense, the Gothic Revival was a return to common usage in the nineteenth century of a style obsolete in high architecture since roughly the sixteenth, and by 1800 only incompletely remembered. What we call routine facts about Gothic are almost all nineteenth-century discoveries, of which the earliest Gothic Revivalists were largely unaware: the Gothic style's history (a twelfth-century invention by and for the Capetian monarchy of France); its real names (*opus modernum*, meaning "new work" or "modern art," and so distinguished from the preceding Romanesque *mos romanorum*, the way of building like the Romans promoted by Charlemagne; and outside France *opus francigenum*, "French work"); how it transformed Romanesque by creating far greater height and effects of light through open skeletal construction, pointed arches; and its rib vaults and buttresses balanced by pinnacles, often "flying" to the ground free of outer walls. "Gothic" in 1800 was often called "Gothick," implying a quaint assemblage of non-classical forms that seemed, in contrast to the reigning Classical Revival forms, at best whimsical, at worse crude, outlandish, barbaric. The assemblage included pointed arches perched on spindly stilt-like columns with no hint of classical proportions and with caricatures of

4.11. Basic elements of Gothic (or any) style often appear most obviously in naive or vernacular forms. Here the full range of pointed arches and spiky pinnacles, spindly columns and cardboardy crenellations is displayed on the parish church of Sainte-Anne de Lapérade on the Saint Lawrence, built 1855–69 by Casimir Coursol in emulation of Montreal's huge Gothic parish church of Notre-Dame, in turn inspired (in this author's opinion) by Sainte-Croix d'Orléans, a Gothic cathedral destroyed in the sixteenth century and rebuilt consciously in Gothic over succeeding centuries, until finished in 1829. (IMG:NAL)

4.12. Gothic structural forms could not only be faked in wood and plaster building, but could also be applied decoratively, as in this "Modern Gothic Sideboard" from Harriet Spofford's 1878 Art Decoration Applied to Furniture: *crenellations run along the tops, ribs support shelves, traceried windows adorn sides, and cathedral doors give majestic access to lower cupboards.*

4.13. One of the early sights of the affluent "improved community" of Grosse Ile on the Detroit River in Michigan was Samuel Lewis's Wedding Cake House, built about 1850 of "brick with external walls of wood veneer," as William Woodward described it in A Tour Guide to Grosse Ile *(1963). Gothic Revival ornament was very commonly "veneer"—often prefabricated and detatchable. (IMG:NAL)*

classical capitals; and roof lines marked by crenellations ("castellated" was a common synonym for Gothic well into the century), with pinnacles stuck along roof lines here, there, and all over. In fact, composition of Gothic Revival architecture and furniture by assemblage long continued *[4.11, 4.12]*. But around the turn of the nineteenth century a change of mood and thence of attitudes toward Gothic occurred. By the 1780s the Romantics had begun calling the style "horrid" in a pleasingly exotic sense, and soon thereafter "Gothic" came to be a collective synonym for imagination, emotion, faith, spontaneity, naturalness, and a host of other qualities sadly neglected by classical insistence upon Reason.

Comparably, the Gothic Revival in due course came to be a catch-all for an enormous variety of nonclassical styles. R. M. Newton in *Town & Davis* (New York, 1942) describes Alexander Jackson Davis, the country's leading Gothic Revivalist, in the 1840s and 1850s offering clients "American Log Cabin, Farm Villa, English Cottage, Collegiate Gothic, Manor House, French Suburban, Switz Chalet, Switz Mansion, Lombard Italian, Tuscan from Pliny's Villa at Ostia, Ancient Etruscan, Suburban Greek, Oriental, Moorish, Round, Castellated."

It sounds chaotic, but it actually was not. Though any number of exotic new styles were introduced on paper, most of them were represented by relatively few executed examples. The Gothic Revival's rarer and more exotic substyles were easily distinguishable from one another by a few distinctive details: Moorish by horseshoe-shaped arches and flat overall patternings that looked vaguely Islamic; Oriental by curved roof shapes; "Switz" by boards cut out into decorative patterns, and so forth. And no matter how diverse their nomenclature and details, all shared a common set of qualities that could be summarized as simply contrasts with the dominant Classical Revival:

• All emphasized visual effects of verticality, in contrast to Classical horizontality. In substyles of the Gothic Revival proper these effects were achieved by details taken directly from medieval sources: pinnacles, tall narrow pointed windows with thin tracery (instead of stolid classical mullions), tall narrow niches, panels carved into trefoil or quatrefoil patterns, decorative crockets on eaves or door frames *[4.13]*. Sometimes the source was medieval architecture, via line drawings most often, sometimes borders of illuminated manuscripts, and sometimes medieval furniture. In others, vertical effects were achieved with bargeboarding imitating Gothic effects or with predominantly vertical proportions in windows, towers, and elevations generally.

• All emphasized asymmetry rather than balance.

• All emphasized textures made eye-catching by colors contrasting to classical whiteness and roughness in contrast to classical smoothness.

4.14. "Veneer" could also apply to the silverwork on this goblet and pitcher made by Zalmon Bostwick in New York City in 1845; its array of Gothic Revival motifs—pointed arch arcades, cusps, leaf bosses, lozenges—gives the work a very ecclesiastical look. (The Brooklyn Museum, gift of the Estate of May S. Kelley by exchange)

4.15. This main or center block of the Canadian Parliament Buildings in Ottawa was built in High Picturesque Gothic style between 1859 and 1866 to designs by Thomas Fuller and Chilion Jones of England; it was later modified by Fuller in collaboration with Charles Baillairgé of the distinguished Québécois family of architects and sculptors. Destroyed by fire in February 1916. Its existing Academic Gothic replacement was undertaken as a statement of determination to prosecute a war and was brought to completion with a Victory Tower (now called Peace Tower) in 1919. (Public Archives of Canada)

• Colored glass for windows was often employed, providing pleasing effects of mysterious gloom to contrast with the crystal clarity of classical glass. Sometimes these windows actually imitated medieval Gothic glass; sometimes they were just colored panes.

So interrelated were these characteristics that almost from the beginning Gothic Revival substyles were mixed up with each other. And this is a major difference. If Classical Revivalists mixed up Roman and Greek, and both with Egyptian, it was from combinations of ignorance and necessity; their professed intent was to keep them separate. Gothic Revivalists mixed elements from different sources naturally, because they aimed at very general sorts of effects and allusions. This attitude led directly to the Picturesque, which swallowed up the Gothic and all other historicist styles indiscriminately (see chapter 5).

Mixing began earlier in interior design and furniture than in exterior architecture. In the first (1828) American edition of her *Domestic Duties; or Instruc-*

tions to Young Married Ladies on the Management of Their Households, Mrs. William Parkes urged her readers to judicious mixing (it seems that furniture, once as much a man's concern as architecture, had already become primarily a woman's concern, to be chosen on loosely symbolic lines):

> Every room should be furnished in a style not inconsistent with the use for which it is set apart. The dining-room, the place of rendez-vous for the *important* concerns of the table, should not be furnished in the light and airy style which you may adopt in your drawing-room, in which amusement and ease are the objects desired. . . . The furniture most usual in the dining-room is of a substantial kind; for instance, mahogany chairs, tables, and sideboards. . . . A solid simplicity generally characterizes the style of the dining-room, rendering it less subject to the variation of fashion than in some other parts of the house. . . . The style of the drawing-room furniture is almost as changeable in fashion as female dress; sometimes it is Grecian, then Egyptian, and now Turkish.

Furniture in the Gothic Revival style proper did exist, of course: armchairs modeled more or less loosely on the Coronation throne in Westminster Abbey, with high narrow backs edged in spiky cuspings; side chairs ornamented with lozenges copied from fourteenth-century tombs; knickknack holders adapted from *prie-dieus,* and so on *[4.14].* But it was always rare; an atmosphere of "special occasion" clung to it. It was something you ordered if you had a mansion on the Hudson, exalted cultural pretensions, and a taste for unconventional posings; if you were furnishing the chancel of an Episcopal church or the vestibule of a bishopric; if you wanted to give your Lodge hall a touch of class. The Gothic Revival's social function was always limited.

Social Function

The basic social function that made revival of Gothic architecture and allied arts into the serious cultural movement that it became in Britain was to create an antirevolutionary metaphor of continuity and stability. A second social function, sometimes though not necessarily related to the first, was to create images calling to mind what its proponents considered a more moral—usually meaning Christian—social order; this was the source of its greatest appeal in America. Obviously the operative context of such endeavors would vary according to times and places; it follows that to understand properly how the Gothic Revival functioned in American so-

ciety requires an awareness of its quite contrasting role in British.

In Britain the Gothic Revival began around 1725 as a frivolous taste among what would today be called avant-garde connoisseurs. But during Britain's long wars with revolutionary France, it became more serious. Gothic began to be associated with the survival and stability and endurance of hereditary institutions. An age when the church had been strong and nobles respected began to look very attractive to lords and churchmen in England, who saw their counterparts in France despoiled and guillotined; the distinctive architecture style of that age became correspondingly more attractive too. Gothic styles came to be seen as means of making antirevolutionary statements, ideological ripostes to the Classical Revival styles adopted by revolutionaries in France and America both.[4] For half a century thereafter Gothic continued to make effective images of an establishment that survived wars with two revolutionary powers and preserved continuity of past and present.[5] It functioned in fact as the *de facto* official style of the Second British Empire from the 1820s at least through the 1860s.

Gothic Revival became therefore the *de facto* official style of Canada into the 1870s, and as such it was the natural choice of style for government buildings; compare Ottawa's Gothic Revival Parliament Buildings, begun in the mid-1850s and completed in the early 1860s, with Washington's Roman Revival Capitol, enlarged over the same years *[4.15].* It was also the preferred and popularly approved style for mansions of establishment figures, and was the style of the majority of farmhouses *[4.16, 4.17].* But in the United States it was none of these things. American Gothic Revival had a different and contrasting social function which, by logical implication, had subversive associations.[6]

For in the United States, where the official establishment was revolutionary—that is, proclaimed a new order *(novus ordo seclorum)* in which ties of past to present are ruptured—the Gothic Revival, with its connotations of continuity, necessarily had an anti-establishment stance. It could function to imply if not actually promote subversion. Gervase Wheeler complained in his 1851 *Rural Homes* that "many persons of pure taste are frightened when the idea of 'Gothic' is presented to them as the style suggested for their home." And it probably is not entirely by coincidence that the only two departures of state capitols from the Classical Revival norm of the national Capitol were Georgia's at Milledgeville

4.16. Crenellated roof lines, towered keep, pointed windows, and turrets together proclaim the residence of a magistrate of the Second British Empire doing his tour of duty in the colonies: Holland House, which stood on Wellington Street in what is now downtown Toronto, was built in 1831 by the Honorable H. J. Boulton, Attorney-General of Canada West, and named for his birthplace, Holland House in Kensington, London. Demolished c. 1900, it is seen here as romantically rendered in a watercolor c. 1880. (Toronto Public Libraries)

4.17. Farmhouses like this one in Fergusonvale near Georgian Bay, built c. 1860, were visual metaphors of the settlement origins of Ontario. Their erection in great numbers from c. 1835 to c. 1860 (with more Picturesque versions common for another twenty years) stamped permanence and prosperity on the land, after its pioneer era. The basic plan—symmetrical, with gable eave affording pronouncedly vertical (Gothic) accent—is American, probably derived from Downing's cottages. The elaborately patterned brickwork derives from industrial and lower-middle-class Gothic Revival usages in northern England, southern Scotland, and Ulster; the elaborate gable tracery and pinnacles were ordered from stock books and attached. The whole comprises a highly distinctive vernacular, with regional variations within Ontario: west of the Thames Valley yellow brick trimmed with red is most common; eastward from London, red trimmed with yellow (and occasional blue or black accents), as here. (IMG:NAL, 1950)

and Louisiana's at Baton Rouge, both of which housed Confederate legislatures a dozen or so years after completion [4.18–4.20].

Certainly Gothic Revival functioned to promote eccentric departures from cultural norms. It tended to be the particular passion of romantic intellectuals out of step with solid American citizenry, of Episcopalians rather than old-line Colonial Protestant Dissenters, of aesthetes, of lukewarm democrats. (Conversely, of course, the Classical Revivals tended to have a comparable function in Britain after Gothic became the establishment style in the 1830s.) In farmhouses Gothic promoted ideas of Old World permanence, disguised under words like "snug." There was nothing subversive or eccentric

about that in theory; but in actuality somehow again Gothic went contrary to the American ethos—for whatever their occasional rhetorical professions of love for home and fireplace, Americans were not peasants tied to the same plot or village for generations, but ever ready to move in hopes of betterment.

Finally the Gothic Revival in America was used to defend and promote religion in general—that is, the Christian Western tradition as against those secular materialist attitudes of mind deriving from science that, with vacillations and vicissitudes, still continued to gain ground throughout the nineteenth century. The dim religious light and massive solidity of medieval architecture, seemingly witness

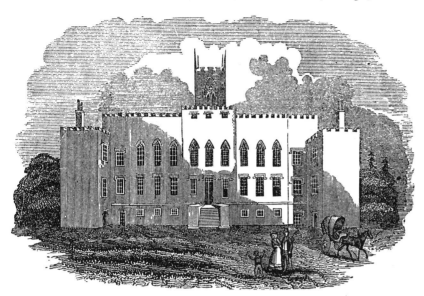

4.18. Between 1827 and 1830 the brick building that served as Georgia's capitol at Milledgeville was whitewashed and provided with crenellations, pinnacles, and pointed arches by an unknown architect, whose efforts were not universally appreciated: "I visited the State House," wrote a tourist in the 1830s. "It is a brick building which some blockhead of an architect has thought fit to Gothicize." Nor has a motivation for this startling departure been recorded. However, remodeling coincided exactly with the Nullification movement in South Carolina, with which legislators of Georgia warmly sympathized. (Robert Sears, Pictorial Description of the United States, *1848)*

4.19. Louisiana's Old State Capitol as seen from the river is essentially the building completed in 1849 to designs of James H. Dakin of New York. Like most American Gothic Revival buildings, it is sited in a Classical Revival spirit, commanding a bluff like the Virginia capitol at Richmond; it is also painted in classical white and beige. Abandoned after the Civil War, restored in the 1880s, it served as the capitol until replaced by the present splendid abstract Classical Revival capitol in 1932. (IMG:NAL)

4.20. Interior of the Old State Capitol at Baton Rouge was completed in the 1880s under William Feret of New Orleans. Its perpetuation of Gothic Revival probably had some ideological motivation: few Confederate states suffered as much in and from the Civil War as Louisiana. Visually it recalls Mark Twain's description of "Steamboat Gothic," in Life on the Mississippi: *"curving patterns of filigree work touched up with gilding, stretching overhead all down the converging vista . . . an April shower of glittering glass-drops; lovely rainbow-light falling everywhere from the colored glazing of the skylights; the whole . . . a bewildering and soul-satisfying spectacle."*

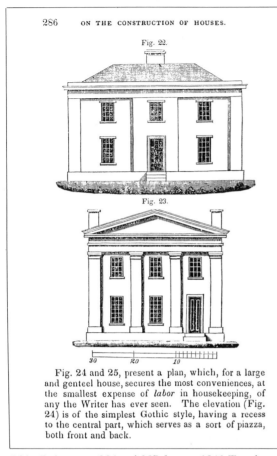

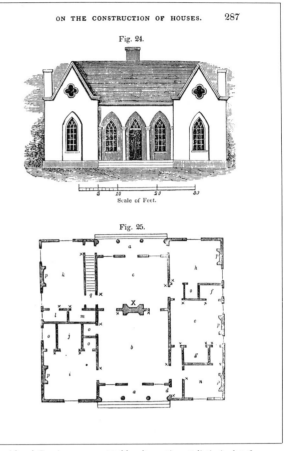

4.21. Facing pages 286 and 287 from an 1841 Treatise on Domestic Economy: for the use of Young Ladies at Home and in School, *"by Miss Catharine E. Beecher, Late Principal of the Hartford Female Seminary." At this point Beecher still considered Grecian an acceptable alternative stylistic jacket for a similar plan. Notable is her advocacy of parlors (usually a set family-icon space) doubling as bedrooms at night; by the 1860s convertible furniture to facilitate such conversions was common.*

of past devotion and ages of faith unshaken, comforted the spiritually unsettled, for whom skepticism was not religion enough. In this sense too there was something antirevolutionary and therefore subversive about the social function of its revival.

In the United States the Gothic Revival was necessarily more associated with religion than in Britain, where it had begun more as a national style than a religious expression. Westminster Abbey and major cathedrals were restored with parliamentary grants, for example, not because they were Anglican churches but because they were national monuments. But in the United States national monuments properly took Classical Revival forms. It followed that churches represent a much larger proportion of Gothic Revival architecture in the

United States than in Britain. Arguments for and against Gothic Revival usage in the United States were very often arguments about the nature and form of religion.[7] For example, when Ithiel Town designed a little stone church in Gothic Revival style for the Episcopalians of New Haven, Connecticut, and another, bigger, Congregational church next to it in forms close to replicating Gibbs's Saint Martin-in-the-Fields *[2.99,]* the difference was not one of aesthetic taste but of religious opinion. The best American example of Gothic used to promote Christian moral values is probably Catharine Beecher's writings and thought. In her *Treatise on Domestic Economy: for the Use of Young Ladies at Home and in School* of 1841, and more explicitly in her last book, *The American Woman's Home Companion* of 1869, she assumes that women were in charge of homemaking in order to function as "ministers of a Christian commonwealth . . . the home church of Jesus Christ,"[8] for which Gothic would obviously be the best style *[4.21, 4.22]*. But there are other examples almost as striking *[4.23]*.

Applications of Gothic Revival Styles to Architectural Types

Overwhelmingly, American Gothic Revival was conceived and used as a style for churches, with overtones of dissent from the establishment. That is not to say it was necessarily quite out of the mainstream of American life in its time; clearly there was some connection between the great popular ferment that put Andrew Jackson in the White House and the great ferment of evangelical religion in the 1820s–40s that put so many Gothic Revival churches on the landscape.[9]

Connotations of "apartness" that made the Gothic Revival a satisfactory style for churches also commended its use for jails. Visual associations with castle-fortresses made Gothic seem comfortingly protective to law-abiding burghers outside—a rationale that led to its widespread application to armories as well *[4.24–4.27]*.

"Apartness" and "special occasion" made Gothic Revival forms appropriate for the layout of cemetery parks, here meeting a central need of any society, regardless of revolutionary professions, for some establishment of continuity with the past *[4.6]*. Gothic was also widely used for cemetery gates and chapels. But complementary usage of Gothic for mausolea and other sorts of memorials

II.

A CHRISTIAN HOUSE.

In the Divine Word it is written, "The wise woman buildeth her house." To be "wise," is "to choose the best means for accomplishing the best end." It has been shown that the best end for a woman to seek is the training of God's children for their eternal home, by guiding them to intelligence, virtue, and true happiness. When, therefore, the wise woman seeks a home in which to exercise this

4.22. Page 23 of The American Woman's Home, *published in 1869 by Catharine E. Beecher and Harriet Beecher Stowe. Now Gothic is ideologically predominant; this model has a cross over the gable peak. Both the 1841 and 1869 plans have been cited as anticipations of Frank Lloyd Wright's focus on a central hearth with other areas radiating axially from it.*

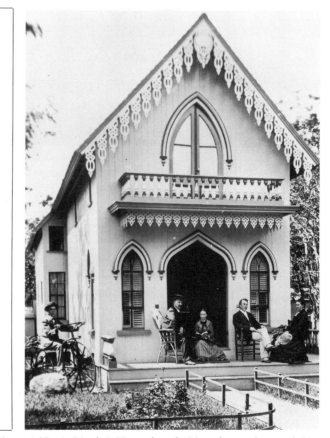

4.23. At Martha's Vineyard on the Massachusetts shore a whole village of little Gothic cottages grew up, whose style expressed their origin in Methodist summer camp meetings. (Photograph c. 1870, courtesy of Dukes County Historical Society, Edgartown, Massachusetts)

4.24. Montgomery County Prison, Norristown, Pennsylvania, built in 1850 with Early Gothic symmetry. Architect Napoleon Lebrun freely adapted from T. U. Walter's Moyamensing Prison in Philadelphia. Two flanking buildings were designed at about the same time: on one side Saint John's Episcopal Church in complementary Early Gothic style (still standing); on the other, a courthouse, long gone, in Greek Revival. (IMG:NAL)

4.25. The castellated grandeur of Cincinnati's Workhouse and Jail, built 1866–69 to designs of Samuel Hannaford, still loomed over I-75 in the late 1980s. A small city in itself, containing tiers of cells for prisoners, institutional offices, and personnel quarters, it also dominated other buildings on the same grounds, including a hospital and offices where baking, laundering, and sewing were taught. (IMG:NAL)

never overcame Classical Revival appeal *[3.11, 4.7]*, despite impressive endorsements *[4.28, 4.29]*.

For collegiate buildings (especially for the many new colleges begun under evangelical auspices), use of Gothic could be justified by references to "Christian education" made through general medieval forms and specific allusions to "ancient seats of Christian learning" (Oxford, Cambridge, Heidelberg), or simply by implicit contrast of mossy, vague, blurred, erratic visual effects to the neat, ordered regularity of Classical Revival forms, with their evocations of arid, if not godless, Reason. But though there were some early examples (New

York University's main building of 1830) and some spectacular later ones (College Hall at the University of Pennsylvania in 1871), Gothic Revival never became very common on American campuses until the Academic Revival of it began in the late 1880s (chapter 6). The reason probably has to do with the fact that collegiate architectural types share a social function fundamentally similar to that of government architectural types—to form the officially acceptable culture—and for this nothing could make Gothic fully appropriate in the United States.

In fact the only architectural types where Gothic Revival enjoyed any widespread popularity, other

4.26. Cornerstone of Hagerstown's main firehouse bears the date 1892, showing that the Picturesque Gothic substyle remained popular, at least in remoter areas such as western Maryland then was, almost into the twentieth century. (IMG:NAL)

4.27. Montana authorized a state prison at Deer Lodge in 1870; begun in 1893, it was completed in 1912, using convict labor and a local designer. (IMG:NAL)

4.28. George Washington's will specified that his and Martha Washington's bodies were to be buried at Mount Vernon in a new tomb. Congress hoped his tomb would be in the Capitol and had a sarcophagus prepared for it (still there). But in the end the will was respected; executors provided a brick tomb in simple Early Gothic style some distance from the main house. It was not begun, however, until 1831, and not completed until 1837. (IMG:NAL)

than for churches and cemetery parks, was for small farmhouses—what its chief promoters, Andrew Jackson Downing, Alexander Jackson Davis, and Gervase Wheeler, liked to call "rural cottages." Associations with "roots," "heritage," and "Christianity" had appeal to some homemakers on this level *[4.30]*.

The appeal of Gothic Revival for mansions, on grounds of "superior taste," was even narrower. Gothic Revival mansions have, however, received a good deal more attention than their numbers warrant, mainly because of the personality and writings of their chief proponent, Downing. Downing was charismatic enough to get a contract from his fellow New Yorker, President Millard Fillmore, to redo the Mall in Washington as a Picturesque park—celebrated by Millard Fillmore clubs to this day as their hero's greatest, and perhaps only perceptible act, and memorable chiefly as explaining the capital's one Gothic Revival public building, the Smithsonian "Castle" *[4.31]*.

Writings like Downing's 1841 *Treatise on Landscape Gardening*, 1842 *Rural Cottages*, and 1850 *Architecture of Country Houses* had plenty of appeal for a snobbocracy emerging in the Hudson Valley as successor to the slaveholders and patroons, whose privileges had been abolished only in the 1820s and

4.29. In Honolulu another "king" was provided a Gothic tomb, in Picturesque vernacular, this time. The Lunalilo tomb, designed by Robert Lishman for the last male of the Kamehameha line, who died in 1874, and his father, Kanaina, was completed in 1876. It stands in the ground of the vaguely New England–Gibbsian Kawaiahao Church, built by the missionary Hiram Bingham in 1842. (IMG:NAL)

PRINCIPAL FLOOR.

4.30. Alexander Jackson Davis, who provided plan and perspective for this "Bracketed Cottage" appearing in Downing's Country Houses *of 1850, claimed to have introduced to America (in 1832) the "English perpendicular Gothic Villa with Barge Boards, Bracketts, Oriels, Tracery in Windows, etc." His Gothic styles, though never rivaling Classical Revival high styles*

and vernaculars, were quite widely used, often in unexpected contexts—as for all the buildings at Fort Dalles on the Columbia River in Oregon, hurriedly authorized in the early 1850s to control Walla Walla Indians, following the "Whitman Massacre" in 1847 (of which one "Bracketed Cottage," housing the Surgeon's Quarters remains).

1830s. But it had little appeal for the Age of Jackson's surging egalitarian democracy. Downing was too fond of pointing out how "modern landscape gardening owes its existence almost entirely to the English," how it "has been developed and carried to its greatest perfection in the British Isles," and how, unfortunately, "in the United States, it is highly improbable that we shall ever witness such splendid examples . . . here the rights of man are held to be equal." He could write eloquently about great wealth being "contrary to republican institutions, wholly in contradiction to the spirit of our time and people" and how "intelligent working men in America ought . . . to feel . . . the superior beauty of a cottage home which is truthful and aims to be no more than it honestly is." But the objects of his greatest admiration were not such as to encourage mass adoption of Gothic Revival styles by the population at large: Hyde Park, whose grounds are "finely varied . . . including, as they do, the noble Hudson for sixty miles in its course"; the Manor of Livingston, "commanding prospects for sixty miles around"; Kenwood, near Albany, "a country residence of much picturesque beauty, erected in the Tudor style . . . there are about 1200 acres in the estate, and pleasure grounds." Gothic Revival mansions came in fact to be a signal of great

riches: Lyndhurst at Tarrytown began a string of status symbols running far up the Hudson to Rhinebeck; the Lockwood/Mathews mansion at Norwalk was in another string, along Long Island Sound through Rye to New Haven *[4.32]*

For architectural types with public connotations—government buildings, public works, public amenities—Gothic Revival usages in the United States were almost exactly opposite to those in Britain and Canada. There, Gothic Revival for such types was the norm; in the United States, so rare as to make examples instant monuments when erected, almost invariably proclaiming an English immigrant designer: the City Hall in Holyoke, Massachusetts, for instance; or the Jefferson Market Police Station on Sixth Avenue in New York *[4.33]*; or Point of Rocks station on the Baltimore & Ohio going out of Maryland into West Virginia. In Britain and Canada, Classical Revival was the style for buildings with connotations of "culture," as distinct from everyday life and living (a British Museum, an exclusive Royal High School in Edinburgh, or a great public auditorium in Liverpool), whereas in the United States Gothic proper, and variants, was most commonly used for such situations: major galleries and museums in Philadelphia (Academy of Fine Arts) and New York (original

4.31. *"The Castle," original building of the Smithsonian Institution, was begun in 1849 to a design by James Renwick. James Smithson, an Englishman who never had been in America, founded the Smithsonian with a bequest in 1829 to encourage* science in the new Republic; appropriately, Renwick's chosen style referred to German Romanesque—it was as much Romanesque as Gothic—in homage to German scientific accomplishments. *(IMG:NAL)*

4.32. Mansions built with New York City money began lining the Hudson River and Long Island Sound shores during the 1850s. Given their social function to proclaim how acquisition of culture follows upon acquisition of wealth, high style up-to-dateness was imperative. So for successful Connecticut speculator LeGrand Lockwood, Austrian-born Detlef Lienau designed a mansion in Norwalk that added to a Gothic frame elements from Italianate and incoming French Second Empire styles, thus presaging the High Picturesque styles of the 1860s and 1870s, and Richard Morris Hunt's "Vanderbilt Gothic" of the 1880s and 1890s. Only four years after Lockwood's mansion was completed in 1864, he lost his fortune and it passed into other hands; it is now the Lockwood/Mathews Museum. (IMG:NAL)

4.33. The Jefferson Market Police Station, Jail, and quasi-firehouse (its tower functioned as a fire lookout) was built in 1875–77. Later it served as a courthouse; it was, and remains, a striking sight on Sixth Avenue (at West Tenth Street) in New York. Like so much American Gothic Revival, it was designed by an Englishman, Frederick C. Withers. It was restored in 1967 (under Giorgio Cavaglieri) and is now a library, a function much more appropriate for Picturesque Gothic building in America. (IMG:NAL)

Metropolitan), country fair buildings, traveling circuses, and Mississippi steamboat saloons.

Likewise, Gothic was a great style for commercial buildings in England, but not in the United States. Because of associations with Venice's great seaborne empire, the Doge's and other Venetian palaces inspired innumerable structures from Manchester to Madras, not to mention counterparts in Canada (the Canada Life Assurance [Birks] Building in Hamilton). But in the United States Gothic commercial buildings tended to be freaks. Notable in their own time for that reason were the 1850s Jayne Building and Furness's 1870s banks in Philadelphia, or the Syracuse Savings Bank of the 1880s, which was "a textbook illustration of the style" (Picturesque Gothic) precisely because that style was so rarely used.[10] The buildings' special allusions, if any, are mostly to architects' eccentricities; we are not surprised to find that the Syracuse Bank was by Frank Lloyd Wright's mentor Lyman Silsbee, who had connections with Frank Furness.

Substyles

Five principal substyles of the Gothic Revival can be identified: Early Gothic, General and Specific; Picturesque Gothic; Exotic or Non-European Medieval; Denominational Expressions (Episcopal, Catholic, Presbyterian); and Technological.

Early Gothic Revival Substyles, General

Early Gothic Revival is generally identifiable by the general practice of adding distinctively Gothic features like pinnacles, crenellations, or pointed arches to basically symmetrical, balanced, Classical/Colonial plans and bodies.

These distinctively Gothic forms derive from a miscellany of medieval sources: manuscript illuminations, furniture, tapestry, stained glass, as well as architecture. They are applied arbitrarily with little consideration of what function (physical or otherwise) they may originally have played in a design or what relationship they may originally have had to structure *[4.13]*.

Compared to their models, Early Gothic Revival forms tend to be thin and linear, what architectural critics call "dry." Plans of buildings to which they are applied are usually symmetrical and often indistinguishable from eighteenth-century Classical Revival plans for the same building types; proportions too tend to be similar to classical ones—that is, designers still mainly think in terms of scaling elements to human measure, of columns with Vitruvian ratios of base to shaft to cornice.

Early Gothic Revival first appeared in America in its eighteenth-century "Gothick" phase. In architecture, examples are rare; the best known is the south front porch William Buckland added to Gunston Hall in northern Virginia, with ogee arches in Palladian-proportioned frames. But in furniture it was common and found expression in such styles as Chippendale Gothic.

Of nineteenth-century Early Gothic, good examples were the County Jail in Norristown, Pennsylvania *[4.24]*, the City Armory in Cincinnati, the now-vanished Old Georgia Statehouse at Milledgeville *[4.18]* and, of course, innumerable churches—all with symmetrical plans and elevations, pointed windows, crenellated roof lines, and pinnacled towers *[4.34, 4.11]*.

Churches increasingly came to feature spires, often added later in conformity with a mid-nineteenth-century taste for them as "pointers to

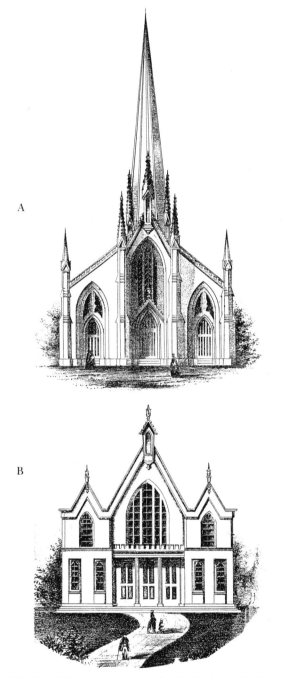

A

B

4.34. Incredibly enough, these two facades (and several others) appearing in C. P. Dwyer's Economy of Church, School, and Parsonage Architecture *(Buffalo, 1856) are intended to be interchangeable: they fit onto the same rectangular box behind. Of course this is only possible because the structure behind is a box, and the facade are elements absolutely regular and symmetrical. The intent is that (A) should be what we would call Picturesque Gothic (because of its lavishness and vertical spire), while (B) would be simpler, Early Gothic. But in terms of basic symmetrical concept there is little difference.*

4.35. "A cottage in the English or Rural Gothic Style," Figure 9 in Downing's Cottage Residences *(1857), is also a stylistic jacket, with perfectly symmetrical elements applicable to a symmetrically disposed box behind. It is also intended to be more Picturesque than earlier styles of cottage [4.30] and was conceived in symmetrical Early Gothic terms.*

Heaven" and indications of "Christian community" which was so strong that by 1859 even *The Congregational Quarterly* was carrying such assertions as: "Erase our church towers and spires, and what a cheerless heathen aspect would our landscapes take on."[11] Of this taste Trinity Church on New Haven Green is a conspicuous memorial. As originally designed by Ithiel Town and/or Asher Benjamin, it had a stolid crenellated tower. To this in 1859 a spire was added, which quite altered its appearance;

in 1903 the spire crashed and was put up again, this time reinforced with steel; but when damaged again in 1928, it was removed for good, so that the church looks now as it did when first erected in 1814 *[2.99].*

This general kind of Early Gothic Revival was easy to design and build with local skills from guidebooks. Many small Episcopal churches were built from models of the sort Richard Upjohn supplied free to Episcopal parishes as a contribution to that faith. It was equally simple to transform a British cabin or New England homestead type into a Gothic farmhouse by inserting a straight-framed pointed gable, with or without a round-framed pointed window inside it, into the long side, above the main door. For the slightly more ambitious, Downing and Davis promoted several varieties of medieval-looking cottages as a substitute for Classical Revival temple-houses, all of them following the basic Early Gothic Revival formula *[4.35].*

Early Gothic Revival Substyles, Specific

Until very near the end of the nineteenth century, specific styles from the Middle Ages were differentiated much more purposefully and precisely in Britain than in America. Under the rubric "Gothic Revival" Charles Eastlake's 1872 *History of the Gothic Revival* specified Elizabethan, Tudor, and Jacobean as a matter of course. But in the United States, only one medieval style apart from Gothic was widely recognized. This was Romanesque, which in its own time was often carelessly called a Round Style (in fine disregard for confusions with the Italianate, also called The Round Style because of its round

4.36. Warrens Corner Methodist Church outside Lockport, about thirty miles east of Buffalo, is a typical mid-nineteenth-century Protestant church: rectangular box with vertically proportioned windows (built 1858). Methodist churches were in general designed as simpler versions of Episcopal ones, inasmuch as Methodism originated as a movement toward evangelical simplicity within the Church of England. Here, for example, the windows are round-headed, vaguely Italianate or Romanesque instead of pointed Gothic, and illuminations are lighter and plainer in color, with simple emblematic illustrations (wheat sheaves, lilies, crowns, and anchors). Oak pews and wood-grained furnishings also represent simplified versions of Gothic Revival usage. (IMG:NAL)

arches [see chapter 5, Picturesque Substyles]), and sometimes also Lombard.

There were probably far more examples of this kind of Romanesque than have been recognized. Certainly it was used by all the leading architects of the day—James Renwick, Leopold Eidlitz, even Richard Upjohn—almost as a routine alternative to Gothic proper. In church styling, Romanesque allowed Methodist or Baptist or Congregational congregations to be fashionably medieval without Episcopal or Catholic associations. Romanesque also perhaps had appropriate ethnic associations for Lutheran congregations, as it had special associations with German history. It offered economic advantages: churches could be in good Romanesque style yet be only boxes with a few round-arched doors and windows; there was no need to apologize for the absence of the side aisles, chapels, apses, and chancels that Gothic proper required [4.36]. As Romanesque was at this time under enthusiastic revival in Germany as a national expression[12], it was often revived in America for ethnic associations with "German heritage."[13] Also, most dramatically, Romanesque was used for its associations with advanced science, in which Germany held a lead throughout the nineteenth century; the most notable example is James Renwick's styling of the Smithsonian Institution "Castle" in Washington, D.C. [4.31].[14]

Much of this early Romanesque was so visually close to Italianate that on occasion it passed as an acceptable alternative to Gothic proper for civic types like courthouses (for example, the one in Syracuse, by Horatio Nelson White, 1855) or city halls (Springfield, Massachusetts, by Leopold Eidlitz 1854–55). But by that very process it inevitably dissolved into the Picturesque pot and was lost for a couple of decades. Reformed by H. H. Richardson, it reappeared as the greatest and most American of all Picturesque substyles.

Picturesque Gothic Revival Substyles

A number of substyles fall within this general category; none is absolutely distinct from the others, and demarcations between them are often arbitrary. They are Early Picturesque Gothic Revival, Picturesque Gothic Revival High Style, Picturesque Gothic Vernacular, and Vestigial Picturesque Gothic.

Early Picturesque Gothic Revival. Elements of picturesque asymmetry appear on an otherwise Classical

4.37. The most famous Gothic Revival monument of its time was Trinity Episcopal Church on Broadway in New York, now buried in the financial district but when built (1839–46) set on spacious grounds with fine mansions not far off. Here it is illustrated in Putnam's Magazine *for 1853. Architect Richard Upjohn replaced a vaguely Early Gothic building (old Trinity, 1788–90) with a splendid evocation of great English parish churches of the fourteenth and fifteenth centuries. It is still basically symmetrical, however Picturesque its elaborate detail.*

Revival or Colonial frame, in addition to the usual few pointed windows or pinnacles that mark Early Gothic. Most commonly the mark of Picturesque Gothic was an asymmetrically placed tower and/or drum and/or spire, of pronouncedly vertical proportion, often with some medieval-derived detail. There was, by definition, no uniform practice about placement of towers, but they were usually on one corner or at the join of projections. Given more than one tower, they might be of different sizes and shapes. Towers and spires being especially vulnerable to time and storm, the Picturesque Gothic style of many extant buildings was originally much more obvious than it is now.

A good representative of Early Picturesque

4.38. The capitol intended to give Connecticut one legislative center produced controversy tremendous even by normal capitol-building standards. It was finally erected in 1873–79 with

Gothic detail designed by Richard Mitchell Upjohn, but on the conventional capitol plan of central dome with end blocks and connecting wings. (IMG:NAL)

Gothic Revival is the famous Trinity Church on Broadway in New York, designed by Richard Upjohn and built in 1839–46 to replace a simple Early Gothic Revival church (one of the country's earliest) on the same site *[4.37]*. Trinity's combination of showy Gothic detail and dramatically vertical proportions with a basically symmetrical—that is, inherited eighteenth-century classical—plan, corresponds nicely to Page Smith's description of the denomination that built it:

> The Episcopal church, the American variation of the Church of England, or Anglican Church, was as fashionable [by the 1830s and 1840s] as the Unitarian. The alliance between success and religion was consummated in the Episcopal Church, which discerned exactly the right balance between piety and worldliness that would appeal to the urban upper class and those aspiring to it.

To the decorum of a lucidly rational plan, that is,

4.39. A gem in the pretty northern California town of Yreka, Saint Mark's Episcopal Church was completed in 1880 and restored in 1975, complete with sandstone effects on its vertical bargeboarding. It is typical of vernacular styles to emphasize signal features: here, oversize pointed windows. (IMG:NAL)

Upjohn aspired to add awe—effects of the numinous, of soaring verticality, of mystery. How well he succeeded, and to what extent there is truth, if any, in Page's implication that the Episcopalian church was founded on pious hypocrisy or self-deception, are matters of personal interpretation.[15]

Certainly application of the kind of combination of rational and numinous which Picturesque Gothic could create was not limited to churches. Richard Upjohn had a son, Richard Mitchell Upjohn, who like his father specialized in Picturesque Gothic, though his detail was a bit more florid. In that style Richard M. Upjohn executed a number of commissions, most notably the new Connecticut State Capitol at Hartford in 1872–78 *[4.38].* Here again a rigidly symmetrical and traditional plan—a normal capitol's main block, flanking wings, and central cupola—is given a "spiritual dimension" by lavish Gothic detail; and here again the alert, or the cynical, might perceive an expression of the perennial recipe for political success: combine calculating adherence to mean practicalities and the main chance, with soaring rhetoric about high ideals and noble motives.

Picturesque Gothic Revival High Style.   This is the category for buildings in which Gothic details and/or effects (like pronounced asymmetry) give a dominant character, although details from other styles can be found mixed in. Clearly the line between this substyle and a substyle of Picturesque proper is fluid, depending on the point at which Gothic elements cease to dominate and represent just one element in an eclectic mixture. It took a trained and sophisticated architect to use this style properly; its presence usually indicates one.

High Picturesque Gothic is also sometimes called Ruskinian Gothic, after its great English champion, John Ruskin. It was most dramatically represented in the United States by Memorial Hall, Harvard's tribute to her Civil War dead. Memorial Hall's present fate and appearance, a truncated white elephant, perhaps best express the failure of this style ever to find a real place in American life. It looks odd wherever you find it. Cincinnati's Workhouse and Jail is now and always was grotesquely out of scale to its surroundings *[4.25];* the same is true of the Jefferson Market Police Station *[4.33].*

Picturesque Gothic Vernacular.   There are far more buildings in this category than in the High Picturesque Gothic style; the great bulk of Gothic Revival

4.40. The model at several removes for Saint Mark's in Yreka could have been Saint Mark's in Philadelphia, built in 1847–51 to designs of John Notman, premier English expert on Gothic Revival and Italianate throughout the Delaware Valley and New Jersey. At Saint Mark's he may have had some collaboration from a leading Ecclesiologist in England, R. C. Carpenter. Like Saint Mark's in Yreka, this church is a gem in its setting, though the setting is very different. (IMG:NAL, 1971)

churches built between 1840 and 1900 in the country and small towns belong to it. It is the work of builders who have a vague idea that the effect their clients desire will be produced by something picturesque in outline, with pointed windows and a pinnacle or two or an asymmetrical turret. And the line of demarcation between it and substyles of Picturesque proper is just as fluid, just as dependent on degrees of mixture with other, nonmedieval details.

To the extent that Gothic was ever fully Americanized, it was in the Picturesque Gothic Vernacular substyle. In general that is best represented by small Episcopal churches from the 1850s to 1900. They are usually the best, and often are unique examples of architectural art in their communities *[4.39, 4.40].* But of course plenty of other denominations, and bigger churches, used it as well.[16]

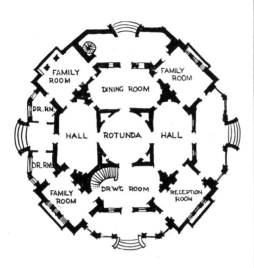

4.41. Longwood outside Natchez is often called an octagon, and so, basically, it came out; but as this plan of it shows (published as "A Villa in the Oriental Style" in Godey's Magazine, *1861), its basic concept was a whole series of geometric shapes arranged on a criss-cross axis; the "Oriental" detailing was all jacket. (Plan redrawn by George L. Hersey in "Godey's Choice,"* Journal of the Society of Architectural Historians *18/3 [1958]:108.)*

4.42. The exterior of Longwood was handsomely restored in the 1970s; but the interior, begun in 1858, remains to this day unfinished as workmen left it on the outbreak of the Civil War in 1861. (IMG:NAL)

Picturesque Gothic Vernacular was a reasonably popular, and natural, style for summer homes, not least because of the consistent associations of Gothic with something going against the norm. Owning both a city and a country residence was decidedly a privilege of wealth until almost the end of the nineteenth century; a Gothic Vernacular cottage expressed this exclusiveness. A special and ultimate Americanization of Gothic was represented, perhaps, by the summer cottages in the Methodist camp-meeting village on Martha's Vineyard built in the post–Civil War decades; here all the special connotations of Gothic—social exclusivity to the point of eccentricity, dissent, religion—were perfectly blended [4.23].

Vestigial Picturesque Gothic. The odd remnant of Gothic Revival detail tacked irregularly onto some standard body—this is the style of a good deal of later nineteenth century building, most notably mass-prefabricated suburban housing in "Tudor."

Revivals of Exotic Non-European Medieval Styles

In the early-nineteenth-century American mind, much more was encompassed under the term "Gothic" than is now. Thus in this category would be found the Moorish-style Brewster Burke house of 1849 in Rochester, which still stands, and P. T. Barnum's Iranistan in Bridgeport, which does not (designed for him in 1848 by the Austrian Leopold Eidlitz, it burned in 1857). It would also include Nathan Dunn's "Chinese cottage," which stands sadly mutilated in Mount Holly, New Jersey, designed around 1840, along with its grounds, by John Notman, another British Gothic Revival specialist. Like Notman's Italianate style, his "Chinese" included lots of Gothic detail. By far the most striking example of this substyle is Longwood near Natchez, Mississippi, recently restored to its unfinished condition as of 1861, when workmen decamped at the outbreak of the Civil War [4.41, 4.42]. Longwood had those eccentric and dissenting connotations so consistently typical of Gothic; Roger Kennedy in *Architecture, Men, Women, and Money* has movingly described the tribulations of Unionist Haller Nutt trying to cooperate with architect Samuel Sloan of Philadelphia amid the Deep South's increasingly hostile atmosphere.

This substyle survived well into the twentieth century as peculiarly appropriate for the architecture of fairs, spas, circuses, and the like, which are by their nature exotic, set apart from everyday norms. Abundant at the turn of this century, few now survive. The Historic American Buildings Survey published its records of Saltair near Salt Lake City in its 1947 *Utah Guide;* the 1906 Bath House at Ocean Park, California, is best seen in postcards *[5.31].*

Denominational Expressions

"Among all the diversities of what may properly be called ecclesiastical architecture, something may be found appropriate to all varieties of Christian sentiment, and possibly some outward form answering to every inward type of Christian character and experience." So the Committee of the Congregational Church introduced its statement on *Plans for Churches* in 1853, for which designs had been submitted by most of the eminent architects of the day, certainly all with major Gothic Revival reputations: Richard Upjohn, John Renwick, Henry Austin, Gervase Wheeler, and John Wills. It is a sentiment not easily comprehensible in an era like our own. Modern Americans generally find the idea of religious denominations distasteful and have trouble understanding how important it seemed in the nineteenth century for Catholic parents to make sure their children married Catholics and for Protestants to marry within their own denomination; only among Jews and more recently arrived groups has some sense of this kind of denominationalism retained much strength. Once grasp the earlier situation, however, and it will not be surprising how many distinctive denominational substyles can be recognized within nineteenth-century Picturesque Gothic churches. Not, of course, that these were used with anything like absolute consistency; what appears instead is a discernible pattern.

The predilection of evangelical Protestant denominations like Methodists, Congregationalists, and Baptists for Romanesque/Round/Lombard has been noted earlier. A style about as far from it as possible was adopted (perhaps predictably) by Roman Catholics, as nineteenth-century immigration began to increase their numbers dramatically. This can be called Catholic Gothic Revival. There was also a distinctively Episcopal kind of Ecclesiological Gothic; and, I think, a Presbyterian Gothic as well.

Catholic Gothic Revival. This was essentially the creation of an Englishman, son of a French royalist emigré, Augustus Welby North Pugin, whose polemical promotions began to appear in the 1820s. Influenced by his father's experiences, Pugin was devoted to Gothic as the cultural expression of an older, nobler, merrier England (and Europe), whose happier state he attributed mainly to the beneficent influences of Gothic architecture and the Catholic Church. Enthusiastically he set himself to revive both, as a means to restore that earlier, better society. To that end he devoted books like *Contrasts,* which set images of bleak eighteenth-century buildings and life opposite pageants of medieval glory, and in others gave innumerable demonstrations of the kind of Gothic Catholics ought to use to display their faith. But at home his efforts were of little avail; "the huge Irish immigration into England was accommodated in the cheapest possible fashion" by variants of Italian Renaissance and Baroque.[17] It was in North America that Pugin's ideas had the most success, applied by architects of Irish origin, like Patrick Charles Keely, "the patriarch of Roman Catholic architecture in the United States" or Joseph Connolly of Ontario (often borrowing from church architecture in Ireland). From the 1870s on Catholic Gothic began to bulk large on landscapes, most prominently but by no means exclusively in New England and New York City; everywhere the great wave of Irish immigration of the 1840s and 1850s touched, churches in this characteristic style were to be seen. And in great numbers; architects like Keely and Connolly were never without commissions. Catholic Gothic was distinguished by exaggeratedly vertical effects, great barnlike naves (deliberately or by accident emphasizing the size of Catholic congregations), and a general thinness of proportion in the details. Red brick was a very common material for parish churches; cathedrals tended to be in stone *[4.11, 4.43].*

Episcopal or Ecclesiological Gothic. This was the style for High Church Episcopalians. It was promoted (and often judged) by the Camden Society of Cambridge (England), founded in 1841, reorganized in London as the Ecclesiological Society in 1846—an organization of self-appointed Gothic experts who undertook to promote throughout the Anglican world their approved standards. Correct Gothic was for them Gothic as it was in England around 1300: asymmetrical, with piled-up masses, and richly colorful (gold and scarlet, the English royal colors, were much favored; to this day you can still tell Episcopal churches by their scarlet doors). Cor-

4.43. The biggest Gothic church on the continent was for many decades Montreal's premier parish church—Notre-Dame, La Paroisse, begun in 1824 to plans of Irish architect James O'Donnell. It opened for services in 1829, but between 1872 and 1880 its interior was completely done over under the direction of local architect Victor Bourgeau. Bourgeau smothered O'Donnell's galleries and vaults in tight, thin, garishly painted Gothic detail; installed a huge altar and retable; and inserted elaborately traceried skylights. The result, and undoubtedly the motivation, was to make the church look much more Catholic than O'Donnell had. There are strong visual resemblances between the interior effect achieved here and in Catholic churches from these same decades in New England, where denominational expression was so essential. It is hardly coincidental, then, that while Bourgeau was so transforming Notre-Dame into "Catholic Gothic," he was also commissioned by the Bishop of Montreal to build a new basilican cathedral for Montreal as a scaled-down model of Saint Peter's. (IMG:NAL)

4.44. Nobody could mistake an Ecclesiological Gothic interior like this one of the Anglican Cathedral of Newfoundland in its capital city of Saint John's—all severe "good form"—with the lavishness of Catholic Gothic. It was built over many years (1843–1900), *interrupted by several fires, to plans supplied by George Gilbert Scott, the leading English Gothic Revivalist, and his son Gilbert Scott. (IMG:NAL)*

respondence flowed freely from the society's office to any parish, no matter how remote, which undertook to build a new church—Saint John's in Newfoundland *[4.44]*, Galle Face in Colombo, the cathedral in Lahore, and the cemetery of Saint James the Less in Toronto.

Understandably the best examples of Ecclesiological Gothic tended to be in the British empire. New York architect John Wills carried out one of the continent's best examples in the 1840s for the Anglican Cathedral in Fredericton, New Brunswick *[4.45]*. But there were a number in the United States as well. Here the fate of Ecclesiological Gothic depended very largely upon the attitudes of the clergy, and its history is a fine demonstration of the axiom "architecture is politics in three dimensions." Its spread corresponded almost exactly, as Phoebe Stanton pointed out in *The Gothic Revival*, to the distribution of American Episcopal bishops sympathetic to the High Church doctrinal position initiated by John Henry Hobart, Bishop of New York from 1816 to 1830: from the Philadelphia/New York axis into Maryland and North Carolina, Pennsylvania, upstate New York and Vermont.

Of the two most famous examples, one was Saint James the Less, built in New York in 1846–49 to plans actually supplied by the Cambridge Camden Society and therefore enthusiastically approved by it. It had an elaborate high altar at the far end of an elevated chancel, which contained a chanting choir, all far removed from the congregation. The second was Saint Mary's Cathedral in nearby Burlington, New Jersey, built in 1846–48. It was the work of the publicity-seeking, eccentric, progressive Bishop George Washington Doane, who looks, in a famous portrait by Henry Inman, the very image of an American Gothic Revivalist. Doane's stance in clerical politics was also indicated by the rectory he commissioned from architect John Notman of Philadelphia, which was to be a small episcopal palace in the fashionable Italianate villa style of the day.

But the spread of Ecclesiological Gothic also corresponded to something else—to the political stance of the states at the outbreak of Civil War in 1861. Only in one Southern state did it appear—North Carolina, most lukewarm of the Confederacy—and the leading bishops opposed to it came precisely from that state which came to lead the Confederacy. As early as 1839 Bishop Moore of Virginia attacked the Oxford Tracts, the High Church movement that produced the Cambridge Camden Society. His successor was that same

4.45. *Nor could this massy pile climaxing in lofty spire be anything but an Anglican church; indeed a principal goal of the Camden Society was to emphasize the superiority of English Gothic to all others, and thus, incidentally, to promote the British Empire; hence there are so many great examples in Canada. But Ecclesiological Gothic had many American admirers and practitioners. The architect of this example, Christ Church Cathedral (1845–53) in Fredericton, capital of the Canadian province of New Brunswick (Gothic cathedrals appeared in the Canadian capitals like Wren/Gibbs churches in capitals of the old American colonies), was John Wills, from 1822 to 1856 architect to the Camden Society's New York branch. Though to most eyes he would seem to have produced here one of the continent's great works of architectural art, Wills was criticized by Ecclesiologists for taking as his model Saint Mary's Snettisham (Norfolk) instead of one of the society's approved models (Saint Mary's Arnold near Nottingham, All Saints Hawton, or Saint Andrew's Hickington). An 1850 contributor to* The Ecclesiologist *sniffed: "It would be far better for persons wishing to build churches in the colonies to send, at first at least, for designs from England." (New Brunswick Tourism)*

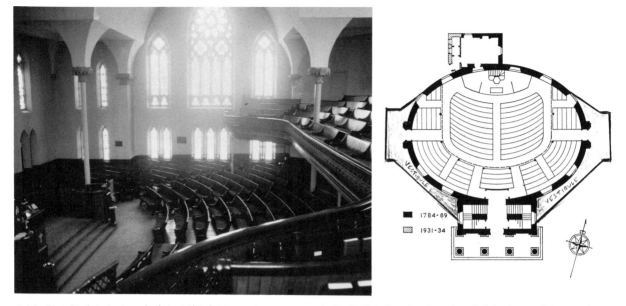

4.46. *First Presbyterian was built in 1878–79 to occupy a position on the central green next to the court house, in the Ontario town of Brockville on the Saint Lawrence. But architect and contractors came from upstate New York, across the river: J. P. Johnston from Ogdensburg, Moore and Fields from Canton. Perhaps they were Scots by birth. In any event this is a perfectly preserved church, complete with original pews and glass. There are some counterparts in the United States (First Presbyterian at Albion, New York, is one), but they did not dominate towns as Presbyterian churches had in Canada. (IMG:NAL)*

4.47. *Presbyterian churches adopted their characteristic curved seating arrangements in the 1860s and 1870s after the practice of dispensing communion from long tables was discontinued. So, for example, the seating for this 1785 church of Saint Andrew's in Edinburgh dates from 1878, though the plan itself is a typical Adamesque oval. This church was architecturally important because the "Disruption," or Free Church movement to which most North American Presbyterian churches adhered, began in it. Derivations usually had straight exterior walls. (Plan from George Hay,* The Architecture of Scottish Post-Reformation Churches *[Oxford, 1957], p. 98.)*

Bishop Meade who spoke so eloquently in praise of King Carter's Church—"a house whose sacred form and beautiful arches seemed to give force and music to the feeblest tongue beyond any other building in which I ever performed"—and who led the first movement to renovate and restore to use the Colonial Southern Plantation style churches which in a sense sacramentalized the older slave-holding society of his Virginia diocese.[18] Bishop John Johns, Meade's successor, remained so opposed to Gothic that the style never appeared in Virginia until after his death in 1876; "apparently, no clearly neo-Gothic Episcopal Church building was built east of the Blue Ridge until the 20th century."[19] Ostensibly the reason was fear of Romeward drift. They could cite High Church priest Newman becoming Cardinal Newman, or they could cite Bishop Doane's own older son becoming Roman Catholic coadjutant Bishop of Newark, New Jersey. But the real reason was political: Ecclesiological Gothic was a mark of Northern liberals,

prone to foreign ideas that were subversive to their religious heritage.

For Low Church Episcopalians, who thought of themselves more as Protestants than Anglo-Catholics, Picturesque Gothic Vernacular was more commonly used; but it was by no means limited to them. That style could be, and was, used by all sorts of Protestants. Nevertheless, here too Ecclesiological Gothic left its mark; its influence was undoubtedly responsible for Episcopal churches, even in Picturesque Gothic Vernacular, being so consistently superior to others in architectural quality.

Presbyterian Gothic.   A distinctively Presbyterian sort of Gothic was not the result of a transplantation of Scottish culture in any colonial sense, but was instead the reflection of nineteenth-century Presbyterian Church history. In 1843 the established Church of Scotland was split by a sizable "Free Church" movement, whose adherents frequently had money and will enough to make architectural statements of their convictions in the form of a distinctive kind of church building. Counterpart to Pugin's Catholic Gothic and the Episcopalians' Ecclesiological Gothic was the style developed by Frederick Thomas Pilkington during the 1850s and 1860s for Presbyterian churches at Ayr, Irvine, Kelso, Dundee, Penicuik, and Barclay Church Tolcross in Edinburgh. In the 1870s comparable churches were commissioned for Presbyterian congregations all over North America. A fine example is First Presbyterian in Albion, New York, but by far the most dramatic were in Ontario—often called "the British Empire's Scotch colony." Especially noteworthy were Central Presbyterian in Galt of the 1880s and First Presbyterian in Brockville of 1878–79 *[4.46, 4.47]*.

Presbyterian Gothic is distinguished by centralizing plans. It has squarish, lozenge, oval shapes (sometimes expressed on the exterior, sometimes encased in a more conventionally rectangular shell) with curving banks of pews in two or more tiers; the whole is focused on an oval platform, which formed the base of the composition (characteristically, the minister was at a level lower than the congregation), and on which stood pulpit, communion table, and an organ with exposed pipes. These traditions (except for the organ) derived from seventeenth- and eighteenth-century Presbyterian usage; now they were given vertical proportions and Gothic details: narrow pointed windows, with distinctive colored glass set in nonfigural patterns derived from such medieval sources as illuminated manuscript borders; pews whose ends were pointed with inset traceried roundels. Presbyterian Gothic could have quite a lot of vaguely or explicitly medieval woodcarving, but it characteristically avoided features like floor tiles that suggested cathedrals or monasteries.

In the 1880s Presbyterian Gothic was displaced by an almost equally distinctive form of Romanesque, wherever heavy Scots and Scots–Irish populations were concentrated: in the Shenandoah valley and southwestern Virginia, for instance (Lynchburg Presbyterian, now United Methodist [1888]), or Ontario (from Chatham in the southwest [1892–93] to Winchester [1889–90] in the extreme east).

Technological Gothic Revival

This final substyle of the Gothic Revival differs from the others fundamentally. Its frame of reference was no longer the old religion of the West, but the new religion of human perfectibility through science, and it was manifest more in an attitude toward what architectural art entailed than by specific outward forms. The Technological Gothic Revival began to appear in the 1840s and 1850s. Those were the pivotal decades when mechanistic causality came to dominate advanced thought in the West; when Marx's allegedly scientific theory of social history appeared, alongside Darwin's allegedly scientific theories of prehistoric evolution, and the Impressionists' allegedly scientific theories of painting appeared as investigations of light, color, and psyches.

Already in his 1862 *Discourses on Architecture,* the celebrated French archaeological restorer Eugène Viollet-le-Duc had spelled out, in the spirit of his time, a new approach to historic architecture as the scientific study of early technology. He claimed no interest in any associations of Gothic with Christianity; he was interested in the technology of Gothic construction, in buttresses, rib vaulting, and the like. The whole idea of architecture projecting an image of social or religious or political conviction, as it had for thousands of years past—the basic principle inherent in Greek temples and Versailles, Holy Wisdom in Constantinople and Angkor Wat in Cambodia, the Colosseum and Chartres and Cluny—seemed simply to have vanished from his consciousness. In its place had come an idea of architecture as a work of art. Both implicit and explicit in the religion of human perfectibility through science was the idea of "men as Gods" (the phrasing H. G. Wells made famous); artists and architects were now to share in that aspiration. Their works were to be understood and appreciated as outward manifestations and proofs of the deification process. They were to be judged not by outward frames of reference, but by principles derived from the art itself, independent of social context.

Viollet-le-Duc's students, coming out of French humanist traditions, found his ideas barbaric. They objected; they protested; they drove him from his professorial chair. But his attitude proved to be the wave of the future. Already by 1872 it was enshrined in Charles Eastlake's *History of the Gothic Revival.* Whereas Eastlake's early chapters marshaled documentary evidence to show that the impulse behind the early Gothic Revival was its perceived ability to provide visual metaphors of continuity, his later ones argued a case for the Gothic Revival on fundamentally different grounds. The

4.48. *Begun in 1874, officially opened 24 May 1883, the soaring Brooklyn Bridge over New York's East River was one of three famous suspension bridges designed by John Augustus Roebling (the others are over the Niagara at Niagara Falls, 1851–66, and over the Ohio at Cincinnati, 1857–67). This section of Beal's Panoramic View of Lower Manhattan in 1876 from the Brooklyn side shows the Gothic towers under construction; their scaffolding creates an effect of tracery. (New-York Historical Society)*

4.49. *A view of the Brooklyn Bridge from Peck Slip on the Manhattan side in February 1982 (IMG:NAL). Colonel Washington Roebling was in charge after his father's death; later his wife Emily took over after he in turn was disabled by working too long on caissons. The bridge was a notable technological feat (first major use of steel for cables); its "poetry resides in its ability to soar free of its context and to be seen as an independent object apart, a freedom reinforced at the symbolic level by the aspirational Gothic gateways of its piers. At the practical level the bridge's functional aloofness was only too obvious to the commuters forced to cope daily with its absolutely unconsidered connections to the cities at either end." (Alan Trachtenberg,* Brooklyn Bridge: Fact and Symbol *[New York, 1965])*

most influential art critic of his day, John Ruskin, had proposed that Britain have as a national style something like Pisan Romanesque, or Venetian Gothic, or Trecento Florentine Protorenaissance. Instead of pointing out that such styles were ludicrously inappropriate for the proposed purpose, because they had no associations with British national history, and presented no image at all relevant to British society or the continuity of British institutions, Eastlake said they were ludicrous because Ruskin had failed to understand the principles of "good architecture." These, he suddenly announced, meant honest use of materials and direct expression of structure. On these grounds he defended the Ecclesiologists' long-standing preference for Northern Gothic as the best of all medieval styles. What Eastlake apparently failed to realize is that on these grounds *no* eclectic style whatever could be defended for long. It is not so much that one could easily imagine a kind of building that emphasized materials and structure and space for their own sakes to a degree impossible in archaeologically correct Gothic—indeed, the Crystal Palace for the Great Exhibition of 1850 in London had already provided an example; it is that on these grounds *all* historic architecture is and must be "bad." No historic style was ever created on the basis Eastlake assumes; none could ever be justified on his criteria. Eastlake has not only forgotten the social function that originally motivated the Gothic Revival; he has forgotten that architecture everywhere was invented to fulfill a distinct social function—most especially the original Gothic of the Île-de-France. And at this point we realize that Eastlake is taking for granted a fundamentally new concept of what the art of architecture is all about, one that seems to have developed quite suddenly in the twenty years 1840–60, and with such a sense of inevitability that few were conscious of the change taking place.

The logical consequence of this new concept is that whatever reason medieval people may have had for wanting tall buildings is of no importance to us; all that's relevant for moderns is the technology used to put them up, including the use of metal for spires and other details. *That* we can copy. *That* is all we need to copy, to create great buildings appropriate to our own era, the era of technology: structures consisting solely of exposed bearing elements—flying buttresses and rib vaults on piers without all the historicist freight of a cathedral. An immediate consequence of such thinking was the

Eiffel Tower, duly appearing in the 1880s and, after an initial shock, being accepted, then famed, then beloved as a monument to technology, an icon of applied science. The Gothic Revival, having shown us how such monuments might be built, has no more to offer.[20]

In America, monuments to technology were anticipated by a series of great bridges, of which the Brooklyn, begun in 1872, was and remains the most famous *[4.48, 4.49]*. It actually has Gothic arches, of course, but is revered—the centenary of its completion was observed with enormous pomp and fanfare in 1983—as a monument to technological accomplishment. Other bridges have Gothic elements too. Whether on this account they belong somehow in the Gothic Revival or whether they are utilitarian structures because elements like pointed arches have no associational meaning in this context, is possibly an arguable point. Spiritually they belong with Modern architecture, as was recognized by Siegfried Giedion, who so publicized them in the bible of Modernism, his *Space, Time, and Architecture.*

Viollet-le-Duc's concept of Technological Gothic as no more than a solution to structural problems thus appears a direct anticipation of the Bauhaus and the Radiant City, not to mention those semiotic and structuralist sorts of architectural writings that rest upon a premise that, as to understand the processes of thought is to understand reality, so to understand the processes of architecture (how its parts work, how architects perceive their operative processes) is to explain everything important about architecture. From *opus modernum* to Modernism: the Gothic Revival then, in addition to its other interests, forms a bridge or transition from romantic revivalist styles, with their allusive and associative meanings, through Picturesque styles, whose effects are primarily visual, to that Modern transformation in the whole concept of what architecture involves that we still live with—a continuing cultural expression.

The Gothic Revival as Continuing Cultural Expression

The Gothic Revival, like all movements in American architecture, corresponded to and manifested certain deep currents in American life that remain part of the ongoing stream. One, certainly, is religion in general, and evangelical religion in particular. Among intellectuals, that impulse has long been secularized into faith in salvation on earth via good works in some field of scientific endeavor (politics, technology, self-consciously Modern arts). But the Gothic Revival as such has survived, and in the service of a social function comparable to the original, in Popular/Commercial building. Here it is to be found especially in churches and funeral homes that proclaim adherence to Christian principles, built by people who fly in the face of the intellectual mainstream quite as defiantly as did many of the original users of American Gothic (see substyles in chapters 7 and 8).

Gothic persists, along with the patterns of thought it serves and expresses, for much the same reasons that it originally appeared on the American landscape: as an alternative to styles of life and art—in this case scientific/materialist/mechanistic-abstract-causal patterns of thought, and their architectural expressions—that fail to satisfy emotional needs or to correspond very closely to actual life experiences. As long as this situation continues, the demise of the Gothic Revival that has been so long and so often predicted will no doubt continue to be deferred.

Notes

1. At this time it was very much a non-mainline movement (for example, Saint Mary's Chapel for Baltimore Catholics in 1806, by Maximilien Godefroy; Old Saint Patrick's for New York Catholics in 1809). The versatile Latrobe, as an avant-gardist, also worked in Gothic, notably in Sedgeley outside Philadelphia as early as 1799 and Saint Paul's Episcopal in Alexandria, Virginia, in 1818–19. Saint Paul's may well have been the formal inspiration for the most important of all examples of this phase of the Gothic Revival, Irishman James O'Donnell's famous design for *La Paroisse,* Montreal's huge parish church of Notre-Dame, built 1823–29 *[4.43].* But Notre-Dame's ideological inspiration was quite different—the Cathedral of Orléans, also completed in 1829, a symbol of restored and resiliant Catholicism. I have summarized the argument in "Sainte-Croix d'Orléans," *Gazette des Beaux-Arts* (September 1988).

2. *Creating Central Park: The Papers of Frederick Law Olmsted,* III (Baltimore: Johns Hopkins University Press, 1983); see also David Schuyler, *The New Urban Landscape* (Baltimore: Johns Hopkins University Press, 1986). Such studies in depth of a few decades are relatively rare and provide an indispensable background for understanding stylistic change, since so far from a matter of simple shifts in "taste," it involves the total fabric of society. (Incidentally such studies also document how far back urban problems go; already in the 1850s and 1860s New York

was suffering from pollution, urban blight, encroachment of commerce on residential areas and the consequent collapse of land values, not to mention political strife on an ethnic basis—in this case, Irish displacing WASPS.)

3. Communication to author from David Schuyler, November 1987: "In *The New Urban Landscape,* pp. 114–28, I . . . attempt to interpret the parkway as innovation. There is no evidence at hand to *prove* this, but I believe the very term 'parkway' was chosen for two reasons: first, because it was meant to convey the meaning of approaches to the park [Central], though Olmsted (and perhaps Vaux) gave it a much broader meaning; second, because parkway was a different word than Haussmann's "avenue" or "boulevard," which A. H. Green and the Central Park Commission used to describe the streets they were constructing in Manhattan north of 59th Street in the 1860s." A detailed discussion of the matter is given in Glenn S. Orlin's "Roads and Parks in Harmony," *Washington History* 1/1 (1989): 59–70.

4. "Once understand that the function of revived medieval forms was to create a symbolic image of British nationalism, and you will realize that it was no accident that Tennyson should have chosen to write an epic poem about King Arthur; 'Idylls of the King' and Gothic Revival buildings like the Houses of Parliament are both facets of a single symbolic image of British institutions descending unbroken from a misty medieval past. This same image is the distinctive characteristic of Turner's paintings—ancient castles and towers . . . all painted 'upsun', dissolved in timeless haze. Nor is it any accident that Constable first achieved popular success with his pictures of Salisbury Cathedral shrouded in its ancient elms. Nor that alongside the Gothic Revival in architecture, a distinctive new linear drawing style filled with medieval allusions and borrowings should have been adopted by all the leading popular illustrators—Cruikshank, 'Phiz', Seymour, Doyle, Tenniel; these are all aspects of the same process of creating a symbolic national image." Alan Gowans, "Taste and Ideology: Principles for a New American Art History," in *The Shaping of Art and Architecture in Nineteenth-Century America* (New York: Metropolitan Museum of Art 100th Birthday Symposium, 1972), pp. 156–87.

5. By the 1850s specific associations of Gothic Revival with national British institutions lost their urgency, because monarchy and parliament were very stable and ideological support for them correspondingly less important. But a cult of chivalry derived from Gothic Revival impulses continued to flourish in Britain, manifested in such diverse ways as public-school games, Boy Scouts, and Boys' Brigade, right down to the Great War of 1914–18 (whose memorials were so often in Academic Gothic Revival styles). Mark Girouard has gone into this theme richly in *The Return to Camelot* (New Haven, Conn.: Yale University Press, 1983).

6. Some perception of this quality no doubt contributed to Mark Twain's indignation over Louisiana's old state capitol: "It is pathetic enough that a whitewashed castle . . . should ever have been built in this otherwise honorable place; but it is much more pathetic to see this

architectural falsehood undergoing restoration. . . . By itself the imitation castle is doubtless harmless, and well enough; but as a symbol and breeder and sustainer of maudlin Middle-Age romanticism [noble Southern knights easily routing crass Northern clerks] . . . it is necessarily a hurtful thing and a mistake [people start wars only when they think they can win]" (*Life on the Mississippi*, 1874, ch. 38).

7. Illustrative is the controversy over introduction of Gothic Revival into Virginia Episcopal Church architecture, recounted by James McAllister, "Architecture and Change in the Diocese of Virginia," *Historical Magazine of the Protestant Episcopal Church* 45/3 (1976):297–323.

8. Home as a place where offspring were inculcated with ideals of "work and sacrifice for the common good" was for Beecher "the true Protestant system . . . the Heaven-devised plan of the family state." In 1865 she described in a *Harper's New Monthly Magazine* article ("How to Redeem Woman's Profession from Dishonor") how plan and furnishings (often set in niches with pointed arches) are alike to be determined in the light of the idea that the home is a kind of church, its round of daily, weekly, and seasonal chores a kind of church year. All this is admirably described by Dolores Hayden, "Catharine Beecher and the Politics of Housework," in Susana Torre, ed., *Women in American Architecture* (New York: Whitney Library of Design, 1977). Hayden argues that the ultimate effect of Beecher's advocacies was, ironically in view of her career as a single woman and professional writer, to set a pattern for women as suburban housewives.

9. "Americans of the time, as well as foreign visitors, noted again and again the ideological affinity between Jacksonian democracy and the various species of revivalistic religion so prominent in the period, yet no one has yet worked out the details of that affinity and tested to what degree egalitarianism in religion carried over into social preferences, by studying the political and economic behavior of regions most affected by evangelical religion" (John William Ward, "The Age of the Common Man," *The Reconstruction of American History*, ed. John Higham [New York: Harper & Row, 1962], p. 97). As far as I know, the comment is still valid, at least in regard to a logical catalyst, the Gothic Revival in architecture.

10. See Thomas J. McCormick, "The Early Work of J. L. Silsbee," *In Search of Modern Architecture: A Tribute to Henry-Russell Hitchcock* (New York, 1982), p. 172.

11. H. M. Dexter, "Meeting Houses Considered Historically and Suggestively," *Congregational Quarterly* 1/9 (1859):206. This important article is that rarity in nineteenth-century (and for that matter twentieth-century) architectural writings, an attempt to associate styles with ideas and ideological stances. It is cited, for example, in Carroll L. V. Meeks's pioneering "Romanesque before Richardson," *Art Bulletin* 35/1 (1953).

12. Some decades before the restoration of Ottonian architecture in the Rhineland after Germany was unified in the Empire of 1871 (for example the cathedrals of Mainz, Worms, Speyer, abbey of Maria Laach), revival of Romanesque as a German national expression was well

under way: Munich's Ludwigskirche was built 1829–43; Potsdam's Friedenskirche in 1845–48; and between 1832 and 1835 Schinkel built four suburban churches in Romanesque style for rapidly expanding Berlin.

13. A climactic example is the magnificent German Romanesque Crouse Memorial College, the second major building at Syracuse University in upstate New York, built 1887–89 by donor John Crouse (grandson of Jacob Krauss, emigrant from Saxony, probably purchaser also of Leopold von Ranke's library for Syracuse). A local architect was nominally in charge; see Evamaria Hardin, *Archimedes Russell: Upstate Architect* (Syracuse: Syracuse University Press, 1980).

14. Robert Dale Owen's *Hints on Public Architecture* of 1849, whose principal subject was Renwick's Smithsonian design (Renwick apparently helped with both text and illustrations), especially mentioned the influence of two books published in 1835: William Whewell's *Architectural Notes on German Churches*, with Maria Laach featured as a frontispiece, and Thomas Hope's *Essay on Architecture*, which praised and illustrated Romanesque churches from many European countries, but especially Germany.

15. Page Smith, *The Nation Comes of Age* (New York: McGraw-Hill, 1981), pp. 504, 505.

16. The variety of small Episcopal and Anglican churches of Picturesque Gothic Vernacular style is astonishing. All over the continent you commonly find small towns with two little architectural jewels—a bank and an Episcopal (or Anglican, in Canada) church. Western Canada, and especially British Columbia, where in the nineteenth century the Church of England was a kind of colonizing agent, is remarkably rich in them.

17. "The huge Irish immigration into England was accommodated in the cheapest possible fashion; in those Catholic areas where funds were available the influence of certain religious orders of an Italian origin or character . . . the Redemptorists, the Oratorians, the Passionists . . . worked towards an Italian style, and the famous and powerful Cardinal Wiseman's tastes were directly at variance with Medievalism, and . . . most of the churches erected under his authority were of a quasi-Italian character" (Charles Eastlake, *A History of the Gothic Revival* [1872; reprinted 1975 by American Life Foundation, Watkins Glen, N. Y.], p. 347).

18. Quote from Bishop William Meade, *Old Churches, Ministers, and Families of Virginia* (1855), II, 116–24, referring to notes made twenty years earlier. The context is presented in my *King Carter's Church* (Victoria, B.C: University of Victoria, 1969).

19. James McAllister, "Architecture and Change in the Diocese of Virginia," *Historical Magazine of the Protestant Episcopal Church* 45/3 (1976): 321. McAllister cautions that there may be exceptions to his statement; what is striking is that such a claim could be made at all.

20. There is a coincidental American connection: Viollet's *Entretiens* was published in 1881 in Boston in an English translation by Henry Van Brunt of Boston's patrician Ware & Van Brunt architectural firm. Since by Boston came Viollet-le-Duc, so also by Boston came the Bauhaus.

5.3. North American cities great and small, old and new, and coast to coast took pride in a bustling Main Street lined with new Picturesque commercial buildings; prints of them constituted a form of civic advertising. This view of King Street in Toronto c. 1880, from **Picturesque Canada,** is typical. Take away the flags bearing the Union Jack and it could be anywhere on the continent.

5
PICTURESQUE IMAGERY OF
A COMMERCIAL REPUBLIC, c. 1845–c. 1885

Picturesque Styles
in Their Time and Place

"Where Moses Yale Beach, in the 1840's, had found barely a score of New Yorkers worth a million dollars or more, and contemporary researches in other cities may have uncovered, all told, another score, a careful tally by the *New York Tribune* in 1892 disclosed that the number of American millionaires that year had risen above 4,000. Beach's gauge of wealth had been $100,000. By now, estates in the millions had become much more common than those one-tenth as large only fifty years before."[1]

What relation the dramatic increase of wealth in America between the 1840s and the 1890s had to the Civil War of 1861–65 has long been debated. Whether under specious cover of concern for oppressed slaves, Northern capitalists got a conquered agrarian South to exploit; whether the quarrel over slavery was exacerbated by the great shift from handicraft artisanship to serflike factory labor during the 1840–60 decades, which induced massive increases in Northern immigration and population growth not matched in the South; whether Southern society preserved older values lost in the North's vulgar scramble for money—all these questions have been endlessly argued. But about the relationship of Picturesque styles to these processes there can be no argument. They were its expression and to some degree its instrument.

So much more of the furniture that survives in Picturesque styles is mass-produced, compared to earlier times. And there is so much of it! Some pieces are preserved and displayed in museums *[5.1, 5.2]*, but the majority has remained in use in old houses. For every one or two craftsmen who produced furniture in the 1820s, there were a hun-

dred hired hands at work on machines in great factories by the 1880s, turning out pieces by the thousand for shipment on the new railroads to cities and hamlets all over the continent.[2] Once upon a time individuals stood some chance of knowing who—if not themselves—made their chairs and cupboards (not to mention their clothes, carriages, carts, and crockery). Now they knew as much about the manufacturers as we do today—that is to say, nothing; it was all done in factories owned by amassers of great capital, who neither knew nor cared about the work process so long as it returned a profit.[3]

The Picturesque architectural past is best recaptured in old prints and photos—Main Streets with their bustling horse-drawn streetcars and carriages and carts, with their gay striped awnings and flags all flying, with their sprouting cornices and jungles of poles and wires *[5.3, on p. 164]*; residential areas with spacious houses and sweeping lawns in front, and generously proportioned carriage houses behind *[5.4]*.

Of such scenes patches survive here and there: in small towns close enough to a metropolis to draw some economic lifeblood from them, yet not so close as to be swallowed up in suburbs *[5.8–5.10]*; commercial buildings and churches and row houses still in use downtown *[5.11, 5.12, 5.70]*; slummy ruins urban and rural alike, become picturesque now in the original early romantic sense, like blasted trees and ancient tumbledown castles *[5.13]*.

Sometimes sanitized versions have been preserved, neatened and tidied, or frozen into museums—often with admirable correctness, but only feeble approximations to the feels and smells and noises of everyday life: cigar smoke in the drapes, macassar oil on chair backs, horse manure on the

5.1. A Classical infrastructure still consistently governs proportions and creates a unified visual effect in this Italianate parlor from the Robert J. Milligan house, built in Saratoga Springs, New York, in 1853, and reassembled in the Brooklyn Museum. But it is characteristic of this first of the Picturesque styles, as of later ones, that all edges and outlines—of chairs and tables, of windows and doors and fireplace—look as if they were seeded with ornament somehow, sprouting and growing independently of its setting, as its Rococo prototypes never did. (The Brooklyn Museum, gift of Sarah Milligan Rand, Kate Milligan Brill, and the Dick S. Ramsay Fund)

5.2. A Classical sense for symmetry still underlies much of the furnishing of this smoking room from the John D. Rockefeller houses, built in New York City in 1864–65 (on a site now occupied by the Museum of Modern Art), remodeled in 1884, and reassembled in the Brooklyn Museum. But now the proportions have been affected by Gothic verticality, so that the general effect is quite different from the Italianate Milligan parlor; there is a mixture of diverse stylistic traditions here. And ornament has spread over everything, leaving no surface plain. (The Brooklyn Museum, gift of John D. Rockefeller, Jr., and John D. Rockefeller III)

5.4. Plate 19 from Exterior Decoration: A Treatise on the Artistic Use of Colors in the Ornamentation of Buildings, *a new edition of a house-painting guide first published in 1885 with twenty color plates and fifty paint samples. (Athenaeum of Philadelphia, 1976)*

5.6. The mansion that Reuben Fenton had built for himself in 1863 outside the western New York center of Jamestown, by local architect Aaron Hall, is now maintained by the Fenton Historical Society, chartered in 1964 by the University of the State of New York as a local educational institution and historical center. As such, it has preserved the mansion's exterior and three interior rooms—kitchen, parlor (with hallway), and Nanny's room. Other rooms have been devoted to a research library, Swedish Heritage, Italian Heritage, pioneer tools, and the like, so visitors are necessarily aware that they are in a museum rather than a reconstruction. The most prominent exterior object is Fenton's life-size statue on a tall plinth, executed by Bryant Baker and erected in 1932 by Fenton's daughter, in part to help rehabilitate his reputation. As the first post–Civil War Governor of New York and later United States Senator, Fenton (one of the founders of the Republican Party) was popularly known as "The Soldiers' Friend," but toward the end of his career he had to resign under a cloud of scandal. (IMG:NAL)

5.7. An icon of High Picturesque American architecture, perhaps its most famous example, is the William Carson house in Eureka, California, built by San Francisco architects Samuel and Joseph Cather Newsom between 1884 and 1886. Inordinately and mindlessly damned during the decades of Modernist supremacy, it seems threatened now with inordinate and mindless praise. Although never intended to be inconspicuous—Carson, like Reuben Fenton, made his fortune in lumbering, and his mansion originally overlooked the vast lumberyards he owned and operated—it never had anything like its present Versaillesque approach either: a formal, terraced avenue that makes a public monument of it. (IMG:NAL)

5.5. View along Fourth Street from the intersection of Main, in the Iowa town of Grinnell, famous for its college and as site of Louis Sullivan's Merchants' National (now Poweshiek County) Bank of 1913–14. Sullivan's bank is at the far end of this view; in the foreground appears a typical shop (store with apartments above) of the 1890s. Such a view could illustrate Robert Twombley's contention that Sullivan's late bank commissions were basically a result of cultural lag; these little towns still liked Sullivan's Picturesque style and the idea of getting work by a nationally known architect, without realizing that he had gone "out of fashion" in reputation and style both. (IMG:NAL)

drive; carriage wheels squeaking and horse hooves clopping and frantic buzzings from houseflies trapped on sticky streamers *[5.5–5.7]*. Nor can we easily recapture the kind of thrill they produced on those who first built and saw them.

The contemporary Postmodern city, like its predecessors, has striking eye appeal. To fly in at night over a city swathed in multicolored strings of light is to behold a sight unique to our generation. But it is not Picturesque in the nineteenth-century sense. Only old photographs or prints can suggest the kind of awe that people living in the 1860s and 1870s felt before the Picturesque skyscrapers and mansions of their cities or the Main Streets of their small towns *[5.14]*. Sinclair Lewis captured something of it in his description of Gopher Prairie seen through the eyes of a Scandinavian girl from a remote Minnesota farm:

And the stores! . . . more than four whole blocks! The Bon Ton Store—big as four barns. . . . A drug store with a soda fountain that was just huge, awful long, and all lovely marble; and on it there was a great big lamp with the biggest shade you ever saw—all different kinds colored glass stuck together. . . . A hotel, awful high, higher than Oscar Tollefson's new red barn: three stories, one right on top of another; you had to stick your head back to look clear up to the top. . . .

How could they have so many stores? Why! There was one just for tobacco alone, and one . . . for pictures and vases and stuff, with oh, the dandiest vase made so it looked just like a tree trunk. [*Main Street*, chapter 4]

Main Street's heroine felt a good deal less ecstatic about it; but she was from big cities like Chicago and Saint Paul and had Progressive social notions. Sinclair Lewis, a Progressive himself, described in *Babbit* a mansion "in the 'nice parts' of Zenith as they appeared from 1860 to 1900" as

a red brick immensity with gray sandstone lintels and a roof of slate in courses of red, green, and dyspeptic yellow. There are two anemic towers, one roofed with copper, the other crowned with castiron ferns. The porch is like an open tomb; it is supported by squat granite pillars above which hang frozen cascades of brick. At one side of the house is a huge stained-glass window in the shape of a keyhole. But the house has an effect not at all humorous. It embodies the heavy dignity of those Victorian financiers who . . . created a somber oligarchy by gaining control of banks, mills, land, railroads, mines.

Such are the mansions appearing alongside biographies of the self-made men in the *National Cyclopaedia of American Biography* or on borders of bird's-eye views of burgeoning new industrial towns from the 1880s and 1890s.

5.8. Port Townsend on the Olympic Peninsula in far northwest Washington had so good a harbor and prospects of becoming metropolis for the region that many fine buildings were erected there from the 1870s through the 1890s. Then it turned out Seattle on Puget Sound had an even better harbor. Main railroads chose to terminate there, and Port Townsend's growth stopped. But it still served its own peninsula, rich in fish, timber, and fruit and so remained more or less intact. Today it is one of the best places *to sense what a burgeoning town of the late 1880s and early 1890s felt like. In this view the town is dominated by the Jefferson County Courthouse, built in 1892 in Richardsonian style by a young architect with offices in Seattle, Willis A. Ritchie. From its 124-foot tower a clock constructed in 1892 by the E. Howard Watch and Clock Company of Boston has ever since been booming out the hours from a 3500-pound, 6-inch-thick bell. (IMG:NAL)*

5.9. *Cape May on the seacoast of southern New Jersey was a famous nineteenth-century resort, accessible from what was even then becoming the Philadelphia/New York corridor. Its popularity never waned, but competitors kept it from growing too fast;* *consequently it has remained another "living museum" of Picturesque architectural landscape, though still very much a popular and prosperous resort as well. (IMG:NAL)*

Such associations are worth keeping in mind these days, when nostalgia for life in a mid-nineteenth-century small city is running so high. Disneyland began Main Street's rehabilitation with its neatly scaled down and wholesomely sanitized image of that Main Street in Missouri where once the child Walt walked. Disneyland did for middle-class taste in the 1970s what Williamsburg had done for middle-class taste in the 1930s. Time did the rest. As The Gilded Age (its own critics' name) receded into a golden past, so did recollections of the price to be paid for competition unregulated by law or social custom: insecurity and greed and cruelty and corruption.[4] One sweet lingering scent was left hanging in the mental air: of dear hearts and gentle people living dear, gentle, and above all un-regulated lives. Not for those folks the trammels of income-tax forms, zoning restrictions, anti-discrimination laws. O happy age that knew nothing of telephone surveys, of inflation, of nuclear war!

O admirable too the architectural memorials to such innocent hopes and dreams! For such purposes classical forms would no longer do. Already in the very first years of the nineteenth century a distinguished American classicist had mournfully predicted that study of Greek and Roman texts must soon decay in the United States, for a variety of reasons but chiefly because "The spirit of our people is *commercial.* It has been said, and perhaps

5.10. *Courthouse squares often retain a pristine character if no explosive growth occurs; so the Clarion County Courthouse square in central Pennsylvania still feels very much as it must have in 1900. The courthouse was designed by local architect E. M. Butz and built in 1884–85; it has the period's pronounced verticality and mixture of motifs from a wide range of sources. The Civil War monument dates from 1896 (many small towns could not afford a monument until thirty years after that devastating conflict), but it is still strongly Picturesque, with its emphasis on variegated textures and clumsy confusion of bulk with monumentality. (IMG:NAL)*

5.11. Seven out of the nine buildings in this view of downtown Milwaukee taken in February 1974 were still in Picturesque styles. (IMG:NAL)

5.12. Part of San Francisco's legendary charm derives from rows of Italianate frame row houses from the late 1870s through the 1880s that have somehow survived earthquake and escaped fire, like these on Gough Street looking east from Chestnut. (IMG:NAL)

5.13. This abandoned row of contiguous town houses in French Second Empire style from the 1870s, on Front Street three blocks from Main Street in Binghamton, New York, had "seen better days" when this photo was taken in August 1980. But even in ruin it had a kind of grandeur. (IMG:NAL)

with some justice, that the *love of gain* peculiarly characterizes the inhabitants of the United States."[5] That Americans more than other people have some detestable preference for being rich over being poor is not a dubious proposition, merely absurd.[6] But the American system undeniably has made it possible for more Americans to get rich than people elsewhere. And because more Americans got richer, architectural displays of wealth were undeniably more widespread and lavish than elsewhere. Whence all those Picturesque county courthouses and town halls and stores, simultaneously both grand and quaint, with their brickwork patternings and frilly tinwork, their flamboyant cornices, their slender flagpoles with big shiny balls on top. Whence no doubt another reason for late-twentieth-century Americans wishing to recapture something of that past Picturesque age: they had been starved for richness for so long, by an architecture proclaiming "less is more" and extolling beatitudes of starkness and barrenness, the visual virtues of poverty, that reaction was inevitable.

Wishes being parents to deeds, Picturesque architecture is duly reappearing, sometimes through restoration, sometimes reconstruction, sometimes disguised as Postmodernism[7]—all demonstrating still, as Macaulay said in the 1840s, that

> we are under a deception similar to that which misleads the traveller in the Arabian desert. Beneath the caravan all is dry and bare; but far in advance, and far in the rear, is the semblance of refreshing waters. The pilgrims hasten forward and find nothing but sand where, an hour before, they had seen a lake. They turn their eyes and see a lake where, an hour before, they were toiling through sand. A similar illusion seems to haunt nations. . . . We too shall, in our turn, be outstripped, and in our turn be envied. [*History of England* I, chapter 3]

It is an incongruous end for a movement that began in Europe with the delicate elitist writings of eighteenth-century aesthetes[8] and was fortified by early-nineteenth-century self-conscious "sensibility."

Picturesque taste first became apparent in avant-garde English and continental architecture around 1800–10, and Picturesque styles remained popular there throughout the nineteenth century. American Picturesque styles began to appear considerably later.[9] The fashion for Italianate, the first major Picturesque substyle in the United States, did not displace Roman and Greek Revivals in popularity until the period c. 1845–60. But when they did come in, Picturesque styles flourished in the United

5.14. The glamor of Picturesque skyscrapers lasted well past 1900—witness this illustration from Scribners *in 1909 (no. 46, September 1909, p. 259), showing Richard Morris Hunt's Tribune Building of 1873–76 as enlarged with additional upper floors in 1905 and George B. Post's World Building of 1889–90. The Singer Building was built as late as 1906–8. All are now gone.*

States with unparalleled exuberance, partly because they took wooden forms, which allowed freer imaginative treatment than stone or brick, partly because democratic institutions and attitudes overcame inhibiting traditional discipline much more easily, partly because wealth was more easily amassed in this vast, rich new country.

French Second Empire style was all the rage from the 1860s on. By c. 1870–85 Picturesque taste was at its height. Thereafter it was superseded by Academic taste in architecturally educated circles, though it survived on popular and vernacular levels for another few decades at least; in Popular/Commercial and Postmodern forms it still thrives.

Picturesque styles were particularly lively in the Midwest, the Rocky Mountain states, and the West, for there were found those new towns where the Picturesque was most at home. There were found that rawness and naiveté and naked love of gain that it expressed so well. Not that Picturesque was limited to those regions. It was the first visual manifestation of American culture expanding across the whole continent, so that a "boom-town" store front or High Picturesque villa will look much the same

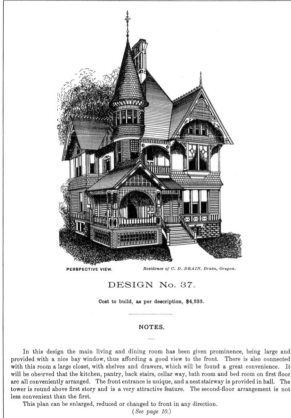

PERSPECTIVE VIEW.   *Residence of C. D. DRAIN, Drain, Oregon.*

DESIGN No. 37.

Cost to build, as per description, $4,535.

———

NOTES.

In this design the main living and dining room has been given prominence, being large and provided with a nice bay window, thus affording a good view to the front. There is also connected with this room a large closet, with shelves and drawers, which will be found a great convenience. It will be observed that the kitchen, pantry, back stairs, cellar way, bath room and bed room on first floor are all conveniently arranged. The front entrance is unique, and a neat stairway is provided in hall. The tower is round above first story and is a very attractive feature. The second-floor arrangement is not less convenient than the first.

This plan can be enlarged, reduced or changed to front in any direction.

(See page 10.)

5.15. *So pervasive was the fondness for breaking sharp outlines that it was carried out even in mass-prefabricated houses, where such details added incalculable extra expense. This is a house advertised in the catalogue of George F. Barber of Knoxville, Tennessee, probably the first offerer of a house totally prefabricated in every way. It is described as the home of C. D. Drain; it was in fact built in 1892 in the Oregon town of Drain and still stands there, unrecognized as a prefab until recently. Originally the house cost $4,535—by no means cheap in those days—and required over three hundred crates to ship. But all the necessary features to break up outlines were included: peak ornaments, turned and carved decoration throughout, internal gable ornaments, dentils, horizontal bands, fish-scale and other kinds of decorative shingle, turned portico balustrades, carved panels, clapboard sidings, beveled or leaded glass transoms, small window panes, carved panels of many sorts, tower finials, and the rest.*

in Missouri or Montana or Maine. Because of the mysteries of cultural lag, the dates vary uniformly from east to west.[10] But that is all part of a broader uniformity that is the Picturesque styles' most lasting legacy on the American landscape.

Definition and Identifying Characteristics

Ordinary usage in American architectural history does not admit the term "Picturesque style." There are a multitude of styles—Italianate, French Second Empire, Richardsonian Romanesque, Queen Anne, to name only the most obvious—to which picturesqueness is fundamental, but there is no generic term covering them all. "High Victorian" has been used on occasion, or just "Victorian," and there is historical justification for that. "Picturesque Eclecticism" is more exact. But it would seem logical to put under one umbrella all those styles whose common picturesqueness is far more significant than differences in detail or emphasis. For picturesqueness was *the* key quality in architecture over many decades. The transition that had begun in the Gothic Revival, from the historic and traditional understanding of architecture as an art of creating purposeful visual metaphors to an assumption that the art of architecture is first and foremost a matter of visual effects, was consummated by the Picturesque attitude dominating all design for so many decades.

"Picturesque" architecture, as the name implies, was inspired by pictures, via idealized landscapes admired by eighteenth-century romantics for giving beholders a thrill. Their thrill derived in part from pleasing visual combinations of spaces, colors, textures, and ornament; and in part from a variety of pleasing nostalgic sentiments derived from associated ideas of every sort—literary, patriotic, religious.[11] But during the earlier nineteenth century, that associational side of the Picturesque began evaporating. By mid-century, specific associations began to matter less and less, eye appeal more and more. At that point, specific Revivals of Gothic or Greek or Chinese or anything else began to dissolve. Distinctions among them were impossible to maintain, and pointless, too. What followed should be called phases rather than substyles. They are identifiable as much by how they used ornament as by what ornament they used.

Phases of Picturesque usage are roughly identifiable by (1) increasingly indiscriminate mixings of ornamental motifs; (2) an overall increase in the amount of ornament; (3) increasing use of ornament to produce effects of age and stability. Over the period c. 1860–c. 1885 these three developments go on simultaneously.

Indiscriminate mixing of all sorts of preceding styles is the most obvious characteristic of Picturesque generally. By the 1870s and early 1880s every imaginable ingredient had been stirred into the generic pot: textures and motifs of every sort from every past style, many of them mass-replicated. A royal array of domes and mansards, pilasters and pinnacles, urns, balconies, and balustrades was available for any who wished to evoke the splendors of Baroque France, Renaissance Italy, Gothic Flanders, or Elizabethan England on any Main Street in any prairie town. The field for borrowing was limitless. At the time it looked like a chaos of ostentation, and much of it was; yet in retrospect a pattern is discernible in the process.[12]

Amounts of ornament increased steadily throughout the Picturesque decades by a kind of inner necessity: once ornament was used for display and eye appeal rather than for some specific ideological or emotive association, every fresh increase in it *had* to be emulated, matched, and surpassed. So roof lines were edged in increasingly lavish cast-iron "gingerbread," window frames and door frames surrounded with increasingly lavish jig-sawed wooden ornaments *[5.15]*. Arrays of little knobs and tassels fringed the bottoms of furniture, arms and backs were covered by fussy little panels full of floral sprays or lacy antimacassars. Elaborately patterned wallpapers covered interior walls, a mass of ornamental detail into which merged motifs from bric-a-brac crowded onto plate rails.

Color contributed to lavishness of ornament, for color too was increasingly used in purely decorative ways, long gone past the associations or restraints of any specific historic style *[5.4]*. Rusticated gray stonework, mixed with polished red brick walls, might be picked out by touches of tile and wood contrasting in color and texture and plane. Roof tiles in green and purple patterns abounded; shingles stained fern green (later "garage green"), chocolate, mahogany, and rust sheathed not only parts of roofs but also walls, chimneys, verandas. Spindly white Colonial balusters might be found next to squat sturdy pillars in speckled red granite. Patterned floorings in different shades of brown and yellow ornamented interiors, along with

5.16. *Drawing by Stanford White published in the 1875* New York Sketch Book of Architecture, *of the William Watts-Sherman house in Newport, Rhode Island, built to Richardson's plans in 1875–76 (in 1879–81 White did some redecorating and an extension there). A remarkable example of the emerging architectural type of "summer cottage" for a leading New England family; in style, a remarkable example of masses of decorative effects and colors (pink granite in random ashlar with sandstone trim; shingles and half-timber in darkish reds and greens; stucco panels) producing a cumulative effect of monumental stability.*

stained glass windows of all sizes and sorts—some sporting elaborate figural compositions, others with no more than a chaste floral tendril or two; tiny amber bull's-eyes and ovals, huge floor-to-ceiling combinations of every glowing color on earth *[5.16]*.

The cumulative result of this increase in mixing and amounts of ornament was, paradoxically enough, to increase effects of age. Drawing on all styles, blurring all edges, basing color use on self-referential decorative schemes meant that no distinct reference to any one era in the past could be made. Picturesque buildings seemed to trail off into indefinite time, into pastness in general, rather than referring to any specific time or place.

Heaping ornament into masses that covered both exterior and interior forms meant that they became perceptible again as solid masses. Already in the 1850s the elaborate masses of carved ornament on Belter furniture began to produce this effect, and thereafter furniture came to rest on bases and legs ever more bulbous and ponderous. By the 1870s similar effects were everywhere perceptible in High Picturesque architecture as well—buildings ever

5.17. *"Solid" is the word for this house, designed in fashionable Richardsonian Romanesque style by Frank Freeman and built in 1889 on Riverside Drive at 108th Street in New York. (From* A History of Real Estate, Building, and Architecture in New York City, *1898)*

more steadily anchored to the ground by lower stories made ever more massive in effect by combinations of stone foundations, *porte-cochères,* and spreading verandas. This trend climaxed in Richardsonian Romanesque *[5.17].* Whether in wood or stone, Richardsonian Romanesque buildings were really masses of textural or morphological ornament cumulatingly producing an effect of tremendous solidity.

Whence the style's sudden and enormous popularity: here, finally, was the ultimate formula for carrying out the deep social purposes of Picturesque styles: creation of visual metaphors of the stability of newly rich capitalist families and of the promise of the capitalist system to provide maximum egalitarian opportunity consistent with personal liberty.

Social Function

To identify the characteristics of Picturesque styles is to describe their social function: they were determined, consciously or not, by an urge to legitimize wealth as democratic. It was to advertise wealth and so multiply it by conspicuous waste that ornament was so indiscriminately mixed, so abundant, ultimately so massive in effect.[13]

The idea of advertising wealth by conspicuously wasteful displays of ornament was not new; far from it. Kings and princes and spiritual potentates had long used this method of advertising their powers and resources: witness Chambord and Versailles, the Bishop's palace at Würzburg, and the Elizabethan country house. Seventeenth-century Dutch merchants made their prosperity manifest by the elaborate brickwork and scrolled gables of their town houses; drops on the overhangs of big New England saltboxes, and the elaborate turned balusters and spindles of the furniture inside, must have served something of the same function. The new element in nineteenth-century Picturesque styles was what could best be called the urgency of its luxuriance. There was something hysterical about it, as if the post–Civil War bourgeoisie somehow felt compelled to display how untrammeled they were from interference and constraint by any other class; how the equality in which they so earnestly believed had not been jeopardized by inordinate amassings of wealth.

It was important to affirm egalitarianism at a time when a class of the very rich was forming concomitant with a new class of the very poor, produced by an unprecedented volume of immigration, and when the possibility of passing from one to the other seemed increasingly difficult.[14] This social function too was admirably fulfilled by Picturesque styles. Their dissolution of all historicist ornament into one great indiscriminate bath meant that *everybody* could understand Picturesque architecture. There was nothing *to* understand. No literary allusions, no subtleties of meaning. You just took in the visual effects. Rich and poor, educated and illiterate, cultured and barbarian, colonial patrician and raw immigrant, all were equal before the Picturesque.

The massiveness of later Picturesque styles also functioned to alleviate the age's intellectual malaise. During the decades between 1840 and 1860, what was called then the "conflict of science with religion," long incipient, came to focus in intellectual circles, and began spreading among the educated everywhere. It aggravated other social and economic uneasinesses, so that the "massy piles" with satisfying intimations of stability that Picturesque styles began producing in the 1870s and 1880s not only shored up the social pretensions of merchants and industrialists fresh off the farm, or Southerners dispossessed in rank, but also those in all stations of life who felt their traditional religious beliefs imperiled by the steady drift toward scientific thought in general and Darwinism in particular. Never before or since have American churches been built so massively.

Applications of Picturesque Styles to Architectural Types

Picturesque styles were especially well suited to the social functions of two architectural types—mansion and shop—which set the tone for all others.

Whereas mansions in National Democratic Classical Revival styles proclaimed that within there dwelt a virtuous, patriotic citizen with civic responsibilities, country villas and grand town mansions in Picturesque styles proclaimed that within there dwelt a rich, materially successful citizen, responsible to nobody. Successive substyles drew out that central theme. Italianate of the 1840s and 1850s retained some vestiges of the Classical style's public coding both in architecture *[5.18]* and furniture *[5.1]*: there is a formal front door and a formal front parlor. High Picturesque mansions of the 1860s

5.18. New York State Senator William Johnson's fine Italianate mansion on Cayuga Street in Seneca Falls was built in the late 1850s in the first of the fashionable Picturesque styles, with appropriate eave brackets and pairs of round-headed windows, a squarish tower with flattish pyramidal roof, and a spreading veranda. But it retained a Classical sense of symmetry appropriate to the dignity of a public figure; manifestly still, like Classical Revival temple-houses, home of a Virtuous Citizen of the Republic.

5.19. Corresponding to the Picturesque mansion's inconspicuous entrance was the tendency toward totally private use of its interior spaces. For this family portrait, international financier Andrew Allen, based in Montreal but operating out of New York and London as well, commissioned a composite—separate images of family members informally posed were pasted onto an interior of the main drawing room, then rephotographed. The room is very grand: crammed with Picturesque ornament, its ceiling palatially high and its dimensions enormous compared to counterparts only a few decades earlier. Yet the room does not function as a formal reception area, as such spaces had until very recently; the royal family is not "receiving" anyone, but posed as if merely enjoying each other's company. For this king—and his powers of course are kingly—need not show himself and his family to his subjects; the big capitalist's relationship to his subjects and the outside world is never direct, but through intermediaries—front companies and corporations, political appointees, and the like. (Notman Photographic Archives, McCord Museum, McGill University)

and 1870s visually denied public access, as their entrances were hidden in swathes of veranda and within and behind towers *[5.5, 5.6]*, and the formal front parlor became as private as every other room *[5.19]*. And Richardsonian Romanesque mansions of the 1880s were mighty fortresses for defending privacy behind bastion-like walls, complete with turreted donjon towers *[5.17]*.

Besides mansions proper, two subtypes of mansion first appeared on the American scene in Picturesque styles: hotel (including summer hotel, a very large category in the mid- and late-nineteenth century)[15] and later, motel. Both were variants of "The Mansion You Can Rent." As all distinctions within such types were determined by wealth, they became emblems of an era when wealth was increasingly the measure of success, happiness, and status, and Picturesque styles were correspondingly appropriate to them.

Thanks to Picturesque styles, the small hotel acquired distinctive features, most notably long porches extending across the widest side and sometimes around all sides, thus forming a transitional space from street to lobby or bar and spelling out "restricted public space" and ornamental cornices proclaiming "commercial function" *[5.20]*. As for bigger hotels, Picturesque lavishness advertised claims that only money was now required to command luxuries reserved in earlier ages for princes

and nobles *[5.21, 5.22]*. And indeed palatial hotels that began to appear in American cities after the Civil War did offer luxuries unmatched anywhere else in their own time, and by only the greatest palaces of earlier ages. They were a distinctive glory of American cities and were the first type of American architecture to be truly world famous, not least because of the lavish Picturesque styles applied to them.[16] Postmodernism has rehabilitated their fame (cf. 9.25).

Applied to apartments, Picturesque styles could establish by amount and variety of ornament what class of renter was expected, therefore what class of neighbors to expect in any given building. Lavish ornament inside and out proclaimed the availability of a mansion fit for royalty *[5.23]*; its absence indicated a tenement. And "apartments," by their name and its contrast to the English "flat," testify to a demand for privacy or "apartness" from society. "Flat" implies some variant of the urban row house, being in origin and conception the horizontal unit that results when you rent a two-to-five-story row house by stories. "Apartment," by contrast, is a suite of rooms feeding off a central space (which need not be and originally often was not all on one story); in other words, a separate sort of unit, conceived as a conveniently located and serviced counterpart to the freestanding palatial villa/mansion that developed from the late 1850s on.[17] Architec-

5.20. *The Holbrooke Hotel in Grass Valley opened for business in 1851; the present building, with bar, was completed in 1862. It also is a valuable demonstration of how the older concept of hotels as inns, defensive shelters for travelers (like the* caravansari *of the Ottoman Empire, or the mile houses on English highroads), was subsumed by the modern concept of "luxury mansion for rent" and so identified by such architectural symbols as a long porch and, in this case, "boom-town [commercial] front." (IMG:NAL)*

5.21. *This wood engraving of the inner courtyard of the Palace Hotel in San Francisco illustrated George Augustus Sala's 1883* America Revisited. *Guests' carriages are arriving in the court through an entrance archway from the street, just as visitors were admitted to the great palaces of Renaissance Italy. That "Palace" was one of the commonest of all names for American hotels is by no means accidental; palaces were their prototype. Introduction of elevators in the 1860s made their size almost limitless; this one, built around 1870, already was big enough to accommodate twelve hundred guests.*

5.22. *Two famous sights in the United States, dating from the 1870s, not to be omitted from any picture book were New York's Grand Union hotel (right) and Grand Central Depot, as seen in Asher and Adams's* New Columbian Railroad Atlas and Pictorial Album of American Industry, *1884.*

5.23. Among the first apartment buildings in Washington, D.C. was Portland Flats at Thomas Circle, begun in 1879 (demolished 1962). Its luxuriousness (at 150 dollars per month, as contrasted to average rentals of 50 dollars for an entire house) was proclaimed by ornamental details borrowed more or less directly from famous hotels like the Arlington (1868) and Ebbit House (1872). (Kiplinger Washington Collection, photograph c. 1950)

5.24. A surprisingly large number of early office buildings have survived on back streets of deep downtown New York. This is 75 Murray Street, off lower Broadway, built in 1858 with James Bogardus as the architect. Once upon a time the commercial areas of Manhattan and other American cities were lined with such low-rise offices in Italianate jackets. (IMG:NAL)

tural character again was developed in order to express degrees of wealth.

Picturesque styles as proclamations of wealth were as effectively applied to commercial architecture as to mansions—even more so, perhaps, since if shop types are to carry out their social function, displaying wealth is mandatory rather than optional.

Two broad sorts of social function are served by Picturesque styles on commercial buildings, developing through the century from the 1850s onward. One is to promote an image of business associated with culture; that is, being a successful moneymaker is not incompatible with discriminating taste in cultural matters. This takes the form of associating commercial buildings with great past ages of world culture by means of architectural detail borrowed from them. The other is to show that culture (in this case, familiarity with art and architecture of the past) is not incompatible with technological progress. This takes the form of devising appropriate stylistic envelopes for the new kind of tall commercial building made possible by development of elevators and metal-cage construction.

By the 1850s it had become common already to deck shops and offices of all kinds with details taken from architecture associated with the merchant princes of Florence and Venice—usually Italianate, more rarely Gothic. Much of it was simply attached facade, often prefabricated in iron [5.24]. Siegfried

Giedion in *Space, Time, and Architecture* cited such buildings as evidence of how mid-nineteenth-century architecture anticipated twentieth-century technological potential, but also of how blind to that grand future were "Victorian" designers in their insistence upon casting those prefabrications in historicist, eclectic, borrowed forms. Apparently he could not or would not realize that these were not Modern buildings to be valued by how well they manifested work (the workings of parts with each other, the process of construction, in a scientific materialist or Marxist sense). Their intent was to manifest Culture. And they did so by eclectic detail. What made them successful—fulfill the social function required—were references to precedents for combinations of culture with business (look at the Medici of Renaissance Florence, who were great art patrons, great businessmen, great public benefactors too!) and combinations of art with technology (the metal cage is a great technological advance, but it does not therefore require you to jettison all traditional culture).

Picturesque styles applied to tall buildings had the social function of integrating with past human culture a kind of building otherwise in danger of being made into some soulless sort of upended egg crate. To so define them was the great merit of

Louis Sullivan's theories. "Picturesque" was a term Sullivan often used about his own work, and it is therefore not derogatory to classify his style in the Picturesque category.[18] For Picturesque designers generally had a humanizing intent. How well they succeeded is another matter: the Academic designers who followed them thought their effects too lavishly crude, and the Moderns who followed them despised the effort altogether. But in fairness, and for historical understanding, that kind of judgment needs to be suspended. They were meeting a kind of design problem quite new in the world.

Already from the 1830s commercial buildings of great size, sometimes occupying whole blocks, had begun to appear in American cities in response to new possibilities of concentrating raw materials and processing operations in one place, brought about by new ease of transportation (railway networks) and communications (mail, telegraph). The large commercial buildings were in turn concentrated in a few cities, preeminently New York. They were limited in height by the difficulty of renting offices more than seven floors up when stairs were the only access. Installation of safety elevators, from the late 1850s on, changed all that. Now the higher floors were the easiest to rent, because of their light, air, and prestige ("high" or "tall" has always had con-

5.25. *The rise of New York City to unchallenged financial mastery of the nation was marked by a transformation of its skyline. A forest of tall towers began pushing up over the low blocks punctuated by spires that here as elsewhere in the world had been the norm throughout history. The process was well under way when J. H. Beal made his panoramic views in 1876. Captions below this panel identify spires of Trinity Church at far left and Saint Paul's at far right, and between them new and huger structures challenging and surpassing them in height: the Second French Empire bulks identified from left to right as the Equitable Life Insurance, Western Union, and Park Bank buildings. (New-York Historical Society)*

5.26. *As noblemen once displayed their rank through prints of their palaces, so nineteenth-century corporations displayed theirs via prints of their office buildings. This 1875 lithograph shows the Western Union Telegraph Building on Broadway, begun in 1872 on designs by George B. Post. At ten stories it was the tallest building in New York City (thanks to partial steel frame and elevators), and, depending on how "first skyscraper" is defined, was a strong contender for that honor.*

5.27. *William Le Baron Jenney designed Chicago's Manhattan Building in 1889 and completed it, in collaboration with engineer Louis E. Ritter, in 1890. Technologically it was very advanced—the first building, in fact, to embody full metal skeleton construction calculated to support all loads without masonry support. But still masonry textures are used to provide a humanized perception (rough as if thicker below, smooth as if thinner above). For this designer, technology is not yet an end in itself and technological expression not yet a proper theme for architects; their proper role is to make buildings practical to use (maximum light through bay windows, and so on) and comfortable to see. (IMG:NAL)*

5.28. *The Singer Building of 1906–8 in New York was taller than anything in Chicago and the technology correspondingly advanced. That technology is expressed to some extent by banding devices, but architect Ernest Flagg insisted on maintaining visual humanization via a crowning section still in quasi-mansard and other French Baroque forms and ornament taught in the Paris Ecole des Beaux-Arts, where he had trained. From the late 1930s, Modern theorists routinely vilified such "historicist confections" and extolled the "purer" structural expression in Chicago's tall buildings.*

notations of power and prestige in every language). Developments in steel making, spurred by the Civil War, completed the incentive to build offices ever higher—"skyscrapers," they were called in the admiring and wondering era that beheld them first *[5.14, 5.25]*. (Moderns called them "tall buildings" because that was more "scientific.")

The resultant vertical cages in theory need not have had any ornament; certainly they would have been much more economically erected bald and bare from the factory. Instead, architects of the 1870s and 1880s left plain only the middle section. Bottom and top they swathed in ornament. Their skyscrapers were most commonly crowned with forms drawn from the great seventeenth-century palaces of France, via revivals of them introduced by France's Second Empire, founded by Louis Napoleon in the 1850s. Their bases most often carried variants of Second Empire forms but with more allusions to Classical Revival details: colonnades, pediments, niches, and the like, appropriate for a building's public face *[5.26]*. By the 1870s a tripartite formula for tall-building design had been devised that lasted until the 1930s: street level with elaborate entrances and show windows; long unadorned shaft containing working floors; and a crowning element with some kind of palatial allusions. What determined this composition was how human beings actually perceived the building, what it should do for them, rather than cerebral assumptions of some imperative need for open expression of materials and structure *[5.27, 5.28]*.

Picturesque skyscrapers have almost all been demolished or totally altered. But innumerable photographs and prints were made of them, because in and for the society of their time they were many of the same things that cathedrals had been in and for medieval society—visual metaphors of community aspirations and seats of municipal pride (which is why they so soon became obsolete).

Gone too are most of the factories in Picturesque styles. "Picturesque factories" seems a contradiction in terms; yet they derived from the same social logic that felt Picturesque shops and offices to be entirely appropriate: all were suppliers of the era's economic fuel, all accordingly deserved glorification *[5.29]*.

The range of Picturesque styles, and their basic character, made them particularly suitable for amenities. And the range of Picturesque buildings in the class of amenities was correspondingly wide. At one end were works like the Auditorium Build-

5.29. The warehouse (or more precisely, wholesale store) that Henry Hobson Richardson built for the Marshall Field Company in Chicago (1885–87) was hailed as a model of organic simplicity for a succeeding generation of Progressive architects. But this simplicity was in reality best suited to the social functions of a warehouse, and the wiser of its admirers extravagantly praised but rarely imitated it, except for comparable architectural types. It was demolished in 1930 when Marshall Field's wholesale division ceased business. (Chicago Architectural Photo Company)

ing, sometime wonder of the great city of Chicago—combination hotel, office tower, and concert hall *[5.30]*. At the other were outright pleasure palaces, great and small, like the Bath House at Ocean Park, sometime world wonder of southern California and the Venice area in particular *[5.31]*. Inbetween came all sorts of libraries, opera houses, hospitals, benevolent society halls, clubhouses for rich and poor; most privately funded, all in Picturesque styles conveying allusions to a blend of cultural pretension and egalitarian assumptions: great wealth can not only assure culture, but make great philanthropists out of anybody *[5.48, 5.68]*.

For the palace type proper—government buildings—Picturesque styles proclaimed much the same sort of union of culture and wealth under the aegis of business as they did for mansion and shop. The most famous example is Philadelphia City Hall, whose ambitious program of sculptural references to all times and continents complements its sophisticated French Second Empire architectural forms *[5.32]*.[19] Its loads of treasure borrowed from Periclean Greece and Bourbon France, Caesar's Rome and Dante's Florence was the tangible counterpart of the lyrical exhortation by Walt Whitman (a great admirer of the building, as his 26 August 1879 diary entry suggests) to

> Sail, sail thy best, ship of Democracy
> Of value is thy freight, 'tis not the Present only,
> The Past is also stored in thee . . .
> Earth's resume entire floats on thy keel.

From this era there are government buildings with comparable styling and with allegorical sculptures to create similar visual metaphors all over the country, with the Midwest, and particularly Ohio, being especially rich in them *[5.33; cf. 5.10].*

In this era a new subtype of palace government building begins to develop: the post office. It arises in the decades after introduction of adhesive postage stamps in the 1840s. Makeshift buildings were common at first, with few attempts to rival custom houses in showing forth the grandeur of government. But by the 1880s it had become evident that in post offices, government met the governed in a more direct and positive way than any other, and the subtype took on appropriate Picturesque forms. A climax was the 1899 Old Post Office in Washington, dominating Pennsylvania Avenue between the Treasury and the Capitol; as "The Pavilion" it still dominates, thanks to another of the preservation movement's greatest triumphs.

5.30 (right). Another major icon of American architecture is the Auditorium Building, occupying the whole Wabash/Michigan block of Chicago's downtown. Commissioned from the firm of Dankmar Adler and Louis Sullivan in December 1886, its construction began in October 1887 and was completed in the spring of 1889 to a chorus of superlatives: the biggest mass of masonry ever built and the biggest structure in Chicago up to that time, with the tallest tower. Actually it was Adler's structural and acoustical engineering that was most appreciated; Sullivan's design tried to combine expressions of commercial enterprise, inspired by Richardson's new Marshall Field warehouse, with expressions of culture and festivity appropriate to an amenity—an impossible combination. His decoration for the music hall itself and the main bar was much admired, but the main facade was at best confused in character. It was a failed essay in Picturesque without the unity of Richardson's Marshall Field warehouse or the coordinations later Academics would achieve, which helps explain the disastrous decline in his career that soon followed. Since 1946 the Auditorium Building has been occupied by Roosevelt University. The music hall proper was refurbished and reopened in 1967. (IMG:NAL)

The Bath House, Ocean Park, Cal.

5.31. Post–Civil War America abounded in new cultural establishments accommodated in Picturesque buildings. New York had its Booth Theatre (1869), Metropolitan Museum, and Metropolitan Opera, Wilmington its Grand Theatre and Opera (1880), Milwaukee its Pabst Theatre (1895), and so on through practically any town of importance from the Midwest to New England. Many have survived, especially buildings by famous architects, like Richardson's Crane Memorial Library in Quincy [5.68]. Many have not, like this Bath House from 1906 in Ocean Park, California. It has the generous archway signaling openness to the public that Sullivan employed in his Transportation Building at the Chicago world's fair, but here backed up by the array of domes and pennants and flags and arcades necessary to make a holiday metaphor fully effective. (IMG:NAL)

5.32. A Philadelphia committee in 1869 commissioned a grand combined city hall and county courthouse from Scottish immigrant architect John McArthur, to open coincident with the fair commemorating the Centennial of Independence. In style it was to recall Napoleon III's New Louvre in Paris, in height to surpass any other in the world. In fact the city hall was not begun until 1872, the 37-foot statue of William Penn not hoisted atop its 548-foot tower until 1894, the whole not officially opened until 1901—by which time the Eiffel Tower in Paris at 984 feet and the Washington Monument at 555 feet stood taller. A favorite target for Modernist vituperation in the 1940s and 1950s, Philadelphia City Hall was saved from demolition by the report of an AIA committee (whose members were Kenneth Day, Louis Kahn, Vincent Kling, Morton Keast, H. Mather Lippincott, and Sidney E. Martin), which called the building "perhaps the greatest single effort of late 19th-century American architecture. Its absence would weaken the continuity of architectural tradition of the whole country." (IMG:NAL)

5.33. The 1886 Presidio County Courthouse dominates the small Texas town of Marfa, like hundreds of courthouses in its era, each with vertically proportioned dome, flanking wings with French Second Empire mansards, and a statue of Justice, blindfolded with her scales, nobly capping the whole. The nearer and later buildings along Main Street are Colonial Spanish. (IMG:NAL)

5.34. When "Old Main" (University Hall) was built in 1873–76 for what was then the Arkansas Industrial University at Fayetteville, it was 150 miles from the nearest railroad station and 60 miles from the nearest port, Van Buren on the Arkansas River. The architect was John M. Van Osdel, who here repeated his 1868 "Old Main" for the Illinois Industrial University (later University of Illinois) at Urbana of 1868. During the 1860s and 1870s one college after another—particularly the new land-grant institutions created during the war—erected such fine towered, mansarded, gingerbreaded buildings dramatizing an American concept of higher education as comprehensive and democratically available. (Courtesy of University of Arkansas)

5.35. Hebert Hall was built at Tulane University in 1894 as a physical laboratory to specifications of physics professor Brown Ayres. To render Romanesque in brick, as architects Harrod & Andry here did, was then common (more so in city residences than official sorts of buildings). Other nearby Tulane buildings were and are stone, among them Tilton Hall (formerly Library), with its Tiffany windows (1901–2, annex 1907), and Gibson Hall of 1894. They form an impressive complex, one of the few to preserve an idea of what most leading American campuses looked like in the 1890s.(IMG:NAL)

Picturesque styles worked perfectly for the kind of collegiate buildings characteristic of the later nineteenth century, because culture grafted onto wealth was exactly what colleges and universities in this age were about. Many older American colleges have an "Old Main" in some Picturesque style, commemorating a fresh start after the Civil War *[5.34]*; but the great collegiate monuments to post–Civil War wealth appeared on those comparatively few colleges specially favored by the newly rich of those decades. It was at this time that the "Ivy League" schools began to pull decisively ahead of the miscellaneous pre-war pack. Their good fortune was owed in large part to the American tradition of philanthropy; with few exceptions it was those schools endowed by private wealth, rather than land-grant colleges established in the 1860s, that acquired lasting prestige. By the 1880s they had accumulated enough to begin trying to emulate old European universities. Perfect for this purpose was the climactic Picturesque substyle, Richardsonian Romanesque, with its effects of venerability and stability and, not least, allusions to that Ottonian Romanesque that had become the national style of a new German Empire famous for rigorous academic standards. Old prints show how many campuses were built almost exclusively in this style by 1890; Princeton was an outstanding example. In succeeding decades many of these buildings were replaced by Academic Gothic inspired by English precedents. But there are many survivors; the Tulane campus in New Orleans preserves an especially noteworthy assemblage [5.35].

Richardsonian Romanesque was also much fa-

vored for high schools—academically much more prestigious then than now. A splendid example is Old Central School in Grand Rapids, Minnesota, once attended by actress Judy Garland and in part preserved as a memorial to her.

Just as Picturesque styles could cover the stark technology of metal-cage skyscrapers with a veneer of culture, or turn defensive inns into palatial hotels, so they could attempt to "humanize the iron horse" by transforming railroad stations from mere passenger-sheltering sheds into spaces related by ornament to human history, tradition, feelings, and reactions. They achieved best results in small stations [5.36], with a climactic development in the "Railroad Beautiful" stations designed in the 1880s for the Boston & Albany by Richardson, where

5.36. A station in Italianate style on the Rutland Railroad at New Haven, Vermont, built c. 1875, still preserved its dull red, dull green, and dull yellow color scheme in this photograph taken in October 1954, shortly before the line went out of business. (IMG:NAL)

5.37. Chestnut Hill "station beautiful" on the Boston & Albany commuter line near Newton, Massachusetts, built 1883–84 to designs of Richardson with grounds landscaped by Olmsted. This view shows the porte-cochère *that allowed passengers to get from their vehicles to the waiting room, thence to platform. Dignified and attractive; but not enough, apparently, to prevent its demolition for a parking lot in 1960. (IMG:NAL, 1957)*

Frederick Law Olmsted provided many landscape settings *[5.37].* [20]

Bigger stations were at first conceived either as a commercial type, glamorized with exotic towers, marble floors, and masses of polychromatic ornament, or as palatial villas treated much the same *[5.38].* Combining both concepts resulted in the "railroad hotel"; its elements were first effectively integrated at London's Saint Pancras station and then brought to maturity in the "château-style" hotels that dominated Canada's seaward approaches both east and west. By the 1890s big-city railroad stations especially were being conceived as public monuments, and again Richardsonian Romanesque proved the first effective stylistic vehicle, combining great towers to signal public monument

5.38. Union Depot when built in 1847–48 to designs by precocious Brown University student Thomas Tefft was one of the glories of Providence, Rhode Island; here it appears in vignette on the frame of a big 1857 city view. Tefft preserved the symmetrical dignity of Classical styles but added picturesqueness via Italianate towers with spiky roofs, corbel tables, brackets, and round-headed arches, thus making a nice comparison to James Renwick's Smithsonian "Castle," built around the same time with some similarities in plan and elevation, but with medieval detail. In a country where Classical was still the national style, Italianate was appropriate for public works like railroad stations, but medieval for such a public amenity as the Smithsonian research institute and museum. (Courtesy of the Rhode Island Historical Society)

5.39. The Northwest Railroad Station in Milwaukee was built in 1889 to designs of Charles Sumner Frost. Its body shows complex spaces directed by a long unifying roof line (anticipated by a folk aesthetic in smaller and less self-conscious stations: cf. 5.36), but the strident gables, along with the surging tower that announces the railroad as a major community building, preserve Picturesqueness. (IMG:NAL, 1965)

5.40. A memorial to President Garfield in his hometown was conceived after his assassination in 1881, built in Cleveland's Lakeview Cemetery and dedicated Memorial Day, 1890. The commission was awarded in competition to George W. Keller, and Clevelanders were very proud of possessing, as a result, the first true mausoleum in America (combining tomb and memorial functions), counterpart to those of Mausolus at Halicarnassus and Hadrian in Rome. The memorial is lavishly ornamented with relief outside, gold and marble mosaics inside; at its core is Garfield's statue in white marble. (Courtesy of the Western Reserve Historical Society)

5.41. "Woman is a jewel, at her loveliest in the setting of the home," announces an inscription on this 1898 tombstone, which consists of ponderous intersecting white granite arches with a reddish granite ball suspended ominously above. It was erected in memory of a Mrs. Hall in Pittsfield, Illinois, and leaves no doubt that Mr. Hall was well-to-do. (IMG:NAL)

with roof lines so designed as to visually unite utilitarian train shed and shop-cum-villa passenger spaces *[5.39]*.

Picturesque styles did not really suit homestead types. A contradiction was involved. If you were wealthy enough to afford conspicuous waste, you wouldn't be living in a homestead. Nevertheless, the general ambiance of the era was reflected in homesteads to the extend that the average house kept growing steadily larger. What would count as a big Gothic Revival or Classical Revival homestead—over two stories—would count as a small one in Picturesque; otherwise most of the houses in American towns by c. 1885 would have to be classified as mansions. To qualify as a mansion—that is, to connote superior social status—by then, a house needed to be surrounded by ample grounds, with

attendant outbuildings (carriage houses, gatehouses, and so on). The era's wealth was attested to very well in a new subtype of amenity that began to proliferate after the Civil War: summer cottages, frequently as big or bigger than homesteads in earlier eras had been. For them the lavishness of Picturesque styles was ideal, because possession of a summer home at Newport or Cape Cod was so very much a conspicuous luxury *[5.16, 5.43]*.[21]

There was one architectural type for which Picturesqueness was not suited at all: monument. In contrast to its premier role in the Classical Revival, monument in Picturesque styles became the feeblest and least convincing of all building types. Big Picturesque monuments looked bombastic and pompous, like the Civil War monuments in Detroit or Indianapolis; little ones necessarily looked stolid

5.42. In 1879 directors of the Union Pacific Railroad commissioned a monument from Richardson to honor their sometime chairmen, financiers Oakes and Oliver Ames, and to memorialize a Supreme Court decision vindicating them of Credit Mobilier scandal charges. It stood on a huge empty plain at Sherman Station in south-central Wyoming, between Cheyenne and Laramie, three hundred feet south of the highest grade on its line. Richardson designed a large quasi-pyramidal cairn with broken Picturesque outlines, carrying on two of its faces portrait medallions in relief by Augustus Saint-Gaudens, of Oakes Ames on the east face, and Oliver Ames on the west. It was built between 1879 and 1882. In 1901 the line was moved to avoid unnecessary grades and the town of Sherman disappeared, leaving the monument in lonely majesty with Buford, some dozen miles away, its nearest community. Then around 1970 Interstate 80 came through along the old railroad route, bringing a good many visitors and, alas, vandals. (IMG:NAL)

or trivial, or both *[5.10]*. Sometimes a Picturesque monument contrives to be all three at once; the Garfield Monument was one such *[5.40]*, and there are all sorts of private examples *[5.41]*. An era whose highest ideal was the making and possessing of money could find adequate monumental expression only in extraordinary situations and circumstances *[5.42]*. The era's few effective monuments were in a "Picturesque Classical" style, retaining some fundamentally Classical features and proportions, betraying the reigning taste of their time sometimes in a distinctive verticality, sometimes a tendency to fussy accumulations of detail, sometimes in distinctive ponderousness. Grant's Tomb and the Statue of Liberty are major examples; a good minor example is the monument to Union soldiers at Finns Point National Cemetery in southern New Jersey.

Substyles
(Phases of Picturesque Styling)

Since the very essence of Picturesque styling was to mix details from past sources, clear distinctions between and within substyles are hardly to be expected. Substyles to some degree can be determined by a given prominent feature, like bracketing or mansard roofs or massive stonework. But it really would be more sensible to speak of "phases," various mixes that "phase in and out" of fashion. Six of them can be discerned:

1. The earliest such phase is Italianate, which becomes prominent on the American architectural scene well before the Civil War and includes such variants as Italianate/Gothic and Italianate/Romanesque in several high-style (such as Lombard) and vernacular versions.

2. Then comes French Second Empire, with such variants as Italianate/Second Empire in high-style and vernacular combinations, Second Empire/Renaissance ("General Grant").

3. Next come High Picturesque mixes, in which no single source is predominant; these climax in the so-called Queen Anne style.

4 and 5. Coincident with High Picturesque mixes—largely, perhaps, because they were so poorly suited for architecture needing a credible public face—there developed (4) a Picturesque Classical styling, widespread in application but rather overlooked in architectural history, and (5) the so-called Richardsonian Romanesque, which

likewise ranges widely from high-style to local variants.

6. A last phase of Picturesque is represented by vestigial survivals of a wide range of motifs and features, from brackets to turrets, which pass over into vernacular and mass-produced commercial building, ultimately to reappear in Popular/Commercial form.

Italianate

Italianate was the dominant mid-nineteenth-century North American architectural style. Under the general rubric of Italianate went in its own time, and sometimes still in ours, a wide variety of manners or modes, including Italian villa, Tuscan villa, Early Renaissance Revival, Swiss Bracketed, Romano-Tuscan, North Italian, First Renaissance Revival, Round, Antique, and some aspects of High Victorian and Norman. In furniture the style was often called Rococo, also Renaissance, in its own time; in ours Belter, after its most successful proponent. In church architecture Italianate was often combined and/or confused with Romanesque, Lombard, and Gothic.

Principal influences on Italianate generally came from the architecture of rural Italy—country villas, vernacular buildings, country churches.[22] Two particular features identify most Italianate buildings, great or small: brackets, especially under the eaves or supporting them (in its own time Americans often called Italianate "the bracketed style"), and round-headed arches, most often used above windows and doors, singly or in arcaded pairs or triples; but also on occasion appearing as blind arches in walls or corbeling along gables [5.43].

Other common features are verandas extending along facades of houses and often wrapping around one or more sides as well, frequently with round-headed arcades; squarish towers with low-pitched hipped or pyramidal roofs; chimneys with prominent horizontal ledges; and belvederes, that is, tiny towers atop the peak of roofs, supplied with windows all around and pinnacled or pyramided rooflets [5.6, 5.18].

Noteworthy about these features is that they are almost entirely matters of visual effect. They have little or no other function. That is, they are decoration (most commonly added to a body with a Georgian plan) for which no practical, ideational, or symbolic need is apparent: brackets not actually supporting anything (being in fact available precut, to be added after a building was erected); belvederes letting in no light below and often accessible only by ladders—certainly never intended as places to live or work. Yet this is not yet the simply vulgar ostentatious ornament of later Picturesque

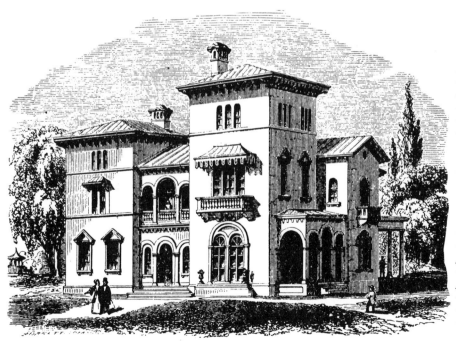

5.43. In 1845 Richard Upjohn built a villa—what later might be called a summer house—for Edward King in Newport, Rhode Island. It was obviously considered an appropriate alternative to Gothic both by Upjohn, whose specialty was Gothic churches large and small, and Andrew Jackson Downing, who illustrated the villa in his 1851 Country Houses *as a model of "Tuscan, or American style." Downing referred to the combination of "the Swiss and bracketed cottage, and the different highly irregular forms of the Italian villa." In social function the King villa was a direct ancestor of Newport's fabled and fabulous late-nineteenth-century summer palaces; their climactic example, The Breakers (cf. 6.37), was designed in an Academic version of Italianate style.*

substyles. These brackets still generally retain a humane function of improving the look of the house by providing visual support to its eaves; these belvederes provide an articulating visual focus for the total composition; these arcaded verandas are proportioned to the whole.

For Italianate still had ideological overtones. One source of its great popularity was precisely the fact that it could be considered as a variant either of Classical or of Gothic Revivals. If you wanted to think of Italianate columns and gables and pediments as symbolic of classical Italy and the great civic ideals of the Republic, you could. But if you wanted to find in its towers and arches and assymmetrical plans evocations of the Early Christian and Romanesque Middle Ages—a "Christian" style but without the Gothic Revival's shrillness—it could be

that too. This flexibility explained a good deal about its history.

Italianate appeared in England considerably earlier than in the United States. John Nash's "Italian" villa Cronkhill was built near Shrewsbury as early as 1802, and his Regents Park Village outside London in the 1820s; by the 1830s, when editions of J. C. Loudon's *An Encyclopaedia of Cottage, Farm and Villa Architecture and Furniture* began appearing, Italianate was a well-established English style. In the States, by contrast, Italianate architecture was still avant-garde in the 1830s, represented by a few details on Washington Irving's Sunnyside at Tarrytown (1832), the Italianate villa A. J. Davis exhibited in 1833, or John Notman's Riverside for Bishop Doane of New Jersey in 1837 or 1838. Italianate furniture began to be popular in the 1840s—

5.44. *John Henry Belter of New York City made this laminated rosewood bed around 1860, now exhibited in the Brooklyn Museum. The fussy, frilly pillowcases and sheets perfectly complement the furniture style, as do, of course, the bedclothes of the period. Sociologically, such beds, like hall stands and other distinctive items of the period [5.54], are as emblematic of the bourgeois family founded on money as were the great canopied state beds of older noble houses founded on land. (The Brooklyn Museum, gift of Mrs. Ernest Vietor)*

5.45. *Italianate row houses on Chestnut Street at the corner of Lombard in San Francisco. In the nearest houses, Postmodern remodeling of the lower story may be observed; ogee arches are an entirely appropriate stylistic mix. (IMG:NAL)*

the transition from the more vulgar and mass-produced forms of Empire ("Butcher Phyfe," for example) to Italianate was easy, as Joseph Meeks's famous catalog suggests, and soon quite lavish Italianate furniture in Rococo Revival and Belter substyles was becoming accepted, becoming all the rage by the 1850s *[5.44]*. [23] Architecture was a different story; in America Italianate was not really established until the 1840s.

As long as it was merely a variant of the Classical style, Italianate had no particular place in America, where the roots of the classical tradition were so deep and the symbolical associations of Greek and Roman almost a cult. But considered as a variant of Gothic (as it was already at Riverside, where Doane's library within his Italianate villa was in Gothic and the whole matched his Ecclesiological Gothic Cathedral), Italianate took on another aspect entirely. In this capacity it was a very welcome and extremely convenient means of realizing some aesthetic aspirations of progressive-thinking Gothic Revivalists, without accepting what seemed in America to be the eccentric and foreign character of Gothic forms as such.

An Italianate mansion, that is, could project an image of increasing wealth via superfluous ornament, without implying eccentric departures from Classical norms appropriate to the dignity of the virtuous republican. It follows that many larger Italianate mansions were Gothic castles in thin disguise. Reuben Fenton's in Jamestown, New York *[5.6]* was one such; a classic was A. J. Davis's 1853–55 Litchfield house in Brooklyn, with its wonderfully complicated interior spatial vistas. Others combined primmer detail with pleasing but not extravagant assymmetry; for example, the one Henry Austin designed on Hillhouse Avenue in New Haven for a Yale professor, based on a plate in Downing's 1841 *Treatise on Landscape Gardening* of "The Tuscan or American Villa."

For those more comfortable with closer allusions to Classicism proper, there were Italianate/Renaissance mixes; these were common on commercial structures *[5.24]*, but were occasionally used on residences too (Austin's 1859 Victoria Mansion for R. S. Morse in Portland, Maine), or on special occasions, like the Athenaeum building John Notman designed in Philadelphia in a Renaissance/Italianate style alluding to Charles M. Barry's designs for cosmopolitan clubs in London.

The most frequent manifestation of Italianate was in row houses appearing in American cities from the mid-1840s on. They came in a wide range, from palatial to vernacular to primitive. New York and Brooklyn had famous "brownstones" with all details—pediments, lintels, sweeping entrance steps complete with balusters and newel posts—carved out of purplish sandstone. Cincinnati had blocks with one-third and two-thirds Georgian plans. Early developers filled San Francisco streets with wooden versions of them *[5.12, 5.45]*. [24] And Chicago had blocks of "Chicago cottages"—tiny, built for quick construction, quick sale, quick abandonment, a direct precedent for mass-prefabricated suburbs at the end of the century, yet withal having a distinct stylistic character provided by bits of Italianate bracketing on the eaves, curved window frame and transom, bull's-eye in the gable *[5.46]*.

Combined and/or confused with Romanesque, Italianate was a popular style for small churches (cf. 4.36); for grander religious buildings, Italianate

5.46. *Standing high on a brick foundation (because of a high water table and frequent changes of street level) is the balloon-framed "Chicago cottage," utilizing a technique invented in Chicago and sheathed in clapboard. The narrow houses were infinitely replaceable; each customarily had two stories and an attic, as here. Not until the very end of the nineteenth century were such houses mass prefabricated, strangely enough. (From* Mid-North District, *Chicago Historical and Architectural Landmarks Commission, 1974)*

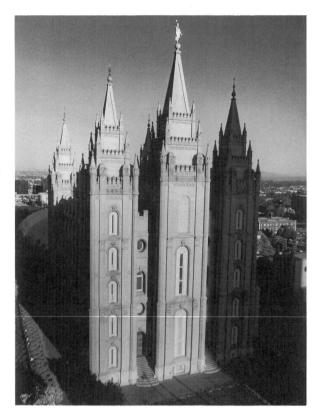

5.47. The Great Temple at Salt Lake City in Utah, the Mormons' Promised Land, succeeded earlier temples at Kirtland, Ohio (1836) and Nauvoo, Illinois (1846). Its site was designated by Brigham Young in July 1847; cornerstone laid 1853; completed with its six granite towers in 1893. It was designed by Truman O. Angell, the Saints' chief architect, who here employed a mixture of Italianate and Gothic elements much commoner in the nineteenth century than survivors would indicate—though not, of course, on this scale. For Italianate elements, Angell seems to have drawn upon William Ranlett's The Architect *(New York, 1849); Gothic crenellations, pinnacles, and spires he seems to have invented himself. In this view, a morning sun hits the Temple's west front, gleaming off the statue of Moroni on the main tower; the tall shadows are cast by the Hotel Utah across Main Street, one of the church's later commercial enterprises. Temples represented visual metaphors of central ideas in Mormon thought: they were used for "sacred ordinances" that bound the community together—"sacred" in the sense of referring to a spiritual dimension of time, for the ceremonies here performed, such as marriage, were considered binding not only in this life ("until death do us part"), but through all eternity. (IMG:NAL)*

could be combined and/or confused with Gothic— Mormon temples at Manti and Salt Lake are famous examples *[5.47]*. But its most lasting popularity was as a style for commercial buildings. Italianate dispossessed all others in this field during the 1850s. It was the style for the first great office blocks, the first great department stores (A. T. Stewart's of 1862 on Broadway being in its day the best known), and the first fireproof office buildings (James Bogardus's prefabricated metal skeletons in Italianate style, complete with glassed facades *[5.24]*, are but the most famous of thousands). It also provided the basic ingredient in the "boom-town front" that through the 1870s and 1880s proved the most lasting of all images of how a prosperous store—often combined with offices and lodge halls for Odd Fellows or Masons or Woodmen of the World—ought to look *[5.5, 5.48]*. By then Italianate had long been mixed with elements of the succeeding phase of Picturesque styles, French Second Empire.

Second Empire

Second Empire proper—the high style—is distinguishable by several characteristic features, often in

combination: mansard roofs *[5.49]*; composition by pavilions; outlines set off by intricately detailed cast-iron railings (gingerbread); shallow arcades composed of ornamented columns and entablatures variously drawn from diverse classical sources, characteristically lighter and more intricate than their models, decoratively attached to walls, windows, and entrances. But there is no sharp line separating Second Empire from Italianate; it has most of the same elements, only more elaborate and more vertical; Second Empire towers, for instance, tend to be higher and narrower and end in variants of mansard roofs *[5.32, 5.34]*. Very high style Second Empire has mansardic pavilion or dome terminations *[5.50, 5.51]*.

The mansard roof proper was a seventeenth-century invention that was picked up and developed in the France of Louis Napoleon, who established a "Second Empire" (Napoleon Bonaparte's being the first) in 1852, for its obvious allusions to the great age of Louis XIV, when French culture had dominated Europe without challenge. Simple mansards began to appear on American roofs by the 1850s, and by the 1860s and 1870s more elaborate

5.48. *In early Los Angeles, as in many other new small towns of the time "with prospects," prosperity and culture were proclaimed by spanking new city blocks in Italianate style, each identified by cornice and crestings known colloquially as a "boom-town front." Here on North Market Street may still be seen (left to right) the* 1868 *Pico Theater (attributed to Ezra F. Kysor), the Merced Theater of* 1869, *and the old Plaza Firehouse of* 1883. *If it seems hard to tell firehouse from theater, and either from stores, that's the spirit of the age: commerce was its common denominator. Seen here in* 1966, *as recently restored. (IMG:NAL)*

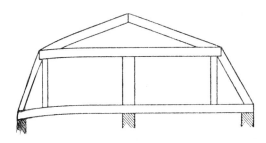

5.49. *Diagram of a mansard roof. (From* Dictionnaire Larousse*)*

5.50. *From* 1871 *to* 1888—*for seventeen years and four months—Alfred Bult Mullett worked on a huge four-winged replacement for the old executive buildings that used to flank the White House (cf.* 3.34*) —the new State, War, and Navy (now Old Executive) Building. Nothing so dramatically illustrated the nation's transformation by Civil War. Instead of the older naive Classical Revival boxes came a dramatic stage set proclaiming a bigger, stronger, more cultured nation capable of rivaling, say, France; its successive stories were each in a different order, and its mansarded roof line recalled the Tuileries or New Louvre. The view here, with ornament further enhanced by flags of the United States and the homeland of visiting dignitaries, shows how the building functioned (and still does) as an appropriate backdrop for state appearances ever farther from the simplicities of Lincoln's or Jackson's times. (IMG:NAL)*

5.51. Providence's city hall, completed in 1878 to designs of Samuel Thayer, followed the specific forms of Boston's 1862–65 city hall by Bryant and Gilman and the general urbanizing spirit of the era. This view shows its mansardic dome climaxed by a gingerbread crown—a motif traceable to Bernini's seventeenth-century Louvre palace, but now honoring the sovereign people. (IMG:NAL)

5.52. The Iolani Palace in Honolulu was built for the reigning Hawaiian sovereigns by California architects Thomas J. Baker and C. S. Wall, and looks it, with its cast-iron railings and columns. It is another visual manifestation, perhaps, of how slim was the distinction in this era between having been born royal and having become rich. Begun in 1879 and finished in 1882, it was turned over to cabinet officers and the legislature after the monarchy was overthrown in 1893. Restored in the 1970s. (IMG:NAL)

versions had come to constitute, along with super-imposed rows of columns or pilasters attached to facades, the mark of truly up-to-date public buildings. Fine surviving examples include the city hall in Philadelphia *[5.32]*, the Old Executive Building in Washington, the city hall in Providence, and the Iolani Palace in Honolulu *[5.50–5.52]*. But, as might be expected in this era, plenty can be found on mansions as well *[5.53]*.

Given the nature of the Picturesque, the mansard roof rarely remained faithful to French models. It was early and often mixed up with Gothic roof forms; and when put to such novel uses as capping the era's new skyscrapers, it displayed such truly astonishing inventiveness *[5.25, 5.26]* as still to be chosen for major early twentieth-century buildings (for example, Ernest Flagg's Singer Building of 1906–8 *[5.28]*).[25]

Every sort of combination of Second Empire with Italianate could be found, sometimes mixed up too with more specifically Italian Renaissance revivals. The "General Grant villa," as commonly built for upper-middle-class clients, belongs in this category and is one of two famous representatives of it *[5.4]*.

The other is the commercial store facade, so distinctive a sign of this era. Varieties range from elaborate designs by well-known architects, to sheet-metal prefabrications, to mere boards put up in front of some shed to provide a public face *[5.6, 5.48]*.

As the "boom-town front" for blacksmith's shops, pool halls, and taverns, this form has become the Old West's very image, especially since it made such easily erected movie or television stage sets.[26]

In furniture, the logical counterpart to Second Empire architecture ought to be Louis Quatorze style; but logic was not what Picturesque designers were after. Their most admired quality was inventive variation on mixed motifs *[5.54]*. Some writers of the time advocated consistency of style within rooms, but evidence suggests that this ideal was rarely attained, and indeed seldom attempted; at most a few pieces matched, when bought as sets. Office furnishings were most commonly in variants of the Italian Renaissance, consistent, more or less, with Italianate/Second Empire combinations on exteriors. What interior designers of the era really

5.53. In 1878 Hoag, Wade and Company's History of the State of Rhode Island *featured the residence of James O. Inman at Burrillville, as it looked when brand new around 1870. As befitted a prominent citizen, classical tradition governed the plans of house and grounds, but outlines were another matter—these are* Picturesque. *The main house has mansards; the carriage house is mansarded to match, with cupola and weather vane; and the fence is Italianate. As for the birdhouse for purple martins with its own little drum and cupola carried on high ironwork stilts—words fail!*

5.54. *Hall stands, like this one made about 1865 and now owned by the Rock County Historical Society of Janesville, Wisconsin, had an important social role in American life from the 1860s through the 1890s. Their use was part of an etiquette that helped restore to social life an order whose destruction had been a Revolutionary ideal yet proved necessary after all. Visually such a piece matches Second Empire architecture to the extent that it combines Italianate elements (such as the marble tabletop) with robust and sweeping Baroque forms. (Photo courtesy Kenneth Ames)*

5.55 *(below, left).* The Art Journal *for 1876 published this vignette of a house in Newport, Rhode Island, built for Charlotte Cushman a few years before (1871–74). The Cushmans were a Brahmin family, and their architect was the young Richard Morris Hunt, who here produced a typically Picturesque display of wealth through a mass of walls patterned by slats and shingles and clapboards, swathed in verandas all strutted and gabled, capped by a forest of medieval turrets and chimneys. Hunt's later style changed to a model of Academic restraint and correctness; his clientele always remained the very rich. (From S. Landau, "The Continental Picturesque and the 'Stick Style,'"* Journal of the Society of Architectural Historians *42/3 [1983]:283)*

5.56 *(below, right). Only a tiny fraction of American architecture was built for the very rich, and American architectural history is not simply a record of the styles displayed in that fraction, which often changed as capriciously and for reasons as trivial as changes in dress fashions. The deep meaning of American architecture is to be sought rather in vernacular renderings of major styles and their phases: for example, this house in Independence, Missouri, has the same basic elements in the same basic mix as the Cushman house [5.55] but on a less pretentious and more rational scale. From 1919 to 1972 it was the home of Harry S Truman, one of the less pretentious and more rational American presidents. The house was bought in 1867 by Bess Truman's grandfather, who had it remodeled and enlarged to its present appearance in 1885, by some local contractor. (Harry S Truman National Historic Site, National Park Service)*

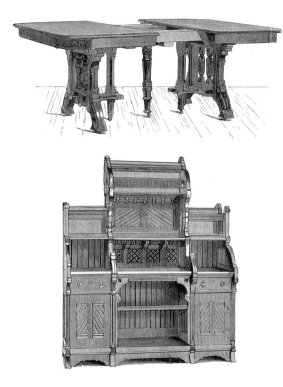

5.57. *Charles Locke Eastlake's* Hints on Household Taste *first appeared in England in 1868, then in the United States in 1872. It produced an Eastlake style boomlet in furniture and interior design just before and after the 1876 Centennial. Illustrating some pieces in her* Art Decoration Applied to Furniture *(New York: Harper & Brothers, 1878), Harriet Prescott Spofford remarked that Eastlake had shown "readers how to furnish their homes picturesquely, yet with reference to modern ideas of comfort." Thus an Eastlake dining table followed his dictum that "mouldings should be carved from the solid, not made of detached slips of wood glued on a surface [like wicked dishonest Belter]," yet provided for convenient extension unknown in the Middle Ages (a point refuted by Spofford). An Eastlake sideboard followed his dictum that "surfaces should be left in their native hue, never varnished, but if painted at all, painted in flatted color, with 'a line introduced here and there to define the construction, with an angle ornament (which may be stencilled) at the corners'." An Eastlake chair eschews curves—"this detestable system of ornamentation . . . called shaping" that is "a weakener of the fibre of the wood"—hence its resemblance to Stick Style [4.12].*

wanted was in fact much the same as the architects, only more so: rejecting more totally the old principle of specific copyings from earlier historical styles as somehow naive and unimaginative, they made even more general images of pastness, which were even more vague, indiscriminate, and obsessed with miscellaneous visual effects. Already in the 1860s furniture was anticipating the High Picturesque mixes characteristic of mid-1870s architecture.

High Picturesque Mixes

Once elements of medieval origin get stirred into the Italianate/Second Empire/Renaissance Revival mix, all stylistic coherence vanishes. This is the kind of architecture that the term "Victorian" brings to most people's minds—not so long ago, with a knee-jerk repulsion; now, often, with knee-jerk adulation.

Categorization of buildings so styled becomes quite arbitrary. Names like Eastlake, Queen Anne, or Stick Style can be attached to this or that combination of forms and ornament; but exceptions to any rule *are* the rule. And this is not merely in hindsight. In 1880 one T. D. G. of Carson, Iowa, wrote to the editors of *Carpentry and Building* magazine to ask, "Would you be kind enough to illustrate

through the columns of your journal the characteristics of 'Queen Anne,' 'Elizabethan,' and 'Eastlake' styles of architecture? Volume One of your journal treats the subject briefly, but I cannot distinguish the different styles from what I find there." "It is quite impossible," the editor replies, "to say nowadays where one style begins and another ends . . . at present they are rather names than styles, and architects use them without any very clear idea of their meaning, in a great many cases. Any attempt at classification would, we fear, be misleading." Wise advice.

But minds crave order, to the extent of imposing structure on the world, as semioticians tell us; so one can at least suggest some general trends in mixing, to which some of the more common stylistic names can with some reason be attached. Nowadays the principal examples of them are houses, partly because High Picturesque mixes were most often found on houses, partly because they were so offensively ineffective on public buildings that few have survived. There are high-style Medieval/Renaissance combinations that occur consistently enough to justify Vincent Scully's having christened them "Stick Style" some decades ago [5.55] and vernacular counterparts [5.56].[27] There are interiors that use a distinctive kind of medievalistic detail

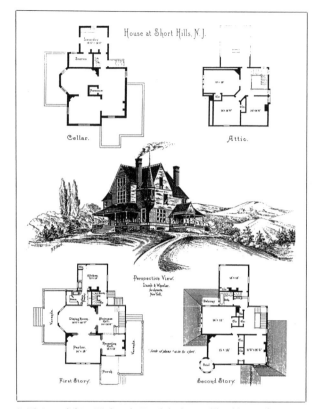

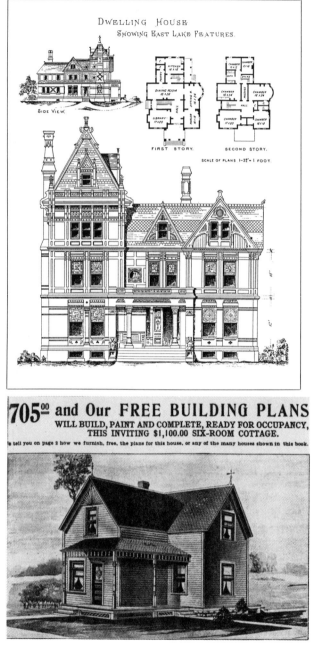

5.58 *(top, left). High-style Eastlake houses like this one from William Comstock's 1881* Modern Architectural Designs and Details *(reprint, American Life Foundation, 1976) are comparatively rare; but such examples demonstrate how it primarily consisted of assemblages of allegedly "honest" medieval details on a kind of latticework pattern: tiny roundels in square blocks, lozenges within triangles, cusps within squares. It also demonstrates one source of Medieval/Renaissance mixes: confusion between Quattrocento ("Pre-Raphaelite"—note facade plaque) and medieval-derived details proper. Though the Eastlake boomlet per se was short-lived, its influence was lasting: the Arts and Crafts movement of the 1890s that was one matrix of the Prairie School and much else, resulted from maximizing Eastlake's "honesty to materials" and minimizing his "picturesqueness." And Eastlake's prejudice against convertible furniture as dishonest helped discourage technological innovation.*

5.59 *(top, right). The essential concept of Queen Anne as a "country house" style is brought out in this "Perspective View of a House at Short Hills New Jersey" by Lamb and Wheeler of New York, appearing in Comstock's 1881* Modern Architectural Designs. *Four floor plans accompany it, from which we learn that the second-story projecting bay window with peaked turret is to be called an "oriel," but, more significantly, that central heating from a basement furnace allows great flexibility in room arrangements: the central hearth is gone, leaving only a few ornamental corner fireplaces fed off the chimney stacks. Far more common in America were vernacular versions of Queen Anne as a city villa (cf. 5.15).*

5.60. *It seems a long way from Lamb and Wheeler in Short Hills to Sears, Roebuck's 1908* Book of Modern Homes *advertising "$705 and Our Free Building Plans Will Build, Paint and Complete Ready for Occupancy, This Inviting . . . Cottage," but it really isn't. This house sports the lowest common denominator of Eastlake and Queen Anne features—Eastlake detailing around the windows, a Queen Anne–like spindled porch—on a plan derived, at great vernacular remove, from the Classical Revival temple-house with wing.*

consistently enough to constitute an Eastlake style *[5.57]*, and, more rarely, exteriors comparably detailed *[5.58]*. And then there is Queen Anne, a "Picturesque Renaissance" mix.

As invented in England by Norman Shaw, Queen Anne style took its name from an alleged resemblance to English rural architecture in the time of Queen Anne; that is, a kind of early-eighteenth-century vernacular version of the "English Renaissance." This muddled prescription was confounded further by American practice. American Queen Anne, both high style and vernacular *[5.15, 5.59, 5.60]*, turned out to be most commonly in wood rather than brick, as Shaw had intended. Its basic elements were actually drawn from English country houses over a wide range of time: Palladian windows (its only really eighteenth-century feature, and in American usage much commoner in vernacular than high style); great two-story window banks, which are actually Elizabethan or Tudor; and turrets with witch-cap towers. It also featured round arches and arcades which sometimes seemed to look back to Italianate, sometimes sideways to Richardsonian Roman-

esque. Picturesque Renaissance Revival is in fact an obvious contradiction in terms, picturesqueness being surely the very antithesis of Renaissance. That is, no doubt, precisely why it had such appeal in an era that equated novel combinations with stylistic inventiveness.

Inventiveness is the key quality in the furniture styles that correspond to High Picturesque mixes in architecture. Furniture perhaps gives a better indication than architecture of the appeal of these styles in their own time. Taste in the 1860s and 1870s reveled in the kind of novelties that could be produced by machines. With steam-driven presses and saws, furniture manufacturers forced their will impartially upon wood, papier-mâché, metal, and marble; furniture was bent, beaten, punched, twisted, steamed and laminated into every conceivable shape—scrolls and knobs and lacework and sinuous moldings. All sorts of new combinations of types were invented too—beds with desks, desks with tables, tables with bathtubs, chairs that folded and hung and turned into hat stands *[5.61]*. Such furniture novelties were a kind of craze in some ways comparable to the computer/semiotics craze

5.61. Page 263 of Paine's 1891–92 furniture catalog shows how a child can with one finger convert a living-room fireplace into a double bed, an arrangement whose desirability was recommended as early as 1841 by Catharine Beecher (cf. 4.21). The room shown is still generally Eastlake style, with notable exceptions, like the obviously Colonial Revival alcove table.

5.62. An easy chair made c. 1885, perhaps by the Newark, New Jersey, firm of Kirk & Jacobus, entirely expressive of its era. Stylistically it is a typical mélange—mahogany frame sporting a range of terminations from near-classical capitals and flutings on the upper front legs to quasi-Gothic crockets on their bottoms, and Baroquish acanthus elsewhere; upholstered in gray and taupe cut velvet with bold floral patterns. Technically it is a marvel of inventiveness, with its back adjustable to five different angles simply by moving a rod. (The Newark Museum, gift of Mr. and Mrs. Percy Ballantine, 1946)

5.63. *Provident Life and Trust Company, built 1876–79 to Frank Furness's designs in Philadelphia, stood on Chestnut Street opposite the Second Bank of the United States until its demolition in the twentieth century. Extravagantly praised by twentieth-century architectural critics, ostensibly for "boldly scaled" elements kept under "tough-minded" geometric control, and other aesthetic excellences, but perhaps subliminally because it defied its setting in much the same arrogant way as early Modern buildings defied theirs.*

5.64. *James D. McCabe's* Illustrated History of the Centennial Exhibition *(Philadelphia, 1876) showed among other modern wonders of the city, a "Provident Life and Trust Company" building on Chestnut Street which appears to be an alternative to the one built to Furness's design. It is an up-to-date Picturesque Classical version of the Greek Revival bank across the street.*

of the 1980s, fueled perhaps by something of the same deep expectations of salvation through science [5.62].[28]

Given mixing on this scale, it is something of an idle exercise to distinguish between high style and vernacular, certainly with any consistency. If the only real rule is inventiveness, one can hardly say that a High Picturesque building designed by an architect is necessarily more high style than one not. What one can say is that some of the most extraordinary buildings of this era were produced by local builders, fitting prefabricated ornament to traditional plans in many cases [5.60].

In 1888 a writer for *American Architect and Building News* declared: "Queen Anne relies upon the variety and vivacity of rapidly changing effects from different points of view; on sharp contrasts, and the piquancy of small detached masses; on quick transitions of form, color, and materials. It seldom inspires homage but often commands applause." Not, of course, during the Modernist regime. High Picturesque classics like the Carson house in Eureka [5.7] were precisely what Modernist taste makers most loved to trash. What they called bourgeois incoherence to another mind seems an image of free invention, an avenue of escape from Modern-

5.65. *The present First National Bank in the small Minnesota town of Sauk Centre, where Sinclair Lewis grew up, in some ways justifies the low opinion of small-town culture that pervades his novels. Its facade, designed by local architect Tom Tudar, has a fine array of classical elements, but they have curiously attenuated proportions and seem assembled on Picturesque principles. (IMG:NAL)*

5.66. *This mix of classical with Picturesque (in this case Richardsonian Romanesque) elements constituted an image of stability plus enterprise for the 1908 Maryland National Bank in Cambridge, on the eastern shore. (IMG:NAL)*

ism's sour seriousness. Fickle taste is no guide to lasting reputation; what can be lastingly admired is the way this architecture fulfilled a social function in and for its own time.

Picturesque Classical

Use of the Classical Revival as the national style for major monuments persisted into the 1850s, 1860s, and 1870s, long after Picturesque styles had become not only fashionable, but the norm elsewhere. By the 1870s, both famous examples like Grant's Tomb and humbler ones like the iron Federal lighthouse at Finns Point in southern New Jer-

sey show an attenuation of individual elements and total proportions distinctive of the era. And on the vernacular level admixtures of Picturesque eye-catching elements like bits of rustication or foliate decoration, or textured panels and outbursts of ornament generally, were evident even in designs whose basic elements were still drawn from a recognizably classical matrix of columns, pediments, entablatures, and porticoes.

This distinctive Picturesque Classical mix was particularly common on small banks. Not that full-fledged Picturesque banks could never be found; those by Frank Furness in the 1870s and 1880s

5.67. *The main facade of People's Federal Savings & Loan bank in the small Ohio town of Sidney sets a classically lettered exhortation to THRIFT in a lavishly ornamental setting that could be by none other than Louis Sullivan. It was one of his last works (1917–18) and is still as fundamentally Picturesque as in the 1880s. (IMG:NAL)*

spring to mind *[5.63]*. But such essays were relatively quite rare; they are more famous than they deserve in American architectural history, perhaps, because Furness's early efforts to create architecture expressing his own personal tastes at least as much as any client's wishes earned him a place in the pantheon of Modern progenitors. Indeed Furness's eloquence and conviction may have been as responsible for acceptance of his extravagant Picturesque designs as any widespread liking for them; Picturesque Classical alternatives seem to have existed even for his most famous works *[5.64]*. And certainly it was classical elements used in a Picturesque way, or with a picturesque admixture of non-

classical elements, combining effects of richness (to get rich you should look rich) with intimations of stability, that had the most lasting appeal, especially to bankers in small towns, well into the first dozen years of the twentieth century *[5.65, 5.66]*. This may explain in part, as Robert Twombley has argued convincingly, Louis Sullivan's later problems getting commissions; by the early 1900s his kind of extravagant Picturesque style was long out of fashion in capitals, and had never been strong in the provinces *[5.67]*.

Richardsonian Romanesque

Richardsonian Romanesque is the most famous of Picturesque substyles and has been so, uninterruptedly since Richardson's lifetime. As almost all writers about the matter have observed, Henry Hobson Richardson was not the style's inventor, but rather the *re*finer and *de*finer of a Romanesque before Richardson (cf. chapter 4, "Substyles"). He made Romanesque into a style still Picturesque, but so appropriate and successful for big public buildings as to sweep all rivals away by the 1880s and into the 1890s; and because it appeared in that role at just the moment when the United States was recognized as already a great world power, Richardsonian Romanesque became the first American architectural style to be emulated as such abroad.

Two varieties of his distinctive style were developed by the master himself, and both were extensively imitated on both high-style and vernacular levels. For mansions and luxurious summer cottages, Richardson devised what later generations would call the Shingle Style; it had some stonework, especially for foundations, but also featured great expanses of wood, brick, and tile *[5.16]*. Richardsonian Romanesque proper was primarily intended to be executed in stone, for public buildings; but given the nature of the age, it is not surprising to find its monumental forms soon and often applied to mansions as well *[5.17, 5.68]*.

The Richardsonian Romanesque high style consists primarily of stone buildings with heavy round arches and rough cuttings to emphasize stone texture, associated either directly or closely with the office of Henry Hobson Richardson. Richardson was the second architect (after Furness) to self-consciously promote a personal stylistic signature—an attitude picked up and carried much further by Sullivan and Wright, both in some ways his disciples. His vocabulary was enormously varied. The heavy

5.68. *The public library at Quincy, Massachusetts, was built as a memorial to Thomas Crane, local mason and stone dealer, on plans (including furniture) by H. H. Richardson, 1880–82. It is an archetypal Richardsonian library, with functions of the several parts easily read off plan and elevation. A reading room for research (right) is separated from a stack wing by a controlling central area (whose importance is indicated by monumental arch and turret), where circulation and research both can be monitored; the whole is unified by generous roof. Appropriately for a monument to a mason, Richardson used three varieties of stone: Quincy granite (base), North Easton granite (walls), and Longmeadow brownstone trim. (IMG:NAL)*

5.69. *Allegheny County Courthouse in Pittsburgh, built to Richardson's plans in 1884–88. The building is in some ways a remarkable contrast to French Second Empire public buildings like the Philadelphia City Hall and Court House (planned twenty years before and still under construction when this was finished); but not in others: the plan (around a central court) is similar in essentials, and Picturesque effects are still a preeminent consideration. (Carnegie Photo)*

round arches and massive textural stonework might derive from early Christian or Syrian sources or from Italian Byzantine architecture. The characteristic squat colonnettes and arcades usually come from Romanesque monastic or cathedral architecture in the West. Other elements have antecedents in the Gothic Revival: many characteristic Richardsonian roofs; polychromatic effects made by stones of different colors and textures set against variegated brickwork. Still others are more typical of High Picturesque mixes than anything else: polished granite attached columns that pop up here and there; windows grouped in twos and threes with stubby medieval-looking columns in between but nonmedieval sash openings (rather than casements with pointed or round heads, as you might expect).

The most famous Richardsonian Romanesque building is the Allegheny County Courthouse and Jail in Pittsburgh *[5.69]*, "conceded on every hand to be among the preeminent monuments of American architecture—national treasures of the first magnitude. . . . Not only are both buildings venerable facets of Richardson's genius, they are part of the very bone and flesh of Pittsburgh—in short, they *are* Pittsburgh," as James D. Van Trump wrote in "Project H. H. Richardson," in *The Charette* for April 1962. It's hard to realize that this tribute was part of a campaign to save the Allegheny County Courthouse from demolition and replacement by some glass box—one of many last-ditch defenses of Richardsonian buildings in the 1960s.

The massiveness that made Richardsonian Romanesque so effective for public buildings also made it effective for warehouses, where intimations of fortress were appropriate. The most famous example is a warehouse designed by Richardson for Marshall Field's wholesale division goods storage in Chicago; it was vastly admired by Sullivan for aesthetic reasons and by Moderns as anticipating their own brand of simplicity, but demolished nonetheless *[5.29]*. Many emulations survive, however.

For churches, Richardsonian Romanesque massiveness also had much to offer. Trinity Episcopal in Boston's fashionable Back Bay, built in the 1870s, was in fact Richardson's first great success *[5.70]*. This kind of Picturesque style did much more than express the wealth of those who commissioned it; it provided them with an image of something they did not have and wanted very much—venerability. Who could guess that so

mighty and massy and richly textured a pile stood upon brand-new land, only a decade or two earlier cut laboriously out of downtown Boston hills, carted here, and dumped as fill into a shallow inlet? Who could tell that a denomination with enough wealth and social clout to get such a church erected had through most of Boston's early history been a beleaguered, outnumbered minority? Or how very recently the Episcopal Church had become a powerful cultural establishment in Boston?

Furthermore, Richardsonian Romanesque could imply, as no other Picturesque substyle could, something of the awe and decorum requisite in sanctuary types. And that surely was also part of its appeal, why it seemed the right choice for Trinity Episcopal in Boston as well as for Faith Presbyterian in Cairo, Illinois, First Presbyterian in Lynchburg, Virginia, or First Congregational in Malone, New York.

Richardsonian Romanesque had less to offer commercial buildings; its massiveness tended to obstruct effective functioning for small office buildings and for tall ones was a positive handicap. There are points to admire in skyscrapers like John Welburn Root's Monadnock Building or Jenney's Manhattan in Chicago *[5.28]*; but in fact heavy walls made their first-floor masonry so thick as to be rendered virtually useless for commercial purposes, so that practical arguments in favor of glass curtain walls in the Modernist manner, with all weight being carried on a steel cage, were overwhelming.

Even less appropriate was Richardsonian Romanesque massiveness applied to mansions, even those designed by the master himself. Montgomery Schuyler's famous criticism of the Glessner House in Chicago, in *Harper's Magazine* for 1891, is still generally apropos: "Richardson's domestic architecture . . . arrests attention and prevents apathy. . . . A granite wall over 150 feet long, as in the side of this building, almost unbroken, and with its structure clearly exhibited, is sure enough to arrest and strike the beholder . . . but . . . the merits of the building as a building . . . are much effaced when it is considered as a dwelling [i.e., in terms of appropriateness of style to social function], and the structure ceases to be defensible, except, indeed, in a military sense" (cf. 5.17).

We certainly find it so. As for Richardsonian Romanesque furniture, it too seems far too ponderous for everyday domestic use *[5.71]*. It looks as if it all should belong in a city hall somewhere. To appreciate the original appeal of Richardsonian Roman-

5.70. *Copley Square was the showpiece of Boston's new Back Bay area. A fashionable tone was set for it by Richardson's Trinity Church (far left), built 1872–77 of Quincy granite with Longmeadow brownstone trim and other decorative stonework, on a Greek cross plan to accommodate the preaching of its popular rector and later Episcopal Bishop of Massachusetts, Phillips Brooks. A number of later visual alterations produced the building now seen. The west facade and towers were remodeled in the 1890s by Richardson's successor firm, Shepley Rutan & Coolidge.*

In the 1910s the Copley Plaza hotel appeared on another side of the square (right), then an office building of the 1920s in the background (left of center). Famous Catholic architect Charles Donagh Maginnis designed a new chancel, installed 1937–38. But nothing changed the effect of the church like the 1970–71 John Hancock Tower, designed by another famous Boston architect, I. M. Pei, on a totally different scale (center). This photograph of April 1973 shows the tower with most of its windows blown out, temporarily replaced by plywood. (IMG:NAL)

5.71. *Richardson's furniture design had an intrinsically public character; a good deal of it was in fact designed for public buildings, like this chair and benches for the Public Library of Woburn, Massachusetts, in 1878. A highly eclectic mixture, they combine elements of William and Mary and seventeenth-century "Pilgrim" (from the reigning Queen Anne taste) with other historic references—medieval golden oak, velvet, and the like. Not the least*

aspect of Richardson's historical importance is his designing of furniture appropriate to his architecture; that is, to complement exposed ceiling beams, rich textiles, and massive structural forms. Sullivan and Wright followed his lead in this as in so many matters. Photos of Richardson's Brookline studio show him sitting in furniture like this—the famous "my god, how he looks like his own buildings!" applies to his furniture too.

5.72. *In expanding western cities, especially during the years 1900–15, houses were popular that evoked effects of permanence and stability (despite prefabricated wooden construction), combined with hints of wealth via Picturesque touches. So here: set into the basic big foursquare here—double cube with pyramidal roof and*   *broad one-story facade porch—are turrets with flagpoles, extra projecting entry porch, splayed Queen Anne–like roof eaves and widow's walk on the roof peak. These examples were built on 17th Street SE in the archetypal North American western city of Calgary, Alberta. (IMG:NAL)*

esque furniture, we need to keep in mind what contemporaries were comparing it to; again, we find stability and venerability is what they valued.

High Picturesque furniture had reveled in novelty. Not only did it display ever-changing combinations of eclectic ornament, but it also delighted in effects made possible by machinery. The result had been curiously unsubstantial. Richardsonian Romanesque furniture, by contrast, looked as if it would last forever. It was characteristically made of heavy materials—oak, by preference. Its carved ornament emphasized mass rather than void. Where High Picturesque designers delighted in deceiving the eye, treating stone like wood and wood like stone, piling up forms to dizzy heights and unexpected projections, Richardsonian Romanesque projected impressions of solidity, stability, security—or what Richardson himself called "quiet"—through a truth to materials quite foreign to High Picturesque mixes.

"Truth to materials" linked Richardsonian Romanesque to the preceding Eastlake, and to the succeeding Arts and Crafts movement, thence to Sullivan and Wright. But that of course is not an explanation of its importance in its own day, only a historiographic distinction. In its own era Richard-

sonian Romanesque, both in furniture and architecture, met an intensely felt need for environments at once picturesque and solid, environments, that is, which let immigrants to cities from remote farms or far-off countries enjoy some satisfying sense of participation in an exciting world of technological change, along with some reassuring sense of permanence too. Hence its amazing popularity.

And amazing is the word. Within fifteen years of Richardsonian Romanesque's maturation in the early 1870s, every part of the country had regional versions of it. It was practiced by local builders and by the country's leading architects. Then, just as suddenly, it fell out of favor—first in the pacesetting Northeast, then gradually in the West, following the mysterious dictates of cultural lag.[29]

Vestigial Picturesque

Long after Picturesque styles had gone out of high fashion their appeal continued on middle- and lower-middle-class levels. Suburban houses best evidence it; turrets and other Picturesque features were quite common in them until around 1910 [5.72]. Neater, more Academically refined versions of Picturesque styles could be found through the

1920s.[30] And the whole taste for Picturesque effects came back to uproarious life in Popular/Commercial strips that began to preface approaches to every city and town from the 1940s on (see chapter 8). Though Postmodernists seldom admit it, in fact their ideas owe a lot to vestigial Picturesque styles. Plainly, Picturesque styles corresponded to something deep in the American psyche, and still do.

Picturesque Styles as Continuing Cultural Expression

In Picturesque styles may be read a record of all sorts of processes that continue in late-twentieth-century North American life. Most obvious is the economic shift from production by individuals and small groups to production by corporate groups and large factories, as expressed in machine-replicated ornamental detail on architecture and furniture entirely made by machinery, with counterparts in the rise of political "machines" in agribusiness. Ernest Hagen described it in his *Personal Experiences of an Old New York Cabinetmaker* from the 1870s; Steinbeck described it in *Grapes of Wrath;* and today you can see the process extending, in advertisements of a host of popular magazines for prefabricated "authentic period details," even to what was once the last bastion of rugged domestic individualism: historic house renovation and restoration.

Underlying it all is the steady ascendancy of science. As Americans of the 1860s, 1870s, and 1880s compensated themselves for eroding individual identity with delight at the promise-crammed progress of science—manifested in astounding new demonstrations of applied technology in their Picturesque architecture loaded with lavish prefabricated ornament, in convertible furniture that could transform living rooms into bedrooms and back "in a jiffy," in a wealth of new luxuries available to all in every store—so Americans of the 1980s reveled in the promises of computers, even though their most immediate promise was to abolish individual privacy and liberty of action in yet more areas. We speak of computers the way they spoke of machinery, as if some manifestation of godlike human power were involved.[31]

Satisfying demonstrations of power over the past—that's a cultural expression continuing from the Picturesque era. Science's early tools provided the untrammelled masses of ornament that gave Gilded Age Americans their heady sense of control over history, which was proof that the historical past was literally in their hands (on all levels, from the specific iconography of government buildings like the Philadelphia City Hall to miscellaneous booty from all the ages assembled on the Carson house at Eureka). Science's later electronic machines seemed to provide comparable satisfactions for Americans of the 1980s: all knowledge can be codified, organized, used. The belief may be illogical and the satisfaction illusory, but that's irrelevant. It's real while it lasts.

Notes

1. William Miller, "The Realm of Wealth," in John Higham, ed., *The Reconstruction of American History* (New York: Harper & Row, 1962), p. 141.

2. From the census of 1810 it appears that something like 1,000 persons were engaged in making cabinets and chairs. By 1850 there were 37,359, with 83,580 in "furniture making and allied trades."

3. Mass prefabrication began earlier in furniture than in architecture, for obvious reasons, but both developments proceeded along quite similar lines. Top-quality items continued to be "hand-made" or "architect-designed (and supervised)"; but individual craftsmen trained according to the old apprenticeship system were steadily forced by economic circumstance to go into some form of mass production. They could either found small companies of their own that employed labor-saving machines capable of using standardized patterns (e.g., Duncan Phyfe or John Hall's 1840 *Cabinet Maker's Assistant*), or they could go straight into mass production with a big factory, making a smaller profit per item on a far bigger volume. Naturally the long-term advantage was with the bigger factories: led in the 1830s by New York firms like Joseph Meeks and Sons, or Tweed & Bonnell, or Graham & Montgomery of Pittsburgh, in the 1840s by Bird & Burrows of Cincinnati and Birge & Brothers in Troy, New York. As the companies expanded, the older individualistic craftsmen were pushed out, a poignant personal account of the process being *Personal Experiences of an Old New York Cabinet Maker*, written in 1908 by a seventy-eight-year-old immigrant from Hamburg, who after twenty years of practicing his craft around Rivington, Norfolk, and Suffolk streets in New York, found himself unable to meet competition from "Western factory work," which "drove everything else out of the market." The notebook was first published by Elizabeth Ingerham in *Winterthur Newletter* 8/1 (1962):1–7.

4. All too often the mid-nineteenth-century city was a place of what seems in retrospect incredible corruption—physical, aesthetic, and political. So we read in the *Cleveland Leader* for 5 March 1861: "A petition is now before the City Council praying for the repeal of an ordinance, which was passed four years ago, making it unlawful to

pour any slops, filth, &c., into the Cuyahoga River within the city limits, and which in effect shuts off manufactories and refineries from being established upon the river banks. This petition should be granted. To refuse to do it is to pursue the same policy toward manufactures that has diverted trade and business to other more favorable points, and has greatly retarded the legitimate growth of our city."

The history of American Picturesque styles is really inseparable from a history of American morality.

5. Samuel Miller, *A Brief Retrospect of the Eighteenth Century* (New York: T. and J. Swords, 1803).

6. If one wished truly to comment in classical terms, one would attribute loss of virtue not to some vulgar lust for commercial gain, but rather to the moral confusions of a great civil war, and would recall Thucydides's lament over what happened in Greece as the Peloponnesian War dragged on indefinitely: "Proper shame is now termed sheer stupidity; shamelessness on the other hand is called manliness; voluptuousness passes for good tone; haughtiness for good education; lawlessness for freedom: honorable dealing is dubbed hypocrisy and dishonesty, good fortune." It sounds like the description of a General Grant mansion.

7. The precise relationship between Postmodernism and Popular/Commercial styles, especially in the matter of using elements from Picturesque historicist styles for commercial purposes, is dicey. Architects and furniture designers may no longer be as sure about what they like and what good taste is as they were in the heydey of Modernism; but most still seem sure that Popular/Commercial building is what they ought *not* to like and what *bad* taste is. Yet in Popular/Commercial styles are to be found forms they need. See further, chapters 8 and 9.

8. A. J. Downing, first great American advocate of the Picturesque, who devoted many pages of his *Treatise on Landscape Gardening* to defining it, drew his ideas chiefly from *Three Essays: On Picturesque Beauty, etc.,* by William Gilpin (1724–1804), and the *Essay on the Picturesque* of 1794 by Uvedale Price (1747–1829).

9. What could be called Picturesque ostentation appeared in America much earlier than the 1840s, of course. You can sense it very well in a mansion like Linden Place in Bristol, Rhode Island, built by George De-Wolfe as the last of three houses built by brothers of the same family, each grander than the last. It is described and illustrated in Roger Kennedy's *Architecture, Men, Women, and Money* (New York: Random House, 1985): a pile of bracketed balconies and mullions, fanlights, giant pilasters—about as Picturesque in spirit as one could go without obviously abandoning Classical principles altogether.

10. There is a regular pattern here comparable to that which obtains in Colonial English (see chapter 2). It could be demonstrated by comparing the dates when any given Picturesque substyle or its variants (Italianate, Second Empire, etc.) began appearing in a given region (East, Midwest, West) on any given subtype (palace/courthouse, mansion, shop/bank).

11. As Uvedale Price wrote in his 1791 *Essay on the Picturesque:*

> We have already described the difference between the beautiful landscapes of Claude and the picturesque scenes painted by Salvator. . . . The Beautiful is an idea of beauty calmly and harmoniously expressed; the Picturesque an idea of beauty or power strongly and irregularly expressed. . . . Architecture borrows . . . the same expression. We find the Beautiful in the most symmetrical edifices, built in the finest proportions, and of the purest materials. It is on the other hand in some irregular castle . . . , some rude mill nearly as wild as the glen where it is placed, some thatched cottage, weather stained and moss covered, that we find the Picturesque.

12. The pattern can be seen plainly by tracing any sequence of substyles through a single subtype—Italianate through High Picturesque to Richardsonian Romanesque, say, on mansions or department store blocks.

13. The idea has become associated with Thorsten Veblen, though it is, for all intents and purposes, endemic in American culture. Roger Kennedy's *Architecture, Men, Women, and Money* has many fine passages on this theme; for example: "Fine houses, conveyances, and costumes . . . were, and are today, a part of an elaborate and subtle process akin to that in chemistry called seeding. A crystal is placed in a saturated solution and seems to attract to itself, out of that solution, more crystals like itself. . . . In the same way, the appearance of prosperity . . . attracts prosperity" (p. 114).

14. People born in the 1820–40 decades had the best chance of parlaying hard work and a bit of luck into riches. After the Civil War this was much less likely. The *Dictionary of American Biography* tells the story. Fewer and fewer are the "rags-to-riches" success stories in the generations after 1850.

15. By the later nineteenth century all big Northern cities had their mountain resort areas with clusters of elegant summer hotels—Catskills for New York, Poconos for Philadelphia, Adirondacks for New England. Seaside resorts began displacing them in popularity early in the twentieth century, and the mountain hotels, being all wooden, rapidly fell into ruin. Only a few remain; but the most famous of all, the Coronado outside San Diego, has largely survived; it is the subject of a good article by Ann Halpenny Kantor, "Hotel Del Coronado," in *Victorian Resorts and Hotels,* ed. Richard Guy Wilson (Philadelphia: The Victorian Society, 1982).

16. On descriptions by foreigners of American hotels in the post-Civil War decades, see especially the amusing chapter by John Maass in *Victorian Resorts and Hotels.*

17. On evolution of the apartment type, see James Goode's *Best Addresses: A Century of Washington's Distinguished Apartment Houses* (Washington, D.C.: Smithsonian Institution Press, 1988).

18. Awareness of this need to humanize the new tall office buildings constitutes Louis Sullivan's primary importance as an architectural theoretician, it seems to me. Robert Twombley has put the case with his usual acuity in *Louis Sullivan* (New York: Viking, 1986), p. 132:

He did not question America's commitment to "free" enterprise, its choice of businessmen as cultural heroes. Since their energy fuelled the nation, it was only fitting that their buildings be the occasion for a new architecture. . . . Sullivan felt that by working out its aesthetics he could make a real contribution toward an American style.

19. The Philadelphia City Hall was arranged, like many other large Picturesque buildings, around an open court that provided settings for a mass of sculpture allegorizing American and Philadelphian history. All of it, as well as the statue of William Penn, was by a single sculptor: another Scottish immigrant, Alexander Milne Calder, whose work marked, as John Maass observed in his definitive "Philadelphia City Hall: Monster or Masterpiece?" (*AIA Journal,* February 1965), "the very end of a long Renaissance tradition of stereotomy and stone carving" that had been particularly tenacious in Scotland.

20. Many of these stations were completed by Richardson's successor firm, Shepley, Rutan & Coolidge. Appellation of "The Railroad Beautiful" to the B&A seems to have been initiated by Charles Mulford Robinson, an acknowledged leader of the "City Beautiful" movement. These stations are illustrated and discerningly discussed in James O'Gorman's chapter "Commuterism" in *H. H. Richardson: Architectural Forms for an American Society* (Chicago: University of Chicago Press, 1987); and by Jeffrey K. Ochsner in "The Boston & Albany Railroad," *Journal of the Society of Architectural Historians* 47/2 (1988), as well as *H. H. Richardson: Complete Architectural Works* (Cambridge, Mass.: MIT Press, 1982).

21. An excellent idea of their variety and how they came into being is provided by Sarah Bradford Landau's article, "Richard Morris Hunt, the Continental Picturesque, and the 'Stick Style'," *Journal of the Society of Architectural Historians* 42/3 (1983):272–89. The subtype includes such famous examples as the Watts-Sherman house in Newport, designed by H. H. Richardson with Stanford White in the mid-1870s *[5.16].*

22. Claudia Lazzaro has usefully explored the "country" background of Italianate in "Rustic Country House to Refined Farmhouse," *Journal of the Society of Architectural Historians* 44/4 (1985). In many of the villas and hunting lodges she illustrates there are intimations of the American foursquare form so popular at the turn of the twentieth century, as well as of the squarish Italianate villa with belvedere.

23. "Belter" in modern usage tends to be a generic name for combinations of Rococo curves with lavish masses of fruit and flower ornament intricately molded in rosewood, produced more or less indiscriminately by John Henry Belter (1804–63), Charles Baudouine, and Alexander Roux in New York; George Henkels and Daniel Pabst in Philadelphia; A. Eliaers in Boston; Seibrecht and Mallard in New Orleans, and many others.

24. See Anne Bloomfield, "The Real Estate Associates: A Land and Housing Developer of the 1870s in San Francisco," *Journal of the Society of Architectural Historians* 37/1 (1978):13ff.

25. As Leland Roth nicely observed in his *Concise History of American Architecture* (New York: Harper & Row, 1969); "Though . . . under virulent attack during the 1950s and 1960s, they served a very necessary visual function . . . a visual reward" (188). His writings were among the first to appreciate them properly.

26. Recognition on the popular level long continued. For instance, when a hulking 1890s school at Lafayette, Oregon, was abandoned in the late 1960s and taken over for use as a flea market, its change of function was signified by a large boom-town front erected across the eave lines.

27. Vincent Scully, *The Shingle Style* (New Haven, Conn.: Yale University Press, 1955; reissued in 1976 as *The Shingle Style and the Stick Style).* The nature of High Picturesque mixes invites such amoeba-like divisions.

28. The connection has been nicely made by David Hanks in his book accompanying the Smithsonian exhibition *Innovative American Furniture from 1800 to 1980* (New York: Horizon Press, 1981). Rob Krumm, *Working with Displaywrite 3* (TAB Books, 1986), used for his first demonstration text: "It was only with the advent of computers that people actually tried to create 'thinking' machines. . . . As a result, we have acquired, in the last twenty years or so, a new kind of perspective on what thought is, and what it is not."

29. James Goode's *Capital Losses* (Washington, D.C.: Smithsonian Institution Press, 1979, pp. 93–96) tells a revealing story of millionaires George and Phoebe Hearst moving to Washington from the west, buying a fine late Georgian house in 1883 and proceeding to remodel it at great expense into what they thought was still fashionable Richardsonian Romanesque—only to discover that, by the time their house was ready for them, everybody *au courant* in the east was building in new Academic versions of the Georgian style they had just obliterated.

30. Chapter 9 of *The Comfortable House : North American Suburban Architecture 1890–1930* (Cambridge, Mass.: The MIT Press, 1986) gives an extensive treatment of this subject.

31. A fine recent treatment of this theme at length is provided by Thomas Hughes, *American Genesis: A Century of Invention and Technological Enthusiasm 1870–1970* (New York: Viking, 1989, p. 3). "This history argues that inventors, industrial scientists, engineers and system builders have been the makers of modern America. Their numerous and enthusiastic supporters from many levels of society believed their methods and values applicable and beneficial when applied to such other realms of social activity as politics, business, architecture, and art. . . . The invention of a method of invention was the greatest invention of the [post–Civil War] era. Men and women assumed, as never before, that they had the power to create a world of their own design." All too often it hemmed them in.

6.37. At the turn of this century, palatial mansions built as summer homes lined the Newport shore, as Roman villas and estates lined the coasts of Italy in imperial times. Nowadays egalitarianism has made such ostentatious displays of wealth unseemly, and graduated income taxes have made great wealth a little harder to possess. So Cornelius Vanderbilt's The Breakers, in the foreground, is now a museum, and the larger villa behind it, real-estate developer Ogden Goelet's Ochre Court, is now Salve Regina College. Both were built to designs by Richard Morris Hunt, in 1895 and 1890 respectively, the one in an Academic Renaissance variant (based on sixteenth-century Genoese palaces), the other in a variant of Academic Gothic inspired by châteaux on the Loire. (Photograph by John T. Hopf, courtesy of Newport County Chamber of Commerce)

6
A WORLD POWER AND ITS ACADEMIC ARCHITECTURE, c. 1890–c. 1930

Academic Styles
in Their Time and Place

Until around 1890, Europeans generally thought the United States as much a curiosity as a world power. After 1900 that changed. Quite suddenly, the rest of the world discovered a nation whose population in the 1850s had been less than France's but now surpassed in numbers all Western nations but Russia; which had become the world's leading exporter of food and coal, a major producer of iron and steel, and a financial center rivaling London; which had begun building a navy as big as Germany's, and in the Spanish-American War had shown a disposition to use it for empire building in far parts of the globe; and which claimed the status of international arbiter in settling the Boxer Rebellion in China, the war between Japan and Russia, and the Morocco crisis—previews of the role Woodrow Wilson was to play in the 1919 Peace of Versailles and League of Nations.

Contemporaries were struck by the sudden change of status. Ivy League professors began writing books about it; two in 1908 alone: *America as a World Power 1897–1907* by John H. Latanbe of Johns Hopkins; *The United States as a World Power* by Archibald Cary Coolidge of Harvard. Soon "World Power" had to be a standard concluding chapter heading for line-of-progress American histories of all sorts.

Put another way: the national posture acquired a new dignity. The Gilded Age's nouveau-riche clownishness and provincial vulgarity were no longer tolerable. Nor were the styles of architecture and furniture that had been produced for and by it. An era with new national dignity demanded more

dignified artistic expressions. The response was an Academic architecture and furniture, whose styling showed, by a new sense of restraint and discipline of ornament, the results of systematic training in professional academies of art and architecture.

Not that such training was unique to America, of course; far from it. The first great American exemplars of Academic styles were trained in Europe, especially France. Nor was the idea of expressing national pride unique to America either; a Romantic nationalism which thought of nations as having personalities like individuals, personalities that could and should find expression in a national architecture, pervaded all advanced Western culture at the end of the nineteenth century. One of the qualities distinguishing Academic styles from the preceding Picturesque is precisely their relationship to broader international movements, expressing a more mature nation's broader outlook.

Cities continued to grow rapidly in the years between 1890 and 1930; confident and dramatic images of new world power appeared in downtowns and suburbs alike. The most confident and dramatic of these images were in New York. This was New York's great age. Its national leadership in matters financial and commercial was everywhere acknowledged; New York claimed cultural leadership as well, and commissioned architecture correspondingly. True, the great showpiece for what could be accomplished in Academic styles was created at Chicago's 1893 World's Columbian Exposition—urban architecture appropriate to the new era, great white and gold reincarnations of Imperial Roman grandeur, the National Democratic Classical Revival on a grander, more sophisticated, more majestic scale. But New York architects set the tone

6.1. Liberty Enlightening the World, *looking south from the tip of Manhattan Island. Fabricated in Paris by Frédéric Auguste* *Bartholdi and set up on a base designed by Richard Morris Hunt in 1886; restored and reopened 4 July 1986. (IMG:NAL)*

6.2. The Woolworth Building, begun 1911, here seen from Broadway. From its completion in 1913 until 1931 this was New York's tallest building, and many believe it the greatest embodiment of Louis Sullivan's skyscraper ideal, a distinctly American building type that ought to be "every inch a proud and soaring thing." Architect Cass Gilbert used Gothic forms to achieve this effect, and he sheathed the building in terra cotta using a technique first introduced by the famous Gothic Revivalist James Renwick. Restored in 1980 by Ezra D. Ehrenkrantz Associates of San Francisco. (IMG:NAL)

for this world's fair, and New York tried hardest, in the most unpromising circumstances, to realize the new Academic ideals.

Public architecture in New York City spanned the widest range of Academic taste *[6.1, 6.2]*. It included many of the earliest as well as many of the most famous monuments in Academic Classical styles: from the Statue of Liberty in the 1880s to the New York Public Library, the Natural History Museum, Metropolitan Life, the Municipal Building, and Columbia University's main campus, to the abstracted Art-Deco sort of classicism displayed by the Chrysler Building and Rockefeller Center in the 1930s. It also included the Academic Gothic Revival's most famous single example: the Woolworth Building of 1913, which Paul Goldberger has happily called "the Mozart of skyscrapers." There are countless other demonstrations of the Academic style's versatility and variety, like the Sherry-Netherland, Pierre, and Savoy-Plaza grouping of hotels around Central Park. Much of this city still stands, some happily preserved (see 6.15, 6.16, 6.28), some in sad ruin *[6.3]*. But however decayed, in popular mind and memory they all live a forever-youthful Dorian Gray existence in countless movies, posters, paintings, and novels.[1]

Academic styles were introduced into New York with the Statue of Liberty in the mid-1880s. Along with Liberty the statue celebrated the nation's recovery from Civil War division and self-doubt; celebrated too New York's definitive rise to supremacy in national affairs, its role as gateway to opportunity. Architect of the base and setting for Bartholdi's gigantic statue was Richard Morris Hunt, first of the great Academic architects of the nation and moving spirit of the World's Columbian Exposition in Chicago a decade later. Funds for final completion were provided by a genuinely grassroots campaign, so thoroughly had the whole idea seized popular imagination. For patriots, pleasing associations with the Revolution were aroused—part of a Colonial Revival just getting underway. For progressives, pleasing associations with democracy were reinforced, especially by Emma Lazarus's poem about the Golden Door offering a refuge from wretched Europe's teeming shores. This statue instantly became a prime image of national aspirations in Popular/Commercial arts of every sort from ashtrays to needlepoint, and has remained so. Still in the 1980s you found spontaneous folk-art replicas on lawns *[8.19]* and official reminders on New York license plates; Chinese students demonstrating for democracy wheeled a big model of the "Goddess of Liberty" into the main square of Beijing. It remains the prime monument to spirit and forms of the Academic era.

The Academic spirit was genuinely national; that is to say, its sentiments were widespread throughout the middle class, in an era when middle-class sentiments were the ones that set public taste. Streetscapes of new dignity began appearing, even in small-town strongholds of the Picturesque *[6.4, 6.5]*. Smaller cities with aspirations openly emulated New York: Salt Lake's "Wall Street of the West," Oakland's mini–Times Square *[6.6, 6.7]*. But the American spirit of that time was most monumentally expressed where, according to all social logic, it ought to have been—in the capital, Washington, D.C.

Not all visitors to Washington understand that the city's truly monumental area, the whole mall between the Washington Monument and the Lincoln Memorial, with the Memorial Bridge across the Potomac behind it, is a creation of the first decades of the twentieth century. Before that, much of that area was water and swamp, and much else ruined by a century of mindless improvisation. Academic city planners in the McMillan Commission of 1909, determined to reaffirm the intentions of George Washington and his French classical planner L'Enfant to create a new Rome on a new Tiber, made Washington what it is today. And it is a great sight. The grand row of museums, the monumental facades of Constitution Avenue, the Pan-American Building, the Vietnam Memorial, and the First Divi-

sion Column—there's nothing like it anywhere.

To those grand monumental vistas created for American cities by high-style Academic architects, there is a counterpart: the "comfortable house," built in countless numbers between 1890 and the 1930s, memorials to the one and only attempt ever made by any nation in history to provide homes of their own for all its citizens *[6.8, 6.9]*. These enduring monuments to the spirit of the era can be seen everywhere. Tiniest towns, deepest country, fashionable suburb, and industrial slum—no place is without its complement of suburban-type houses from this period. They were built by architects, near-architects, and non-architects; by contractors and handymen; by big companies like Sears and

6.3. Frederick Douglass Boulevard at 154th Street in Harlem. Apartment houses with store fronts on ground level, built c. 1895–1910. The inherent dignity of Academic architecture is perceptible despite dilapidation: elements of Academic Classical, Academic Italianate, even Romanesque are coordinated, restrained, interrelated. (IMG:NAL)

6.4 (top). *This view of State Street in Harrisburg looking toward the Pennsylvania state capitol is dominated by Saint Patrick's Church, built c. 1900 in Academic Italianate forms; its dome recalls Saint Peter's in Rome (also the state capitol, begun 1901), and its facade recalls Jesuit-style facades of sixteenth-century Italy. Its scale and sophistication make neighboring Italianate row houses and the 1871–74 Gothic Revival Methodist Episcopal church look somehow small and naive. (IMG:NAL)*

6.5 (left). *Small-town banks in simple classical-temple forms were as typical of Academic architecture as little Episcopal churches had been of Gothic or boom-town cornices of Picturesque. This one was built in 1915 in the small Ohio town of Sidney, two years before Sullivan came there to design the People's Federal Savings Bank [5.67] on the opposite side of the courthouse square, in his much more personal, much subtler, lingeringly Picturesque manner. (IMG:NAL)*

"Sorely throb my feet, a-tramping city pavements (Ah, the springy sod upon an upland moor!)"

6.6 (opposite, center). "Wall Street of the West": intersection of South Main, Broadway, and Exchange streets in Salt Lake City. In the background appear the heavy Academic Classical blocks of the Boston and Newhouse buildings, designed by New York architect Henry Cobb and named after Jewish entrepreneur Samuel Newhouse, whose fortune was based on the Boston Mine and who was the moving force behind the development between 1900 and 1910 of this "gentile" (in Mormon terms) business district some blocks away from the Saints' business district around Temple Square. Just behind them is the Salt Lake Exchange, again consciously recalling New York. In the foreground is the Judge Building, more similar to Louis Sullivan's 1890 Wainwright Building in St. Louis. (IMG:NAL)

6.7 (top, left). The convergence of Broadway, Telegraph Avenue, and San Pablo Street creates a succession of triangular sites in downtown Oakland, occupied by the Broadway (foreground) and Cathedral buildings. Seattle also has a triangular "Times Square building" at the intersection of Olive Way and Stewart Street, as do many other cities. All were under way between 1905 and 1915, all were tributes to New York's commercial glamor in general and particularly to the Flatiron Building. (IMG:NAL)

6.8 (top, right). Illustration for a 1929 promotional brochure by the Van Sweringen Company of Cleveland advertising "Peaceful Shaker Heights." The company developed not only such elegant suburbs, but also much of downtown Cleveland's city center.

6.9 (above, right). "Low Cost Homes designed especially for Industrial Purposes": front and back covers of a brochure put out by the Aladdin Company of Bay City, Michigan. This manufacturer of mass-prefabricated homes was prepared to—and did on numerous occasions—lay out entire towns on short notice. Though this working-class suburb promised no such idyllic escape from city stresses as Van Sweringen's Shaker Heights, it does offer an escape from barracks-like conformity, through a comparable variety of stylistic forms.

Wards; by smaller ones like Aladdin of Bay City, Michigan, and Southern Homes of Shreveport; by fly-by-nights. Some recognizably relate to Academic high styles. Others seem generated by some quasi-vernacular aesthetic. But all in one way or another bear the stamp of their times.

Definition and Identifying Characteristics

"Academic" here includes as substyles Beaux-Arts, Colonial Revival, Arts and Crafts, Mission, Moderne, Prairie, and many more which have in common a new self-conscious attitude toward "Art" (whence "Academic," where art is self-consciously taught, rather than learned by apprenticeship, as had been characteristic of architectural education heretofore). This Academic attitude involved a distinctively restrained and sophisticated rehandling

6.10. *Illustration from promotional brochure for the R. Guastanino Company showing adaptation of ancient Catalan light clay vaulting techniques in recent (1897–1911) buildings. Among notable users, duly numbered: (1) Heins and La Farge for their [Byzantine/Gothic] Cathedral of Saint John the Divine in New York, 1908–9; (2) Hornblower and Marshall for their 1906–10 Natural History Museum on the Mall in Washington; (9) H. Van Buren Magonigle for the 1905–6 McKinley National Memorial in Canton, Ohio; (12) McKim, Mead and White for their 1897 restoration of the Rotunda at the University of Virginia. (From George R. Collins, "The Transfer of Thin Masonry Vaulting from Spain to America,"* JSAH 27/1 [1968])

of architectural composition and forms, from wherever derived, hence nearly all earlier styles have Academic counterparts (see "Substyles" and Appendix).

Aggressive Modernists in a later generation were fond of denouncing Academic architecture as mere copying of historic styles. This is to misunderstand it. Academic architects were never mere copyists; they thought of their goal as to "be in the boots of" architects of earlier times—to think like the creators of Gothic cathedrals or Renaissance palaces or Georgian mansions and in their turn to create new designs out of older elements, appropriate to the needs of contemporary life.[2] The classic example of this attitude was Julia Morgan having all her papers burned when she retired, because of her belief that modern architects should be like the anonymous builders of the Middle Ages, with buildings as their proper monuments, not biographies. Thus far—and thus far from copying—the new self-consciousness took Academic architects; it did not yet take them to the point of realizing that architects of earlier times were never self-conscious in the sense that they were, hence moderns could never "step into their boots."

"Academic" does not itself refer to a style; it is a way of handling other, earlier styles, refining and correcting them according to rules or, more precisely, according to attitudes learned "academically."

Four basic attitudes distinguish Academic styles from the Picturesque styles that precede them and the Modern ones that follow: a willingness to use applied ornament; generous scale; systematically disciplined adaptation of past styles; and a vague, generalized sort of associationism. All of these are evident in most Academic works. These characteristics, plus a shared self-consciousness, explain how such outwardly different substyles as Beaux-Arts Classical, Georgian, and Arts and Crafts can belong together in the single category of Academic.

Willingness to retain applied ornament is the primary characteristic that distinguishes Academic from Modern. In the 1880s a crisis occurred in concepts of design, comparable in many ways to what has happened in the 1980s. Central to it was the role of ornament. What was to be done about the excess of meaningless ornament that was making all design farcical? In essence, three solutions were proposed. One, in retrospect leading directly to Modernism, was to abolish ornament altogether, as decadent (in the sense of having lost its object, repeated by rote) and nonscientific. A second, essentially the Beaux-Arts position, was to discipline ornament by careful study of historical models. A third was to let ornament be dictated by the nature of materials and the uses of given buildings; this was called by its practitioners the "progressive" or "organic" concept. The second and third positions were perceived as antithetical at the time, and certainly later writers often made much of the "great war" between Progressives and Beaux-Arts advocates.[3] Yet historical perspective reveals much more in common between, say, Frank Lloyd Wright and Richard Morris Hunt, than in dispute between them. What they shared—a willingness to keep ornament a vital part of architecture, and through it maintain a vital continuity between past and present—was in the long run far more significant than any superficial quarrels over how ornament ought best to be used.

Where Academic styles are most strikingly distinguishable from the preceding Picturesque, Classical Revival, or Gothic Revival styles, and therefore most strikingly express the culture of a newly self-conscious world power, is in generous scale. Academic liking for bigness, both relative and absolute, often demanded new technologies, whether for vast vaulting schemes *[6.10]* or simply to produce the great expanses of single-paned windows demanded on all levels. For this taste was pervasive. Thanks to more widely distributed wealth, larger-dimensioned elements of all sorts were available: high ceilings, big fireplaces, spacious verandas with sturdy columns, heavy plate rails, massively coffered doors—all apparent, in relative proportions, in bungalows as well as mansions, carriage houses and courthouses.

Such scale was appropriate to a country so much bigger than it had been, especially in the pre–Civil War era. That earlier America of small towns and tidy courthouses and simple citizen-farmers seems very, very far away, and architecture shows it. In place of the neat residences illustrated by Downing or Minard Lafever, or Mark Twain's little house in Hannibal, come those spacious high-ceiling, many-roomed, wide-porched houses of the prosperous middle-class suburbs around 1900—hard to heat, costly to paint, with cramped kitchens and minuscule chambers for the hired help, but pretentious parlors for entertaining the rector, the literary circle, or dinner guests. In place of temple-houses like Jefferson's Monticello or Biddle's Andalusia, the upper class now built like Theodore Roosevelt's Sagamore Hill—"a home with elbow room. . . . Ten bedrooms on the second floor and two on the third, besides maids' rooms. . . . The architects gave him . . . eight fireplaces . . . foundations twenty feet thick; joists, rafters, and roof-boards . . . in proportion."[4]

This age likewise built factories of a complexity, and office buildings on a scale, unimaginable earlier. Compared to the gargantuan complex of plants the Ford Motor Company spread around Detroit in the early decades of the twentieth century, for instance, little new England factories like Slater's Mill appeared as ridiculously primitive as the bicycle shed where Henry Ford built his first car. Nor could the 1830s generation who hailed Isaiah Rogers's Tremont House in Boston as the wonder of an age have dreamt of the scale normal for hotels of any pretension in any middling early-twentieth-century American city: the Hotel Utah in Salt Lake, the Traymore in Atlantic City, the Monteleone in New Orleans, the Jefferson in Richmond *[6.11, 6.12]*.

And such big-scale buildings were put into settings of comparable grandeur: Daniel Burnham's 1912 motto "Make no little plans!" ruled city planning everywhere. The age agreed, "They have no magic to stir men's blood. . . . Make big plans." It was Burnham who set the colossal scale of the 1893 Chicago world's fair. In his offices was designed (probably by Charles G. Atwood, 1849–95) the first fair building: the temporary railroad station behind the Administration Building site, which ultimately begat a mighty progeny of vaulted and columned Roman baths serving passengers from Seattle to Philadelphia and which was so immediately popular that, as Carroll Meeks remarked in *The Railroad Station*, "a scale nearly that of Michelangelo at St. Peter's was considered normal for public buildings in the early part of this century" *[6.13]*.[5] Sheer bigness was a principal ingredient in the appeal of skyscrapers to this age also: from 1908 to 1930 Burnham's 1901 Flatiron Building in New York was featured as the apex of the "Tree of Architecture" frontispiece to successive editions of Sir Bannister Flight Fletcher's *History of Architecture on the Comparative Method*, an architectural history text which in Academic architectural offices carried the same sort of quasi-biblical authority enjoyed by Giedion's *Space, Time and Architecture* in Moderns' *[Introduction A, 6.7]*.

Such grand structures were meant to be seen at great distances, of course, which led to the ever-

6.11. Rotunda Mezzanine Lobby of the Jefferson [Jefferson Sheraton] Hotel in Richmond, Virginia, completed 1898 on designs of Carrère and Hastings. This room alone afforded nearly 7500 square feet of reception space, and the Empire Room next to it had over 4000. The lobby proper is in the Palm Court, where now stands a statue of Jefferson, once erected in the Rotunda of the University of Virginia. Vlastomil Koubek directed a total refurbishing in the mid-1980s. The original commission came to Carrère and Hastings a few years after completion of their famous Ponce de Leon Hotel in Saint Augustine, and this version of Beaux-Arts Classicism was likewise given a Mediterranean cast—vaguely Italian sixteenth century—no doubt to suggest Southern expansiveness. (Courtesy Jefferson Sheraton Hotel)

6.12. Mezzanine floor plan of the Jefferson Hotel suggests more of its size and complexity. Besides the Rotunda there were five other public spaces plus a nearly 5000-square-foot Grand Ballroom with stage and retail shops below, added in 1928. (see also 9.32.)

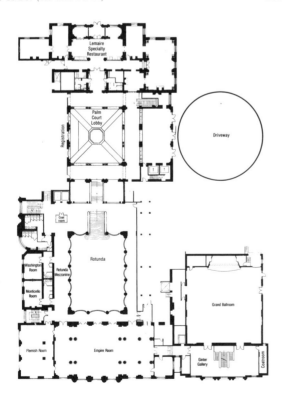

increasing scale of Academic city plans. Burnham led the way, with his replanning of Cleveland, San Francisco, Manila in the Philippines, and especially Chicago (his 1906–9 plan was so comprehensive that as simplified in the Wacker Manual it was used to teach local history in Chicago schools). Ironically, the most lasting and effective result of all this planning was restoration of the L'Enfant plan for Washington, D.C. (by the McMillan Commission, on which sat Burnham, sculptor Augustus Saint-Gaudens, and old Frederick Law Olmsted)—the one American city where tall buildings in the city core were forbidden by law!

Academic styles are further distinguished from the preceding Picturesque by correct and restrained adaptation of past styles, exteriors that are usually all in the same style, and interior rooms that are occasionally in diverse styles but consistent within themselves. "Restraint" is a relative quality, obviously. In this case, its meaning is first of all relative to the preceding Picturesque styles. No more vulgar pilings of one floor on another, each heaped with ornament indiscriminately. As for

6.13. The grand scaling of Academic styles works admirably to proclaim the hugeness of a country whose Confederation was inconceivable before transcontinental railroads. In this vast hall announcements of departures to exotic far-off places boom and reverberate all round, complementing the encircling frieze bearing their names in grand Roman majescules on the encircling frieze: Toronto's Union Station (1914–29, architects Ross & MacDonald, Hugh Jones, and John M. Lyle). Immediate model was New York's Academic Roman Revival Pennsylvania Station, completed only a half-dozen years earlier—another of the innumerable echoes of New York to be found in Toronto, at once the most British and most American of Canadian cities. (IMG:NAL, 1950)

6.14. Entrance loggia with view to the courtyard and second-floor galleries in the Dade County Art Museum, built as Vizcaya, James Deering's mansion near Miami, by F. Burrall Hoffman, Jr., and Paul Chalfin, 1913–16. (Courtesy of Dade County Museum)

"correctness," it can mean either incorporation in a design of exact replication of whole buildings or parts of buildings taken from specific sources, or use of stone or wood or brick so as to express its natural qualities; often it means both simultaneously.

At one extreme, "correctness" often went so far as incorporation of actual historical material. In the Louis XIV room at Cornelius Vanderbilt's Breakers, R. M. Hunt put one or two original seventeenth-century chairs and matched them with copies so exact that a casual glance couldn't tell which was which. Vizcaya re-created a Mediterranean palace *[6.14]*. A short and logical step led to historical museums like Winterthur and Colonial Williamsburg—one a late-eighteenth-century house enlarged by early-twentieth-century additions of actual early American rooms and furniture painstakingly selected with the most expert advice then available *[2.37, 3.54]*; the other a 1920s town carefully restored and rebuilt back into an eighteenth-century past *[2.73, 9.14]*. Both are mythical pasts, to be sure, where leaders were more heroic and cultured, followers more docile and unobtrusive than soberer history suggests—but created with strict scholarly accuracy within those limits.

"Correctness" could also include the earliest furniture by Gustav Stickley at the turn of the century, made with such fidelity to eighteenth-century forms and materials that all examples seem to have vanished. Obviously the line between designing with such "Academic" accuracy and outright restorations of buildings was always thin. William Strickland's restoration of the tower of Independence Hall in 1827 might well be taken as the beginning of the Academic Colonial Revival as distinct from Colonial survivals *[2.5]*; certain it is that after the Civil War, complementary patriotic enthusiasms fueled both Academic restorations and Academic re-creations, setting a precedent for the restoration/rebuilding/preservation syndrome that so promoted Postmodernism in the 1970s.

Academic architecture retained a vague and generalized associationism distinguishable alike from the naive ideological associations of Classical and Greek Revivalists who consciously used past styles to promote present ideologies; from those older traditions of architecture as metaphor which took for granted use of certain shapes and styles for given purposes and occasions and was still alive in the colonial era; and from the Modern assumption that architecture should keep no literary or romantic associations whatever.

Academic Gothic Revivalists like Ralph Adams Cram, Henry Vaughn, or Bernard Maybeck loved the Middle Ages as deeply as earlier Gothic Revivalists like Pugin or Upjohn; but they also knew sufficiently more about medieval architecture that they could no longer maintain their naive notions of Gothic being specifically and exclusively devised to express Christian ideas. They could see that Gothic was also the product of economic and social conditions. When they called Gothic Christian and Catholic, they meant not that it made dogmatic statements about some specific form of religion, but rather that in Gothic architecture, as in Catholic Christianity (including Anglo-Catholic), was to be found the highest principles of truth and beauty that constituted the good life. A statement like the following from Cram's *My Life in Architecture* perfectly exemplifies the Academic attitude:

> After all, Gothic is no isolated style with its own individual laws wrought out of nothing for its own original ends. The *forms* of beauty vary from age to age; the

creative and controlling laws are ever the same, and it is because these were recognized in [1870s designs like] Trinity [Episcopal church, by Richardson], in [1880s designs like] the McKim Library [i.e., Boston Public] and in St. Augustine [i.e., Ponce de Leon Hotel by Carrère & Hastings] that they are all good.[6]

Similarly, whereas for earlier Classical Revivalists the "American" connotations of classical architecture were precise and specific—Roman Republican virtue, Greek democratic liberty, and so on—Academics understood the "American" implications of Imperial Roman railroad stations or Louis XVI mansions, Cape Cod cottages and Georgian college dormitories in a far more general way. Fifty years of intervening scholarship presented past styles in a perspective of given times and conditions in American history, understandable as general manifestations of the American past rather than specific statements about American character.

At the same time, Academics still could not equate functionalism with physical convenience, the way their Modernist successors would; in Academic architecture, styles still had a social function. Thus, for example: to build all of Pennsylvania Station in New York with the same frankly exposed frame of steel and glass that could be seen in the train shed would have seemed barbaric to them. It would have reduced the building to a utilitarian structure, a mechanical contrivance, and so destroyed the principal social function of this or any other public building—to proclaim the grandeur of the city, to help citizens perceive themselves as part of it, to make individual lives somehow nobler by being set in relationship to a grand past *[6.13, 6.16–6.18]*.

This vague attitude to associationism was exemplified in, and perhaps founded upon, the Academic habit of reading architectural history apart from any specific meanings inherent in actual built forms. Mimetic forms, inherited symbolic forms like the sacred and royal dome, *architecture parlante*—all these were never, for all practical purposes, acknowledged; they belonged, so Academics believed, to times when people could not read and had to be taught by pictures instead, hence were inappropriate in more enlightened ages, especially in this, the most learned and enlightened of all. Higher art, so the argument ran, really began when symbolism ended. So you got such stuff as this, from AIA Gold Medal winner Charles Donagh Maginnis, quoted in his *Dictionary of American Biography* entry: "The high distinction of Greek architecture was the sensitiveness with which it manifested its primitive system of construction," and "Romanesque . . . was an episode of the great Gothic system which seized a latent structural principle and carried it forward to astonishing integrity." How such a definition differed from Corbusier's concept of classical styles involving no more than judicious manipulation of solids and voids in light, or Giedion's exaltation of utilitarian bridges into Great Architecture, who could say? Such Academic attitudes plainly provided a catalyst to precipitate the Modern revolution that destroyed them. But in its own time Academic was the great stylistic vehicle for proclaiming the values and goals of a society newly aware of itself as a world power.

Social Function

Within American society, Academic architecture in all its substyles reinforced the status quo in the years c. 1890–c. 1930; it confirmed the pretensions of a new upper class emerging in the post–Civil War years, based upon second-generation wealth. In a broader perspective, Academic architecture served to create visual metaphors of distinctive American nationality, comparable to those being created for other nations in Western civilization; it was part of a climactic enthusiasm in Western society for "Romantic Nationalism." In the course of the nineteenth century almost all Western nations had seen reforms of their institutions carried out along democratic and rational lines, by various means and with varying degrees of success. All sorts of architects who thought themselves progressive and high-minded were trying to create visual metaphors of their respective varieties of this new nationalism; there was a romantic British architecture (Edwin Lutyens being its most notable exponent, in retrospect at least); a romantic Dutch architecture (Petrus Berlage's Stock Exchange of the 1890s); German (Peter Behrens's AG Farben factory expressing German industrial might); Swedish (Ragnar Östberg's 1923 Stockholm City Hall), and so on. Creating appropriate American counterparts was of concern to American Academic architects of every persuasion. Wright, Burnham, Sullivan, Hunt, Maybeck—they all talked about expressing "Americanism" in architecture. But they differed about how this social function was to be realized in practice, how exactly "American democracy" was to be translated into architectural form.

In general they all agreed that Academic architectural practice, as distinct from the preceding Picturesque, required greater discipline and sophistication to achieve its goals. Whether it was to proclaim the cultural superiority of inherited wealth over mere money grubbing, or to create visual metaphors of those values from the past from which the new nation's distinctive institutions had been drawn, and on which they rested still, architecture would have to be far more discriminating, far more correct, in its usage of earlier styles. Concepts of "correct usage" might vary widely. Frank Lloyd Wright's interpretation was a long way from Richard Morris Hunt's and both from, say, Julia Morgan's or Irving Gill's. But all would agree upon the general principle of correctness and restraint (indeed Wright called his architecture "The Cause Conservative") because all agreed in principle upon what architecture ought to do in and for society.

All shared too a sense of exhilaration at creating a new and significantly American architecture. In his 1936 autobiography *My Life in Architecture,* Ralph Adams Cram spoke for them all when he looked back upon his arrival in Boston in 1881 to begin an architectural apprenticeship. He found American architecture in a "general condition . . . of confusion worse confounded. . . . Prior to 1830 nothing really bad had been done . . . hitherto, the Republic had been explicitly aristocratic, selective, even fastidious in the choices it made . . . from then on nothing good, except sporadically, came into existence, and for fifty years architecture in America fell to a lower level than history had ever before recorded." Even Richardson, as Cram saw him in retrospect, was not the "saviour" he had seemed, but had only added one more confused and illogical eclectic style to the heap: "It was evident that, compared even with contemporary Europe, we were artistic barbarians, and that for our own national credit that condition of things would have to be changed."

Then came what seemed to him the miraculous transformation. "The American Institute of Architects . . . took on a new life; schools of architecture, notably those of Massachusetts Institute of Technology and Columbia University, began systems of consistent training, and more and more students began going over to the French Ecole des Beaux Arts, at that time the one great and effective center of architectural training. The 'American Renaissance' . . . !"

That meant, in practice, usage of eclectic styles would be determined by "the right thing to do" as understood by consensus within a fairly tight group of wealthy cultural leaders, critics, teachers, writers (including architectural historians), and practitioners—often related by family, often playing several roles (like practicing architects Cram, Russell Sturgis of Boston, or Talbot Hamlin, who all wrote definitive textbooks and criticism). Always understood, though seldom explicitly stated, was the role of these refined Academic styles in and for this tight little society: to proclaim the cultural sophistication of a generation come into inherited wealth, grown into superior social status, taking wealth and status for granted and so feeling no need to flaunt it to the world, only to their peers. What this generation wanted architecture to do for them was to proclaim to their peers how well educated they were, how polished their manners, how adroit their *savoir faire*—in a word, how they were no longer *nouveaux riches* like their parents, but long-time establishment. They wanted their architecture to demonstrate how risible, to people like themselves, familiar with Athens and Westminster Abbey, were little wooden Greek Revival houses of the 1830s or Gothic Revival churches of the 1850s; how provincial and crude, to frequenters of Flanders and Provence, were bits and pieces of Renaissance and medieval ornament piled together by California lumber barons, or piratical merchants trading out of Boston. They wanted the real thing, made out of the real materials, even if only bits and pieces of the real thing were available. Whence the somewhat ludicrous spectacle of American millionaires trotting all over the world with a crowd of dealers and agents and experts strung out like pack mules behind, buying here ancestral busts, there tapestries and paintings and furniture, all for shipment by the boatload back to the States to stock "instant museums"; or being cheated at home by a passel of smooth, sharp-talking dealers with stables of experts ready to fake Old Masters on demand. In later times it would be asked often and rhetorically, What was "American" about all this? There was an answer: to provide environments that would express and create a hereditary American aristocracy. Deering's Vizcaya is only one among many examples:

On Christmas Day, 1916, when the late James Deering opened the doors of Vizcaya in Miami, Florida, he saw a dream come true. For 25 years he had collected in Europe architectural backgrounds, rare period furniture, textiles, sculpture, and ceramics. To enshrine them he built Vizcaya . . . *[6.14]*. The architects, F. Burrall Hoffman, Jr., and Paul Chalfin, designed a building to accommodate the remarkable collection. . . . Mr. Deering leased large warehouses in which he and the architects, over and over again, experimentally laid out and furnished room after room. The height of the second floor was determined by the size of a tall entranceway . . . from the palace built for Niccolò Pisani and his son, Vettor, daring Venetian admirals of the 14th century when Venice was a great sea power. . . . The tall, graceful doors at either end of the loggia once stood in the vestibule of the Hotel Beauharnais in Paris. . . . occupied by Napoleon's stepson Eugène. . . . The library shows . . . a fine Corinthian mantel, over which an ancient Roman mosaic has been set into the wall. . . . The style of Vizcaya's 18th-century salon is Louis XV . . . [the] size of the room determined by the plaster ceiling, which once graced the Palazzo Rossi in Venice. . . . In the music room . . . ornate ceiling and paneled, painted canvas walls came out of a Milanese palace.[7]

What is "American" about all this? Simple: it makes James Deering into a member of an American aristocracy.

To find late-nineteenth-century American capitalists in silk hats and frock coats stepping out the doors of French Renaissance palaces on Fifth Avenue was to Louis Sullivan, in a once-famous passage from *Kindergarten Chats,* "a paradox, a contradiction, an absurdity." But in terms of this architecture's social function, it is Sullivan's comment that is absurd.[8] For people like Deering or the Vanderbilts or the du Ponts, whose power and social position in turn-of-the-century American society was entirely comparable to anything enjoyed by the Medicis or Valoises, to appropriate their architectural symbolism was entirely logical and proper. Furthermore, these visual metaphors were never aimed at people like the author and readers of *Kindergarten Chats.* They were addressed to inferior members of the peer group: to the Carsons of Eureka, the Crockers of San Francisco, the Hearsts newly moved to Washington, D.C., nerds of great wealth who still lived in vulgar, unsophisticated Picturesque mansions.

For the rich, Joy Wheeler Dow put the case very well in a collection of essays he published in 1904 under the title *American Renaissance:* a Vanderbilt mansion in New York, Newport, or Asheville, despite any original inspiration in European palaces, already was "gradually grown to look to us what it really is, i.e., good American Renaissance."

For the middle classes, the case was put more

implicitly but just as effectively in blurbs for prefabricated suburban houses from the period. Hear Sears, Roebuck and Company advertising an "Exclusive Magnolia" model in the 1918 edition of its *Modern Homes*: "A colonial type of residence which from the days of George Washington to the present time has housed the greatest figures in American history, science, and literature." Such a group you, for a mere five thousand dollars, can join. And why should a twentieth-century middle-class American live in an eighteenth-century style of house? For the same reason that the rich wanted to live in Genoese palaces and French châteaux—because it shows how much more you know about history, science, and literature than your parents, who were immigrants living in a tenement, or grandparents, who were busting sod in Nebraska or staking claims in some godforsaken Rocky Mountain mining camp. Not to mention how much more American you are!

So Academic styles functioned on all social levels to provide requisite images of sophisticated dignity, personal and national: for middle-class homeowners just risen from the ranks of laborers, for high-school graduates whose parents never went to school, just as well as for the Yale or Harvard man whose father trundled a pushcart around Boston streets like Bernard Berenson's, or ran a Hudson River ferryboat like the Vanderbilts'.

And for the poor? What about them, made all the more conspicuous by contrast with such wealth (as hundreds of reformers and activists constantly tried to keep before the public mind)? What did Academic styles do for them? Well, insofar as they were conscious of architectural styling at all—and that would at best be only subliminally—it gave them a similar message: things are getting better, slowly, steadily, by some mysterious law of progress uniquely applicable in this best of all possible lands. Sooner or later inequities will be done away with; the poor will inherit the earth, including its past treasures, just as the rich are now doing. Implicit in the general shift from Picturesque to Academic styles in American architecture was the message that the unrestrained individuality of preceding decades was no longer generally acceptable. No vestige was left in Academic styles of that ancient contrast between palace and homestead which was still perceptible in Picturesque.

Evelyn Watson put the case admirably in a 1910 article on bungalows: bungalows, she thought—and in her context that meant "workingmen's housing"—in their "adaptability and adjustment that is as ingenious as the American himself" were images of democracy on its way to fulfilment, to "a time when the houses of the rich will be recognized to have the same fundamental lines as the houses of the poor."[9] In that sense and on that level, one cultural counterpart to Academic architecture was passage of an income tax law around 1908. Prior to that time, proposals for an income tax, except in the war crisis of 1863, had routinely been defeated because so many believed that everyone could eventually get rich.[10] Now it passed; and a monument to its passage were those rows of little suburban houses which now came increasingly to be occupied by working-class people. Not that anything like equality had been achieved, or that passing the income tax had anything immediate to do with the appearance of working-class suburbs; but the same styles of architecture now began to apply to all. To create such promises of future equality was another social function of Academic architecture, part of the image of "Americanness" its high-style exponents were concerned with ("One nation . . . with justice for all"), and part of its continuing cultural legacy.

Application of Academic Styles to Architectural Types

How Academic styles were applied to architectural types was determined by nationalism and urbanism; that is, by basic social function—the self-conscious assertion of a new, more dignified American nationality—and by the changing configurations of American cities.

Buildings composing public presentations of the new national image were of premier importance for Academic architects, beginning with government buildings proper. The era felt a need and impulse to proclaim, more assertively than ever before, the virtues of the United States' distinctive principles of government. By the 1920s it was a poor American community indeed that had not acquired a dignified courthouse or city hall or, at the very least, a distinguished-looking post office. Dozens of new state capitols date from the Academic decades, always dramatically sited—sometimes on hills majestically overlooking their sites, like Rhode Island's in Providence or Utah's in Salt Lake City; sometimes climaxing newly laid out urban vistas, like Arkansas's in Little Rock (where the new capitol faces the town and not the river, as the old one had); sometimes smack in the center of town, like Idaho's in Boise.

Post offices are particularly characteristic of the Academic era, because this subtype decisively displaced the Custom House (of which it had been a humble part) as a statement of government presence; it displayed flags and current presidents' photographs, just like the public schools. But many other types were perceived as contributing to the national public image as well.

In remarkable contrast to the covert appearance of mansions in Modern times, when prevalent ideology disparaged displays of great wealth, mansions in Academic style were perceived as public architecture, lending refined aristocratic pretensions not only to their rich builders, but also to the towns where they stood. New York's mansions for Vanderbilts and Fricks were only the most famous of many all over the country. The close connection between mansion and public amenity was evidenced by the easy transition of so many from residence to museum or library; the Frick Collection is typical *[6.15]*.

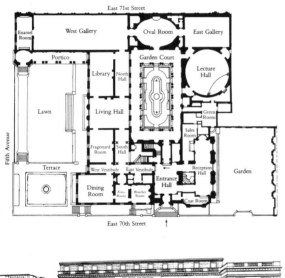

6.15. Henry Clay Frick, coke and steel industrialist from Pittsburgh, adorned Fifth Avenue between 70th and 71st streets with a grand Italian palazzo, built 1913–14 to designs of Thomas Hastings of Carrère and Hastings. It took only addition of a wing in the 1930s to turn mansion into museum, as is illustrated by these drawings on folders distributed to Frick Collection visitors: elevation of Fifth Avenue mansion facade and museum plan with addition shaded.

The same is true of collegiate architecture: "Princeton in the Nation's Service" is not a concept confined to that one institution, but applies to all the Ivy Leagues and to state schools as well. Collegiate architecture manifested it in all manner of Gothic quads and Roman squares, elegantly composed to recall the role in national life played by Oxford and Cambridge, Heidelberg and the Sorbonne, and not least Jefferson's model American University, the University of Virginia *[6.19, 6.20]*.[11] A comparable impulse is apparent on all levels. It was in this Academic era that pledges of allegiance to the flag and the display of presidents' pictures became obligatory in every public school. Setting elementary and secondary schools on hilltops became common practice *[6.21]*, along with a loose kind of stylistic code: elementary in various Classical modes, secondary often in Gothic (collegiate Gothic, Elizabethan, etc.). Hilltop settings and coded styles alike recalled usage for churches in earlier eras, as schools largely took over the primordial communal functions of churches in traditional societies: instilling that common language and outlook on which all enduring institutions eventually must stand.

Public works attained unprecedented status as statements of national achievement. That great cities demand approaches by splendid bridges was a given, and they duly appeared over the Potomac, the East River, the Bay in San Francisco, and the Susquehanna at Harrisburg. That great railroads should build monumental city railroad stations likewise went without saying, and they too appeared everywhere: Grand Central and Pennsylvania in New York *[6.16, 6.17]*, Union in Toronto *[6.13]*, Washington, Salt Lake City, Portland, Vancouver, Cincinnati *[6.18]*. Majestic viaducts also appeared, not only in cities but in remote places as well; the Lackawanna Railroad's over the Tunkahannock Gorge at Nicholson, Pennsylvania is perhaps the most spectacular example *[6.22]*. Federal power stations, generators, and dams were also perceived as appropriate occasions for architectural displays of national greatness—usually in vaguely Academic Classical modes—as were local fort types like police and fire stations.

Comparably perceived in terms of sober community responsibility were amenity types like hospitals, libraries, art galleries, and museums. Whereas in Picturesque styles they were monuments to the wealth and/or arty taste of private philanthropists, now all became contributing members of the City

6.16. *Grandest of all North American railroad stations was Pennsylvania Station in New York, built 1902–10 to designs of McKim, Mead & White. Its destruction in the 1960s spurred the preservation movement and ultimately Postmodernism. From this view of it made c. 1915 can be read the sequential experiences it provided. A grand colonnade fronts the street, transforming still squalid and cramped streets into a monumental visual experience* evoking an American republic growing to emulate ancient Rome; *then arcades, also grandly Roman, lead to the main waiting room whose outline rises behind. It is a vast interior suggestive of the baths of Caracalla or the basilicas of Constantine, but, unlike them, built not with tax money but by private enterprise. Something of its grandeur can still be experienced in surviving progeny all over the country (cf. 6.13).*

6.17. *Presentation drawing from the office of McKim, Mead and White for Pennsylvania Station's concourse, with stairways to tracks, published in the* New York Times *for 20 May 1906. Here deliberate contrast was made with the Academic Roman grandeur of the facade and waiting room; technological expertise was left exposed for all to admire, a prelude to experiencing the marvels of railroading, climactic American industry of the age, on the track level forty-five feet below. This largest railroad station of its time, indeed largest building since the Pyramids constructed in a continuous operation, was demolished in 1963 to make way for a bland Modern Madison Square Garden that promptly went bankrupt. (From Lorraine Diehl,* The Late, Great, Pennsylvania Station*)*

6.18. *The cornerstone of Union Terminal in Cincinnati was laid in 1931 and the building completed in 1933, to service seven trunk lines with 22 buildings, 287 acres of railroad yards, and 94 miles of track. In railroading history it is remarkable as the last of the grand City Beautiful terminals, complete with approach plaza 1400 feet long and 500 feet wide edged in formal flower beds of cannas, tiger lilies, and gladioli, climaxed by an ornamental stepped fountain and curving automobile access on both sides. In architectural history it is remarkable evidence for the relationship of Art Deco to Academic Classical Revival: a legitimate descendant of New York's Pennsylvania Station. New York architects Alfred Fellheimer and Steward Wagner collaborated with classicist Paul Cret, architect of the Philadelphia and Detroit art museums. The building was successfully recycled as a commercial center in the late 1970s. (IMG:NAL)*

6.19. *Rotunda/Library of the University of Virginia at Charlottesville, as completed in 1898 by McKim, Mead and White after a 1894 fire, following instructions of the university building committee and Board of Visitors, who also specified closing off Jefferson's previously open campus with Cabell Hall at the other end.*

6.20. *The Graduate College at Princeton University, completed in 1913 (far quadrangle added 1937), was conceived as a kind of monastic complex physically distanced from the undergraduate campus. Appropriately enough, it was designed by the great Academic Gothic Revivalist Ralph Adams Cram. Princeton's president, Woodrow Wilson, had wanted something more democratic and egalitarian; when Graduate Dean Andrew West's views prevailed, after a bitter quarrel, Wilson resigned and went on to lesser things. A life-size bronze statue of the dean, visible in this picture taken from the College tower, still stands in the first quad, attesting to his triumph. (Photograph by Clem Fiori, courtesy of Princeton University Communications/Publications)*

6.21. *In medieval towns, eminences were normally occupied by a cathedral or church, emblematic of the community's authority, laws, and cohesion. In early-nineteenth-century America, town halls or courthouses normally occupied such sites and fulfilled a similar role; in the early twentieth, schools. In the old southwestern Pennsylvania town of Washington, four of five hills have schools on them (Washington County Courthouse has occupied the other since c. 1820). Here is Old West Washington School, begun 1904, defining a neighborhood of prefab and vernacular houses, built around the same time. Its shape is the old New England meeting house, with central belfry (partially demolished when this picture was taken in 1982). (IMG:NAL)*

6.22. *The sign says "Welcome to Nicholson, Population 1000, Hospitality for a Million," and we come in sight of a bunch of little prefab and spec houses in a variety of vernacular and commercially generated Academic styles: that is one image of the era. Another arches over the scene: the Tunkahannock Viaduct, built in 1912–15 by the Lackawanna Railroad to haul coal from central Pennsylvania to seaboard industry. Unlike earlier utilitarian viaducts in this area (earliest was the Erie's Starrucca near Susquehanna, Pennsylvania, of 1847–48), this one was consciously intended to recall Roman constructions, and indeed designer A. Burton Cohen and engineer G. J. Ray have brought Segovia or the Pont du Gard to mind. (IMG:NAL)*

Beautiful, matching other apparel appropriate to the culturally well-turned-out community. And it was true not only in big "Cities Beautiful," but in the remotest towns as well, with Carnegie libraries especially providing neat Academic accents on Main Street [6.23].

Churches and synagogues were also designed to be adornments to urban space. The more their spires and towers were displaced on the skyline by soaring commercial buildings from the 1890s on,

the more they were conceived in terms of visual units relating to uniform street fronts or occupying visual focal points on grids [6.4], with correspondingly less emphasis on relation of style to denomination.

Commercial buildings were, of course, the new nation's most famous manifestation, primarily those tall office buildings which the era itself proudly called skyscrapers. No longer isolated mushrooms popping up here and there, they rose now in shining clusters out of the heart of every city. How much they were considered cultural amenities is suggested by their frequent incorporation of concert halls (Adler and Sullivan's Auditorium Building is a famous, but by no means unique, example). And their quasi-religious character is suggested not only by fondness for Academic Gothic styling, but also by the era's veneration of the profession of life insurance. Ollie M. James's *Splendid Century: Centennial History of the Union Central Life Insurance Company of Cincinnati, Ohio* gives a reverential account of how business and evangelical motives were interwoven in the founding of this typical company, in which clergy were employed to sell life insurance on pastoral calls (thus caring at once for this world and the next).[12] Robert Cruden's *Ministers of Reform* tells how "life insurance had a self image that was religious to the point of unctuousness. . . . George W. Perkins told a correspondent, 'Our profession requires the same zeal, the same enthusiasm, and the same earnest purpose that must be born in a man if he succeeds as a minister of the Gospel.' Composer Charles Ives wrote a pamphlet . . . in 1912 in which he equated insurance tables with science, science with progress, progress with democracy."[13] Not coincidentally, insurance companies' towers were among the first to surpass church spires. But

6.23. *The small town of Livingston in central Montana spent a Carnegie grant of $10,000 on this public library in 1903. Until 1908 each recipient community was free to build whatever form it liked. Most, like Livingston, chose to be as up to date as possible—a very typical neat Academic Roman Revival design, with some Italianate admixtures (as usual in this substyle) resulted. After 1908 plans had to be submitted to a Carnegie committee for approval; in 1911* Notes on Library Buildings *was published as directions, with a written text and suggested plans. The results were not, interestingly enough, markedly different in quality. (IMG:NAL)*

all commercial towers were styled with a new dignified grandeur, befitting structures everywhere taken to be America's most conscious and conspicuous images of modernity. Which indeed they were: when the era's theorists tried to define truly American architecture, it was the skyscraper that they most often cited; when the new Soviet rulers sought to create convincing visual metaphors of Russia's emergence from feudal darkness into the marvelous light of scientific modernity, it was the American skyscraper that they copied—and specifically, those that capitalism had built in Academic styles just before the 1917 revolution.

But Academic commercial buildings were by no means all tall offices. Department stores were equally considered ornaments to urban life, and were styled accordingly. In this age they achieved a refined maturity of design in terms of both social and physical function; they became in fact practically self-sufficient mini-cities, containing within themselves restaurants and lounges and theaters in addition to shops of every possible description.[14] Smaller cities had commercial buildings similarly styled, on appropriately smaller physical scale; conspicuous in this category were the nicely and generously scaled Classical Revival banks that graced Main Streets everywhere *[6.5]*.

Application of Academic design concepts to the factory subtype—a proliferating category in this age of expanding mass-production industry—brought especially dramatic results. Picturesque crestings indicative of wealth in general would no longer do. Nor would a sophisticated academic sense of associations accept for factories the kind of Colonial Revival appropriate for mansions or Classical Revival for banks; obviously some kind of refined and proportioned utilitarian forms were called for, along the lines already suggested by Richardson's Marshall Field warehouse *[5.29]*. One of Frank Lloyd Wright's greatest achievements was the solution to this problem represented by his buildings for the Larkin and Johnson's Wax mail-order distribution businesses *[6.24, 6.25]*. Another solution, even more significant perhaps, was provided by Albert Kahn's Dodge Half-Ton Truck plant in Detroit of the same year, which was the culmination of twenty years spent working out factory designs. From abstract classical forms Kahn finally came to a structure of technically utilitarian aspect and form, but in fact proportioned with exquisite refinement *[6.26]*. That this was a conscious solution and no accident is evident from Kahn's

6.24. When built in 1936–39, Frank Lloyd Wright's design for the administration building of the S. C. Johnson & Son company in Racine, Wisconsin, was hailed for its modernity—eschewing applied ornament, using "modern" materials like glass brick, taking curved "organic" forms. In retrospect it is more praiseworthy for its persistent humanism. Not, like European Modernist buildings, conceived as a machine to house other machines, it was designed to provide a home away from home, for a kind of community. All its basic effects were intended to make those who spent a third of their lives here feel comfortable—the scale, the ornament deriving from familiar materials and textures, and above all the famous molded "golf-tee" supports. Many of them do not in fact touch the ceiling; their function is visual and psychological, to make the interior space feel well supported to those inhabiting it. (Courtesy of S. C. Johnson & Son, Inc.)

6.25. Exterior of the often misnamed Johnson's Wax Factory (actually an office building) is imbued with but never dominated by twentieth-century technology. Its social function and form alike represent a climax of the refinement and subtleties of Academic design in later nineteenth- and early twentieth-century architecture, not a prelude to mechanistic European Modernism. (Courtesy of S. C. Johnson & Son, Inc.)

6.26. As early as 1917 Albert Kahn was the published authority on factory design in the United States; ultimately he was responsible for over two thousand. One of his climactic efforts was this Dodge Half-Ton Truck plant in Detroit, finished in 1937. Here utilitarian forms appropriately expressing mechanical efficiency are refined and proportioned by the controlling architect to scale for human beings—a classic reconciliation of mechanization and humanization. But Kahn also understood that utilitarian forms were not all that architecture ever required; for other types he used eclectic styles carrying associations to human history and past aspirations.

6.27. Hugh Ferriss worked in Cass Gilbert's office while the Woolworth Building was being designed [6.2], and there was imbued with a vision of grand new cities full of soaring, dramatically lighted commercial towers. Here is a rendering in his distinctively elegant charcoal technique of the Chicago Tribune Tower, as built to the Academic Gothic designs of competition winners John Mead Howells and Raymond Hood, 1922–25. Its set-back crown (imposed by Chicago's zoning laws) was modeled on the "Butter Tower" in Rouen.

an interplay of economic, technological (transportation modes especially), and demographic forces. It was in fact being literally turned inside out. The architectural types principally affected by this change were, of course, homestead and mansion, and all their subtypes.

For most of Western history, city-center was the desirable place to live. However noisy and dirty conditions there, you were at least close to everything; you did not have a long, tedious, and dangerous trek in to work every morning. Toward the end of the nineteenth century that pattern altered drastically. Easy commuting made the difference. First trains, then electric streetcars, then automobiles made it easier and faster to have it both ways— escape the noise and dirt, yet profit from being at the center of everything. In consequence, the whole morphology of the city came to be perceived differently, on every level—from idealistic visions of city centers as a sort of dramatic theater (Hugh Ferris's 1929 *Metropolis of Tomorrow* is the classic of this genre [6.27]) to promotional literature by suburban developers, like the Van Sweringen Company's "Peaceful Shaker Heights" brochure of 1929 [6.8]. Architectural styling altered accordingly.

City-center now was not a place where you lived, it was a place where you came to work in the morning and left in the evening. Or more precisely, you lived there only if you could not avoid it. If you were a transient, somebody in town for a few days on business, you stayed in a downtown hotel, in the luxury of a "mansion you can rent." If you were *lumpenproletariat,* down and out, a street person, or one of the masses of immigrants streaming into cities from the ghettos of Europe, or the South, you stayed in the shadow of city-center's glittering towers, in decaying row houses abandoned in the flight suburbsward, in tenements put up speculatively for the purpose, or in alleys full of garbage and rats. Your aim in any case was not to stay long. If you were what the era called "the deserving poor," your goal was like every other city dweller's—to get out to the suburbs, to move away from city-center into one of the residential rings that were beginning to surround it.

Those rings grew in predictable sequence. First, what once had been the desirable residential neighborhoods close-in to town, with mansions in Picturesque or earlier styles, were divided and subdivided into ever smaller units until they fell into total decrepitude and under wreckers' balls, to make way for commuter parking lots and yet more offices.

deliberate use of Academic historicist styles for other types of buildings with different social functions, such as the Clements Library in Ann Arbor [6.58]; he was almost unique for his time in demonstrating how styles of buildings should be determined by their function in and for society, rather than being the expression of the architect's personality.

The changing American city also determined how Academic styles were applied to building types. The city was being changed not simply by designers holding Beaux-Arts ideals of a City Beautiful with broad avenues, parks, and impressive monuments everywhere—though their efforts often did transform whole areas. Rather, the American city's fundamental form was being changed by

Then came middle-class areas of single-family homes and apartment houses spreading out to the city limits.

The apartment house was a type characteristic of the Academic era, though invented earlier (see chapter 5). Its very name implied a class difference. "Flats," the English word, implied identical minimum-facility units all stacked up, either deliberately as in tenements or as a result of subdividing floors in older one-family homes; "flats" were for the poor, and so the word soon disappeared from an upwardly mobile society's vocabulary. "Apartment houses" were created for the rich, and so the word, originally French, was adopted by everybody. They had been introduced to New York from Paris, tenta-

tively in the 1860s by Lienau, effectively in the 1870s by Richard Morris Hunt. Each apartment house contained a set of mansions, complete with living rooms for entertainment, fireplaces, libraries, numerous bedrooms, even quarters for servants. These early luxury apartment houses long remained desirable—in fact still are—and so by demographic process came to be in or near city centers, close to the hotels to which they were generically so similar; New York's Dakota and Sherry-Netherland are fine examples [6.28, 6.29]. Practical adaptations of them created middle-class apartments. They were usually as identical and standardized as flats, often indeed turning into tenements by demographic processes, but they al-

6.28. *The Dakota Apartments in New York City was built 1881–84 to designs of Henry J. Hardenbergh, in Academic French Gothic inspired by the Loire châteaux ("the castle you can rent"). Luxury features included elevators powered by steam pumps. (IMG:NAL)*

6.29. *A more refined and sophisticated version of the Dakota's Academic Gothic is represented by the Sherry-Netherland apartment hotel on Grand Army Plaza at Fifty-ninth Street, built 1926–27 to designs of New York's premier firm of hotel builders in the 1920s, Schultze and Weaver. Their Hotel Pierre still stands nearby, but the Savoy-Plaza, which once completed a triad called in Paul Goldberger's admirable* The City Observed *"as potent a symbol of romantic New York as ever existed anywhere," is gone, replaced in the 1960s by "the hard lines of the General Motors Building [which] jeer at the delicacy of the two old hotels and [whose] mass is belittling to them." (IMG:NAL)*

6.30. The Maplewood, built in 1906 in Cincinnati, was a typical small apartment building for middle-class professional people working in nearby offices. Its lobby, however, still plainly suggested its prototype, "the mansion you can rent," in its elegantly marbled "presentation" staircase, with mahogany handrails; the lobby floor is mosaicked, and the stairwell receives light through stained glass windows. (IMG:NAL)

ways kept some vestigial indications of their origins, through ornamentation in entrance lobbies or facades *[6.30]*. Curiously, the transition from sets of mansions to standardized flats can be best traced in arrangements for garbage disposal: separate disposal facilities for each unit (as dictated by the original concept of a rentable mansion) were replaced first with separate facilities connected by a common chute, then by disposal entirely outside the units, via common chutes on each hallway. Social status was most commonly indicated by amount of ornament, as in Picturesque styles, but Academic styles had some typically vague associations that often apply—Colonial French often had connotations of luxury, for example.

Beyond these districts came the suburbs proper. They also proliferated according to predictable patterns. Earliest were upper-middle-class suburbs, most of whose houses were designed by architects. Then middle-class suburbs, designed by near-architects, non-architects, and speculative builders imitating each other's work. And between the more desirable tracts were blue-collar, working-class suburbs, mainly built out of catalogs. Furthest out of all came architecture for those wealthy enough not to commute, either retired persons of means or those able to maintain both country and city residences. In this category came seasonal cottages and villas,

and casinos, a new sort of sports club with styles that ranged over a few decades from lingering Picturesque playfulness to ponderous Academic dignity.[15] All were gradually replicated on middle-class levels within a few decades, and most were swallowed up in a few decades more by urban sprawl.

Substyles

In theory there could be an Academic version of every preceding substyle in the nation's architectural history. And in practice, to some extent, there was. But the resultant diversity was not so pointless a welter as Modernists were fond of supposing. Correlations between style and type were vaguely defined but consistent enough in usage to make Academic landscapes meaningful in terms of life.

Take, for example, the Academic habit of trying to design post offices in regional forms. Whereas Academic capitols stressed how each state was part of the union, by stylistic concurrence with the national capitol, Academic post offices stressed by their styles—and in murals with regional subjects—how government was experienced by the people on a regional level *[6.31–6.33]*. Another example is the styling of rest stops on the interstate highway system as begun in 1955. On the Massachusetts Turnpike you find stops modeled on historic New England seventeenth-century homesteads; through Louisiana on I-10, on Acadian farmhouses; on the Pennsylvania Turnpike, sturdy stone Pennsylvania homestead types; on the Kennedy Turnpike through Maryland, adaptations of famous Maryland mansions *[6.34–6.36]*. Even stops designed in full High Modernism, like those on I-80 through Nebraska in the 1970s, continued to display plaques and posters bespeaking the Spirit of the Place: "Here [at Ogalalla] the old emigrant trains Westward divided, one to Oregon, the other to California." And from the 1920s onward the practice of regionalizing roadside restaurants by style was actively pursued.[16]

Another instance of how Academic substyles and architectural types interrelated is provided by the common Academic practice of having exteriors uniform in style but interiors varied. Surely the most famous example is The Breakers in Newport *[6.37, on p. 210]*: externally, consistent Academic Italian Renaissance (specifically, Genoese palatial); internally, one room stylistically quite different from the next—here Louis XIV (with a mixture of original seventeenth-century pieces and indistinguishable

6.31. The main post office in San Antonio is one element in a complex of structures all dating from 1936: the Alamo Cenotaph, commemorating the hundredth anniversary of the battle (with elaborate sculpture by extraordinarily prolific patriotic sculptor Pompeo Coppini); the restored Alamo itself, and a near-replica beside it combining shrine, museum, bookstore, and souvenir shop. Largest of the group, the post office provides a fine backdrop for them, incorporating numerous allusions to them (grillwork on doors and windows, for example) into a basically Academic Classical design (by Ralph Cameron, following guidelines of Roosevelt-era public works architect Louis A. Simon and consulting architect Paul Cret). This is, however, only a more dramatic version of a concern for regional roots and expression common to most Academic architecture and especially evident in post offices from 1900 to 1950. (IMG:NAL)

6.32. On a dull November day the small Minnesota town of New Ulm is brightened by its 1909 post office, designed in a style alluding to sixteenth-century urban architecture in Germany, homeland of the town's founders. James Knox Taylor was the supervising public works architect; he encouraged regional expressions in post office buildings erected during his tenure. (IMG:NAL)

6.33. A small post office in the New Mexico hamlet of Mesquite, built in 1975 to designs of Gene Sanchez and Edwin Sternklaus, still in the Pueblo substyle. (IMG:NAL)

6.34 (right). A rest stop in Louisiana's Acadian style on I-10 near Grosse Tete, from the early 1960s. This is about as late in time as Academic styling goes. By the later 1960s and 1970s Modernism took over, producing such severely mechanical and "purist" stops as those on I-80 through Nebraska. In the 1980s Postmodernism began reinstating "historical quotations"—not quite the same thing as Academic "revivals." (IMG:NAL)

6.35 (below). Maryland House stop on I-95 near Aberdeen, a studied composition of elements from eighteenth-century English Colonial in Maryland. (IMG:NAL)

6.36 (bottom). Earliest of the interstates was the Pennsylvania Turnpike, completed in June 1940 (designated I-76 in the mid-1950s, when the interstate system was formally established under Eisenhower). It was modeled on the German autobahns, and its rest stops, like theirs, emphasized regional architecture. Here is Hickory Run, featuring Pennsylvania Colonial's distinctive stonework. (IMG:NAL)

replicas), there Louis XV, and so on. How such stylistic variety works was evident in this era's luxurious ocean liners, designed on the same principle. Externally, each was composed of one style, almost utilitarian. Internally, each space took a style appropriate to its social function for passengers on voyage: public areas like dining rooms and smokers were in varieties of High Georgian; bedrooms in middle-class Colonial Revival with chintz curtains and bedspreads; pool in stark Grecian with Pompeian key pattern; on the decks, chairs and tables in wicker with Arts and Crafts touches. Best of all examples are the era's great hotels: formal lobbies in marble and gilt, bedroom styles scaling down according to use (suites, for business meetings or parties, simple bedrooms, etc.).

Academic Colonial Revivals

Revival of styles from the American colonial past began, perhaps, with restoration of Independence Hall tower, as a national patriotic symbol, by William Strickland in 1827. But the movement proper hardly began before the 1876 Centennial Exhibition in Philadelphia, and its real momentum dated from the great exhibition in Chicago celebrating the four-hundredth anniversary of Columbus's voyage. Diverse motivations were at work, as always; and each Colonial Revival had a specific appeal. Colonial English carried comforting associations, for descendants of colonial settlers now threatened by massive Eastern and Southern European immigrations, with allegedly more secure times when English-speaking Protestants were in full control of all the American colonies. Intimations of exotic Mediterranean heritage seemed for many Californians, especially real-estate promoters, implicit in Colonial Spanish. Flattering ties with great dynastic families might be implied by Academic French adaptations of Loire châteaux; if you lived in an Italian palace, you might be taken for a Medici, too. As for "Dutch colonial," it seemed somehow redolent of stolid, peaceful comforts in the old quaint Hudson Valley, so satisfyingly different from present-day lives there. And so on.

Overriding all other specific and local appeals, however, was the impetus for reviving every style from America's colonial past inherent in the Academic era's sense of new national dignity. European nations were being conceived as biological entities; each one demonstrably had a birth, a period of adolescence, and now a democratic liberal

6.38. Archetypal Academic Colonial Spanish suburban house, built in Colusa, California, c. 1923.

adulthood (or soon would have). The United States should have roots too. Academic Colonial Revival substyles would go a long way toward providing them.

Academic Colonial Spanish Revival of what were taken to be forms from colonial Spain had special appeal in Florida, the Southwest, and California, for a number of reasons: visual and textural combinations appropriate to clear, dry, sunny atmospheres; connotations of easy-going, fun-loving lifestyles for stern Yankee workaholics retiring to California or living in Florida for their health; associations with the glamorous life of Hollywood. For settlers coming from older regions like New England, environments built in revived Colonial Spanish styles provided a compensatory sense of historical depth, as well as a pleasingly exotic sense of "difference." And besides, Academic Colonial Spanish *looked* good, attractively colorful even in drab suburbs of northern industrial cities.

The bulk of Academic Colonial Spanish buildings of whatever substyle are generally identifiable by combinations of some or all of the following features: tiles covering all, or at least the visible parts, of roofs; low-pitched roofs (advertising "mild tropical climate"); walls stuccoed or made of the pseudo-stucco "staff" or (less often) in concrete to imitate effects of adobe construction; patches of terra cotta or other sorts of molded ornament; exposed wood (posts, rafters, etc.) stained or otherwise darkened; thin wrought-iron grillwork; round-headed openings [6.38]. These characteristics form the base for specific Spanish substyles.

6.39. *In this 1915 photograph of a spacious Mission-style house in Pasadena, the simple central core is very evident. Features that identify the style are simply tacked onto a big foursquare. (Special Collections, University of California at Los Angeles Library)*

First of these was Mission, launched in the 1890s. Its name and some of its identifying features came from a romantic interest in the churches built by Spanish missionary padres from Mexico between the 1780s and 1820s strung from southern California to north of San Francisco. To general Academic Colonial Spanish, Mission added some elements copied, adapted, or supposed to be derived from the California missions, such as facades with promi-

nently scalloped outlines and clearly recognizable parapets; towers on one or both ends; arcades forming an entranceway or side porch; bell towers composed of tile-roofed cubes with round or elliptical cupolas (usually on public buildings like railroad stations and city halls, but occasionally on mansions); extremely simplified classical details like pilasters and tapering columns. External details like these, applied to a simple core form on a traditional

6.40. *As built to Arthur Benton's designs in 1890–1901, Mission Inn in Riverside, California, was the most famous of a chain of hotels whose Academic Colonial Spanish buildings expressed the good, relaxed life of warm climates (the Royal Hawaiian in Honolulu is another). Later additions that emphasized exposed reinforced concrete walls brought out the proto-Modernism always inherent in that substyle. (IMG:NAL)*

plan, most commonly constituted Mission *[6.39].* A few monuments were exceptional: Mission Inn at Riverside, for instance, was innovatively Mission inside as well as out, which no doubt makes a case for Arthur Benton being the style's inventor *[6.40].*[17]

Mission interiors characteristically had ceilings treated to resemble the open timberwork of missions, which in practice meant beams (or boards imitating beams) stained and exposed. For obvious reasons, there was no Mission furniture as such, since any that missions once possessed had long ago disappeared. Usually Mission houses were furnished in compatible styles, usually some Arts and Crafts variant of Colonial English, but frequently Gustav Stickley's Mission furniture, which otherwise has no direct relationship to Mission style proper (its name came from Stickley's populist obsession with his "mission" to refine and restore American design to good taste).

The Mission substyle was most popular in the period 1890–1910; thereafter it was gradually displaced in popularity by Mediterranean, which was composed of the general Colonial Spanish base plus elements picked up in Mexico, North Africa, Spain, Italy (especially Genoa and Venice), or Greece. In practice it consisted of simulations of Mediterranean atria (patios) by making verandas into arcaded loggias and/or by extending one or two walls to make an entrance into the backyard or garage; sophisticated play upon arches both outside and in (including "Mozarab" scalloped and flattened forms); and much more emphatic color—white or earth-hue walls trimmed in scarlet, orange, azure, and other Mediterranean colors, with random pavings of driveways and walkways to match. In the most elaborate examples, like Coral Gables outside Miami, even Venetian canals and lagoons were recreated, complete with bridges, islands, and other exotica; tiles were imported from Cuba, for authenticity. Other famous representatives of the Mediterranean substyle would include Vizcaya, also outside Miami *[6.14];* San Simeon, the castle-mansion Julia Morgan designed for William Randoph Hearst; and Santa Barbara's courthouse, a wondrous assemblage of cool patios and arcades, elegant Spanish archways and dappled creamy walls, allegedly intended to make government attractive *[6.41].*

Three other movements (rather than substyles proper) are detectable within Academic Colonial Spanish throughout the entire 1890–1930 period, and later: Pueblo, Native American Decorative (mainly Navaho and Aztec patternings); and proto-Modernism.

Pueblo derived from building traditions of New Mexico and Arizona Indians co-opted (as everywhere in New Spain) to complete the peasant element in the Spanish class-structured state (cf. 2.12).

6.41. One of the greatest showpieces of Academic Colonial Spanish architecture in all its variety is the small California city of Santa Barbara, where the style has been mandatory since the 1920s. Santa Barbara not only has the kind of Colonial Spanish railroad station, shopping centers, theaters, and rich array of suburban houses that you will commonly see elsewhere, but a Colonial Spanish airport that is, shall we say, rarer. Its masterpiece is the famous courthouse completed in 1929, on an original design by J. J. Plunket with William Mooser and Company of San Francisco supervising. Myron Hunt and G. S. Wilson made later additions. (IMG:NAL)

6.42. *For the Fred Harvey chain of southwestern hotels associated with the Santa Fe Railroad, chief interior designer Mary Elizabeth Colter made effective use of native American Indian motifs to create an "American" style. She sometimes employed Navaho motifs directly, as in wall hangings, but more often abstracted them in metalwork and textile patternings. How her distinctive combinations related to Pueblo style structural effects (as in ceilings) can be seen very well in this photo of the reception room of the El Navajo Hotel in Gallup, New Mexico, in the mid-1920s. (Courtesy of Special Collections, University of Arizona Library, Tucson)*

It was easily distinguishable from ordinary Spanish Colonial by beam ends projecting through walls at roof level and by corners smoothed off and rounded as if in malleable clay. Originally it functioned to create an ambience separating New Mexico and Arizona from their giant neighbors, Texas and California, on either side; when there was more general consciousness of styles than now, battles were fought to preserve these little states' stylistic identity.[18] Just as Santa Barbara was all Spanish by decree, so Pueblo was all but mandatory in towns like Santa Fe and Las Cruces, for stores and theaters and government buildings as well as houses. As the twentieth century wore on, Pueblo passed imperceptibly from an Academic to a Popular/Commercial substyle, and as such flourishes still *[6.33].*

Related to Pueblo were stylistic allusions to native American cultures, principally in the form of ornament derived from Aztec, Maya, and Navaho motifs *[6.42].* They are part of the era's concern with visual metaphors of "Americanism."[19]

What one can best call proto-Modern versions of Colonial Spanish derive from that flexibility which it shares with all Academic design. David Gebhardt and Esther McCoy have written convincingly about relationships to Modern architecture not only in the work of people like Gregory Ain and Irving Gill, where it is obvious, but also where it is not, in the high-style Spanish Colonial of George Washington Smith and James Osborne Craig in Santa Barbara, or Wallace Neff of Pasadena. All of them share a taste for expanses of unadorned wall, quasi-strip windows, stark massing of shapes, and other intimations of European Modernism proper *[6.40].* There are other, less deliberate interrelationships.

The style lent itself to easy conflations with Art Deco, what Gebhardt calls "Moderne," and Academic Classical too; you can see some spectacular examples in the center of San Antonio, with the post office on one side elegantly combining Roman and Spanish motifs, the Alamo reconstruction in Mission style, and what is popularly called the "Crockett monument" making unmistakable allusions to the reigning Art Deco tastes of the 1930s (cf. 6.31).

Academic Colonial French   Academic versions of Colonial French styles never attained anything like the popularity of Spanish. Strictly speaking, they did not represent revival of any Colonial style, either—certainly not the house forms of Quebec and Louisiana, whose connotations were "peasant." "French" in turn-of-the-century American culture most commonly carried associations with "smartness," "up-to-dateness," "elegance," "sophistication"—a carry-over, no doubt, from old correspondences of Jeffersons and Franklins with Enlightenment philosophers and salons. "French" had overtones of *"châteaux";* indeed the term "châteauesque" is often applied to much of it. "French" is therefore identifiable by features like round turrets *(tourelles)* set in an angle or at corners; steep-pitched roofs, often slate shingled with bell-cast flaring eaves, with dormers set into them like mansards (but the mansard itself was rarely revived, probably because it looked too much like the horribly out-of-fashion Picturesque Second Empire). Tall chimneys with ornamental brickwork patterns were characteristic too; so were rusticated quoins around main openings. Upper-story windows were often casements, and ground-story windows were brought down to floor level ("French windows").

With such connotations it is not surprising to find Academic Colonial French most often represented by mansions for the very, very rich, and of infrequent occurrence further down in social scale. By far the best-known examples were and are the Vanderbilt mansions on Fifth Avenue that so roused Sullivan's ire, and the even bigger Biltmore outside Asheville, North Carolina *[6.43]*. They had a good many emulators. St. Louis had a particularly large number, many still standing. New York of course had even more, but almost none survive; even the fame of Charles M. Schwab did not preserve his mansion on Riverside Drive (Schwab was to be

cited more often than anyone else in Dale Carnegie's fantastically popular *How to Win Friends and Influence People,* classic of its genre, in the 1930s; he was the model employee, it seems, and his mansion exemplified his techniques—in the Vanderbilt style but conspicuously more modest, showing the winning ways of deference). More likely to survive were upper-middle-class suburban houses, and indeed some can occasionally be found in elegant suburbs like Shaker Heights or Chevy Chase *[6.44]*.

Hotels and apartment houses for the very rich also favored Academic French. The Dakota (originally nicknamed for its remoteness) on the west side of Central Park in the 1880s was and remains a famous example—prototype for Canadian Pacific

6.43. *Biltmore, designed by Richard Morris Hunt for George Washington Vanderbilt, a son of "the Commodore," was built in the North Carolina hills outside Asheville in 1888–95, with grounds landscaped by Frederick Law Olmsted. Biltmore was much bigger than its model, the Loire palace of Blois; its facade was a thousand feet long. But then Vanderbilt had more funds than sixteenth-century French nobility or kings, and wielded as much social power, so the style was appropriate. Furthermore, as a* practical extension of the implications of aristocracy expressed in the mansion—and in the Vanderbilt marriages to European aristocrats—Biltmore's grounds functioned as a tree farm as well as a pleasure park. *Noblesse oblige: here Gifford Pinchot developed ideas that led to the federal Bureau of Forestry, after Pinchot had studied German practices in Berlin; a German, Carl Schenck, established the first American school of forestry at Biltmore.*

6.44. Not quite Biltmore, but no prefab either: an upper-middle-class suburban dwelling in Academic Colonial French style in the affluent Washington suburb of Chevy Chase, Maryland. (IMG:NAL)

Railroad's "château-style" hotels, still in the 1980s retaining pretensions elegant enough for John Lennon to live and invest heavily in it *[6.28]*. There were occasional other examples in public architecture: a few "château-style" railroad stations, usually with Canadian associations *[2.20];* [20] the St. Louis City Hall, an oddity to be explained by the city (like Philadelphia earlier) getting a city hall to match a major fair, in this case St. Louis's 1904 exposition emphasizing romantic allusions to a French past.

Dutch Colonial   North European Colonial styles had their Academic representatives, like every other, but most of them are quite rare. That Dutch mercantile high style which had long since disappeared from the Delaware and Hudson valleys found occasional revival—here a fire station in Albany with its characteristic stepped gable; there a row of gables in Philadelphia or Lancaster, Pennsylvania. Occasionally, too, Academic revivals of Colonial High German—or, more precisely, an urban version of high Renaissance/Baroque German style that never had made it to the New World—put in an appearance: the 1904 post office in the Minnesota town of New Ulm, for instance, recalling regional German and Bohemian roots in the Academic way *[6.32];* Harvard's Busch-Reisinger Museum of Germanic culture.

What the era called "Dutch Colonial" was, except for its first appearance around 1900 as an architects' *jeu d'esprit,* a much less learned business. In fact it was hardly learned at all. The post office that Franklin D. Roosevelt helped design in his hometown of Hyde Park is Dutch only in its stonework and could just as easily be called something else. The two most distinguishing characteristics of the 1920s middle-class suburban style that went under the name of Dutch Colonial are a gambrel roof often sweeping out over a porch in front (and sometimes over another in back as well), which was sup-

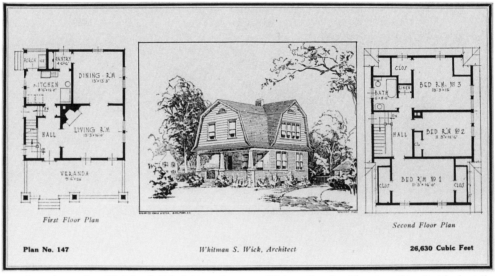

First Floor Plan

Plan No. 147   *Whitman S. Wick, Architect*   **26,630 Cubic Feet**

Second Floor Plan

6.45. "Six-room frame house of modified Dutch Colonial type, by Whitman S. Wick, architect" in The Book of a Thousand Homes *(I, 1923). Houses very similar to this are found all over the country, but are not always designated Dutch Colonial, modified or otherwise. There is nothing Dutch about the miles of streets lined with them in Boston suburbs like Medford and Somerville, built between 1900 and 1925 to house second- and third-generation Boston Irish, for instance.*

posed to derive from farmhouses built by settlers in New Netherlands, but in fact had no precedents in Holland or Flanders *[6.45, 2.34]*, and a combination of gambrel and bell-cast eave with a spacious, inset, dormer-like second floor that was entirely a creation of Academic Revivalist imaginations. Indeed, houses with dormered gambrel roofs often got called Dutch Colonial simply because they happened to stand in regions somehow associated with early Dutch settlement, like northern New Jersey, western Long Island, the Hudson and Mohawk valleys, even if their gambrels occurred in a context of details obviously referring to some other Colonial style such as (most often) Georgian. But what we might call inconsistency, that era tended to admire as flexibility, and Dutch Colonial prospered correspondingly.

Colonial English   The most popular of all Academic substyles was the Colonial English Revival, under which generic title went all sorts of adaptations and reappearances of homestead and high styles from the old pre-revolutionary English colonies. Immigration had been changing American demographic patterns steadily since the Civil War, but "the old stock" still occupied commanding social positions, challenged only enough by changing times and incoming peoples to appreciate reassurances of continuing superiority via architectural and sculptural

forms recalling those days when their ancestors had settled the continent and made the great Revolution.

Early impulses toward Colonial English revival had marked naiveté. Connecticut's quaint pavilion at the 1876 Centennial is an example, as are the curious combinations of motifs that went under the name of Colonial Revival furniture, like halves of spinning wheels used for chair backs; still in 1892 Paine's Furniture Company of Boston advertised some "Colonial" furniture suites that mixed up all phases of eighteenth-century furniture and put seventeenth-century details into the mix as well. But the Academic instinct for correctness and refinement dictated that revival of Colonial English styles would be accompanied by actual study of them, so that by the time Colonial styles were broadly popularized by their use for several major pavilions at the 1893 World's Columbian Exposition in Chicago, they were competently interpreted *[6.46]*, and continued to be so. Instructive books on colonial life and arts continued to multiply along with rows of suburban houses in fairly consistent Homestead Revival styles, public buildings and furniture in fairly consistent High Georgian *[6.47, 6.48]*, and churches in competent Wren/Gibbs and other Colonial styles.

Styles of colonial homesteads given Academic revival included the New England Cape Cod, the

6.46. The Massachusetts Pavilion at the World's Columbian Exposition in Chicago dramatized to what an extent the Academic Colonial English Revival was a Massachusetts creation. It was an expression of that state's claim to be the nation's model of true Americanism because of its role in the Abolition movement and the Civil War and the reaction of its dominant minority to a nineteenth-century immigration so heavy as to produce the nation's highest proportion of non-WASP population. Architect of the pavilion was Robert Peabody, whose Peabody and Stearns firm bore ancient Massachusetts names; his model was measured drawings of the Beacon Hill mansion built for John Hancock, first signer of the Declaration of Independence, which had been demolished in 1863. (From James W. and Daniel B. Shepp, Shepp's World's Fair Photographed [Chicago and Philadelphia, 1893])

6.47. *How competent the Colonial English Revival was in Massachusetts before the Chicago fair is demonstrated by the Bemis Town Hall in Lincoln, built in 1891–92 to designs of Harvard professor Herbert Langford Warren. It complemented a new Unitarian church in Richardsonian Romanesque style built at the same time. Jointly they replaced an earlier church and town hall, which in turn had been built to supersede the old Puritan meetinghouse for combined religious and civic functions, and become obsolete following an 1842 ordinance separating church and state. Bemis Town Hall (named for a donor) subtly recalled the days when church and state were one by a form freely based (in typical Academic manner) upon Old Ship Meetinghouse in Hingham [2.88]. But the elegant brickwork recalls Virginia; this is a visual metaphor of the Union that Massachusetts saved too. (IMG:NAL)*

6.48. *In its 1892 catalog Paine's Furniture Company of Boston advertised this hall clock "in Oak or Mahogany Cases," whose purchasers could revel not only in the Colonial associations of Chippendale-Georgian cresting, pinnacles on globes, and shell carvings, but also in the genuine English associations of "complete equipment" that included "English Cathedral Bells, Westminster Chimes, Whitington Bells, Bowbells . . ."*

6.49. *Colonial ancestry was an asset for politicians down to World War II, and flaunted in various ways. The furnishings of Franklin Delano Roosevelt's Little White House in Georgia, at Warm Springs, where he died, are an example. Pilgrim chairs with rush seats and straight spindled backs, plain-boarded walls, a few simple mementoes on the shelf, a woven rug proclaimed kinship with Dutch, Huguenot, and early English forebears.*

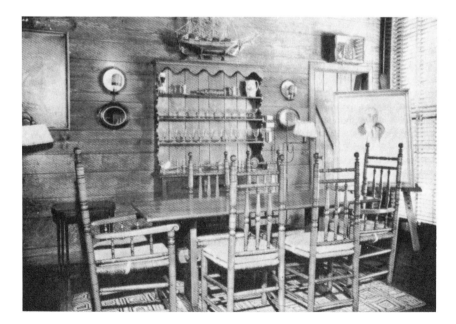

6.50. Henry-Russell Hitchcock, in Rhode Island Architecture *(Providence, 1939), called the 1887 house that McKim, Mead and White designed for W. G. Low near Bristol "a masterpiece among American summer houses, purged of the extreme picturesqueness of the 'Queen Anne' but not bound by the academic discipline of the Colonial Revival. To be compared with Richardson's and Wright's best wooden houses." "Purged" is an interesting choice of word, recalling a prime source of virtue for Puritan and European Modernist alike. (HABS photograph, Library of Congress)*

Southern Hall and Parlor, the Southern Cabin, and one-and-a-half gambrelled subtypes from Delmarva and New England (cf. chapter 2). Their counterpart in furniture used spindles, natural wood, cane seats, and the like to create images of what was supposed to have been New England "plain living and high thinking"; a Pilgrim substyle appeared as early as the 1890s and was still popular for informal use into the 1930s *[6.49].* Popular on upper social levels was an elaboration of shingled walls characteristic of small northern New England homesteads into what was later christened the Shingle Style[21]; Charles Follen McKim's summer place for W. G. Low at Bristol, Rhode Island, was one classic of the genre, Gustave Stickley's Craftsman Farms another *[6.50, 6.51].* At the other end, the I-form retained its popularity as a farmhouse type long enough to be offered in several mail-order, mass-prefabrication company catalogs. Curiously, the New England saltbox was rare.

6.51. The Community house that Gustav Stickley built in 1911 for his Craftsman Farms school outside Morris Plains, New Jersey, drew upon a similar reservoir of Colonial homestead forms and associations with virtue as the Low house; comparing the two, one is struck with how much freedom Academic architects actually exercised on their models, in contrast to the stereotype of them. The main interior room of this house was in a "peeled log" style. (IMG:NAL)

Also common in suburban domestic usage were revivals of Colonial English urban styles—the Philadelphia spec house, the Georgian row house, and a kind of fusion of Georgian and homestead that could best be called the "Williamsburg style," which climaxed popularization of Colonial English on a truly national scale in the late 1920s through the 1940s *[6.52]*; both passed directly over into Popular/Commercial vocabulary.

There was a natural tendency to conflate High Georgian with various sorts of Academic Classical Revival; generally, however, the characteristic Academic sense of appropriateness prevailed: Georgian suited the social purposes and pretensions of smaller post offices and public buildings, but on a bigger scale looked grotesque—cupolas and porticoes invented for two- or three-story buildings stuck onto block-long complexes ten or fifteen stories high, and the like. Therefore buildings of any great size tended to be in variants of Academic Roman Revival, that included elements from the same Italian Renaissance sources as Colonial.

Academic Classical Revivals

Grand-scale compositions of elements from classical antiquity, sometimes borrowed directly and

6.52. "House Plan No. 4B15," published c. 1915 by the Mountain Division of the Architects Small House Service Bureau, the American Institute of Architects' answer to mass-prefabrication of suburban houses by mail-order companies. It combined a vaguely Colonial homestead form ("In Colonial Times this style of house was called a 'cottage'; today it is known as a bungalow," the caption misinforms us) with a bit of Georgian detail to create a popular mix that melded into "Williamsburg Colonial," popularized by the 1930s restoration, and so became a standard small house form for the rest of the country. It was centrally heated, but had a decorative fireplace.

sometimes via the Italian Renaissance, are what "Academic architecture" most commonly brings to mind. Sometimes the whole movement has been loosely referred to as "Beaux-Arts" because Academic Classical Revival was what the Ecole des Beaux-Arts in Paris was most famous for teaching, sometimes as "City Beautiful" because that movement most often took Academic Classical Revival form. Certainly the nation's most dramatic architectural proclamations of its new awareness of itself were made in this style, which more or less consciously evoked both the grandeurs of the Roman Empire and the new Republic which had first revived it.

Academic architects employed three basic varieties of Classical Revival: Classical proper, which meant primarily Roman and Greek, with Renaissance admixtures; Classical vernaculars, which were styles used primarily in mass-prefabricated suburban houses; and a later, more sophisticated and abstracted variant of Classicism that generally goes under the names "Art Deco" or "Moderne." They occurred roughly in that chronological order, Roman/Renaissance being most popular with the first Academics from 1890 to 1910, Greek detailing from around 1910 to 1930, Deco in the 1930s. But in time all varieties overlapped a good deal. In forms, they overlapped even more. Literal replication of Roman or Greek models, or "pure" renderings of either style, were in fact even more impossible than in the Classical Revival proper, both because Academic Classical Revival was seen as particularly appropriate for public use and hence tended to appear on structures of great size, and because the Academic mindset was so much more given to vague generalities.

Academic Roman Revival was the designated style for the City Beautiful, and civic buildings in it proliferated from coast to coast *[6.53, 6.54]*. It was also overwhelmingly favored for the new era's world's fairs: at Chicago in 1893 *[6.55]*, St. Louis in 1904, San Francisco in 1915. Of these, the principal survivor is the Palace of Fine Arts that Bernard Maybeck designed for San Francisco; it is still a major public attraction and an admirable demonstration of how inventive a Classical design can be *[6.56]*. There was of course a reciprocal influence between these fairs and the restoration and elaboration of the Capitol Mall in Washington, and between both of them and the plethora of new capitols belonging to this era.

Academic Roman Revival was the favored style

6.53. *Municipal Building, a vast annex to New York City Hall begun in 1907 and completed in 1914, was the first skyscraper built by the firm of McKim, Mead and White; it was designed by William Kendall of the firm's office. He made reference to the old City Hall in an almost pre–Postmodern manner by creating a U-shaped plan visually embracing it and a crown repeating its dome. Still one of the metropolis's greatest buildings, it is seen here from lower Broadway. (IMG:NAL)*

6.54. *A classic example of public architecture taking the form of a skyscraper with Academic Roman Revival detail, plus some Renaissance admixtures: the City Hall in Oakland, built in 1914 as part of a riposte to San Francisco's City Beautiful grandeurs across the bay. Henry Hornbostle of Palmer, Hornbostle and Jones, was the architect. (IMG:NAL)*

6.55. *The City Beautiful: one of countless contemporary views of the 1893 Columbian Exposition in Chicago that suggest what made it such an inspiration for so many other cities (including variants like Coral Gardens near Miami).*

6.56. *Survivor of one of the many fairs modeled on Chicago's is the Palace of Fine Arts and adjacent buildings from the 1915 Panama-Pacific Exposition in San Francisco, still in active use as a city park, Exploratorium, and Museum of Science and*

Inventions. Typically Academic is architect Bernard Maybeck's imaginative use of classical elements to create subtle plays of space and a freedom in composing them. (IMG:NAL)

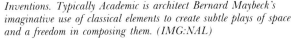

6.57. *Settlement of the Canadian west began in many cases with banks, like this Canadian Imperial Bank of Commerce in Elkhorn, Manitoba, built in 1912. Frequently the first freight carried on expanding railroads were prefabricated bank buildings in classical temple form, to be set down on the prairie at sixteen-mile intervals (determined by an eight-mile estimate for farmers to get produce to markets and back in one day) so as to be available to serve settlers on arrival. Classical details—gable dentils, Ionic pilasters, elaborate doorway pediments, keystoned oculus—were not quite in scale and not quite archaeologically correct either. But they gave dignity to what would otherwise have been a clapboarded box; often, indeed, such banks remained the best-designed buildings in town. (Courtesy of Provincial Archives of Manitoba)*

for grand new city halls; for the viaducts and bridges of national roads; for grand city hotels and railroad stations and viaducts *[6.10, 6.11, 6.16, 6.22]*. It was, not coincidentally perhaps, the reigning style for banks and financial institutions of all sorts. Smaller banks revived the temple-house forms of banks in the early Republic *[6.5; cf. 3.42, 3.60]*; some even prefabricated them *[6.57]*. Bigger banks regularly capped their tall towers with temples, thus in a measure reconstructing an earlier Classical Revival America's streets high in the air. Most of the public libraries Andrew Carnegie spread across the country were in varieties of Academic Roman style, equating the era's faith in education with its ideals of good citizenship *[6.23]*. It was also popular for state universities expanding in this era—Minnesota, for example, or Iowa—Cities Beautiful in collegiate miniature, on axial plans inspired by the 1893 Chicago fair.

Related to Academic Roman and often conflated with it was Italian Renaissance. Except for Roman Catholic churches, where the reference was to sixteenth-century Italian churches *[6.4]*, Italian Renaissance generally meant Quattrocento Italy in general, and in particular the early Renaissance in Florence, and signified "culture." Thus it was ap-

6.58. *Albert Kahn was the greatest proponent in his time of the principle that different types of buildings may demand different styles to evoke qualities requisite to their proper and effective functioning in and for society. This 1923 William L. Clements Library at the University of Michigan in Ann Arbor is entirely and consciously different from the automobile factories for which he* was famous (cf. 6.26). *He understood, in a word, how stylings that expressed mechanical efficiency would be inappropriate for a library dedicated to humanistic scholarship, just as it would be absurd to associate a factory with the Italian Quattrocentro renaissance of learning via forms from the Pazzi chapel used here.*

propriate for those quite numerous mansions whose owners' cultural inclinations tended toward Italy—Frick's in New York City, housing his considerable collection of Italian Renaissance art, was only the best known of many—and for libraries, ranging from the specialized Clements Library that Albert Kahn designed for the the University of Michigan *[6.58]* to the Umatilla County Library at Pendleton, an outpost of culture in eastern Oregon's ranching country.

Yet another variant was eighteenth-century French Classical. Its most famous architectural example was the Vanderbilt house in Newport, based on the Grand Trianon in Paris; ultimately more significant were the interior design concepts of Elsie de Wolfe, who has sometimes been hailed as founder of the art of interior design in the United States. The style was particularly popular for those lavish costume balls held in the era's pretentious mansions to boost hostesses' standings in "high society." Thence it easily worked its way to lesser social levels; throughout the twentieth century "French provincial" has been a "safe" style for middle-class living rooms and hotel bedrooms *[6.59]*. Admirers have seen anticipations of Modernism in de Wolfe's light, white, simple eighteenth-century

6.59. *Elsie de Wolfe's ambience, if not her direct influence, is to be seen in this 1892 advertisement by Paine's Furniture Company of Boston. For husbands, a "Gentleman's Chiffonier" is offered in vaguely Georgian style (brass handles, urns on mirror holder); for wives, a "Ladies' Dressing Cabinet" in a much lighter and more delicately detailed, vaguely Rococo style.*

6.60. *Tennessee's gradual return to prosperity after the Civil War was celebrated in an 1897 Centennial Exposition at Nashville, whose centerpiece—appropriately enough for a city with great Greek Revival traditions—was a replica of the Parthenon (it housed an art gallery), built of temporary materials on designs of Colonel William Smith, CSA, and sculptor George J. Zolnay. A replacement in permanent materials was constructed between 1921 and 1931, supervised by Professor William B. Dinsmoor, reigning authority on Greek and Roman architecture, with associated sculptors Leopold and Belle Kinney Scholz. It was completed about the same time as another major Academic Classical Revival monument in Nashville, Tennessee's World War I Memorial. (Photograph by Paul A. Moore, Tennessee Conservation Department)*

6.61. *The Lincoln Memorial is symbolically sited on the western end of the Mall axis to balance the Capitol, with the Washington Monument equidistant between them. It was completed in 1922; the architect was Henry Bacon and the sculptor Daniel Chester French. This premier example of Academic Greek Revival displays the style's splendid flexibility: its recessed attic recalls classical mausolea design (for example, Hellenistic tomb monument of Mausolus at Halicarnassus) without copying any literally; entrance on the long side creates a main facade which faces the Capitol, closes off the Mall, provides a columnar system emphasizing the unity that classical colonnades naturally provide, and affords places for emblems of all the reunited states in the cornice. (IMG:NAL)*

French effects, but nowadays they seem so chiefly as exemplification (like de Wolfe herself) of the era's uncritical adulation of European culture.

Greek was a considerably less common Academic Revival. It usually preserved something of the original Greek Revival's special associations with Liberty; in the Academic version this translated into "patriotism." The country's first famous example was the Parthenon in Nashville, Tennessee, whose authenticity—down to color—was assisted by none other than William B. Dinsmoor, professor of classical art at Columbia [6.60]. Its effect derives from that authenticity; people come prepared to laugh, and leave it strangely moved, for this is as close as anyone is ever likely to get to the experience of being in a Greek temple as originally built. However, it is also this kind of copying that gave Academic its bad name among later Modernists. Similar criticisms could be leveled, with some justice, at Masonic temples of the 1920s, like the Washington National Masonic Monument in Alexandria, Virginia, where a well-designed Greek temple forms the base, but looks distorted by stories piled on above. By far the fairest test of what Academic architects could do is the Lincoln Memorial in Washington [6.61].

The Lincoln Memorial is Academic Classicism at its best. It is not a copy of any one specific Greek or Roman building, nor intended to be one, but a new and original combination of classical elements. Yet to experience the Lincoln Memorial—to climb the steps and find the great cult image looming into view level by level, so perfectly proportioned to the space; to walk around the monument on its elevated terrace; to feel how each column relates to the colonnade and then to the whole panorama of Mall and Reflecting Basin and Memorial Bridge—is to understand something of how successive generations of Greeks and Romans experienced the presence of divinity. There is about the Lincoln Memorial an unmistakable religious quality; perhaps that is why it has always been the most popular place for visitors on the Mall despite there being nothing to *do* there. But what is worshipped here? Surely not Lincoln the man. Rather, the idea that became an article of faith in early-nineteenth-century America, that the United States is not a nation like others, under judgment by God and history, but rather the culmination of history (as indeed it figures in a number of "universal histories" written in nineteenth-century America) and an instrument to be used by God to bring about His purposes. Lincoln apparently thought of his historical role in some such terms. And when you consider the follies that led up to the calamity of a five-year Civil War, the idiocies and pusillanimity of the media, the petty ambitions of politicians, the stupidities of the generals throughout that conflict who so often brought catastrophe so close, then survival of the nation does seem some sort of miracle, explicable only in terms of a divine favor that could use fools to further some grand plan of human redemption.

To compare the Academic Greek Revival of the Lincoln Memorial with other monuments nearby is to confirm is effectiveness. The perfection of its proportions is pointed up by the Jefferson Memorial, created a dozen years later in part as a Democratic party riposte to commemoration of the first Republican president. Its forms are too thin somehow, its interior a curious combination of baldness with fussy detail, the statue somehow too big for its setting—the whole dramatizes how very rare is the kind of proportion achieved by the combination of French's statue and Bacon's building. The Lincoln Memorial's meaning has only been deepened by setting the Vietnam and Kennedy memorials in proximity. The one, with a wedge pointing directly at Lincoln and another at the Washington Monu-

6.62. *A foursquare at Mill Run on Pennsylvania State Road 381. It was built as a prefabricated house c. 1910, probably supplied by the Aladdin Company of Michigan, which provided many houses in this vicinity, including a summer cottage for the Edgar Kaufmann family of Pittsburgh, later replaced by Frank Lloyd Wright's Fallingwater. (IMG:NAL)*

ment, seems a reminder that the United States is not, apparently, foreordained to win all wars; the other is a kind of monumental media event intended to associate the two presidents, but in fact merely pointing up the differences *[7.61]*. (The Kennedy Center is not only similar in general shape and layout, with over-sized statuary of the martyr inside, but carries on its outer terrace walls inscriptions from JFK's campaign speeches in Roman script identical to that of Lincoln's Gettysburg and Second Inaugural addresses on *his* Memorial walls.)

Just as suburbs were counterparts to the Academic era's great planned city spaces, Classical Revival vernaculars created in and for middle-class suburbs were counterparts to the high-style Academic Classical Revival of great city monuments. Most common were stylistic shapes, identifiable more by forms vaguely deriving from classical precedent than from any ornament consistently drawn from classical sources. One, easily recognizable, is the big foursquare, whose common or regional names—double decker, double cube, Seattle Box—suggest how it is perceived as a geometric shape (cube with pyramidal roof) traceable through Italianate intermediaries back to the Classical Revival proper *[6.62; cf. 3.74]*. Other derivations from

Classical Revival origins include the small four-square (from the "classical cottage" *[cf. 3.73]*) and the temple-house, which also comes large and small, often with quasi-porticoes added.[22]

Academic Classical Revival also includes a great variety of Late Abstract Classical substyles, whose distinctions are so fine as to warrant collective consideration under the generic title "Art Deco." They include Art Deco proper, which stylized classical forms into straight lines, zigzags, and vertical accents; Moderne, which emphasized round shapes and horizontal accents; and a combination of these two sometimes called PWA Moderne, seemingly a bureaucratic creation favored for Public Works Administration structures of the 1930s. Art Deco derived its name from the 1925 Paris *Exposition Internationale des Arts Décoratifs et Industriels Moderne*—a

show most notable in retrospect for its near-total exclusion of representation from either the Weimar Bauhaus or the closely related De Stijl movement in Holland, the two most potent sources of that European Modernism which after 1945 made so swift and so total a conquest of the American art world.

Unlike Bauhaus Modernism, Art Deco's prime concerns were with perceived American realities and needs in the 1920s and especially the 1930s. No matter how abstracted, how varied in degree of lavishness or economy of execution, its forms were still recognizably drawn from that classical past embodied in the old American National Classical Revival *[6.63, 6.64]*. The nation's last great railroad stations, like Union Terminal in Cincinnati, were in Art Deco *[6.18]*. The same is true of furniture and interiors *[6.65, 6.66]*, whose whole range has been

6.63. How variously Academic designers could adapt and abstract classical elements is suggested in this photo of the upper part of the Chrysler Building (completed 1929) with part of the New York Public Library (1904) in right foreground. (IMG:NAL)

6.64. 30 Rockefeller Plaza, in the complex of twenty-one buildings that make up the "city within a city" that is Rockefeller Center, opened in 1934; Wallace K. Harrison was general architect. Broadly abstracted classical sculptures of Wisdom flanked by Light and Sound by Lee Lawrie and Leon V. Solon helped humanize the otherwise overwhelming buildings as consistently as classical traditions early and late (cf. 3.1, 9.1). (IMG:NAL)

6.65. *Worgelt Study designed by Alavoine of Paris and New York City, 1928–30, as set up in the Brooklyn Museum. The room is designed as a whole: the furniture, paneling, lamps, and sculpture all contribute to the total Art Deco effect and show the range of Academic Classical, from representational to abstract forms. (The Brooklyn Museum, gift of Mr. and Mrs. Raymond Worgelt. Photograph by Paul Warchol, 1987)*

6.66. *Vanity table and matching stool, of chrome-plated tubular steel, wood, and glass. Designed by Kem Weber; made in Michigan by the Lloyd Manufacturing Company of Menominee, 1934. However "modern" the materials, the forms are not dictated by them but by proportions descended from the classical tradition. (The Brooklyn Museum, Modernism Benefit Fund. Photograph by Jerry Kobylecky)*

so nicely summarized in the 1987 exhibition and accompanying catalog *American Art Deco* by Alastair Duncan. At one end of the scale are what resemble anticipations of Bauhaus European Modernism, at the other, clumsy classical pastiches; but the bulk, the whole middle range, from Donald Deskey to Elsie de Wolfe, is solidly based on simplifications and abstractions of the Classical Revival tradition.

Furthermore, Art Deco designers addressed problems growing out of the Great Depression, whose impact upon American life and culture seems so deliberately minimized in immediately succeeding decades as to suggest a kind of induced cultural amnesia. That was particularly evident in the two great fairs of the 1930s—Chicago's Century of Progress in 1933 and the New York World's Fair in 1939. What the American industrial designers represented there were concerned with—and the stars were predominantly Americans and not Europeans despite the Bauhaus radiance already lighting the elitist firmaments of Harvard, Yale, and IIT—was practical, Depression-beating devices: Buckminster Fuller with his Dymaxion auto at the Century of Progress; Walter Dorwin Teague and Norman Bel Geddes with their "Futurama" and Henry Dreyfuss with his "Democracity" at the New

York fair; Raymond Loewy popularizing streamlining. Ultimately their innovations were all intended to improve the industrial fabric and provide jobs for everybody again. They were not glorifications of machines or subordinations of human interest to theories of scientific materialism, but "streamlined" practical solutions to problems plaguing human life: superhighways that would make driving easier, cars that would make driving safer and easier, better-looking and better-working radios and clocks and washing machines. Streamlining referred not to some mystical "new Modern spirit," but to the reduction of complexity to simple, easy-flowing shapes for the benefit of beholders and users in every aspect of life—machines, buildings, furniture. Streamlining expressed and coped with Depression economies; it justified harsh necessities in terms of aesthetics, showing how the efficiencies of exposed steel-cage construction or factory-made materials like glass brick could be made attractive to users (the dogmatics would come later).[23]

These considerations operated on all levels. They very largely account for the great popularity of Nebraska's skyscraper-capitol in Lincoln, stripped down from its original conventionally lavish Academic program to a much simplified version

6.67. How "skyscraper ideals" dominated the Academic era is evidenced in its adaption for even the most tenacious of all architectural subtypes, the capitol. Here is Nebraska's, built 1922–32 to designs from 1919–20 by Bertram Grosvenor Goodhue. (Division of Nebraska Resources, Lincoln)

6.68. California early introduced the idea of combining several movie theaters under a single roof; here, the combined Esquire and Plaza theaters in Sacramento, built in 1940, with William B. David as architect. But Art Deco was found everywhere as a theater style, because association with motion pictures universally carried connotations of "modernity." In theater architecture, Art Deco frequently coalesced with Colonial Spanish and its implications of leisure, fun and sun, et cetera. (IMG:NAL)

of the classical portico plus dome *[6.67];* much the same happened also in the Oregon state capitol at Salem, completed roughly at the same time.

So speaking to American needs in forms still comprehensibly American, Art Deco had extraordinary appeal in its own time, and an even more extraordinary nostalgia boom in post-Modern times. There is some irony in nostalgia for those Depression years, so helpless, so hopeless, so gloomy with darkening clouds of World War II; but it is understandable in terms of Art Deco's frivolity, its refusal to take itself seriously, hence its usefulness as an escape vehicle—from the Depression in the 1930s, from Modernism in the later 1970s. It is no accident that Art Deco should be so closely connected to and so obvious an expression of the American radio and movie industry during the decade 1928–38 especially, of which the crowning exemplar is of course the Chrysler Building's "microphone" cresting *[6.63],* matched in effects by movie theaters in every small town *[6.68].* And there was a further appealing contrast with the Modern that succeeded Art Deco: it was not primarily addressed to an elite establishment.

Art Deco was not primarily a gallery style, dependent for promotion on media hype; it could also address the sensibilities of apartment dwellers in small towns, people who ate in diners and shopped in five-and-dime stores *[6.69–6.71].* [24] It could make business look glamorous *[6.72a, b].* But it was not necessarily Popular/Commercial. Sociologically diverse, Art Deco was also ideologically divided. For it could not only function as a middle-brow vernacular (like its Classical Revival progenitor), but could also serve as a vehicle for high-brow social protest. Art Deco can be seen, among other things, as a visual metaphor for precisely the sort of compromise between radical collectivism and the old American individualism that a whole generation of people educated to liberal opinions and dedicated to social progress were trying to make in the 1930s. It corresponded to the attitudes of "Parlor Pink" people, fond of praising and promoting socialist and communist ideas for reorganizing society along lines supposedly more scientific than those that brought about World War I and the Depression, but hoping to keep their own freedom of action; people who talked about social order without regimentation, especially theirs; the sort who felt everybody was equal but some more equal than others, hence got a warm egalitarian glow from calling their black servants "cleaning ladies." In short, Art

6.69. *Parkside Manor was a small Eureka apartment house built in 1937 in the California version of Art Deco called Streamline Moderne—all simple geometric lines and shapes, and so a standing challenge to the famed Carson House a dozen-odd blocks away [5.7]. It was in fact a small visual metaphor of the "reverse mirror image" on which so much Modern theory was based.*

6.70. *Miami's first big boom, in the 1920s, found architectural expression in Academic Spanish Colonial with "sun and fun" connotations; after the 1929 bust, the city's recovery in the 1930s produced the nation's greatest single concentration of Art Deco, in its famous Art Deco District. The style's appeal was its frivolity and escape from seriousness. These are typical low-rise apartments-cum-shops on Collins Avenue. (Courtesy of Miami Design Preservation League)*

6.71. *A beneficiary of Depression era penny-pinching was the chain of Samuel H. Kress & Company 5-10-25 Cent Stores; during the years 1929–54 the firm's principal architect Edward F. Sibbert designed dozens of stores all over the country in basic Art Deco with variant motifs, most notably Maya/Aztec Revival inspired by Kress's personal enthusiasms for the Land of Mu. This one was built in Hilo, Hawaii, in 1932. (Courtesy of Don Hibbard, Hawaii State Preservation Office)*

6.72. Chandelier, ceiling, and elevator doors—a few specimens of Lincoln Rogers's elegant Art Deco detailing for Honolulu's Dillingham Building, 1928–29. (Courtesy of Don Hibbard, Hawaii State Preservation Office)

Deco created visual metaphors of a mentality not altogether unlike stock 1980s liberalism; whence, perhaps, one source of those curious similarities between much Postmodern furniture design and, say, Elsie de Wolfe's chairs.

Academic Medieval Revival Styles

In theory there could be an Academic version of every previous medieval substyle, as there could for preceding Colonial and Classical substyles. And a few examples of each can indeed be found: an Academic French Romanesque and an Academic Italianate Romanesque, with more refined and correct forms drawn from sources, from which came Henry Hobson Richardson's more picturesquely robust Romanesque, for instance. Just as Academic Classical had its late abstracted Art Deco form, so Academic Gothic had its late abstracted form in Dom Bellot's attempt to combine intimations of Modernity with ancient religious tradition, seen at its best in Canada [6.73]. But in basic practice Academic Gothic was as much or more limited in usage and application than the Gothic Revival proper had been.

For religious buildings an Academic Gothic high style flourished, led by prolific self-convinced and convincing propagandists like Ralph Adams Cram and Henry Vaughan. Its most famous example was Cram's redesign of the 1892 Byzantine Episcopal

Church of Saint John the Divine in New York City. He created a contemporary cathedral in purest High Gothic style, with mighty cross vaults of authentic construction, rose windows and lancets, applied sculpture, all in technique as authentically medieval as possible, however contemporary in political and social themes. From there the style descended in social scale, shedding extravagances as it went; but it was usually elaborate enough, given the era's emphasis on establishment values that translated into favor and funds for the more established churches and synagogues. (Temple Emanu-El on Fifth Avenue was another composition of revived medieval elements.)

Its counterpart was the Academic High Gothic (with Picturesque admixtures) now favored for campuses of Ivy League universities, wherein Cram also played a large part [6.20]. Exquisitely refined Academic versions of English and French medieval university Gothic, corrected and improved, neater and more consistent and better scaled than the originals, making sophisticated allusion to "ancient, stable institution", gave Yale and Princeton (especially) settings to rival Oxbridge, with student capers resounding through "quads" and "commons," porters' lodges, spired towers, compulsory chapel under mighty Gothic vaults—the works.

For these few universities, Academic High Gothic style was appropriate; it marked them off as defenders and custodians of the ancient tradition of universities providing social polish and polite accomplishments rather than job training, places whose students' livelihoods and spheres of activity were determined by birth. But for most others it was not.[25] To be sure, a good deal of "collegiate Gothic"—scaled down, less elaborate, more domestic—was built. There was always some trumpery about it—false notes, because most colleges in the country were not developing on lines anything like European universities. They were in fact in-

creasingly modeled on business corporations, for the very good reason that they had to raise money to survive. Fluttering gowns and wisteria'd quads and quaint student capers were ever further from the realities of most American universities. Preston Slosson's 1930 contribution to the History of American Life series cogently pointed out what had happened:

> Faculty control does very well under European conditions, where an anciently endowed institution has only routine administrative tasks and can devote its main

6.73. *Exterior and vestible of the monastery of Saint-Benoît-du-Lac in Quebec, just north of the Vermont border at Richford. It is the best example on the continent of the Dom Bellot style, which aimed to reconcile Academic Gothic Revival and "modern spirit." Commissioned in 1935, completed in 1939 on plans of Dom Bellot associated with Dom Claude-Marie Côté and Félix Racicot. (IMG:NAL)*

6.74. Sunshine glances off the upper stories of the 1927 "Cathedral of Learning" at the University of Pittsburgh, an architectural metaphor of a distinctively American concept of education conducted in the image of business that appeared in the 1920s. "A great symphony . . . of upwardness" is how the building program described it—an expression of the university's new aspirations to serve a multiplicity of social purposes. Architect Charles Z. Klauder was also responsible for the 1933 Heinz Chapel in the foreground, dedicated to older religions. Another, later architectural metaphor of the social-service multiversity can also be seen at Pitt: Forbes Quadrangle, a huge office/factory complex built by the state of Pennsylvania's engineering department in the 1970s. (IMG:NAL)

energies to teaching and research. But where an institution is rapidly developing from a college of a few hundred to a university of ten thousand, where millions of dollars must be raised within three or four years, where a rigid classical curriculum is being rapidly broadened into an elective system which offers every imaginable course from aeronautics to cemetery planning, where the university is expected to serve a whole state with extension courses, correspondence work, loan libraries and agricultural demonstration

stations, there is imperative need for an executive of the "captain-of-industry" type. Under such conditions the president becomes a general manager responsible to a board of regents or trustees as "directors," the deans are managers and division superintendents, the department heads are foremen, the rank and file of the teaching staff employees, the students are the raw material, and the alumni the manufactured product.[26]

What would the appropriate image for such an institution be? One might be factory-like "Depression buildings" such as the two from 1935–36 that appeared at George Washington University in Washington, D.C., during the tenure of President Marvin (a classic demonstration of Slosson's case, who within a year of his appointment in 1927 had abolished the school's ancient [1821] constitution and put himself in direct charge of a mammoth expansion along business lines):

> Buildings C and D . . . were identical in appearance . . . improvised by the president . . . designed for the utmost economy in their original cost and maintenance. Built of used brick, later painted white, they were essentially cubes, four stories and basement, with hollow-tile room partitions, and exposed pipes and wiring. Walls were unfinished and the ceiling design was derived from the cement forms of the floor above. Rooms could be changed in size, practically overnight, by moving the hollow tiles of the walls. Exposed pipes and wiring made repair easy. In this highly ingenious fashion, classrooms and laboratories were provided at amazingly low cost.[27]

That was an honest expression of the educational situation. A better one—in fact one of the era's most revealing and significant buildings—was the "Cathedral of Learning," whose erection in 1927, in the form of an Academic Gothic Revival skyscraper obviously similar to commercial structures like the Woolworth Building a decade earlier, signaled the University of Pittsburgh's dramatic expansion in the 1920s [6.74; cf. 6.2].

The most widespread and ultimately important of Academic medieval styles was Tudor. Its uses were principally domestic. It was found on quite elaborate mansions with very correct copyings of sixteenth-century Tudor proper, Elizabethan, or Jacobean forms, all the way down through "Stockbroker Tudor" to prefabricated mail-order suburbans whose styles could most charitably be called not very correct [6.75]. It no doubt appealed to the owners' lingering tastes for picturesqueness. In architectural history it has another importance. From this style, which eschewed overt Gothicisms like pointed windows but embraced a basic medieval peasant building emphasis on the nature and textures of materials, came that extraordinary style that goes under the names of Arts and Crafts, Prairie, Wrightian, and the like, the style in which one of this era's most central metaphors of "Americanism" was created—a style that is, in fact, a rarified, Academically refined version of the Picturesque.

The Progressive Styles

In American architectural history, the early-nineteenth-century Gothic Revival's inherent picturesqueness made it a natural catalyst for creating Picturesque styles proper by mid-century; so again, in the 1890s, the expression of materials and structure inherent in Academic Medieval Revival styles made them a natural base for creating a style that would be at once modern and American. The result was a series of styles that in their own day went under names like Craftsman, Organic, and Prairie. A good generic name for them is Progressive, for they were closely related to the Progressive movement of the 1890–1930 period, not least to its "advanced" political and social attitudes and their heavily moral implications. "Progressive" would generally cover the wide range of styles practiced by Frank Lloyd Wright and his Prairie School group (George W. Maher, Robert C. Spencer Jr., Dwight Heald Perkins, Claude Bragdon, Myron C. Hunt, Walter Burley Griffin, Marian Mahoney); the delicate variations on Japanese practiced by Charles and Henry Greene in California; Bernard Maybeck's free interpretations of Gothic at First Church of Christ Scientist in Berkeley and Academic Roman at the Palace of Fine Arts or the Packard Showrooms, with their Spanish admixtures, in San Francisco; Irving Gill's proto-Modern variants on Academic Spanish Colonial; the Scandinavian version of Arts and Crafts exemplified by Eliel Saarinen and the Cranbrook School in Bloomfield Hills; and the Populist version promoted by Gustave Stickley—to mention only some of the more prominent.

In their own time and since, much was made of how Modern Progressive architecture was, compared to the undisguised Academic eclecticism by the likes of Hunt, McKim, or Cram, or even the freer eclecticism of, say, Julia Morgan. And by that standard Progressives, eschewing applied ornament and deriving ornamental effects exclusively from what they considered to be the nature of mate-

rials and plans they were using, were Modern indeed. Compare Wright's conception of a country villa with Morgan's, from whatever periods of their respective careers *[6.76, 6.77]*. Morgan's Hearst Castle is full of eclectically derivative forms commanding the site, while Wright's Fallingwater takes forms dictated by their nature and seems to grow naturally out of the earth. In the one, ancient materials—ashlar, tile, stucco—are traditionally structured; in the other, modern materials—ferroconcrete slabs—cantilevered out from a core. The one has windows traditionally conceived as framed openings punched in a wall; the other has windows in strips of two, three, four, or more units, often set in corners as well as if to display skeletal steel structure.

Above all, Progressives prided themselves on democratic populist attitudes. Not that they would necessarily have scorned to work for those Vanderbilts or McCormicks or Hearsts who were the eclectic Academics' prize clients, had commissions from them been forthcoming; rather, they were willing and happy to work on middle-class designs on occasion *[6.78, 6.79]*. Like the old Quakers (and indeed such Protestant religious strains ran strong in them) Progressives would be "plain, but of the best sort." And this, they believed, was to be modern.

European Moderns, who began to arrive in force during the 1930s, thought otherwise. Their mouthpieces, like Siegfried Giedion and his canonical

6.75. Darkened oak framing stands out against white stucco walls, sun glances off diamond-mullioned window bank of this grand Tudor suburban house, built in 1911 on a cross-axial plan by British Columbia's premier architect, Samuel Maclure, in Victoria's elegant suburb of Oak Bay. Like all too many of its kind, it has been internally split into apartments since the 1950s. Samuel Maclure, trained in Philadelphia, was a correspondent of Frank Lloyd Wright, some of whose first houses were in this Tudor style. (IMG: NAL)

6.76. In 1919 architect Julia Morgan and media magnate William Randolph Hearst had their first meetings over what became one of the most elaborate mansions of the 1920s: Hearst Castle at San Simeon, on the California coast fifty-odd miles from San Luis Obispo. Its construction occupied the next dozen years. Components were complex (including guest cottages, classical temple, colonnaded loggia, swimming pools, greenhouses, and zoo), and so was its style: a distinctively Academic mix of Colonial Spanish with medieval elements. "Casa Grande," seen here, was the main house, built 1922–26; the facade was reinforced concrete faced with stone. (Photograph by Ken Raveill, courtesy of Hearst San Simeon State Historical Monument)

6.77. Fallingwater was built for Edgar J. Kaufmann, Sr., of Pittsburgh, as a weekend home. Frank Lloyd Wright secured the commission through Kaufmann's son, who had studied in the Taliesin fellowship, and made of it a mature statement of his architectural philosophy. The living room floor is solid rock, and the various parts cantilever out from that central core. Since 1963 administered by the Western Pennsylvania Conservancy. (IMG: NAL)

Space, Time and Architecture, treated Wright with frigid courtesy, but always in the past tense, as a precursor of sorts for their own revelations. Of the other Progressives they spoke hardly at all. For all Progressives in their eyes were guilty of the unforgivable, inexcusable sin of being unscientific—which meant, among other things, designing in a historical context, with references and allusions in form and proportion to past styles. And indeed it was so.

All sorts of allusions and borrowings could be recognized in Progressive styles. Decorative details, shapes, proportions, black-and-white patternings that could be Japanese, maybe even lingering, covert, Tudor *[6.80]*. Proportioning that suggested an underlying classicism, like Art Deco *[6.81]*. Out-

right borrowings from Gothic and Classical, sometimes both *[6.82]*. And all that medieval allusion and insinuation lurking about—linen-fold effects carved into wood panels; ornament in colored terra cotta, sometimes painted, even; heavy, round entrance arches decidedly reminiscent of Romanesque; extensive use of stained-glass windows with leaded mullions, sometimes used in skylights as well. Even when the Progressives' motifs might not be historicist, their total effect most certainly was. Supremely reprehensible, of course, was the very retention of ornament at all. No matter if it derived from the nature of materials or structure, it was still ornamental; and ornament was for European Modernists the ultimate and absolute taboo. For them this American Progressive Modernism was in fact

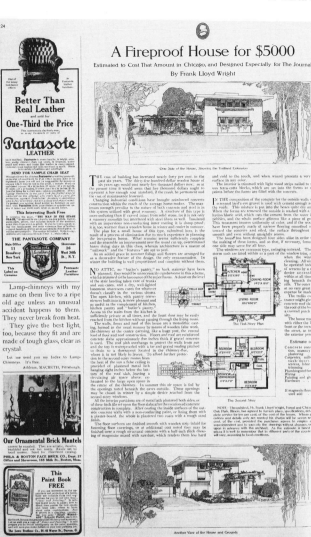

A Fireproof House for $5000

Estimated to Cost That Amount in Chicago, and Designed Especially for The Journal

By Frank Lloyd Wright

One Side of the House, Showing the Trellised Extension

The First-Story Plan

The Second Story

Another View of the House and Grounds

6.78. *This house by Frank Lloyd Wright was published in the April 1907 issue of* The Ladies' Home Journal *as one of a series of presentations on domestic architecture sponsored by publisher Edward Bok. Its plan featured that central core with other elements spreading out from it from which Wright rarely departed.*

6.79. *Many elements of Wright's Prairie houses had wide appeal and were often copied on social levels lower than his clients'. In this house, built c. 1920 in the central California town of Grass Valley, may be recognized the horizontal lines, window ranges with colored glass, and some approximation to Wrightian columns. The typical Prairie plan, requiring lots far more spacious than were usual in suburbs, was copied much less often. Usually Prairie features were tacked on to standard large or small foursquare plans, as here. (IMG:NAL)*

6.80. Living room of the Isabel Roberts house in the Chicago suburb of River Forest as built in 1907 shows intimations of eclectic taste: the two-story arrangement with vases, from Japanese inspiration; the linen-fold effect of desk and side chair, from medieval; the stuffed chair by the fireplace, from Picturesque styles of the more recent past. (An indication of its source occurs in the advertisement published beside Wright's The Ladies' Home Journal *offering [6.78].)*

no more than old Picturesque Eclecticism disguised; for them, Wright was no more than "the greatest architect of the nineteenth century."

But the European Modernists' case against American Progressives went deeper than ornament. It had to do with what architecture fundamentally is *about.* The overriding preoccupation of American architects, whether Academic or Progressive, was to create a visual metaphor of American nationalism. The Europeans, by contrast, made their debut, at the famous 1929 show at the Museum of Modern Art, as promoters of the International Style—that is, as above petty national considerations. By contrast, if American Progressives quarreled with their Beaux-Arts counterparts over eclecticism, the question was whether or not borrowings from foreign parts could ever be sufficiently acclimatized to create the requisite American image. On the appropriateness of creating such an image both agreed.

Not that Progressives were narrow; far from it. They thought of themselves as culminating a change in Western civilization generally, and in the formative basis of architecture in particular, begun with the late-eighteenth-century revolutions in America and France, the Reform Bills of 1832 and 1867 in Britain, and comparable changes elsewhere. As inherited traditional institutions were challenged and discarded, so were inherited traditional architectural forms. Increasingly civilization came to be conceived as a man-made thing, to be shaped by human hands, governed by human will. It followed that, as human beings differ, so must

nations. Each has a character, a personality, a biography—each a birth, a childhood, an adolescence, and now a rational democratic maturity. What that character is, national arts define: narrative paintings of historical events, national tastes in design, presentations of national life and character on stage and in song. But for such a purpose, architecture is *the* art, obviously. Only, it took perceptive architects to realize their role, to accept the greatness historical destiny had thrust upon them. Architects of Progressive persuasion in the United States considered themselves perceptive. They realized what they had to do. After all, their countrymen had led the world in shaping a new rational democratic state. Now at the end of the nineteenth century perfection was in sight. A great Civil War had been fought, slaves freed, a wilderness tamed and populated, government by popular referendum introduced, Pure Food laws passed, trusts busted.[28] It remained only to create a new national architecture, counterpart to national architectures elsewhere in Western Europe, to be sure, but of a character unique to America.

The country being so various, naturally its National architecture would be varied too. Nothing more appropriate than that some of it should contain eclectic echoes—intimations of Spanish culture in California, of sturdy pioneers' log cabins; or that it should, like mid-century Picturesque sculptural programs, take all world cultures into its embrace. Hence "disguised eclecticism," and the persistence of Picturesque in Academic guises were perfectly all right.

Nothing could be more appropriate, either, than that aspirations toward a new American national architecture should be centered in the Midwest. The impulse was general, of course; but it was felt most deeply and imperatively in those territories created by the Northwest Ordinance of 1787, which had been transformed within a century from wilderness to one of the world's centers of heavy industry. According to William N. Parker:

> The heady spiral of solidly based growth in supplies and in demand gave to the Midwest's economy and culture in the late 19th century a vigor, a zest, an optimism and self-assurance which made further accomplishment easy and growth apparently endless.... The Northeast had been "cabinned, cribbed and confined" by valleys and hillsides, by peculiar beliefs, by history and class structures; the South by the foul blight of slavery and racial prejudice, an ill-motivated work force, and an idle and ignorant aristocracy. From 1880 to 1930, the Midwest *was* America.[29]

And the Academic Progressive styles invented in that region were with like certitude understood to be the real American architecture. That is what comes through in all the Progressives' writings and pronouncements. That is why the first and most lasting expression of Progressive architecture was the Prairie style, with its overriding horizontality consciously referring to the Great Plains: low spreading eaves, long balconies, and flattened-out porches; low walls functioning as property barriers or space arrangers, punctuated by parapets (especially slab parapets projecting so as to produce special horizontal emphases); roofs, if not absolutely flat, rarely gabled either *[6.83]*. These Midwest forms never entirely lost their primacy in Progressive thinking.

But for the Progressives, forms were only means to an end. The goal was to create effective visual metaphors of the institutions of the newly matured American nation. That was what Wright's architecture—from beginning to end, in houses and offices, courthouses and apartments—consistently was *about.*[30] His houses, from Prairie in Illinois to Fallingwater in Pennsylvania to Usonian in Arizona, are visual metaphors of the American pioneer institution of family, as Wright's own pioneer Midwest family experienced it in Spring Green, Wisconsin: centered around common fireplace-hearth core, so that no matter how far off each wing may go on its own each retains always that central contact *[6.77, 6.84, 6.85]*.[31] His office buildings—both the Larkin in Buffalo *[6.86]* and the Johnson Wax in Racine

6.81. *Frank Lloyd Wright was an early and enthusiastic advocate of architects' designing their own furniture and interiors generally, considering buildings as total works of art. This furniture was commissioned from him by Herbert Fisk Johnson for the S. C. Johnson & Son Administration Building in Racine, Wisconsin [6.24, 6.25], executed by Steelcase in enameled steel, walnut, and fabric. Japanese and Art Deco influences are detectable. (Courtesy of S. C. Johnson & Son, Inc.)*

6.82. *The 1909–10 Christian Science Church in Berkeley, California, designed by Bernard Maybeck, combined elements of Gothic and Romanesque styles with contemporary structural techniques (cast concrete columns, hinged timber trusses), appropriately expressing that denomination's tenets, but also creating a visual metaphor of worship in general. (IMG:NAL)*

[6.24, 6.25], are visual metaphors of American business centered on and concerned with people—workers who are independent and self-reliant parts of a kind of commercial community.[32] Unity Temple in Chicago is a visual metaphor of liberal, quasi-secularized Protestantism as it had evolved in the Midwest: It has the common core space to which individual parts relate as independent elements, like a congregation without a creed, each finding spiritual satisfaction in a personal way.

The Larkin office and so many other creations by Wright have been demolished; many others were never built (few have realized how many until the extensive series of publications by Bruce Brooks Pfeiffer of drawings and projects in the archives of Wright's last home, Taliesin West). Wright, in his last years especially, proclaimed himself to be, and to have been, the greatest architect America had yet produced or ever would produce. This view did not sit well with contemporaries. Most of them contrasted it unfavorably with the apparent modesty of Gropius and Mies, who insisted upon ascribing their works to vague collaboratives and associates. Yet it was mainly exasperation at the success of the Bauhaus in America that provoked the exaggerations of Wright's late utterances. The more time elapses, the better we can understand Wright's mood. How *could* the architectural establishment have made such a choice? How could the nation have preferred sterile boxes to these marvelously colorful, playfully picturesque city blocks, with department stores and civic centers, self-service garages and YMCAs, laundries and city parks and skyscrapers? When Wright said he could have remade America, it was perfectly true—and how much better might the country have looked had he been given the commissions denied him! But that of course is still a matter of opinion.[33]

Wright was of course far from the only one out to remake America in the 1890–1930 years. This was the Progressive era, and reformers of all kinds abounded, on every level. One of the most interesting was Gustave Stickley, with his self-proclaimed "mission" to educate middle-class Americans to good design practices, especially in furniture.[34] If we can with some justice speak of Wright's style as Elitist Arts and Crafts, then Populist Arts and Crafts is the term for Stickley's far heavier, rougher, rawer Craftsman version of it *[6.87, 6.88]*. Stickley's architecture and furniture had little of Wright's subtleties. Its characteristics were obvious and immediately perceptible: use of wood so as to bring out how it was sawn or split, and how wooden structural members function to support roofs as struts, rafters, or projecting beam ends; big shingles; rough stucco, often with bits of colored glass mixed in for textural effect; pergolas; cobblestone or split field-stone (instead of the sandstone so commonly favored in Richardsonian Romanesque) for veranda steps, railings, or posts; clinker brick; on interiors,

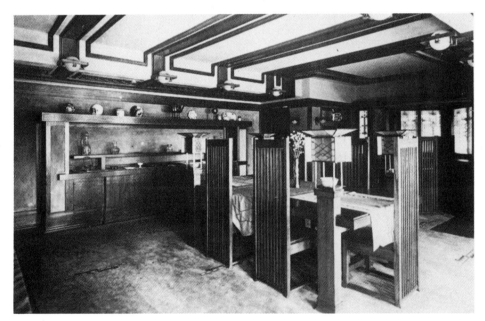

6.83. The house that Frank Lloyd Wright designed for Frederick Robie on South Woodlawn Avenue in Chicago has often been considered the archetypal Prairie house for its low, extended horizontal lines, emphasized by chimney and terrace cappings, and his characteristic urn shapes. The interior is likewise a classic example of assimilated medieval and Oriental borrowings.

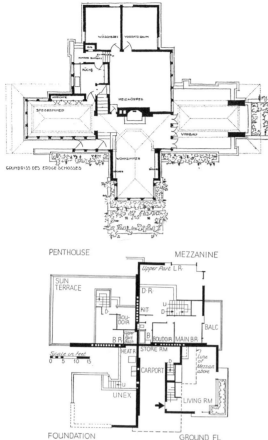

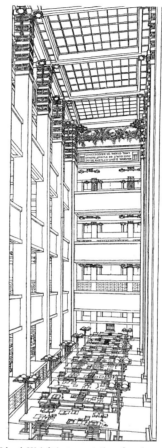

6.84 (top). Ground plan of Frank Lloyd Wright's house for Isabel Roberts in River Forest, 1907. (From Hermann Muthesius, Frank Lloyd Wright: Ausgeführte Bauten *[Berlin: Wasmuth, 1911])*

6.85. Vestiges of the basic "windmill" plan, with central core and radiating wings, was preserved even in the low-cost four-family housing unit Wright designed for the Suntop houses at Ardmore, Pennsylvania, in 1939. Plumbing, heating, electricity, and ventilation were in the central core; the inner brick walls separated different apartments. (From Architectural Forum, *August 1939)*

6.86. Frank Lloyd Wright's presentation drawing of the interior of the Larkin Company Administration Building, built in Buffalo in 1904, demolished in 1949 when collapse of its mail-order business made the building redundant. Dominating this interior is an inscription in Wright's beautiful Arts and Crafts lettering, an admonition from Jesus Christ: "Whatsoever ye would that others should do unto you do ye even so unto them." Such evangelical intrusions into public buildings were common Progressive practice. The design is very close in formal spirit and severe simplicity to Unity Temple, designed a year later. This is a sanctuary community for work—much as Catharine Beecher had perceived the home in an earlier generation. (From Frank Lloyd Wright: An American Architecture *[Horizon Press, 1955])*

prominent fireplaces with big metal hoods. Craftsman was, as its name suggests, predominantly addressed to a clientele that still thought in sexual stereotypes. "Fairly bristling with maleness,"[35] it brings to modern minds an image of the 1910s and 1920s paralleled in comic strip couples, where the Man of the House is so often pictured in shirt sleeves and vest, the Wife in a housedress; the one prone to spend evenings in his basement on some suitably masculine project like Stickley chairs—planing boards, boring decorative holes—while above, something suitably dainty is going on: tatting, tending the house plants, mending lingerie. The era to which such furniture belongs is gone *[6.89]*. Vanished too, we might suppose, is the ethos behind Stickley's furniture: that the production of art should involve, and proclaim, moral values like honesty, integrity, forthrightness, via direct expression of plain materials and straightforward structure.

But more of it remains than might at first be supposed.

6.87. The "Plaza" model, from the Aladdin Company's 1919 catalog of mass-prefabricated houses. Craftsman was a popular architectural style on this social level (though not necessarily deriving from Stickley himself); it could be realized by adding to a basic plan and exterior (see oval) such features as fieldstone chimneys and foundation, shingled walls, pergola, and eave rafters extended with prominent acute-angle cuts. Into such a house, furniture handcrafted from Stickley's designs would fit very well.

6.88. Furniture and interior ideas from Gustav Stickley's magazine The Craftsman dominate this c. 1915 photograph from a promotional brochure for Herbert J. Hapgood's affluent Mountain Lakes development, begun in 1911 in Morris County, New Jersey, not far from Craftsman Farms: oak furniture, wicker chair, Tiffany desk lamp, dark ceiling beams and wall panels, American Indian rug. Most of Mountain Lakes survives in almost pristine state; living rooms like this can still commonly be seen. (Courtesy of John W. Steen.)

6.89. Last great architectural monument to the old Progressive impulse was Timberline Lodge on Mount Hood in Oregon, built 1936–37 by U.S. Forest Service architects directed by Gilbert Stanley Underwood. On the outside all shingle and fieldstone in great swooping roofs and massive buttresses; inside full of heavy

Arts and Crafts sorts of fittings and furniture: great rough-hewn posts, some made from old telephone poles; heavy hardwood chairs and tables, unpainted; wrought iron grilles; hammered copper and leather lamps; mosaics; and much more. (IMG:NAL)

Academic Styles as Continuing Cultural Expression

Upon first reflection, the years that produced Stickley furniture and the Woolworth Building, Woodrow Wilson's idealistic speeches, John Philip Sousa's "Stars and Stripes Forever," and all the other intimations of a happy and prosperous, liberal and democratic America, ever Progressive, ever moving toward political and social perfection, seem to belong in some mythical past. Nor is this just fallible memory. Statistics bear the differences out. In 1890, according to David Klingaman:

> By far, the major occupation was . . . jobs directly in agriculture . . . approximately forty percent of the male workers. The percentage of . . . "manufacturing and mechanical" jobs was about 22 percent. . . . About 83 percent of these were males. . . . It is interesting that the occupations of 1890 were not much different than they were in 1850. . . . The occupations of women were dramatically different from those of men. . . . Fully one-third of working women were servants, including waitresses and housekeepers. . . . The next largest occupation was that of dressmaker, milliner, and seamstress . . . one out of eight working women in the United States and one out of five in the Midwest did this kind of hand work for a living. Nationally, agricultural labor employed about 11 percent of the women who worked. However, these people were overwhelmingly southern blacks. . . . Nearly 10 percent of working women in the Midwest were schoolteachers. . . . Many women also worked as musicians and music teachers, nurses and midwives, and boarding and lodging-house keepers. . . .

> In the Midwest, 98 percent of the population was white; for example, only eight thousand black people lived in Chicago out of a population of one million.[36]

Has this world totally receded into myth? Hardly. Eras in human history are not and never can be like stops on an airline, that leave no trace on planes arriving and departing there. Just as no event in any individual's life can ever be totally forgotten, every one leaving an impression somewhere, on some level of mind and body, so with societies: whatever a nation has been, in some sense it will always be.

America in the 1890–1930 years was a country dominated by white middle-class pluralistic attitudes and outlook. And that was manifested in all its institutions. In contrast to the preceding Gilded Age, the most typical Americans were no longer nouveaux-riches or homesteaders on the frontier, but solidly middle class. And the arts most characteristic of this age were made for them[37]: the comics, wherein are chronicled the middle-class lives of Maggie and Jiggs, Toots and Casper, Blondie and Dagwood, Gasoline Alley's dwellers, and the rest (with a sprinkling of rich and poor at either end, like Daddy Warbucks and Moon Mullins); middle-class magazines, the most famous being the *Ladies' Home Journal,* founded in 1902 by Edward Bok, featuring a "Good Taste/Bad Taste" column ("good taste" = disciplined restraint; "bad taste" = excessive ornament and pretentiousness—Academic doctrine encapsulated, that is); novels like Willa Cather's *My Antonia* and *O Pioneers!,* Theodore Dreiser's *An American Tragedy,* Sinclair Lewis's *Main Street* and *Babbitt* (at the time taken for attacks on the middle class, in retrospect appeals to reform it). But most of all, middle-class suburban architecture in all its variety, from spacious, elegant architect-designed neighborhoods like Shaker Heights to the numberless subdivisions built up by spec builders, developers, and individuals from prefab suppliers. This era, rather than Gilded Age vanities, are usually "the good old days" that later twentieth-century nostalgia calls to mind.

At its best, this was a culture of pluralism, acceptance, and tolerance, not nearly so exclusively created by and for the rich as the era preceding, nor by an elite, like the Modernism that followed. Its arts spoke of and for a broad range of the population, who moreover confidently assumed that everyone *in* that society ultimately would be *of* it, as they were. Such a culture, and such assumptions, are what the infinite adaptability and variety of Academic styles most plainly expressed.

That architects like Maybeck or Maginnis, Howe or Cret could design now in Beaux-Arts Academic Roman, now in Elitist Arts and Crafts, now in Colonial homestead or Georgian, admirably manifested a society on the surface pluralistic but at core holding a solid body of common agreement about fundamentals. Those courthouses and post offices, some in majestic Doric, others in charming Mediterranean or Palatial Georgian or gabled German; those rows upon rows of suburban bungalows and foursquares and temple-houses, in every variety of Dutch Colonial and Georgian and Prairie, in cities and suburbs and villages from the 1890s through the 1930s, are the very image of pluralistic liberal democracy as promised in Fourth of July rhetoric over the preceding century, now come to pass.[38] Progressives and Beaux-Arts proponents fight for prestige, commissions, and the privilege of remaking America to their image, but never in any knock-down, drag-out spirit. For just as the same designer may do one commission in Mediterranean and the next in Craftsman with no real inconsistency, so in the politics of this age one side may gain an ascendancy and make some laws to promote its interests for a few years, then the other takes over and promotes *its* interests for a while, both however always keeping common ends in view. Like baseball—that truly democratic game, depending on skill and brains instead of physical accidents of height or weight—this society was governed by an agreement that sooner or later the other side would always get another chance to bat, another inning to see what they could do; and its architecture expressed this kind of culture precisely. Has this society vanished? It seems to reappear every four years.

And Academic architecture, has it vanished too? True, a new attitude would soon enough appear and a very different kind of architecture with it, expressing the convictions of people who want to play by a different set of rules; who intend, if and when they get an inning, to begin by tearing the ballpark down, metaphorically speaking. Practically speaking they mean, if they can, to ensure that all eclectic styles will be dumped into the "dustbin of history." Their efforts constitute a new stylistic category altogether—Modern, the subject of chapter 7.

To read some books one might get the impression that the Academics puddled along according to their dim historicist lights until one day True Enlightenment from Europe hit them, and poof! they were gone forever. Especially the Progressives. Progressives had imagined they were very different from and far ahead of their Beaux-Arts rivals, by which they meant that they were more "modern." But in fact both sides in this contest shared fundamentally similar social purposes—to create images of America, its life, its institutions, its ideals. Both were, then, fundamentally non-Modern, or, more precisely, pre-Modern. They were not as yet ready to think of architecture, or any art, as an end in itself, making its own rules, appealing neither to past nor present, but to a promised future. Neither side, that is to say, yet had a truly Modern cast of mind. Progressive painters—the Ash Can School and related movements—learned this sad truth first, when they organized the Armory Show of 1913 and innocently invited participation from what they took to be their allies in the modernist cause against Beaux-Arts eclecticism: the European Moderns. It was like the Britons inviting Anglo-Saxons over to help defend their island. By the time the show ended its tour, almost no American "modernism" was left in it. Academic architects had to wait for their corresponding sad moment of truth until the late 1930s, when forward-looking leaders of the American establishment invited Gropius to Harvard and Mies to IIT.

But did all Academic architecture thereupon disappear from the American landscape? Of course not; it survives all around. Much of it endures as Popular/Commercial, surviving first tenaciously and timorously, then lustily and ever more confidently in the teeth of all Modernist pontifications (chapter 8). Nor is that all. Especially after the first wave of European Modernism had been spent, toward the end of the 1950s, Academic styles began to reappear in the form of Subliminal Eclectic substyles, right within the Modern establishment itself. Postmodernism revived many Academic elements too. But for the moment, in the 1940s and 1950s, Modernism arrived, to constitute a new era.

Notes

1. And they have been marvelously recalled in Robert A. M. Stern, Gregory F. Gilmartin, and Thomas Mellins, *New York 1930* (New York: Rizzoli, 1977).

2. The phrase is from Bernard Maybeck, quoted in Esther McCoy's *Five California Architects* (New York: Reinhold, 1960), pp. 112–13, with reference to his attitude toward design of the Christian Science Church in Berkeley 1909–10.

3. "Progressive" ornament was at all times rooted in a matrix of ornamentalism, subliminal yet unmistakable, whether manifest in urns derived from classical tradition or pergolas from medieval or patterns from Aztec or plays of texture deriving from Picturesque usage. European Moderns perceived this self-contradiction immediately, whence their jibe at Wright as "the greatest architect of the nineteenth century."

4. Quote from Hermann Hagedorn, *The Roosevelt Family of Sagamore Hill* (New York: Macmillan, 1954), p. 6. Awareness of Academic "bigness" as a quality seems first effectively to have been defined by Frederick Gutheim,

One Hundred Years of Architecture in America, 1857–1957 (New York: Reinhold, 1958), pp. 64–74.

5. Carroll L. V. Meeks, *The Railroad Station* (New Haven, Conn.: Yale University Press, 1956).

6. Ralph Adams Cram, *My Life in Architecture* (Boston: Little Brown, 1935).

7. Quotation from brochure distributed to visitors to Vizcaya (Dade County Museum), c. 1962.

8. What really outraged Sullivan was not architectural principle but affront to his democratic egalitarian principles. In *McCall's Magazine* for 1903, fifty-seven marriages were listed to date between American heiresses and foreign noblemen. It never seemed to occur to Sullivan, and only rarely to his readers, that the Valois kings in their times were parvenus too. Furthermore, they married for money and rank just like millionaires in the nineteenth century.

9. Evelyn Watson, "Historic Aspects of the Bungalow," *Keith's Magazine* 24 (December 1910):369.

10. This was observed by perceptive contemporaries; thus Jan Cohn in *The Palace or the Poorhouse* (East Lansing: Michigan State University Press, 1979), p. 115, quotes J. W. Ghent's *Our Benevolent Feudalism* of 1902: "The imaginations of most men are fired by the spectacle of the few achieving great fortunes; each believes that a like fortune lies somewhere within his own reach, and with blind fatuity he tolerates conditions which he instinctively feels to be inequitable, simply because he expects himself to master them." On Academic styles functioning in lower-class housing, see my *The Comfortable House* (Cambridge, Mass.: The MIT Press, 1986), *passim*.

11. On the function of Academic styles on campuses, see especially Donald D. Egbert, "The Architecture and the Setting," in *The Modern Princeton* (Princeton, N.J.: Princeton University Press, 1947), pp. 86–121 (including an account of the controversy over the Graduate College); abridged and focused in *On Arts in Society: Selections from the Periodical Writings of D. D. Egbert, A Festschrift Reader* (Victoria, B.C.: University of Victoria, 1970), pp. 45–55. On the University of Virginia Rotunda, and the firm's motivations, see Leland Roth, *McKim, Mead & White* (New York: Harper & Row, 1983), pp. 196–97.

12. Ollie M. James, *Splendid Century: Centennial History of the Union Central Life Insurance Company of Cincinnati, Ohio* (Cincinnati: Union Central Life Insurance Company, 1967).

13. Robert Cruden, *Ministers of Reform* (New York: Basic Books, 1982), pp. 125–26.

14. The department store as a type originated in the mid-nineteenth century, and developed largely by appealing to the needs of women for a respectable place to go on their own. This theme figured in a major exhibition held by the Strong Museum in Rochester, New York, on the life of women in this era, and an accompanying book by Harvey Green, *Light of the Home: An Intimate View of Women in Victorian America* (New York: Pantheon Books, 1983).

15. Richard Guy Wilson has written on this subject with his usual perspicacity in, among other places, "From Informality to Pomposity: The Resort Casino in the Later

20th Century," Richard Guy Wilson, ed., *Victorian Resorts and Hotels: Essays from a Victorian Society Autumn Symposium,* ed. Richard Guy Wilson (Philadelphia: The Victorian Society, 1982). Originally published in *Nineteenth Century* 8/1–2 (1982):111–16.

16. On regional murals, Karal Ann Marling has written eloquently in many contexts. On regional Academic highway architecture, William Rhoads has written with comparable eloquence; see, for example, "Roadside Colonial: Early American Design for the Automobile Age," *Winterthur Portfolio* 21/2–3 (1986):133–52.

17. Benton also did the California Building in Mission style at the 1893 Chicago World's Fair. Other candidates have included his sometime partner, A. Page Brown, Lester B. Moore of Los Angeles (nominated by *The Craftsman* magazine in 1903), and Willis Polk. The truth is, no single individual was actually responsible; Mission Revival was an idea whose time had come. The Mission Inn was conspicuous as the most successful of a great number of successful vacation hotel designs in Mission and later Colonial Spanish styles, from Florida to Honolulu; the style was *made* for this type of building.

18. At the beginning of the twentieth century there was a movement to call Pueblo the "Santa Fe Revival" style. *The Craftsman* magazine for 1911 (19:4, 404–6) recounted a struggle over the style for new University of New Mexico buildings. Its first ones had been in the "style of Indian pueblos" inspired by the researches of university president W. G. Tight, but a new president, hired from California, wanted the style changed to what he termed the "more civilized" Mission style. Native New Mexicans will tell you that Texas several times tried to annex the much poorer territory of New Mexico, but was foiled by freedom-loving New Mexicans opposed to slavery in Texas. Driving west from Texas into New Mexico, a shift from Spanish to Pueblo styles is still perceptible on the landscape.

19. Native peoples were, of course, the "first Americans"; and Progressives of all sorts put heavy stress on the unity, as contrasted to the diversity, of mankind. *Pièce-de-résistance* of the Aztec Revival boomlet of the 1920s was the 1925 Aztec Hotel in Monrovia (which still stands) by British architect Robert B. Stacy-Judd. Cf. Benjamin Keen, *The Aztec Image in Western Thought* (New Brunswick: Rutgers University Press, 1971), and Marjorie I. Ingle, *The Maya Revival Style* (Layton, CA: Peregrine Smith, 1984), and "The Maya Revival Style in the USA," *Cuadernos de Arquitectura Mesoamericana* 9 (1987):69–79. See further note 32.

20. Duluth, Minnesota, is one example; Albany, New York, another. See further Harold D. Kalman, *The Château Style* (Victoria, B.C.: Maltwood Museum-Studies in Architectural History 1, 1968). Strictly speaking many of these (such as the Frontenac in Quebec) are not stations but they were railway hotels, built by and for the railroads.

21. The *AIA Journal,* in a 1918 obituary, called William Ralph Emerson "creator of the shingle country house of the New England coast" and declared that he had "taught his generation how to use local materials without apology, but rather with pride in their rough homespun character." Arthur Little was another important progenitor. Credit for naming and defining the style goes to Vincent Scully's *The Shingle Style* (New Haven, Conn.: Yale University Press, 1955; reissued in 1976 as *The Shingle Style and the Stick Style*). At that time Scully thought (perhaps no longer) of Shingle Style, with its emphasis on naturalness of materials, as a precursor of the Modernism then sweeping into favor, and consequently of McKim as a kind of failed Frank Lloyd Wright (for having abandoned Shingle in favor of more pretentious Academic revivals).

22. The case for such stylistic "trickle-down" is made at length in *The Comfortable House;* another school of thought—complementary as much as contradictory to it—maintains that below a certain level of awareness, stylistic forms in mass-produced arts develop out of a "commercial aesthetic" matrix, by a process analogous to that which produced folk vernaculars. See, for example, the writings of Jan Jennings, *American Vernacular Design, 1870–1940* (New York: Van Nostrand Reinhold, 1985; reissued Ames: Iowa State University Press, 1988), and *American Vernacular Interior Architecture,* with Herbert Gottfried (New York: Van Nostrand Reinhold, 1988).

23. Later generations would blame the Bauhaus Blitz for putting fine architectural craftsmen out of work. Tom Wolfe's *From Bauhaus to Our House* (New York: Farrar Straus Giroux, 1981) movingly recalls skilled craftsmen shaking their fists as they passed the Museum of Modern Art, which they blamed for their unemployment. But the tendency to dispense with elaborate ornamentation dates back to the onset of the Depression; much of the early 1930s ornament had been commissioned in the late 1920s, and much from the middle 1930s was unemployment relief. "Honest expressions of construction" from the 1930s often were accidental, like the exposed steel on the George Washington Bridge over the Hudson above Manhattan, whose covering masonry was deleted from its plans while construction was actually under way. Store and bank walls were opened up by using glass instead of plaster and lath, not influenced by any dogma or mystique of Modern curtain walls, but simply in hopes of improving sales through higher visibility. And so on.

24. Prominent Art Deco designers (Donald Deskey is a prime example) were always being pilloried by Modernists for their "popular success" and being compared to people like Friedrich Kiesler, whose "Endless House" made no concession or compromise to popular taste, and achieved no acceptance outside elitist circles, despite every sort of promotion in the Modernist media.

25. It was during the immediately post–Civil War years that the relative status of American universities solidified, via an academic "wheel of fortune" that lifted some to pinnacles of Ivy League exclusivity and dropped others into relative obscurity. During the 1890–1930 decades the manifestation of status by architectural style was most obvious. After 1950 the full impact of opening higher education to all translated into a factory image for all universities (make universities look like value-producing

units of society), which could be conflated with "up-to-date," "scientific ideology," and the like, so that state college and Ivy League buildings became much less stylistically distinguishable.

26. Preston Slosson, *The Great Crusade and After, 1914–1928* (New York: Macmillan, 1930), p. 337.

27. Elmer Louis Kayser, *Bricks Without Straw* (New York: Appleton Century Crofts, 1970), p. 265. The buildings, now dignified as Alexander Graham Bell and Gilbert Stuart halls, still stand on G Street.

28. The best exposition of the Progressives' creed and motivations that I have read is Robert M. Crunden, *Ministers of Reform* (New York: Basic Books, 1982). He makes a convincing case for Progressivism being a secularized Protestantism in every aspect, including music (Ives) and architecture (Wright).

29. William N. Parker, "Native Origins of Modern Industry," in *Essays on the Economy of the Old Northwest,* ed. D. C. Klingaman and R. K. Vedder (Athens: Ohio University Press, 1987), p. 210.

30. Norris Kelly Smith's *Frank Lloyd Wright: A Study in Architectural Content* (New York: Prentice-Hall, 1966; reprinted with emendations, Watkins Glen, N. Y.: American Life Foundation, 1979) remains the best study of the social function of Frank Lloyd Wright's architecture, and the most persistently misunderstood book about him.

31. From the closed classical form of the Charnley house of 1891 in Chicago, Wright progressed in steady stages toward the mature prairie house of centrifugal plan and freely interpenetrating exterior and interior space—the Winslow house in River Forest (1893); the Helen Husser house in Chicago (1899); the "model home in a prairie town" published in the *Ladies' Home Journal* for 1901; the Ward Willits house in Highland Park (1902); Dana in Springfield, Illinois (1902–4); Darwin D. Martin house in Buffalo (1903–4). The idea is prefigured in Catharine Beecher's plans *[4.22]*. Wright's classic form was achieved by 1907–9 in the Isabel Roberts house in River Forest, the Avery Coonley in Riverside, and the Frederick Robie in Chicago; and it was as its creator that Wright was celebrated by Ernest Wasmuth's 1910 publication in Berlin: *Frank Lloyd Wright: Ausgeführte Bauen und Entwürfe.* And thereafter, except for a few aberrant experiments in southern California, that was the Wrightean formula, given climactic high-style and populist expressions in Pennsylvania in the 1930s: Fallingwater and the Suntop houses in Ardmore, respectively.

32. The Larkin Building was not a factory but an office building, specifically designed with the company's special sort of mail-order business in mind. It is noteworthy for furnishing Wright an occasion to write about how style and type are related, specifically in the Larkin, but by implication in all buildings. This statement occurred, characteristically, in a bit of throw-away literature: *The Larkin Idea* 6 (1906):2–9, of which 250,000 copies were printed, according to a footnote in Jack Quinan's "Frank Lloyd Wright's Reply to Russell Sturgis," *Journal of the Society of Architectural Historians* 41/3 (1982):238.

33. What damaged the conservative cause of American architecture more than commonly admitted was Wright's efforts to regularize his domestic affairs. He could not just go from woman to woman like a sophisticated *Bauhäusler;* no more could the kind of women he preferred, devoted to Higher Things and Lofty Thoughts, glide easily in and out of relationships like, say, Alma Mahler Gropius Wertel. Thus he had to spend critical months and years of his career hiding out from divorce lawyers and court summonses in obscure spots, his efforts to promote an American style and outlook versus a European one correspondingly interrupted and permanently damaged. Perhaps, given the scientific temper of the era, the European Moderns would have superseded him no matter what he did; but his highly publicized matrimonial discords helped them along.

34. There were of course all shades of Arts and Crafts design between the extremes of Wright and Stickley. The Roycrofters of East Aurora in far western New York, led by Elbert Hubbard, were as famous at the time, but they always had something faintly precious about them (it comes through in the middle-brow pap of Hubbard's *Scrapbooks*). Stickley was the most honest, a man of principle who put his "good design for the masses" doctrine into practice by mass-producing furniture, at which he failed. But his magazine *The Craftsman,* founded in 1901, was one of the most influential publications of the period; famous architects like Goodhue and Cram were not too proud to write for it.

35. The phrase is from John C. Freeman, *Forgotten Rebel* (Watkins Glen, N.Y.: Century House Press, 1966).

36. David Klingaman, "The Nature of Midwest Manufacturing in 1890," in Klingaman and Vedder, *Essays,* p. 215.

37. I have written about the social function of comics and other Popular/Commercial arts in several works, among them: *The Unchanging Arts* (Philadelphia: Lippincott, 1971); *Prophetic Allegory: Popeye and the American Dream* (Watkins Glen, N.Y.: American Life Foundation, 1983); *Learning to See: Historical Perspectives on Modern Popular/Commercial Arts* (Bowling Green, Ohio: Popular Press, 1981).

38. That the laws of good taste were applied to the buildings of rich and poor alike, were employed alike by major architects and mean spec builders, made the domestic architecture of this age especially—but all its building to a considerable extent—an instrument for promoting the ideal of "freedom and justice for all." It was of this, surely, that Evelyn Watson was thinking when she declared (as quoted by Mabel Chilson, "Historical Aspects of the Bungalow," *Keith's Magazine* 24 [December 1910]:369) that bungalows were images of democracy on its way to fulfillment, of "a time when the houses of the rich will be recognized to have the same fundamental lines as the houses of the poor."

7.8. *Aerial view of the junction of Pennsylvania and Constitution avenues, Washington, D.C., showing East and West buildings of the National Gallery in relation to the Capitol and Mall. East* *Building (upper left) by I. M. Pei, completed 1976; West (lower right) by John Russell Pope, completed 1939. (Courtesy of National Gallery of Art)*

7
AMERICAN IMPERIAL MODERN,
c. 1950–c. 1980

Modern Styles
in Their Time and Place

In 1945 the United States became an empire. Nobody had quite planned an American empire, but there, like the comparably unpremeditated British and Roman empires, it suddenly was. For a century and more, to be sure, patriotic arts had been prophesying something like it—the grand sculptural programs on Philadelphia City Hall and countless American courthouses, Whitman's poetry, orations like William Henry Channing's "the worships and legislations, colonizations, and empires of all ages have been steps to . . . progressive conquest of good over evil" culminating in the American system . . . "this nation is manifestly summoned to prove the reality of human brotherhood."[1] But this was not exactly what had come to pass. America's leadership in world science could hardly have been predicted as late as, say, 1939. Nor America's becoming and remaining the world's foremost military power—as late as 1944 at Yalta, President Roosevelt was still talking about the United States pulling out of Europe after the war, quite in the Washington Farewell Address manner, and the Vietnam War of the 1960s showed how many Americans were still unreconciled to the idea. But the situation was not theirs to control.

Equally strange, unexpected, and unintended was "Modern" becoming America's chosen stylistic vehicle for its new imperial stance. However variously "Modern" might be interpreted,[2] it surely had not been invented to make visual metaphors of imperial power, let alone American power. Yet that was indubitably its role in the United States. From its first appearance on the American landscape in the 1940s through the 1970s, Modern coincided with and came in great part to express the nation's rise to imperial superpower.

Any reigning style is in its own time excessively praised and, in the next, excessively denigrated. Each era says to the preceding, "How *could* you?" So with Modern. Style-conscious people back in the 1940s looked at Academic styles with disdain and took up Modern as a sacred cause; in the late 1970s Modern in its turn began to be derided.

For some of its architectural legacies, deservedly so. Those great tracts of urban desolation created with the admirable intention of clearing out old, decaying sections of cities and replacing them along Modern, scientific plans, for instance. In theory well-intentioned, in practice disasters. Nothing much like Corbusier's Radiant Cities appeared; awful scarrings from "urban renewal" remained— witness, most dramatically, the Pruitt-Igoe and Darst-Webbe projects in St. Louis *[7.1, 7.2.]* They were often explained as unintended results of applying European solutions in peculiarly American situations; in fact comparable ruins are to be seen in Europe–for one dramatic example, Pruitt-Igoe's remote ancestor the Narkomfin project in Moscow by Moses Ginsburg, famed for communal kitchens and other glories of 1920s scientific housing, adulated by Moderns for decades, now just as horrible a slum, with just as sad a record of muggings, rapes, and general moral collapse.

Modernism left other, less dramatic sorts of urban blight. The style so lent itself to insensitive bureaucratic handling, that thousands of structures survive from those years when Modernism was mandatory for any kind of official building, intended to serve the poor and unfortunate and disadvantaged, actually affronts to human dignity, unnecessary humiliations for the very public they were supposed to serve *[7.3]*. As historical records of a moment in American civilization they have some value. But the nation could do with fewer.

More distinctive and historically interesting are those monuments—not nearly so common—from Modernism's early sweep of the country's institutions. A particularly good example can still be seen at the University of Cincinnati. Here the university's first postwar buildings, erected for the School of Architecture and Interior Design *[7.4]*, directly face the last building erected before the war, Wil-

son Hall for Drama, Oratory, and Music. They make an instructive contrast. Drama, Oratory, and Music had a building (like earlier ones on this campus) with textured brick walls, a formal entrance, and a program of sculptural ornament intended to relate the discipline taught in it to past ages—in this case, figures like Demosthenes and Shakespeare, Daniel Webster and Cervantes and Mozart, who would remind entering students that they were not just residents of a remote American town with a funny name, but part and kin of a high human en-

7.1 *(top). An ideal: "Ville Contemporaine pour 3 Millions d'Habitants" published by Le Corbusier (Charles-Edouard Jeanneret) in* Urbanism, *1922.*

7.2. *A reality: the enormous Pruitt-Igoe housing development in St. Louis, condemned in 1972 as unfit for human habitation, undergoing demolition by implosion in April 1976 (its raw*

ferroconcrete cages and slabs proved difficult to destroy otherwise). Built 1952–55 by Corbusier disciple Minoru Yamasaki and named after two sponsoring politicians, Pruitt-Igoe and its companion Darst-Webbe had long been abandoned by demoralized inhabitants, terrified by the crime encouraged by open-stilted ground floors, exposed stairways, and unsupervisable size.

terprise extending back across the centuries to Athens and Vienna, London and Rome. With the Architecture and Design building all that ended. Nothing "historicist" here. All is stark utility, or made to look so, via exposed steel-cage structure, undisguised concrete slabs, pole-like pillars, strips of plate glass windows with factory vents. The reference is entirely contemporary, to the supposed efficiencies of modern applied science. All over the country in the late 1940s and 1950s buildings like Architecture & Design were rising on American campuses; everywhere they affronted and put down older architecture; rarely has that moment been so nicely preserved as here.

Modernism left clusters of glass and steel towers at the heart of every big American city between 1950 and 1980. In its time the climactic example seemed to be New York's Seagram Building [7.5], pinnacle of a line of progress toward exquisite minimalist perfection in a branch of architectural art called Purism, hence an admirable visual metaphor of Modernism's dependence upon science, whose

7.3 (above). From State of Washington Social Security Offices like this one, on 26th Avenue South in Seattle, are dispensed not only social security but also probation and parole papers, plus food stamps. A typical mid-1960s orthodox Modern building: metal-cage construction revealed by hung panels and exposed stilts on ground floor, mandatory flat roof, and drab industrial color. (IMG:NAL)

7.4. The Frederick and Eleanora C. U. Alms Building (left) contiguous with the School of Architecture and Interior Design at the University of Cincinnati, built 1948–50 by James E. Allen, Architect-Engineer, and George Roth, Architectural Consultant. (See 7.19.) (IMG:NAL)

7.5. Masterpiece of Ludwig Mies van der Rohe was the headquarters of Seagram Whiskey Corporation in New York, commissioned by a family founded by Prohibition bootleggers in Saskatchewan, built 1954–58. Thanks to the influence of family member Phyllis Bronfman Lambert, an architect and later founder of the Canadian Centre for Architecture, Mies (with Philip Johnson collaborating) had almost full freedom to perfect visions from the 1920s of a brave new world sheathed in Crystal Towers. Here an unbroken shaft, sheathed in amber panes so as to shine dull bronze by day and gold by night, is sited (at great rental loss) far enough back from Park Avenue to allow a sheer rise without setbacks and to hide a shift of ground plan in its upper stories.

triumphs derive from hypotheses of abstract conditions purer and more perfect than anything in the material earthly world. But in the perspective of cultural history, by far the two most memorable are the United Nations Building in New York and the East Building of the National Gallery of Art in Washington.

The United Nations Building *[7.6]* is a great historical document, not least of early Imperial American politics. Locating the UN and its permanent delegations from all over the world in an already overcrowded New York was obviously a matter of political image more than convenience or practicality.[3] Crystalline it stands by the East River, occupying a site–as the *UN Visitors' Guide* is quick to point out—"formerly a rundown area of slaughterhouses and light industry." Still all around and contrasting to it is what Modernists were wont to call the disorder of capitalist enterprise. No hint or recollection of that here. No ornamental allusions to a pre-scientific or bourgeois past—most especially not to UN predecessors like the Hague's Peace Palace or the League of Nations Building at Geneva. Here all is sheer block, monumental abstraction, smooth concrete, and smoother glass. All cold, all rational, outward and visible sign of the difference between those earlier foredoomed efforts to keep peace among states conceived on romantic national bases, and the UN Charter based on political science. There are to be sure a few jarring notes. The Soviet Union's *Swords into Plowshares* and Yugoslavia's *The Hero* statuary is in an idealized classical naturalistic style that is hardly scientific. But those lapses are offset, surely, by the rationalism of the UN Meditation Room *[7.7]*, where a single smooth stone block and a single Swedish abstract painting provide ecumenical satisfaction for any spiritual yearnings not met by the Foucault pendulum swinging in the Public Lobby "to offer visual proof of the rotation of the earth."

Nothing quite like this stunning visual effect had ever been seen on earth before, when the UN Building first went up. Nothing like the extravagant hopes and dreams for everlasting felicity had ever been seen on earth before either, and the lightness, clarity, and sheen of the building's Modern style perfectly image them. This architecture takes its meaning and commands applause from a dedicated conviction that "all men"—or, more precisely, all members of the UN—must and "will live here without sin and in timeless harmony with one another." In this place life is perpetually sunny side up; here

7.6. *Original block of United Nations Headquarters Building seen from the East River. Begun in 1948 on designs of a team headed by Wallace K. Harrison; first occupied in 1950. A design by Le Corbusier on which he worked during a visit to the United States in 1946–47 was not accepted, but his ideas were always influential and he served on an advisory board during construction. (IMG:NAL)*

7.7. *Meditation Room in the United Nations Headquarters—"a room of quiet devotion to peace," runs the official description, "and those working for it." Meditations furthered through a fresco by Swedish artist Bo Beskow, and a six-ton polished block of Swedish iron ore. (Courtesy of Office of Public Information, United Nations)*

7.9. Library well in the East Building, showing chairs following a 1919 design by Mies, collaborating with Lily Reich (Courtesy of National Gallery of Art)

is memorialized the triumphant liberal mindset of the 1945–65 period. Forgotten are the unfortunate events of 1935–40, when appeasement and feckless optimism brought the whole world to the brink of immeasurable ruin; forgotten too those primeval emotions of patriotism and self-sacrifice that alone saved it. This architecture speaks of progress made inevitable by human reason, unaffected by human frailty or historic prejudices, of poverty and starvation and ignorance and tyranny all to be ended by scientific provision of money and food, teachers and sanctions. Onward and upward progresses humanity, into boundless light—like the UN's towers soaring into the pure azure of Manhattan's skies. Everywhere in those years liberal ideologues met in luxury hotel, spa, or castle retreat to solve a united world's few remaining problems—as far removed from them as generals from the trenches in World War I, and having about the same success. But the architectural monument they left is still in place, still a marvelous testament to the faith of an era.

Counterpart to the UN Building in many ways was the kind of art-historical surveys that appeared in New York at this same time. As the one proclaimed New York a new world economic capital, so the other made New York out to be a predestined culmination of all the world's artistic strivings over the past six millennia. From caveman to Northeast Corridor—all art of all the ages was here seen as a line of progress coming to miraculous climax in the art galleries of midtown Manhattan.[4]

Complement to the UN building is the East Building of the National Gallery of Art in Washington *[7.8, on p. 270; 7.9]*. It occupies one of the world's most impressive sites, right where Pennsylvania and Constitution Avenues join and proceed to the Capitol, right on the Inaugural and other parade routes. As the UN celebrated America's new primacy in geopolitics, the East Building—especially as seen in its context of museums to every sort of human endeavor lining the Mall—celebrated America's new assumption of primacy in arts and sciences.

Scant decades before any such idea would have seemed preposterous. Through most of history the world's great cultural centers had been Rome, Paris, London, Peking, Baghdad, Athens, Cairo. As late as 1930 Boston, New York, and Washington were remote provincial places, outposts in the marshland of Western civilization as America had been from the beginning. No more.[5] A new era began in 1945, and its premises and convictions stand large on the landscape still.

The East Building is not really a work of architecture in any traditional sense. It is a collection of exquisitely proportioned and crafted sculptural shapes, joined together by steel struts and a glass roof. Its forms are not to be judged by earlier standards; they have to be enjoyed at a new level of aesthetic appreciation. But its social function is nothing new. Many of the world's great architectural monuments have been built for a fundamentally similar purpose in and for society: consecration. Under the great dome of Holy Wisdom in Constantinople its builder, Justinian, stood alone, and had his powers justified and sanctified. Under the great dome of the Pantheon, uneasy and dispirited citizens of the Roman Empire could feel their faith restored. So here. Only the object of consecration is different. The National Gallery's great interior space functions not to impart grandeur and permanence to fallible beings or institutions, but to certify Art.

The West Building of the National Gallery—forty years older—was designed by John Russell Pope in Academic Classical Revival forms to house objects certified as treasures and collected as such. Not so the East Building. About the merits of its collections there was and could be no such agreement. Since Courbet's time, a hundred years before, artists had begun claiming an exclusive right to define what art might be; that definition was enshrined in the 1950s surveys: art is what artists create. What, then, defines artists? Presumably they must be people who create art. So obviously circuitous a definition needed reinforcement; and that is precisely what a structure like the East Building was built to provide. Art, it declares with all the awesome power at architecture's command, is What Is Exhibited in Art Galleries.

Nor can anyone who has attended one of the East Building's grand openings deny that. So grand an interior, so vast, so beautiful, so bathed in warm, indirect light; tiny bulbs twinkling from tall fig trees in alabasterine pots; high above, mighty mobile swaying; below, an ever-shifting panorama of color, bright dresses, shirts of spotless white and jackets of spotless black, the whole surging ceaselessly around ceremonial tables of food and drink—whoever has experienced such an event knows what it was like to communicate at high feast days in a grand medieval cathedral, to celebrate a royal Candella occasion in the temple complex at Khajuraho,[6] to reach the goal of a pilgrimage to Nara or Mecca. All Faith restored, all doubts put to rest.

Here in one grand visual metaphor all the beliefs of the Modern era are made manifest. Its purity of artistic intent: off-white throughout, smooth and lustrous. Its dedication to human creativity, with every human a potential artist, an original: see, on the floor of the library, how the originality of Mies van der Rohe's furniture in the 1936 Barcelona pavilion has been faithfully transmitted and replicated. Its conviction that a scientifically ordered society is one that demands equality: all seven floors of the administrative and library block are identical in plan, decor, and furniture, with never an unseemly display of superiority, save, perhaps, the thicker plush rugs and private office washroom facilities on the seventh floor, where the museum's director and president have their offices. All of which is made convincing by the superb selection and handling of materials and the exquisitely sensitive proportions, which makes the East Building, quite apart from anything else, a magnificent visual experience and the climactic monument of Modernism.

Modernism by the 1970s was already a couple of centuries old. The mental attitude that brought it into being—and all great architectural styles in the world have begun as mental attitudes—appeared early in the eighteenth century, part of that "water-

shed of the European mind" which brought the modern world into being. Roughly between 1685 and 1715, it came to be understood, by some osmotic process among the "educated public," that historical processes were motivated by confidence in Progress rather than faith in Providence and that confidence in Progress was justified by the seventeenth century's "Scientific Revolution." To be sure, the era's greatest scientists themselves tried often enough to explain that they were only accounting for appearances, that they were only proposing theories about theories. But eighteenth-century enthusiasts would have none of that.[7] Like their predecessors the Averroïsts of the Middle Ages, and like their successors the nineteenth- and twentieth-century materialists, they preferred to believe that scientific theories represented some real entity in a real world. They acclaimed Sir Isaac Newton for showing up medieval Aristotelian physics as mere hypotheses (and thereby presumably discrediting traditional religion). Never imagining that twentieth-century physics would do the same to Newtonian mechanics, they hailed Newton as a discoverer of Truth finally and forever, the truth that would make them free. So great a faith in science demanded a comparably great scientific kind of architecture.[8]

Some hints of it—all abstract geometric forms and anticipations of bold new technology—appeared in the later eighteenth century, in America as well as in Europe (see chapter 3). But there and everywhere early impulses toward scientific abstraction were soon subsumed in the Classical Revival. Throughout the nineteenth century architecture was predominantly shaped by Romantic Revivalism, the Picturesque, and Romantic Nationalism (see chapters 4–6). Mixed up within the latter, proto-Modern scientific attitudes began appearing in the early twentieth century, especially in France and Germany. It took the First World War to revitalize the movement toward basing architecture on science, or what were assumed to be scientific verities.

The Great War discredited romanticism of all kinds, at least among the "educated opinion makers" who took on vast new prominence thanks to an enormous expansion of mass media during the war. And what these people claimed to have learned from the catastrophe was not that wars are preventable by making sure nobody imagines they can win one, not that science had demonstrated a potential for exterminating a large part if not all of the human race, but that wars could be prevented, and human perfectibility assured, by restructuring politics, society, arts, and everything else along more scientific lines. In the 1920s and early 1930s an architecture responding to such arguments and convictions began to appear—in historical perspective, a second-wave Modernism. In those interwar years it had the character of an underground movement, full of messianic and chiliastic enthusiasms. Its appeal was greatest, predictably, in the ravaged, ruined, and reconstructed states of Soviet Russia and Weimar Germany. European Modernism—or the International Style, as its American admirers called it—was presented as "the style to end all styles," somehow seen as a counterpart to the immutable truths science was supposed to have discovered. In 1920s Modernism all that strain in Western life represented in earlier times by the Crusades and Calvin's Covenants and the Oath of the Tennis Court—so deeply irrational, so highly emotional—came bubbling up to the surface again in the service of a scientific materialism promising to transform human life. In that service architecture and furniture were of course enlisted, along with Modern painting, Modern poetry, Modern music.

Aesthetic attitudes shifted along with intellectual ones. The nineteenth century's utilitarian bridges and factories now were invested with messianic significance, proclaiming a new scientific civilization; those few structures that actually did have such significance, like London's Crystal Palace and the Eiffel Tower in Paris, centerpieces of great fairs dedicated to progress in general and specifically to scientific advance from tools to machines, became objects of adulation. Soon it came to be taken for granted that true architecture was no longer to be concerned with literary allusions and visual metaphors or conventions of taste, as it had been almost since architectural history began. Now architecture was to be determined by scientific technology. The prime if not sole concern of architecture was how buildings were constructed, how their parts worked together. Workings and motivations were assumed to be the same thing—and all anybody ever needed to know. And by the end of the 1920s anyone in America who hoped to be considered progressive and up-to-date was advised to conform to that consensus, especially after its articulation in Henry-Russell Hitchcock's *Modern Architecture* in 1929.[9]

By the early 1930s theory was being translated into practice. The new International Style had begun to make sporadic but well-publicized American appearances, most dramatically in the PSFS Building in Philadelphia *[7.10]*. By the 1940s European Modernism had taken over the country's intellectual establishment and become mandatory in every field of endeavor, not least architecture *[7.11]*. Its leaders occupied key positions throughout the American educational system. From the fabled but recently defunct Bauhaus alone Walter Gropius and Marcel Breuer went to Harvard's School of Architecture, Mies to the Armour Institute in Chicago (soon to become the Illinois Institute of Technology), László Moholy-Nagy to the Art Institute of Chicago, Joseph Albers to Yale. Their impact on the American architectural land-

7.10. *Philadelphia Savings Fund Society Building, built 1929–32 on plans by local architect George Howe, an early believer in Modernism, in collaboration with William Lescaze, an early practitioner of it, trained at the Zürich Technische Hochschule. A truly pioneer work, it kept only a few traces of Art Deco, let alone anything else Academic, and so anticipated by fifteen years the Modernist takeover of American architecture. (Courtesy of Philadelphia Savings Fund Society)*

7.11. The Alcoa Building, though completed in 1949–51 (on plans by UN architects Harrison and Abramovitz), still makes a strong contrast with surrounding Academic-styled structures in downtown Pittsburgh. Its thirty stories are sheathed in a curtain of prefabricated aluminum sheet panels, six by twelve feet, suspended from hooks on the beams. It is an old American technique: eaves had been hung (pent) from hooks in colonial Philadelphia, and a system of metal panels hung from the framework was patented in 1928 for standardized White Castle Hamburger stands. (Courtesy of Alcoa Corporation)

7.12. Almost immediately upon arrival at Harvard, Walter Gropius began a home on a two-acre plot on Baker Bridge Road in the posh Boston suburb of Lincoln. This, the earliest constructed American showplace of his ideas, was completed in 1937–38. As usual, Gropius attributed the design to a collaborative, in this case consisting of himself and old Bauhaus colleague Marcel Breuer. (IMG:NAL)

7.13. The housing area of the Illinois Institute of Technology, seen from the Commons Building. Small brick box at right is the IIT Chapel. All are part of a twenty-three-building master plan designed by Mies in 1939, carried out in the 1940s and 1950s. (Photograph c. 1955, courtesy of Illinois Institute of Technology, Hube Henry, Hedrich-Blessing)

scape was immediate and lasting *[7.5, 7.12, 7.13].* American intellectual perspectives were similarly affected, as prestigious Ivy League and humble state universities alike scrambled for European art historians to expound these new wonders of science-structured humanity.[10]

What happened is epitomized by three monuments on the American landscape from the same 1937–38 years, all thought by their builders to represent modernity in architecture.

Near the timberline on Mount Hood in Oregon a bevy of populist Arts and Crafts men were just completing Timberline Lodge, a project sponsored by the Depression-fighting Works Progress Administration to employ out-of-work artists and craftspeople *[6.89].* Their dedication to expressing American nationalism included old telephone poles carved into railings and furniture and animal-head finials, boulders picked up off the mountainside and artfully piled into massive fieldstone buttresses, and thick shingles split from local fir trees patterning high, swooping roofs. They thought of themselves as part of an ongoing effort to find truly American architectural expressions. The new Europeanized art world was no longer interested; it found fieldstone walls and fir logs provincial, swooping roofs bourgeois.

In the backwoods of south-central Pennsylvania Frank Lloyd Wright's Fallingwater was rising in those same years *[6.77].* By an incomparably more sophisticated use of Arts and Crafts principles it created a richly colored and textured visual metaphor of the American home and the American relationship to land and the land's resources. To the new Europeanized art world that meant Fallingwater was Romantic, hence nonscientific, hence non-Modern.

And then there was the scientifically white, concrete and steel mansion with prefabricated factory windows that Walter Gropius was building in the suburbs of Boston *[7.12].* It was an object of veneration in the new Europeanized art world as soon as—no, even before—it was built. And it still is. Today its prime venerator is the Society for the Preservation of New England Antiquities, whose prim white Colonial signboard, capped by Colonial broken cornice complete with pineapple, swings in front to tell you so. The Gropius house is nowadays, in fact, a demonstration of the sad truth that the only sure thing about the future is that it will inevitably turn into the past. But when built it was a fabulous futurist icon of scientific architecture—

which meant, the only really truly Modern there was. The immediate future—the next forty years or so of high-style architecture built by and for established institutions of the United States—belonged to the style it represented.

What motivated Americans to transfer their architectural future into European hands has been the subject of much recent debate. In *Images of American Living* I wrote that "it was simply a case of their being better attuned to the 'climate of the times,'" and so I think still. An architecture and furniture which claimed to be so resolutely based on the harsh realities of scientific materialism seemed somehow better adapted to the needs of Depression times than Romantic Nationalism, however modernized. Modernism kept the streak of escapism inherent in the scientific endeavor on which it was supposed to be based: Science does not concern itself with meanings and purposes of life, of society; all you need think about is how things work, and by extension how they look. Why things should work as they do is not at issue—and that was comforting in the world of the 1920s and 1930s, wracked by incomprehensible economic depressions, fears of war, mad dictators Left and Right. Just believe in science, follow her rules, and all will be well. But most of all European Modernism also corresponded to a strong streak of messianic zeal endemic in American culture, especially the latter-day form of old Puritan zeal in that Harvard/Cambridge region that played much the largest part in bringing European Modernism to the United States and establishing it there. By the end of the 1940s European Modernism had in fact consolidated its American position, and during the 1950s outposts of "traditional" or "conservative" opposition to it were fast crumbling. By 1960 European—that is, Bauhaus—Modernism held the field imperiously, with alternatives derided by all means. What wasn't Modern wasn't "serious."

During the 1950s Modernism also became steadily less "modern." It changed from a politically and socially revolutionary to an aesthetically chic movement, and then to a visual habit. Such an aging process is common to all sorts of movements in the realm of ideas; the history of the Classical Revival affords another American example. What was unusual about Modern, however, was an accompanying collapse of its basic rationale. It swept the country just as its most fundamental propositions were becoming unviable.

Just at the moment when Gropius and Breuer

were at the peak of their power at Harvard, the Harvard University Press published A. C. Crombie's seminal and pivotal reevaluation of the history of science, *Augustine to Galileo* (1953). "From the end of the 19th century," Crombie's conclusion ran,

> physicists found that they could meet certain difficulties arising in physics only by abandoning some of the basic principles they had derived from Newton. . . . It is seen that there can never be any finality or certainty about a scientific theory, because it can never be shown that the particular facts or limited generalizations of facts which a given theory is constructed to explain, could not equally well follow from some other theory. . . . It can be seen clearly now in the 20th century, though it did not altogether escape notice in earlier times, that a scientific theory of itself never provides grounds for denying a belief held in a context outside the range of the scientific method. . . . There is nothing in the scientific method that either denies or affirms the validity of other methods of making sense of experience, or the attainability of objective truth. Science can provide no capital for either theologians or atheists, moralists or libertines. It has nothing to say about aesthetics or ethics, about the existence of God or miracles.

"Nothing to say about aesthetics," when a whole generation was being sold Modern as more scientifically accredited, somehow? Apparently so. If anything at all applicable to architecture or furniture styles could be deduced from the scientific method, it was surely that just as there is no line-of-progress inexorably culminating in Man, so there could be no such thing as a line-of-progress inexorably culminating in European Modernism as practiced in the 1950s in the Northeast Corridor, no matter how many new surveys of art and architectural history were being written to map it. If any system of evaluation could be deduced from experimental science, surely it was that every individual phenomenon has to be valued and judged by fitness for its own purpose, not against some arbitrary standard outside itself. Fish are perfectly fitted to swim and are not superior or inferior to birds thereby, and vice-versa. Similarly you cannot properly speak of one architectural style being "better" than another without speaking in terms of social purposes; you cannot call the Seagram Building better than a Pizza Hut without defining your context—because what one does in and for society the other cannot. If a scientific attitude is applicable to arts at all, surely what it inculcates is pluralism, a readiness to examine each separate form on its own

merits. At the very least, the logic of science dictated the demise of orthodox Modernism. But that took decades to happen.

Promoters of Modernism from the eighteenth through the twentieth century were not and, by the nature of their own definition of creativity, could not be expected to be profound thinkers or great scientists. Because they were popularizers, adapters, purveyors of ideas rather than creators of them, Modernism remained triumphant in the media and the consensus stratum of academic life for a quarter-century after its fundamental ideological props had been kicked away and its sociological promises all faded and foiled.[11] Only by the 1980s did Modernism begin generally to be perceived as a style like its predecessors, with a beginning, middle, and end; only then could a range for Modernism be described as effectively c. 1910–40 for its formative, persuasive phase (disregarding eighteenth-century Early Modernism), c. 1950–80 for an established phase, c. 1980+ for Late Modern substyle.

But at no time did Modernism ever become an endemic, indigenous style the way its Classical Revival or Picturesque predecessors had. Below a certain level of American society Modernism never, for all intents and purposes, penetrated. Modernism was the style of the university-educated, of culture-aspiring corporations, of big government; it was never the style for residential homes or for small businesses or for religious denominations speaking for lower-middle and lower classes. It was never a style for the bulk of the population, that is to say. Those needs were met by surviving Academic styles, which turned into Popular/Commercial, as described in chapter 8.

Definition and Identifying Characteristics

In the quite recent past, "modern" and "contemporary" meant much the same thing, and both were definable in terms of contrast with "traditional," "old," "backward," and "Victorian." By "Modern" is meant here a style that was novel around 1900 and going out of fashion by 1980.

Of course early nineteenth- and twentieth-century creators and promoters of Modernism never defined it as a style. They claimed it was a kind of art altogether new in history, above and beyond style. Modern architecture was defined by two fundamental premises, which it shared with all other truly Modern arts of its age. First, that there was such a thing as a Spirit of an Age, a *Zeitgeist,* that had to find artistic expression and that "Modern" was the style in which the twentieth century found its expression.[12] Second, that any art derives importance not from any associated ideas, nor from any function performed in and for society, but simply from being art. Arts were not defined by *doing* anything; just for *being.* "Pure" was a favorite word. Modern Architecture came into existence immaculate, the pure product of its own inevitability. As Gropius put it in a 1922 essay, "Idee und Aufbau": "We want to create the clear organic bodies of buildings, naked and streaming forth from their inner laws, which affirm our world of machines, wires, and fast transport."

Modern was the only pure way to build. The leaders and founders of Modern architecture had found enlightenment and created accordingly, following a noble path of self-renunciation in the creative process. All that later promoters and defenders of established Modernism had to do was follow in this path,[13] with appropriate commentaries upon it (semiotic plays upon the necessity of Whiteness or Greyness, deep structure, epistemological deconstruction, and like imponderables), as indeed later followers of other historical religious revelations had done.

But a basic problem remained: all revelations need to be translated into some visible and tangible form. Even the Buddha had to found a *sasana.* So with Modern architecture. From the first, European or Scientific Modern (the terms being early and long interchangeable) was identifiable by certain distinctive forms.

The forms and effects that individually and in combination distinguish Modern styles from others can be succinctly described. First and most obvious, eschewing of all ornament, whether applied or inherent in materials. Where brick must be used for practical reasons, it should display as little textural effect as brickwork can possibly have—smooth, featureless buff, by preference; concrete likewise should be as plain and featureless as possible, preferably gray or white. Anything like representational relief carving and painting was taboo; no column capitals, no articulative wall paneling. Second, use of materials and structural techniques displaying twentieth-century technology, in contrast to techniques and materials characteristic of earlier times. The formula was "natural" as contrasted to "artificial," which in practice meant use of materials as

they came out of early-twentieth-century factories—steel in heavy flanged bars or hollow tubing, concrete poured into slabs defined by reinforcing metal rods or set in forms framed by rough-sawn form boards (preferably showing attachment holes and form-board textures), and strip windows of plate glass set into prefabricated metal frames. Third, display of structure when at all possible, so that viewers could see precisely how the building was made, as well as what it was made of, how its parts work together. Fourth, free-flowing spaces in, around, and through buildings.

Behind these characteristics lay presuppositions derived from a single, simple, basic myth: proletarian virtue versus bourgeois corruption, somehow demonstrable by science. In retrospect its premises were plain in the 1920s and by the 1930s operative even in America (compare 5.7 with 6.69). Of course the original promoters of Modernism denied any such thing. They assumed, implied, and maintained that Modern forms were simply the result of designing scientifically and resolutely rejecting any and all such extraneous motives as still survived in Art Deco and elitist Arts and Crafts (not to mention Academic) styles—association of literary ideas, for instance, emotional responses, historical allusions. But in fact Modern was defined by myth quite as much as any earlier style, and its forms were quite as demonstrably outward manifestations of inward beliefs. The difference, and the difficulty, is that Modern theory refused to recognize its myths, denied that there were any, claimed to be myth-free and sternly objective. Yet they are easily perceived in the self-contradictions and paradoxes inherent in every one of Modern's fundamental characteristics.

Most coolly scientific and least mythical, it might seem, was the ban on ornament that referred to past styles or just to the past in general. "The deprecation of historical fact is deeply, and probably functionally, ingrained in the ideology of the scientific profession," wrote T. S. Kuhn in *The Structure of Scientific Revolutions.* "Why dignify [by recall or perpetuation those errors that] science's best and most persistent efforts have made it possible to discard?"[14] Yet is this really a logical reason for architects to repudiate eclectic ornament? Because science finds history useless for purposes of pursuing investigations, is history thereby rendered useless for everybody? The question answers itself. Ornament was banned from Modern architecture not so much in consequence of logical scientific reasoning as of religious prejudice (in this case, against science's rival religions in earlier centuries, whose persuasive arts employed ornament so lavishly).

Was it scientific or logical to define the natural or normal forms and handlings of materials as what comes out of factories? The normal form of concrete or metal is in the ground; once dug out and treated, no form they are molded into can logically be more normal or natural than any other. All are artificial—the Modernists' beloved slabs and stanchions and bars no less and no more than the Victorians' beloved urns and Ionic capitals. It was not scientific logic that made factory-made materials and factory forms (open ceiling girders and braces, outward-folding plate glass windows, and the rest) seem right to Modernists. It was a combination of ideological associations—on the one hand with the work process and an idealized proletariat, on the other with the kind of abstract forms in which science most "normally" speaks: $E = mc^2$, and so forth.

Do the principles or practice of science dictate that architects must express structure openly and honestly? Of course not; but the myth constructed around science does, because such a characteristic sets Modern apart from the past. No architecture in the world's history ever expressed its structure directly and honestly by deliberate intent. Utilitarian buildings hide structure and materials without hesitation, for protective or other purposes (covered bridges, stuccoed fieldstone walls); Greek forms were mimetic imitations of revered shapes, painted and gilded; exposed Gothic structure was never an end in itself. Modern was then a new art for a new age based on science. That Modern was thereby better than all earlier architecture is of course totally unprovable, least of all by science, which has not and never can have anything to say about such values as "better" or "best." Here in fact is the architectural form of a classic problem crippling all versions of scientific materialism in this age: how to get from a totally objective position beyond good and evil, to advocacy of "better" things—"better" government, "better" society, "better" architecture?[15] You can do it only by faith and enthusiasm; reason and science can never enter in.

Has science somehow shown that free-flowing space is "good" and interior sectioning "bad"? It has not and cannot ever have anything to say about social arrangements being good or bad. What speaks here is a passion for social equality derived from a source in the old religion: as souls were to

be equal in Heaven, so humans should be equal here on earth. It is for this reason that the robber-baron capitalists who amassed more wealth than their fellows were wicked, and by extension that the kind of individuality they represented, and which was expressed in their mansions divided into self-contained private spaces, was wicked. Not illogical, not unscientific, but wicked; wicked in a moral sense.

All the characteristic forms of Modernism thus turn out to be derived from an overriding myth—a morality myth in fact, based on faith that whatever is scientific must be good, whatever is not must be bad. Whence comes it that High Modern style represents a direct reversal of High Picturesque, that its identifying forms are mirror opposites of High Picturesque ones. Their validity and their appeal derive from an underlying assumption of lean, clean proletarian virtue triumphantly superseding bloated, bejewelled capitalist vice.

Thus: instead of complex, intricately organized shapes, there are simple shapes assembled without fuss. Instead of walls colorfully pattened, walls smooth and plain. Instead of surfaces loaded with ornament, iconoclastic blankness.[16] Instead of robust complexes of swelling forms, taut assemblages of blocks, somehow thin even when gigantic in scale. Instead of compulsive verticality, obsessive horizontality (strip windows, cantilevered slabs, etc.). Instead of richness, barrenness. Instead of structure unnecessarily disguised behind layers of ornamental sheathing, structure revealed with unnecessary starkness. Instead of texture hidden by paint and polish, materials displayed in pristine factory form.

In sum, the definition and identifying characteristics of Modernism alike stem from one great ruling myth. That myth is the heart of the Modern movement. All the rest is variation and commentary on it.[17]

Social Function

Just as Modernism was not supposed to be a style, so it was not supposed to have a social function. It didn't *do* anything in and for society, it just *was*. But in fact Modernism had a number of distinctive social purposes, overlapping and intersecting, some recognized at the time and others only in retrospect:

1. Modern architecture functioned at one and the same time as the instrument and the expression

of what was called the scientific mode of thought (mechanistic abstract causality, scientific materialism), which had been coming to dominance in Western society since the eighteenth century. It was a means to inculcate that kind of thought or, more precisely, to focus and formulate the mindset already existing.[18]

2. Expectations that science would give its practitioners new kinds of power over nature and other men were common from its inception. That was a great part of its appeal to spiritual Franciscans, to Leonardo da Vinci and Francis Bacon and Descartes, to eighteenth-century philosophers of the Enlightenment and to nineteenth-century political revolutionaries. Modern architecture offered the same enticement; it was seen as a symbol of new powers for mankind in general, and an instrument to attain and further them.

3. This appeal was more than generalized; it was specifically applicable to those who held power in society. The principal social function of major architecture throughout Western history, perhaps through all history, had always been to create visual metaphors of established belief that served to confirm the power of those that held it; nor was Modern architecture different. Power is what Modern architecture was all about. To enhance and reaffirm power was its social function. Therein is one explanation of the otherwise incomprehensibly sudden acceptance, spread, and establishment of Modern architecture in the United States. But there is another, deeper, more powerful explanation, which is seldom if ever recognized.

4. Underlying all other social functions was the unconscious assumption that Modern architecture could be an instrument to achieve "Heaven on Earth." Such a goal, of course, has nothing to do with science. Science, in sober logic, never could promote or provide justifications for this or any other goal; it only explains how things happen if they happen, never why they should. All unwittingly, for the most part, early Modern enthusiasts (not uniquely in architecture of course, but even more in politics) were in fact driven by deep impulses derived from the older Judeo-Christian religion of the West, specifically its teachings of equality of all human creatures after death and a new world to come after an Apocalypse, when "old things will be done away." They transferred these longings to the present, made them a goal to be achieved in this world, and imagined science to be their instrument for that purpose. Whence the

prevalence of purity, clarity, purgation in early Modern talk and imagery—heavenly qualities, all.

By the mid-nineteenth century the scientific mode of thought had spread so far as to lie behind an intellectual restructuring of universities—Oxford in the mid-1850s, Harvard in the mid-1870s—that would bring them "in line with the modern age" and decisively mark them off from denominational colleges where older thought patterns persisted. Whereas once Oxford professors had to profess belief in the Thirty-Nine Anglican Articles to gain appointments, now they had to demonstrate (in subtler ways, but nevertheless just as certainly) that their thought was grounded in mechanistic abstract causality. Small wonder that in later decades professors played such a large, non-ivory-tower role in promoting Modern architecture. And by the mid-1920s the prestige of science was far advanced in middle-class culture as well; one of the commonest ways of beginning a magazine advertisement or promoting a charity was with something like "Science teaches us . . ."

But the visual culture was as yet largely unaffected. Thirty years later that situation had been transformed. Everything was Modern, from history books with Abstract Expressionist illustrations[19] to scientific city plans that typically made no provision for private life. (Louis Kahn's megastructure to run right through central New York City, Paolo Soleri's interminably expanding City on a Mesa, mammoth complexes that controlled climates by revolving with the sun or by domes arching over whole countrysides—none of them addressed the possibility of continuing needs for private housing or clubs or neighborhood bars; all seemed to assume a State [democratic, of course!] directing every aspect of life, allocating all premises for use in preapproved ways.[20]) How had all this come about?

Modern architects and their supporters often supposed it was their doing, and wrote prolifically to prove so. Not only was Modern architectural practice claimed to encompass sociology and psychiatry, but it also professed the old socialist goal of restructuring life (via the designed environment) so as to take from each according to ability and give to each according to need—with architects themselves arbitrarily deciding who had what needs, who had what abilities.[21] A mighty monument to these pretensions was the new headquarters of the American Institute of Architects in Washington, commissioned in the 1960s from The Architects Collaborative of Cambridge, in whose hulking Bauhaus shadow its predecessor, The Octagon, looked so humble, so small (cf. 3.49).

But architects were not the end beneficiaries of Modern architecture, nor prime users of its power symbols. As ever throughout history, architecture benefited those who commissioned it. Holders of power have always wanted and needed architecture that would confirm and reassure them of the rightness of their possession. So Pyramids set forth the *ma'at,* the divine order of things by which Pharaohs held their powers, the Forbidden City made metaphor of a universe confirming the Mings, Versailles reaffirmed Louis XIV . . . and Modern architecture ultimately had a comparable function of persuasion/conviction. Architecture, furthermore, has always made its greatest affirmations for institutions that are troubled, shaky, in need of support; and Modern demonstrates that principle too.

In *The Crisis of the Old Order, 1919–1933,* Arthur M. Schlesinger, Jr., described how in the early 1930s, as a result of the Great Depression, "a fog of despair hung over the land":

> One out of every four American workers lacked a job. Factories that had once darkened the skies with smoke stood ghostly and silent. . . . In February 1933 the Senate Finance Committee summoned a procession of business leaders to solicit their ideas on the crisis. Said John W. Davis, the leader of the American bar, "I have nothing to offer, either of fact or theory." William W. Atterbury of the Pennsylvania Railroad: "There is no panacea . . ." "Our entire banking system," said William Gibbs McAdoo in exasperation, "does credit to a collection of imbeciles." . . . [In his inaugural address F. D. Roosevelt said that] the rulers of the exchange of mankind's goods "have failed through their own stubbornness and their own incompetence, have admitted their failure, and have abdicated."[22]

Not quite. The verdict was premature. Only a few years later these same "rulers of the exchange of mankind's goods" were becoming the principal patrons of a European Modernist architecture that would create a much needed new image of them as scientifically efficient organizers, once more in control of their nation, and now of the world. Especially effective was the tall building in Modern style, so unequivocally displaying a totally ordered environment, so prophetically envisaging the enormous enhancement of powers over all areas of life that computerization would bring only a few decades later. But in every architectural situation Modernism offered visual metaphors of that total ethical relativity upon which dominance of a scientific/industrial Establishment in all developed countries

necessarily depends—proclamations that all values are relative except the worth of science, whose values were taken as axiomatic, especially the powers over Man and Nature which it professed to bestow upon those who patronized it. The promise of "Salvation through Design" therefore had irresistible, almost instinctive appeal, even if American corporate capitalism were not exactly what Modernism had been created to save.[23]

Once grasp how Modern in all its substyles functioned as a reinforcing power symbol in and for society and the "mystery" of its sudden acceptance dissolves. How could Modernism have become accepted doctrine in almost all American architecture schools and the normal style of building for government and official commissions, for big corporations, in the astonishingly short space of a few years after 1940? According to Tom Wolfe,

> The reception of Gropius and his confrères was like a certain stock scene from the jungle movies of that period. Bruce Cabot and Myrna Loy make a crash landing in the jungle . . . They are surrounded by savages with bones through their noses—who immediately bow down and prostrate themselves and commence a strange moaning chant: *The White Gods! Come from the skies at last!*[24]

But it was not voodoo. European Modernism succeeded in America, as all great historical styles have succeeded, because it fulfilled a perceived need in and for its society.

Application of Modern Styles to Architectural Types

Each style throughout American architectural history proved to be better applicable to some architectural types than to others. Modern was no exception. But here the disparity was more dramatic. Some historic types and subtypes could accomplish the function mid-twentieth-century American society required of them only in Modern; others could not accomplish it in Modern at all. For example, the kind of power symbols that commercial and government tall buildings became in Modern style would have been inconceivable in any other; conversely, Modern was an impossible style for small suburban homesteads. In the Academic era the stylings of these two types showed a common, unified American culture; now there were two cultures, a Modern and a Popular/Commercial, and it was as if they had been produced by two different kinds of society.

Once an understanding of Modernism's conceptual principles had begun to spread in American society, Modern was the inevitable and invariable style for all architectural types and subtypes made directly by and for big government and big business: tall commercial buildings, government offices, apartment and condominium complexes, and public amenities of all kinds. So it was for types and subtypes associated with them: monumental parks in city centers, Presidential libraries, media buildings, subway stations, and other subtypes of public works. Factories in Modern styles were more prominent on the landscape than before; conversely, mansions for the very rich were far less so—both reflecting an egalitarian ideological climate. As for sanctuary types, a few in High Modern substyles received inordinate publicity, but in fact the overwhelming majority of this type were in some Sub-

liminal Eclectic substyle of Modern, when not in some outright historicist late Academic or Popular/Commercial substyle. The same was true of most restaurants, bars, regional banks, small stores, private residential housing and the like.

To study application of Modern styles to architectural types is in fact to reveal something quite new happening in American civilization—a split between cultural classes. No longer is taste a matter of cultural lag, of the lower and middle classes following the upper at various removes. There is a fundamental divergence. Popular taste is not following Modern taste at all. And this in turn reveals deep differences about ultimate values.

It was in tall buildings—no longer to be called "skyscrapers"; the word's connotations were too Romantic—that Modern could create its most triumphant power symbols. Once in their ambience you were totally under their control. Your light, your air, your heat, all were directed from a single, central source. The Modern tall building was in fact a microcosm of the totalitarian, totally controlled society.[25] Some Modern substyles—Brutalist, High-Tech—created effects of absolute control painfully close to those environments commonly known as penitentiaries. But all other factors apart, Modern technology made it possible for tall buildings to overwhelm by sheer size. They were the stuff of legend, and legends about them abounded. How the PSFS cracked conservative Philadelphia as early as 1929 *[7.10].* How Lever House started the glass-box conquest of the continent. How the Hancock Building terrorized Copley Square when artificial wind-canyon effects tore sheets of plate glass out of its sides onto and through Trinity Church below and its great weight made the whole square sink, yet how the reputations of insurance company and architect alike not only survived but were enhanced when the Massachusetts chapter of AIA awarded the design a special, late prize for excellence in 1984 *[5.70].* How Mies, with an entire Chicago city block on which to site only two buildings—one of them a single-story post office on a raised basement—put a forty-three-story Federal Building directly in front of the historic Monadnock—"an insidious way of destroying a city's architectural heritage." How invaders from Outer Los Angeles dropped an enormous pyramidal rocket onto downtown San Francisco, which promptly cloned a skeletal twin on Mount Sutro *[7.14].* How J.R. struggled for power over the Ewing Oil Tower in Dallas—but that's fiction.[26]

7.14. *By 1973, when the TransAmerica Building was completed on Montgomery Street in downtown San Francisco by the firm of William Pereira and Associates, glass boxes had long lost novelty and become boring clichés; a substyle of Modern created by geometric patternings and shapes offered one alternative. Here it is seen shortly after completion, from Clay Street in Chinatown. (IMG:NAL)*

7.15. *A quadruple row of gigantic slabs marches down the plaza as on temple processional ways at Karnak, Luxor, and Giza. At one head stands the old New York State Capitol, at the other an art gallery. It is the Governor Nelson A. Rockefeller Empire State Plaza at Albany, authorized 1962, begun 1965, named and dedicated 1978. Harrison and Abramovitz were the architects, in close collaboration with Nelson Rockefeller, who selected the art in the gallery and grounds. (IMG:NAL)*

Throughout history the most dramatic examples of power symbols have been erected by institutions that are threatened or otherwise in need of reinforcement—Versailles, for example. So in our own time. New York's World Trade Towers on Lower Manhattan, which were not just out of scale to their neighborhood like the Hancock Tower in Boston, but out of scale to the whole city, were erected at just the moment when New York began to lose its undisputed commercial primacy. "Pharaonic" was the proper word for them, because it was Ancient Egypt that first built for size alone without regard to scale. And pharaonic is the word too for the enormous steel, glass, and concrete slabs that house New York State's ever-expanding bureaucracies (so paradoxically engendered by mechanized office routines) in Albany *[7.15]*, which also appeared at the precise moment when New York lost its electoral supremacy among the states, unchallenged since the 1840s.

The smaller the commercial building, the less imperious its Modernism; the contrast between big and small banks is very instructive *[7.16, 7.17]*.[27] For government buildings, strict Modernism was a natural: government is Power, after all, and in the imperial American age there seemed no such compunction to hide the fact, as earlier.

And in this age too there seemed less reluctance to hide the normal affinity between government and education. Universities had been prime agents for spreading Modernism when it was new; they continued to defend it long after any modernity, even up-to-dateness, had ceased. By 1970 or so every self-respecting institution of higher learning had constructed complexes almost as pharaonic as government or business *[7.18, 7.19]*. Explanations could be offered in terms of the enormous prestige and pampering of scientific endeavor on campuses: in any typical later-twentieth-century university, the departments of Biology, Physics, Chemistry, and Psychology (and their spinoffs like Biochemistry) account for something like 80 percent of the total budget; their buildings are the biggest, the most expensive, and the most prominent. But it was not science faculties who supported Modern architecture earliest or most ardently. Perhaps humanities faculties felt that somehow, by promoting Modernism, they could attract some of science's prestige and pampering to themselves. Perhaps a scientific-looking campus architecture made universities

7.16 (left). Twentieth-century Canadian cities tend to be dominated by bank buildings, in contrast to American ones, where corporations loom largest—witness this view of the Royal Bank building in Calgary, completed in the late 1960s. Its impact is deliberately diminished, however, first by using reflective mirror walls that dissolve into background and sky, then by an opaque slab that bisects the whole, thereby concealing its real shape—as if the bank were not wishing to intrude on the landscape, nor advertise its presence more than necessarily. (IMG:NAL)

7.17 (below). Typifying how a Subliminal Classical substyle of Modern was used for small banks is the Queen at Ward branch of Liberty Bank in Honolulu, built 1966–69 to designs of Rohrig, Onodera, and Kinder. (IMG:NAL)

7.18 (opposite, top). The idea of a collegiate skyscraper initiated at Pittsburgh's Cathedral of Learning in the 1920s continues in Geometric Modern forms for the Earth Sciences building at the Massachusetts Institute of Technology (also known as the Green Building or Building 54), built in 1962–64 to I. M. Pei's designs. Pilotis are already thickening in anticipation of 1970s taste for gigantesque piers and cavernous accesses, disguised somewhat by Calder's abstract stabile. (Courtesy of MIT News Office)

7.19 (opposite, bottom). By the mid-1970s science buildings typically dominated American campuses. Compare the Brodie Science complex on the Cincinnati campus completed in 1976 (A. M. Kinney and Associates; Charles Burchard, designer) with the earlier Arts and Architecture complex, the Wolfson unit of which can be seen at left [cf. 7.4]. (IMG:NAL)

seem less ivory-towerish, better able to fulfill the democratic promise so recklessly being made of college degrees for everyone.[28]

Public amenities in Modern styles include those great public galleries and museums that will surely be among the most enduring of all Modern accomplishments. Strictly speaking these are not creations by and for a political and social elite, of course; they are for the public. But then the public paid in the end for all the great commercial and government buildings, too; the difference is, perhaps, that the public was in theory under no compulsion, direct or indirect, to partake of the artwork which museums consecrate. And the poor could in no way be construed as beneficiaries of the activities carried on in them.

Nor can the views of the poor or minorities be said to have been taken into much account when hospitals and welfare offices and housing projects were designed in Modern style. A promising beginning was made in some New Deal housing projects, most notably Langston Terrace in the Anacostia district of Washington, designed by black architect Hilyard Robinson—an image of the best in the New Deal, it has justly been called *[7.20]*.[29] But after the 1940s, a wholly inappropriate display of power

symbolism took over, as may be seen in almost any project of the 1950s and 1960s *[7.21]*, the wretched Pruitt-Igoe being symptomatic of a general failure *[7.2]*. It took a long time for practical failures to overcome idealistic theory. Hospitals were another example of inappropriate power-tripping: sickness and accident do indeed deliver us suddenly and helplessly into the power of scientists, but who wants or needs to be reminded of that by architecture? One may indeed observe that the more pri-

vate a hospital, the less Modern its design will tend to be, outside and especially in.

For the great fair of the 1960s, Expo 67 in Montreal, on the other hand, Modernism was entirely appropriate. Like Chicago's in 1933 and Philadelphia's in 1876, Expo 67 celebrated a century of progress (Confederation occurred in 1867), but it was closest in spirit to the Great Exhibition of 1851 in London—an exaltation of science as the instrument for achieving human brotherhood, in this case

7.20. To help replace the notorious "Alleys" in which some of Washington's then-segregated black population lived, Franklin D. Roosevelt's Public Works Administration funded Langston Terrace (one of fifty-one housing projects), built in 1936–38 about twenty-five blocks south of the Capitol. It has only a few Art Deco touches (most notably a relief mural over the main entrance, **Progress of the Negro Race**); black architect Hilyard Robinson drew primarily on early Modern housing experiments in Europe for his forms. But his designs show little of orthodox Modernism's preoccupation with scientific formulae; they were based rather on study of the needs of people living in such projects and consultation with them. The result was a design with variety and free spaces that is still not only in use but maintained by its inhabitants with pride. Top: Interior of first court with surfaced playing fields (note picket fences with Popular/Commercial garden ornaments on the lawns at right). Bottom: Spacing of units, and free hillsides. (IMG:NAL)

7.21. *Superficially, Genessee Gateway Public Housing, built in Rochester in 1975, bears some resemblance to Langston Terrace. But it is a very different kind of place. Partly the cause is a confined site: on a narrow strip of land between Mount Hope Avenue and the river, it has few open spaces, and those are asphalted over. Partly it is the materials: not warm brick but cold, gray concrete dominates. Partly it is size: "the project" goes on and on endlessly, unit after unit. All combine to make it look like a prison, feel like a prison, be a prison—a dangerous, demoralizing, dehumanized environment. That is Modernism at its most insensitive. The designs were provided by a state architect working out of New York City. (IMG:NAL)*

not merely technology (though its miracles were chief credentials of belief) but also psychology and political science. "Man and His World" was the main theme; the main mood, that same sunny, optimistic confidence in coming social perfection that informed the UN Building, by now was becoming part of the Canadian psyche in general, an unbeatable electioneering stance for liberal premiers Pearson and Trudeau. For such a context no style could have been more appropriate than High-Tech in the early form of Buckminster Fuller's geodesic globe, which constituted the United States Pavilion; technological bravura was as perfectly suited to the needs of this commission as it had been sadly misplaced in homestead design *[7.36].*

In Modern thinking, traditional monument/memorial/park architecture was conceived as auxiliary to commercial, government, and amenity types. Every great steel-and-glass commercial and governmental tower had its little street-level plaza with appropriately self-referential, ethically neutral sculpture. Among artists there was more or less continuous agitation to have works of art automatically figured into every building contract. To this the public put up by far the most objection. As far as corporate and government power wielders and budget makers were concerned, abstract sculptures and paintings blended in well with Modern architecture, both aesthetically and in terms of social function; nothing in all the great collection of abstract sculptures chosen by Nelson Rockefeller for inclusion in the Empire State Plaza complex could possibly incite a seditious thought, for instance. A similar observation could be made, with some nota-

ble exceptions, about Modern designs for center-city parks; generally they complemented the architecture perfectly, rather than affording relief from or contrast to it *[7.22, 7.23].*

Most dramatic of the monument types in Modern styles were memorials to Imperial Presidencies of the 1960s and 1970s. In keeping with the Modernist ethos, they consisted not of colonnades and statues and domes, but of combinations of libraries, research centers, and exhibition halls, officially dedicated to Work: private scholarship and public education. Harry Truman's memorial was in Independence, Missouri, and Dwight Eisenhower's in Abilene, Kansas, but these are quite modest affairs compared to the sprawling and cadaverous Lyndon Baines Johnson Library and Museum on the University of Texas campus in Austin, designed by Skidmore, Owings and Merrill and opened during his lifetime. Most famous are the two honoring John F. Kennedy: the Library and Museum on Columbia Point in Boston, and the Center for the Performing Arts in Washington. These are in fact antithetical in effect: whereas Edward Durrell Stone made a heroic effort to break out of mandatory European Modernism with a center featuring huge, awkward proportions, spindly columns, and glittery materials *[7.61],* I. M. Pei's Columbia Point monument is one of the era's best examples of Mies's "Less is More" doctrine: outside, a great black shape intersecting with two or three white ones; inside, overwhelming vacuity *[7.24, 7.25].*

By the 1960s Modernism had become mandatory for most subtypes of public works, in particularly harsh forms—presumably to project an image of

7.22. The largest Modern complex in San Francisco is the Embarcadero, begun in 1971 and completed in 1975, a series of high-rises (some Miesian boxes, one John Portman's lavish Hyatt Regency hotel) with interconnecting spaces punctuated by such monumental abstract sculptures as Willi Gutmann's Two Columns with a Wedge *(1971) and Louise Nevelson's* Sky Trees *(1977). The Justin Herman Plaza, or Ferry Park, laid out in 1978 by Lawrence Halprin Associates, contains other sorts of Modernist sculptures, most notably Jean Dubuffet's playful* Chiffonière *and Armand Vaillancourt's sober constructivist* Fountain, *seen here. Nowhere in the country can orthodox Modernism's range be better experienced than in the Embarcadero. (IMG:NAL)*

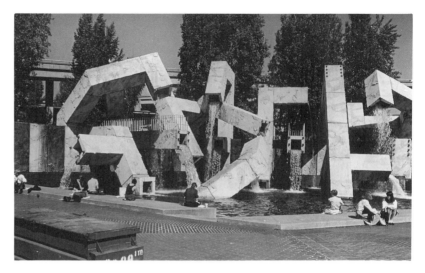

7.23. Central Tulsa has two civic parks that offer a wide range of Modern styles. First Place is an orthodox Modern part of Downtown Mall; the only relief from its barrenness are murals painted on blank walls that show trees. Dewey Bartlett Square from the late 1970s has, by contrast, lots of trees, and big ones, that overlook waterfalls on two levels. It is, if you like, a variant of the cave metaphor so common in the Sculptural substyle of Modernism, but also could be interpreted as Subliminal Picturesque. Architects: Hudgins, Thompson, Ball and Associates (HTB) of Tulsa. (IMG:NAL)

scientific efficiency in transportation. Opinion makers savagely derided any attempts to humanize travel; Eero Saarinen lost his good standing as a serious Modernist when his TWA terminal at Idlewilde airport (later renamed JFK), somehow suggested a bird in flight and thereby appeared attractive to the traveling public. Through the 1970s severely mechanistic Modernism dominated airport, railroad, and highway architecture alike *[7.26, 7.27]*. But thereafter, despite a stubborn rearguard defense—the 1986 Alewife station on Boston's MBTA subway line is an example—public pressure forced modifications: Washington's Metro stations were in a Subliminal Classical style, Portland's MAX ones outrightly Postmodern.

American factories from the 1940s on were more beautiful than ever before in history. They were also more conspicuous on the landscape than they had ever been—certainly than in the preceding era, when they were customarily hidden away as "utilitarian" (even though, in the person of Albert Kahn, America had probably the world's leading factory designer, who built over a thousand plants and was invited to train Soviet factory designers *[6.26]*). For Modernist theory gave factories new ideological prominence. Special values and meanings attached

7.24. *Chaste, outside and in, is the word for the John F. Kennedy Library and Museum, built 1978–79 on Columbia Point on the south side of Boston Harbor, to the designs of MIT-trained architect I. M. Pei. Exterior shapes and colors are of minimalist simplicity. (IMG:NAL)*

7.25. *In clip from a* **Sixty Minutes** *television show at the Kennedy Center, Pei explains the great hall, the building's principal feature: "There's nothing in the interior—that's so each individual visitor can fill it with his own thoughts." He felt it would have been presumptuous to attempt any exactitude in the face of so great a theme as the memory of John F. Kennedy. Less reticence was shown in a "history line" that runs around the top of the nine small, low, almost hidden ground-floor galleries; there, Ada Louise Huxtable noted, "epochal world events are paired with parallel Kennedy family events: Lincoln issued the Emancipation Proclamation and John Fitzgerald was born in Boston's North End; Queen Elizabeth II succeeded to the British throne and John F. Kennedy announced for the Senate. Personal history becomes cosmic history. There is no fudging of pantheistic intent." (Commentary of 28 October 1979, from* Architecture, Anyone? *[New York, 1986], p. 205) (IMG:NAL)*

to building types associated with the work process in European Modernist theory, even if not so regularly in practice.[30] More factories were built in Modern in America than in Europe; all over the place you could see factories rising in the 1950s with long, low lines, clean white blocks, and crisp strips of window in metal and glass that proclaimed "modernity" *[7.28].* But the resemblance to European factories was superficial, because American factories were seldom if ever conceived as, say, Gropius's Fagus Works of 1908 had been, in terms of one whole machine, with the workers being only one of the elements that signified "factory," along with movable partitions, open struts, louvered windows, or dun brick and tile. The underlying concept of American factories was far closer to those expressed in Frank Lloyd Wright's Larkin and Johnson's Wax offices *[6.24, 6.81, 6.86],* whose focus was on people more than process, on employees and management psychologically part of an integrated working community.

Ideology dictated that Modern subtypes of fort should generally be as invisible as possible. Modernists in the 1920s and 1930s preferred not to acknowledge their existences; jails and police stations and fortress bunkers were distasteful to them.

7.26. *By 1971, when Metropark station was built for New Jersey commuters at Iselin, the Academic splendors of Pennsylvania Station in New York and in Philadelphia lay far back in the past, the Postmodern splendors of Washington's refurbished Union Station lay far in the future. The Pennsylvania Railroad had metamorphosed into AMTRAK, and architect Murray Liebowitz was instructed to image only efficiency and economy in the new convenience, which is just what he did. (IMG:NAL)*

7.27. *The "Golden Link" stop on I-80 near the historic central Nebraska junction of Sidney has a plaque to commemorate Nebraska's here becoming, in 1974, the first state to complete its portion of the interstate system as authorized by Congress in 1955. The name is of course a romantic allusion to the golden spike driven at Promontory Point in Utah to celebrate the completion of an intercontinental railroad a century before. But there is no romance in the minimalist Miesian box that houses the comfort station here—nor comfort either, except in the word's euphemistic sense. (IMG:NAL)*

They wanted love and peace, not war. As who did not? But wars and crime persisted all the same, and some of history's most remarkable fort architecture was built in Modern styles. France's Maginot Line of forts against vengeful Germany was begun in 1930, for instance; Alastair Horne's 1969 *To Lose a Battle* described how

> these new concrete and steel monsters were veritable wonders of the modern world. . . . When troops passed through their cavernous gates . . . they entered into a Wellsian civilization in which they could live, sleep, eat, work, and exercise for many weeks without ever seeing the surface of the earth. . . . Electric trains whisked them from their underground barracks and canteens to their gun turrets; vast power stations, equally underground, provided them with heat and light; powerful compressor plants supplied them with air.[31]

America had nothing to match these wonders until the nation began building nuclear defenses in the 1950s, and it soon had all too many. Avant-garde Japanese planned something like them in their science-fiction underground cities. But the United States produced a truly extraordinary reminder of how well suited Modern was to create metaphors of the fact that soldiers and police forces are integral parts of the apparatus of state anywhere: the FBI building in Washington, completed in 1979 *[7.29]*. So far from invisible, this huge fortress stands right on Pennsylvania Avenue near the Mall. Behind its stark masses of concrete cast in Modern block-like shapes are readily perceptible the subliminal outlines of battlement and keep, moat, even drawbridge. The letter of the forms may be Modern; the spirit is primeval. Here is a contem-

7.28 *(above). The Kent Manufacturing Company, one of many new businesses moving into South Carolina after World War II, advertised its new Runnymede Plant at Pickens with this publicity photo, made c. 1952, showing the New South's modernity and efficiency. Indeed the form and materials of the watertower were dictated strictly by utilitarian efficiency, and Modernist aesthetic convention dictated beige brick blocks for almost any human activity.*

7.29. *The J. Edgar Hoover Building, headquarters of the Federal Bureau of Investigation, was completed 1978–79 to designs of John Burgee. It occupies an entire city block, fronting on Pennsylvania Avenue, the national processional way. (IMG:NAL)*

porary version of the Within/Without process of experience that has made fort subtypes generate feelings of security in and for societies throughout all history. To behold such defenses is also, however, to feel for the Duke of Wellington when he muttered about his troops, "I don't know if they terrify the enemy, but they surely terrify me!"

Comparably invisible were examples of mansions proper, the homes of the very rich. Here sociological motives were operative. Earlier generations customarily strived for great wealth precisely in order to flaunt it, by displays of clothes, jewelry, yachts, and most of all in splendid mansions—lavish in Picturesque style, restrainedly tasteful in Academic. Now things were different, especially after the Depression. Vulgar new rich, like Hollywood celebrities, might revel in having multitudes gape at their mansions on guided tours, and if they gaped at daring Modernism like Martha Raye's house or Philip Lovell's *[7.30]* so much the better. But established wealth came to feel, like the Policemen's chorus in *Pirates of Penzance*, "our wisest course is now to hide"—and so they did, screening their mansions behind leafy lanes and hedges, fieldstone walls, and intervening acres of fields and woods. As for style, Modernism was gauche. The wealthy might patronize Modern architects, invest in Modern tall buildings, and collect Modern art; for living, they preferred something comfortable: varieties of Academic substyles outside, inside a bit of Louis XVI or French provincial for formal rooms, otherwise nondescript rumpus-room furnishings. Anything else would be as *declassé* as neatly pressed three-piece IBM suits.[32]

7.30 (right). Dr. Philip Lovell advertised his modernity by commissioning a "Health House" from Richard J. Neutra, Viennese promoter of "human survival through design." It was completed in 1928, with every sophisticated technological feature: one two-story wall of glass, the rest of thin concrete shot against expanded metal; balconies suspended by slender steel cables from the roof frame; furnishings including chair seats suspended from metal tubing. But its ostentatiously dramatic site above Los Angeles was not sophisticated. Truly Modern mansions, like Corbusier's villas outside Paris, were hidden away on suburban estates, so as to protect owners' and architects' egalitarian illusions. (IMG:NAL)

7.31 (above, center). The famous Glass House on Philip Johnson's estate in New Canaan, Connecticut, was built in 1951. In this photograph it is occupied by a touring group of architectural historians. (IMG:NAL)

7.32. Just up the hill from the Glass House is an eighteenth-century farmhouse comfortably refurbished and enlarged by Philip Johnson, the kind of unostentatious and informal mansion deemed proper for a man of wealth in the later twentieth century. (IMG:NAL)

Great examples are on Philip Johnson's Connecticut estate outside New Canaan. There, by special invitation, you may see what might superficially seem an exception to the anonymity of Modern mansions: the famous Glass House *[7.31]* copied most immediately from a Miesian model in Illinois—his Edith Farnsworth house in Plano—but ultimately from the pavilion that Mies designed for the Barcelona fair in 1929. But this is less a mansion to be lived in than an exhibition pavilion itself; it is "not," as Leland Roth said of the Farnsworth house, "designed to be a home at all but the realization of an architectural ideal, existing somewhere between the world of things and the world of dreams."[33] The real mansion on Johnson's New Canaan estate is a rambling early Connecticut farmhouse just up the hill from the Glass House and in full view of it, but so nondescriptly refurbished and so inconspicuously enlarged—with that infallible sensitivity to correct attitude in any given situation which has marked Johnson's whole career—as to be rarely noticed *[7.32].*

For two of the great traditional architectural types, sanctuary and homestead, Modern hardly worked at all. Contrary to common assumption, an extraordinary number of sanctuaries were built in the decades 1950–70; in fact it was a great age of sanctuary building. But very few were in European Modern style. For style and type were in this case antithetical. To design a building in Modern style that purported to induce reverence and decorum before some kind of authority over and above the natural (that is, scientific) order would be a contradiction in terms. For outside of man there was, to the Modernist believer, no order. Mankind creates its own order, or more precisely, the creative element within mankind creates an order which is to be imposed upon the uncreative, while the scientist element within mankind defines a system whose bounds define how all energy in the universe is to be understood. The place where such creation and definition properly occurs is not a sanctuary in the traditional sense, but a research laboratory (like the Salk Institute outside San Diego *[7.52],* or an art gallery (like the East Building of the National Gallery of Art *[7.8, 7.9]*). Indeed, one of the most famous of sanctuaries in Modern style is, in all but name, an art gallery: the Rothko Chapel in Houston *[7.33].* The convergence of art and supernatural religion is effected in it by minimalizing both. Art—specifically fourteen nearly identical minimalist black-on-black paintings of nearly the same size—is a residuum left when all particularities of color and shape and line have been reduced to sheer (or "fulgitudinous") flatness. Religion is the spiritual residuum left when all differences between historic religious revelations have been canceled out. What results is an aura of awe toward mankind's creative potential and feelings of goodwill toward everybody and everything in general.

7.33. The Rothko Chapel in Houston is sited directly contiguous to the campus of Saint Thomas University, in part because the administration of this Catholic school felt it would be inconsistent with their professions to sponsor a nondenominational, multireligion center of the sort Mrs. de Menil proposed to donate, whereupon she paid for its erection in 1971 as "a sacred place open to all." Plans were drawn by Philip Johnson (still in his Miesian phase, as comparison with the IIT chapel shows [7.13]) in collaboration with Houston architects Howard Barnstone and Eugene Aubrey and painter Mark Rothko, who directed permanent installation of fourteen of his minimalist black-on-black paintings, the sole interior contents. Facing the chapel across a reflecting pool is a 1967 sculpture by New York artist Barnett Newman, acquired in 1968 as Broken Obelisk, *later dedicated as a monument to Martin Luther King, Jr. (IMG:NAL)*

7.34. *Lawrence Melillo designed the Interdenominational Center, built on the University of Louisville campus 1972–73. In principle it is another of Modernism's mirror reversals of Victorian values: where High Picturesque chapels towered skyward in masses of colorful, eclectic ornament, the Modern chapel's simple raw gray concrete forms keep low to the ground, indeed sink into it. (IMG:NAL)*

For expressing such a belief, the ethical neutrality of Modern forms was ideal; the Rothko Chapel thus creates an admirable visual metaphor of contentment with the world and everything in it. But possibilities for further architectural expression of such a religion were necessarily minimal also. The logical consequence of continued reduction to essences was simply disappearance—as for all intents and purposes occurs, for example, in the Interdenominational Center at the University of Louisville, which consists of minimal underground spaces with only a low, mound-like structure remaining above [7.34].

Call for minimal sanctuaries of this sort was necessarily minimal also, because the religion they served had very limited appeal. It could presumably speak to those who already have enough of this world's goods and power, so that sanctuaries in Modern style complemented power symbols like Modern tall corporate offices and government buildings. It could also speak to those content with little or none of this world's goods and power. For everybody between, for all those people who understood sanctuary in anything like a traditional sense of churches, synagogues, mosques, or temples where people actually believed they were worshiping some supernatural force with some claim on their lives, it offered little or nothing. Their needs were served in part by outright eclectic Popular/Commercial styles but most effectively by Modern Subliminal Eclectic substyles that retained an outward letter of Modernism—being devoid of applied ornament and using steel and glass and concrete as preferred materials—but departed totally from its spirit by evoking external emotions and ideas as earlier styles had done. Already in the 1950s Marcel Breuer had defied his own Bauhaus rules in just this way for a Benedictine abbey church in Minnesota,[34] and the era is filled with others—some, when architectural history comes to be rewritten, numbering among its most outstanding creations [7.35].

A successful homestead was never designed in Modern style. This was not for lack of trying. Gropius had a "dream of a factory-built house" as early as 1914, whose hopeless failure was much lamented, and in 1919 Bruno Taut proclaimed, "The pride of the social Republic shall have its monument in dwellings for the people (*Volkshäuser*)."[35] Thereafter "model homesteads" dreamed up by various inventors seemed to come along on a regular beat every decade or so: in 1929 Buckminster Fuller's Dymaxion House [7.36], in 1949 Wallace Neff's concrete bubble house, in 1959 Friedrich Kiesler's Endless House, in 1968 Ralph Drury's house of burlap balloons sprayed with polyethylene. Each in its day proclaimed as destined immediately, if not sooner, to replace the despised spec-built suburbs, to transform the American landscape. Each in its day bringing great publicity to its proponent. All soon and totally forgotten.

Many were the famous names in the Modern movement who built famed houses for themselves, their friends, or relatives—Gropius and Breuer *[7.12]*, Johnson *[7.31]*, Louis Kahn. But these were more showpieces of Modernism than homesteads proper—mansions if anything, in the sense that their primary social function was to display class status, membership in a cultural elite. Much the same could be said of Bruce Goff's personally styled houses.[36] As for Louis Sauer and Associates' 1969 complex of fortress-like town houses on Locust Walk in downtown Philadelphia, they were consciousness-raising demonstrations of the viability of inner-city living for the class that later would be called Yuppies, not homesteads where small families might be raised. For the population at large none of these ventures held any interest. Their failure was indeed inherent in Modern theory. If you think in terms of vast abstract forces rather than particular entities, calculate statistics about marriage and population rather than design spaces where husbands and wives and children could most comfortably live together, then what you are designing is housing, not homesteads. Modernists specialized in design for controlled units; the family was not one of those. Furthermore, the population at large was not interested in inhabiting technological experiments; they held atavistic notions of what homesteads ought to be and look like, and only homestead designs that took them into consideration were widely acceptable. That meant, in practice, homesteads in Popular/Commercial styles.

Substyles of Modernism Proper

Like all other styles, Modern had a number of substyles and recognizable groupings within them. The basic division is between Modern proper, and Subliminal Eclectic Modern substyles.

Within Modern substyles proper there was a division between earlier and later, which involved a difference of social function—the earlier being more persuasive, the later more established. And within the established substyles there were variants identifiable by specific forms, or characteristic combinations of forms and textures. These established substyles, and the distinctions between them, have been the subject of extensive critical and semiotic writings. By contrast, Subliminal Eclectic substyles within Modern have been only lightly touched upon, perhaps because their obvious compromises with realities of social usage and public taste took them so far from the ideals early Modernists professed, and critics so long upheld.

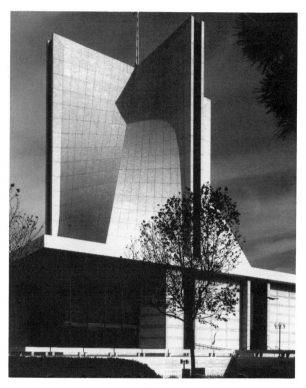

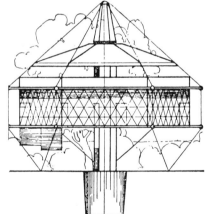

7.35 (top). Saint Mary's Cathedral, occupying a dramatic hilltop site in San Francisco, was completed in 1971 on the designs of Pietro Belluschi; consulting architects were Pier Luigi Nervi of Rome and the local firm of McSweeney, Ryan, and Lee. Complexly intersecting paraboloids create the effect of a steep cross vault without imitating Gothic forms as such; on the interior lighting, mosaics, marble, and gold leaf recall effects of San Vitale in Ravenna, again without copying. In line-of-progress architectural history this structure descends from Breuer's Saint John's Abbey Church and anticipates I. M. Pei's East Building of the National Gallery. (IMG:NAL)

7.36. Buckminster Fuller, dedicated Modernist Utopian, designed this "Dymaxion House" in 1929; by living in such, man may emerge "from the darkness of complete and awful weight to eternal light which has no end."

Proto-Modern Utilitarian

The matrix of this substyle was nineteenth-century utilitarian building in steel, glass, concrete, and brick. It came to be considered architecture partly by misunderstood applications of Modern principles, partly in reaction to the Depression, partly by the unconscious ideological appeal of those spartan structures where scientists were conventionally imagined to toil, wholly concentrated on their work, oblivious to comfortless surroundings: sixteenth-century alchemists amid their retorts, nineteenth-century Faradays on stools in their bare-floored, bar-windowed, barren-walled labs, Star Warriors on old orange crates in their huts at Livermore.

By the mid-1880s steel, glass, and concrete had long been used regularly for utilitarian purposes in America, in architecture and furniture both.[37] The European Modern contribution was to glorify their use as an end in itself. Thus metal fire escapes or the inner workings of elevators might appear indoors as part of an aesthetic ensemble. Folding and portable stools patented in the 1860s and 1870s, made of wood or tubular metal for temporary uses on beaches, military campaigns, and the like, reap-peared in the 1940s transformed into Hardoy, sling, Barcelona, or Eames chairs, the most veritable images of fashionable Modernity[1.4, 7.9, 7.37–7.39].

Counterpart to these developments was an early-appearing and long-continuing sort of Modernism best classifiable as Proto-Modern Utilitarian: essentially, boxes with holes punched in at regular intervals. The utilitarian starkness of its matrix was self-consciously emphasized; it rarely had any systematic combinations, or any use at all, of identifying clichés of early Modernism like strip windows, stilts, exposed struts, or beige-brick curtain walls. All sorts of apartments, hospitals, and diverse small public buildings appeared in this stripped-down style from the 1930s on [7.40].

International Style

This is the substyle that still means "Modern" to the public at large. Its most obvious features were so simple, so easily replicated in semi-prefab structures, as to provide a reservoir of easily pilferable clichés: walls and overhanging roofs composed as light slabs or panels; prominent cantilevered construction; strip windows with steel or aluminum frames, louvered or horizontally sliding; flat or

7.37 (left). Today chrome-plated tubular steel chairs are routinely associated with the Bauhaus—Mies or Breuer. This one, however, was designed by Nathan George Horwitt of Geneva, Illinois, in 1930, and distributed by the Howell Manufacturing Company. (The Brooklyn Museum, gift of Nathan George Horwitt. Photograph by Scott Hyde)

7.38 (center). In 1946 Charles and Ray Eames designed this lounge chair, whose molded ash plywood is still quite reminiscent of a generally Arts and Crafts, if not specifically Scandinavian,

tradition. It was made by Herman Miller, Inc., of Zeeland, Michigan, in association with Evans Products Company, Los Angeles. (The Brooklyn Museum, gift of Barry Friedman)

7.39 (right). By 1950, when Charles and Ray Eames designed this armchair of fiberglass stands and plastic, they were moving more decisively into the European Modern orbit of ostentatious emphasis on industrial materials; it took one further step—black metal legs fitting over the plastic seat—to produce infinitely stackable chairs. (The Brooklyn Museum, gift of Mr. and Mrs. Anthony W. Roberts)

7.40 (above). The Mary Fletcher Hospital in Burlington, Vermont, built in 1940 by architect William Freeman, displays only a few faint hints of stripped-down abstracted classical forms, only a few faint hints of Modernism (something like strip windows on the ends). Otherwise it is a brick box with holes punched into it—a kind of Proto-Modern utilitarian typical of its stylistically transitional time. (IMG:NAL)

7.41. The Van Ness Apartment-Condominium complex in northwest Washington, D.C., with over a thousand units, was built in 1964–68; this is Van Ness North. Architect Joseph Abel specialized in apartment building, and over his long career went from Academic through Art Deco to the standardized International Style of this, his last work. Even in this place and time, the monotonous repetition of stock forms and the choice of drab materials recall early European Modernist ideals of proletarian housing. (IMG:NAL)

near-flat roofs; white walls, usually achieved by stucco or painted brick; "cubist" effects achieved by such devices as keeping windows in the same plane as walls instead of recessing them; and the famous "stilts" whereby a building's structural cage was expressed on its ground level. Effectively promoted by an exhibition at the infant Museum of Modern Art in 1929, with accompanying book by Henry-Russell Hitchcock and Philip Johnson, this "International Style" (a name they later wished to repudiate) was the dominant form of Modernism for the succeeding two decades *[7.3, 7.4, 7.6, 7.12, 7.28, 7.30]*.

The 1929 presentation was superbly geared to the prejudices and enthusiasms of its audience, those wealthy patrons who founded and funded the Museum of Modern Art. Hitchcock and Johnson made it seem an entirely aesthetic movement, like a new fashion in Modern painting, offering the naughty excitement of participation in something

parents would never approve of. The word "socialism," along with all the other ideological baggage endemic in European Modernist writings, vanished from theirs. Yet the appeal of Modernism to mid-twentieth-century intellectuals is unintelligible without that background. What became International Style clichés originated as means to express a "new mindset."[38]

Established Modern

No matter what its ideological undertones, the International Style as established taste among intellectuals and opinion makers was preeminently understood in aesthetic terms. Anyone seeking acceptance in a cultural establishment had to "like Modern" everything—art, literature, dance, architecture, whatever. And so the style spread, rapidly, irresistibly overriding all protests, especially those pointing out its undeniable ugliness. Objections were to be overcome through education. But the

7.42 *(top). Paul Rudolph, professor and then dean of architecture at Yale, was an important figure on the Modern architecture scene in the 1950s and 1960s. This Jewett Art Center at Wellesley College outside Boston was his first big project actually built (1958). It is textbook International Style (including triumphs of theory over practicality resulting in college carpenters having to cut quasi-transoms to get light into studios and halls), spiced up by upper-story screens, boldly (following dictates of exposed construction) bolted into outside walls. (IMG:NAL)*

7.43. *This small office building on the main square of Brinkley, an old Arkansas railroad town, was originally (c. 1955) a beige-brick International Style box with concrete-slab roof. Somehow the design seems not to have appealed, for the facade was soon Permastoned and then hidden altogether by screens made of openwork tiles. (IMG:NAL)*

more widespread the style became, the less well educated were its practitioners, so that subtleties were steadily eliminated. Very soon Modern came to consist of a handful of clichés; in the early 1950s buildings in that style of whatever sort, wherever in the country, looked monotonously similar *[7.41].* The situation invited invention of substyles based on clichés, and they were not long appearing.

"Screen"

Earliest conscious effort to break away from the monotonies of utilitarian effects, the "Screen" substyle was identifiable by open-work screens applied to facades and walls of buildings, especially over windows, which disguised structure and gave effects of richness. Screens were most often of metal. Famous early examples are the Reynolds Aluminum building in Detroit by Minoru Yamasaki (1957) and the Jewett Art Center at Wellesley College by Paul Rudolph (1958) *[7.42].* But screens could also be of concrete (sections of tile pipe laid together sideways, for example), or brick laid with open interstices; in such forms it was often seen in humbler situations relieving Modernism too stark for ordinary tastes: fences and walls, courtyards and atria in everything from highway police stations and small office buildings to parking lots *[7.43].*

The "Screen" substyle so modified the more utilitarian aspects of Established Modern as to make it appropriate where images were wanted of something "up-to-date" and "lavish" at the same time. So it was used in works by Edward Durrell Stone and Morris Lapidus in the late 1950s, and most effectively on the interiors of John Portman's luxury hotels in the 1970s *[7.44, 7.45].*

But enhancement of visual effect by rich texture was never an acceptable justification for high-style use of screens, of course. They were supposed to be utilitarian devices for light control or for effecting economies of ventilation. As soon as it became obvious that screens were being used primarily for visual enrichment, the "Screen" substyle became unacceptable to ruling taste. Thereupon a "Mirror" substyle appeared.

"Mirror"

Inherent in Modernism's classic glass box from its beginnings was the fad for making whole walls of reflective materials, which developed in the early 1960s. Like "Screen," it proved an immensely popular relief from the rigors of Modernist orthodoxy and was widely adopted for all sorts of situations

7.44. *Rejuvenation of Detroit's derelict downtown was symbolized by the shining silver tubular tower of the Renaissance Center Westin hotel, completed in 1977 to designs of John Portman, seen here from the Canadian side of the river, surrounded by its four office towers. The scale contrasts dramatically with the older city.*

Other tubes by the same architect, likewise symbolizing rejuvenation and also created by leveling many old downtown blocks, include Atlanta's Peachtree Plaza (1976) and the Bonaventure in Los Angeles (1977). (IMG:NAL)

7.45. *The interior of Portman's huge hotels evoke effects quite different from their exteriors—appropriately, because their social functions are different. Whereas the exteriors proclaimed solutions to urban problems through technological powers, interiors (here the seven-story lobby of the Bonaventure in Los Angeles) were designed to evoke qualities appropriate to the hotel subtype throughout its history—luxury and class status. Originally such effects were attained by use of Modern materials to produce subliminal Picturesque effects; latterly, as in the 1985 remodeling of Detroit's Renaissance Center, by Postmodern usages. (IMG:NAL)*

[7.16]. Like "Screen," "Mirror" too was quickly perceived to be ornamental, and so denounced by the establishment. And its afterlife was even more fruitful; in retrospect the "Mirror" substyle might be seen as an early intimation of Postmodernism.

As originally conceived, mirror walls were supposed to reflect surrounding buildings in older, "traditional," styles. In that way, something of the novel impact that Modernism enjoyed when it first appeared on American cityscapes might be recaptured. But as things turned out, what usually got reflected was another Modern building. One reaction was the illusionistic paintings that began to appear on blank Modernist walls; Richard Haas's illusionistic *trompe l'oeils* are perhaps best known. But sooner or later the thought was bound to occur: if you want "traditionalist" buildings on the landscape, why rely on survivors? Build some of your own!

"Brutalist"

"The New Brutalism" was the first of a series of substyles that periodically attempted to recall Established Modernism to its utilitarian and/or ideo-

7.46. One of the leading exponents of Brutalist (and later of Hi-Tech) substyles of Modern in North America was the Australian architect John Andrews. Here is his Brutalist mode: Scarboro College, a satellite of the University of Toronto, planned 1963 (with Michael Hugo-Brunt of Cornell), completed 1965. This is the north side, in Führerbunkerstil, *complete with protruding snorkel. On the south is a sheer expanse of slanted glass wall like Andrews's later Gund Hall at Harvard. Admirers of*

Brutalism, like Paul Russell, to whose essay on Scarboro a special issue of Artscanada *(September 1967) was devoted, called it "a hill shelter, warm and inviting. . . . Scarboro is more than architecture; it is city planning. . . . The pathways, iron chimneys and the great indoor ducts—the vital functional elements of the structure are also its key aesthetic factors." Users held other opinions. (IMG:NAL)*

logical roots. Its most famous monument was Peter and Alison Smithson's Hunstanton School (or, more properly now, the Smithdon High School) in Norfolk, finished in 1954. Of their efforts British critic J. Mordaunt Crook wrote "the New Brutalists talked humanity and built barbarism."[39] But imitations abounded in North America. The substyle corresponded to a fashionable stance among sixties youths of "brutal honesty," "no faking," "nothing plastic." And imitating this substyle was so easy. One had only to realize that it was the most ruthless and uncompromising of all Modern reverse-images of Victorian Picturesque to produce something like it. It had nothing easy or pleasant or attractive at all; everything was hard, unyielding, uncompromisingly nonsensuous, the British version of the Bauhaus's "Back to Zero."

It was a substyle of harsh imperatives: steel and concrete and glass are to be handled this way only, and never that. Steel must be inert, concrete pudgy gray, glass hard; all nakedly exposed on floors, walls, roofs. It was the ugliest of all Modern styles; therefore it was a style to be employed only where users had no say—in schools, where teachers and pupils could be counted upon to accept with meek-

ness whatever designers said was good for them *[7.46]*; in housing projects, whose inmates' opinions were never consulted about anything *[7.21]*; in public hospitals; in jails. A substyle too that could only get uglier with time.[40] But having this great merit: it expressed without equivocation what a world would look like whose every aspect was dictated by uncritical believers in mechanistic causality. By such believers, the "Brutalist substyle" in variant forms has continued beloved *[7.54, 7.55]*.

Arrested Rust Sheathing

A logical cliché developing out of Brutalism was artificial imitation of those harsh effects of rusting which exposure of metal structure naturally produces. For such effects considerable technological expertise was required, surfaces actually being so artfully treated as to rust a certain fraction of an inch inward, no more and no less. The rusting is therefore very even, in contrast to utilitarian buildings proper, where corrugated tin, for example, rusts in streaks that run down the walls. This substyle had some vogue in the late 1960s and early 1970s, but it never became widely popular, for reasons partly of expense, and in part some dislike (atavistic, perhaps) for intimations of ruin and neglect *[7.47]*.

Better than any other, however, this substyle manifests how thoroughly ambiguous and convoluted was the relationship between art and science in Modernist ideology. In it, a true wonder of technology is called upon to simulate primeval crudity, which is supposed in turn to derive from scientific materialism. The contradiction goes back, as so many Modern motivations do, to the eighteenth-century notion, derived from popularized science, that nature and natural processes all conform to reason, hence all must be good, hence the closer anything may be to raw nature the better. Arrested Rust Sheathing is by no means the only manifestation of this conviction, of course. For example, it informs Armand Vaillaincourt's constructivist essay *Fountain* in the Embarcadero Center plaza *[7.22]*, where a most complicated hydrostatic system is employed to produce what looks (to the uninitiated) like rust, algae, and assorted crud streaking the broken slabs of a ruined millwheel—shades of Marie Antoinette and her rustic "Hameau" on the grounds of Versailles!

"Geometric"

The 1960s repeated the 1950s pattern of stylistic development in Modern proper: formalistic features originating by ideological motivation somehow, despite all resolutions, became visual signs and thence identifiable substyles. The earliest manifestations of Geometric substyle was, inevitably, in two-dimensional patternings. Two classic early instances stood beside each other in Chicago: Mies's Lake Shore Drive Apartments of 1948–51 and the John Hancock Center by Skidmore, Owings and Merrill of 1965–70 *[7.48]*. In the first, a surface pattern was created by slender I beams attached to the facade with only a decorative function; it in fact disguised the building's structural realities (a contradiction of Modern principles ingeniously defended by Mies's admirers).[41] In the other, a dominant visual pattern is created in the process of affixing external X-braces to the outside tower walls (deliberately exposed in accordance with Modernist dogma) for practical support against winds. Soon such practices became design preoccupations for their own sake *[7.14]*.

Geometric became an unmistakably recognizable substyle when curved forms appeared along with rectangulars—beginning perhaps in the Carpenter Center for the Visual Arts, designed for Harvard by

7.47 *(top). For his most famous glass box, the Seagram Building in New York [7.5], Mies is recorded as promising "I will give you the soul of technology." He could have made the claim even better for a late (1974) work like this American Life and Accident Company Building on the Louisville waterfront, for its amber color contained no possible allusion to whiskey, but derived entirely from the high technology of anodizing metal so as to create an arrested rust effect. (IMG:NAL)*

7.48. *Lake Shore Drive Apartments by Mies (far right, 1948–51) and John Hancock Center by Skidmore, Owings and Merrill (1965–70, center) are two early instances of two-dimensional patterning giving Modern buildings ornament in spite of dogma. Holabird and Root's 1928–29 Palmolive Building's set-back tower provides a visual pattern predetermined by human needs and will.*

7.49. *Carpenter Center for the Visual Arts was commissioned from Le Corbusier in 1959, finished in 1962, inaugurated in 1963. It sits next to the Academic Georgian Fogg Art Museum; farther down Quincy Street is James Stirling's Postmodern Sackler Museum. (IMG:NAL)*

Le Corbusier, built in 1961–62 *[7.49]*. It has been implied that Corbu merely dished up a bouillabaisse of stock forms from his obsolescent repertoire, good enough to impress "the timid ones" who gave him this commission, while reserving the innovative energies that created his dramatic Sculptural substyle for Ronchamp. In this there may be some truth,[42] but not the whole. The clients were looking for something more ostentatiously novel than orthodox Modernism, and the Carpenter Center seemed to provide it: a work of Geometric art, a series of great ovoids and angles that dramatized Harvard's commitment to scientific education since Conant's time, both by contrast with the Fogg Art Museum's Academic Georgian next door, but also in tandem with the Science Center built by Modernist celebrity Josep Luis Sert, Gropius's successor, just a block away.

Perceiving the excellences of Modernism as great geometric forms in space made it far more compre-

7.50. *The Baltimore Harborfront—revitalized from the late 1970s in one of the most successful feats of Modern city planning—can show several noteworthy pieces of architecture, not least the National Aquarium. Originally intended to be built on the Potomac in southwest Washington and relocated by the adroit political maneuvering of Maryland's senators, it was built in 1981 to designs by the same Cambridge Seven responsible, along with Buckminster Fuller, for the United States Pavilion at Expo 1967 in Montreal. To geometric forms the Aquarium's architects added fashionable triangular terminations, one of them containing a tropical garden. (IMG:NAL)*

hensible than as visual metaphors of radical social and political stances held in Europe forty years before. It provided a far more feasible point of departure for analyzing the often minute differences between formalistic compositions than the necessarily subjective sensibilities of professional critics.

In the later 1960s and 1970s Modern buildings classifiable as Geometric substyle were among the most common of all Modern creations, small and large. Not only did classic Modern materials like steel, glass, or concrete create readily perceptible geometric shapes and patterns, so did such traditional materials as wood and brick. Orthodox architects were not supposed to do such things deliberately, and orthodox critics were not supposed to perceive them, but there they were nonetheless. Part of this substyle was a fad not only for sharp, triangular terminations on tall buildings, like Johnson and Burgee's Pennzoil Place in Houston (1972–76) or Stubbins's Citicorp Center in New York (1973–78) or the National Aquarium in Baltimore *[7.50]*, but also for sharp geometric shapes on summer and country houses, which originally catered to avant-garde taste around San Francisco's shoreline, then spread to Lake Tahoe and other fashionable vacation resorts throughout the West *[7.51]*.

"Sculptural"

The human mind so naturally perceives representational configurations in visual forms even where

nothing of the sort was intended that preserving the purity of Modern elements from such contamination always demanded a vigilance and subtlety that only the greatest masters possessed. Very early in the Modern movement, while it was still a Revolutionary Socialist style in Europe, Erich Mendelsohn had begun exploring the potentialities of molding concrete into great abstract sculptural shapes, most notably in his Einstein Tower at Potsdam in 1921, in some ways as significant a monument to the second phase of Modernism as Boullée's Monument to Newton had been for the first—and actually constructed, furthermore (destroyed 1933). But the shapers of orthodox Modern opinion always resisted these potentialities of concrete. Mendelsohn's name appeared in no editions of *Space, Time and Architecture* despite an impressive range of accomplishments, from Maimonides Hospital in San Francisco to Park Synagogue in Cleveland. They were afraid of something like Ledoux's *architecture parlante* reappearing—something easily interpretable as representational, hence unabstract, hence unscientific.

Almost alone among American Moderns, Louis Kahn worked in the 1950s with this idea–one reason admirers ranked him along with Richardson and Wright. But Kahn had to cloak his sculptural bent in mysterious arcane language and talk about creating utilitarian forms that somehow involved a primeval Spirit of Architecture—*Urformen,* to use

7.51. A perfect expression of 1960s radicalism is this Sea Ranch condominium complex built in 1965–66 on the Pacific Coast Road (U.S. 101) north of San Francisco, to designs of Charles Moore. Every sort of variant of this style—high, vernacular, self-consciously naive—was soon scattered all over this coast. Its appeal to radical chic fashion was irresistibly delicious: weathered sidings, simulations of crude palisading, and triangular roofs like industrial sheds corresponded to faded blue jeans, unkempt hair, rude manners, and black speech patterns affected by affluent upper-middle-class whites to signal proletarian sympathies and primitivistic proclivities.

7.52 (above, left and right). Among the best examples of the essential architectural forms Louis Kahn was famed for creating are the buildings for the Jonas Salk Institute near San Diego, built 1959–63. They are customarily photographed in sunshine, which emphasizes their sculptural character; but rainy gloom better brings out the primeval mystical quality for which Kahn was striving. (Courtesy of Salk Institute)

7.53. Always latent in Modernism was a picture of prehistoric man from the religion of science's version of Eden, in a state of innocent response to stimuli. Its reconciliation with realities of scientific practice could involve elaborate forms of architectural deceit. Here in the inner courtyard of a multimillion-dollar Medical Center built in 1966–70 at the University of Toronto (Summerville, McMurrich and Oxley, architects), entered through a contrived cave lined with great "fallen" blocks of rock made out of concrete, are artificial mounds of dirty, melting snow made out of plastic by a sculptor (Ted Bieler). It is a trompe l'oeil all the more interesting because the pavement actually is heated electrically, via underground wires, precisely to prevent snow from accumulating. (IMG:NAL)

the appropriate German word. This of course laid his work open to criticism. His 1957–62 Richards Medical Laboratory complex at the University of Pennsylvania was extravagantly admired as an Architectural Idea in the spirit of Frank Lloyd Wright, but it was not particularly efficient as a laboratory. At Kahn's best, his kind of Sculptural substyle could be remarkably effective; there is an awesome quality about his Jonas Salk Institute near San Diego [7.52]. But all too often it came close to a primitivistic form of Arts and Crafts, like the Erdman Hall dormitory at Bryn Mawr College in the early 1960s, with raw concrete reminiscences of inglenooks and pergolas.

The breakthrough that made a Sculptural sub-

style broadly effective came, as usual in Modern, from Europe. At Ronchamp in east-central France, Le Corbusier designed a chapel (built 1953–55) that finally followed Mendelsohn's lead and employed the capacity of molded concrete to make massive, irregular shapes with more visual impact than ever attainable in those orthodox straight lines and sharp edges to which Kahn had largely conformed. Ronchamp had plain overtones of the primeval. There was imagery in it recalling megalithic dolmens and prehistoric caves, and otherwise alluding to that composite picture of early man which science, by popular consent, had authenticated. Onto this the Modern mindset grafted a subliminal association with primeval innocence drawn from older Judeo-Christian traditions. "Primeval" thus came to have associations with both scientific outlook and the natural goodness of mankind. Small wonder the new substyle associated with it flourished. Its massive molded concrete forms could be understood not only as power symbols, but also as symbols of inherent goodness.

By the 1970s the Sculptural substyle had acquired irresistible appeal for projects of any size. The AIA Headquarters in Washington *[3.49]* illustrates it. The kind of smooth, finished concrete Corbu had insisted upon at the Carpenter Center, his own Ronchamp rendered entirely passé; rough pebbly raw (primeval) grained effects were now *de rigueur*. Entrances were set back beneath second stories, so that buildings in this substyle were seemingly accessed through narrow slits or series of holes overhung by massive second-story concrete walls—in other words, through a kind of cave. Sometimes entrances had artificial rocks strewn about; the Ford Foundation building in New York featured a primeval landscape complete with trees and pools artfully assembled inside on the first floor. Indeed, expressing so artificial a union as primeval innocence with high technology called for impressive displays of ingenuity, endlessly varied *[7.53]*. To what precise degree such imagery was understood in specifics, or intentionally created, was and is not ascertainable, of course.

"Hi-Tech"

The last phase of Utilitarian Modern, and its principal representative in the late 1980s, has been "Hi-Tech." This fanciful and elaborately mannered exaggeration of the technological infrastructure of Modernism began appearing in the 1970s. It emphasized not only naked structure and materials, but also heat ducts, water pipes, and wiring starkly revealed for the admiration of technological enthusiasts. Its ancestry was in the Russian avant-garde of the 1920s: Tatlin's Monument to the Third Internationale and especially the 1922 Pravda building in Leningrad, with exposed outside elevators to dramatize how a proletarian state could achieve what in the bourgeois world had proved only slogans: "open covenants, openly arrived at," "all the news that's fit to print." This last feature now reappeared in contexts wildly divergent from its origin: on a Portland City Parking Garage *[7.54]*; elegantly gilded on interior atria walls of John Portman's luxury hotels; on Toronto's Canadian National Tower, for some while reputedly the continent's tallest structure. Obviously the Hi-Tech substyle was most appropriate on buildings where specific references to science seemed called for, and there it was often and effectively found: science centers at universities (Wellesley College has a nice example); advertisements of public devotion to science following the lead of Paris's Pompidou Center in Paris; or proclamations of science as an instrument of world cooperation and peace, like the Intelsat Building in Washington *[7.55]*.

Hi-Tech involves then, as earlier substyles did not, a conscious element of *architecture parlante*: the more so, the more it necessarily elides into, and becomes, a substyle of Postmodern—that is, mak-

7.54. Bright apple-green exterior elevators provide a dramatic touch of technological symbolism to the otherwise grimly utilitarian City Parking Garage, built 1977–79 by Portland Development Commission designers in downtown Portland, Oregon. (IMG:NAL)

7.55 (top). The Intelsat Building was erected on Connecticut Avenue in northwest Washington, D.C., as home for a consortium of 180 nations cooperating on International Satellite Telecommunications. A scientific image obviously seemed in order, and John Andrews seemed a logical choice to produce one; it was built in 1983–84. Seen here in June 1984, before completion of its landscaping or broad, brick-paved ramp approach, it does indeed uncannily resemble a huge spacecraft just landed on some barren planet. (IMG:NAL)

7.56 (above, left). New York state architect Charles A. Kawecki adhered scrupulously to his Modern mandate for this State Office Building in Watertown, built in 1969–71. It could never be described, like some designs as late as the 1950s, as lingering, stripped-down Academic Classicism or Art Deco. Yet in this facade survives the ghostly outline of entablature and columned portico, picked out by recessed window surfaces, set upon an elevated platform. (IMG:NAL)

7.57. Oral Roberts University in Tulsa, Oklahoma, is the most striking monument to a revival of fundamentalist Protestantism that began in the 1950s and continued into the 1980s. The 500-acre campus was laid out in 1963 and by the 1980s had over twenty major buildings, beginning with this 1963 Prayer Tower. Most buildings were designed by Frank Wallace, who emphasized materials and shapes that were Modern in their technology and abstractness (reflective gold glass, sharply pointed triangles). Some critics saw in them no more than Eisenhower-era middle-class notions of classy surroundings—a fusion of Florida pool and Ramada Inn fixtures. Others recognized how subtly Gothic effects permeated the whole, recalling especially how many Gothic buildings were originally just as brightly painted and gilded. But of primary significance, these buildings had a social function comparable to medieval religious architecture: the Prayer Tower as focal point of the campus kaleidoscopically reflecting all other buildings functions as a visual metaphor of a campus centered on and built by the power of prayer. (IMG:NAL)

ing a characteristically Postmodern kind of self-conscious statement of devotion to the ideals of Modernism.

Subliminal Eclectic Modern Substyles

More than any other style, Modern demanded from its serious practitioners a commitment to a more than intellectual position—to quasi-religious belief, in fact. In due course mere adherents to the faith appeared, borne along on the stream of approved taste; but from beginning to end only truly committed believers could create architecture that was truly Modern. Other practitioners were constantly falling into varieties of heresy, deviationism, or outright unbelief. The frequent human and artistic tragedies that resulted were only rarely noted, if at all.[43] It took the sudden appearance of Postmodernism to demonstrate how uneasy the majority of Modernists had always been with their orthodox creed; wholesale adoption of Postmodernism was so sudden as to leave the remnant of true believers stunned: "I never thought I'd live to see historicism practiced again." But in fact it had been practiced all through the heroic era of Modernism, in two ways: directly, in Popular/Commercial forms, and subliminally, within forms that were nominally Modern.

All through the Modern era, a Popular/Commercial architecture openly flourished. Popular/Commercial could be readily dismissed as cultural lag that time and education would soon dispose of—even if in fact it never showed signs of going away (chapter 8). Subliminal Eclectic styles within Modernism were something else again. Through most of the Modern era they were neither denied nor derided. They simply were not recognized. Rarely written or talked about, their existence was all but ignored. Only in retrospect has it become apparent how much Subliminal Eclecticism was practiced within Modernism, often by its most reputable practitioners, who subscribed to the letter of Modernism while keeping the spirit of traditional styles supposedly gone forever.

Subliminal Eclectic substyles had all the outward characteristics of Modernism. They eschewed applied ornament. They did not rely on texture for ornamental effects. They made prominent play of steel, glass, and concrete materials and construction techniques. Yet the forms and combinations of elements so created had recognizable affinities with forms and combinations of elements characteristic of given historic styles, rather than the identifying shapes and characteristics of Modernism.

Such recollections were not necessarily conscious. In fact, they probably proceeded, in the main, from artists' subconscious (a creative process for arts of all eras, not least Modern). It follows that their wide appeal proceeded from a subconscious source also. What makes people feel, deep inside themselves, "I really like this" or "I really don't like that," in spite of all explicit pressures dictating "You should dislike this," "You ought to like that"? Nobody knows, or can ever know, exactly, since it is our own minds that are in question. But the cause must lie in the operations of a sort of atavistic mind or memory.

Atavistic memory can be recognized easily on a broad scale in the characteristic style of great world civilizations: even the rankest amateur can tell Egyptian from Mesopotamian art forms throughout history, and nobody ever confuses either with Islamic or Japanese or Hindu, even though orthodox art history might carelessly label them all "Oriental." On a narrower scale it can be recognized best in the stylistic forms (as distinct from high styles or their derivatives), such as appear in vernacular and early popular arts. Good examples are the four-square and temple-house forms appearing in suburban houses in the 1890–1930 years; these are not "derived" from corresponding Classical Revival shapes in an ordinary way, but reappearances in response to popular taste elicited by speculative builders through trial-and-error processes (see 6.62). But its most dramatic, because most unexpected, manifestation is in the comparable persistence of unconsciously remembered stylistic shapes in subliminal forms within orthodox Modernism itself.

Predictably, Subliminal Eclectic styles within Modernism occur most often where a collective mind is most operative; that is to say, where those who commissioned and paid for the architecture had most say in its design, where any blatant display of Modernism's power imagery would be obviously inappropriate and resistance thereby more possible: homestead, sanctuary, buildings for smaller and more local governments, amenities privately or locally controlled. Surprisingly, examples can be found among works by the greatest Modern masters.

For example, Subliminal Classical effects abound within Modernism, once you look for them; all over the country are to be seen basic shapes and proportions and scale that are instantly recognizable to any knowledgeable eye as shadowy, ghostly images of classical porticoes and pediments, features of the old American national style, no matter how officious their outward observance of Modernist taboos on applied ornament and historicist shapes *[7.17, 7.56]*. But not only in smaller towns, on local government buildings and banks; they appear also on new state capitols (Reno, Honolulu), in new mass transit stations designed for BART in San Francisco and the Metro in Washington, D.C.; *and* they appear in the work of leading architects—not only in Philip Johnson's addition to the Boston Public Library, where conformity with the older building might have been imposed, but also in the New York State Theatre at Lincoln Center, where it was the architect's own expression. Even Mies did a bank in Subliminal Classical substyle.

Subliminal Gothic effects within Modern also abound, especially though not exclusively applied to sanctuary types. Their range is extraordinary:

7.58. Subliminal Eclectic styles within Modernism were an obvious bridge from Academic Revivals to Postmodern "historicist references." At what precise time the shift occurs depends on circumstances. For example, Westminster Benedictine Abbey chapel of Christ the King at Mission in British Columbia built in 1980–85 to designs of Osborne Gathe could be an example of Postmodernism: its vaults display what could be called "quotes" from isometric sections of Gothic ones, and the ferroconcrete skeleton somehow produces openings with quasi-Gothic arches—not to mention the medieval effect of whole walls of colored windows shifting gradually from blue to purple to red to orange to yellow. Yet Gathe's design goes back far beyond the 1980s; a model of this chapel was on view in the monastery in the late 1960s. (IMG:NAL)

7.59. The cornerstone of a synagogue for the First Hebrew Congregation in Peekskill, New York, was laid in 1957 and its design shows all the marks of 1950s Modernism: no applied ornament, stilt-like columns, flat roofs, dun brick walls. Yet another image obtrudes. Tall slit windows with colored glass suggest a sanctuary; the entrance portico is latticed; lettering in the manner and style of Frank Lloyd Wright adorns the facade, along with a Star of David. Within this Modern body lurks a medieval spirit. (IMG:NAL)

7.60 (left). Yale's Academic Gothic tradition was carried on in subliminal medieval forms despite the mandatory Modernism imposed by imitation of Harvard from the 1950s. Marcel Breuer's Becton Engineering Building of 1971 is one example, but the best is the Beinecke Rare Book and Manuscript Library which Gordon Bunshaft designed in 1961 (completed 1963). Its glowing amber walls created a most un-Modern reverential atmosphere that strikingly recalled the effects of mosaics and windows of early Christian basilicas, most especially San Vitale in Ravenna. (IMG:NAL)

7.61. Brendan Gill's John F. Kennedy Center For the Performing Arts *(New York, 1981, 32) remarks in passing how architect Edward Durrell Stone's design "paid tribute, in a contemporary form, to the nearby Lincoln Memorial"—an early example, perhaps, of respect for surroundings not common among Modernists of the time. (Stone was commissioned in 1959, his model approved in 1962, the center opened in 1971.) The center is seen here looking south from Harborfront on the Potomac in Georgetown; the Lincoln Memorial is just behind. (IMG:NAL)*

from extreme Protestant colleges (Oral Roberts University at Tulsa, Oklahoma *[7.57]* to Benedictine monasteries *[7.58]*; from Catholic cathedrals *[7.35]* to Jewish synagogues *[7.59]*. And of course all sorts of collegiate buildings *[7.60]*.

Then there was Subliminal Picturesque, perhaps the earliest, certainly the most prominent, deviation from Modern canons. It was the style for lavish hotels by Morris Lapidus, John Portman, and others *[7.44, 7.45]*. It was also the style devised by

Edward Durrell Stone for the Kennedy Center in Washington—at once wholly orthodox concrete, steel, plate glass, and wholly unorthodox colorfulness and glitzy textural effects *[7.61]*. At such points the ever-present, ever-persistent Popular/Commercial underground of the Modern era became manifest, even though corresponding reconsideration of American attitudes toward its past was suppressed until Postmodernism forced it into the open.

Notes

1. Quoted in Page Smith, *The Nation Comes of Age* (New York: McGraw-Hall, 1981), p. 526.

2. For example in Canada, Modern architecture was most commonly perceived (among the country's cultural elite anyway) as a visual metaphor of scientific rationalism in general and in particular of the kind of ideal egalitarian democracy structured along rational lines promoted by the British Left (H. G. Wells, Kingsley Martin, Bernard Shaw, etc.) in the 1920s and 1930s. A new kind of Colonialism, if you like; but also an ideal that supplied English Canadians with an identity to replace the one lost when the British Empire collapsed in 1945–50. So may be explained why Modernism was adopted in Canada so early and so enthusiastically, with far less cultural lag than had been the case with preceding styles; and why there was more than the usual cultural lag in adopting Postmodernism.

3. Political maneuverings to get the United Nations located in New York, and on its particular site, are well described in chapter 2 of Samuel Bleecker's *The Politics of Architecture: A Perspective on Nelson A. Rockefeller* (New York: Rutledge Press, 1981)—a book commissioned by Nelson Rockefeller, whose publishing house Rutledge was. It is admirably reviewed by Carol H. Krinsky in *Journal of the Society of Architectural Historians* 4/2 (1982):168–70.

4. In 1939 the principal resource available to those very few people teaching what was in those days almost universally called "art appreciation" in American universities was a small book with smudgy black-and-white illustrations called *Art Through the Ages*, written by Helen Gardner in 1926. It ended with a reference to the regionalist American painter Grant Wood of Iowa.

5. The comparable process in making New York a literary and intellectual center is detailed by Thomas Bender, *New York Intellect* (Baltimore: Johns Hopkins University Press, 1987). Its theme: New York is and always was less provincial than New England because of continuous and heavy Jewish immigration from the nineteenth century onward, which put New York uniquely in touch with the "ancient intellectual centers of Europe."

6. "The whole is an artifical heaven, formerly even more bewildering, when it showed in many colours, reflecting the light. . . . When His Majesty the Paramarabhattaraka Maharajadhiraja attended the service accompanied by his queens, ministers, and other relatives and friends, all in costly, fashionable attire, when a choir sang, accompanied by a great number of instruments, when beautiful dancing girls displayed their art before the idol, furtively throwing amorous glances at the visitors, it must indeed have been a magnificent spectacle. A spectacle, a masterpiece of refined showmanship built up around the divine presence in the idol. What it was worth as genuine religiousness, is another matter." (Hermann Goetz, *Art of India* [Baden-Baden: Holle, 1964], pp. 164–65).

7. "It has been the failure to appreciate this hypothetical and conceptual character of scientific theories that has been mainly responsible for the 'crisis of conscience' following the Scientific Revolution in Europe. . . . From the end of the 18th century things were made worse when the same naive realism, now in the form of materialism, led some scientists and popularisers of science to speak as if 'matter' was the only 'reality' there was" (A. C. Crombie, *Augustine to Galileo* [Cambridge, Mass.: Harvard University Press, 1953], p. 310).

8. Studies of Modernism's eighteenth-century ("First Phase") origins began in the 1930s with Emil Kaufmann's pioneering works, especially *Von Ledoux bis Le Corbusier* in 1933. Contemporary treatments range from Joseph Rykwert, *The First Moderns* (Cambridge: MIT Press, 1980) to Klaus Lankheit, *Der Tempel der Vernunft: Unveröffentlichte Zeichnungen von Boullée* (Basel and Stuttgart: Birkhauser, 1973), which focuses on the ideological significance of the subjects of First Phase Modern monuments. A key monument is Etienne-Louis Boullée's proposal for a gigantic monument to Sir Isaac Newton. Naive in concept—celebrating Newton as a second Savior for the human race, who had discovered the laws whereby the world works, and, even more important, whereby Man can work it, and recalling Pope's famous lines recasting Genesis: "God said, Let Newton be, and all was light"—it was also naive technologically. So bold as to be unbuildable, it was nevertheless put forward (like many other Modern projects) in a confident expectation that Scientific Progress would render it buildable soon, first of many temples to Reason covering the land, replacing the old religion's obsolete cathedrals.

9. This key document in Modernism actually was a catalog, accompanying the exhibition Hitchcock and Johnson arranged at the newly founded Museum of Modern Art to celebrate "the architecture of the New Pioneers, the international style of Le Corbusier, Oud and Gropius, of Lurçat, Rietveld, and Mies van der Rohe." Its effects were immediate. In the early 1920s, for example, R. M. Schindler, who had been one of the first European Modernists to work in the United States and had worked in Frank Lloyd Wright's office intermittently from 1914 to 1921, called the International Style "an expression of the minds of a people who had lived through the World War, clad in uniforms, housed in dugouts, forced into utmost efficiency and meagre sustenance, with no thought for joy, charm, warmth." After 1929 he began to practice it. Eliel Saarinen followed a similar pattern, shown plainly enough in a comparison of his Cranbrook Academy of Art Crafts Building in 1928 or his 1929 Kingswood School at Cranbrook (Bloomfield Hills, Michigan) with the Crow Island School at Winnetka of 1939 or the First Unitarian Church in Columbus, Indiana, of 1940.

10. Most famous of these was Erwin Panofsky, who had an Institute of Advanced Study created for him to study in at Princeton, which he shared with Einstein (the connection of art with science is of course significant). Panofsky was celebrated for analyzing the iconography of historic art with an objectively scientific eye, void of subjective appraisal. What this means, you can easily see by comparing how Panofsky and, say, Emile Mâle, wrote about medieval arts and architecture—*Gothic Architecture*

and Scholasticism, say, compared to *La Fin du paganisme en Gaulle* or *Les Vieilles Eglises de Rome*. Mâle is concerned with *why* medieval arts and architecture appeared where and how they did, with the human factors, with the society that created them; Panofsky in *Scholasticism* and all his other works is concerned with *how* they work and with solving neat little puzzles of authorship, fine points of *Kunstwissenschaft*.

11. By 1931, when Kurt Gödel published his incompleteness theory and Bertrand Russell had abandoned his mammoth project to find absolute truth, mathematicians realized the futility of searching for absolute proofs of truth. If Le Corbusier (for example) was aware of these developments, there seems no evidence of it in all the complex internal intellectual life that Tim Benton describes in "The Sacred and the Search for Myths" (*Le Corbusier: Architect of the Century* [London: Arts Council of Great Britain, 1987], pp. 238–45).

12. *Zeitgeist* (Time/Spirit) is an idea that went back to Early Modern times and was first consistently formulated in Gianbattista Vico's *New Science of History*, written between 1725 and 1750: world history moves in stages and to each stage there is an appropriate expression. By 1900 it had begun sinking into the popular mind, enough to make a bestseller out of a gloomy apology for Germany's defeat in 1914–18, Oswald Spengler's *Untergang des Abendlandes*, her ruin being part of a general inevitable decline of the West. Paradoxically the *Zeitgeist* idea became the favorite single argument for European Modernism: Romanticism was not only out of date, it was out of joint with the times:

> All the drive of our age is directed toward secular building. The efforts of mystics will remain mere episodes . . . we will build no cathedrals. Nor will great romantic gestures mean much to us, for we perceive only empty forms behind them. Our age is unsentimental, we don't esteem great emotions, but the reasonable and the real.

It could come right out of Vico or Spengler, but is from Mies's 1924 *Baukunst und Zeitwille*. The New Age demands a New Architecture: Modernists chanted this litany in the 1910s and 1920s like monks in a cell.

13. The idea of a select band possessed of new truths originates (like so much Modern art theory), in the ambience of what Daniel Boorstin so nicely described as the "Parliament of Scientists" in the seventeenth century, whose spokesman Henry Oldenburg was writing in 1656, "I have begun to enter into companionship with some few men who bend their minds to more solid studies, rather than to others. . . . They are followers of nature itself, and of truth . . ." (cited in *The Discoverers* [New York: Random House, 1983], p. 388). So Moderns from the 1920s organized themselves into *cénacles*, and when they took over in the U.S., ascribed their creations not to individuals but to "cooperatives" or "associations," the most famous being TAC, The Architects' Collaborative in Cambridge. Such demure collectivism added immeasurability to their fame, contrasting favorably as it did to the pretensions of surviving Victorian individualists like Frank Lloyd Wright.

14. Thomas S. Kuhn, *The Structure of Scientific Revolu-*tions (Chicago: University of Chicago Press, 1970), p. 138.

15. An extended treatment of this complex problem that I have found useful is *Breakout from the Crystal Palace* by sociologist John Carroll (London: Routledge & Kegan Paul, 1974).

16. Modernism's protagonists were fond of claiming that they had somehow rescued North American architecture from the horrors of uncontrolled Picturesque Eclecticism; they cited such writers as the Austrian Adolf Loos, who in 1902 called ornament a "crime" and defined the true mark of civilization as unornamented utensils and furniture such as he, coincidentally, designed. In fact the trend toward disciplined restraint in ornament had set in with Academicism and by 1902 High Picturesque was long out of date.

17. In 1927 Le Corbusier defined "Five Points of Modern Architecture" that later became International Style dogma (conveniently assembled by Stanislaus von Moos, *Le Corbusier: Elemente einer Synthese* [Zürich: Huber, 1968; English translation, Cambridge, Mass.: The MIT Press, 1975]): free interior plans; strip windows; free (irregular) facades; flat roofs; *piloti* stilts at ground level. Corbusier implied they were all incontestably logical derivations from ferroconcrete building: once you have a ferroconcrete cage, no inner walls bear loads, so you can plan interiors with complete freedom; put windows and doors in however and wherever you want; install rainwater drains at the center of a flat roof, and leave the cage's stilts open so as to avoid the resultant dampness at ground level. A much more physically functional house results, he implies. That is not demonstrable; what demonstrably does result is a house that looks different from any other house type in history. And why would one want that kind of house? To achieve a visual metaphor of a cherished myth.

18. Or as the critic Susie Gablik defined Modern art: "Art is not a descriptive statement about the way the world is, it is a recommendation that the world ought to be looked at in a given way" (*Progress in Art* [New York: Rizzoli, 1980], p. 159).

19. Schoolbooks of the 1950s . . . beside the current texts . . . look as naïve as Soviet fashion magazines. . . . Recent texts are paragons of sophisticated design. They look not like *People* or *Family Circle* but, rather, like *Architectural Digest* or *Vogue*. One of them has an Abstract Expressionist design on its cover, another a Rauschenberg-style collage. . . . Inside, almost all of them have a full-page reproduction of a painting of the New York School—a Jasper Johns flag, say, or "The Boston Massacre" by Larry Rivers. But these reproductions are separated only with difficulty from the overall design, for the time charts in the books look like Noland stripe paintings, and the distribution charts are as punctilious as Albers' squares in their colour gradings.

(Volker R. Berghan and Hanna Schissler, *Perceptions of History: International Textbook Research in Britain, Germany, and the United States* (Oxford: Oxford University Press, 1987], pp. 22, 23).

20. Modern attitudes toward private amenities and

public services, commercial or otherwise, were set early: "When [Tony] Garnier was asked why there was no law court, police force, jail, or church in his famed 'Industrial City' [1904], he replied that in the new society under socialist law there would be no need for churches, and that as capitalism would be suppressed, there would be no swindlers, thieves, or murderers" (Donald D. Egbert, *Social Radicalism and the Arts in Western Europe* [New York: Knopf, 1970], p. 268). Amusing pretensions—except that right through the 1970s American cities were being designed on such presuppositions; and Pruitt-Igoe was not amusing to live in.

21. The most remarkable example must be the International Style architect John Andrews, an Australian who worked extensively in North America and other continents in variants of the New Brutalism and High-Tech substyles. About one of his characteristic works of the 1960s, Scarboro College in Toronto, he made a statement that could just as well apply to Gund Hall, which he designed at Harvard in the 1970s, or Intelsat in Washington from the 1980s: "The focus is people," he declared. "People moving, standing talking, loving, people with their aspirations and frustrations, living and dying, needing. Only architecture that meets the needs of people endures." Yes, but as Carol Moore Ede (who recorded this statement in *Canadian Architecture, 1960–1970* [Toronto: Burns and MacEachern, 1971], p. 24), observed, the architect made little effort to discover what the people wanted from the people themselves. He *knew*, and he dictated. "Scarboro College has been hailed by many as an exceptional interpretation of contemporary human needs. By others, especially by some of students [who have to live in it], it has been called inhuman."

22. Arthur M. Schlesinger, Jr., *The Crisis of the Old Order, 1919–1933* (Boston: Houghton Mifflin, 1957), pp. 4, 5, 7.

23. The reference is to *Salvation by Design*, written by one of the stars of the Bauhaus, László Moholy-Nagy, after its diaspora. The book's combination of the English language and Utopian German ideas from the 1920s Bauhaus produced enormous impact, and became required reading along with Giedion's *Space, Time and Architecture* for anyone with pretensions to fashionable modernity. The shifting concept of whom Modernism was to save of course reflects its shift from being a persuasive art in the 1920s, trying to convince a hostile society, to being an art of established conviction.

24. Tom Wolfe, *From Bauhaus to Our House* (New York: Farrar Straus Giroux, 1981), p. 72.

25. Arguably, all these technological developments were inherent in the skyscraper as an architectural type. Dependence on elevators began with their invention in 1856 and standardization by the 1870s; likewise the first fully air-conditioned building was the Academically styled Milam in San Antonio, of 1927. Yes; but in earlier tall commercial buildings technology was subordinate to human uses, whereas in Modern counterparts technology dictated the style.

26. Non-fictional quotes: Donald Hoffmann, "John Root's Monadnock Building," *Journal of the Society of Architectural Historians* 26/4 (1967), especially 130, n. 29;

and the entry on the Transamerica Pyramid (1972, William Pereira & Associates), in David Gebhard et al., *A Guide to Architecture in San Francisco and Northern California* (Santa Barbara: Peregrine Smith, 1973), p. 63.

27. Peregrination of styles applied to bank types deserves a book to itself. So suited was the Classical Revival's temple image that examples persisted even through the domination of Picturesque tastes and reemerged in subliminal substyle forms even in major Modern works like Mies's 1963–69 Toronto-Dominion Center in Toronto. There the two principal slabs—a black 56-story monster for the Toronto-Dominion head office bank and a slightly humbler 46-story Royal Trust tower framed a one-story bank pavilion proportioned like the old temples; its purpose, we are told, was to "identify the banking functions" of its giant companions. Smaller and local banks were strongholds of Popular/Commercial styles (see chapter 8). Following 1960s agitations, banks generally began breaking with both images to adopt mirror walls and so become inconspicuous, or even fortress images—the latter represented not only by a chain of small banks designed in St. Louis entered over small bridges across moats with keeps in the center (for example, First Federal Savings, Louisville), but by the International Finance Corporation of the World Bank on the G/H 18th–19th block of downtown Washington surrounded by massive ramparts.

28. Professor T. J. McCormick drew my attention to an interesting early essay on this subject by Albert Bush-Brown, comparing the Graduate Colleges at Princeton and Harvard: "Cram and Gropius: Traditionalism and Progressivism," *The New England Quarterly*, March 1952, pp. 3–22. Bush-Brown perceived Gropius's appointment and subsequent design for the Harvard Graduate College as a return to a primacy of German standards and ideas dominant from the 1870s through the 1890s, rejected in the 1890s at Princeton under Woodrow Wilson and Dean Andrew West, now reasserted by Harvard President J. B. Conant. "The society for which students are to be trained," Bush-Brown wrote, quoting Conant's *Education in a Divided World: The Function of the Public Schools in Our Unique Society* (Cambridge, Mass., 1948), "is that industrial society which Cram avoided" but for which Gropius's Bauhaus was an educational model.

29. So called in Barr Weissman's film on Langston Terrace, documented by Glen Leiner, narrated by Wolf von Eckhardt. Langston worked, according to the film, for three basic reasons. One, paradoxically, was that it was segregated, and so avoided the demographic problems at Pruitt-Igoe; a kind of "neighborhood watch" was always in effect, older residents insisted in interviews. Another, perhaps more basic, was its low-rise design: no unit over four stories, most only two. The film quotes Oscar Newman's maxim in *Defensible Space:* the higher the rise, the higher the crime rate. Third, it had an abundance of open space, not token parkland in the Corbusian sense, but free fields for unstructured play (in addition to designated sports areas). Early Bauhaus housing theory is discussed by J. Joedicke and C. Plath, *Die Weissenhofsiedlung* (Stuttgart, 1968).

30. Early books puffing Modernism always included the 1908 Fagus Shoe-Last factory at Aelfeld by Gropius and the 1927–30 Van Nelle Tobacco Company in Rotterdam by Brinckman and Van der Vlugt. But in fact, as Adolf Max Vogt wrote in *Revolutionsarchitektur* (Cologne: Dumont Schauberg, 1974, p. 148), "that generation which stamped almost every kind of building with the 'face' of industrial building, occupied itself with industrial buildings themselves very little." That is because they thought of it as temporary; soon, come World Revolution, no architectural type would be more industrial than another.

31. Alistair Horne, *To Lose a Battle: France, 1940* (London: Macmillan, 1969), p. 61.

32. "The apartment's living room . . . was enormous, but it appeared to be . . . stuffed . . . with sofas, cushions, fat chairs, and hassocks, all of them braided, tasselled, banded, bordered and . . . stuffed. . . . Even the walls . . . the walls were covered in some sort of padded fabric, with stripes. . . . The windows . . . were curtained in deep folds of the same material, which was pulled back to reveal its rose lining and a trim of striped braid. There was not so much as a hint of the twentieth century in the decor" (Tom Wolfe, *The Bonfire of the Vanities* [New York: Farrar Straus Giroux, 1987], p. 340).

33. Leland M. Roth, *A Concise History of American Architecture* (New York: Harper & Row, 1979), p. 319. Roth admirably analyzes the designs of the Farnsworth and Glass houses, noting how daringly Johnson "introduced a circle into a rectilinear scheme [for a toilet], a filip Mies avoided since he said he had not yet perfected the straight line. Even more significant is the huge fireplace for it throws into sharp relief one of the seven crutches Johnson liked to ridicule—comfort." In the 1970s it was mandatory to do such solemn analyses; one gathers from the context that Roth was no believer, even back then. He does not, however, mention the farmhouse. But it was there!

34. A monument of major importance in any line-of-progress history of Modernism, Saint John's Abbey Church anticipated Corbusier's Ronchamp in many significant ways and was complete by 1958 (commissioned in 1953). Breuer described his goal in good mechanistic causal language as "to defeat gravity and lift the material to great heights over great spans. . . . This is also true for its bell banner—a slender cantilevered slab on parabolic supports" (*Design Quarterly,* 1961). The word "Gothic" was not, of course, mentioned. But anyone who visits can see how subliminal Gothic effects are produced by ostensibly Modern materials and structure.

35. See, for example, Gilbert Herbert, *The Dream of the Factory-Made House: Walter Gropius and Konrad Wachsmann* (Cambridge, Mass.: The MIT Press, 1984). The Taut quote is from "Für die neue Baukunst," *Das Kunstblatt,* 1919, sec. 20.

36. Interesting though David DeLong has made them in *Bruce Goff: Towards Absolute Architecture* (Cambridge, Mass.: The MIT Press; and New York: Architectural History Foundation, 1988).

37. They are treated at length in most early books on Modern architecture, such as Giedion's *Space, Time and Architecture.* Much research has been done since. It seems that large-scale architectural use of iron was first introduced in the 1830s; by the 1850s cast-iron facades were common and by the 1860s a number of competing manufacturers of architectural iron were well established in New York. By the late 1860s and 1870s steel was being used for big bridges and then for ever-taller buildings, once elevators let them soar (1856+). The first complete metal frame is supposed to be William LeBaron Jenney's Home Insurance Building in Chicago, of 1883–85. Broad-paned glass too appeared early: Russell Warren's Providence Arcade of the late 1820s was so roofed. By the 1880s Chicago skyscrapers had strip windows; by 1915 Willis Polk's Hallidie Building in San Francisco had an all-glass facade. Likewise concrete. Natural cement rock was used on the Erie Canal in the 1820s; poured concrete structures appeared in the 1830s; by the 1850s concrete was common for fireproofing. Irving Gill's poured-concrete houses, Wright's Unity Temple, as well as William A. Radford's *Cement Houses and How to Build Them: Perspective Views and Floor Plans of Concrete-Block and Cement-Plaster Houses* (Chicago: Radford Architectural Company, 1909), were all presaged by technological developments from the 1870s and 1880s.

38. "Socialism," or anything else ideological, is rarely mentioned in the other early classic of Modernism, Nicholaus Pevsner's *Pioneers of the Modern Movement* (London and New York, 1937), either. It became somehow tasteless to even mention the matter, as Donald D. Egbert discovered when he published *Social Radicalism and the Arts in Western Europe* (New York: Knopf, 1968), showing how totally interconnected were ideas of social, political, and artistic revolution; his book was quickly remaindered.

39. J. Mordaunt Crook, *The Dilemma of Style* (Chicago: University of Chicago Press, 1987), p. 260.

40. Nor could time improve its practicality; what Martin Pawley observed about Hunstanton could be applied to almost all buildings in this substyle: ever since its opening in 1954 windows have always been popping out and replaced by plywood, doors come unhung for structural reasons, noise is almost unbearable, additions are necessary to make the place workable as a school rather than a monument to Modern Utilitarianism.

41. See the discussion in William Curtis, *Modern Architecture* (London: Phaidon, 1982), p. 218.

42. According to Tim Benton in "The Era of the Great Projects," (*Le Corbusier: Architect of the Century,* 181–84), Corbusier assembled "a sort of dictionary of Corbusian discoveries, from casual observations made fifty years before, through a lifetime's *recherche patiente . . .* the design of the Carpenter Center became explicitly self-referential."

43. Gregory Ain is a striking example; his memory has been preserved, and his problem insightfully analyzed, in *The Architecture of Gregory Ain,* catalog of an exhibition at the University of California at Santa Barbara Art Museum, by David Gebhard, Harriette Von Breton, and Lauren Weiss (Santa Barbara, 1980).

8.2. By the mid-1980s Popular/Commercial effects were being introduced (on selected occasions) even to monumental Modernist creations like Rockefeller Plaza in Albany. (Courtesy of New York State Office of General Services and Public Affairs; photograph by Donald Doremus)

8
AN IMPERIAL UNDERGROUND: POPULAR/COMMERCIAL STYLES IN ARCHITECTURE AND FURNITURE, 1940s–1980s

Popular/Commercial in Its Time and Place

Fast-food stands and shopping malls, big signs on poles and little signs shaped like busboys and bowling balls, parking lots and discount stores, and, as their weekend ads always said, "much, much else," all jostling and weaving, competing, complementing—this is the approach to almost any city or town or village, all over the country *[8.1]*. Lo what Henry Ford hath wrought: the strip, created by and for a culture based on mass-produced automobiles, serving that section of the American people known by the 1980s as the "silent majority."

"The strip" in the course of its evolution from the 1930s on kept some resemblance to old Main Street's mad variety of colors and shapes, its bustlings and whirlings; kept a family resemblance as well to its bigger and brassier cousins in Las Vegas and Reno; also, perhaps, a hint of Times Square at night. What no strip resembled was New York's, or any other big city's, downtowns—those big business areas that Modernism built. Nothing here like their relentless conformity; nothing here to recall those somber, stilted concrete corridors, those empty windswept plazas with those coldly abstract blobs of sculpture deposited in them, those colorless and eyeless sheets of glass wall. Only in the 1980s did the stark contrast begin dissolving, with Modernism's clandestine courtship of Popular/ Commercial, under the veil of Postmodernism *[8.2, on p. 318]*.

Wherever you leave the strip, suburban housing developments begin. Strips and suburbs belong together; both are served by, and were creations of, the automobile. Together they have drastically altered the traditional American landscape in one

sense, blurring the clear distinction between town and countryside always in evidence before, and still common in Europe. But in another, deeper sense they have preserved that landscape, for the architectural styles of strips and suburbs, and the social functions of those styles, are not Modern. For all their overt garishness and vulgarity, they are profoundly traditional.

This is an America familiar to every American who owns or rides in a car—and that is most of the population. But it is an America foreigners rarely, if ever, see or hear about. Not only have American media presented the country as if everyone in it lived in, and everything of consequence happened in, New York, Los Angeles, or Dallas, but when references to suburbs do occur, they have tended to be hostile or derisive.[1] Cars in America are used, were television to be believed, for cops-and-robbers chases or for chauffeuring rich and important people about, against a backdrop of megalomaniac skyscrapers, luxurious ranches outside Dallas, or old row houses in Queens. The world could hardly guess what a huge percentage of Americans live in suburbs and use cars to get to work, go shopping, or take the kids to a drive-in. Least of all could they suspect that most Americans do not live their personal lives in Modern architectural settings of mirrored walls and brutalist monoliths, do in fact dislike the Modern power-image intensely and had steadfastly rejected it from the beginning. Yet it is so.

A very great percentage of the American built environment is in fact not Modern, nor even Subliminal Eclectic Modern substyles. Nor can it be dismissed, as it was for so long, as merely representing the survival, in vulgarized vernacular forms, of obsolete Academic styles, something per-

8.1. *Commercial strip on the main approach street to Manketo, Minnesota (which happens to be called Madison Avenue), October 1980. The historical process of which it is the end product is nicely described in Chester Leibs's* Main Street to Miracle Mile *(Boston: New York Graphic Society, 1985): first detours around an old town center choked with traffic; then a formal bypass; then shopping centers appear on the bypass, and lo! "Miracle Mile"! (IMG:NAL)*

petuated among rednecks that disappeared as soon as artistic education brought elitist taste to the far provinces.[2] It represents a style in its own right, with distinctive social function, characteristics, and substyles—a style popular in the sense of liked and favored by the people, commercial in the sense that it was dictated by buyers of its buildings: Popular/ Commercial, therefore.

Precisely when Popular/Commercial styles began cannot be fixed. One root goes back to the early nineteenth century, to the kind of *architecture parlante* endemic to popular democracy; but while French Revolutionary essays in this direction are well known, American counterparts have been ignored *[8.3–8.5].* Another obvious root is roadside architecture, beginning in the 1920s or even ear-

8.3. *Harvard School of Veterinary Medicine building erected c. 1885, from Edmund V. Gillon, Jr.,* Early Illustrations . . . of American Architecture *(New York: Dover, 1975). Function was identified by a huge horseshoe entrance, two-story horseshoe spikes on the facade, horseshoe-shaped niche in the gable peak containing a stylized horse head, and a very literal cow's head projecting from the corner. So prestigious an institution would hardly have commissioned a freak without any other parallel throughout the nineteenth century.*

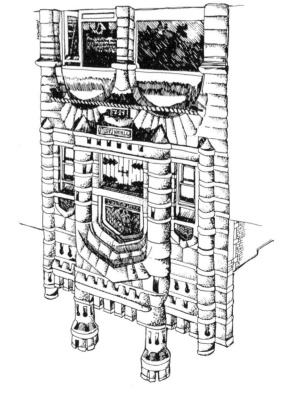

8.4 (left). Knights of Pythias Hall, built in 1904 on Main Street in Weiser, Idaho, is a three-story replica of the stage set for Damon and Pythias, an Elizabethan play whose 1821 version by John Banim inspired the order. (From Don Hibbard, Weiser [Boise, 1978], p. 8)

8.5. The Corn Palace in Mitchell, South Dakota, is a 1921 replacement of 1892 and 1905 buildings. But like the sacred shrines at Ise, this commemoration of harvest is regularly renewed. Each year, says a brochure, "Individual cobs are sawn lengthwise by small power saws, the halves are then nailed, flat side in, to wooden panels which are fastened to the brick walls of the building." Thus "the entire exterior and portions of the interior are covered with corn—red, blue, yellow, and white—arranged in geometric patterns and outlined with grasses and grains [composing ornament and pictures of] wild game, hunting, pioneer history, etc. Along its roof are Moorish minarets and towers which, with their bright colors, add greatly to the design and appearance of a palace." Picturesque architecture parlante, you might call it. (Photograph c. 1958, by Rodney E. Prather)

tion of Academic styles in the late 1950s and early 1960s, as older Academic practitioners retired or died off and nobody was professionally trained to replace them [8.6]. But since demand had not diminished, the free market law of supply began operating. A new kind of commercial designer appeared; and instead of Academic styling, disappearing from the landscape, metamorphosed into a distinct new style. Popular/Commercial was conditioned, as all styles before it had been, by usage; specifically, it appealed to middle- and lower-middle-class tastes and attitudes and was applied to architectural types needed in middle- and lower-middle-class life. These created its identity.[4]

Definition and Identifying Characteristics

Defining Popular/Commercial is first a matter of distinguishing it from "Pop," and "kitsch," from folk building, and from lingering vernacular Academic and emerging Postmodern styles.

Popular/Commercial is the opposite of "Pop." "Pop" was a brief Modern Art fad. In the 1960s elitists set everyday useful objects upon pedestals (literally or metaphorically), applied the formula "art is what artists say it is," and thereby transformed the objects into uselessness and so into art. In the 1970s Pop became a springboard for demonstrating sign systems beloved of European semioticians; for example, James Wines used roadside architecture whose forms he could deconstruct. "De-architecture" the result might be called; Post-modern it could conceivably be; but Popular/Commercial, never.

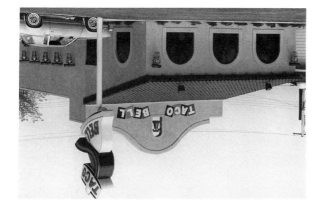

8.7. This Taco Bell outlet in the eastern Michigan town of Lapeer can be dated to the late 1960s, because it is still in the "old" style originating in California, which was a very simplified Mission style, identified by a conglomeration of features: the roof, round arches, stucco walls, Mission facade with bell, protruding beam ends. Later the company literally changed its image to something less obviously Spanish or Mexican. (IMG:NAL.)

lier; but for a long time most of this could be classified as vernacular Academic rather than a style on its own [6.34–6.36, 6.42]. What brought these roots into blossom as Popular/Commercial styles proper was the near-total takeover by 1960 of all schools of architecture and furniture design by Modernists, mainly European, coupled with the continuing rejection of Modernism by most of the population for any kind of architecture or furniture in whose style they had any say.[3]

The most immediate result of this coincidence was a barbarization, vulgarization, and amateuriza-

8.6. A new Baptist church for the small Kentucky community of Crab Orchard was dedicated 18 June 1951, replacing a church burned in 1948, for a Baptist congregation in existence since Kentucky became a state. A Wren/Gibbs style signifying "leading denomination" since Colonial times was appropriate, however severely simplified. (IMG:NAL.)

8.8. *A date of c. 1955 is indicated for Maser's Motel in Frederick, Maryland, both by its comparatively small-scaled rooms and by an exterior that tried some Academic approximation (proportions, porch, outside chimney) to the Maryland Colonial* style *of its region. Nascent Popular/Commercial styling comes out, however, in a generally amateurish effect and in the vertical bargeboarding of the walls. (IMG:NAL)*

Nor is Popular/Commercial a kind of folk art. Folk art was peasant and preindustrial; Popular/Commercial is middle- and lower-middle-class urban, the product of an industrialized civilization. But in some respects Popular/Commercial continues aspects of folk art, especially that deep sense of the "rightness" of certain shapes and combinations of forms over others which made true folk art an agent in the endurance of traditional cultures.[5]

Nor should Popular/Commercial be confused with what gallery elitists call "kitsch." Kitsch is a kind of decorative art that perpetuates styles out of current high fashion—not for sophisticated "quotes" in the Postmodern manner, but under a naive illusion that they constitute "Fine Art": little statuettes like nineteenth-century Rogers groups, or cheap prints of Gainsborough's *Blue Boy*. Popular/Commercial art and architecture, by contrast, used past styles to perform obvious and easily identifiable traditional functions in and for society: substitute imagery, illustration, beautification, persuasion/conviction.[6]

Popular/Commercial originated in an Academic matrix and shows it by being not so much itself a style, as a way of handling other styles. The identifying details of Popular/Commercial are always less learned, less exact than those in any professional Academic style. Contrary to Postmodernism, it never involves in-house jokes, that system of short-

8.9. *Advertisement for Popular/Commercial English Colonial furniture from a Washington, D.C., newspaper in the summer of 1982.*

hand references to or quotations from historic styles rather than reproductions or adaptations of them. Expertise in architecture was not needed to recognize Popular/Commercial stylistic details. They represented a lowest common denominator, always; mass-produced, oftener than not.

For example, you could create Popular/Commercial Colonial Spanish by using simplified and usually not very correct agglomerations of details drawn from high-style variants [8.7] or by prominent use of particular details. The same is true for Colonial English: a Popular/Commercial version could sport a whole form (usually misconstructed in some way [8.8, 8.9]), bits and pieces incorporated into a nondescript "soft Modern" structure [8.10], or anything between, from a few aluminum shutters nailed to walls, to simplified cupolas stuck on roofs and plastic muntin bars snapped over big-paned windows (see 8.18).

Gothic also came in every range from entire buildings to bits and pieces of detail [8.11, 8.12]

8.10 (top, left). One of the "dining rooms," in a McDonald's outlet off the mid-Montana stretch of I-90 near Bozeman. Though featuring the generally muted colors of the new-style McDonald's introduced in 1969, it keeps Popular/Commercial stylistic allusions—most obviously, in this case, to Windsor chairs. In the 1930s Windsors had been pronounced peculiarly American (strong, easily moveable, comparable to balloon framing) in Siegfried Giedion's *Space, Time and Architecture*, which was still canonical when creators of 1970s and 1980s Popular/ Commercial design were in architecture school. So here we have Windsors, swiveling on fixed metal bases. (IMG:NAL.)

8.11 (top, right). Traditional Gothic architecture is recalled in this wedding chapel in the Nevada section of South Lake Tahoe by plastic and plywood pointed arches, some affixed to the wall. Other traditions available to patrons are on-the-spot rental of bridal gowns and bouquets, pastel tuxedos with boutonnieres, cocktail glasses, and the wedding photographer. Otherwise, normal period Modernity of c. 1973 reigns. (IMG:NAL.)

8.12. In this sign identifying a Kingdom Hall of Jehovah's Witnesses near Perry, just off I-69 in southeastern Michigan, the historic style of Saint-Denis and Durham, Wittenburg and Assisi has been reduced to a single simplified identifying element. Yet "castellation" still signifies "fortress of God" effectively enough to convey the denomination's concept of itself. (IMG:NAL, 1981)

Other styles tended to be created entirely out of details, notably Tudor, identified as any display of white walls with black slats nailed over them in big patterns [8.13]. Picturesque, of course, always was created from assemblages, so Popular/Commercial designers followed good precedent when on Modern, even utilitarian, frames they hung every sort of bracket, towerlet, molding, spindle, balustrade, mansard, porch, arcade, and cornice [8.14].

All such usage plainly distinguishes Popular/Commercial from Subliminal Eclectic substyles of Modern. Nothing like the taboos on applied ornament or the disguising of structure that were still observed in Subliminal Gothic or Subliminal Classical applied to Popular/Commercial. Furthermore, Popular/Commercial rejected, especially in domestic architecture, that free-flowing space so beloved of Modern theories: in commercial architecture it rejected as well the whole concept of "megablocks" in favor of retaining the identity of separate units, like the old Picturesque Main Street. Popular/Commercial also resisted Modern scale, keeping traditional proportions and behavioral space wherever possible. Above all, there was nothing minimalist about Popular/Commercial. Its 1950s gaudiness might be toned down in the later 1960s and 1970s—strident scarlets, golds, royal blues, and screaming pinks were superseded by quieter rusts, chocolates, muted pinks and blues.[7] But Popular/Commercial from first to last eschewed the barren, the meager, the empty.

Distinguishing Popular/Commercial from Postmodernism is complicated by blurrings of their more obvious points of interrelationship. Not by Popular/Commercial designers; they would as cheerfully borrow from Postmodern quotes, including semiotic allusions to Modernism, as from any other source, if it suited their social purposes. Rather it was Postmodernists who were diffident about the extent of their learnings from Las Vegas; but that complicated situation is best considered in the context of social function.

8.14. Interior of Pietro's Gold Coast Pizza Parlor in a shopping plaza outside Oregon's capital, Salem, built in 1965 as the third in what came to be a twenty-four-restaurant chain in the Pacific Northwest. Scarlet, gold, and white tinsel contribute to the festive atmosphere; arcades give a hint of Old Italy. (IMG:NAL.)

8.13. A mobile home on Dungeness Point in sight of the Strait of Juan de Fuca in Washington becomes an example of a Tudor mansion by addition of a jutting bay stuccoed in white with black boardings attached. (IMG:NAL, 1969)

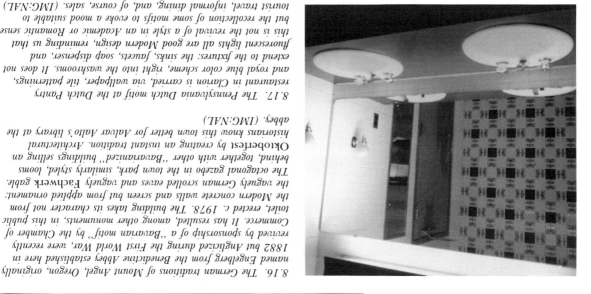

8.17. The Pennsylvania Dutch motif at the Dutch Pantry restaurant in Clarion is carried, via wallpaper, the patternings, and royal blue color scheme, right into the washrooms. It does not extend to the fixtures: the sinks, faucets, soap dispenser, and fluorescent lights all are good Modern design, reminding us that this is not the revival of a style in an Academic or Romantic sense, but the recollection of some motifs to evoke a mood suitable to tourist travel, informal dining, and, of course, sales. (IMG:NAL)

8.16. The German traditions of Mount Angel, Oregon, originally named Engelberg from the Benedictine Abbey established here in 1882 but Anglicized during the First World War, were recently revived by sponsorship of a "Bavarian motif" by the Chamber of Commerce. It has resulted, among other monuments, in this public toilet, erected c. 1978. The building takes its character not from the Modern concrete walls and screen but from applied ornament: the vaguely German scrolled eaves and vaguely Fachwerk gable. The octagonal gazebo in the town park, similarly styled, looms behind, together with other "Bavarianized" buildings selling an Oktoberfest by creating an instant tradition. Architectural historians know this town better for Alvar Aalto's library at the abbey. (IMG:NAL)

8.15. The first Dutch Pantry restaurant was opened in the 1960s at Hummel's Wharf in Pennsylvania's Lancaster County and took its motifs from there: royal blue ("Dutch") color predominating; ornament adapting Fraktur motifs, including wallpaper and various "Villcum" icons signed by Rip Rossman. A ghostly image of Pennsylvania German barns supplies roof line, cupola, and hex signs, more or less. This one is off I-80 in central Pennsylvania, at Clarion. (IMG:NAL)

awareness of the past not recognizable by psychol- ogy based on mechanistic assumptions.

Popular/Commercial styles have preserved the rich variety of American life, in response to de- mands that the design of buildings and furniture be dictated not by their structural systems, but by their human use. Popular/Commercial styles are capable of creating buildings that can provide an appropri- ately reverent atmosphere for worship or for burial, as older sanctuaries had, and the kind of cozy atmo- sphere for lodges and evening gatherings of friends that old taverns once had; buildings that can satisfy small businesspeople's needs for advertisement, needs of the poor for comfort, needs for ethnic self-awareness, even needs of indigenous cultures for survival. It is Popular/Commercial arts that tell you when you are in Pennsylvania Dutch country, when you are in the South, when you are in Ha- waii[8]—the very sort of variety and color Modernism tried so superciliously to blot out [8.14–8.16]. A standard Modern argument against this kind of de- sign was always the incongruity of mixing "tradi- tional" and "modern": Why should a nation that sends astronauts to the moon live on earth amidst fake folk imitations? The answer was always the same: pluralism responds to the human condition. Humans live their lives on many different emo- tional and psychic levels, so that the feelings and moods a launch pad evokes are by no means neces- sarily the ones you want evoked in restaurant and privy, shop and home [8.17, 8.41].

Though the needs thus satisfied in Popular/ Commercial styles are immediate and local, and their means often crude and vulgar, the social func- tion that they addressed is timeless and primordial. Throughout history architecture has been the prime means of creating visual metaphors carrying the values and beliefs, conscious as well as sublimi- nal, that underlie all the institutions of any society. Architecture (in itself and as the frame for furniture and murals and statuary) has been the principal instrument for promoting the endurance of civiliza- tion, for preserving human continuity.

That Modern had lost this function was recog- nized early. "Unless we preserve human continu- ity," Lewis Mumford said in 1968, on the somewhat incongruous occasion of his being awarded the American Institute of Architects' Gold Medal for service to the architectural profession in general and Modernism in particular, "our scientific and technical advances will be not merely menacing but meaningless. Modern man must restore his self-

Social Function

Popular/Commercial architecture has functioned in and for American society on three interrelated levels. First, it could be seen as a regrettable, but temporarily necessary, concession to the money- grubbing propensities of a lower sector of Ameri- can society determined to resist all high-minded efforts to restructure the United States and the world on scientific egalitarian—that is, noncom- petitive—lines. Second, it could be seen as an effort to maintain humane variety in American life, against all the pressures of leveling, conforming, mechanistic Modernism. Third, it could be seen as deliberately, albeit not always consciously or de- perpetuating the traditions and values of a Classical/Ju- daic/Christian civilization against a secular/ materialistic/scientific mindset. As with all historic styles, its several social functions have operated simultaneously on all three levels.

Most obviously, Popular/Commercial styles have been used to sell buildings, furnishings, and related services to those uneducated in cultural matters by universities or art schools. It has been argued that Modern designers might have succeeded in pro- ducing salable homesteads or successful restau- rants if only Popular/Commercial competition had been suppressed, if only "bad" design had been somehow stopped from driving out "good." Sober reflection refutes such contentions. Crude compul- sion might force people to eat in some cold, gleam- ing machine for nutriment-consumption; nothing on earth could make them prefer it to some spot made homier by stylistic tags taken from familiar Colonial or Tudor forms. Even fast-food stands soon switched from walk-up counters and cafeteria- line efficiencies to booths, plastic ruffled curtains, mimetic oak paneling, muted skylighting, and plants. "Soft" Popular/Commercial effects won every contest with hard, sharp, intractable "Mod- ern." The same is true of homesteads. Crude com- pulsion might force people to live in "the projects," so stern, so efficient, so minimal in land and crea- ture comforts; nothing on earth could make them prefer such housing to suburban houses or mobile homes that looked like a traditional homestead, no matter how tacky the Tudor, how gawky the Classi- cal, how crude the Colonial [8.13, 8.18]. It was a dumb instinctive preference, which even in the 1940s was beginning to be supported by research into the human psyche that posited an atavistic

respect. . . . In that process, architecture has been one of the chief means." In stubborn ways Popular/Commercial arts retain this function of telling human beings who they are, where they have been; of providing framework and roots for life. They continue, that is to say, to carry out one of the crucial social functions of all historic arts and architecture. This is the source of their continuing appeal and endurance.

For its own survival every society has to have arts of substitute imagery, illustration, beautification, and persuasion/conviction. If what a society calls its Art fails to do those things, then something else must be invented to do them, whether called Art or not. And so it has happened. What are called collectively the Popular/Commercial arts—visual arts like photography, movies, comics, television, advertising—have done in and for twentieth-century American society what used to be done by portrait painting, commemorative statuary, narrative reliefs, allegorical pageants. Popular/Commercial architecture likewise carries out social functions that are immemorial, that every society has always needed done.

Throughout human history, architecture has functioned to create humanly meaningful environments, by creating recognizable visual metaphors of basic institutions: palace, homestead, fort, sanctuary, monument, shelter. Each successive style has interacted with these types to make them more meaningful, more relevant to its era's perceptions and experience. The Modern style functioned in

8.19. On Michigan Route 60 near Burlington stands this ten-foot-high image of the Statue of Liberty, made in the 1960s. Not commercial because not for sale, not art in the Modern sense because no personal aesthetic or artistic or creative expressions are involved, it is a monument in the popular sense of conveying an idea held in common, or assumed to be so held, throughout society at large. And this is a principal function of monument as an architectural type. To such popular imagery—mostly on a tiny scale—has one of the great social functions of historic architecture throughout history been reduced. (IMG:NAL, 1980)

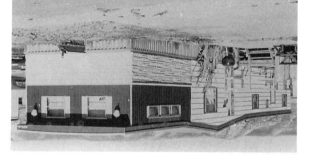

8.18. "Mobile home" is a contradiction in terms. Homestead is the one architectural type that should not be mobile. For the institution of the family, which it houses, demands stability and roots. And Popular/Commercial design provided metaphors of them—even for this mobile home parked on a pad in one of central Wyoming's desert stretches near Rock Springs. In a trailer park serving a temporary construction project, nobody expected to dwell long. Yet the mobile home's wheels are covered by corrugated steel skirts scored to look like concrete blocks; its metal walls are sheathed in plastic Permastone and aluminum siding imitating wood clapboards and paneling; its windows are framed by shutters; its prefab metal garage is painted to resemble the old wooden kind. The purpose of this architecture is obviously not to exhibit truth to materials or display construction, but to create an image of Home, to preserve the institution of family under adverse circumstances. Critics might better appreciate its social function if they tried to live in similar conditions. (IMG:NAL, 1975)

this way too, of course. But it presupposed perceptions and experience that were not common, nor even actual, but rather envisioned in part of some mythical future. Environments in Modern style were therefore drained of meaning for a majority of the population. But Popular/Commercial styles, no matter how trivial or incongruous their outward forms might be, could still make traditional architectural types comprehensible to the populace at large: homesteads that in some sense were still visual metaphors of the principle that the primary agent for stability and endurance of society is, and cannot be anything other than, the family [8.18]; sanctuaries that could function as visual metaphors of the historic role of religion to provide societies with some ideals of decorum and reverence, however elementary [8.11, 8.12]; monuments that proclaimed shared social values in broadly accepted symbolism [8.19]. Popular/Commercial architecture was still capable of creating environments meaningful in the sense that they transmitted the kind of values societies have always had to maintain in order to survive: common denominators of the collective mind, some inheritance of mental habit, on which all the traditions that go together to make up a given society—architectural, linguistic, behavioral, sexual, whatever—ultimately have to depend. In carrying out traditional social functions, Popu-

lar/Commercial architecture perpetuated many traditional means otherwise lost, among them mimetic replications of shapes and textures for associated ideas. However trivial their content and social significance, structures like the Roadside Mammy near Natchez, the Big Duck on Long Island, or restaurants shaped like chuck wagons and lobster pots [8.20][9] were informed by a principle comparable to the impulse behind the pyramids at Giza and Uxmal, the Sun Temple at Konarak, or the Sainte-Chapelle on the Ile-de-France. When Popular/Commercial designers treated concrete to look like canvas or feathers, or simulated effects of dark-grained wood by enamel baked on aluminum, they perpetuated practices of simulating effects of reed and wattle in mud brick and cut stone common in architecture from remotest antiquity.[10]

A more sophisticated architectural device for conveying meaning in traditional architecture was use of similar shapes to convey uniform fundamentals in diverse situations. Throughout the American republic until Modernity, for instance, architectural imagery of state capitols corresponded to that of the national Capitol to proclaim reasoned adherence to the laws and beliefs of their common Union (cf. 3.5, 3.6): in earlier Colonial times, architecture had been used to proclaim reasoned adherence to the common beliefs and obligations of British sub-

8.20. The Chuck Wagon on the Kirkwood Highway between Wilmington and Newark, Delaware, was built c. 1955 in a shape made familiar from television: the Conestoga wagon of the West, from which rough cooks dispensed hot coffee, steaks, and other plain foods for plain folks. A coffee pot forms its door, spoked wheels form its windows, and a concrete shell over mesh simulates a canvas roof. In Postmodernism such details would be called witty quotes; here they are part of Popular/Commercial architecture parlante. Latterly the Chuck Wagon had a much more restrained appearance, having lost much elegance in a rebuilding, following upon brake failure in a sixteen-wheeler attempting to park in front. (IMG:NAI, 1958)

jects via Anglican churches of similar Wren/Gibbs form in every provincial capital [2.90–2.99] and was long remembered [8.6]. So in the design of chain-store outlets, whether fast foods or cosmetics, whether on roadside strips or fashionable boutiques, correspondence of architectural imagery proclaimed correspondence of quality [8.21, 8.22]. In this case, the values involved were material and trivial: the kind of hamburger or fish-sticks or cosmetics you get in one outlet would be of a standard uniform with what you could expect in any other shop similarly shaped and styled. But the principle involved was one of architecture's important functions until very recent times. What was trivial about Popular/Commercial architecture was not its principles, then, but what those principles were applied to: the primordial powers of architecture were applied to: the primordial powers of architecture were applied to unify nations and empires, and thereby promote their endurance, somehow has come to be employed to advertise uniformity of fish sticks and cosmetics and hamburgers. Why that should have happened is not explicable in terms of architecture, Modern or Popular/Commercial, but is a matter for investigation by sociologists or political scientists.

Latter-day defenders of Modernism in general argued that perpetuation of these older functions and forms was a regression. Modernism had been a gigantic step forward for mankind, a climb to a new plateau of aesthetic experience and creativity, in which Popular/Commercial failed to participate. Defenders of Popular/Commercial argued that the Modern contention rested on two false premises. First, it assumed that once you had built to great heights, you could kick foundations away. Twelfth-century philosophers claimed that they could see further than their predecessors because they stood on the shoulders of giants; their twentieth-century counterparts claimed to be giants themselves, needing no platform to stand upon. Yet a present or a future that claims not to rest upon a past is a paper planning, a verbose mental construct, signifying nothing. Second, the notion of a giant step forward for Mankind presupposed not only a new kind of architecture but a new kind of society as well. But while the new forms duly came into existence and were everywhere successfully imposed, the new society supposed to accompany and justify them had conspicuously failed to materialize. Popular/Commercial architecture, by contrast, continued to serve real, ongoing needs in a real, on-going society.

8.21 A McDonald's fast-food outlet, opened August 12, 1985, off I-90 near Bozeman, Montana. Its prototype was designed by Don E. Miller for owner Ray Kroc and first introduced in 1969. Parabolic arches from the older type and its bright colors survive as the logo on a huge sign, designed to attract attention from miles away on the interstate. The arches were designed in the 1950s by Charles Fish, a young University of Cincinnati graduate in architecture, working as draftsman for Stanley C. Meston; his inspiration could well have come from Giedion's Space, Time and Architecture, there as everywhere a required text. (IMG:NAL)

8.22 Siegfried Giedion was a great promoter of Robert Maillart's ferroconcrete arches, illustrating almost all of them in Space, Time and Architecture. Figure 220, reproduced here, showed a construction diagram for Maillart's Cement Hall for the Swiss National Exhibition at Zurich in 1939. Maillart may not have gained proper fame in Switzerland, but if, as is likely, this diagram was Charles Fish's inspiration for the Golden Arches of the original McDonald's outlets, which later became McDonald's logo, then indeed Giedion's efforts to redirect taste in American architecture were successful.

Application of Popular/Commercial Styles to Architectural Types

Popular/Commercial styles were created by and for the private sector of the economy and responded to a demand for art forms corresponding to middle- and lower-middle-class perceptions of the world. It follows that Popular/Commercial styles naturally were applied to types of private architecture directly paid for by individuals, rather than public architecture indirectly paid for through taxation and tax breaks. That meant Popular/Commercial styles applied to a very high percentage of home-steads and small businesses, but never, for all intents and purposes, to architectural types commissioned by big corporations and state or federal governments, including universities. Application to other architectural types was split between Popular/Commercial and Modern styles and substyles, roughly by social class and clout: Modern for the bigger and more powerful, Popular/Commercial for the rest.

In the later 1960s and 1970s cultural geographers and sociologists began devoting intensive attention to the suburban homestead in its then Popular/Commercial form.[11] Apparently the conviction that families ought to be founded, and land is what you found them on, went too deep in Western civilization to have been killed by twentieth-century technological and sociological changes; only its manifestations had changed. Although the characteristic family estate had been suburbanized, and become measurable more by what could be earned in salaries than from farming or trade (sec-ondary rather than primary production), still it remained a joint enterprise to which everyone contributed: husband, wife, older children. And its visual metaphor remained a self-contained dwelling on a piece of land, with forms, ornament, and be-havioral spaces still determined in relationship to owners and inhabitants.[12] In other words, the ideal that produced the ''comfortable house'' suburbs of the 1890–1930 period was by no means gone. Still in the 1970s Amos Rapoport (in *House Form and Culture*, 126) reported that to be ''socially and cul-turally valid'' in America, housing had to be free-standing. And to be so valid—that is, to ''work''—on a middle-class level or lower, housing also had to be decked out in some recollection in forms or proportions of historic styles: Tudor, Picturesque, Colonial above all. How can we account for such persistence? One theory would have it that built environments evoke either cognitive or affective at-titudes, corresponding to inhabitants' back-grounds: people educated or learned in architec-ture have cognitive responses to buildings, in terms of styles they recognize, whereas others have affec-tive attitudes—gut responses.[13] Obviously it is with that latter and by far larger segment of the popula-tion that Popular/Commercial styles work. Or it may be that the appeal of historic styles in Popular/Commercial (or Academic or Subliminal Modern) forms has to do with some kind of atavistic sense for things having a right ''look.'' On some deep level they seem to further that continuity with the human past which the whole function of homesteads in modern society entails, which might explain, for

8.23. *Advertisement from 1974 brochure for Tamarron Doublewide Mobile Homes, built by ''Champion Home Builders Co. with 63 Coast-to-Coast plants,'' supplies a complete image: dark bargeboarded walls with white ornamental patterns, diamond-mullioned windows, vaguely old- and solid-looking interior with drapes and mimetic oak panels on the walls; Dad on the patio firing up the barbecue for the three kids, Mom fixing salad in her kitchen. ''Share in the Great American Dream . . . A spacious home of your own . . . Nearly 50% of all new single family homes sold in the United States in 1973 were mobile homes. Because the costs of conventional homes are out of reach of the majority of Americans . . . the mobile home way of life will soon be dominating the American housing scene.'' (IMG:NAL)*

8.24. Picket fences, flamingos, and birdbaths establish "the private home" and so function even in a public housing project, here Langston Terrace in Washington, D.C. (IMG:NAL, 1988)

example, how insistently the Popular/Commercial style focuses on immemorial elements in the homestead: door, porch, hearth/chimney.

The humanizing function of Popular/Commercial styles was most dramatically evident in "mobile homes," a subtype of homestead which every year from the 1940s through the 1980s accounted for a greater percentage of new single-family units. Product almost entirely of the private sector, mobile homes were the era's most obviously democratic architecture. Available to all, mobile homes came in what at first seemed wildly diverse Popular/Commercial styles—something to suit every conceivable individual or family preference [8.13, 8.23]. At first sight they seem the very image of all the restlessness associated with American life from frontier days onward—impermanence, insistence on individual freedom to move on and try to find a better life. Yet closer analysis reveals that what was created by the mobile home's most characteristic stylistic elements (mimetic effects of stone, clapboard, sheathing, and timberwork; outdoor lamps; pedimental door and window frames) was an image of stability and permanence. And the reason must be obvious: "mobile home" is a contradiction in terms. A "home" cannot be "mobile." The very idea of "home" implies roots. Home is where your roots are. Popular/Commercial styles worked to make it look so [8.18] [14]

For houses in the large-scale developments of the 1950s like the famous "Levittowns" on Long Island and in Bristol, Pennsylvania, Popular/Commercial

humanization was effected by other means than architectural styles proper. On its first appearance—in quick and effective response to the enormous demand for postwar housing—the "development house" was the very symbol, for sophisticates, of middle-class conformity. A much-reproduced New Yorker cartoon of the late 1940s showed two householders standing on the sidewalk of an endless street of absolutely identical houses, gazing up at a single weathervane affixed to a single one of the monotonous row of front gables: "I hear he's eccentric in lots of ways," reads the caption. But the cartoon turned out to be prophetic. Very soon, conformity was replaced by infinite variety. Diverse plantings, paint, rock gardens, ornaments on walls, fountains, flamingos, and every sort of yard art transformed the scene, so that no two identical spec-built units in suburbs anywhere looked alike. Every prefab house, every mobile home in trailer parks, even public housing units, by such means could acquire individuality and become, to that extent, a homestead [8.24, 8.25].

Yard art belongs in the category of monument/memorial, an architectural type to which Popular/Commercial styles were applied to great effect. It includes not only homeowners' arts like groupings of mass-produced elves and deer, junk sculpture like old painted bathtubs set upright to serve as niches for a statue of the Virgin Mary and hubcaps nailed around stumps,[15] such garden arts as trimmed hedges or scalloped flower beds, but also roadside art: gigantic signs visible for miles across

deserts, blinkering lures on the strip, graffiti on rocks and bumper stickers, welcoming signs and categorilla[16] announcements ("approaching the World Center of Gopher Farming," etc.), giant fiberglass statues of Indians and busboys and chickens, and the statuary of theme parks. Some of this art might be classifiable as advertisements straight and simple, some as a kind of art for art's sake [8.26]. Some is in the category of folk art survivals and some entirely a product of twentieth-century merchandising. Some is created by communal concern [8.27]. But all of it performs that basic social function which the later twentieth century relegated to Popular/Commercial arts, to create an environment that is intelligible and responsive to human needs—"beautification," in the ancient sense.

In that perspective, these later Popular/Commercial monuments and memorials have had a considerable lineage in the United States: signboards projecting from Colonial street fronts; statuary and oversized architectural ornament naively advertising the status of newly rich merchants in the naive New Republic: arrays of abstractly stylized figures from classical mythology defining Rockefeller Center in the 1930s as no mere mercantile venture but a cultured combination of commerce and art [6.64]. For cemetery and funereal sorts of monument/memorial types. Popular/Commercial had the field pretty much to itself, as Modernism found the idea of death quite as distasteful as war, corruption, or inequality, and ignored it even more, if possible. It must be said the best-known example, Forest Lawn in Glendale, California, reaches no great heights either, sharing to a great extent the Modern delusion that Heaven can somehow be re-created on earth [8.26].[17] But Popular/Commercial arts here at least admitted that there is a problem. They re-

8.26. Statue of Motherhood flanked by replica of sixteenth-century Florentine wrestlers and an early-twentieth-century "thinker," with Michelangelo's David poking head and shoulders above a split fieldstone wall, in Forest Lawn Cemetery's Mystery of Life Garden, in the Glendale district of Los Angeles. But it is really a theme park, brought to forested lawned life out of a treeless, grassless tract, like Disneyland and King's Island giving the people what the people want. Only in this case, different kinds of needs were to be satisfied: the theme here is "Contemplation." (IMG:NAL)

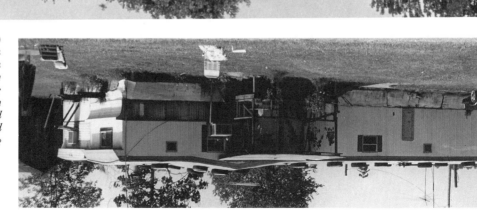

8.25. The additions of a porch and lawn furniture, plus the car in front, create the air of a traditional Southern homestead out of two big, interconnected mobile homes off U.S. 70 near Biscoe, Arkansas. (IMG:NAL)

call to some degree architecture's primordial function of providing space for contemplations of First and Last Things, the whys as well as the hows of life. Forest Lawn's patriotic effusions, however awkward, at least preserve some vestigial notion that arts ought to go beyond individual expression, to keep before mind and eye some idea of states and societies being composed of the living, the dead, and the yet-to-be-born. Ethnic cemeteries recall such a function too, of course, but in general only to the limited extent of keeping ethnic traditions alive.

Popular/Commercial styles allowed sanctuary

types to keep such functions also. Their perpetuations of Colonial (early and late) and Gothic, however rudimentary, at least provided houses of worship that were not easily mistaken for gymnasia or supermarkets or the town hall; their activities are correspondingly differentiated [8.6, 8.11, 8.12], and so is ethnic distinctiveness [8.28].

Application of Popular/Commercial styles to shelter types was a common way to produce garages and sheds, privies and tents and bus stops that recalled human continuity by mimetic textures or traditional shapes.   Application of Popular/Commercial styles to ho-

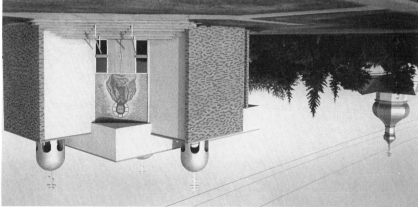

8.28. Ukrainian Colonial style of c. 1920 on the old church of Saint Vladimir (left, behind) contrasts with its replacement of 1965—no longer a style used to transplant a culture from Old to New Worlds, but a style used to transmit ethnic traditions from one New World generation to another. This church is one of a truly remarkable row of Popular/Commercial structures on 48th Street in the central Alberta town of Vegreville, otherwise famous for its Ukrainian Easter Egg enlarged one hundred times by the technological skill of an engineer from Colorado. (IMG:NAL)

8.27. Local citizens aroused by governmental apathy toward a suddenly narrowing "killer" section of U.S. 15 between Gettysburg and Heidlersburg banded together to memorialize its victims in "Accident Row." "Death cars" were sprayed silver-white (ancient death color) and erected on poles beginning in late 1983. By 1986 the state of Pennsylvania had begun a sped-up program of widening this stretch; it was completed, and "Accident Row"

removed, in 1988. This project makes an interesting comparison in social junction to "Cadillac Ranch" from the 1960s, on old Route 66 near Amarillo, Texas. There "Ant Farm," a self-styled Counter-culture Collective of Art Persons, embedded ten Cadillacs in a wheatfield as a work of art supposedly commemorating the myth of Route 66; their work was funded and acquired by a wealthy Texas art collector. (IMG:NAL)

tels and motels was dictated by travelers'—not architects'—perceptions of what travel and accommodation away from home involve. Routine business travelers, or families en route to some regular destination, preferred familiarity; for them Popular/Commercial provided an image of ''homi-ness'' through plans that laid out tonight's room as much as possible like last night's and tomorrow night's (phone, bed, desk, bathroom all in about the same places; same pictures on the walls; same bland and nondescript style applied to everything; traditional proportions and behavioral spaces)—materializations of what sociologists would call the ''con-

servative impulse'' to maintenance of continuity. By contrast, travelers for pleasure were offered a huge range of accommodation, from lavish Subliminal Picturesque substyles of Modern [8.29] to every variety of Colonial courts [8.8], Tudor villas, Sleeper Teepee wigwams, Seven Dwarfs cottages; motels gorgeously adorned with coach lamps and interior bargeboarding and plastic knights in plumed armor on their doors. And of course every variety of regional expression [8.30, 8.31].

Likewise dependent upon circumstance was application of Popular/Commercial styles to commercial buildings. On roadside strips they were pretty

8.30. *Westward Ho Motel in Grand Forks, North Dakota—the name tells it all. Though it had a large layout for the time when it was built, 1954–55, it is really a small theme park, complete with main house and guest rooms connected by a Western-style covered sidewalk. The sidewalk also leads to a dining room (with wagon-wheel chandeliers, naturally), gift shop, arcades, and other buildings. The whole is addressed to tourists for whom The West meant ''ranch.''* (IMG:NAL.)

8.31. *Westward Ho has small-scaled rooms of the 1950s motel variety, furnished in a Popular/Commercial version of that populist Arts and Crafts whose high-style climax was at Timberline Lodge in Oregon [6.89]* (IMG:NAL, 1980)

8.29. *Tom Penny Inn in El Paso, built c. 1977, is one of a chain of three motels in Texas, with rooms bigger than the usual hotel rooms, luxurious furnishings, and a style so vaguely Colonial Spanish, so vaguely Classical Revival Southern Plantation (higher arcades above, lower below) as to be practically Subliminal Modern.* (IMG:NAL.)

8.32. *Independence Mall on Concord Pike, U.S. Route 202, Wilmington, Delaware, designed by and for Emilio Capaldi in 1963, appeared on postcards as one of the sights of the city. Its layout is typical of 1950s shopping centers, in which a squared U*

recalls a village green and tries in some way to recapture a village atmosphere. Uncraded sidewalk preserves the old Main Street effect.

8.33 *(above). Postcards describe Independence Mall as ''a stroll through Historic Philadelphia'' with its quaint shoppe fronts [they are in fact facades over plain brick boxes] and colonial atmosphere. . . . Independence Hall [complete with a replica of the Liberty Bell made in Baltimore, installed 1965], Betsy Ross House, Library Hall, Letitia Penn House . . . all recreated from golden moments of the past to implement and serve the present.'' In a Philadelphia Inquirer Magazine article for 26 July 1964 Capaldi explained that he wanted to pay tribute to the institutions of the country that had enabled him, an immigrant's son, to prosper in business. Both in concept and details the mall has resemblances to Disneyland and Henry Ford's Greenfield Village Museum at Dearborn. (IMG:NAL.)*

8.34 *(left). Ala Moana shopping center in Honolulu has no specific style but, intended by developer John Graham to reproduce the feel of an old Main Street in scale and plan, in fact recalls something of its picturesqueness. This 1959 center repeated Graham's success with Northgate in Seattle: ''Its concept—a long, straight, tightly compressed pedestrian mall lined on both sides with a dense array of stores and services—doubled the number of stores while reducing the distances the public had to walk, and at the same time it enhanced the opportunity for impulse sales'' (Meredith Clausen, ''Northgate Center,'' p. 160).*

well mandatory; small businesses had to attract attention or die. They were common in smaller shopping centers also—Independence Mall north of Wilmington, Delaware, was a famous example of how Popular/Commercial styles could cushion "future shock," the transition to technologically advanced merchandising machines from the old small-town Main Street and familiar department store *[8.32, 8.33]*. Already in the 1950s shopping centers had begun developing a Popular/Commercial bland style that did not scream at potential customers but lulled them into comfortable vulnerability.[18] "Bland, inoffensive, geared neither to elevate the spirit nor to gain the architect fame, but simply to generate sales," Meredith Claussen called it, describing Northgate in Seattle, earliest of developer John Graham's mini-cities.[19] Nonetheless, considerable local flavor was maintained—Graham's Ala Moana in Honolulu could hardly be anywhere else, for instance *[8.34]*. Furthermore, rows of shops facing each other across sidewalks separated by plantings and trees produced an uncanny resemblance to Main Street, with its concomitant picturesqueness, and prepared the way for resurgent Postmodernist historicism.

Application of Popular/Commercial styles to restaurants has been determined by users—specifically, by their styles of eating. Quick lunches, family meals, elegant dining—each demanded an appropriate setting for commercial success, and got it.

The famous roadside diner of the 1930s and 1940s was (despite its name)[20] styled to express efficiency in serving quick, life-sustaining meals, by emphasis on glass and stainless steel in more or less Art Deco forms. But historicist stylings were never abandoned and indeed soon came to flourish—witness the famous White Castle chain *[8.35]*.[21] And as the quick lunch spot metamorphosed into a family restaurant, thanks to more mothers having regular jobs and families eating out more often, the features imaging efficiency were altogether replaced by mimetic approximations of wood panels and ruffly curtains and traditional dining room furniture. By the 1970s distinctions between Popular/Commercial and high architecture were beginning to blur *[8.36, 8.37]*, again presaging postmodernism.

Quite in contrast was the development of Popular/Commercial applied to bars—taverns proper, bars in lodges and clubs. Here the requirements were different: windows boarded up or glass-bricked in or left out altogether, so that the outside world is shut out almost entirely. There was an air of subversion about them. Not, as was sometimes thought, lingering whiffs from Prohibition days, but chills from an official elite culture˘which frowned instinctively on individuals setting themselves off in groups apart from approved collective activities: what are they up to inside, those people in murk, smoking and drinking and staring up at television sports evening after evening, those Elks and Eagles, those X-6 clubs and ladies at Male Stripper nights and Mystic Knights of the Sea? Why aren't they

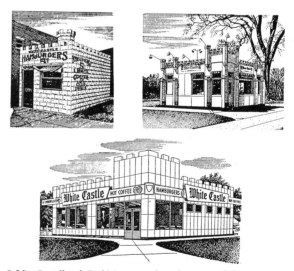

8.35. *Castellated Gothic seems to have been one of the most popular of all historic styles with the public, if not with architectural historians. Its peregrinations can be traced instructively in the designs for White Castle hamburger stands. Borrowing from the Chicago Water Power of the 1880s (top), the first stand (middle left) appeared in 1921 in Wichita as a 15 by 10 foot cement-block box with five counter stools. By the 1930s it was of metal skeleton construction, from which hung prefabricated enameled porcelain panels, a process patented in 1928 (middle right). In the 1930s castellation merged into a distinctive kind of Art Deco. (From* All This from a 5-cent Hamburger*)*

8.36. *This Chart House restaurant was built in 1978 in Rancho Mirage, outside Los Angeles. Designed by architect Kendrick Kellogg of San Diego and costing two million dollars, it is a far cry from Wichita's White Castle. Yet it too is one of a chain (of fifty, founded in 1962) that has stubbornly rejected Modernism as an appropriate restaurant style. In fact stylistic ancestry here is plain: this is not at all far from Taliesin West in feel. All weight is supported on 156 posts so that the walls can be glass and nature almost literally incorporated into the design. That Frank Lloyd Wright's style should be carried on by a chain restaurant (in turn descended from others, such as the late 1960s style of Denny's and the Snack on Kalakaua Avenue in Honolulu, also featuring stone and wood textures) has a certain democratic aspect he should have found congenial, especially since few from the mobocracy would likely be found dining in a place like this. (IMG:NAL)*

8.37. *For comparison, Frank Lloyd Wright's Taliesin West outside Scottsdale, Arizona, designed in the 1930s (begun 1938). (IMG:NAL)*

improving their minds in some art gallery, enjoying the free-flowing space and the factory-strutted ceiling and chaste white walls—that's what their taxes go for!

Speaking of Amenities—although this architectural type was in general one of Modernism's great strongholds from the 1950s onward, a surprising number of local museums, put together by community effort, were in Popular/Commercial styles. Sometimes that styling is disguised by a pretense that the museum, however recent, was a restoration of a historic structure. Such was the Davy Crockett Tavern in Morristown, Tennessee; such too in a sense is Disneyland's reconstruction of Walt Disney's childhood village, whose back-door approach to reviving historicism proved so effective as to be counted a major influence in American Postmodernism. But often it was genuinely Popular/Commercial. An outstanding example was the Air and Space Museum erected to honor Neil A. Armstrong, "first man on the moon," on I-75 outside his hometown of Wapakoneta, Ohio, designed by

Arthur Klipfel in 1972, when Modernism was at its height *[8.38]*.

Why Popular/Commercial? First, because it is people oriented. In contrast to the usual museum of Science, which shows what Science can do, this one shows what an individual can do with Science. It emphasizes human qualities of courage, fortitude, and daring rather than abstract calculations; it has the same kind of appeal as *Star Trek,* therefore. Second, because technology is servant and not master of the design. It has not been dictated by the properties of steel and glass and concrete, but, rather, steel and glass and concrete have been molded by the architect into a representational shape—the famous view of Earth from the surface of the Moon, to be exact. Materials were used here, in other words, as materials were used throughout all the pre-Modern history of architecture, as instruments and not determinants of design. Third, just as the design process has been determined by beholders, so the building is sited to present its best view from the interstate; that is, in terms of how the populace at large will best see it, in marked contrast to tall buildings designed without concern for whether anyone could ever see them as a whole. Furthermore, the image is not wholly man-made; it takes snow on the ground to become completely effective. Every style has its masterpieces; this is one of Popular/Commercial's.

Substyles

Popular/Commercial substyles are easily distinguished from Subliminal Eclectic substyles of Modern, with which they are contemporary, because Modern recalled only effects of specific older styles without reproducing specific details (soaring space and radiance, say, without pointed arches), whereas with Popular/Commercial it was almost the opposite: specific details were what counted, and oftener than not the effects of the original style are ignored and lost (pointed arches were enough, never mind space or radiance!). Not always so easy is a distinction between Popular/Commercial and Academic, since the one derived directly from the other; here the difference was one of quality. Popular/Commercial details were simpler, more abstract, less historically accurate; the whole poorer and meaner, more vulgar, less subtle. But in whatever forms, Popular/Commercial perpetuated all the older Academic styles and added a few deriving from Modern.

Popular/Commercial Utilitarian

In this category are a great number of monuments consisting of plinths or pads on which actual pieces of machinery, implements, or vehicles have been set up for commemorative associations with events: guns (field pieces and machine guns, most commonly) serving as war memorials; locomotives commemorating the Age of Steam or history of civic progress in general; bicycles, mining cars, airplanes, even wrecked autos to serve as warnings at dangerous stretches of road; the list is long *[8.27]*.

Related is a Primitive style, usually created by covering plain surfaces with split logs (real, or mimetic imitations in aluminum or plaster), or rough weathered boards, to provide summer cottages or

8.38. Neil A. Armstrong Air and Space Museum, on I-75 in mid-Ohio at the Wapakoneta exit. Earth as seen from the moon: a kind of high-style roadside architecture parlante. *(IMG:NAL)*

taverns or restaurants with pleasing allusions to rugged outdoor life, pioneer wholesomeness, and escape from routine generally.

Popular/Commercial Spanish Colonial

A dab of red-tiled roofing, a simulated stucco wall, a round-headed arcade or even a single round arch, a touch of black metalwork, and you have the Popular/Commercial version of Spanish Colonial. In contrast to Academic, Popular/Commercial Spanish Colonial tended to be confined more to its heartland in California, Florida, and the Southwest *[8.29]*; its ventures into northern regions were usually occasioned by proclamation of Mexican cuisine, exotic or otherwise *[8.7]*. Philip Langdon's account of the evolution of Taco Bell stands admirably compliments earlier (1971) observations by Reyner Banham in *Architecture of the Four Ecologies,* despite failure to recognize that Academic Spanish Colonial had long since turned into Popular/Commercial:

The predominantly Anglo-Saxon culture of Los Angeles ("built by the British, financed by the Canadians") is deeply entangled with the remnants of Spain and has been so ever since an early-arriving Yanqui like Benjamin Wilson could translate himself into a "Don Benito" by marrying into the Yorba clan, and thus into a ranching empire that spread over vast acreages to the east of the Pueblo [of L.A.]. This ancient entanglement is still deeply felt . . . still provides the psychological support for the periodical outbursts of pantiled roofs, adobe construction, arcaded courtyards, that constitute the elusive but ever-present Spanish Colonial Revival style, in all its variants from the simplest stuccoed shed to fantasies of fully-fledged Neo-Churrigueresque. Such architecture should never be brushed off as mere fancy-dress; in Los Angeles it makes both ancestral and environmental sense, and much of the best modern architecture owes much to its example.[22]

8.39. *El Calvaro Methodist church was designed, according to a plaque on its wall, in 1976 by the Building Committee with contractor G. B. Smith and engineer Orlando Cervantes. It incorporates some elements from an earlier church (presumably its Methodist predecessor), most notably Gothic windows identifying it as "church." Arcade and mission-style gable identify it as "Spanish," and projecting beam ends as "pueblo," specifically "New Mexico," like the rest of Las Cruces, in whose downtown area it stands. (IMG:NAL)*

8.40. *The very image of a retirement home in New Mexico is this little house and garage, with matching "Pueblo" beam ends projecting, built in the 1950s in Las Cruces. (IMG:NAL)*

Popular/Commercial Spanish flourished in the years after 1970 because of the great Hispanic immigration into California and the Southwest, and it created striking visual metaphors of various sorts of assimilation *[8.39]*.

Popular/Commercial Pueblo

Even more than its Spanish counterpart, Pueblo tended to be a regional expression, continuing to give New Mexico towns a sense of identity separate from Texas, even if often reduced only to its most obvious single feature, the exposed beam ends *[8.40]*. More elaborate—indeed the most striking single example in the country—is a complex of buildings in Taos's main square dating from the 1950s and 1960s.

Popular/Commercial French Colonial

Another example of Popular/Commercial preserving regional identities, this substyle derived directly from Academic precedents in the Acadian parishes of Louisiana *[6.34]*, mainly for self-built or locally contracted homesteads, but also often for small banks and restaurants, (for example, Landry's Seafood chain), occasionally on shops ("Le Mah Gah Ze," Erath), small government buildings, even public works (Cajun Electric, New Roads). Of course it was very common in Quebec during the Nationalist/Secessionist agitations of the 1970s and later; "Maisons du Patrimoine" popped up everywhere.

Popular/Commercial Dutch/German Colonial

As Academic Spanish persisted in Popular/Commercial form in California, Academic Pueblo in New Mexico, and Academic French in Louisiana, so Academic Dutch Colonial homesteads persisted in Popular/Commercial form in the valleys of the Hudson and the Delaware, comparably reduced to essentials, usually a gambrel roof. "Pennsylvania Dutch" is another matter. Here Popular/Commercial usage has continued the conflation of "German" and "Dutch" begun in Colonial times, combining motifs from the old Germanic settlements of Pennsylvania with such motifs popularly associated with Holland as tulips and royal Dutch blue color schemes *[8.15, 8.16]*. Much the same occurred in Popular/Commercial treatments of "German"; for example, in the "theme towns" of Mount Angel in Oregon *[8.16]* or Leavenworth in Washington, "Bavarian" and "Batavian" appear oddly intermingled.

8.41. Advertisement for New England house forms built from standardized plans—a kind of housing that can be traced in American history back to the 1840s or 1850s. (From Yankee *magazine, December 1987)*

Popular/Commercial Colonial (English)

"Colonial" in Popular/Commercial terminology almost invariably meant "English Colonial," and in usage regularly conflated forms or ornamental clichés from homestead and palatial (Palladian) substyles. Only a pedant would care to disentangle them, or note in any detail the range from bare style signs—like shutters nailed to walls, detachable plastic molded window muntin bars and cupolas, aluminum baked-paint clapboards and tiny cupolas, prefab door crestings complete with pineapple centerpiece—to superficially complete ensembles *[8.32, 8.33]*, fairly close regional forms *[8.41]*, and,

8.43 (left and above). *Exterior and interior of Carter House Bed & Breakfast Inn, built by Mark Carter in 1985 as a reproduction of the 1884 Murphy mansion in San Francisco, which was destroyed in the 1906 catastrophe. Carter worked from the original designs of its architects Samuel and Joseph C. Newsom to "faithfully recreate it on a hillside in Eureka with views of the bay and of the nearby Carson Mansion," according to Jacqueline Killeen's* Country Inns of the Far West: California. *On the interior "Mark did depart from the Victorian tradition of interior design by painting the walls a stark white and elminating the frills and clutter associated with the period." He made it "country," in other words, with "decor . . . beautifully understated . . . paintings and ceramics by local artists and baskets of flowers and potted plants strategically set about."*

8.42 (top). *Country living in a Bed and Breakfast: furnishings of a bedroom in Pearson House at Montross in northern Virginia near Stratford. The lamp has a bonnet, the eighteenth-century wing chair type has an antimacassar, the butcher Phyfe type round table has trailing lace cloth and doilies. The house itself is a foursquare, c. 1915; the furnishings were acquired regionally. (IMG:NAL)*

in furniture at least, fairly accurate replications *[8.9]*. Popular/Commercial Colonial would also include an amazing proliferation of "reproduction Colonial antiques" *[8.42, 8.43]* and magazines promoting them.[23]

Popular/Commercial East and South European, Far Eastern

Here the distinction to be made is between Late Colonial and Popular/Commercial usage, espe-

cially in sanctuary types *[8.28]*. In general, homestead and sanctuary as erected by first-generation immigrants were Late Colonial in social function and reproduced Old World details and forms as accurately as resources permitted. Popular/Commercial styles—generally concentrating on a few easily recognizable details from the original models—were employed where there was a commercial function, as for restaurants where the style advertised Italian or Greek or Japanese food, or buildings styled for tourist appeal, such as telephone booths or theaters in contemporary Chinatowns *[8.14]*.

Popular/Commercial Colonial/Classical

Occasionally it is possible to say, "This is a Popular/Commercial building and it is definitely supposed to be Greek (or Roman)—you can recognize the Orders (or something else)." Edwards Department Store in Pittsford Plaza outside Rochester, New York, has a big Greek Revival portico front (befitting the region). Or you could acquire a mobile home whose street front sports a two-columned portico in Tuscan or Doric or put on an addition with Egyptian pylon motif (featured especially at Bing Crosby's "Blue Skies" park near Palm Springs). Banks modeled on Monticello are not uncommon *[8.44]*. The form of interstate markers recognizably derives from Academic Roman shields. But such clarity of stylistic definition is, shall we say, rare. Colonial/Classical mixtures are much more the rule.

Popular/Commercial Medieval Revivals

The pointed arch is easily recognizable; buttresses with sloping ends are easy to make out of wood and tack on to side walls; even the clumsiest carpenter can whack out a few crenellations on demand. Plus, Gothic in North America was always preeminently a "churchy" style. This combination of circumstances ensured a lusty survival of Gothic in Popular/Commercial forms, for churches, for wedding chapels, for funeral homes—anywhere a "religious connotation" was required *[8.11, 8.12]*. Colored glass in pointed windows is common in Popular/Commercial Gothic; representational windows can be found on occasion (sometimes simulated in translucent plastic). Use of Gothic for nonreligious allusion practically disappeared with the demise of White Castle hamburgers *[8.35]*. Among variant medieval styles, Tudor has thrived in Popular/Commercial form. Patterns simulating its black-on-white half-timbering patterns pop up everywhere—on apartment houses, suburban dwellings, restaurants, small hotels, mobile homes *[8.13, 8.23]*. Their builders were no more bothered by what might be called shortfalls in historical authenticity than were *their* predecessors, who built mass-prefabricated suburban houses in the 1890–1930 years—perhaps because there often was some correspondence between outward patternings and the balloon framing used to construct gables with windows in them, but more likely because a house so patterned looked more like a "home" somehow. More "picturesque," if they could have put their feelings into words.

8.44. *Bardstown Road branch of the First National Bank of Louisville, built c. 1965, evokes the same icon as every five-cent piece minted in the United States since the 1930s. In such styling, small banks maintained the same great tradition of stubborn* *resistance to mandates of current high-style authorities that permitted creation of Sullivan's small banks fifty years before. (IMG:NAL)*

8.45. *"Splash-down" sports parks began appearing in the late 1970s in the Pacific Northwest. This one was built (along with tennis courts, picnic areas, etc.) in 1982 outside Spokane, in full view of I-90. Hi-tech features convey implications of efficiency, but this is no Modern substyle; its bright color scheme of diverse blues and grays is decisively Popular/Commercial. (IMG:NAL)*

Popular/Commercial Picturesque

Identifying signs for this vast category might include fairly accurate recollections of at least the basic distinguishing features of Italianate; psychedelic repaintings of High Picturesque houses and shop fronts (gables painted orange and magenta, scarlet doors and pink railings and baby blue walls); Second Empire mansards shingled in the Arts and Crafts fashion; Disneyland's artificial cityscapes; accurate reproductions of High Picturesque models *[8.43].* Here is one obvious source of Postmodern taste.

Popular/Commercial Academic

In a general sense all Popular/Commercial styles are in this category, since Popular/Commercial *is* Academic, prolonged through the era of dominant Modernism and adapted to survive it. The specific substyle referred to here is, however, the "bland" Popular/Commercial that developed around 1970 for McDonald's outlets and many other sorts of commercial uses, especially big shopping centers. Though the effect remains strongly picturesque and usage of forms and colors is ornamental, no one historicist reference dominates, and sometimes

8.46. *Illusionistic painting by Richard Haas of imaginary New York cityscape, including a Brooklyn Bridge (with the real Brooklyn Bridge appearing behind in this photo), completed 1981–82. Visually it destroys the blank wall of a Con Edison power station at South Street in lower Manhattan (Peck Slip) like a mirror wall. Among other projects Haas proposed painting a "shadow" of the Chrysler Building on walls of the World Trade Center to relieve its montony. (IMG:NAL)*

there is no effective historicist reference at all *[8.10, 8.21]*. Here is another obvious Postmodern source.

Popular/Commercial Modern

Popular/Commercial Modern is not a contradiction in terms, but a deliberate use of Modern effects (steel structure, plate glass, concrete slabs) for associative purposes, in situations where some sort of reference to mechanical efficiency seems appropriate. "Splash-Down Pool" chains in the West are good examples; the historicist reference is not to something from the past but to Modernist forms. What distinguishes the style as Popular/Commercial and not Modern proper is, in this case and most others, use of color. While the image of efficiency (and hence safety) is appropriate for a popular taste and commercial purpose, orthodox insistence that concrete must be gray or white and tubing must be metallic is not, and is therefore abandoned *[8.45]*. It looked, by 1990, as though this substyle might soon dominate the landscape; it appealed both to those who still thought that to be Modern was to be up to date, and to those who knew Modern was passé but were too timid to adopt Postmodernism unreservedly.

Popular/Commercial Representational

This substyle includes buildings of representational sculptural shapes as well as buildings that have representational paintings on their walls which change their character (for example, Richard Haas murals, as on the Con Edison Building in New York *[8.46]*). Included in this category is representational sculpture associated with buildings, since it furthers the social function of its architectural environment: yard sculpture defining the individuality of a house owner, giant sculptures promoting commercial success on roadside strips and festive atmospheres at fairs (like those giant toys featured at the 1933 Century of Progress in Chicago—coaster wagon, elephant, Tin Woodman and Scarecrow from Oz); and so forth *[8.1, 8.21, 8.25]*.

Popular/Commercial as Continuing Cultural Expression

And so, in such underground channels, a traditional architecture with historicist references continued to lead a clandestine existence through the 1950s to the 1980s. Popular culture is indeed the only visible and audible evidence for the existence of a great majority of the American population, otherwise effectively ignored both by professional literature and the media. What such a state of affairs has to tell us about the state of the nation as a whole in those years is still a field of speculative study. Popular/Commercial architecture will provide prime data.

Notes

1. What Ellen Weiss in *City in the Woods* (New York: Oxford University Press, 1987) called "American intellectuals' annoyance with the middle class" has been manifest in media at least since the late 1950s, when education at an elitist liberal college became almost a prerequisite for professional media success. It is "so consistent," she writes, "as to suggest the need for a study that might be called 'The Intellectual Against the Suburb,' a modern sequel to the Morton and Lucia White classic, *The Intellectual versus the City.*" Of course much of this represents the familiar belated American importation of old European Modernist attitudes, so well described, for example, in Erich Auerbach's chapter "Germinie Lacerteux," in Mimesis (Princeton, N.J.: Princeton University Press, 1953), pp. 434–61.

2. One of the first to recognize what had been going on was Henry A. Millon, in a symposium on architecture of the 1930s in *Journal of the Society of Architectural Historians* 24/1 (1965): 54:

> It is becoming increasingly clear, also, that in spite of their denials, the historians of the modern movement were not only chronicling the emergence of a new way of analyzing, relating, and achieving architecture, but were themselves involved as apostles of the new order. Their mission was persuasion and conversion to the new faith. . . . About architecture other than rational, as a consequence, there was a virtual information black-out, or at the very least, it was simply ignored by the official publication of the propaganda arm of the modern movement. Today we still find very little written about the 'other' architecture of the 1930s.

3. In this process four basic phases are discernible:
(1) native naive *architecture parlante* (for example, figures 8.3, 8.4); and small churches built by and for black congregations throughout the Deep South (for example, Free African Baptist of Kingsland, Georgia)—a wonderful subject, unstudied to my knowledge;
(2) roadside architecture, product of the emerging automobile culture from the 1910s onward, with a first crescendo in the 1930s (see note 9);
(3) routine and sometimes hysterical denunciations by fashionable tastemakers from the 1940s into the 1960s of whatever Popular/Commercial architecture came to their attention (classic: Peter Blake's *God's Own Junkyard*, applying to this roadside efflorescence the thesis of Tunnard and Pushkarev's *Chaos or Control*);
(4) tentative and then enthusiastic appreciation, and serious study of it (see note 4).

4. A critical factor in changing establishment attitudes was Reyner Banham's *Los Angeles: Architecture of the Four Ecologies* (Penguin, 1971), with its sympathetic perception of the social function of popular Spanish Colonial, which gave him lasting status as resident expert on vernacular among the intellectuals (not always lived up to). Admiration from establishment critics followed, most notably in Robert Venturi's *Learning from Las Vegas* and *Dimensions* by Charles Moore and Gerald Allen. A decisive event for serious study was the foundation of the Society for Commercial Archaeology in 1977, pioneered especially by Chester Liebs, who in 1985 published *Main Street to Miracle Mile.* But by that time it was one of many excellent works on Popular/Commercial architecture; between 1978 and 1987 over twenty-five titles appeared. To name only a few of the best: Philip Langdon, *Orange Roofs, Golden Arches* (1986); Karal A. Marling, *The Colossus of Roads: Myth and Symbol Along the American Highway* (1984); Phil Patton, *The Open Road* (1986); Thomas J. Schlereth, *U.S. 40: A Roadscape of the American Experience* (1985); Dell Upton and Michael Vlach, eds., *Common Places: Readings in American Architecture* (1986).

5. The basic relationship between folk, vernacular, and Popular/Commercial arts has nowhere been better explored than in Henry Glassie's essay "Folk Art" in the collection *Folklore and Folklife,* ed. Richard M. Dorson (Chicago: University of Chicago Press, 1972), p. 278.

6. *Kitsch* is a German word that seems to have been imported into the language along with such detritus of Marxism as "lackeys of the bourgeoisie" and *"lumpenproletariat."* See my "The Case for Kitsch: Popular/Commercial Arts as a Reservoir of Traditional Culture and Humane Values" in *Reading the Visible Past* (Ann Arbor, Mich.: UMI Research Press, 1990).

7. "The designers of a chain restaurant," wrote Philip Langdon in "Burgers! Shakes!" *Atlantic Monthly,* December 1985, p. 75, ". . . unlike the architect of a church, a museum, or . . . some . . . serious cultural monument, can respond wholeheartedly to the spirit of the times, without worrying about how the colors, textures, and forms will look 30 or 50 years in the future." Significantly, Langdon's study of McDonald's and competing fast-food chains is entitled *Orange Roofs, Golden Arches* (New York: Knopf, 1986).

8. At a June 1985 conference sponsored by the Division of State Parks, Hawaii, on the survival of Pacific native cultures, the point was made that it had been in Popular/Commercial forms that native traditions had been most effectively perpetuated, and that self-conscious "art in native styles" imitated the letter of older culture but lost its spirit; that is, the social function in and for Polynesian societies for and by which the distinctive art forms of those societies had been created was gone forever. Popular/Commercial perpetuations were in fact closer to the original spirit of self-awareness than gallery art could be. See my "Conserving Cultural Traditions through a Humane Modern Architecture," *Problems and Issues in Cultural Heritage Preservation: Proceedings of the first HAPI [Heritage of South Asia and the Pacific] Colloquium,* ed. Don Hibbard (Honolulu, 1986). See further, note 17.

9. The most famous single example has to be The Big Duck erected in 1931 in Riverhead on Long Island, moved in 1941 to stand in front of a restaurant featuring Long Island duckling. Legend attributes its discovery to, among others, Henry-Russell Hitchcock, author of *The International Style* and famed promoter of Modernism. Panned by Peter Blake, beloved of Venturi, Denise Scott Brown and Steven Izenour; constructed of cement spread over wire lath. Its story is told at some length in Phil Patton's *Open Road* (New York: Simon & Schuster, 1986), illustrated with commentary in Chester Liebs's *Main Street to Miracle Mile* (Boston: New York Graphic Society, 1985). The most famous collection has to be along U.S. 1 and U.S. 22 in the New Jersey part of the New York-to-Washington corridor strip, now largely in ruins or gone altogether. Michael Aaron Rockland has preserved something of their memory in "The Double Deuce," *New Jersey Magazine* (April 1978). He tells of the once famous "flagship," a battleship huge and gray with "decks, railings, portholes, even a sailor aloft, flashing signals," which became "the biggest hot dog stand in the world, then a nightclub where Frank Sinatra used to sing, now a furniture store." He describes the Leaning Tower of Pisa (= pizza), explains that the "ghoulish-looking building in Watchung shaped like a concrete casket" is "the Norwalk Vault Company, and they make concrete caskets there."

10. As one example, consider how early automobiles perpetuated the shape of buggies and carriages (vehicles for the rich and socially elevated), even down to sockets for no longer existent horses with power-plant in front despite all mechanical logic. Automobiles took their standard form in the 1930s, and they have remained unchanged in essentials for the past fifty years. When social function does not change, the forms of traditional arts (unlike Modern ones) do not change either; hence the enormous longevity of traditional art styles. The change around 1930 reflected the coming of age of a new generation for whom carriages were merely antiquated forms of transportation they had never been in, and which consequently had no prestige associations. The old form lost its social function and changed accordingly. For extended treatment of such themes, see my *Learning to See* (Bowling Green, Ohio: Popular Press, 1982).

11. As early as 1917 Jan Lavinsky in *The Origin of Property* (London, 1917) considered the detached house in sociocultural terms as "an oasis of individualism" (p. 55); outstanding among recent treatments of the theme has been Amos Rapoport, *House Form and Culture* (Englewood Cliffs, NJ, 1969), who sees the free-standing single family house functioning as a symbol in several different ways: for security, for prestige, for the ideal life, for territoriality. Other studies include Julian Cavalier, *American Castles* (New York, 1973); S. O. Clark, *The Suburban Society* (Toronto, 1966); Oscar Newman, *Defensible Space* (New York, 1973); Humphrey Carver, *Cities in the Suburbs* (Toronto, 1962).

12. "The need for ownership of territory can be traced back to pioneer days. The 'image' is still simple and clear. A tract of land with a free-standing house, a picture of the individual in his paradise, where he owns everything from

the ground to the sky" (Lars Lerup, "Suburban Residential Environments Analysis," *Ekistics* 31/183 [1971], p. 198). "The single family house set on its own piece of land, isolated from its neighbours by as little as six feet, has been the traditional expression of arrival in almost every Western culture" (Newman, *Defensible Space,* p. 34). That the house is still an extension of the owners' selves, as perceived on the banks of Alloways Creek in eighteenth-century New Jersey and in blurbs for mass-prefabricated suburban houses in the 1890–1930 decades (see Gowans, *The Comfortable House* [Cambridge, Mass.: The MIT Press, 1986], pp. 9–13, and bibliography), is affirmed by sophisticated existentialist and Gestalt theory and by behavioral psychologists (Jean-Paul Sartre, *Existential Psychoanalysis* [Chicago, 1953]; Frederick Perls, *Gestalt Therapy Verbatim* [Lafayette, Calif.: 1969]). In Jean Piaget's developmental paradigm the house "accommodates" the self; the more anyone is "at home," the more can his/her environment be defined. Thence to the theories of Christian Norberg-Schulz, *Existence, Space, and Architecture* (London, 1971, esp. pp. 11, 30).

13. A most useful but apparently overlooked contribution to this problem is the paper by P. E. Murphy and R. G. Golledge, "Comments on the Use of Attitude as a Variable in Urban Geography," Discussion Paper 25, Ohio State University Department of Geography (Columbus, 1972).

14. There have always been two basic concepts of the portable house. One has been admirably expressed in John Brinckerhoff Jackson, *Discovering the Vernacular Landscape* (New Haven: Yale University Press, 1984): "The temporary dwelling . . . has always offered, though for a brief time only, a kind of freedom we often undervalue: the freedom from burdensome emotional ties with the environment, freedom from communal responsibilities, freedom from the tyranny of the traditional home and its possessions; the freedom from belonging to a tight-knit social order; and above all, the freedom to move on to somewhere else" (pp. 100–101).

The other was expressed by Elmer Frey, writing in *Trailer Dealer Magazine* in 1953 to defend the Trailer Coach Manufacturers' Association change of name in that year to the Mobile Home Manufacturers Association: "When you see a man towing his home, why do you call it a trailer? . . . Why not call it exactly what it is—a home which is mobile, hence a MOBILE HOME."

15. On the social function of yard art, see particularly Gerald L. Pocius, "Newfoundland Yard Art," in *Flights of Fancy* (St. John's, Newfoundland: Memorial University Art Gallery, 1983), pp. 6–11; for a pioneering survey, see Fred E. H. Schroeder, *Outlaw Aesthetics* (Bowling Green, Ohio: Popular Press, 1977), chapter 6.

16. Invention of the term "categorilla" is attributed by Wilbur Zelinsky to John K. Wright and is "most briefly defined as the claim to eminence or primacy in some trivial department of human endeavor" ("Where Every Town Is Above Average," *op. cit.,* p. 8).

17. Barbara Rubin's small book *Forest Lawn* (Santa Monica, 1979) nicely describes how the living and the dead keep contact via all sorts of visits and offerings at grave sites, including tributes in Babyland, where the last interment was forty-five years ago. Ethnically, Forest Lawn is WASP; in it the attitudes of a dominant minority around 1917 have a fly-in-amber preservation. Popular/Commercial funerary arts also preserve Italian, Greek, Chinese, Polish, Ukrainian, and other traditions, either in ethnically-separated cemeteries (in Frackville, Mahanoy City, and other towns in the anthracite-mining area of Pennsylvania there are dozens) or in separate areas of existing cemeteries. Late Colonial styles here meld directly into Popular/Commercial.

18. Philip Langdon, in *Orange Roofs, Golden Arches,* attributes this change to market research on the part of the companies, using devices like tachistoscopes, which flash images on screens and record instant reactions and thus test the effectiveness of logos and designs.

19. Meredith Clausen, "Northgate Regional Shopping Center," *Journal of the Society of Architectural Historians,* 43/2 (1984):155–67.

20. See Michael Aaron Rockland, "The Rest of America may belong to the Fast-Food Chains but New Jersey is proud to be its Diner Capital," *New Jersey Magazine,* October 1977, p. 53.

21. "To make the business distinctive, I suggested that we use the name White Castle, because 'White' signifies purity and cleanliness and 'Castle' represents strength, permanence, stability [the building being in fact highly portable, made by hanging panels over a frame as in the later Alcoa Building in Pittsburgh, so that in case of dispute over rental of the land it could be transferred to another site with a more amenable landlord]. The building itself was of cement block construction, designed with battlements and a turret in keeping with the Castle idea, a style of architecture still in use." (C. W. Ingram, *All This from a 5-Cent Hamburger: The Story of the White Castle System,* Newcomen Society of New York/Downington/Princeton/Portland, 1970).

22. Langdon, *Orange Roofs, Golden Arches,* p. 27.

23. *Country Home,* published in Des Moines, Iowa, and sent to subscribers scented to smell like the sachets in old country clothes closets and chests, is one of a proliferating genre (another is *Yankee,* published in Dublin, New Hampshire) that not only appeals to deep-seated rural and small-town fantasies, but also actively brings them to pass. Such magazines both reflect and have helped create what could well be called Fantasy Farm suburbs, which came into existence during the 1970s and are now (1989) a striking new feature of the American landscape. Anywhere within fifty or sixty miles of an American city you find every road lined with fantasy farms—houses of 1950–70 suburban form set on plots of anywhere from two to ten acres, complete with sheds and barns and apple trees and plump middle-aged men riding power mowers. They have created a market for what countless highway shops advertise as "new antiques"—country rockers, quilts, pseudo-kerosene lamps. Their history and background, from Jefferson's Arcadia to Downing's *Rural Cottages* to *Green Acres* with Zsa Zsa Gabor, await study and analysis.

9.36. PPG Plaza in Pittsburgh, completed to the designs of Johnson/Burgee in 1982 as world headquarters for Pittsburgh Plate Glass Industries. Most obviously it is an echo or quote of Pittsburgh University's famous Cathedral of Learning, with a Heinz Chapel at its base [6.74]; but the details are imaginatively abstracted and set in a new context of Modern mirror walls. (Courtesy of PPG Industries)

9

NEW OPPORTUNITIES AND EXPECTATIONS: POSTMODERN STYLES, c. 1975–

Postmodern in Its Time and Place

You turn onto Fourth Avenue in the center of Portland, Oregon, and there, amid the usual core cluster of glass boxes and concrete bunkers, is the Public Service Building addition to City Hall—what a contrast [9.1]! Color and design make the building, hardly a decade old and already a famous city landmark, look much bigger than it really is: rich blues and oranges and tans instead of dirty grays and glints; insets and proportions not just subliminally but recognizably referring to monumental classicism. Centered above its entrance is a glittering copper sculpture, over life-size, likewise classical—*Portlandia,* the city emblem, gleaming like newly minted pennies. It takes some visual literacy to recognize all the influences: among others, hints of the Revolutionary Classical substyle of the early American republic in the architecture, and in the sculpture a pose from Blake's *Ancient of Days* and technique from the Statue of Liberty. But anyone can see the contrast between this building and the surrounding Modern monoliths. Anyone can see that the American landscape, ever changing, has begun to change again. But this is not a change like Modern, that began in one or two seminal places and spread outward from them. This time the landscape has seemed to change everywhere at once. Postmodern is what these new buildings are generally called. Nobody likes the name; but there is no agreement on a better one.

You would not, in earlier eras, have thought of a city so remote from the old national centers as Portland, Oregon, becoming a center for a new style. Nor Houston, Texas. Yet entering Houston's commercial downtown from the Medical Center area, you come upon a cluster of towers in fantastic shapes and colors breaking the skyline, climaxed by a soaring mass of flamed granite, ultramarine glass, and light concrete patterns, composing filigree like the creations of stonecutters and mosaicists in Hindu and Muslim India [9.2]; at the other end of the district, a rich and colorful hall immediately recalling the fabled Paris Opera [9.3]. Elsewhere in Houston you'll find an experimental tall building complex by Johnson/Burgee, suburbs rich with new Postmodern house imagery [9.27–9.29], and diversity and novelty unimagined in what not long before was dismissed as a cultural backwater. No city can be so dismissed any more. The elitist "line-of-progress" apexing in one place, time, and architectural style is gone; you find new exciting work everywhere. It's the Postmodern era.

So you may be driving in extreme southwest Virginia, going from upper to deep South, and come across what seems at first to be one of those big advertisements that used to be painted over the blank brick side walls of commercial buildings, ancestors of the billboard [9.4]. But this is no antique relic; this is a contemporary image, drawing textures and color combinations from that older material culture to create something new and of the 1980s—Postmodernism, come to Troutville, Virginia, about the same time as anywhere else!

Or you're in Moorestown, New Jersey, and come across a new fire station named, in keeping with the times, "Emergency Services Building." And it's styled in keeping with the times too—to match the gracious old Second Empire and other High Picturesque structures that line Main Street [9.5]. Its design is in response, so an article in *Architecture* magazine tells us, to a coalition of citizens voting down a bond issue to "put another concrete bunker on the Victorian Main Street."[1] Or you're in Chicago,

and find a library with furniture molded and colored and sculptural as furniture has not been since High Picturesque times *[9.6]*.

Not that you don't see new buildings in Modern styles on the landscape any more. You do, and lots of them; they win prizes, they are admired, and they are admirable. Along with Houston's Plaza and Wertham Theatre you can see the Menil Collection building in handsome Late Modern—or rather Postmodern Modern, because now Modern is self-consciously adopted, no longer the only possible high style for a new contemporary building. Its proponents can no longer dictate to everyone else. Pluralism is now acceptable, and the new landscape shows it. Postmodernism, Modernism, Popular/Commercial, they all coexist; acceptance of the right to coexist is what is new.

Nowhere is the new scope, variety, and vitality of American architecture better displayed than in the nation's capital, Washington, D.C. In place of the sleepy old Southern city that older visitors remember is an expanding metropolis taking full advan-

9.1 (above, left). "Portland Building," a.k.a. Municipal Service Building, a.k.a. Public Service Building, was begun in 1980 and completed in 1982; its design was a winning competition entry by Michael Graves. A larger than life-size statue of Portlandia *was commissioned separately from Ray Kaskey, executed by a three-dimensional pantograph, shipped from the sculptor's studio outside Washington, D.C., to Oregon by rail in six pieces, and then assembled in a Portland shipyard. "Thanks to this building," Vincent Scully wrote, "the word 'citizen' takes on a special physical credibility. In this way the building brings some not-so-old but almost forgotten American traditions to life. To that end Graves carefully studied the heart of downtown Portland as it was before it was struck by the International Style. . . . At one stroke, everything has returned, the monumental community building and its colossal figural sculpture: the human environment and the human act together"* (Michael Graves: Projects and Buildings *[New York: Rizzoli, 1982]). (IMG:NAL)*

9.2 (above, right). Heritage Plaza in Houston, as completed in 1987 by developer Wortham and Van Liew, on plans by architect Mohammad Nasr and Partners of Houston, incorporates and so preserves Houston's 1929 Federal Land Bank, which provided long-term, low-interest loans to farmers and ranchers who in the nineteenth century developed the surrounding lands. The complex stands on property purchased in 1836 by the founders of the city of Houston (who in 1858 lost it, in a sheriff's sale). (Courtesy The Webster Company, Houston)

9.3 (right). Houston's Wertham Opera Hall, designed by Eugene Aubrey of the Houston firm of Morris/Aubrey to house the Houston Grand Opera and the Houston Ballet opened in 1986, on the 150th anniversary of the city's founding. It was funded entirely by private contributions. The exterior includes a proscenium arch of vaguely Palladian derivation, deep pink granite and striated pink brick walls, and a dark burgundy steel structural system. The interior makes vague allusion to traditional opera houses, but like the exterior copies nothing in particular. The sculptural elements were designed by Albert Paley of Rochester, New York. (IMG:NAL)

9.4 (below). Distribution and office building for General Cinema Beverages, designed by Homer Daniels of Boston, in southwest Virginia south of Troutville. (Holland) (IMG:NAL)

9.5 (bottom). This view of the Moorestown Emergency Services Building shows different stylings for different elements of the complex: at left, utilitarian Modern for the garage housing firetrucks; at center, Postmodern Picturesque for the station's main front, with a high style appropriate for its role as a public building on the main street of this small town; at right, Second Empire for a town house of ca. 1870 refurbished to serve as offices. The style in each case is determined by social as well as physical function. Completed 1985, on designs of Herman Hassinger, with Gary Wagner, of Moorestown. (IMG:NAL)

9.6. *Furniture in the Conrad Sulzer Regional Library in Chicago was designed by Tannys Langdon to recall folk furniture of the Pennsylvania and Shenandoah Germans and so complement the exterior of the library, designed by Thomas Beeby of the Chicago firm of Hammond Beeby and Babka, which recalls German Renaissance style of the Berlin Arsenal (1695–1706). Completed 1986. (Courtesy of Hammond Beeby and Babka)*

9.7. *The Vietnam Veterans Memorial Fund, Inc., a nonprofit, charitable organization, was incorporated in April 1979; Congress authorized a Mall site for the monument in July 1980. Inevitably, memorializing a conflict that generated such tremendous controversy would be controversial as well. The final design solution was a compromise between those wanting an easily recognized figurative monument and those wanting a Modern expression, those who wanted to honor the brave fallen and those wishing to express guilt over a "bad war." One part of the monument, designed by Yale architecture student Maya Ying Lin in 1981, was a starkly angled trench with polished black granite walls on which were inscribed names of the fallen soldiers. Near it was added, in 1982,*

a three-man group, life-size and very literally rendered, by experienced popular sculptor Frederick Hart. By such a fusion of Modern and Popular/Commercial excellences, contact has been restored between two fundamentally different concepts of what public art and architecture involves.

Left: View of wall in winter showing its reflectivity, how visitors can make personal contact with the inscriptions, and how one arm of the wall points to the Lincoln Memorial (the other points to the Washington Memorial). (IMG:NAL, February 1982)

Right: View of the figures in the heat haze of summer. (IMG:NAL, July 1985)

tage of Postmodern design opportunities, indeed leading the way.

Nowadays most visitors come first to the Vietnam Veterans Memorial, to see a sort of monument unprecedented in the United States. It not only commemorates a lost war, and the loss of ill-advised imperial pretensions at the same time, but also accepts pluralistic attitudes toward these events. Its conception was a compromise between contending parties and concepts of public art, and the result is a monument neither Modern nor Popular/Commercial but a combination of the two, that could only be a creation of that 1980s pluralism which is one essence of the Postmodern *[9.7]*.

The whimsical, "quoting" side of Postmodern architecture abounds—in small banks composed by sophisticated arrangement of selected Colonial elements *[9.8]*; in block-long offices blending in with older settings through suitable allusion and reconstruction *[9.9, 9.10]*; in a Postmodern Canadian Chancery almost on the Mall *[9.11]*. [2]

When did all this begin to happen? Is Postmodernism traceable to some particular influence? To writings, such as Robert Venturi's *Complexity and Contradiction* or Charles Jencks's *Language of Post-Modern Architecture* or Jane Jacobs's *Life and Death of Great American Cities*? To dramatic demonstrations of the new style like Charles Moore's Piazza d'Italia

9.8 (above, left). Georgetown office of the Madison National Bank in Washington, D.C., by local firm of Isaiah Martin and David Jones, 1981. (IMG:NAL)

9.9 (above, right). Michler Place at 1777 F Street, office building designed by David Childs of Skidmore, Owings and Merrill, 1981–82, to incorporate restored and reconstructed facades from the block of twelve brick Second Empire houses developed in 1870–76 by Boss Shepherd, second governor of the District of Columbia—but so treated as to leave no doubt they are actually from the 1980s. They also match (though not exactly) mansards on the Old Executive Office Building just down the street [5.50]. SOM/Washington "turned eclectic" independently of, and long before, the firm's other offices. (IMG:NAL)

9.10 (left). 2000 Pennsylvania Avenue office building, an investment of George Washington University, incorporates some actual 1880s buildings from Red Lion Row and some with refurbished facades. Begun 1981, completed 1983, on plans by the same John Carl Warnecke who designed Hawaii's capitol in a Subliminal Classical substyle of Modern. (IMG:NAL)

in New Orleans or Philip Johnson's AT&T Building in New York *[9.12]*? But these are only two examples, and not necessarily the earliest; what about Citizen's Federal Savings and Loan in San Francisco, by Charles Moore; Laclede Town in St. Louis, by Cloethiel Woodard Smith; Guild House in Philadelphia, by Robert Venturi *[9.13]*? And what about all the innumerable parallels in Popular/Commercial architecture, long before and contemporary with these high-style ventures?[3] To disputations on priority there can be no end. Probably it's truer, and certainly simpler, to think of these and so many others as indicators of an ongoing shift in mindset rather than creators of it.

Could the semiotics of the late 1960s and 1970s have induced architects to think about buildings as sign systems within themselves? If so, it inadvertently reintroduced the possibility of buildings having some meaning outside themselves, and thereby led architects to historicist architecture by a backdoor route.

Certainly the preservation/restoration movement was influential. It had become well established in America by the 1960s[4] and played an incalculable part in saving cities from the indiscriminate

9.11. Given its physical and ideological setting, the new Canadian Chancery, begun in 1983 at the intersection of Constitution and Pennsylvania avenues, afforded opportunities for a Postmodern Classical design with a nod to Modernism across the street (I. M. Pei's East Wing of the National Gallery of Art). Instead, it is Modern (the architect's losing entry in the Portland Public Service Building competition, in fact) with a nod to Postmodernism, in the form of a few hastily added quasi-symbols of Canadian nationalism.

ruin Modernism was wreaking on them, thereby repudiating Modern attitudes toward historicist styles—a repudiation begun, interestingly enough, in Germany after 1945, when wrecked cities were rebuilt in traditional German forms to restore an older, pre-Nazi, heritage.[5]

Influential too was a continuing study of American architectural history that defied the "Bauhaus Blitz." The Colonial Revival begun in the 1890s achieved a first climax in the 1930s at Colonial Williamsburg, whose sophistication is paradoxically most apparent in Merchants' Square, in retrospect an anticipation of Postmodernist attitudes *[9.14]*.[6] But it did not cease there; despite high-style Colonial Revival being temporarily forced into Popular/Commercial forms, the scholarly research that had fueled it only accelerated. The Society of Architectural Historians was founded in the 1940s to provide a group identity independent of the College Art Association, taking special interest in American buildings[7]; by the 1970s, thanks in part to its efforts, books on American national, state, and regional architectural history were appearing by the dozens each year. This activity too involved an implicit repudiation of Modernist attitudes.[8]

But when all is said and done, Postmodernism is more than anything else a product of disenchantment with Modernism and all its works—aesthetic, intellectual, emotional. It is not just a revulsion to its physical ugliness, or even to its moral ugliness, with its associations with and expressions of crude power. First apparent in reaction to the wastelands of "urban renewal," that revulsion became focused during the Vietnam War, when the nation lost all stomach for imperial muscle-flexing and its concomitant architectural style. Circumventing Modernist dogma by Subliminal Eclectic stylings could not remain an acceptable solution forever.

For underlying everything else was a shaking—perhaps only temporary—of the intellectual premises underlying Modernism: its faith in scientific materialism as the one, the only, basis on which to build; its claim to be civilization's only alternative to kitsch; its assumption that some line of progress led ever onward and upward from caves to Corbu and the culture critics of New York. In the sense of a reaction to loss of Modernist faith, Postmodernism dates back to the 1930s, before Modernism itself had even become "establishment." The foundation for belief in science as the great and ultimate source of truth had been undermined beyond repair in the 1930s, when mathematics, queen of Modern epis-

9.12 (top, left). Model of the AT&T Corporate Headquarters, which on its appearance in 1978 constituted another dramatic announcement of a new stylistic era (much as its predecessor the Western Union had been a century before). Color and the old tripartite division of tall buildings now reappeared: clad in pinkish granite, the bulk of office space came in the thirty-seven floors above the entrance colonnade and beneath a crown with broken pediment. Most of all, eclectic ornament, described by Progressive Architecture *in 1978 as "more or less Renaissance Revival in character," reappeared, very prominently. Wrote architect Philip Johnson later, "What Post-Modernism is really doing is legitimizing eclecticism. . . . I am . . . a functionalist; but . . . also an eclectic." (Photograph by Louis Checkman, courtesy of Johnson/Burgee Architects)*

9.13 (left). Guild House, Home for the Aging, built 1961–65 to designs of Robert Venturi (Venturi and Rauch, Cope and Lippincott). The building is famed for its mix of motifs adapted from traditional Philadelphia brick row-house architecture, elements from Popular/Commercial (white painted strips and prominent lettering reminded many of supermarkets), and semiotic indicators (most notably the gold antenna on the roof, signifying the inhabitants' occupation), all on a Utilitarian Modern frame.

9.14 (top, right). The most obviously Postmodern element in Colonial Williamsburg is this "blind" wall with trompe l'oeil *roof line. It covers a scar left when a church was demolished in the late 1970s and is, according to Vice-President for Research Cary Carson, a "genuine Postmodern whimsy awaiting new construction on the site." (IMG:NAL)*

temologies, proved its inability to prove anything with certainty, and concurrently, psychology demonstrated reason's inability to function apart from emotion, the subconscious, the unconscious—that tradition, in short, can never be shaken off, but must be taken into account somehow.[9] Once scientific materialism, including Freud's, was shown to be only one of many bases for understanding life, any movement built exclusively upon it could not stand scrutiny; and indeed the word

Postmodernismo does seem first to have appeared in the 1930s.[10]

So when did the Postmodern era begin? Arbitrarily put: Postmodernism was first perceptible in the 1930s, in both positive and negative reactions against Modernism in the realm of ideas. Its earliest practical architectural manifestation was in impulses from the late 1940s on to preserve older eclectic architecture and to perpetuate it via Popular/Commercial styles. During the 1950s and

9.15. Like medieval cathedrals, shopping malls in later twentieth-century America have taken form over many decades in successive building campaigns. Often a transition can be traced in them, from Modern to Postmodern via Popular/Commercial. Thus, for example, the earliest part of the mall in the historic southern Pennsylvania town of King of Prussia, from the 1950s, is weakly Modern in style; a second Plaza section, added c. 1970 and centering on John Wanamaker's department store, shows reappearance of Main Street picturesqueness; a third, in 1981, centering on Bloomingdale's and Abraham & Straus, is Postmodern. Bloomingdale's, as designed by Hellmuth Obata and Kesselbaum, "quotes" the Crystal Palace from London's Great Exhibition of 1851. (IMG:NAL)

9.16. Print from the 1850s of the interior of the Crystal Palace that appeared as figure 107 in Siegfried Giedion's Space, Time and Architecture; *there were several other illustrations of it and a considerable discussion.*

1960s, Postmodern principles infiltrated Modernism in the form of Subliminal Eclectic substyles. And finally, Postmodernism became a self-conscious architectural movement during the 1970s.

Definition and Identifying Characteristics

Postmodernism has been defined by necessity more than anything else—the necessity of living up to its name. The implication that people who criticize Modernism are old fogies has been upended; now the old fogies are people who defended Modernism. How long could a style go on being revolutionary; how long could a "new mind-set" remain new?

Times change. Just as Moderns had once insisted we must be Modern to meet the spirit of our age, it was now argued we must be Postmodern to keep up with the times. A style that called itself "modern" in 1895—so the apologia ran—could hardly be called "modern" in 1975; our era too calls for a "style of its own." Definitions of what is or is not Postmodern flow naturally from that premise.

The most general and obvious of Postmodern characteristics is the reemergence of applied ornament, in defiance of Modern taboos. This ornament is eclectically derived, but not miscellaneous; it is usually though not infallibly recognizable by a few specific qualities and handlings: (1) use of pastel, psychedelic, or other color schemes at variance with orthodox Modern usage *[9.1, 9.2]*; (2) insistent exaggeration of elements that serve as semiotic signals, like "door" or "window," a usage particularly encouraged by the works of Robert Venturi and Denise Scott Brown, both buildings *[9.13]* and writings (especially *Learning from Las Vegas*); (3) use of applied ornament drawn from earlier styles, but with deliberate distortions to ensure that it is not mistaken for copying *[9.8]*; (4) within this ornament, preference for certain kinds of historical quotes over others. As might be expected, the preceding thirty years when Giedion's *Space, Time and Architecture* was canonical reading in architectural schools had its impact; probably it is thanks to this bible that the Crystal Palace seems so prominent among Postmodern inspirations *[9.15, 9.16]*. But a good Postmodernist always draws on diverse sources *[9.17, 9.18]*. Abstracted Palladian windows are very common (as indeed they were in prefabricated suburban houses long before; cf. 9.26). So are vaguely Greek, Tuscan, or Roman details—enough for Postmodernism at times to be tagged "the New Classicism." However, all historical styles can be found represented in Postmodernism somewhere (see "Substyles").

But most of all Postmodernism is definable by and distinguishable from Modern, Academic, or Popular/Commercial by the way its elements are put together. The rule is that elements from older styles, however transposed, whenever borrowed, must be set in relationships that can only be of *now*—that is, their own, Postmodern, period. Two factors are operative here. The first is a very conscious awareness of artifice, of architecture as art. J. Mordaunt Crook in *The Dilemma of Style* has tellingly quoted Philip Johnson to this effect: "For Mies," Johnson said,

> Beauty was Truth and Truth beauty—a thing I have always hated John Keats for, and always will, because as Nietzsche very properly replied, "Art is with us that we not perish from the truth" . . . Art is artifice, the opposite of Truth; it's innovation, it's lying, it's cheating the eye, it's subverting the psyche. That's what art is.[11]

This kind of artifice is particularly operative in integrations of new with historic buildings ("facodomy" *[9.9, 9.10]*) and in "transitional" furniture.[12] It is of course particularly suitable to furniture treatment *[8.11]* and readily distinguishes Postmodern furniture from High Picturesque or Progressive Arts and Crafts furniture with superficially similar forms *[9.19–9.21]*.

The second factor operative here, determining

9.17 (top). Llewellyn Park in West Orange, New Jersey, was one of America's first and most elegant suburbs. It was filled with Romantic houses (cf. 4.8, 4.9); in the late 1970s elegance and romance of a Postmodern sort appeared there, with Robert A. M. Stern's Pool House. This view of the pool itself shows palm-tree columns derived from the 1820s Regent's Palace and abstracted colorful versions of the stubby, simple Doric columns so admired by avant-garde Classicists of that same period (cf. 3.10). (1981 photograph © Peter Aaron/ESTO)

9.18. Figure 61 in Giedion's Space, Time and Architecture *is this print, "JOHN NASH. Royal Pavilion, Brighton. The kitchen."*

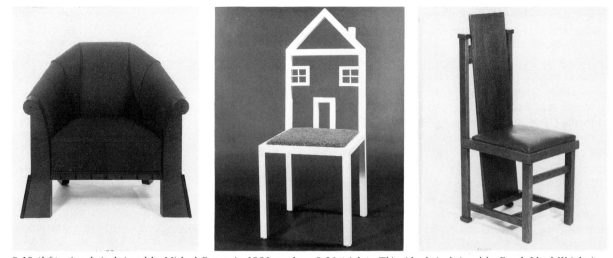

9.19 (left). Armchair designed by Michael Graves in 1981, made for SunarHauserman in 1982, combining reminiscences of the eighteenth century and Art Deco mixed with touches of Arts and Crafts and the Bauhaus to produce a new and distinctively Postmodern object. The materials also represent a distinctively new combination: pomele-burled mahogany veneer over hardwood frame; silkscreen decoration; wool, nylon, and polyester fabric. (The Brooklyn Museum,. gift of SunarHauserman)

9.20 (center). "One Family Chair" designed by Kate Loye in 1984 (this example from 1986). Though the chair looks as if it could be made from cardboard, the materials are steel tubing, electrostatic paint, and astroturf over plywood. (The Brooklyn Museum, gift of Ms. Riane Eisler)

9.21 (right). This side chair designed by Frank Lloyd Wright in 1904 has some superficial resemblances to Postmodernism, in that its daring juxtaposition of shapes breaks with conventional furniture of its period and suggests the personal style of an artist. It also relates to Modern in its concern for physical function above comfort. But the materials are oak and leather—nonindustrial, so non-Modern, and ultimately deriving from romantic Arts and Crafts recollections of the Middle Ages via Morris and Ruskin. The honest expression of structure and consistent use of materials has no trace of Postmodern whimsy or artifice. In the Wrightian circle, only Bruce Goff was an artist of the Postmodern kind. (The Brooklyn Museum)

how eclectic elements would be arranged in Postmodernism, is the doctrine of *Zeitgeist.* Because Postmodernism was the idea that "each era must have its own style" to justify breaking with a Modernism that had outlived its own time, it is stuck with the necessity of avoiding any suggestion of reviving a past style, as Academics had; otherwise its rationale would collapse, and it would become simply a reaction, a reversion to nineteenth-century historicism. Whence an apparent contradiction with the great defiance of Modernism that reintroduction of applied eclectic ornament seemed to represent. You can borrow ornament from the past, you can borrow stylistic forms from the past, but you must not use them in combinations used in the past. You must always emphasize your own distinctiveness. The result often looks like whimsy or eccentricity, and often is; but it proceeds naturally from the premises.

Put another way: Modernism was governed by an overriding conviction that in scientific materialism lay all the answers to design (not to mention social) problems. From this it derived two cardinal rules: no applied ornament, because literary allusions and emotional associations are not justifiable by objective—that is, scientific—analysis; and strict observance of *Zeitgeist,* it being understood that there is only one true spirit in any age, and ours is the spirit of scientific materialism. Postmodernism broke decisively with the first rule, but not with the second.

The variety of applied ornament reintroduced by Postmodernism, then, is neither result nor expression of any conviction that an era could have more than one kind of spirit. Neither are its different sorts of eclectic forms necessarily associated with any variety of social functions. Rather, Postmodernism's diverse and inventive ornament expresses a pluralism resulting from increased, ever-exaggerated emphasis on that equality which in Modernism had been only a pious formula. One big factor in the changed attitude was the upheavals of the 1960s, which emphasized minority rights of all sorts. Feminism especially played an important part in developing Postmodern pluralism, as it correctly identified the elitist assumptions behind Modernism's egalitarian facade, focused on accomplishments of women in the Modern movement that had gone largely unacknowledged, and insisted on women's rights to a larger part in the architecture profession generally.[13]

In sum, Postmodern is distinguishable from Academic by its insistence on making clear the differences between past and present. Any and all suggestions of "reviving" some past style, of "getting into the shoes" of a designer from some past era and recreating its spirit, as did Bernard Maybeck or Julia Morgan, is contrary to the guiding Postmodern principle of *Zeitgeist,* of being always in the spirit of your own time and no other. Whence in general the qualities that distinguish Postmodern from Academic styles: juxtapositions of ornament in bizarre combinations, self-consciously declamatory "quotations" from earlier styles of ornament, ostentatious separation of "real restored" from "artificially recreated" parts of buildings that involve any degree of reconstruction.

Arbitrary combinations of forms and details also separate Postmodern from Popular/Commercial. Postmodernists have taken from Popular/Commercial many formalistic elements—its colors, its contradictory complications, its lightness (or, if you prefer, its thin, abstract, pasteboardy effects and general flatness; its penchant for shapes cut out of flat surfaces or whimsically indented). But they have not taken over or even barely acknowledged its overtly commercial functions. They reject as resolutely as any Modern the whole idea of forms dictated by sales appeal—that is, appeal to sentimental associative values. What they borrow is dictated by their persistence in seeing Popular/Commercial not as an appropriate response to a particular social need, but as a kind of failed version of high serious architecture, a lode of details that can be mined for light-hearted or whimsical ornament on serious architecture, or for identificatory deviations from Academic norms.

Further, Postmodernism is distinguishable from Popular/Commercial by attitudes of self-consciously artistic creation that contrast markedly to the anonymity of all who designed the Popular/Commercial world.[14] For Postmodernists, indeed, anonymity is a horror. They thrive on publicity, especially publicity identifying them as creators of Works of Art. Philip Johnson appeared on the cover of *Time* magazine cradling a model of the AT&T

Building, like some medieval master builder with a cathedral model under his arm (though his cloak looked more Wrightian than medieval, an appropriately Postmodern juxtaposition). Scott Johnson appeared in a similar pose on the cover of *Pacific Southwest Airlines Magazine* in fancy suit, viewed from below, with his Fox Plaza rising behind; an interview explained how he thought of his architecture in terms of light and space art, like James Turrell's *[9.22].*

More than any preceding styles, Postmodernism has been conceived in terms of works of art. This

9.22. The thirty-four gray-tinted glass and salmon pink granite stories of Fox Plaza, corporate headquarters of Twentieth Century Fox, were completed in January 1987 to designs of Scott Johnson of Johnson Fain and Pereira, successor firm to Pereira and Associates. Standing alone in a low-rise area, it invites contemplation as a work of architectural art and thereby comparison with William Pereira's TransAmerica Building in San Francisco of a dozen years before, one of a cluster of tall buildings jostling for preeminence as demonstrations of technological power [7.14]. The building displays the conscious effort to establish historic continuity with the architectural environment through visual recollections of Los Angeles "Moderne." (Courtesy of Johnson Fain and Pereira Associates)

9.23. *"The Artist Surrounded by His Creation," a favorite theme in avant-garde painting since Courbet and in semiotic art criticism since the 1960s, appears now in Postmodern architecture: Frank O. Gehry of Santa Monica outside his Cardboard House of 1980; Experimental Edges Chaise Lounge is in foreground, Lead Fish exterior in background. These installed designs from a 1986–88 traveling exhibition recall various Gehry works: a thick-walled corrugated cardboard construction recalls the Ron Davis house (and holds a selection of cardboard furniture, which John Pastier [*Architecture,* November 1986] called "a poker-faced transformation of a typical modern-art museum display of high-pedigree design products for upscale consumers"); a colonnade of "vigorously skewed plywood prisms" recalls the entrance to an office building by Gehry in Venice, California. (Photograph courtesy of Walker Art Center and Frank O. Gehry Associates)*

characteristic is perhaps most obvious in furniture; all aspiring architects now produce furniture intended to be perceived primarily as works of art *[9.23].*[15] But it is also apparent in a new concept of architectural drawings produced for sale and collection, like paintings. For the first time in history, specialized galleries are devoted to the exhibition and sale of sketches, elevations, presentation drawings, and plans that make no practical distinctions between works executed and unexecuted or even between commissioned projects, competition pieces, and works made with no thought whatever of translation into built form.[16]

All such developments proceed from roots deep in historic Western culture. The idea of a work of art severed from social function goes back as far as the Renaissance, originating first with music in late-sixteenth-century Venice, perhaps. The idea of Architect as Creative Genius is also not new—Andrea Palladio, *né* stonemason Andrea di Pietro, had himself borne about by flunkies on a ceremonial litter. But it is from Modernism that Postmodernists chiefly have derived these attitudes: from the notion of Men as Gods that underlay it, formulated by the likes of H. G. Wells, believed to be manifest in the inspired creativity of painters basing their work on science, from Impressionist physics of light to Surrealist psychology to the *Gestalt* of Abstract Expressionism. From Modernism too they have learned how to attract and manipulate media by

gimmickry, and a weakness for semiotics. Perhaps that is why predictions of the imminent demise of Postmodernism have always been so rife. But Postmodernism has abandoned the more arcane aspects of Modern semiotics, partly because of their absurdity—by the late 1970s architectural semiotics had become reminiscent of nothing so much as Late Scholasticism in the waning Middle Ages[17]— but mainly because of an increasingly different concept of social function.

Social Function

Charles Jencks, who has done as much as anyone to make Postmodernism a reality, wrote in 1987:

> After more than twenty years the Post-Modern movement has achieved a revolution in Western culture without breaking anything more than a few eggheads. It has successfully challenged the reign of Modern art and architecture, it has put Positivism and other twentieth-century philosophies in their rightfully narrow place, brought back enjoyable modes in literature without becoming populist, and slowed, if not halted altogether, the wanton destruction of cities.[18]

Two basic goals are recognizable here: first to change the concept of what architecture is; then, with this new definition, to change what architecture does or should do in and for society.

Postmodernism's first goal was to make architecture once again an art shaped by all sorts of human needs—mental, emotional, psychological, as well as physical—rather than by its own materials and processes. Architecture was to be no longer a master, but a servant. Architecture was to be no longer a self-referential art whose critics addressed only each other, whose practitioners spoke only in oracles, and whose public existed, like the public in Courbet's *Studio* and *Bonjour Monsieur Courbet,* only to render homage to the Great Artist. Now the two worlds of architectural criticism and user feedback, so long estranged, were to recognize each other's existence once again.

An architecture so conceived could have humanizing functions in and for society, which was impossible as long as architecture was so equated with technology that palaces presented design problems identical to bridges and architectural history in consequence denied all practical significance.[19] An architecture so conceived could become an agent to make cities more livable, through variety, scale, color, and ornament proportioned to life and reestablishing a continuum with the past. Admittedly, Postmodernism has, of this writing, not fully achieved all these goals. Artistic self-consciousness has all too often been excessively pursued. Nevertheless, Postmodernism has functioned more like a traditional art in the service of civilization than like Modernism bound to its own rules, and to that extent its eclecticism, eccentric as it may be, is praiseworthy:

> To abstract the mind from all local emotion [as orthodox Modernism tried to do] would be impossible, if it were endeavoured, and would be foolish, if it were possible. Whatever withdraws us from the power of our senses, whatever makes the past, the distant, or the future, predominate over the present, advances us in the dignity of thinking beings. [Samuel Johnson on Iona, *Journey to the Western Islands of Scotland,* 1775]

Most of all, an architecture so conceived could promote pluralism in society. Its perception of history not as a line of progress culminating at one point, but as an ongoing process of self-realization for more and more people, made it both instrument and expression of the principle that there is not just one way of doing, one way of perceiving, one way of voicing the realities of the human condition. Free choice once again became an element in architectural composition. Postmodernism has thus functioned to bring American architecture more in line with the pluralistic realities of American life, to make it part of the "Age of Discovery" apparent in so many other fields.[20] This social function deter-

mined the style's application to architectural types, and its substyles.

Application of Postmodern Style to Architectural Types

In theory, given its dedication to pluralism, Postmodern styling should be indiscriminately applicable. In theory, reintroduction of eclectic styles should have made it possible to create genuine visual metaphors in all types, of a more sophisticated sort than was possible in Academic styles. In practice, this has happened only sporadically. In practice, Postmodern has been like every other style, more applicable to some types than to others.

Thus Postmodern's most dramatic successes have been with commercial building types. Tall office buildings—no longer mighty power symbols but instead eye-catchingly silhouetted and picturesquely color patterned—both new and in tandem with restoration/preservation projects, have added immeasurably to the humanization of American cities *[9.1, 9.2, 9.9, 9.10, 9.12].* Postmodern styles have also melded easily with Popular/Commercial in banks and comparable smaller commer-

9.24. *Steven Izenour designed this summer place in 1985–86 for George and Hildegard Izenour on Thimble Island Road on the Connecticut coast at Stony Creek, overlooking Long Island Sound. Historical references and quotes include a granite base recalling pier for Stony Creek Granite Company once operative here (it supplied granite for the base of the Statute of Liberty), the patterned shingles recalling oyster sheds once here also; and a big wheel referring to nautical industry on Connecticut shore generally. (IMG:NAL)*

9.25. *Postmodern versions of Second Empire style roofs at the Willard International Hotel, Washington, D.C., are carefully distinguished from the originals by slight differences in shape, introduction of oriel windows, abstraction and lighter color schemes for supporting details. Multiplication gives a sense of richness and luxury compatible with but not imitating the famous landmark designed by Henry Hardenbergh in 1901 to replace the original of 1818, remodeled in 1850, where Grant, Lincoln, and other notables stayed. Renovation and addition of office complex was carried out 1984–86 on designs by Hardy Holtzman Pfeiffer of New York, with design modifications by Vlastomil Koubek. (IMG:NAL)*

9.26. *General view of Franklin Court, part of Independence National Historical Park in Philadelphia. Begun in 1973 and completed 1976 by David Vaughan and John Milner of Venturi, Rauch and Scott Brown, the monument consists of a ghostlike outline of Benjamin Franklin's long-vanished house, set in a garden space enclosed by five restored houses on Market Street, with access and exhibition space below ground. It makes an interesting contrast to a nearby 1971 monument to Franklin by Reginald E. Bauchamp, an oversized bust made of pennies contributed by children in honor of the one hundredth anniversary of the Philadelphia Fire Department, which tries to convey an idea of "great man." The Venturi firm's monument is conceived differently. Perhaps because Postmodern is characteristically erudite, and recent erudition has revealed a Franklin with rather more than his share of human foibles and frailties, it emphasizes the aspect of archaeological and biographical discovery, plus public amenity. (Photograph Copyright Mark Cohn, courtesy of Venturi, Rauch, and Scott Brown)*

cial buildings *[9.8]*, with Utilitarian Modern in bigger ones *[9.15]*. All sorts of shelter types, from factories to municipal bus stops, have also been effectively humanized by Postmodern stylings *[9.4]*, as have many sorts of public works (such as Portland's MAX transit stations). Postmodernism's light touch is admirably suited for most forms of theater *[9.3]* and for summer homes *[9.24]*.

Postmodern has also been able to provide a lavishness appropriate to mansions *[9.17]* and hotels,

melding easily as required with that High Picturesque that made America's first big hotels so world renowned *[9.25]*.

For other types, limitations have been apparent. Postmodernism's characteristic whimsicality of detail and pastel color preferences are ill-suited to evoke either awe or decorum, hence various Subliminal Eclectic substyles of Modern continue to work better for sanctuaries. The same is true for small-scaled palace (government) types, for which

9.27. Postmodern town houses recalling mass-prefabricated suburban houses of the 1890–1930 years often have pleasing continuities of past with present. This is William F. Stern's Wroxton Street Residences in the West University district of Houston of 1985–86. (Another fine example is Arvid Elness's Harriet Square of c. 1986 in Minneapolis, which simulates a street of homestead temple-house forms.) Such designs require great architectural skill, because however similar the forms, in social function such buildings are quite different from their models. The older suburban houses were set on good-sized lots with garages (if any) put separately behind or beside; their purpose was to provide space for raising families. Living in typical Postmodern town houses, by contrast, are working couples with two cars, so each unit needs a two-car garage, built in for protection, occupying a large proportion of otherwise potential living space. (Photograph by Paul Hester, courtesy of William F. Stern Associates)

9.28. Interior designs of Wroxton town houses owe a good deal to the famous 1963 house in Chestnut Hill designed by Robert Venturi for his mother; that too was not intended for family living, shown by its abstract white-walled forms, deriving from Corbusier's Pessac and Palais de l'Esprit Nouveau inspirations, which turn the houses into little museums. "No children live here" is the message; instead, it is inhabited by members of the "aging children" generation, lovers of the Good Things in Life: antiques old and new, Americana genuine and reproduction. (Photograph by Paul Hester, courtesy of William F. Stern Associates)

Postmodernism works well *[9.5]*, but on a larger scale the requisite weight is hard to reconcile with its basic qualities *[9.11]*, the Portland Municipal Building's great success notwithstanding. Indeed it was the trimming of Graves's original design for budgetary reasons, which led to the elimination of its more frivolous details, that gave that building the dignity requisite for such types. A similar sort of serendipity made the Vietnam Veterans Memorial effective; Postmodernism alone rarely succceds

in creating those effects of reverence, awe, and inspiration requisite for monument types and so evidently operative on visitors here. Much more within Postmodernism's effective range are the kind of light-hearted, whimsical recollections of the past evoked by Venturi, Rauch and Scott Brown's Franklin Court in Philadelphia or Western Plaza in Washington; the serious thoughts they raise are about the nature and social function of arts in public places *[9.26]*.

9.29. "Richard Meier's Framework for the Decorative Arts" is how an Architectural Digest *article (41 [1984]: 126–33) describes the 1983 High Museum in Atlanta. Here the Postmodern version of Hi-Tech Modern (less hard, less harsh, rounded edges and curiously rubbery effect reveal that this is not* echt *Modernismus, but the building's guts still hang out) is effectively used to insist that the objects from the Virginia Carroll Crawford Collection of American furniture and decorative objects are to be seen not as historical documents, but as Works of Art—which the building certifies as such. (Photograph by Ezra Stoller, © ESTO; courtesy of High Museum of Art, Atlanta)*

Application of Postmodern styles to the homestead type is of special interest as a reflection of shifting economic trends in the later 1970s and 1980s, to some degree at least in reaction to insistent efforts to legislate social equality. Despite, or because of them, single-family homesteads on a new, very grand scale have become common—quasi-mansions, really, designed in Postmodern versions of French châteaux and Virginia plantations. Concomitantly the older sort of modest middle-class mass-produced homestead on its lot has become steadily rarer in urban areas, because of steeply rising land costs. In its place have come rows of contiguous town houses, requiring less land

per unit, yet still affordable, as often as not, only by couples with two incomes; Postmodernist designs for them often recall the older mass-produced suburban "comfortable houses" with nostalgia *[9.27, 9.28]*.[21]

For buildings associated with the theory or practice of science itself, Hi-Tech Modern substyle has persisted, seeming more natural than any Postmodern alternative. That includes a good many tall buildings, as well as research institutes like Intelsat or collegiate science buildings. It also includes art galleries. Postmodernism's touch has been too light for the solemn business of certification and sanctification of artifacts as Works of Art; that is evident from the positive reception accorded Richard Meier's High Museum at Atlanta *[9.29]* or his new wing for the Getty, compared with generally negative reactions to the Postmodern style of James Stirling's Sackler Museum at Harvard *[9.30]*.

For effects of stability, permanence, or reliability demanded by the social function of fort subtypes—jail, police station, wall, fence, or Public Works—some form of Modern seems to work best: either the Hi-Tech substyle, or a close Postmodern variant of it. A strikingly successful example is the United Terminal walkways in O'Hare by Helmut Jahn *[9.31]*.

Substyles

Postmodern practice encourages deliberate elusiveness, pluralism, and a use of ornament as visual embellishment not altogether removed from the kind of indiscriminate ornamentation that brought Picturesque styles into disrepute and encouraged early Modernism. Nevertheless, substyles are discernible here as in every other style, especially when Postmodernist design has been applied to preservation and restoration projects that "conform to the character" of neighborhoods or regions.

Proto-Postmodernism

All sorts of stylings from the 1940s onward are in retrospect recognizable as anticipating Postmodern, which at the time seemed merely eccentric. There are a great number in the monument category especially, because Modern was so ideologically inhibited from recalling the past. One example is the Pearl Harbor Memorial in Honolulu, which utilizes the half-sunk battleship *Arizona*. It is not Popular/Commercial because not commercial; not

9.30. A principal declared function of Postmodern design, to create buildings compatible with their environment, is achieved brilliantly in the 1984–85 Arthur M. Sackler Museum at Harvard University. The messages encoded in James Stirling's design correspond to the dominant social mode of the Cambridge academic community from the 1960s on: here is an architectural metaphor of radical chic, of the soft semiotic sort of Marxism that proclaimed academics, proletarians, and street people sisters under the skin. The evocation of old British industrial building in the Midlands produces a sort of architectural equivalent to fur-lined blue jeans. How well it suits the functions of a university art museum is another matter, of course. (IMG:NAL)

exactly Populist, since commissioned from above by the government; not Modern either because it is an actual object preserved for romantic and historical associations. In fact, it anticipates Postmodern habits, both of "quoting" bits from the past and dramatically juxtaposing artifacts with architecture.

Another sort of anticipation of Postmodern occurred in connection with restoration projects, often very early; the mall at Colonial Williamsburg is a classic example.

Early premonitions of Postmodernism can be recognized in the work of "eccentrics" coming out of the Academic Arts and Crafts traditions; Bruce Goff in Oklahoma is the best known. They persistently broke rules, both Academic and Modern, for emotive effect, though without much if any semiotic concern; a well-known Postmodern representative of this kind of artist is Frank O. Gehry *[9.23]*, and it was entirely appropriate that Gehry should have provided an introduction to David DeLong's *Bruce Goff: Towards Absolute Architecture* (New York: Architectural History Foundation, 1988).

Postmodern Colonial

By its nature and definition Postmodern does not use any past style with archaeological or scholarly accuracy, for fear of confusion with a revival and contradicting the *Zeitgeist*. But often you find elements fairly consistently drawn from given past styles and substyles, rearranged in distinctively late-twentieth-century combinations. Thus designs by Bart Prince of Albuquerque show his debt not only to Bruce Goff but obviously to Colonial Span-

9.31. Walkways in the new (completed 1987 by Helmut Jahn and others) United Airlines terminal at O'Hare airport in Chicago provide a typically Postmodern combination. Their Postmodern version of Hi-Tech Modern conveys the idea of scientific efficiency, but running bands of neon also create the effect of a kind of art of light in which travelers are involved as performers. Jahn's airport station for the Chicago Rapid Transit employs similar effective styling. (Courtesy of United Airlines)

ish and Pueblo. At LaClede Town in St. Louis, Clothiel Woodard Smith combined elements from several Colonial homestead substyles. For their Madison National Bank in Georgetown, Isaiah Martin and David Jones rearranged elements picked fairly consistently from Palladian Georgian *[9.8]*. Palladianism has provided the most consistently used single motif in Postmodernism (for example, 9.27). Designers of Postmodern furniture, especially on a wholesale basis, often make very similar unique combinations *[9.32]*. Every variant of New England Colonial substyles has been echoed in Postmodern summer houses and permanent homes along the coasts of the region *[9.24]*, and other regions are comparably represented. Also Postmodern has been able to provide identity for all sorts of ethnic groups in the United States, just as Later Colonial proper, and Academic and Popular/Commercial Colonial, did in their time.

Postmodern Classical

Those who see "Postmodernism" and "New Classicism" as nearly interchangeable terms generally ex-

9.32. The television cabinet in a guest room of Richmond's refurbished Jefferson Hotel, opened 1986 (original hotel opened 1895). Hochheiser-Elias Design Group of New York produced for the occasion a combination of various eighteenth-century elements (chest of drawers, secretary, vaguely ogee-arched cabinet doors) in a late-twentieth-century, Postmodern setting. (IMG:NAL)

tended "Classical" to include everything from eighteenth-century through Greek and Roman Revivals to Italianate and Beaux-Arts. But in practice "Classical" tended to be more specifically defined. The phase of Classical Revival represented by its Revolutionary Democratic substyle had the greatest appeal for early Postmodernists. Though long ago faded from popular favor and never reaching vernacular levels, its memory had been revived by Modern historians, with their admiration for abstract cubistic forms. By the mid-1980s Johnson/Burgee were reproducing LeDoux's paradigm for an education building in his ideal city of Chaux almost verbatim for an education building at the University of Houston; Leon Krier made a considerable reputation ringing whimsical changes on Schinkel's heroic German Romantic classicism *[9.33]*.

Americans generally were more comfortable with the Palladian brand of early classicism espoused by Jefferson; Robert Stern gave a fine demonstration of how to do it right at the University of Virginia *[9.34]*.

For more monumental Academic Classicism, there was admiration throughout the Modern era too. As early as 1962 Philip Johnson was among the picketers protesting demolition of Pennsylvania Station. The Museum of Modern Art's 1976 exhibition on the Ecole des Beaux-Arts was a landmark in the shift away from orthodox Modernism. By the mid-1980s architects could order prefabricated classical columns from several sources: the Hartmann-Saunders Company, for instance, offered Corinthian, Doric, Tuscan, Ionic, or all four, in heart redwood with fiberglass capitals, bases, and plinths. But chances to employ the visual power of classical orders were few, because commissions for the kind of major government buildings where it could be displayed were limited; the Canadian Chancery was a unique opportunity *[9.11]*.

Postmodern Italianate

Twentieth-century Italian architecture always resisted the extremes of CIAM French and German Modernism. The country had known enough about military conquests not to invite a cultural one. And it was secure enough in its cultural heritage that Fascism and its concomitant stripped-down classicism never seemed as reprehensible in Italy, where it had been a fact, as in the United States, where it had been made so terrifying a bogy. Therefore Italian postwar architecture, abstract yet retaining recognizable shapes like arches, pilasters, and vaults, infused furthermore with semiotic overtones via De Chirico and the old Futurists, became during the 1970s a natural focus for discontent with Modernism. Italian furniture and industrial design exerted a continuing influence.[22] It is no accident that among Postmodernism's most notable American successes is the Piazza d'Italia in New Orleans, built 1976–79 by Charles Moore and Perez & Associates on commission from an Italian community wishing to reinforce its cultural identity *[9.35];* nor that the single event that most firmly "established" Postmodernism was the architecture section of the 1980 Venice Biennale, organized by Paolo Portoghesi and called "The Presence of the Past."[23]

But these were learned *jeux d'esprit.* Workaday Postmodernism picked up more on that Italianate which had been for so long in the nineteenth century the country's single most popular Picturesque substyle (see chapter 5). Round-arched windows and arcades, squarish towers, and pyramidal roofs proliferated. This "New Tuscanism" was more colorful than the old "Tuscan or American" style (as

9.33. Model for a building by Leon Krier in the town of Seaside, Florida, a suburb planned by Andres Duany and Elizabeth Plater-Zyberk in "stripped classical style," where visions of the American past by European typologists were to be assembled. It is based on the kind of piled-up intersecting temples Karl Friedrich Schinkel sketched for the 1818–21 Berlin Schauspielhaus, but with early American Greek Revival naiveté of scale, attached pilasters, and shingle-style walls. (Courtesy Leon Krier)

9.34. Robert A. M. Stern's design for Observatory Hall Dining Room at the University of Virginia of 1982–84 (remodeling of an older and smaller Modern building on this famous campus) naturally invites comparison with Academic additions in the 1890s by McKim, Mead and White—the Rotunda at one end of the Lawn, Cabell Hall at the other (cf. 3.47, 3.48). The comparison *comes out very much in Stern's favor, for he kept the scale of the Lawn buildings, did not attempt to produce something more archaeologically correct, and used motifs from Jeffersonian architecture to produce a new combination expressing late-twentieth-century perceptions. (Photograph by Whitney Cox, courtesy of R. A. M. Stern Associates)*

Downing had called it)—witness Thomas Gordon Smith's Tuscan houses "in the spirit of Pliny's villa" at Livermore, California (1971) or Thomas Hall Beeby's "House of Virgil to be built in anticipation of a return of the Golden Age to Midwestern U.S." But there was an unmistakable resemblance. Romanticism, overt and covert, was the link.

Postmodern Gothic and Picturesque

The old Gothic Revival had considerable appeal for certain kinds of Postmodernists, not for its religious associations, of course, but for its air of eccentricity (conveyed by a certain thin artificiality of form) and especially its romantic picturesqueness. Postmodern Gothic is in essence a substyle of Picturesque, just as Gothic had become in the 1870s and 1880s, and has been so used, even when primarily motivated by quotes and echoes from the past, as by Philip Johnson in both the Pittsburgh Plate Glass building *[9.36, on p. 348]* and in the Republic Bank of Houston. The romantic side of picturesqueness, fueled by the enormous success and appeal of Dis-

neyland, produced a comparable series of small-scaled villas, often in otherwise incompatible settings *[9.37].*

In their times the old Picturesque styles had expressed that exuberant commercialism which was such a basic quality in American civilization. Suppressed by the austerities of orthodox Modernism, that quality now burst out again and was luxuriantly manifest on the streetscapes of all American cities by the later 1980s. Turrets, flags, varicolored textures and wall patternings, ornament of all sorts, burst out uproariously, on every architectural type from skyscrapers to parking garages *[9.38; cf. 9.2, 9.9, 9.10].* It was almost as if things were picking up where Louis Sullivan had left off, and to much Postmodern Picturesque you could apply Robert Twombley's apt description of Sullivan's basic principles:

> However reductionist his approach may have been, it left ample room for architectural flourish. . . . unlike "modernism" later on, it did not reject history. Sullivan was no historicist, no dutiful copier or adapter of

9.35. One of the most dramatic announcements of Postmodernism was the Piazza d'Italia in New Orleans, built 1976–79 to designs of Charles Moore, with Allen Eskew and Malcolm Heard, Jr., of Perez and Associates and Ron Filson. According to Jencks's Language of Post-Modern Architecture *its intent was to "reinforce the urban fabric while changing its meaning." That refers, apparently, to the way a Postmodern design like this is set off from a comparable Popular/Commercial work like Pietro's Gold Coast Pizza Parlor in Salem [8.14]: Popular/Commercial elements and colors are handled to recall the cross section of an architectural drawing, thereby proclaiming its primacy as a Work of Art. (Courtesy of Charles W. Moore)*

9.37. The Robert Leefeldt house stands at the head of Mathews Drive in Chico, a California university town whose principal historic building, the Bidwell mansion of 1865–67, it "quotes." Its grounds recall, without reviving, a High Picturesque villa and are better appreciated from them, perhaps, than from the long street of suburban houses in 1960s and 1970s versions of Popular/Commercial Spanish Colonial. Designed by Robert Leefeldt of Piedmont, California. (IMG:NAL)

ancient styles. But . . . he did not disguise his architectural references. . . . Like all artists, Sullivan borrowed ideas, feelings, even actual fragments, to work into new syntheses.[24]

Late Modern: The Postmodern Version of Modern

Modern in the 1980s was practiced in a way inconceivable in the 1950s, because of the kind of self-conscious analysis and delicate distinctions that had grown up in the intervening decades.[25] Such Late or Postmodern Modern, chosen with deliberate conviction, for specific purposes, has often produced highly satisfying prize-winning works *[9.29, 9.31]*.

Postmodern Popular/Commercial

The 1980s brought a quite new self-conscious use of Modernism for purposes of commercial appeal. At one end of the scale this produced a sort of prole chic, popular especially in regions where cultural

lag meant that "modern" was still equated with "up to date" and "efficient" and so some vulgarized version of Hi-Tech was supposed to have customer appeal. At the other, it tacked onto otherwise nondescript buildings that in another era might have been called "Modern utilitarian" a few highly conspicuous elements that looked vaguely to be in the new fashion (Palladian windows outlined in neon, for example). This is one point where Postmodern melts into Popular/Commercial. It happened as well at another, opposite pole, where Popular/Commercial reproduction melted into Postmodern conscious recombinations. The distinction also blurred at or below a perceptible social level.

All this—the pluralism of Postmodernism proper, plus the survival of Popular/Commercial and Modern in some respects on their own, added up to a cultural expression new in one way, yet in another inherent in the very essence of the American republic.

9.38. New headquarters for the old Cincinnati firm of Procter & Gamble was designed by the firm of Kohn Pedersen Fox and built 1982–85. In it something of the spacious feeling of old Classical Revival Cincinnati can be detected [3.1] as well as diverse references to surviving historic architecture. The design thereby constitutes a visual metaphor of the opening statement in its descriptive brochure: "For nearly 150 years since the founding of Procter & Gamble its heart and its headquarters have found a home in Cincinnati. Together, both the City and the Company have prospered. The Tower Building addition to our General Offices complex is testimony to our ongoing commitment . . . to the city."

Postmodernism as Continuing Cultural Expression

Many are the theories purporting to explain social or cultural or intellectual factors contributing to Postmodernism's appearance and/or to its early demise. Its appearance has been attributed to a breakdown of faith—the utopia promised by science has failed to arrive, therefore nothing can be taken seriously any longer; our spiritual insecurities are expressed in a "flimsiness" in 1980s architecture. Or we know too much to take anything seriously any longer; theories believed today will be disproved tomorrow; the whole world will be deconstructed and prove as evanescent as the cat that ate its own tail.

But there never has been an age without insecuri-

ties; that indeed is one reason why religious faiths arise and endure all disillusionments. Nor is a joking, whimsical attitude to life anything new, especially in America. It has in fact always been a particularly distinctive feature of American civilization—necessary for its workings, even. In the 1840s and 1850s, Page Smith wrote in *The Nation Comes of Age:*

All people knew . . . in at least one part of their consciousness, that American politics was a vast, immeasurable humbug, a swindle on a gigantic scale. And yet, seen in another perspective, it was the means of survival, the only hope of the republic, the shield against an always threatening chaos, the only game in town. Perhaps humbug was the antidote to tragedy. Moreover, humbuggery had in it a measure of self-mockery, while it was commonly free of any corrosive sense of shame. . . .

In other countries people tried to save face. In America letting the laugh be on you showed you were a good democrat.[26]

Still in the 1980s the President of the United States carried on this tradition; according to the *Washington Post* for 30 March 1987, President Reagan began Washington's annual Gridiron Club dinner, where leading figures were invited to make jokes at their own expense, with the following remarks:

"With the Iran thing [controversy over clandestine arms sales to Iran] occupying everyone's attention, I was thinking: Do you remember the flap when I said, 'We begin bombing in five minutes?' Remember when I fell asleep during my audience with the pope? Remember Bitburg? . . . Boy, those were the good old days." The audience loved it. Reality, in fact, gave the evening its best lines.

As these passages reveal, whimsicality can and often does serve a deep purpose in American life— among other things, serving to equalize in some deep way governors with the governed. Postmodernism's whimsy and self-deprecation likewise serves an equalizing purpose: it promotes pluralism. Overt, dedicated pluralism is what constitutes the novelty of Postmodernism in American cultural history. Not, of course, that pluralism was something new in American society; obviously it is inherent in the nation's institutions. What is new is its conscious and deliberate architectural expression.

In Frank Lloyd Wright's battle with Modernism's simplistic line-of-progress to itself as the end and meaning of history, he was once driven to exclaim, "Nothing, to my mind, could be a worse imposition than to have some individual, even temporarily, deliberately fix the outward forms of his concept of beauty upon the future of a free people or even a growing city."[27] He lost that battle. Not until the later 1970s did America begin developing an overtly democratic architecture corresponding to its basic values and culture. Those values and culture were nowhere better described than by the enthusiastic democrat Carl Schurz, just arrived from a lost revolutionary struggle in Germany, writing in 1852:

It is true, indeed, that the first sight of this country fills one with dumb amazement. Here you see the principle of individual freedom carried to its ultimate consequences: voluntarily made laws treated with contempt; in another place you notice the crassest religious fanaticism venting itself in brutal acts; on the other hand you see the great mass of the laboring people in com-

plete freedom striving for emancipation, and by their side the speculative spirit of capital plunging into unheard of enterprises . . .—all these in complete liberty, moving in a confused tumult, one with the other, one by the side of the other. The democrat just arrived from Europe, who has so far lived in a world of ideas and has had no opportunity to see these ideas put into actual, sound practice will ask himself, hesitatingly, Is this, indeed, a free people? Is this a real democracy? Is democracy a fact if it shelters under one cloak such conflicting principles? . . . Finally he will arrive at the solution of the problem. Yes, this is humanity when it is free. Liberty breaks the chain of development. All strength, all weakness, all that is good, all that is bad, is here in full view and in free activity.[28]

"All strength, all weakness, all that is good, all that is bad . . . in full view"—he could be talking about the Postmodern era.

Notes

1. Michael J. Crosbie, "Firehouse Inserted Discreetly into Victorian Main Street," *Architecture* 74 (October 1985): 70–71.
2. Postmodernism's complexities and contradictions are nowhere better exemplified than by the Canadian Chancery. It was commissioned by the government of Pierre Trudeau, who had consistently professed a policy of distancing Canada from the United States yet who finally proclaimed instead a "special relationship" embodied in a Chancery that sits, unique among all foreign embassies, surrounded by American government buildings and practically in the American Capitol's shadow. The building's architect, Arthur Erickson, ends his autobiography (*The Architecture of Arthur Erickson,* New York: Harper & Row, 1988) by professing astonishment that Philip Johnson should admire it as a monument to Postmodernism, whereas he himself would remain forever philosophically unsympathetic to Postmodernism, forever faithful to that Modernism which had so well and so profitably expressed Trudeau's (and his own) profession since the 1950s.
3. Popular/Commercial precedents are literally too numerous to mention. Churches are especially rich in what might, in a Postmodern context, be called "quotes." El Calvaro in Las Cruces is an example *[8.39].*
4. How advanced the movement was in the late 1970s is evident from books like Barbaralee Diamonstein's *Buildings Reborn* (New York: Harper & Row, 1978), but a full history remains to be written of its complex interrelationship with Modernism. Many early and enthusiastic advocates of Modernism were also advocates of preservation, maintaining their paradoxically dual activities by appeal to *Zeitgeist:* Greek Revival was in keeping with the spirit of the 1830s, but the spirit of the 1950s demands another style. When Modernism turned out to be a style limited to a particular time and outlook like every other,

it was hard to take for many who, such as James Marston Fitch, had spent a lifetime as an active and impressively successful preservationist.

5. During the 1970s *Architese,* published in Zürich under the editorship of Stanislaus von Moos, was an important forum for discussing interrelationships of architectural ideas in Europe and the United States. Volumes, issued irregularly throughout the year, were each devoted to a central theme; number 9 in 1973 described German postwar rebuilding and the theories behind it, especially the 1946 plan for Freiburg im Breisgau by Joseph Schlippe, carried out over a thirty-year period, often in modern materials with "recycled uses": the fifteenth-century Kornhalle metamorphosed into a community building with Ratskeller, for instance.

How curious that at the very moment when German Modernism was taking over the States, German Modernism was being repudiated at home in favor of an architecture with a social function proclaiming roots, traditions, and all those qualities Modernists at Harvard, Yale, etc., were teaching Americans to despise.

6. "Merchants Square . . . is one of the earliest theme malls in the country," writes Cary Carson, Vice-President for Research, Colonial Williamsburg Foundation (letter to the author, 16 September 1988). It was "designed by Perry, Shaw and Hepburn [one of the country's leading Academic Colonial Revivalist firms] and built in the years after 1934." An information sheet distributed by the Foundation quotes its architect Nicholas Pappas: "The Restoration did not want to dislodge the local merchants but, rather, provide them a place to move . . . as their buildings were acquired and restored or demolished on the Duke of Gloucester Street. The buildings are not replications of any particular buildings or places. They are a synthesis of carefully-researched design elements," and an ancestor of Postmodernism in conforming to the earlier architecture of its setting while constantly asserting its differences.

7. In the 1940s, and even later, you often came across books with titles like "The Art and Architecture of . . .", as if architecture needed legitimization by association with "art proper." Indeed it was not until the early 1970s that the SAH started to meet separately, and at a different time of year, from CAA, and even then there were deep misgivings within the Society about it.

8. A landmark of establishment approval was an exhibition at the Museum of Modern Art in New York given full-scale treatment in Ada Louise Huxtable's "Beaux-Arts—the Latest Avant-Garde" in *The New York Times Magazine,* 26 October 1975, and commemorated by *The Architecture of the Ecole des Beaux-Arts,* edited by Arthur Drexler, with essays by Richard Chafee, Arthur Drexler, Neil Levine, and David Van Zanten (New York: Museum of Modern Art, 1977). Another landmark was *The American Renaissance 1876–1917* (Brooklyn: Brooklyn Museum of Art, 1979), with essays by Richard Guy Wilson, Dianne H. Pilgrim, and Richard N. Murray.

9. Henri Bergson's *The Two Sources of Morality and Religion* was published in France in the early 1930s, in New York in 1935: "All around intelligence there lingers a fringe of intuition, vague and evanescent"; this "fringe of intuition" cooperates with intelligence, or the concept-forming faculty in humans, to bring about a progressively more satisfying understanding of life, in "reciprocal interpenetration." His *Creative Evolution* appeared in an English translation in New York in 1944. Jung's vast array of writings were very conveniently summarized in *Memories, Dreams, Reflections* in the 1960s.

10. Charles Jencks, *Post-Modernism* (New York: Rizzoli, 1987), p. 13, claims the word was first used in 1934 in an anthology of Spanish and Spanish-American poetry but in reference to a kind of ultra-avantgardism, so distinguished from "old Modernism." Many writers were still so using it in the 1970s to refer to "Late Modernism." Jencks finds the first use of "Post-Modern," referring to pluralism, in Arnold Toynbee's *Study of History* in 1947.

11. J. Mordaunt Crook, *The Dilemma of Style* (Chicago: University of Chicago Press, 1987).

12. "Transitional" reflects ongoing problems of finding some positive word for what was going on in the 1980s; like "Postmodernism" this is defined in terms of movements outside itself. Under whatever name, "Transitional" represents interesting combinations of Modern with various traditions—with Colonial/Classical in the designs of Ralph Lauren, Juan Montoya, John Masheroni, and Ward Bennett (whose 1967 Adamesque-Federal/Modern "banker's chair" was one of the earliest); with 1930s Art-Deco classicism in the designs of John Widdicomb or Jay Spectre.

13. To realize how fully, and how recently, women came to participate in a formerly all-male field, see Lamia Doumato, *Architecture and Women: A Bibliography documenting women architects, landscape artists, designers, architectural critics and writers, and women in related fields working in the United States* (New York: Garland, 1988).

14. How many architectural historians or students have ever heard of Don Miller, Thomas Wells, Colwell & Ray, or Abraham J. Goldberg? Only readers of Philip Langdon's accounts of the evolution of fast-food restaurant forms (McDonald's, Coco's, Denny's, Dunkin' Donuts) in *Orange Roofs, Golden Arches* (New York: Knopf, 1986). The cause is not just a lack of publicity or elitist disdain, but a whole attitude to design. Architects like Miller, Wells, Colwell & Ray, and Goldberg worked in a traditional relationship to clients: the clients explained their wishes, the architects provided what was asked. So Richard Morris Hunt is supposed to have said that if a Vanderbilt wanted a chimney in his basement, he'd put one there. European Moderns and their followers took a different stance. First they produced a theory and publicized it; then if clients wanted the kind of designs that resulted, they'd provide some. Otherwise, no.

15. In the 1980s it was much more common than ever before for architects to have a "line" of furniture; *Skyline* devoted an issue to this process in April 1983. So Knoll International, upon being taken over by General Felt Industries in 1978, revived the early company's sponsorship of contemporary furniture (it had carried lines by

Mies, Eero Saarinen, Eames, and Breuer in the 1940s and 1950s) by commissioning and promoting Postmodern furniture from architects as diverse as Stanley Tigerman, Richard Meier, Charles Gwathmey, Robert Venturi, and Margaret McCurry. The new Knoll's practice was to get diverse celebrated architects to design their several show-rooms—Venturi designed one, Gwathmey/Siegel another, Stanley Tigerman a third. By contrast, only Michael Graves designed several showrooms for Sunar; the "complete spatial and decorative continuity" thereby achieved "obviously provides a sympathetic setting for Graves' furnishings." You buy such furniture as you would buy a painting or sculpture; the showrooms then function like art galleries, certifying the designs as Works of Art.

16. Selling architects' drawings, models, even blueprints has become a lucrative dealer specialty, according to a dealer quoted in an article by Douglas McGill in *The New York Times* for 31 August 1987: "Important drawings by major architects [how defined is not explained] today range in price from between $2,500 to $20,000 while they sold for between $200 and $3000 in the late 1970s." A reason for this development is suggested by a quote in the same article from Heinrich Klotz, that "architecture has become an art again, not just technology. The models and drawings have become works of art in themselves."

17. Anyone interested in architectural literature of the 1970s can do no better than read the brilliant review by Rosemary Haag Bletter of *Five Architects—Eisenman, Graves, Gwathmey, Hejduk, Meier,* with preface by Arthur Drexler, introduction by Colin Rowe, critique by Kenneth Frampton, postscript by Philip Johnson (New York: Oxford University Press, 1975), in *Journal of the Society of Architectural Historians* 38/1 (1979): 206–7.

18. Charles Jencks, *Post-Modernism: The New Classicism in Art and Architecture* (New York: Rizzoli, 1987), p. 11. The title is unfortunate, for there are many contemporary types to which classical forms in any guise are not particularly applicable.

19. Alfred H. Barr, Jr., quotes in his *Picasso* (New York: Museum of Modern Art, 1946) from one of Christian Zervos's "Conversations avec Picasso" in *Cahiers d'art,* in which the master says: "The Parthenon is really only a farmyard over which someone put a roof; colonnades and sculptures were added because there were people in Athens who happened to be working, and wanted to express themselves" (p. 175). This is no more uncivilized than Corbusier's famous assessment of the Parthenon as "magnificent forms in space and light." What really determined the design of a classical Greek or Roman temple is as incomprehensible and meaningless to these orthodox Moderns as it was to Goths or Slavs or any other barbarians who periodically overran Athens. In such remarks is revealed the underlying mental world of Modern scientificism: barbarism disguised by high technology.

20. The expression is borrowed from Cyrus H. Gordon, who uses it casually in referring to the enormous expansion of knowledge about ancient languages and literatures of the Near East (*The Ancient Near East,* New York, 1966, p.115) and concomitantly deeper and more complex understandings of that world; greater depth, more complexity has been true of almost every field of intellectual activity except established Modernism in the arts, where the focus has consistently narrowed.

21. There is a deep streak of impracticality, not to say unreality, in much Postmodern theory on housing and city planning. It is most obvious in big-scale works, such as Leon Krier's proposed replanning of Washington, D.C., as four Williamsburg-like villages, which won much critical acclaim but obviously involved no expectations whatever of practical implementation—architectural dreaming, in fact, far closer in spirit to Dalí than to L'Enfant, issuing not in bricks and mortar but in fanciful drawings for sale to collectors and foundations. Likewise, Postmodern writings about housing in the 1980s still showed little awareness of the social function of homesteads, raising a family. Overwhelmingly their concern was with childless couples, or couples wealthy enough to hire lots of help and pay for private schooling.

22. Furniture especially has shown the Italian influence: Mario Botta, Giancarlo Piretti, Achille Castiglioni, Vico Magistretti—such names are to be reckoned with in American furniture design. And perhaps it is culturally significant that the handsome cars in the national capital's subway system were designed in Milan.

23. Heinrich Klotz's *The History of Postmodern Architecture* (Cambridge, Mass.: The MIT Press, 1987) claims the Velasca Tower in Milan of c. 1957–60 by Ernesto Rogers as a pioneer Postmodern building, along with the Chase Manhattan Bank branch in Milan of 1969 by the BBPE group. He would see the beginnings of Postmodernism in a speech made by Giancarlo de Carlo at the CIAM meetings of 1959, which called for "pliant and adjustable plans" based "on detailed knowledge of historical data."

24. Robert Twombly, *Louis Sullivan* (New York: Viking, 1986), p. 278.

25. And any sharp separation of these in turn from other kinds of Postmodern stylings would be pedantic too. Thus many different aspects of building in the 1980s are represented in most critical writings of consequence, and readers can discover all sorts of cross connections. For introductions to this field one could hardly do better than Tod A. Marder's *Critical Edge: Controversy in Recent American Architecture* (Cambridge, Mass.: The MIT Press, and Zimmerli Art Museum of Rutgers University, 1986), or Gavin Macrae-Gibson, *The Secret Life of Buildings: An American Mythology for Modern Architecture* (Cambridge, Mass.: The MIT Press, 1986). The first includes critiques of twelve very different kinds of buildings, the second discusses seven.

26. Page Smith, *The Nation Comes of Age* (New York: McGraw-Hill, 1981), pp. 781, 782.

27. Quoted in *Architectural Review* 171 (1982):61.

28. Carl Schurz, letter to Malwida von Meysenburg, in Frederick Bancroft, ed., *Speeches, Correspondence, and Political Papers of Carl Schurz,* I, 1913, pp. 5, 6.

APPENDIX

Styles and Types of North American Architecture:
A Categorization System

The following system was worked out over many years for the National Images of North American Living slide collection, to cover about 30,000 slides—representing perhaps 20,000 different architectural artifacts—assembled over nearly forty years; the first ones were made in 1955, the latest in 1989.* The North American architectural landscape does not consist exclusively of High Style examples, nor does this collection; the system reflects its complexity and richness. Everything artifactual on that landscape can be located in this collection by combinations of codes for Style/Substyle/Type/Subtype.** Besides such practical advantages, the system offers research dividends: it can be used to point up similarities and correspondences between styles and types not always obvious in more conventional systems. The present book owes much to insights thus provided. Individual chapters will, I hope, adequately explain whatever of the system's rationale is not self-evident.

Styles and Substyles

10. Utilitarian

What has no style cannot have substyles. However, utilitarian structures and materials produce certain stylistic effects. These utilitarian stylistic effects may be categorized as follows:

10-001. Sod, earth textures
10-002. Thatch, branch textures
10-003. Log textures
10-004. Timber textures (e.g., half-timber effects)
10-005. Board/siding/picket textures
10-006. Shingles (e.g., wood, asphalt)
10-007. Adobe, mud-brick textures
10-008. Brick (kiln-burnt) patterns, textures
10-009. Tile
10-010. Stone, laid (mortarless)
10-011. Rubble effects
10-012. Fieldstone effects
10-013. Cobblestone effects

10-014. Cut stone, masonry effects
10-015. Sheet metal/iron effects
10-016. Iron construction effects
10-017. Concrete block effects
10-018. Cast/ferroconcrete effects
10-019. Glass effects
10-020. Stucco effects
10-021. Effects of artificial facings, in plastic, Permastone, etc.
10-022. Effects of miscellaneous textures

21. Colonial Spanish

21-100. Colonial Spanish, general
21-111. Colonial Spanish folk vernacular, general
21-112. Colonial Spanish folk vernacular, Pueblo
21-117. Precolumbian survivals, integrations (e.g., Aztec, Maya)
21-121. Colonial Spanish urban
21-131. Colonial Spanish aristocratic high styles
21-141. Colonial Spanish vernacular versions of high or urban styles

22. Colonial French

22-200. Colonial French, general
22-212. Colonial French folk vernacular
22-222. Colonial French urban
22-232. Colonial French aristocratic high
22-242. Colonial French vernacular versions of high and/or urban styles

23. Colonial North European

23-300. Colonial North European, general
23-316. Colonial North European vernacular Swedish/Scandinavian
23-319. Colonial North European Scottish
23-320. Colonial North European Irish
23-321. Colonial North European Dutch/Flemish
23-323. Colonial North European urban styles (Swedish, Dutch, etc.)

---

*National Images of North American Living, Research and Archival Center, 524-2020 F Street, N.W., Washington, DC 20006.
**The numbers for each entry or category are the access codes to the National Images of North American Living slide collection.

23-333. Colonial North European high styles (Swedish, Dutch, etc.)

23-343. Colonial North European vernacular versions of urban and/or high

24. Colonial German

24-400. Colonial German, general

24-414. Colonial German folk vernacular

24-424. Colonial German urban

24-434. Colonial German high

24-444. Colonial German vernacular versions of urban and/or high styles

25. Colonial English

25-500. Colonial English, general

25-501. Colonial English homestead general and folk vernacular

25-502. New England small homestead forms, including Cape Cod

25-503. New England large homestead forms, including saltboxes (see type E)

25-504. New England contiguous style of building

25-512. Small Southern homestead types, including hall-and-parlor and Southern Cabin

25-513. 1½-story Southern homestead styles, including 1½-story Delmarva gambrel

25-514. Larger (2 + story) Southern homestead types

25-516. Georgian (British) Cabin, the Georgianized version of 501, 502, 512

25-520. Philadelphia spec house form

25-521. Colonial English urban, general

25-522. Salem County gambrel-roofed patterned-brick form

25-528. Cross-plan form, signaling "mansion" (type H), but occasionally E

25-530. Basic Georgian, including ⅓ and ⅔ Georgian vernacular

25-532. Early Southern Georgian, erratic and variant forms

25-533. I-form

25-539. Puritan meetinghouse form

25-541. Bawn

25-542. High Georgian/Palladian palace/mansion substyle

25-545. Wren/Gibbs Anglican church form

25-549. Southern Anglican plantation church form

25-550. Vernacular and Late Georgian/Palladian

26–29. Later Colonial Styles

26-600. Colonial East European, general (Ukrainian, Russian, Czech, Polish)

26-626. Colonial East European folk vernacular

26-636. Colonial East European high styles

26-646. Colonial East European vernacular versions of high or urban styles

27-700. Colonial South European, general

27-717. Colonial South European folk vernacular

27-737. Colonial South European high

27-747. Colonial South European vernacular versions of high and/or urban

28-800. Colonial Far Eastern styles

28-818. Colonial Far Eastern folk vernacular

28-838. Colonial Far Eastern high and urban

28-848. Colonial Far Eastern vernacular versions of high and/or urban

29-900. Miscellaneous other later Colonial styles

30. National Democratic Classical Revival Substyles

30-000. Introductory; background; antiquity; Europe; landscape

30-010. Utilitarian buildings with Classical proportions or touches

30-100. Classical Revival, general

30-251. Appended porch/portico

30-253. Appended portico proper

30-254. Palladian used for Classical Revival social function

30-300. Revolutionary Democratic avant-garde, general

30-305. Octagon/round shape dominant

30-315. *Architecture parlante*

30-325. Adamesque-Federal style used for Classical Revival social function

30-331. Roman Revival proper/dominant

30-332. Greek Revival proper/dominant

30-333. Egyptian Revival proper/dominant

30-335. Mixes, variants, vernaculars of 331–333

30-340. Classical Revival with Gothic details

30-600. Classical Square form

30-620. Classical Cottage form

30-640. Shotgun form

30-660. Basilica form

30-700. Vestigial Classical revivals

40. Gothic Revival

40-040. Gothic Revival as an avant-garde style (Gothick)

40-100. Early Gothic Revival, general

40-140. Early Gothic Revival, specific

40-200. Early Picturesque Gothic Revival

40-300. Early Gothic revivals of exotic (non-European) styles (Chinese, Moorish, etc.)

40-400. Catholic Gothic Revival (Puginesque)

40-450. Ecclesiological Gothic

40-500. Picturesque Gothic Revival High Style

40-540. Picturesque Gothic Vernacular

40-580. Vestigial Picturesque Gothic

40-700. Archaeological Gothic

50. Picturesque

50-100. Picturesque, general

50-200. Italianate, general

50-210. Italianate/Renaissance

50-220. Italianate/Gothic

50-240. Italianate/Romanesque (Lombard)

50-280. Italianate/Romanesque vernaculars and variants

50-300. Second (French) Empire High Style

50-340. Italianate/Second Empire combinations, high style, heavy (General Grant)

50-350. Italianate/Second Empire/Renaissance combinations, high style, light (Eastlake)

50-360. Italianate/Second Empire/Renaissance combinations, vernacular (stick style)
50-370. Vernacular commercial Italianate/Second Empire (boom-town front)
50-375. High Picturesque with Renaissance elements predominant (Queen Anne)
50-380. Late Picturesque Classical High Style
50-385. Renaissance/medieval combinations, high style
50-390. Vernacular/variant versions of Late Picturesque Classical (50-380)
50-400. Richardsonian Romanesque High Style
50-410. Richardsonian Romanesque, local variations
50-420. Shingle style
50-450. High Picturesque, medieval emphasis
50-480. High Picturesque, medieval emphasis, vernacular
50-500. Vestigial Picturesque

60. Academic

60-100. Academic, general
60-210. Academic Spanish Colonial Revival; general
60-211. Academic Spanish Colonial Mission Revival
60-212. Academic Spanish Colonial Mediterranean Revival
60-213. Academic Spanish Colonial high styles
60-214. Academic Pueblo
60-217. Revivals of Precolumbian styles
60-220. Academic Colonial French, general
60-222. Academic Colonial French, vernacular
60-223. Academic Colonial French high styles (Château)
60-224. Academic Colonial French urban/high styles
60-232. Academic Colonial North European Revival, general
60-234. Academic Dutch Colonial folk form (suburban houses)
60-236. Academic Dutch Colonial urban form revival
60-250. Academic English Colonial Revival, general
60-251. Academic English Colonial homestead revivals
60-252. Academic English Colonial urban styles
60-253. Academic English Georgian homestead styles
60-254. Academic English High Georgian
60-260. Academic East European
60-270. Academic South European
60-280. Academic Far Eastern
60-290. Academic Near Eastern
60-300. Academic Classical Revival, general
60-310. Academic Classical high style revivals
60-360. Academic Classical vernacular revivals
60-361. The foursquare form, small and big
60-362. The temple-house form, small and big
60-375. Academic Late Abstract Classical (Art Deco, Moderne)
60-380. Academic Late Classical revivals, vestigial
60-410. Academic Medieval Revival styles, general
60-414. Academic Tudor (Tudorbethan)
60-415. Academic Romanesque (French)
60-424. Academic Italianate/Romanesque (Lombard)
60-430. Academic Early Christian/Byzantine
60-445. Academic High Gothic
60-450. Academic Picturesque Gothic

60-454. Academic Picturesque Domestic Gothic
60-460. Late and abstracted medieval revivals (Dom Bellot)
60-480. Academic medieval revivals, vestigial
60-510. Academic versions of picturesque styles, general
60-511. Bungalow forms, small and big
60-520. Academic Italian Renaissance Revival
60-545. Academic Elitist Arts and Crafts (Wrightian, Prairie)
60-548. Populist Arts and Crafts

70. Modern

70-010. Utilitarian Modern
70-070. Revolutionary Socialist
70-100. Established Modern, general
70-120. "Screen"
70-130. "Mirror"
70-140. "Abstract Sculptural," general
70-150. Arrested Rust Sheathing
70-160. "Brutalist"
70-170. "Abstract Geometric"
70-180. "Hi-Tech"

Subliminal Modern Eclectic Survivals

70-200.+ Subliminal Colonial (210 Spanish, 220 French, 250 English, etc.)
70-300. Subliminal Classical
70-400. Subliminal Gothic
70-500. Subliminal Picturesque
70-600. Subliminal Academic
70-650. Subliminal Picturesque Arts and Crafts (e.g., Frank Lloyd Wright influence)
70-700. Vestigial and Vernacular Modern

80. Popular/Commercial

80-010. Popular/Commercial Utilitarian (including monuments made of machines, and the like)
80-200. Popular/Commercial Colonial, general
80-210. Popular/Commercial Colonial Spanish (80-215 Pueblo, 80-217 Aztec, Precolumbian, etc.)
80-220. Popular/Commercial Colonial French
80-230. Popular/Commercial Colonial North European (e.g., Dutch Colonial after 1945)
80-250. Popular/Commercial Colonial English, general (80-251 Homestead, 80-254 Palladian, etc.)
80-260. Popular/Commercial East European
80-270. Popular/Commercial South European (e.g., Italian, Greek restaurant substyles)
80-280. Popular/Commercial Far Eastern (e.g., Chinese, Japanese)
80-290. Popular/Commercial other Late Colonial substyles
80-300. Popular/Commercial Classical Revival
80-400. Popular/Commercial Gothic/Medieval
80-500. Popular/Commercial Picturesque
80-600. Popular/Commercial Academic (e.g., 80-654 Arts and Crafts, Popular/Commercial perpetuation)
80-700. Popular/Commercial Modern (modern forms but Popular/Commercial uses)

80-800. Popular/Commercial representational architecture (including representational art of all kinds used in Popular/Commercial architectural/landscape context)

90 Postmodern

90-090. Proto-Postmodern
90-100. Postmodern, general (including semiotics)
90-200. Colonial stylistic elements (as appropriate, 90-220, -250, -260 for French, English, East European, etc.)
90-300. Postmodern Classical allusions
90-400. Postmodern Gothic allusions
90-500. Postmodern Picturesque allusions
90-700. Self-conscious Modernism (e.g., Corbusian)
90-800. Postmodern Popular/Commercial
90-900. Preservation and restoration projects, facadomy, etc.

Types and Subtypes

A. *Monument and Tomb*

AA. Pillar (Stele)

a. Memorial parks (if containing monuments to wars or heroes; otherwise AC-c)
b. Memorials to wars and war heroes, including victory columns, obelisks (memorial windows = AF-a)
c. Monuments to royalty and rulers (e.g., presidents, colonial governors)
d. Monuments to culture heroes, political figures, historical events (including monuments to art and artists)
e. Architectural monuments to wars, including monumental arches (gates = AC-g or AA-m)
f. Architectural monuments to royalty and rulers
g. Architectural monuments to culture heroes, political figures, historical events
h. Monuments to buildings (e.g., fragments, artificial ruins preserved)
j. Signs and graffiti (roadside markers for traffic, etc. = GC-d, c)
k. Flagpoles
m. Commemorative arches, colonnades functioning as arches, etc.

AB. Tomb

a. Tombstones and grave monuments
b. Funerary sculpture
c. Mounds, tumuli, omphaloi, etc.
d. Mausolea, above ground (including sarcophagi)
e. Mausolea, below ground (e.g., vaults, crypts)
f. Other

AC. Plot/Park

a. Cemetery parks, also churchyards (as appropriate)
b. Cemetery buildings (body storage, chapels, etc.)
c. Civic parks and city plans/views (amusement parks = JK-g)

d. Civic park buildings (bandstands, gazebos, etc.)
e. Lanterns and light standards (in parks, or otherwise monumental)
f. Fountains, monumental and/or ornamental (utilitarian fountains = GB-a)
g. Gates to parks, etc. (ceremonial military gates = CB-b) (commemorative arches/gates = AA-m)

AD. Garden

a. Landscaped grounds, "parks" of great estates (including twentieth-century hotels)
b. Buildings, including ruins, on landscaped grounds
c. Gardens proper
d. Garden ornaments and the like
e. Lawns/yards
f. Other

AE. Popular and Private Sculpture in Public Places (as distinct from AA-e; AA-f; AB-b; government commissions)

a. Commemorative (e.g., monuments by Chambers of Commerce or by local groups to American Indians, historic events, etc.)
b. Commercial (advertising)
c. Historical and idealistic (monuments to motherhood, dogs, etc.)
d. Religious (crèches, Sacre Coeur monuments, etc.; also secular paradise imagery; Christmas ornamentation = AE-j)
e. Decorative (e.g., sculpture attached to buildings)
f. Folk (e.g., snowmen, fiberglass animals)
g. Mailboxes, hydrants, "found" or "invented" folk art
h. Christmas ornamentations, on streets, etc.
j. Sculptural architecture: buildings in recognizable shapes; also, buildings with walls painted three-dimensionally

AF. Architectural Elements with Monument/Memorial Functions

a. Stained-glass windows as memorials
b. Niches
c. Other comparable elements

B. *Shrine and Sanctuary*

BA. Sanctuary Grounds (Grotto, Shrine, Pilgrimage Site, etc., with attendant signs, fences, markers, etc.)

BB. Sanctuary Building (as Synagogue, Church, Mosque, etc.)

BC. Meeting House (not sanctuary, but used for religious observances)

BD. Auxiliary Sanctuary Building (as Parish House, Church Hall, also Office Tower or Bazaar [adjoining Mosque], etc.)

BE. Clergy Residence (as Manse, Rectory, Presbytère, etc., if next sanctuary building or on sanctuary grounds)

BF. Outbuilding on Sanctuary Grounds (as Tool Shed)

BG. Monastery or Convent

BH. Utopian Community (secular or supernatural faith, and its buildings)

BJ. Religious School (on grounds, part of complex [civic school = FG-a, FG-b] including Madrassahs)

BK. Funeral Home

Subtypes (apply to all the above):

  a. Precolumbian religions
  b. Jewish
  c. Roman Catholic
  d. Anglican/Episcopal/Church of England
  e. Congregational/Puritan/Unitarian
  f. Presbyterian/Calvinist
  g. Methodist
  h. Lutheran
  j. Baptist/Evangelical
  k. Other Protestant
  m. East European Orthodox and Catholic (e.g., Ukrainian, Russian)
  n. Muslim
  p. Buddhist
  q. Shinto
  r. Other non-Christian
  s. Nondenominational

C. Wall and Fort

CA. Defensive Works Proper

  a. Fortresses (intended for defense, with resident troops, as contrasted to armories = CC-d, or police stations = CC-b)
  b. Trenches, bunkers, ramparts
  c. Towers and keeps for military purposes
  d. Auxiliary defensive buildings (e.g., radar installations)
  e. Military bases, nineteenth and twentieth century, with barracks, mess halls, etc., not necessarily defending anything, but for training
  f. Other

CB. Statements of Presence

  a. Castles, mainly or primarily ceremonial and/or symbolic
  b. Ceremonial and symbolic gates to fortresses (park gates = AC)
  c. Markers of possession

CC. Civic Protection

  a. Fence, wall
  b. Police station (including guardhouse)
  c. Ranger station
  d. Armory
  e. Jail/penitentiary
  f. Fire hall (firehouse)

  g. Security headquarters (e.g., FBI, Scotland Yard)
  h. Arsenal, magazine

D. Shelter and Shed

DA. Shelter for Humans

  a. Outhouse/privy (cave)
  b. Tent or comparable structure for temporary living
  c. Shanty (pre-homestead, including sod house but not log cabin = EA)
  d. Studio/workshop (private; but artist's studio = KC-b)
  e. Temporary housing for migrants, etc.
  f. Telephone booth
  g. Bus shelter
  h. Other temporary shelter (e.g., parking-lot attendant booth)

DB. Shelter for Beasts and/or Storage for Food

  a. Food storage sheds (roothouse, icehouse)
  b. Barn proper
  c. Storehouse/warehouse
  d. Grain elevator
  e. Silo
  f. Greenhouse
  g. Stable or other animal shelter not part of barn
  h. Doghouse
  j. Birdhouse
  k. Other

DC. Shelter and Service for Vehicles (private, nonsocially essential, as compared to GC: Public Works Transportation, vital to functioning of society)

  a. Storage for farm vehicles and/or tools
  b. Gas station (including repair shop if part thereof)
  c. Repair shop
  d. Private garage (for storing cars); also carriage house (private)
  e. Public garage (also carriage house [public])
  f. Car-wash service
  g. Boathouse
  h. Hangar or other airport storage
  k. Car-dealer service
  m. Other

DD. Shelter for Work

  a. Factory/mill
  b. Factory/office (office buildings proper = JB, JC)
  c. Food/drink manufacture (bakery, dairy, brewery, etc.)
  d. Fishing sheds, drying racks
  e. Kitchen or other separate building for food preparation (e.g., plantation)
  f. Mine buildings
  g. Blacksmith shop/shoe repair shop
  h. Other

DE. Industrial Shelters

  a. Kiln/slash burner
  b. Oil drums, refinery equipment, gas drums

c. Water tanks (e.g., roofs; public waterworks = GB)
d. Bases for machinery and machinery itself (e.g., sugar mills, oil-drill donkeys)
e. Storage sheds

E. Homestead

EA. Single Detached House: Rural, Urban, Suburban

a. Small
b. Big*

EB. Row House

EC. Tenement (usually a multiple family dwelling, distinguished from row house by size [bigger], from apartment proper by social function [built for speculative renting])

ED. Company Housing (including slave quarters, pre-1865)

EF. Suburban Dwelling (now subsumed in and filed with EA)

EG. Mobile Home

EH. "Fantasy Farm" (the play-farm rural/suburban subtype appearing from c.1970 onward)

F. Palace

FA. Palace Proper

a. Governor's palace or other official residence
b. Leading citizens' houses which function as images of some kind of local authority: bawns; tongs
c. Surrogate governors' palaces: homes of chief justices; Royal Canadian Mounted Police homes functioning as offices; Québecois *manoirs*
d. Embassies or consulates

FB. Legislative Buildings

a. Capitols or parliament buildings
b. City halls
c. Courthouses
d. Township halls, municipal offices, etc.
e. Other (e.g., parole center)

FC. Other Buildings Where Government Meets People

a. Government complex, general
b. Mints, Internal Revenue Service buildings
c. Customhouses
d. Post offices
e. Registry offices
f. Office or administration buildings (e.g., Labor Exchange, government banks; other banks = JC)
g. Government Information Bureaux (Chamber of Commerce Information Bureaux = JE)
h. Government liquor stores
j. Archives/records offices and buildings

FD. Communications

a. Telephone building
b. Radio or TV station
c. Telegraph station or building
d. Newspaper building
e. Publishing company building

FG. Schools

a. Elementary/secondary school buildings
b. University/college buildings, including libraries (public library = KA)
c. Research institutes

G. Public Works

GA. Public Works with a Memorial/Monumental Function (Specific)

GB. Essential Public Services

a. Wells and fountains (commemorative/park fountain = AC)
b. Waterworks and water towers (see also DE-c, for industrial water tanks)
c. Aqueducts
d. Windmills
e. Electric plants
f. Atomic energy plants
g. Sewer and other public health installations
h. Dams (for generating power)
j. Irrigation systems, canals, etc.

GC. Transportation

a. Road (road proper—i.e., highway, railroad itself): GC-aa = path; GC-ab = regular road; GC-ac = superhighway; GC-ad = railroad; GC-ae = subway, metro; GC-af = canal (used for transportation; irrigation canal = GB-j)
b. Bridge: GC-ba = flat; GC-bb = suspension; GC-bc = truss; GC-bd = cantilever; GC-be = bascule (lift)
c. Tunnel
d. Road buildings: GC-da = freeway/toll-road buildings, like rest stops, toll booths; GC-db = road service buildings; GC-dc = roadside signs, other such necessary to users of the roads
e. Railroad buildings: GC-ea = stations; GC-eb = railroad service buildings, sheds; GC-ec = railroad signs, signals, necessary for users
f. Air-travel buildings: GC-fa = airport proper; GC-fb = service buildings, like hangars; GC-fc = signs, etc. for users of airways
g. Shipping buildings: GC-ga = terminals, including ferry terminals; GC-gb = service structures like wharves, docks, locks, etc.; GC-gc = signs, etc. for shipping, including lighthouses
h. Subway stations and related subway buildings

---

*Note on a/b categorization: reflecting social function of proclaiming upward mobility, in styles 10–40 a small house (a) will be one to one-and-a-half stories, but in styles 50+, a small house (a) will be up to two-and-a-half stories or about 10 rooms, and a big house (b) will be over that height and number.

H. Mansion

HA. Merchant's House Proper

a. House with goods facilities or shop included (shop proper = J)

HB. Mansion Proper

a. Town mansion (including big Georgian row houses), most commonly eighteenth-century
b. Country/plantation house (e.g., Georgian), most commonly eighteenth-century
c. Upper-middle-class city or suburban "villa," most commonly nineteenth-century
d. Country villa, most commonly nineteenth-century
e. Mansions for the twentieth-century wealthy

HC. Homestead Functioning as Mansion (status symbolized by homestead type; for subtypes use homestead system)

HD. Apartment House ("The Mansion You Can Rent")

a. Commercial apartment, small (lower than six stories)
b. Commercial apartment, big (more than six stories), or twenty units
c. Condominium (institutional housing, old people's, etc. = KA-e)

HE. Hotels/Motels

a. Hotels, small (including inns)
b. Hotels, big (higher than six stories)
c. Motels, small (one or two stories)
d. Motels, big

HK. Hotel/Lodge Combinations

J. Shop and Office

JA. Shops

a. Booth (including photography stand)
b. Shops proper (small, individual or small row, usually with living quarters above)
c. Farmers' markets; antique shops; flea markets
d. Market or supermarket (blocks of stores)
e. Department store or emporium
f. Shopping arcade
g. Shopping center
h. Showroom (e.g., for cars, boats)

JB. Commercial Buildings with Governmental Functions

a. Market/town-hall combinations

JC. Exchange and Bank

a. Stock exchange
b. Bank, small
c. Bank, office tower (over six stories)

JD. Office/Corporation Building

a. Small office (less than six stories)
b. Tall office (more than six)

JE. Public Relations Services

a. Chamber of commerce
b. Information stand
c. Other

JH. Shop/Mansion Combination

a. Shopping center/apartment-house combinations, single building
b. Shopping center/apartment-house combinations, complex of buildings

JK. Commercial Amenities

a. Restaurant
b. Tavern or pub (when principal feature)
c. Shop/lodge combination (hall above, stores below)
d. Casino
e. Resort and associated facilities
f. Disco/dance hall/bowling alley
g. Amusement park
h. Movie set
j. Pornography shop

K. Amenities

KA. Public Service

a. Hospital
b. Orphanage
c. Public library
d. Mental institution
e. Institutional housing (old people's, projects, etc.)
f. Veterinary hospital
g. Clinic

KB. Social/Recreational: Public

a. Club or lodge proper
b. Community center or hall
c. Theater, cinema, or music hall
d. Museum or gallery
e. Fairs/exhibition grounds and buildings
f. Sports arenas/gymnasiums
g. Museums/exhibitions at historic sites
h. Campground
j. Conference center/summer lodge or hall

KC. Social/Recreational: Private

a. Summer cottages and other vacation structures
b. Studio (art, music, etc.)
c. Summer inns and lodges
d. Sports club
e. Summer camp

KD. Philanthropic/Civic

a. Philanthropic headquarters (e.g., foundation building)
b. Boy Scout headquarters and comparable buildings
c. YMCA/YWCA and comparable buildings

KE. Professional/Recreational

a. Union hall

INDEX

Page numbers in italics refer to picture captions.